Purchasing and Supply Chain Management

Purchasing and Supply
Chain Management

Sixth Edition

Kenneth Lysons
MA, MEd, PhD, Dipl.PA, Ac.Dip.Ed.,
DMS, FCIS, FCIPS, FInst M

Michael Gillingham
MBA, DMS, MCIPS, MInst LM, PGCE

FT Prentice Hall
FINANCIAL TIMES

An imprint of **Pearson Education**
Harlow, England • London • New York • Boston • San Francisco • Toronto • Sydney • Singapore • Hong Kong
Tokyo • Seoul • Taipei • New Delhi • Cape Town • Madrid • Mexico City • Amsterdam • Munich • Paris • Milan

Pearson Education Limited
Edinburgh Gate
Harlow
Essex CM20 2JE
England

and Associated Companies throughout the world

Visit us on the World Wide Web at:
www.pearsoned.co.uk

———————————

First published 1981 Macdonald & Evans Limited
Second edition 1989 Longman Group UK Limited
Third edition 1993 Longman Group UK Limited
Fourth edition 1996 Pitman Publishing, a division of Pearson Professional Limited
Fifth edition 2000 Pearson Education Limited
Sixth edition 2003 Pearson Education Limited

© Macdonald & Evans Limited 1981
© Longman Group Limited 1989, 1993
© Pearson Professional Limited 1996
© Pearson Education Limited 2000, 2003

ISBN 0 273 65764 X

British Library Cataloguing-in-Publication Data
A catalogue record for this book is available from the British Library

10 9 8 7 6 5 4 3
07 06 05 04

Typeset in $9^{1}/_{2}$/12pt Stone Serif by 35
Printed and bound by Bell & Bain Limited, Glasgow

Contents

Preface to sixth edition

The first edition of this book appeared in 1981. Advantage has been taken of the publisher's request to include in this sixth edition much new material and to substantially rewrite some important sections. New chapters have been added on logistics and supply chains, global sourcing and transporting supplies. Every chapter has been revised and contains new material.

The present book, now under joint authorship, aims to be both a textbook for students of purchasing and supply chain management and a guidebook for practitioners.

As a textbook, full coverage is provided for the syllabuses of the Chartered Institute of Purchasing and Supply in respect of the Foundation stage subjects 'Introduction to Supply and Materials Management' and 'Legal and Procurement Processes', and the Graduate Diploma, Professional Stage core and option subjects of 'Purchasing and Supply Chain Management I: Strategy' and 'Purchasing and Supply Chain Management II: Tactics and Operations'. It also largely covers the option subjects of 'Stores and Inventory Management', 'Operations Management', 'Commercial Relationships' and 'International Purchasing'. The book may also be useful to students taking the examinations of the Institute of Logistics and Transport. Additional new features are at least one case study and discussion questions at the end of each chapter which may be equally useful for class use or private study. An Instructor's Manual is now available for the use of tutors.

As a guidebook the text should provide a quick source of reference for practitioners on many aspects of purchasing and supply. Of particular importance is the glossary of purchasing and supply terms which should complement in some cases the excellent *Dictionary of Purchasing and Supply* by Compton and Jessop.[1]

As stated in the preface to the first edition, the modern emphasis is on integrated study, and in writing the book the authors have drawn on many disciplines that contribute to a sound knowledge of purchasing and supply chain management practice and techniques. These include financial and management accountancy, economics, ethics, human resources management, law, operational research, marketing, negotiation, psychology, sociology and strategic management. Career progress in the purchasing and supply field increasingly requires the critical thinking that derives from wide perspectives. The range of disciplines referred to above indicates that any person aspiring to become a 'purchasing professional' must be well acquainted with the many fields of knowledge that contribute to efficient purchasing and also dedicated to continuing self-development.

Finally, to complement this book, online lecturer's resources are available, comprising an Instructor's Manual and PowerPoint slides. You can find these at www. booksites.net/lysons.

Note

1. Compton, H.K. and Jessop, D.A., *The Official Dictionary of Purchasing and Supply*, Liverpool Business Publishing, 2001

Acknowledgements

The writers are indebted to many organisations and people.

All writers are indebted to libraries and we would put on record the courteous assistance received from the staffs of the British Library, the Department of Trade and Industry Library, the Institute of Management Foundation, the Chartered Institute of Personnel and Development, the Institute of Logistics and Transport, the Picton Library, the Prescot Branch of the Metropolitan Borough of Knowsley Library Service, the St Helens College, the University of Liverpool, the John Rylands and Business School Libraries of the University of Manchester and the Library of Thames Valley University.

The Chartered Institute of Purchasing and Supply kindly gave permission to use questions and some case studies from papers set at the Foundation and Diploma stage examinations.

It is impossible to mention by name everyone who has contributed to this book, but the authors would specifically thank Ken Burnett, Dr Marc Day and Georgina Sear of the Chartered Institute of Purchasing and Supply, Peter Huggett and Lynn Mayhew of the Institute of Transport and Logistics, Professor Peter Hines of the Cardiff University Business School, Gillian Hern of Thames Valley University, Eric Evans, Nicolas Graham, Howard Jones of Rolls-Royce, Dr David Jones, Peter Kileen, Colette Langley and Libby Howells of the N.W. European Information Centre, Liverpool, Sarah Lim of Purcon Consultants Ltd, Jonathan Lyles and Robert Payne of Market Focus Research Ltd, Irene Marshall and Irene Jones of Prescot Library, Brian McArdle and Rosanne Lynden-Brown of Marks and Spencer, Gerald Morris of the British Electro-technical and Allied Manufacturing Association, Shane Perry of the Qualifications and Curriculum Authority, Professor Michael Quayle, Drs S. New and S. Young, Dr P. Niruwenhuis, Elizabeth Stanton Jones of Partnership Sourcing, John Stevens, Professor John Smith of the Ford Motor Co. and Steve Young.

Kenneth Lysons would again put on record the help given by Jeanne Ashton, a loyal friend and assistant over many years. The authors would also thank their respective wives, Audrey Lysons and Anne Gillingham, for their patience during a lengthy period of writing.

Finally, the book has been expertly word processed by Judith Ray, who has patiently coped with idiosyncrasies of handwriting and changes to the text. And our thanks too, to Jill Birch who project edited the book on behalf of the publishers.

Publisher's acknowledgements

We are grateful for permission to reproduce the following copyright material:

Dr David Jones for Table 1.5 and Figure 1.3. Russell Syson for Figures 2.5 and 2.6. Professor Peter Hines for Figures 3.12, 3.13 and the summary of the aims and objectives of *Kyoryoku Kai* on p 363. The Bourton Consultancy Group for Figures 3.16 and 3.17. Gerry Johnson and Kevin Scholes for Table 4.7. The Chartered Institute of Purchasing and Supply for permission to use questions and some case studies set at previous examinations and also for the example of the Purchasing and Supply Process Model shown in Figure 4.12 and for Table 15.6. The Institute has also kindly allowed Dr Lysons to use CIPS copyright material from his publications *Managing Human Resources in Purchasing and Supply* and *How to Write Specifications*. Jonathan Lyles for Figure 5.11. The Epicor Software Corporation for Figure 6.2 and Active Secretariat for Figure 6.5. The Ford Motor Co. Ltd for Figures 7.14 and 7.15 and Company Policy Publications for Figure 9.11. M. Bensaou and the *Sloan Management Review* for Figure 9.14. Gerald Morris and the British Electro-technical and Allied Manufacturing Association provided Example 10.5. The Institute of Logistics and Transport for Figures 13.6, 13.7, 13.8 and 13.9. Purcon Consultants provided Figures 15.2 and 15.3.

In some instances we have been unable to trace the owners of copyright material, and we would appreciate any information that would enable us to do so.

To Jeffrey Kenneth Lysons, Beth and Wesley Jones and Richard, Gillian and Jonathan Lysons.

To Anne, Mark and Eric Gillingham.

Plan of the book

Part One	Introduction and strategy				
Chapter 1 What is purchasing?	Chapter 2 Purchasing and information technology	Chapter 3 Logistics and supply chains	Chapter 4 Purchasing and supply chain strategy	Chapter 5 Supply organisations and structures	Chapter 6 Purchasing procedures

Part Two	Strategy, tactics and operations (1): purchasing factors		
Chapter 7 Specifying and managing quality	Chapter 8 Matching supply with demand	Chapter 9 Sourcing and supplier information	Chapter 10 Buying at the right price

Part Three	Strategy, tactics and operations (2): buying situations	
Chapter 11 Contrasting approaches to supply	Chapter 12 Global sourcing	

Part Four	Strategy, tactics and operations (3): logistics	
Chapter 13 Storing supplies	Chapter 14 Transporting goods	

Part Five	Strategy, tactics and operations (4): support tools, supplier relationships and purchasing performance		
Chapter 15 Human resources in the supply chain	Chapter 16 Negotiation	Chapter 17 Support tools	Chapter 18 Purchasing research, performance and ethics

Introduction and strategy

What is purchasing?

After reading this chapter you should be able to:

- Discuss several perspectives from which the study of purchasing may be approached.
- Distinguish between such terms as 'purchasing', 'organisational buying', 'procurement', 'supplier management' and 'external resource management'.
- Offer a tentative definition of purchasing.
- Describe some models of purchasing evolution.
- Identify some drivers that are influencing changes in purchasing philosophies, processes and procedures.
- Indicate some changing aspects of traditional purchasing.
- State some characteristics of 'world-class purchasing'.
- Discuss some factors affecting internal and external perceptions of the status of purchasing.

1.1 Perspectives on purchasing

The study of purchasing can be approached from several perspectives. Such perspectives include those of function, process, link in the supplier or value chain, discipline and profession.

1.1.1 Purchasing as a function

In management studies, a 'function' is often defined as a unit or department in which people use specialised skills, knowledge and resources to perform specialised tasks. A function is also that which a resource is designed to do, e.g. the function of a pen is to write. A distinction can therefore be made between the purchasing *function* and the purchasing *department*. The former is to procure supplies.

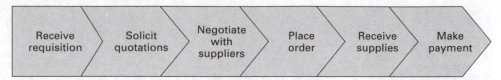

Figure 1.1 The purchasing process chain

The latter is the organisation unit responsible for carrying out the function. In many organisations, purchasing is still part of a segmented, departmentalised structure in which the procurement of supplies is a separate activity in the sequence of production operations. The challenge of global competition has, however, led many organisations to replace segmented by integrated structures in which purchasing is part of a larger grouping such as materials or logistics management. Such structures emphasise the importance of cross-functional decision making.

1.1.2 Purchasing as a process

A *process* is a set of subprocesses or stages directed to achieving an output. The various tasks or stages can be depicted by a process chain. Thus, as Figure 1.1, purchasing can be depicted as a sequential chain of events leading to the acquisition of supplies.

The link in the purchasing process chain is information. Thus, each subprocess in the chain is responsible for capturing or otherwise processing information that enables us to answer the questions 'what are we required to purchase?' and 'where and how can the required supplies be obtained?' A process chain relationship can therefore be also considered as a message chain relationship. Previously, messages both internal (e.g. requisitions) and external (e.g. orders and payments) were transmitted on paper documents through the post. As shown later, electronic transmission has revolutionised the cost and speed of purchasing processes.

1.1.3 Purchasing as a supply or value chain

Purchasing, along with such activities as production, warehousing and transportation, is one of the links in the sequence of processes by which designs and resources are converted into finished goods that satisfy the needs of customers.

1.1.4 Purchasing as a discipline

A discipline is a department of knowledge. The academic content of purchasing lacks the clearly defined focus associated with other fields of study such as mathematics, economics and law and draws heavily on other subjects to build its knowledge base. Such subjects include accounting, economics, ethics, information technology, law, management accounting, operational research, marketing, management and psychology. Purchasing as a sub-area of study often included in wider courses including logistics management, operations management and marketing.

1.1.5   Purchasing as a profession

This aspect is discussed later in the chapter.

1.2   Definitions

Purchasing as an occupation involves a variety of roles and activities differing from one organisation to another and from one level to another within the same organisation. The contingency approach that it is impossible to specify a single way of managing that works best in all situations is particularly relevant to purchasing. All purchasing has common elements including sourcing, suppliers, negotiating with them and evaluating their performance. There are, however, also considerable situational diversities such as strategic importance, amount of spend, contribution to profitability, supplier relationships and the responsibilities and recognition given to those employed in purchasing. Because of such diversities, many organisations are changing the designations of departments and the job titles of people formerly known as purchasing. The diversity of such factors means that any definition of purchasing is open to criticism. Not surprisingly there have been numerous definitions of purchasing and suggested alternative terms. Apart from integrated designations such as materials and logistics management, some definitions are considered below.

1.2.1   The classic definition of purchasing

This defines purchasing from the standpoint of objectives namely:

> **To obtain materials of the right quality in the right quantity from the right source, delivered to the right place at the right price.**

- The term 'right' is situational: each organisation will define 'right' differently.
- What is 'right' will change as the overall purchasing context and environment changes.
- The specified 'rights' must be consistent with corporate goals and objectives from which functional goals and objectives are derived.
- In practice some rights are irreconcilable, e.g. it may be possible to obtain the right quality but not at the right price – 'the best suppliers are often the busiest but also the dearest'.

1.2.2   Purchasing as procurement

Procurement is a wider term than purchasing which implies acquisition of goods or services in return for a monetary or equivalent payment. Procurement, however, is the process of obtaining goods or services in any way including borrowing, leasing and even force or pillage. Since procurement is strictly a more accurate term it is unsurprising that the word procurement is often supplanting 'purchasing' in job titles such as 'procurement manager', 'procurement agents' and 'head of procurement'.

Table 1.1 A typology of organisational buyers

Types of organisation	Characteristics	Examples
Industrial/producer organisations	Purchase of goods and services for some tangible production and commercially significant purpose	Manufacturers: primary (extractive) producers – agriculture, forestry, fishing, horticulture, mining
Intermediate organisations	Purchase of goods and services for resale or for facilitating the resale of other goods in the industrial or ultimate consumer markets	Distributors, dealers, wholesalers, retailers, banks, hotels and service traders
Government and public sector organisations	Purchase of goods and services for resale or use by organisations providing a service, often tangible, and not always commercially significant at national, regional and local levels	Central and local government, public utilities
Institutions	Purchase of goods and services for institutions that buy independently on their own behalf	Schools, colleges, hospitals, voluntary organisations

1.2.3 Purchasing as organisational buying

Organisational buyers have been defined by Marrian[1] as:

> **Those buyers of goods and services for the specific purpose of industrial or agricultural production or for use in the operation or conduct of a plant, business, institution, profession or service.**

Organisational buyers are, therefore, those who buy on behalf of an organisation rather than for individual or family use or consumption. Organisational buyers can, as shown in Table 1.1, be considered as belonging to one of four buying groups each of which can be further subdivided.

Some of the categories in Table 1.1 may overlap. Thus in the National Health Service some supplies may be bought centrally by government agencies, regionally by local health authorities and locally by hospitals themselves.

1.2.4 Purchasing as supplier management

Supplier management may be defined as:

> **That aspect of purchasing or procurement concerned with rationalising the supplier base and selecting, coordinating, appraising the performance of and developing the potential of suppliers.**

Supplier management is a more strategic and cross-functional activity than purchasing, which is transactionally and commercially biased. The relationship between procurement, purchasing and supplier management is shown in Figure 1.2.

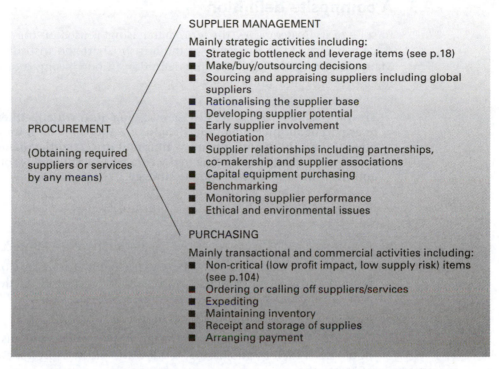

Figure 1.2　The relationship between procurement, supplier management and purchasing

1.2.5　Purchasing as external resource management

This is the view of Lamming:[2]

> The new strategic function will probably not be called purchasing – that is much too limited a word. The connotations of purse strings and spending money have no relevance to the setting up and management of strategic inter-firm relationships. This task is concerned with ensuring the correct external resources are in place to complement the internal resources. Perhaps 'external resource managers' is a term that future purchasing managers will adopt.

The perspective of external resource management is also adopted by Van Weele[3] who defines purchasing as:

> Obtaining from external sources all goods and services which are necessary for running, maintaining and managing the company's primary and support activities at the most favourable conditions.

Against these definitions it may be objected that 'external resources' include people the recruitment and management of whom, as individuals is primarily a human resources management responsibility. Services provided by people collectively as in outsourcing or the procurement of facilities may, of course, fall within the purchasing remit. As a staff manager the purchasing executive will also be responsible for the management of internal resources.

1.2.6 A composite definition

In spite of its inadequacies, the term 'purchasing' is used on the title of this book since it is retained in the name of the British Chartered Institute of Purchasing Management (CIPS). The following definition of purchasing is offered as including aspects of the definitions given above:

> **The process undertaken by the organisational unit which, either as a function or as part of an integrated supply chain, is responsible both for procuring supplies of the right quality, quantity, time and price and the management of the suppliers, thereby contributing to the competitive advantages of the enterprise and the achievement of corporate strategy.**

The significant words or terms in this definition are:

- *Processes* – the chain or sequence of activities involved in procuring supplies.
- *Organisational unit* – this may be a department, team, cost or profit centre responsible for all purchasing activities under the control of a designated manager. An alternative term might be 'responsibility centre'.
- *Function* – a discrete organisational unit.
- *Integrated supply chain* – refers to the absorption of formerly discrete organisational units such as purchasing, production and sales into a continuous flow of interaction.
- *Procurement* – as stated above, this is the process of obtaining goods or services by any means.
- *Quality, quantity, time and price* – these concepts are discussed in appropriate chapters of this book.
- *The management of suppliers* – this is defined above and, as stated, is sometimes regarded as a support activity distinct from the actual procurement of supplies.
- *Competitive advantage* – is a special edge that enables an organisation to deal with market and environmental forces better than its competitors. Purchasing power and well-developed supplier relationships are two ways in which an organisation may obtain a competitive advantage over its competitors.
- *Corporate strategy* – the aims and objectives of an enterprise together with the means by which theses are to be achieved. Functional strategies such as purchasing strategy should be related to corporate strategy.

1.3 The evolution of purchasing

Purchasing represents a stage in evolution of civilised human relationships since it enables a desired object to be obtained by trading rather than conquest, plunder or confiscation. It is a very ancient activity. A cuneiform clay tablet excavated at El-Rash Shamra in Egypt dated about 2800 BC carries an inscription which, roughly

Table 1.2 The evolution of purchasing

Stage	Characteristics
Stage 1 Product-centred purchasing	Product focused – concerned with the five 'rights' which concentrate exclusively upon the purchasing of tangible products and outcome dimensions through which this product can be described and mentioned
Stage 2 Process-centred purchasing	Product focused – moves beyond a concern with outcomes and begins to measure the process through which the outcome is delivered
Stage 3 Relational purchasing	Process and relationally focused – expanded to include purchaser–supplier relationships and how these might be used to manage the quality and nature of the supplier
Stage 4 Performance-centred purchasing	Focused on best product management methods. Employs an integrated methodology to manage relationships, processes and outcomes. Jointly resources this methodology with suppliers

translated, reads: 'HST to deliver 50 jars of fragrant smooth oil each fifteen days after [a starting date] and during the reign of AS. In return he will be paid 600 small weight in grain. This order will continue indefinitely until the purchaser or his son removes his consent'.

Despite its long history, however, it was only in the latter half of the twentieth century that the importance of efficient purchasing was widely recognised. It was even later when its strategic aim as opposed to operational significance was acknowledged with an emphasis on purchasing processes, relationships and performance rather than on products. Stannack and Jones[4] have identified four stages of purchasing evolution, as shown in Table 1.2.

An alternative model of purchasing evolution is provided by Reck and Long[5] who identify four stages of development that purchasing must pass through to become a competitive weapon in the battle for markets (see Table 1.3).

Reck and Long also identify the effect at each of the four stages of 12 non-operational development variables as shown in Table 1.4.

Other attempts to trace the evolution of purchasing are those of Syson[6] and Morris and Calantone[7] who each identify three stages. Syson refers to 'the changing focus of purchasing as it evolves from a purely clerical routine activity to a commercial stage in which the emphasis is on cost savings and finally a proactive strategic function concerned with materials or logistics management'. Morris and Calantone differentiate between (i) clerical, (ii) 'asset management' and profitability, and (iii) 'core-strategic' function stages.

Jones,[8] however, criticises the above approaches on two grounds. Firstly, they are non-operational and merely indicate the stage of development of purchasing activity the criteria for which may differ from one procurement organisation to another. Secondly, the models have a restricted number of development measurement variables. In an attempt to remedy those deficiencies Jones suggests a five-stage development model using 18 measurement criteria. The five stages of purchasing development measured on a scale of 1 to 5 are shown in Table 1.5.

Table 1.3   Strategic stages of the development of a purchasing function

Stage	Definition and characteristics	
Stage 1 Passive	Definition:	Purchasing function has no strategic direction and primarily reacts to the requests of other functions
	Characteristics:	■ High proportion of time on quick-fix routine operations ■ Functional and individual communications due to purchasing's low visibility ■ Supplier selection based on price and availability
Stage 2 Independent	Definition:	Purchasing function adopts the latest purchasing techniques and processes, but its strategic direction is independent of the firm's competitive strategy
	Characteristics:	■ Performance based primarily on cost reduction and efficiency disciplines ■ Coordination links are established between purchasing and technical disciplines ■ Top management recognises the importance of professional development ■ Top management recognises the opportunities in purchasing for contribution to profitability
Stage 3 Supportive	Definition:	The purchasing function supports the firm's competitive strategy by adopting purchasing techniques and products, which strengthen the firm's competitive position
	Characteristics:	■ Purchasers are included in sales proposal teams ■ Suppliers are considered a resource with emphasis on experience, motivation and attitude ■ Markets, products and suppliers are continuously monitored and analysed
Stage 4 Integrative	Definition:	Purchasing's strategy is fully integrated into the firm's competitive strategy and constitutes part of an integrated effort among functional peers to formulate and implement a strategic plan
	Characteristics:	■ Cross-functional training of purchasing professionals-executives is made available ■ Permanent lines of communication are established among other functional areas ■ Professional development focuses on strategic elements of the competitive strategy ■ Purchasing performance is measured in terms of contribution to the firm's success

Source: adapted from Reck, R.F. and Long, B., 'Purchasing a competitive weapon', *Journal of Purchasing and Materials Management*, vol.24, No.3 (1998), pp.2–8

The purchasing profile shown in Figure 1.3 enables the stage of development reached by a particular organisation to be identified and assessed on a scale of 1 to 5. The profile also indicates areas where further development is required as measured by the 18 criteria shown. Appropriate strategies to meet identified shortcomings can then be devised.

1.4   Purchasing and change

At least three drivers have influenced and are influencing changes in purchasing, philosophies, processes and procedures. They are looked at next.

Table 1.4 Stage characteristics – Reck and Long Development Model

Characteristics (variable)	Passive	Independent	Supportive	Integrative
Nature of long-range planning	None	Commodity or procedural	Supportive of strategy	Integral part of strategy
Impetus for change	Management demands	Competitive parity	Competitive strategy	Integrative management
Career advancement	Limited	Possible	Probable	Unlimited
Basis of evaluation	Complaints	Cost reduction and supplier performance	Competitive objectives	Strategic contribution
Organisational visibility	Low	Limited	Variable	High
Computer systems focus	Repetitive	Techniques	Specific	Needs of system
Sources of new ideas	Trial and error	Current purchasing practices	Competitive strategy	Interfunctional information exchange
Basis of resource availability	Limited	Arbitrary/affordable	Objectives	Strategic requirements
Basis of supplier evaluation	Price and easy availability	Least total cost	Competitive objectives	Strategic contributions
Attitude towards suppliers	Adversarial	Variable	Company resource	Mutual interdependence
Professional development focus	Deemed unnecessary	Current new practices	Elements of strategy	Cross-functional understanding
Overall characteristics	Clerical function	Functional efficiency	Strategic facilitator	Strategic contributor

Table 1.5 Purchasing development stages and performance capabilities

Stage of development	Capabilities	Estimated organisational contribution
Stage 1 Infant	Fragmented purchasing	None or low
Stage 2 Awakening	Realisation of savings potential	Clerical efficiency. Small savings through consolidation 2–5%
Stage 3 Developing	Control and development of purchasing price/negotiation capabilities	Cost reduction 5–10%
Stage 4 Mature	80/20 recognised Specialist buyers Cost reductions Commencement of supplier base management	Cost reduction 10–20% Acquisition costs 1–10%
Stage 5 Advanced	Devolution of purchasing Strong central control Supply chain management	Cost reduction 25% Cost of ownership Acquisition cost and supply chain management 30%+ Leverage buying Global sourcing Understanding and practice of acquisition cost and cost of ownership

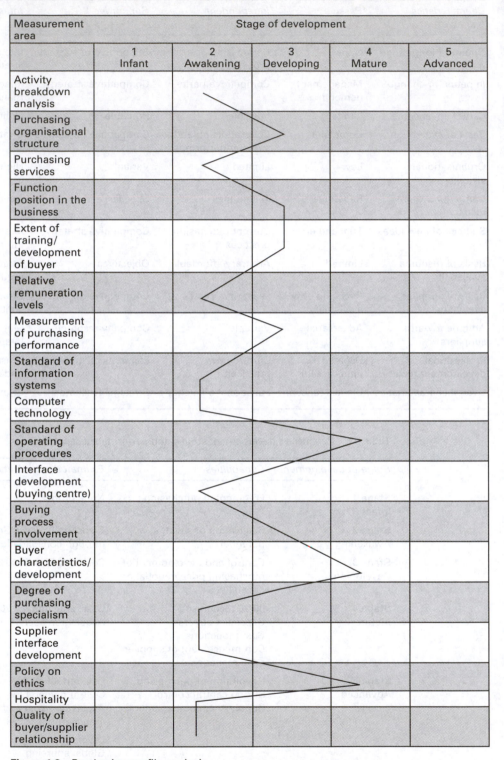

Measurement area	Stage of development				
	1 Infant	2 Awakening	3 Developing	4 Mature	5 Advanced
Activity breakdown analysis					
Purchasing organisational structure					
Purchasing services					
Function position in the business					
Extent of training/ development of buyer					
Relative remuneration levels					
Measurement of purchasing performance					
Standard of information systems					
Computer technology					
Standard of operating procedures					
Interface development (buying centre)					
Buying process involvement					
Buyer characteristics/ development					
Degree of purchasing specialism					
Supplier interface development					
Policy on ethics					
Hospitality					
Quality of buyer/supplier relationship					

Figure 1.3 Purchasing profile analysis

1.4.1 Globalisation

There are numerous definitions of globalisation and considerable controversy regarding its real significance and the extent to which it is really a new concept. A useful definition of globalisation is:[9]

The increasing interdependence across national and geographical boundaries of people, trade and commerce driven in large part by information technology and technology generally.

An even more concise definition is:[10]

The integration of the world's economies.

From the standpoint of this book an important aspect of globalisation is global sourcing which may be defined as:

A process of manufacturing and/or purchasing of components in various parts of the world and then assembling them into a final product: an international division of labour in which activities are performed in countries where they can be done well at the lowest level.

Christopher[11] provides a 'classic' example of global sourcing by referring to the Singer Sewing Machine Company:

It buys sewing machine shells from a subcontractor in the United States, the motors from Brazil, the drive shafts from Italy and assembles the finished machine in Taiwan. It then markets the finished machines in most countries of the world.

Global sourcing is a wider term than 'import purchasing' or 'international procurement' since it involves strategic product life cycle decisions relating to long-term supplier relationships based on such factors as purchase price and lead time reliability, supplier flexibility and political stability. Global purchasing is considered further in Chapter 12.

1.4.2 Information technology

As stated in the above definition, globalisation is driven in large part by information technology (IT). IT comprising computers and telecommunications, especially the internet, has already had a significant effect on purchasing processes and procedures. By sharing information and processing electronic transactions over the internet, suppliers are being converted into e-suppliers. Large undertakings such as Ford have indicated that eventually all their suppliers will be e-suppliers. IT and its applications to purchasing and supply management (PSM) are dealt with in Chapter 2.

1.4.3 Changing production and management philosophies

Green[12] has pointed out that 'as global competition heats up the need to identify and implement strategies that yield competitive advantage increases'. Such

Table 1.6 Philosophy time line

Philosophy	Time line	Advantage	Disadvantage
EOQ	1915	Minimisation of inventory cost for independent demand	Not suited for independent demand
MRP	1965	Minimisation of inventory costs for dependent demand	Required precise information Very difficult to implement
MRP II	1970	Integrated financial and marketing planning with production planning	Required extensive hardware, software and computer expertise
JIT	1975	Elimination of waste by reducing inventory levels and improving process	Primarily cost reduction strategy and within factory focus Heavy dependence on timely supplier deliveries
TQM	1980	Focus on quality and continuous improvement of process	Within factory focus lack of focus on process improvement
TOC	1985	Focus on constraints to improve throughput	Limited focus within the factory on constraints
TBC	1990	Efforts to shorten supply chain Focus on time as competitive advantage variable	Limit to how much chain can be shortened Competitors rapidly adopt similar strategy
SCM	1995	Expansion of focus to include suppliers and customers	

EOQ	economic order quantity
MRP	materials requirement planning
MRP II	manufacturing resource planning
JIT	just-in-time
TQM	total quality management
TOC	theory of constraints
TBC	time-based competition
SCM	supply chain management

competitive advantage may be sought through inventory models such as economic order quantity and through comprehensive planning approaches exemplified by just-in-time, total quality management, theory of constraints, time-based competition and supply chain management. Green states these models and philosophies should not be viewed as mutually exclusive but as part of the evolution of production and operations management, philosophy and practice and provides the evolutionary conspectus shown in Table 1.6.

Green anticipates that the next development will be virtual management comprising a manufacturing core that excels at production while seamlessly integrating external organisations such as suppliers.

The above conspectus shows how production philosophies have developed through focuses on inventory, waste, quality, throughput, agility and flexibility, time and supply chain relationships. All of these have had consequential changes in PSM, some of which are shown in Table 1.7.

In summary, the changes indicated above are from reactive to proactive and from tactical to strategic purchasing. Reactive purchasing is characterised by the

Table 1.7   Changing aspects of PSM

Aspect	Traditional	Changing
Structure	Vertical, hierarchical, functionally oriented Purchasing regarded as a separate function	Horizontal, flatter, involving self-managed teams and cross-managed relationships Purchasing regarded as part of an integrated supply chain
Procedures	Paper-based Slow, high cost All procurement routed through purchasing	Based on IT applications Rapid, low cost Increased emphasis on centre-led, user procurement
Purchase considerations	Price only Buy what we cannot make	Total cost of acquisition and use Subcontract or outsource non-core business
Sourcing	Multisourcing Local or national Little use of purchasing consortia	Reducing supplier base Global Increasing use of purchasing consortia
Supplier relationships	Short-term Adversarial and confrontational Win–lose negotiations Retention of information	Long-term Partnerships and collaborative Win–win negotiations Sharing of information
Quality and specification	Purchaser specifications of design and quality Inspection of goods on receipt	Supplier specifications of design and quality Supplier certification
Inventory and lead times	High to provide security	Low through JIT requirements thus obviating waste through such causes as holding costs, obsolescence etc.
Purchasing performance	Assessed mainly on price differences and savings	Assessed mainly on its value-added activities as part of the supply chain

failure to react appropriately to environmental changes or to develop strategies, plans and policies to exploit new opportunities. Tactical purchasing is characterised by short-term, adaptive, action–interaction approaches directed at limited goals. Conversely, strategic purchasing provides a long-term continuing basis for directing required adaptations towards the achievement of corporate ends. Strategic purchasing is considered in Chapter 3.

1.5   Purchasing in the future

Research in the USA[13] indicates that within the decade commencing 2000 future trends relating to PSM will include:

- An increase in the strategic importance of PSM. Key activities will include supplier evaluation, selection and management.
- Tactical purchasing activities such as ordering and expediting will increasingly be automated and selected low value, non-critical standard commodity purchases are likely to be outsourced to full-service providers.

- Most non-tactical items will be bought under master contracts enabling transactions such as releasing, receiving and accounting to be undertaken by users who will select their requirements from online databases maintained by suppliers and consortiums.

- The internet/World Wide Web will be the main vehicle for electronic purchasing which will be increasingly used for purchase transactions and will also be the key to globalisation.

- While the core procurement organisation will remain, leading organisations will establish strategic purchasing competency centres with highly trained, cross-functional personnel responsible for achieving competitive advantage through their choice of supply chain partners, influencing design, sourcing, production, and integrating the innovations and contributions of suppliers.

- Strategic alliances with suppliers will increase.

- Organisations in the supply chain will increasingly share resources including intellectual properties information, people and other assets.

- Increased coordination of suppliers through Supplier Associations modelled on the Kyoryoku Kai pattern discussed in Chapter 9.

- Global supplier development will be critical to global penetration.

- There will be an increasing emphasis on win–win negotiation.

- Dominant companies in the supply chain will influence the sourcing decision of first-, second- and third-tier suppliers.

- While price paid will be an important measure of purchasing performance this will be considered as part of the overall contribution of PSM to profit.

- Environmental factors will become increasingly important to purchasing considerations.

- The absolute number of purchasing jobs will decrease especially in respect of staff employed on tactical purchasing.

- Personnel employed in PSM will require a higher level of training, including leadership and influence skills.

1.6 World class purchasing

The term 'world class' was popularised by the book *World Class Manufacturing* by Schonberger[14] published in 1986. Schonberger defined world class manufacturing as analogous to the Olympic motto 'citius, altius, fortius' (translated as faster, higher, stronger). The world class manufacturing equivalent is continual and rapid improvement.

Twelve characteristics of world class supplier management were identified by the USA Centre for Advanced Purchasing Studies,[15] namely:

- *Commitment to total quality management.*
- *Commitment to just-in-time.*
- *Commitment to total cycle time reduction.*

- *Long-range strategic plans* that are multidimensional, fully integrated with the overall corporate plan including the organisation's supply strategy and related to customer needs.

- *Supplier relationships* including networks, partnerships and alliances. Relationships include such matters as supply base rationalisation and the segmentation of suppliers as 'strategic', 'preferred' and 'arm's length'. Relationships with strategic suppliers include a high level of trust, shared risks and rewards, sharing of data and supplier involvement in product improvement.

- *Strategic cost management* – this involves a total life acquisition approach to evaluating bids and the use of IT to support a paperless and seamless purchasing process across the whole supply chain.

- *Performance measurements* including regular benchmarking with and across industries. Performance measures are developed in consultation with customers, other organisational units and suppliers.

- *Training and professional development* including identification of required skills for higher-level purchasing posts and the maintenance of employee skills inventories.

- *Service excellence* – purchasing is proactive, anticipates customer needs and demonstrated flexibility.

- *Corporate social responsibility* especially in respect of ethical, environmental and safety issues and support of local suppliers.

- *Learning* – world class purchasing recognises that learning and education are critical factors in continuous improvement.

- *Management and leadership* – although listed last this is probably the most important factor. Purchasing executives earn and enjoy top management support, and recognise the importance of transformational change. Such leaders have vision, foster open communications, treat others with respect and develop the potential of both their staffs and suppliers.

Ultimately, world class purchasing depends on obtaining world class suppliers. World class suppliers will tend to mirror the characteristics of world class purchasing listed above. Research reported by Minahan[16] indicates that while to be considered 'world class' suppliers must excel in such areas as competitive price, quality and lead times, these attributes are 'just the price of entry to get into the game'. The research identified the following three characteristics of world class suppliers:

- *Continuous improvement.* World class suppliers have a formal and proven commitment to achieve year-on-year product and process improvements.

- *Technology and innovation.* World class suppliers are technology leaders in their respective industries, providing customers with next-generation technologies and a 'leg-up' on their competition.

- *Adaptability.* World class suppliers are willing to invest in new equipment, develop new technologies and rework their businesses to better support the strategies of their customers.

World class supplier management is therefore concerned with:

■ searching for suppliers with the above characteristics or the potential to achieve them;

■ providing such suppliers with specifications of the purchaser's expectations relating to products and services and agreeing how supplier performance will be measured against expectations;

■ recognised outstanding supplier performance by such means as the award of long-term contracts and sharing the benefits of collaborative innovation or performance that enhance the purchaser's competitiveness.

Strategic purchasing partnerships are partnerships of equals in which suppliers are regarded as a source of competitive edge responsible for a major share of product costs. As Saunders[17] rightly observes:

> **For a firm to reach world-class standards in serving its own customers, it is vital to achieve world-class standards in controlling its network of suppliers.**

1.7 The status of purchasing and supply management

The status of PSM can be considered from both internal and external aspects. The former is the value placed on PSM within a particular organisation; the latter, with the standing accorded to the occupation by the outside world.

1.7.1 Internal

Within a particular organisation the status of PSM is influenced by (i) leverage, (ii) focus and (iii) professionalism.

Leverage

Leverage in the present context is the power of purchasing to enhance profitability.

The greatest scope for saving lies in the areas of greatest expenditure. For most organisations the areas of greatest expenditure are purchasing and payments to personnel. As a result of technology, labour costs in manufacturing enterprises are tending to reduce substantially. Conversely, manufacturing organisations may find it cheaper to outsource assemblies and components from specialised suppliers that were formerly made in-house. These tendencies are shown by Figures 1.4 and 1.5 which relate to the expenditures of a UK manufacturing company for the years 1979 and 2000 respectively.

The greatest scope for savings lies in the area of bought-out items, which in 2000 had superseded labour as the area of greatest expenditure. It follows therefore that:

■ Assuming other variables remain constant, every pound saved on purchasing is a pound of profit.

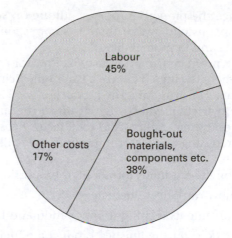

Figure 1.4 Costs of a manufacturing company in 1979

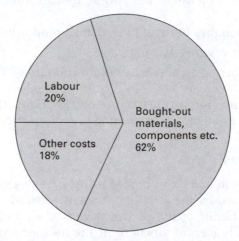

Figure 1.5 Costs of the same manufacturing company in 2000

- For many reasons, e.g. increased defects or poorer deliveries, a pound off the purchase price does not necessarily represent a pound of profit.
- When purchases form a high proportion of total costs a modest saving on bought-out items will result in a similar contribution to profits as a substantial increase in sales. As shown below, a 4 per cent reduction in purchase cost makes the same contribution to profits as a 20 per cent expansion of turnover.

		SALES	
Then	Now	Increase	Extra profit
£	£	£	£
100,000	120,000	20	2,000
			(assuming 10% on turnover)
		PURCHASING	
50,000	48,000	−4	2,000
		(i.e. a saving)	

Since the proportion of expenditure on supplies varies widely between organisations, it follows that there is a corresponding variance in the contribution of purchasing to profitability.

The profit contribution may be low, for example, in the pharmaceutical industry where the ingredients of a patent medicine can be insignificant compared with the costs of marketing the product.

Conversely it will be significant in the motor vehicle industry where the proportion of material costs to total factory costs will be high.

Purchasing as a factor in profitability is likely to be critical where:

■ bought-out items form a high proportion of total expenditure;
■ short-run prices fluctuate;
■ judgements relating to innovation and fashion are involved;
■ markets for the finished product are highly competitive.

Purchasing will be less critical, though still important, where:

■ bought-out items form a small proportion of total expenditure;
■ prices are relatively stable;
■ there is an absence of innovation in operations.

Within non-manufacturing organisations, the savings resulting from value-for-money efficiency purchasing may allow increased expenditure in other areas.

Focus

The internal status of PSM will also be closely related to the stage of development reached by the activity in the enterprise. Thus, using the Reck and Long model, purchasing at the passive stage is likely to be viewed by top management as a mainly clerical function. At the independent and supportive stages, purchasing will be regarded as a significant commercial activity. Only at the integrative stage is PSM recognised as making a strategic contribution.

Syson[18] states that the position of purchasing within a particular organisation depends on whether the focus of the function is transactional, commercial or strategic. Each of these foci is appropriate to sustaining commercial advantage for different types of enterprise: 'in terms of effectiveness, the key question is whether the correct focus exists. In terms of efficiency, how well are the key task discharged?' Over time, the focus of purchasing may, as shown in Figures 1.6 and 1.7, change from transactional to a procedure perspective. The more purchasing becomes involved in commercial and strategic areas the greater will be its effectiveness and consequent standing within the organisation.

In Figures 1.6 and 1.7 it will be noticed that as PSM moves from a transactional to a proactivity focus; performance measures also change from efficiency to effectiveness.

Efficiency is a measure of how well or productively resources are used to achieve a goal. *Effectiveness* is a measure of the appropriateness of the goals the organisation is pursuing and of the degree to which those goals are achieved.

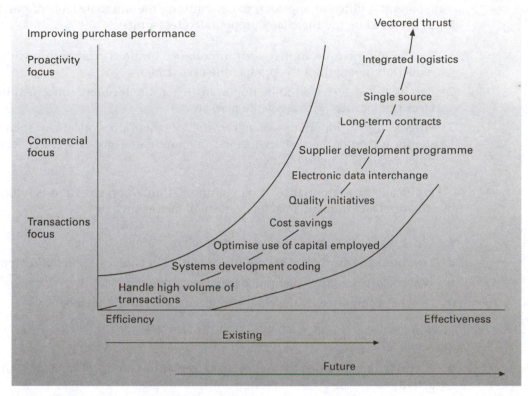

Figure 1.6 Positioning graph: strategies/policies

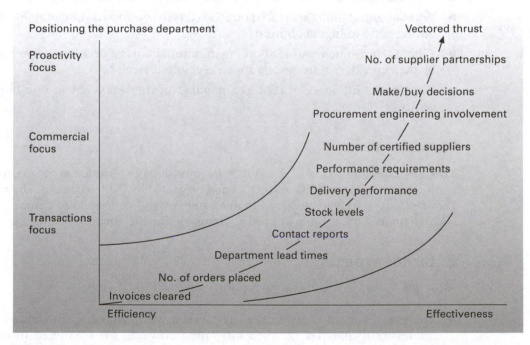

Figure 1.7 Positioning graph: measures of performance

A somewhat different approach to determining the internal status of purchasing is provided by the three laws propounded by Farmer:[19]

1 Purchasing increases in perceived importance in direct relationship with the reduction in length of the product life cycle times.
2 Purchasing is perceived to be important when the business concerned interfaces significantly with a volatile market.
3 Purchasing is important whenever the organisation concerned spends a significant proportion of its income on purchasing goods and services, in order to allow it to do business.

Empirically, the importance of purchasing within an organisation is indicated by structural and influential factors. *Structural* factors include:

- What is the job title of the executive in charge of purchasing?
- To whom and at what level does the executive in charge of purchasing report?
- What salary does the chief purchasing executive receive?
- Of what committees is the chief purchasing executive a member?

Influential factors include:

- Is purchasing regarded by the top management as an operational or strategic activity?
- What is the total annual spend for which PSM is responsible?
- How crucial is effective PSM to the competitiveness of the enterprise?
- What financial limits are placed on PSM staff to commit the undertaking without recourse to higher authority?
- What is the influence of PSM on organisational buying decisions as perceived by persons external to the enterprise, e.g. salespersons?
- What is the influence of PSM as a member of the supply chain or a buying centre?

Professionalism

This is discussed in section 1.7.2. It may be provisionally regarded as the expertise, commitment, responsibility and ethics demonstrated by PSM personnel. The more PSM staff are perceived both by top management and colleagues to demonstrate such attributes, the greater will be the status ascribed to them.

1.7.2 External aspects

Attempts to raise the external perception of purchasing include:

- The establishment of institutions concerned with promoting the concept of 'professional' purchasing. Such institutions include the Chartered Institute of Purchasing and Supply (CIPS) in Great Britain and the Institute of Supply

Management in the USA. In 2000, over 40 national purchasing associations were affiliated to the International Federation of Purchasing and Materials Management.

- The development of undergraduate and postgraduate courses with a purchasing content.
- The establishment of chairs in purchasing or logistics at some universities.
- Research into PSM and related fields.
- The publication of textbooks and specialist journals relating to purchasing. Journals include: *Supply Management (UK)*, *European Purchasing Management* and the *International Journal of Purchasing and Supply Management*. In the logistics field, publications include *Logistics Focus* and the *International Journal of Logistics*.
- Published codes of ethics (see Appendices 1 and 2).

Notwithstanding the enhanced status of purchasing in Britain by the granting in 1992 of a Royal Charter to the Institute of Purchasing and Supply, the occupation has to surmount difficulties in the quest for professional status.

Millerson[20] has defined a 'profession' as:

A type of higher-grade non-manual occupation with both subjectively and objectively recognised occupational status, possessing a well-defined area of study or concern and providing a definite service after advanced training and education.

Millerson lists the essential features of a profession as follows:

- A skill based on theoretical knowledge.
- A skill requiring training and education.
- The denomination of competence by professional by passing a test.
- Maintenance of integrity by adherence to a code of conduct.
- Service provided for the public good.
- The profession is organised.

The difficulties encountered by purchasing in meeting such criteria are:

- No regulation of entry – it is not necessary to have a professional qualification in purchasing to enter the occupation.
- Purchasing practitioners are at all levels of evolution. Persons with only an operational or transactional knowledge of purchasing might experience difficulty in moving to strategic purchasing.
- Limited powers to enforce ethical standards.

The general problem, however, is what constitutes the academic content. Purchasing is a hybrid subject, which draws heavily on other disciplines to build its knowledge base. Such disciplines include accounting, economics, ethics, IT, marketing, management and psychology.

Even topics such as negotiation can be enhanced by the study of negotiation in other fields such as politics or industrial relations. This is not necessarily a weakness since, as Lamming stated, strategic purchasing requires a broad rather than a narrow knowledge base. This consideration led Lamming[21] to conclude:

> The traditional Purchasing Officer is not equipped to manage strategic relationships with collaborators. Such responsibilities can hardly be placed upon the shoulders of those who left school and assume it will last them for the rest of their lives . . . The likelihood is that unless new business skills are developed in these people, they are not going to be able to handle the requirements of the organisation of the future and there will be a steady supply of young MBA graduates with engineering degrees, who would never call themselves purchasing people, ready to move in and run these relationships.

Case study

Hawthorne Engineering is a private limited company mainly engaged in the continuous production and assembly of domestic products. The annual turnover is £200,000,000. The largest area of expenditure is raw materials and components where the annual spend is approximately £70,000,000. The managing director, Bill Maylor, considers that profit margins are too small and has asked you to suggest how profitability might be increased. Bill suggests that this might be done by appointing additional sales staff and by an advertising campaign which would, hopefully, increase turnover and thereby reduce overhead costs per item.

You find that purchasing is little more than a post-office function. Specifications are received from the design or user departments and sent either to suppliers designated by the directors or to the supplier providing the cheapest quotation. The company does, in fact, deal with many suppliers and issues many orders for low-cost items. All purchasing is done by manual means. None of the buying staff has had any specific purchasing training and the head of the purchasing department, who will shortly be retiring, has held the post for over 30 years. Bill informs you that the intention is that he will be succeeded by his present deputy.

You suggest to Bill that profitability might be enhanced by more efficient purchasing. Bill is unimpressed. His retort is: 'Anyone can buy. Buying is only a matter of obtaining three quotations and accepting the cheapest offer. In any event, only the design staff have the technical knowledge to specify what is required, and often, the suppliers from whom it should be bought.'

Questions

1 What general reasons would you advance to convince Bill that efficient purchasing might significantly enhance profitability?
2 What specific recommendations would you make regarding how the efficiency and effectiveness of purchasing at Hawthorne Engineering might be improved?

? Discussion questions

1.1 In certain organisations the functional approach to purchasing has decided advantages. Consider the extent to which this statement is true.

1.2 Prepare a flowchart showing the processes involved in procuring supplies in your organisation. Compare your flowchart with those prepared by other students and consider where and how improvements might be made.

1.3 Supply chain management was initially developed by wholesaling and retailing organisations. Why do you think organisation in the distributive sector led the way?

1.4 In the text an example was given of how it might not be possible to reconcile the 'right quality' with the 'right price'. Discuss some other problems of reconciling the six 'rights'.

1.5 List five ways in which buying for industrial/producer organisations may differ from buying from (i) intermediaries and (ii) institutions.

1.6 Why do some organisations pay insufficient attention to supplier management?

1.7 Consider the four stages of the development of the purchasing function identified by Reck and Long. State, with reasons, the stage reached by purchasing in your organisation.

1.8 Use the purchasing profile developed by Jones to identify the stage reached by your organisation in respect of each of the 18 criteria listed under 'measurement area'.

1.9 Why is 'globalisation' a wider term than 'import purchasing' or 'international procurement'?

1.10 Without referring to Table 1.6, try to arrange the following acronyms in order of time progression TQM, EOQ, JIT, SCM, MRP, MRP II, TOC, TBC.

1.11 Using the format of Table 1.7, compare reactive and proactive approaches to purchasing.

1.12 The absolute number of purchasing jobs will decrease especially in respect of staff employed on tactical purchasing. Prepare a self-development plan to ensure that you will be prepared to take advantage of the career opportunities presented by the move to strategic procurement.

1.13 Rate your organisation on a scale of (1) low, (2) average, (3) high on each of the following criteria relating to world class purchasing.

Characteristic	High(3)	Average(2)	Low(1)
1. Commitment to TQM			
2. Commitment to JIT			
3. Commitment to total cycle time reduction			
4. Long-range strategic plans			
5. Supplier relationships			
6. Strategic cost management			
7. Performance management			
8. Training and professional development			
9. Service excellence			
10. Learning			
11. Management and leadership			

Consider what action you could take to improve the rating on any characteristics you have rated low.

1.14 Consider the following figures relating to a company.

	£'000	£'000
Sales		100,000
Purchases	20,000	
Wages etc.	20,000	
Cost of sales		40,000
Gross profit		60,000
Operating costs		55,000
Net profit		5,000

(a) Assume that there are savings of 5 per cent on purchases and that turnover and operating costs remain constant. What, in percentage terms, will be the effect on net profit?

(b) What increase in sales will have to be achieved to obtain a similar percentage increase in profit assuming no purchasing savings and the same proportionate cost of sales and operating expenses?

1.15 Discuss the following statement:

theoretical study alone cannot make managers. Their success will depend on their innate qualities, acquired knowledge, experience under competent guidance and, above all, on the degree to which they combine these elements into a balanced personality.

(adapted from Urwick Report 1947[22])

(a) Why then study purchasing?

(b) What are the characteristics of 'balanced personality'?

? Past examination questions

1 How is the buyers role likely to change as the buyer becomes more involved with proactive strategic purchasing?

(CIPS, Purchasing and Supply Chain Management I: Strategy, May 1997)

2 Using a purchasing development model or framework with which you are familiar, explain how such a model could be usefully employed in assisting the development of the purchasing activity.

(CIPS, Purchasing, November 1998)

Notes

1. Marrian, J., 'Market characteristics of industrial goals and buyers', in Wilson (ed). *The Marketing of Industrial Products*, Hutchinson, 1965, p.11

2. Lamming, R., 'The future of purchasing: developing lean supply', in Lamming, R. and Cox, A. (eds) *Strategic Procurement Management in the 1990s*, Earlsgate Press, 1985, Ch.3, p.40

3. Van Weele, A.J., *Purchasing Management*, Chapman and Hall, 1994, Ch.1, p.9

4. Stannack, P. and Jones, M., *The Death of Purchasing Procedures*, PSERA, 1996

5. Reck, R.F. and Long, B., 'Purchasing a competitive weapon', *Journal for Purchasing and Materials Management*, Vol.24, No.3 (1998), p.4

6. Syson, R., *Improving Purchasing Performance*, Pitman, 1992, Ch.8, pp.254–5

7. Morris, N. and Calantone, R.J., 'Redefining the purchasing function', *International Journal of Purchasing and Materials Management*, Fall 1992

8. Jones, D.M., 'Development models', *Supply Management*, 18 March 1999. The authors are particularly grateful to Dr Jones for the use of figures 1.6 and 1.7

9. These two definitions (here, and see also n.10 below) are taken from *Globalisation and the Triple Bottom Line*, Australian Public Service and Merit Protection Commission 1999 on http://www.psmpc.gov.au/pps/globe.htm (updated August 2000)

10. Schermerborn, J.R., *Management for Productivity*, 4th edn, John Wiley, 1993, glossary, p.G6

11. Christopher, M., *Logistics and Supply Chain Management*, 2nd edn, Prentice Hall, 1998, Ch.5, p.129

12. Green, K.W., *Production and Operations Management Philosophies, Evolution and Synthesis*, revised August 2000, Henderson State University on http://www.hsu.edu/faculty/green/pomphil.htm (accessed 2000)

13. See, for example, Carter, J.R., *Purchasing and Supply Management: Future Directions and Trends*, available at http://www.capsresearch.org/reportHIMS/tutrs.htm and especially *The Future of Purchasing and Supply Management – A Five and Ten Year Forecast*, Joint Research Initiative of Centre for Advanced Purchasing Studies, NAPM and AT Kearney, 1998

14. Schonberger, R.J., *World Class Manufacturing: The Next Decade: Building Power, Strength and Value*, Free Press, 1986

15. Carter, P.L. and Ogden, J.A., *The World Class Purchasing and Supply Organisation, Identifying the Characteristics*, Centre for Advanced Purchasing Study, University of Arizona, 1999

16. Minahan, T., 'What makes a supplier world class?', *Purchasing On Line*, 13 August 1988

17. Saunders, M., *Strategic Purchasing and Supply Chain Management*, Pitman, 1994, p.11

18. Syson, R., as n.6 above

19. Farmer, D., 'Organisation for purchasing', *Purchasing and Supply Management*, February 1990, pp.23–7

20. Millerson, G., *The Qualifying Associations*, Routledge & Kegan Paul, 1964, p.4

21. Lamming, R., as n.2 above, p.40

22. Urwick, L.F., *Report on Education for Management*, HMSO, 1947

Purchasing and information technology

After reading this chapter you should be able to:

- Define the terms 'information' and 'information society'.
- Distinguish information from data and knowledge.
- State the main characteristics of information.
- Define the term 'information systems'.
- Distinguish between TPS, MRS, DSS and EIS systems.
- Describe spreadsheets and their application to purchasing.
- Explain expert systems.
- Define the term 'information technology'.
- Describe the processes of information capture, input, processing, storage and output in the context of computing.
- Explain the purpose, technology, standards, applications and benefits of bar coding.
- Indicate the benefits of EPOS to customers and sellers.
- Define the terms 'telecommunications' and 'networks'.
- Classify networks according to communication media, technology, ownership, geographic scope and topology.
- Differentiate between e-commerce and e-business.
- Distinguish between intra- and inter-organisational integration.
- Discuss the contributions of ERP and intranets to intra-organisational integration.
- Define the term 'EDI'.
- Describe how EDI is implemented and its advantages, problems and limitations, and discuss how such limitations may be resolved.
- Outline some security and legal issues associated with IT.

2.1   Information

2.1.1   Definition

Information is the foundation of management control. Good decisions depend on having the right people, having the right information at the right time and from the right sources. As shown later, information is a key element in supply chain success since, without information managers are unaware of what customers require, what inventory exists to meet those requirements and when more of a product should be produced or ordered. From a wider perspective, organisations are becoming increasingly information based and we now live in an information society. An information society has been defined as:[1]

> A term used to describe a society and an economy that makes the best possible use of new information and communication technologies (ICTs). In an Information Society people will get the full benefits of new technology in all aspects of their lives: at work, at home and at play. Examples of ICTs are ATM (automatic teller machines) for cash withdrawal and other banking services, mobile phones, teletext television, faxes and information services such as the Internet and e-mail.

2.1.2   Information differs from data and knowledge

> *Data* is unsummarised facts and is the raw material. *Information* is data that has been processed into a form (often a message) that is meaningful to the person who receives it and is of real or perceived value in current or perceived actions and decision.

Knowledge, as Zack[2] states, is 'that which we come to believe and value, based on the meaningfully organised accumulation of information (messages) through experience, communication or inference. Knowledge can be looked at either as something to be stored or a process of acting or applying expertise. *Tacit knowledge* is what is in the minds of persons and what is transportable by the individual. *Explicit knowledge* consists of information formally recorded by such means as procedure manuals, instructions, catalogues and computer software.

The relationship between data, information and knowledge are shown in Figure 2.1.

The distinction between data, information and knowledge is important. One of the uses of information technology (IT) is to help managers transform data into information so they can make better decisions. The conversion of data into information also requires knowledge and by definition knowledge is specialised. Information-based organisations will therefore require more specialists than traditional command and control organisations. As Peter Drucker[3] observes, to 'remain competitive – maybe even to survive – businesses will have to transform themselves into organisations of knowledgeable specialists'.

The relationship between data, information and knowledge can be summarised as follows:

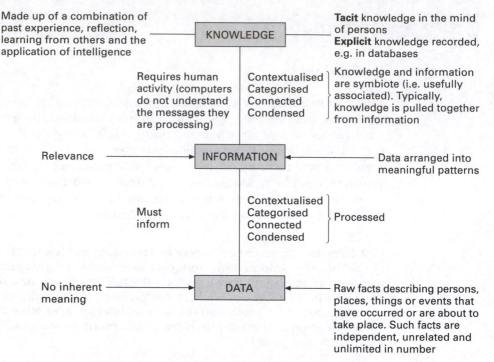

Figure 2.1   The relationship between data, information and knowledge

Data is the reality that a computer records, stores and processes.
Information is what a person is able to understand about reality.
Knowledge is what a business uses to make decisions.

The application of the above definitions to a purchasing decision is given in the following example:

Data: An enterprise has 500 suppliers
Information: The data can be processed to show how many suppliers fall into the following categories:
- high, medium or low spend
- high profit / high supply risk
- low profit impact / high supply risk
- high profit impact / low supply risk
- low profit impact / low supply risk

Knowledge: The information can be interpreted to lead to the decision to reduce the supplier base

2.1.3   Information characteristics

Good information has the following characteristics:

- *Accuracy* – error free.
- *Completeness* – all required information is available.

- *Economy* – the cost of obtaining the information must not be excessive or more than the information is worth.

- *Intelligible* – the information must be preserved in such a way that the recipient can understand it, e.g. information may be quantitative/qualitative, numerical/graphical, printed/displayed, summarised/detailed.

- *Relevance* – the information is necessary to enable the recipient to complete the tasks or make the decision.

- *Simplicity* – the information is not too complex and information overload is avoided.

- *Timeliness* – the information is available when needed.

- *Veracity* – the information can be checked for accuracy or reliability.

Absence of some of the above characteristics can affect the quality of decision making. Wrong or inadequate decisions can usually be traced to such factors as:

- partial or incomplete data;

- lack of accuracy in recording data;

- data may be wrongly processed;

- exceptions to the general rule or perceptions;

- a narrow knowledge base;

- information overload resulting in important information being inadvertently disregarded.

Human beings are often imperfect information processors and are affected by such factors as: lack of sufficient background knowledge to appreciate the value of information; an inability to see relationships between apparently unrelated information; bias in interpreting information; and the deliberate distortion of information. Distortion may take such forms as delay in transmitting information and the filtering or presentation to justify a particular decision.

2.2   Information systems

2.2.1   Definitions

Information systems have been defined as:[4]

> **The means by which organisation and people utilising appropriate technologies gather, process, store, use and disseminate information.**

Information systems may be classified as: transactional processing systems, management reporting systems, decision support systems or executive information systems.

Transactional processing system (TPS)

A transaction is any event which requires a record to be generated for processing in a data processing system such as placing an order or paying an invoice. The data provides the basis for management reporting systems.

Management reporting system (MRS)

This system provides managers with information and support for effective decision making and provides feedback on daily operations. Usually the information provided by such systems is the form of reports generated through accumulation of transaction processing data. Typical purchasing reports might include:

- value of orders placed in a specific period;
- value of orders to any one supplier;
- current expenditure/commitment against appropriate budgets;
- updated expenditure on capital projects;
- vendor rating reports;
- slow-moving and dead stocks.

Decision support system (DSS)

Decision support systems are designed to enable an individual or group to make decisions by summarising all relevant information whether held in the organisations database or externally, e.g. interest rates, currency changes. DSS have four principal characteristics: (i) they use both data and 'models', e.g. a representation of a system, device or process in mathematical form; (ii) they aim to assist managers in solving both structured and unstructured problems; (iii) they support, rather than replace managerial judgement and (iv) their objective is to improve the effectiveness of the decisions not the efficiency with which decision are made.

Two examples of DSS relevant to purchasing are spreadsheets and expert systems.

2.2.2 Spreadsheets

A spreadsheet is a powerful computer program that can be used to design and develop anything from a simple costing sheet for a new product to a large and complicated financial model of a new business. An example of a spreadsheet matrix or grid (often referred to as a worksheet) is shown in Figure 2.2. Although larger spreadsheets are available, a typical program will display about 250 rows and 60 columns. Each row and column is identified by its row number and column letter. The lines drawn to define the rows and columns form 'cells' or 'locations'. Using as many or as few of the rows and columns as are required for the particular application, one of three types of information is entered into a cell by means of the computer keyboard:

- *Text*, such as column or row headings, notes or descriptions. Text columns are ignored when the calculations are performed.

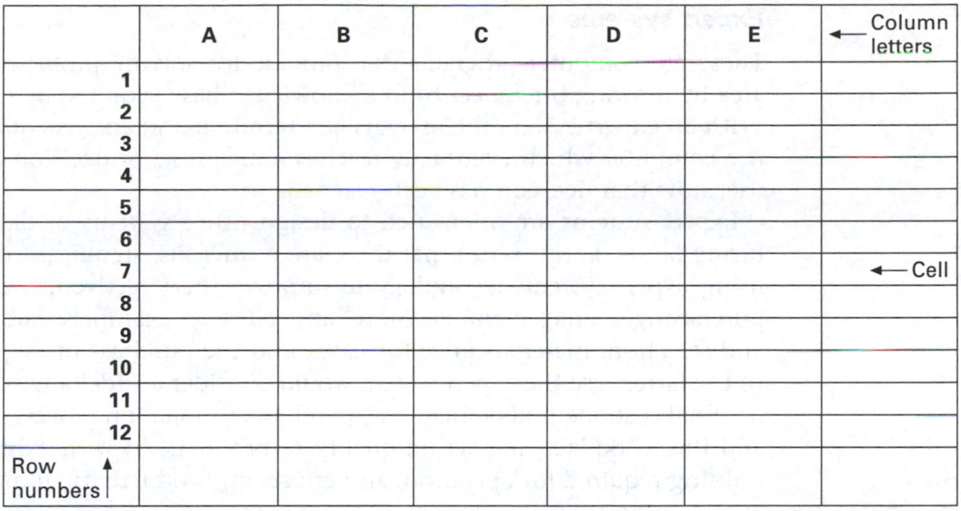

	A	B	C	D	E	← Column letters
1						
2						
3						
4						
5						
6						
7						← Cell
8						
9						
10						
11						
12						
Row numbers ↑						

Figure 2.2   A spreadsheet matrix

- *Numbers*, which can be specified as whole numbers, decimals, straight numbers or currency.
- *Formulae* expressing the relationship between numbers.

The only difference between using a spreadsheet program on a microcomputer and working out problems with a calculator, pen and paper is the amount of effort required to carry out repeated computations. Once the worksheet has been set up on the program, different ideas or models involving changes to the figures can be easily and quickly evaluated.

The list of potential spreadsheet models applicable to purchasing is limited only by the creativity of the individual user. Important purchasing and stores routines facilitated by the use of spreadsheets include:

- project evaluations, such as the centralisation of the supplies function;
- bill of materials evaluation;
- materials requirement planning;
- phasing of projects to meet total cash flow criteria;
- capacity planning for production and logistics;
- evaluation of the effects of changes in sales volume and phasing on stocks, stockholding costs and customer service levels;
- inventory management, e.g. economic order quantity models and extensions, activity-based costing analysis and stocktaking evaluations;
- supplier comparisons when a range of volume-related price bands apply and in relation to quantity discounts and expected failure rates;
- collection and analysis of data for departmental performance operation;
- evaluation of alternative stockholding and purchasing strategies;
- departmental budgeting, reporting and variance analysis;
- time series analysis of data for forecasting purposes.

Expert systems

These are computer programs that provide for solving problems in a particular area by drawing inferences from a knowledge base acquired by human expertise. With an expert system the user sits at a terminal and answers questions posed by the computer which eventually reaches a diagnosis or decision and informs the user how that decision has been reached.

Expert systems are often used to design other systems or diagnose manufacturing faults. Lorin[5] states that there are numerous, significant opportunities for using expert systems technology to improve the effectiveness and efficiency of purchasing management decisions and cites as examples: supplier evaluation and selection, materials price forecasts, and the purchase of major capital assets. In the latter case the expert system would consider a wide range of factors including final cost, method of financing, purchase, installation process, effects on labour and the workplace, impact on quality of products, fit with existing technology, training required for operation, and effects on productivity, to mention a few.

Executive information system (EIS)

This system is an extension of the DSS intended to provide current and appropriate information to support decision making by executives. Such systems emphasise graphical displays and canned reports or briefings intended to save expensive executive time.

While the above four types of system may be separate, in many organisations they are integrated through a common database. Separation of DSS transactions in the database from TPS and MIS transactions may be important for performance reasons.

2.3 Information technology

2.3.1 Definition

Information technology has been comprehensively defined as:[6]

> **Automatic acquisition, storage, manipulation, movement, control, display, switching, interchange, transmission or reception of data or information.**

An alternative definition is:[7]

> **The acquisition, processing, storage and dissemination of vocal, pictorial, textual and numeric information by microelectronics-based combinations of computing and telecommunications.**

The major components of IT are therefore (i) computers and (ii) telecommunications.

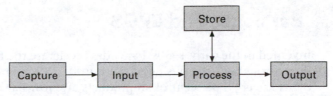

Figure 2.3 The steps in data processing

2.4   Computers

Computerised data processing involves five main steps: data capture, input, processing, storing and output. These steps are shown in Figure 2.3.

2.5   Data capture

Data capture refers to the collection of data for input into a computer. A wide variety of methods are available, including:

- bar codes and light pens
- concept keyboards
- digital cameras
- electronic point of sale registers
- graphic pads
- kimball tags (essentially the same as bar codes but capable of capturing more data)
- laser scanners
- magnetic ink character recognition
- magnetic stripe cards
- mark sensing and optical character recognition
- questionnaires
- scanners
- sensors
- voice recognition

It is important to ensure that the data captured is accurate. Within the present book it is impossible to describe all the above and other methods of data capture. Bar codes and electronic point of sale (EPOS) are, however, of particular importance.

2.6 Bar codes and EPOS

Invented in the early 1950s, bar codes accelerate the flow of product and information throughout the business community. Commencing in the grocery industry (where over 98 per cent of all products are now bar coded), bar coding was soon applied to production and warehousing.

Bar coding applications include lot and process quality control. Warehouse applications relate to receiving, put away, picking and packing. Economic pressures including global competition, with a consequent emphasis on cost reduction, speed and enhanced productivity, have made bar code technology as applied to materials management and logistics an industrial priority. A basic knowledge of bar coding requires an understanding of bar coding technology, standards and advantages.

2.6.1 Bar coding technology

Bar codes work in a similar way to the Morse code except that instead of dots and dashes to create unique patterns representing letters or numbers they use wide and narrow bars and spaces. The number 3 in Morse is represented by ... – – (three dots and two dashes). In one bar sequence the number 3 is encoded in two wide and three narrow elements.

Changing the sequence of the wide elements creates different patterns representing different numbers. The number 8 comprises five elements but the wide elements are now in different positions as shown below:

A sequence of vertical lines and space patterns is used to represent a unique product. This sequence of characters is known as a symbology. To read the code, several different devices called bar code readers, bar code scanners or optical wands are used. These use a laser beam that is sensitive to the reflections from the line and space thickness and variations. By moving the reader, scanner or wand over the surface of the bar code the data is recorded in the computer or a portable hand-held device.

2.6.2 Bar coding standards

There are many different bar codes or symbologies. Each with its own rules for characters (e.g. a letter, number, punctuation) encoding, printing and decoding requirements, error checking and other features. The most prevalent in the UK is the European Article Number (EAN) System for the identification of goods, services and locations and automatic data capture. In 1976 the Article Numbering Association (ANA) became the UK standards authority for bar coding. The ANA was also founder member of the international numbering association *EAN International*, which, together with the USA sister organisation the Uniform Code

Figure 2.4   EAN13 Bar code

Council, directs the use of the system in over 90 countries. In 1998 the ANA merged with the Electronic Commerce Association to form the Association for Standards and Practices in Electronic Trade or the e-centre.[8]

The most commonly used code is EAN13. As shown in Figure 2.4 this comprises 12 codes grouped together as two lots of 6, separated by a centre pattern and guard bits at each end. The first two digits identify the issuing organisation, i.e. 50 the UK, 32 France, 00 the USA. Digits 3–7 identify the manufacturing or marketing organisation. Digits 8–12 identify the product. Digit 13 is a check digit and is used to ensure by the use of the item reference that the complete number is unique to the product or service being numbered.

The above information is read by a laser scanner and sent to the computer. The description of the item is stored in the computer and, in the case of supermarkets, instantly sent back to the checkout where it is printed on the receipt.

2.6.3   Bar coding applications

Some production applications of bar coding are:

- counting raw materials and finished goods inventories;
- automatic sorting of cartons and bins on conveyor belts and palletisers;
- lot tracking;
- production reporting;
- automatic warehouse applications including receiving, put away, picking and shipping;
- identification of production bottlenecks;
- package tracking;
- access control;
- tool cribs and spare parts issue.

2.6.4   Benefits of bar coding

Benefits include the following:

- *Faster data entry*. Bar code scanners can record data 5–7 times as fast as a skilled typist.
- *Greater accuracy*. Keyboard data entry creates an average of one error in 300 keystrokes. Bar code entry has an error rate of about 1 in 3 million.

- *Reduced labour costs* through time saving and increased productivity.

- *Elimination of costly over or under stocking* and the increased efficiency of just-in-time inventory systems.

- *Better decision making.* Bar code systems can easily capture information that would be difficult to collect in other ways. This helps managers to make fully informed decisions.

- *Faster access to information.*

- *The ability to automate warehousing.*

- *Greater responsiveness to customers and suppliers.*

2.6.5 Electronic point of sale (EPOS)

The most familiar example of EPOS is the recording of retail store sales by scanning product bar codes at the checkout tills. The most important purpose of using an EPOS system is to scan and capture information relating to goods sold. An EPOS system verifies, checks and charges transactions, provides instant sales reports, monitors and changes prices, sends intra- and inter-stores messages and stores data. In the context of retailing, the benefits of EPOS to customers and sellers include:

- reduced checkout times;

- provision of information to customers relating to products and prices;

- facilitation of payment by credit card;

- reduction in labour costs by eliminating the need to mark products individually;

- electronic article surveillance (EAS) can assist in the detection and prevention of shoplifting;

- smart shelves which read and transmit data through the internet to store managers and manufacturers, notifying them when stocks are low. Managers are thereby relieved of checking inventory or placing orders since automatically generated purchase orders enable suppliers to produce and replenish goods sold.

- Daily, weekly etc. sales reports.

EPOS also has applications in production supply chain management including vendor-managed inventory (VMI) and collaborative planning, forecasting and replenishment (CPFR).

2.7 Input

Captured data is fed into the computer using such devices as a keyboard, mouse, voice or scanner. Care must be taken to avoid mistakes when inputting data.

2.8   Processing

This phase comprises all the number and character manipulation activities to convert data to information. Such activities include sorting, classifying, summarising and comparing data, performing calculations and executing logical processing activities such as listing information in a particular order.

The key factor in processing is the software. Software is of two basic types: systems and applications.

Systems software consists of low-level programs that control and coordinate the operation of the various types of equipment in the computer system. The most important type of systems software is known as the *operating system*. This contains general instructions that enable the computer to carry out the basic functions common to all computer programs such as loading, storing and retrieving files. The operating system also establishes the interface with the end user.

Once a computer has systems software, applications software (also termed end-user programs) can be added on. The best approach to sorting out complex application systems such as production or purchasing is to split them into modules. As shown in Figure 2.5, commercial software is available comprising a central purchasing module enabling the user to enter purchasing requests. Optional goods receiving, inventory control and remote requisition entry modules expand the capabilities of the system, enabling functions or departments other than purchasing to perform activities or analyse the data.

The prime function of the purchasing module is to process requests from initial entry through to completion. Sophisticated searching and cross-matching

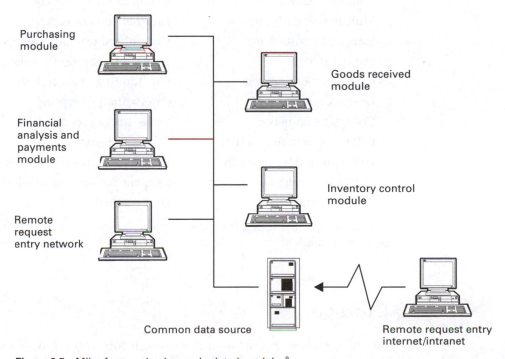

Purchasing module

Goods received module

Financial analysis and payments module

Inventory control module

Remote request entry network

Common data source

Remote request entry internet/intranet

Figure 2.5   Mikrofax purchasing and related modules[9]

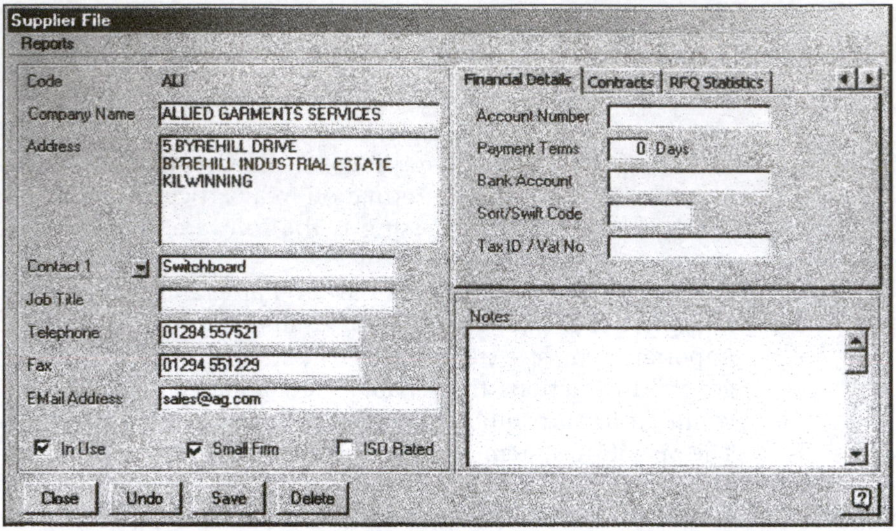

Figure 2.6   Sample screen shot of information from the supplier file

capabilities provide financial analysis including yearly and monthly committed expenditure breakdowns with optional budgetary control. The module provides the following information and reports:

Supplier file	Match invoices
Delivery point	Request for quotation
Item catalogue	Optional budgetary control
Multiple expenditure codes	Internal copy of order
Standard clauses file	Committed expenditure reports
Multicurrency	Management reports (+ data export)
Unique order numbers	Outstanding order reports
Distinct order types	Pareto analysis reports
Contract numbers	Order history report
Extensive item description	Password security
Order authorisation levels	Preview all reports on-screen
Controlled order amendments	Context sensitive online help
Record payments	User manual

An example of information given by the supplier file in the above system is given in Figure 2.6.

2.9   Storage

The storage phase is that in which data, information and processing instructions are stored in computable user form for retrieval as well as updating and subsequent processing as required. What is known as 'main' may be distinguished from 'secondary' storage. The main memory database holds the program instructions and data being processed as well as processed information awaiting transfer to output devices. Secondary storage complements the main memory and is used for data that may be needed on a semi-permanent basis. On modern systems this generally takes the form of a hard drive, floppy disk, tape cartridge or magneto-optical disk.

A *database* is a collection of data so arranged that its contents can easily be accessed, managed and updated. Databases contain aggregations of data records or files such as the supplier file shown in Figure 2.6. Other typical files might be part number and purchase files. A part number file will contain a record for every material item or component manufactured by the user undertaking. Each record would also contain data for each specific part number such as description, use, lead time requirement, minimum stock level, total purchase requisitions and total purchase orders.

Purchase files will contain a record for every part number purchased relating to the most recent quotations received from suppliers and purchasers.

A distinction can also be made between data warehouses and operational databases.

2.9.1   Data warehouses

A *data warehouse* is a central deposit system for all or significant parts of the data collected from the source documents created by the various transactions such as placing orders or making payments. Data warehouses drive decision support systems by enabling decision makers to extract information quickly to provide answers to queries about the business or answer what-if questions. Noel[10] lists six characteristics that differentiate the data warehouse from other database systems in an enterprise:

- The data in the warehouse is separate from the operational systems in the enterprise and is populated by data from these systems.
- The data warehouse exists entirely for the task of making data available to be interrogated by the business users.
- The data in the warehouse is interrogated on the basis of a standard enterprise model.
- It is time stamped and associated with a defined period of time, e.g. calendar or fiscal reporting periods.
- It is subject oriented, e.g. on the basis of suppliers.
- It is accessible to users who have a limited knowledge of computer systems or data structure.

2.9.2   Operational databases

Operational databases, in contrast, are used to process information that is needed to perform operational tasks. They are active for updating in all the hours that

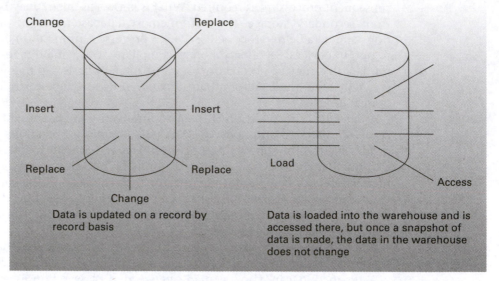

Figure 2.7   Comparison of operational database (left) and data warehouse (right)

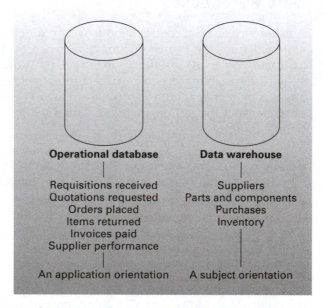

Figure 2.8   Contents of operational databases and data warehouses

business is transacted, whereas the data warehouse is available for accession only during business hours. Some of the differences between operational databases and data warehouses as depicted by Noel are shown in Figure 2.7.

   A comparison of the contents of operational databases and data warehouses is shown in Figure 2.8.

2.10   Output

Output can be provided either for current or future users and can take the form of hard or soft copy. ***Hard copy*** is output printed on paper or output on microfilm and is appropriate for information presented in report form. ***Soft copy*** is presented on a visual display unit (VDU) and is suitable for information that needs to be viewed only occasionally or for a short time.

2.11   Telecommunications and networks

2.11.1   Definition

Telecommunications is the transmission of information over distances by such means as electrical signals usually carried over telephone lines, radio waves or satellite transmission apparatus.

A *network* is a set of devices that can directly access each other by means of a shared directory. Examples of linked electronic devices are computers, telephones and Web TV. The *directory* corresponds to an ordinary telephone directory except that it provides an address to each device comprising the network. To add a new telephone to the public telephone system it is not sufficient to have a handset. A telephone number listed in a directory is also required.

2.11.2   Classification of networks

Networks may be classified as shown in Figure 2.9.

Communications media

Information may only be transmitted by voice, video, data, e-mail, fax and multimedia means (e.g. voice + data + text + image). Initially, public telephone systems were almost exclusively voice networks. Video transmissions were separate from voice and data networks. The increased demand for non-voice dial-up data applications such as e-mail, fax and file transmissions has led to the development of increased integration of different types of information, e.g. voice, data, image and text on the same network.

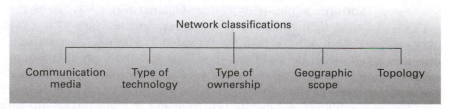

Figure 2.9   Network classifications

Type of technology

The dominant technology for a particular application may be optic, microwave or satellite, either separately or interoperating.

Type of ownership

Networks may be public or private, open or closed. The world's largest public network is the internet, accessible by telephone lines. In essence the internet is a network of networks, linking an ever growing number of networks and users in almost every country in the world. The internet was created in the 1960s by the US military–industrial complex to enable government researchers working on military projects to share computer files. The internet has several uses: (i) to send and receive e-mail; (ii) to transfer files from one computer to another; (iii) to locate information on a global basis for business research or political, educational or business purposes; (iv) to communicate with other computers either one at a time (instant message) or many at once (chat rooms or discussion groups).

■ The *World Wide Web* is *not* the internet but one system running on the internet. Basically, the internet is the hardware and the web the software. The web provides a graphical user interface (GUI) and means for the display of graphical images, pictures etc. The usefulness of the web is that every document embodies someone's efforts to explain what resources are available and to organise them in a way that facilitates their retrieval. The web also allows users to create their own web documents which, in turn, can provide links to further documents. The web is the most common way for businesses to establish a presence on the internet.

■ *Private networks* are those in which the organisation typically runs its own private branch exchange (PBX) and data-switching equipment as well as modems, multipliers and other circuit interface devices.

■ '*Intranet*' is the term applied to organisation-wide systems that operate like an internal internet. Such a system may allow other links in the supply chain to communicate with purchasing, and vice versa.

■ *Extranet* is the term used for an intranet that has been extended to include access to or from selected external organisations such as customers or suppliers, thus making possible collaborative inter-enterprise sharing of information and communication.

Organisations may also set up bilateral, point-to-point transmission schemes with other enterprises who are regular trading partners. Alternatively, organisations use a third-party value added network (VAN) for receiving, storing and distributing their data. The user transmits the data which is routed to and collected in an electronic mailbox provided by the VAN service provider and 'owned' by the user. The right pieces of data are then re-routed automatically by the VAN service to other electronic mailboxes 'owned' by the intended recipients where they are held until the receiving organisation asks for them. This process provides the opportunity for transmission and receipt from multiple partners with a single telephone call.

Geographic scope

Networks are categorised as LANs, MANs and WANs according to the area covered.

- *LANs* (local area networks) are privately owned communication networks linking personal computers and workstations or telephones within a limited geographical area such as a building or group of buildings within a distance of one or two miles.
- *MANs* (metropolitan area networks) are high-speed computer or telephone networks designed to link two or more LANs within a limited geographical region such as the various departments of a local authority.
- *WANs* (wide area networks) extend over a large geographical area such as a whole country. The internet links together hundreds of computer WANs. Most telephone systems are WANs.

Topology

In this context, topology relates to the interconnection or organisation of computers in a network. It may also be defined as the physical configuration of the various *nodes* and the manner in which they are linked. (A node is a point to which a group of devices such as microcomputers or terminals and transmission lines connect.) Most LAN topologies currently in use are star, bus or token ring.

A *star network* means that the arrangement of the LAN resembles a star. A star LAN has a central server (a *server* is a central computer that holds databases and programs for many PC workstations or terminals which are called *clients*). Each computer in the network is connected to the server as shown in Figure 2.10. The disadvantage of a star topology is that if the hub fails then all the computers on that hub fail. If, however, a line from the hub to the computer is broken then only that computer is down. If one computer fails, the rest of the network stays up.

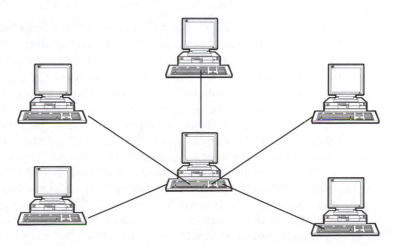

Figure 2.10   A star network

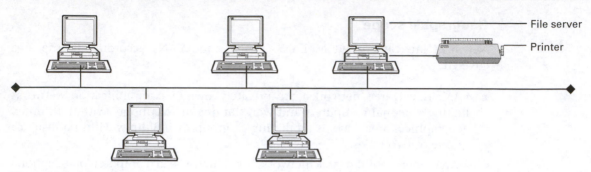

File server

Printer

Figure 2.11 A bus network

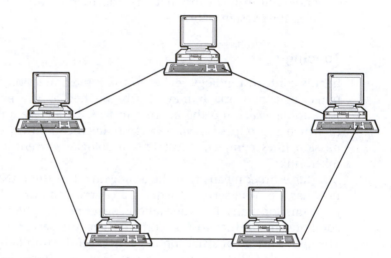

Figure 2.12 A ring network

A *bus topology* means that the arrangement resembles the seating on a bus. Each seat on the bus is a computer and the computers communicate through the passage down the centre of the bus as shown in Figure 2.11. The disadvantage is that cable breaks can disable the whole network.

A *ring network* means that the computers are arranged in a ring as shown in Figure 2.12. With ring networks there is no central server. Computers communicate by passing an electronic token or signal from computer to computer until the token reaches the destination computer that matches the address on the data. Again, a break in the ring can disable the entire network.

Other forms of networks include mesh and hybrid topologies. A *mesh network* is one in which every device on the network is connected to every other device. Such networks are not much used in LANs but are utilised for WANs where reliability is important. *Hybrid networks* are combinations of star, bus and ring topologies. Because each topology has its own strengths and weaknesses several types can be combined for maximum effectiveness.

Table 2.1 Basic types of e-commerce

Term	Definition	Example
Business to business e-commerce	The use of e-commerce between two companies	Online purchasing of supplies by company A from company B
Business to customer e-commerce	The use of e-commerce between an enterprise and a customer	Online sale of a product to a customer
Government to business e-commerce	The use of e-commerce between government and businesses	Government website use by a business to obtain information about state aid to industry
Government to citizen e-commerce	The use of e-commerce between government and citizens	Online submission of tax return

2.12 E-commerce and e-business

2.12.1 Definition of e-commerce

Although there is no internationally accepted definition of e-commerce (electronic commerce) the following definition has been proposed to the Organisation for Economic Cooperation and Development (OECD) by the Department of Trade and Industry (DTI):

> Using an electronic network to simplify and speed up all stages of the business process, from design and making to buying and delivery, e-commerce is the exchange of information across electronic networks, at any stage in the supply chain, whether within an organisation, between businesses and consumers or between the public and private sectors, whether paid or unpaid.

As shown in Table 2.1 there are four basic types of e-commerce.

2.12.2 E-business

Although, as in the above DTI definition, the terms 'e-commerce' and 'e-business' are sometimes used synonymously, the consensus is that e-commerce is rather a subset of e-business.

E-commerce relates primarily to *transactions* or the buying and selling of products or services on the internet. It usually refers to a website that has an online storefront or catalogue and the facility for electronic order processing. It should be noted that e-commerce may also be conducted through more limited forms of electronic communication including e-mail, fax and the emerging use of telephone calls over the internet.

E-business, however, incorporates a wide range of production, customer and internal processes that are only indirectly related to commercial transactions.

■ Production-focused processes include electronic links with suppliers especially manufacturing resource planning (MRP II), enterprise resource planning (ERP) and advanced planning and scheduling (APS).

■ Customer-focused processes include online customer support and customer relationship management (CRM).

■ Internal or management-focused processes include automated employee services, training, information sharing, video-conferencing and recruiting.

There are also many general benefits of e-business such as:

■ provision of 24 hour a day, 7 day a week information access;

■ aggregation of information from several sources;

■ accurate audit trails of transactions enabling businesses to identify areas offering the greatest potential for efficiency, improvements and cost reduction;

■ personalisation and customisation of information.

2.13 Integrated information systems

IT has enabled the integration of functions and the sharing of information at all levels within and between organisations. IT is therefore an important source of comparative advantage in promoting integration both within the organisation and externally. Internally IT can provide comparative advantage by providing employees with rapid access to information thus saving time and enhancing the productivity of employees not only in respect of direct production but also with regard to the various back office activities of invoicing, payments, customer care, authentication and fraud detection.

Externally the integration provided by electronic links can expand the joint capabilities of participating organisations. Sharing of information can provide participants with enhanced efficiency, flexibility and innovation to respond to the competition of global marketplaces.

2.13.1 Intra-organisational integration

Two important means of internal integration are ERP and the intranet.

Enterprise resource planning (ERP)

As shown in Chapter 8, ERP evolved from materials requirement planning (MRP) systems. MRP is a sequential 'push' system in which a master production schedule (MPS) is generated from demand predictions. Based on the MPS, the required quantity of parts is calculated using a part explosion or BOM (bill of materials) package. In the 1970s the concept of MRP II (manufacturing resource planning) evolved. MRP II extended MRP to shopfloor and distribution management activities and later to such areas as finance, human resources and product management and the term 'enterprise resource planning' was coined. Bandwidth ERP solutions address broad areas within any business, including purchasing, manufacturing, distribution, finance, service, maintenance and transportation. Such ERP systems aim to provide the seamless integration essential for ensuring visibility and consistency across an enterprise.

The intranet

An intranet is essentially a private internet operating on a company's internal network.[11]

The purpose of an intranet as Wright[12] states 'is to allow everyone to share information and facilitate group processes'. Like every other network, it holds file directories and allows resource sharing such as printers. A large multinational company may, for example, put all legal contracts on its intranet thus allowing purchasing officers in any division in any country to search and find the legal arrangements made with suppliers. Other applications of intranets are:

- publication of corporate documents, e.g. policy statements;
- publication of individual documents for group discussion, e.g. a proposal by a manager for discussion by other managers;
- providing access to groupware applications, e.g. ERP;
- providing a consistent communication link among colleagues.

2.13.2 Inter-organisational integration

Inter-organisational information systems (IOIS) are 'systems based on informational technologies that cross organisational boundaries'. Inter-organisational integration is facilitated by electronic data interchange and internet applications.

2.14   Electronic data interchange

2.14.1 Definition

Electronic data interchange (EDI) may be defined as follows:

The technique based on agreed standards, which facilitates business transactions in standardised electronic form in an automated manner directly from a computer application in one organisation to an application in another.

A *transaction* in EDI is a term used to describe the electronic transmission of a single document. Each transaction set is usually referred to by a name and number which are defined by the ASCx12 or EDIFACT standards referred to below. Thus a purchase order in x12 is number 850. Each line of a transaction is termed a *segment* and each piece of information in the line an *element*. In a purchase order, for example, the segment is the name and address of the purchaser or supplier. The segment is broken down into such data elements as organisation name, address line 1, address line 2, address line 3, postcode, country.

2.14.2 Standards

Date elements and codes are described in a *directory* relating to the message standard used. By the use of trade, national and international standards, organisations can trade electronically.

Early message standards were developed by group or communities of organisations, e.g. automotive, banking, construction, electronic enterprises which had an interest in trading together. Thus automotive manufacturers in ten European countries, i.e. Ford, General Motors, Saab, Renault, Fiat, Austin Rover and Citroën, and suppliers Lucas, Perkins, Bosch, CKN, SKF and BCS set up ODETTE (Organisation for Data Exchange by Tele-Transmission in Europe) as a collaborative agreement for common messages and protocols.

Although there are still many EDI standards, only two, namely ASCx12 and EDIFACT, have wide use and recognition. ASCx12 standards were created in 1979 by the Accredited Standards Committee of the American National Standards Institute. These standards define the data formats and encoding rules for business transactions including order placement and transportation. EDIFACT (EDI for Administration, Commerce and Transport) was developed by the United Nations in 1985 for the purpose of providing EDI standards that would support world trade. This international standard has been ratified as ISO 9735. UN/EDIFACT directories are published twice yearly by the United Nations.

2.14.3 How EDI works

How EDI is implemented is shown by Figure 2.13. The sequence is as follows:

1 Company A sets up purchase order using its internal business software.
2 EDI software translates the order from the internal format to the standard 850 purchase order document format.
3 Company A sends 850 purchase order to Company B over a third-party value added network (VAN) or encrypted in EDIFACT format over the internet.
4 Company B receives 850 purchase order document and will translate it from EDI to its proprietary format. Typically company A will then send an acknowledgement to company B.

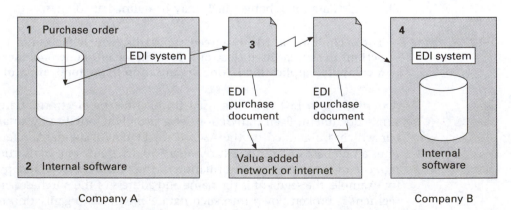

Figure 2.13 EDI Implemention[13]

2.14.4 The advantages of EDI

1 The replacement of the paper documents, e.g. purchase orders, acknowledgements, invoices, etc. used by buyers and sellers in commercial transactions, by standard electronic messages conveyed between computers often without the need for human intervention.

Example 2.1   EDI at the supermarket

One of the best examples of EDI is EPOS (electronic point of sale) at the supermarket. When a product is purchased, the checkout operator scans a bar code on its label which automatically registers the price on the cash till. That same signal also triggers a computer process which reorders the item from the manufacturer, sets off a production, cycle, arranges invoicing, payment and transportation of the new order. EDI effectively puts the product back on the shelf with no paperwork and a minimum of human involvement.[14]

---

2 Reduction in lead times through buyers and suppliers working together in a real-time environment. Armstrong and Jackson[15] provide a real-life example of pre- and post-EDI lead times in which the latter shows reductions of 8 days to acknowledge the order and 5 days to deliver it.

Day 1:   Order prepared and authorised electronically; posted into EDI service.

Day 2:   Order taken from EDI service by recipient and put straight into order processing system; acknowledgement created automatically and sent to EDI service.

Day 3:   Manufacturing process begins (7 days); acknowledgement received by originator and processed automatically.

Day 9:   Manufacturing complete.

Day 11: Delivery complete.

3 Reduction in cost if inventory and release of working capital.

4 Promotion of such strategies as JIT as a consequence of 2 and 3.

5 Better customer service.

6 Facilitation of global purchasing through international standards, e.g. EDIFACT which is compatible with most equipment in most countries. In 1970 Sitpro (Simplification of International Trade Procedures Board) was established 'to guide, stimulate and assist the rationalisation of international trade procedures and the documentation and information flows associated with them'. Sitpro works with the British Standards Institution in connection with EDI standards.

7 Facilitation of invoice payments by the computer-to-computer transfer of money which eliminates the need for the preparation and posting of cheques.

8 The integration of functions, particularly marketing, purchasing production and finance.

9 EDI tends to promote long-term buyer–supplier relationships and increase mutual trust.

2.14.5 **Some potential problems in implementing EDI**

Killen and Kamauff[16] point out that before adopting EDI an organisation should:

- Ensure that exchanging information electronically supports the overall organisational strategy.
- Consider the cost and ramifications of EDI standard tools and techniques including implementation, software maintenance, manpower and participant training and how to promote systems and applications integration.
- Consider the organisational and process changes involved.

In relation to the second point, Norman[17] states that the more data that is being processed and reprocessed the more room there is to save time and money. Potential EDI users should therefore calculate the cost per transaction. If it is cheaper to fax or manually perform the task the buyer probably lacks the volume to invest in EDI. Monczka and Carter[18] propose the following indicators of a reasonable opportunity for the application of EDI in the purchasing environment:

- A high volume of paperwork transaction documents.
- Numerous suppliers.
- A long internal administration lead time associated with the purchasing cycle.
- A desire for personnel reductions, new hire avoidance, or both.
- A need to increase the professionalism of purchasing personnel.

2.14.6 **EDI limitations**

Historically the two principal limitations of EDI relate to cost and inflexibility.

Cost

EDI was, and still is, an expensive option given that, until recently, organisations sent all EDI transactions over a VAN that had high set-up and running costs often on the basis of per thousand characters transmitted. The scope of EDI was also intentionally limited to ensure controlled activity within a closed-door environment. The heavy overhead associated with the EDI infrastructure was prohibitive for many small and medium-sized enterprises.

Internet and extranet approaches can, however, enable small businesses to link into secure EDI networks at a minimal cost. The internet pricing model of flat monthly rates has forced most of the VAN networks to lower their pricing structures. A new market shift is also under way in which organisations are moving from proprietary technology to extranet solutions. A comparison of EDI and extranet technology is shown in Table 2.2.

Small businesses using the internet can compete on a level playing field with large competitors, expand globally and improve their trading partner relationships.

Table 2.2   Comparison of EDI and extranets

Characteristics	EDI	Extranets
Infrastructure	Customised software	Packaged solutions that leverage and extend existing internet technology and intranet investment
Transmission costs	Extensive VANS or leased lines, slow dial-up connections	Inexpensive and fast internet connections
Access	Proprietary software	Web browser, support EDI protocols as well as many other open standards
Scale	Restricted to only the largest vendors who can support EDI infrastructure	Supports real-time buying and selling, allowing for tighter and more proactive planning

Inflexibility

EDI is a cumbersome, static and inflexible method of transmitting data most suited to straightforward business transactions such as the placement of purchase orders for known requirements. It is not suitable for transactions requiring tight coupling and coordination such as the consideration of several possible purchase alternatives or supply chain optimisation. Unlike human beings, computers are poor at interpreting unstructured data and cannot derive useful information from web documents that are not predefined and permanent. The standard document language used to create web pages is hypertext markup language (HTML). While HTML is able to display data and focuses on how data looks, it cannot describe data. While HTML can state what items a supplier can offer, it cannot describe them. Traditional EDI approaches do not, therefore, provide the flexibility required in a dynamic internet environment.

XML (extensible markup language) approved by the World Wide Web Consortium (W3C) in February 1998 is an attempt to meet the above problems and provide a foundation for a whole new way of communicating across the internet and beyond. The major difference between EDI and XML is that the former is designed to meet business needs and is a *process*. XML is a *language* and its success in any business will always depend upon how it is being used by a given application. As a language, XML provides a basic syntax that can be used to share information between many kinds of computer, different applications and different organisations. XML can also describe – as distinct from display – data. It can, for example, enable a purchaser to understand in detail what a supplier has to offer. It also ensures that a purchase order accurately describes what the purchaser requires. It therefore provides a direct route between purchaser and supplier irrespective of the size of either that was unavailable with EDI. Some writers predict that XML, when widely used, will result in the demise of EDI. This will not be the case:

> What XML will do – and is already doing – is to force EDI solution providers to consider how they need to re-engineer the EDI business model to fit into a more flexible framework and also how to leverage the benefits of the Internet.

As far as MRO [maintenance, repair and operating supplies] e-procurement is concerned, XML will become an important element and it will be necessary for both purchasers and suppliers to consider how their applications will work within the XML framework.[19]

In addition to EDI and the internet there are other ways of transmitting data electronically between two or more organisations. For small businesses, encrypted e-mails are very cost effective. Orders can be collected securely online and put into existing in-house systems which automatically e-mail suppliers when stock values reach lower limits. Technology is also changing. Although until recently PCs were the internet access device of choice, preferred substitutes such as cellular phones and personal digital assistants (PDAs) are outselling PCs several times over. As an IBM[20] publication states:

By 2003 the number of cellular phones around the world is expected to exceed one billion, with about 80 per sent of them having some form of access to the Internet. This rapid proliferation of new network access devices is referred to as pervasive computing – migration of the web beyond PCs to a new generation of devices that can access any service utilising both wireless and wired connections.

2.15 Portals

Generally synonymous with gateway the term portal refers to a World Wide Web site that provides a major starting point for web users. A portal is therefore an entry point or homepage for accessing Internet content and services.

Portals may be horizontal or vertical. Typical horizontal or consumer portals include Yahoo!, Excite, Lycos and Microsoft Network. Vertical or 'Enterprise Information Portals' (EIPs) provide information to a particular group or interest who access the customised or personalised portal. As Pimblett[21] states:

Integrating existing systems and new technologies is the real benefit of web portals. In a back-to-front scenario, portals allow analytical processing applications to derive information from databases and other information repositories that were previously unavailable to managers or sales personnel in the field. In a front-to-back scenario, portals allow a greater number of points-of-entry for supply of databases and enterprise resource planning systems.

2.16 Security and legal issues

The many advantages of EDI and the internet are balanced by concern over security and legal aspects. Lack of clarity on these issues is significant reason why many organisations have been slow to adopt e-business approaches. Security and legal issues are too complex for detailed discussion in this book. Some of the relevant issues are outlined below:

2.16.1   Security issues

Security threats to information transmitted by EDI and the internet include:

- Interception and modification by third parties of messages sent, e.g. purchase orders, credit card numbers.
- Loss of messages.
- Messages may be read by persons other than the intended recipient.
- A third party may pretend to be one of the original two parties.
- One of the parties may claim never to have sent or received a particular message.

Approaches to meeting the above concerns include:

- *Encryption technologies*. Encryption is the art of encoding information in such a way that only the holder of a secret password can decode and read it. Encryption is based on an algorithm or mathematical formula that can transform intelligible into unintelligible text, and a key (symmetric encryption) or pair of keys (asymmetric encryption) to decrypt the text.
- *Certification authorities* are entities that certify signatures and provide proof that a signature is valid.

2.16.2   Legal issues

E-business raises legal issues relating to:

- Online contracts, i.e.
  - contracts and types of contracts
  - pre-contract considerations
  - contract creation
  - writing and signature requirements
  - online contract terms and conditions
- International issues:
  - jurisdiction
  - applicable law
  - enforcement
  - reconciliation of territorial law and global reach
- Evidence and security:
  - types of evidence
  - real evidence
  - admissibility and hearsay evidence
  - the reliability of computer evidence
  - good practice i.e. BSI and DISC PC 0008 codes
  - protection of intellectual property

- Data protection
- Webvertising
- Taxation of electronic commerce

Readers requiring further clarification of the above matters should consult ISO and BS specifications 17799 and 7799 in which information security is defined as maintaining:

- *Confidentiality* – personal and business-sensitive confidential information is protected from unauthorised disclosure, loss, damage or use.
- *Availability* – ensuring that information is available to those persons authorised to see, use and process information.
- *Integrity* – information is protected from unauthorised alteration and is reliable.

Other useful sources of information on the security and legal aspects of e-business include relevant publications of the UK government and the European Commission.

2.17 The impact of IT on purchasing and supply

While IT has revolutionised purchasing procedures it does not obviate the need for some human interaction. Complex purchasing and partnerships cannot be put in place without considerable personal negotiation between the parties concerned. It is inconceivable that any critical supply would be selected or purchased purely on the information provided by a website. For such matters, suppliers' appraisal visits and personal negotiation will still be essential. Nevertheless there are many areas in which IT applications are relevant to purchasing and these are covered at appropriate places in this book. Such applications include:

- e-auctions (see Chapter 6);
- business intelligence (see Chapter 3);
- e-catalogs (see Chapter 8);
- continuous replenishment programmes (CRP) (see Chapter 8);
- customer relationship management (see Chapter 19);
- efficient consumer response (ECR) (see Chapter 19);
- JIT (see Chapter 8);
- e-marketplaces (see Chapters 8 and 12);
- vendor-managed inventory (see Chapter 8).

Case study 1

Bonnington Construction is a large company undertaking substantial job contracts such as buildings and road construction. At any given time Bonnington's inventory of tools, equipment and materials purchased for individual contracts is in excess of £5 million which it must be able to track on a job-by-job basis since accurate job costing and inventory control are essential.

Notwithstanding its size, Bonnington's method of tracking and recording inventory are rudimentary. All steel and components allocated to a job are identified by a job order number painted on the particular item. Sometimes, in an emergency, such items are transferred to other jobs.

Records of all tools, equipment or materials requisitioned for a particular contract or job are maintained by employees in written logbooks. These logbooks are subsequently used by costing as a basis for charging all items recorded in respect of the contract. This system means that the costing staff have to decipher the handwritten notes before they can key in the data to computerised costing records. When writing cannot be deciphered the costing staff have to contact the employee who made the record and ask for clarification of the entry.

Often, tools and equipment are lost, broken or transferred to other jobs without being reported. In consequence there is always uncertainty regarding what inventory is available and where it is recorded.

The works manager recognises that the system is antiquated and unsatisfactory and asks you to investigate and make recommendations how the system can be improved.

Questions

1 List the possible losses and adverse effects on profitability of the present system.
2 Suggest an alternative system that will enable tools, equipment and materials to be located in inventory and tracked on a job-by-job basis and records to be maintained regarding the condition of tools and equipment while also improving the accuracy of job costing.

Case study 2

Electronics Ltd manufactures electric domestic appliances. When stores, production or administrative staff require to purchase supplies they complete a requisition form which is then forwarded for processing by the purchasing department.

Several managers complain that the above process leads to needless delays both in purchasing the required items and in their delivery. They therefore recommend that a purchase request should be entered by the requisitioner on an online computer terminal. The purchasing staff would then retrieve on their own terminal, verify the information and forward an order to an appropriate supplier.

The accountant who has been with Electronics Ltd for over 30 years is, however, opposed to the recommendation on the grounds that the paper requisition has to be signed by the requisitioner. This signature provides the purchasing department with the assurance that the purchase is authorised. If an online terminal is used there is no guarantee that the individual inputting the requisition is authorised to do so.

The advocates of the new proposal point out that the person entering the requisition would first have to enter a password that only he or she knows. The accountant counters this argument by stating that passwords are easily misplaced or discovered by those not authorised to requisition a purchase. In contrast a signature is unique to the individual and is difficult to forge.

Question

As the managing director of Electronics Ltd state which argument you would support, giving the reasons for your decision.

Discussion questions

2.1 In the context of purchasing, give three examples in each case of (a) tacit and (b) explicit knowledge.

2.2 What is the practical use to purchasing and supplies staff of the distinctions between data, information and knowledge?

2.3 You have received information from a fellow purchasing professional regarding a possible supplier of an important item. Your informant has no personal experience of dealing with the recommended supplier but states that she has had many favourable reports relating to their prices and quality. What criteria would you apply in evaluating this information and deciding whether to act on it?

2.4 'Human beings are often imperfect processors.' Think of examples from your own experience that would support this statement.

2.5 State three reports that might be useful to each of the following in helping them to make decision.

    (a) A purchasing executive.

    (b) A materials manager.

    (c) A logistics manager.

    (d) A supply chain executive.

2.6 What uses might be made of spreadsheets apart from those mentioned in the text?

2.7 If you were ill, which of the following would you prefer to diagnose your illness and prescribe treatment? why?

    (a) An expert system.

    (b) A doctor using an expert system.

    (c) A specialist not using an expert system.

2.8   Why may organisations need to upgrade or modify their IT systems several times before such systems reach the end of their working life?

2.9   Attempt to set out in tabular form some differences between (a) transactional processing systems, (b) management reporting systems, (c) decision support systems and (d) executive information systems.

2.10   List the main factors you would consider when purchasing a computer system (a) for personal use and (b) for use in purchasing and supply work.

2.11   A survey in the April 1992 issue of *Purchasing and Supply Management* related to the features most commonly sought in systems designed to support purchasing functions. The survey indicated that 77 per cent of respondents identified purchase order generation as an essential feature and 74 per cent the recording of goods received as important. In what order would you place the following?

(a)   Online enquiry

(b)   supplier records

(c)   receipt order matching

(d)   purchase management information

(e)   stock recording

(f)   issue recording

(g)   price records

(h)   receipt order matching

(i)   purchase order status monitoring

(j)   coding/classification

2.12   Consider the computer system at your place of work. Is it organised on a star, bus, ring or some other form of network?

2.13   Intranets can fail to meet specifications because they are poorly marketed internally. How would you market the intranet to ensure that it is successfully used in your organisation?

2.14

Type of purchase	High frequency, low value	Low frequency, low value	High frequency, high value	Low frequency, low planning
Example of product				
Possible e-commerce method				

Complete the above chart by:

(a)   Allocating the following products under the appropriate heading:

    (i)   Incidental items

    (ii)   Raw materials

    (iii)   Capital equipment

    (iv)   MRO (maintenance, repair and operating supplies)

    (v)   Urgently required low-cost items

    (vi)   Insurance and legal services

    (vii)   Product components

    (viii)   Commodities

(b) Allocate the following electronic commerce methods under the appropriate headings (some may be suitable for more than one heading):

(i) Internet for sourcing

(ii) Online catalogues

(iii) EDI

(iv) Procurement cards

(v) E-mail

(vi) ERP systems

(vii) Fax

2.15 What are the advantages to book publishers and customers of bar coding?

2.16 ERP attempts to integrate all departments and functions across a single computer system that can serve all those different departments' particular needs. Yet ERP vendors are finding it difficult to move from streamlining business practices inside a company to those that face outward to the rest of the world. Can you think of reasons why such a transition is difficult?

2.17 Electronic funds transfer (EFT) involves the electronic transmission of receipts and payments between banks and their customers and purchasers and suppliers. When linked with EDI, EFT enables paperless payments to be made, 'money travels but not paper'. What are the advantages and possible disadvantages of EDI/EFT?

2.18 XML offers its users many advantages, including

■ simplicity

■ extensibility

■ interoperability

■ openness

Try to give one example in each case of how XML provides the above advantages.

2.19 A company has acquired a detailed marketing database giving a vast amount of information concerning the ages, past and present occupations, income, spending habits and interests of households within your area. Can you think of ways in which such information might be used unethically?

? Past examination questions

1 Discuss the claims that electronic point of sale systems (EPOS systems) provide a potential for greatly increased efficiency but only if they are fully integrated into the supply chain.

(CIPS, Retail Merchandise Management, May 1998)

2 To improve the efficiency of the supply chain strategically it is imperative that information is communicated quickly to those who need it for decision-making purposes. Discuss how information technology can contribute to efficiency and effectiveness in this area.

(CIPS, Purchasing and Supply Chain Management I: Strategy, November 1999)

3 The use of e-commerce is likely to have a major impact on the way in which buyers conduct business in the future with suppliers. Using an example of your choice, identify the likely scope and benefits of this relatively new development.

(CIPS, Purchasing, May 2000)

4 'E-commerce will change the dynamics of the profession and how we work, and it should be embraced. There will be a shift to methods of working, based on empowering and training users, suppliers and customers. The emphasis will increasingly be on cost, knowledge, management and change' (Melinda Jackson, *Supply Management*, April 2000).

With reference to this quotation explain how e-commerce and information technology in general, have affected the operations of the purchasing function, and how they may continue to do so in the future.

(CIPS, *Purchasing and Supply Management II: Tactics and Operations* November 2000)

Notes

1. Definition by the Information Society
2. Zack, M.H.,'Managing codified knowledge', *Sloan Management Review*, Summer 1999, pp.45–8
3. Drucker, P., 'The coming of the new organisation', *Harvard Business Review*, Jan./Feb. 1988, p.45
4. Definition of the United Kingdom Academy of Information Systems
5. Lorin, R.C., 'Expert systems in purchasing', *Journal of Purchasing and Supply Management*, Fall 1992, pp.23–4
6. Office of Information Resource Management, Office of the Director of National Institutes of Health, USA, 1996
7. Longley, D. and Shain, M., Dictionary of Information Technology, Macmillan, 1992, p.165
8. E-centre UK, 10 Maltravers Street, London WC2 3BX
9. The authors are indebted to Mikrofax, 360 Highgate High Street, London N6 5JT for permission to use the relevant material
10. Noel, R., *Data Warehouses*, 1996, on noelatc.s.rpi.edu. Noel was then a masters student at Rensetier Polytechnic Institute
11. Wright, A., *An Introduction to Intranets*, Institute of Chartered Accountants, 1999, p.5
12. Ibid.
13. Adapted from *Using Technologies to Cross Organisational Boundaries*, Fastwater Library on http://www.fastwater.com/Library/General/cobs/COBS-EDI-fr.php3
14. Sanders, J., quoted by Tyler, G. in 'Is paperless trading finally a reality?' *Purchasing and Supply Management*, Dec. 1991, pp.26–9
15. Armstrong, V. and Jackson, D., *Electronic Data Interchange: A Guide to Purchasing and Supply*, CIPS, 1991, pp.15–16
16. Killen, K.H. and Kamauff, J.W., *Managing Purchasing*, Irwin, 1995, Ch.4, p.60
17. Norman G., Is It Time for EDI?, Logistics Supplement to Purchasing and Supply Management, June 1994, p.20

18. Monczka, R.M. and Carter, J.R., 'Implementing electronic data interchange', *Journal of Purchasing and Supply Management*, Summer 1988, pp.2–9
19. E-procurement, A Report of the Butler Group, Vol. 1 (Aug. 2000), p.38
20. IBM, *Computing in an E-business World*, 2000, p.16
21. Pimblett, A.C., *The Essential Guide to E-Business and Optional Supply Chain Management for the Appraisal and Footwear Industries Worldwide*, Datel White Paper, 2001

Logistics and supply chains

Learning goals

After reading this chapter you should be able to:

- Define the terms 'logistics' and 'supply chain'.
- Identify the main activities comprising logistics.
- Distinguish logistics from materials management (MM) and physical distribution management (PDM).
- Indicate the main activities comprising MM and PDM.
- State the main logistical objectives.
- Explain the term 'reverse logistics'.
- Distinguish between logistics and supply chains.
- Define the term 'network' in a supply chain context.
- Explain the concepts of network 'dynamics' and network 'influence'.
- State the characteristics of the four types of network identified by Zheng *et al*.
- Define the term 'value chain'.
- Discuss the concepts of value chains identified with Michael Porter and Peter Hines.
- Explain the terms 'connectivity', 'integration', 'visibility' and 'responsiveness' in a supply chain context.
- State some planning and execution supply software applications.
- Define and list the main characteristics of lean supply.
- Define and list some main characteristics of agile supply.
- Explain some differences between lean and agile supply chain networks.
- Indicate what is meant by time compression.
- Define and discuss the concept of supply chain optimisation.
- Discuss the impact of the supply chain concept on purchasing.
- Identify some contributions of purchasing to supply chain management.

3.1 What is logistics?

3.1.1 Military logistics

The supply chain approach developed from logistics. Logistics, initially a military term dating from the Napoleonic Wars, refers to the technique of moving and quartering armies (i.e. quartermaster's work). The scope of logistics in a military sense is reflected in the definition adopted by NATO:[1]

> The science of planning and carrying out the movement and maintenance of forces. In its most comprehensive sense the aspects of military operations which deal with:
>
> (a) design and development, acquisition, storage, transport, distribution, maintenance, evacuation and disposition of material;
>
> (b) transport of personnel;
>
> (c) acquisition or construction, maintenance, operation and disposition of facilities;
>
> (d) acquisition or furnishing of services; and
>
> (e) medical and health support.

NATO also distinguishes between two important aspects of logistics: acquisition logistics and operational logistics (Figure 3.1).

The importance of military logistics is apparent from a consideration of the enormous problems relating to the supply of the Allied forces involved in the D-Day invasion of Europe in World War II or the Falklands War of 1982.

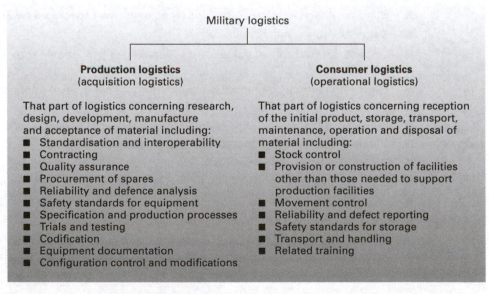

Figure 3.1 The scope of military logistics

Source: NATO, *Logistics Handbook*, 1997, paras 103–104

3.1.2 Non-military applications of logistics

Non-military applications of logistics, although generally less complex, still cover the same ground, as indicated by the following definitions:

> Logistics is the total management of the key operational functions in the supply chain – procurement, production and distribution. Procurement includes purchasing and product development. The production function includes manufacturing and assembling, while the distribution function involves warehousing, inventory, transport and delivery.[2]

> Logistics is the process of managing both the movement and storage of goods and materials from the source to the point of ultimate consumption and the associated information flow.[3]

> Logistics is that part of the supply chain process that plans, implements and controls the efficient, effective flow and storage of goods, services and related information from the point of origin to the point of consumption in order to meet the customers' requirements.[4]

3.2 Material, logistics and distribution management

As shown in Figure 3.2, logistics comprises both materials management and physical distribution management.

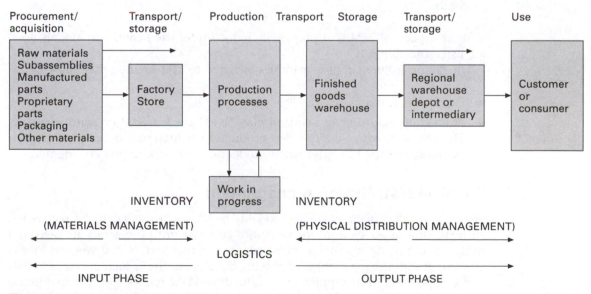

Figure 3.2 Scope of logistics management

Source: adapted from Gattorna, J., 'Strategic issues in logistics', *Focus on Physical Distribution and Logistics Management*, Oct./Nov. 1986

Table 3.1   Materials flow activities

Materials flow	Typical activities
Planning	Preparation of materials budgets, product research and development, value engineering and analysis, standardisation of specifications
Procurement	Determining order quantities, processing of works and stores requisitions, issue of enquiries, evaluation of quotations, supplier appraisal, negotiation, placing of contracts, progressing of deliveries, certifying payments, vendor rating
Storage	Stores location, layout and equipment, mechanical handling, stores classification, coding and cataloguing, receipt of purchased items, inspection, storage or return, protection of stores, issue to production, provision of cost data, stock records, disposal of obsolete, surplus or scrap material
Production control	Forward ordering arrangements for materials, preparation of production schedules and sequences, issue of orders to production, emergency action to meet material shortages, make-or-buy decisions, quality and reliability feedback, and adjustment of supplies flow to production line or sales trend

3.2.1 Materials management

Materials management (MM) is concerned with the flow of materials to and from production or manufacturing and has been defined as:[5]

> **The planning, organisation and control of all aspects of inventory embracing procurement, warehousing, work in progress and distribution of finished goods.**

Some aspects of MM that may be included under the heading 'materials flow' are listed in Table 3.1.

The factors influencing the activities assigned to MM include the following:

- Purchasing is frequently the 'key' activity.
- Production planning and control may be assigned to MM or manufacturing. The former tends to apply when production is materials oriented, e.g. in an assembly factory; the latter when production is machine/process oriented.

3.2.2 Physical distribution management

Physical distribution management (PDM) is often considered to be concerned with the flow of goods from the receipt of an order until the goods are delivered to the customer. An alternative view, adopted in this text, is that whereas MM is concerned with the *input* phase of moving bought out items such as raw materials and components from suppliers to production, PDM relates to the *output* phase of moving finished goods from the production departments to finished goods stores and then through the appropriate channels of distribution to the ultimate consumer. The main activities associated with PDM are inventory control, warehousing and storage, materials handling, protective packaging and container-isation and transportation. Developments such as just-in-time (JIT), where both producers and distributors carry only a few hours' stock and rely on their suppliers to meet their production or sales requirements, have greatly enhanced the import-ance of PDM.

It has been stated that the perspective of the logistician is 'what flows can be made to flow faster?' From this standpoint, the logistician studies the costs incurred by the enterprise, beginning with the initial input factor, spent on the production process and terminating when the customer pays for the product or service received. The longer the time at each stage of the process, the higher the costs incurred. A reduction in the time at any stage will provide an opportunity of cost reduction which can, in turn, lead to a reduction in price.

3.2.3 Some important logistics concepts

Total systems management

Total systems management emphasises a total rather than a limited departmental viewpoint. Total systems management has been facilitated by the availability of information technology.

Trade-offs

A trade-off is where an increased cost in one area is more than offset by a cost reduction in another, so that the whole system benefits. This may give rise to interdepartmental conflicts owing to different objectives. Thus, purchasing may advocate bulk purchases of materials to secure larger supplier discounts. This policy might be opposed by finance because of money tie up in the working cap-ital and by inventory because of the increased cost of warehousing. The conflict should be settled on the basis of which policy yields the greater trade-off. Similarly, purchasing may have to consider whether the security of supply consequent upon having a number of suppliers is offset by the economies resulting from single-source buying. Thus, the effects of trade-offs may be assessed by their impacts on total systems cost and sales revenue.

Thus, higher inventory costs may result from increased stocks, yet quicker delivery may increase total sales revenue. Obtaining the information for com-puter trade-offs requires breaking down of functional barriers which protect departmental 'territory' and discourage information sharing.

Cooperative planning

This can work forwards to customers and backwards to suppliers. The change from product- to customer-oriented supply chains, and thus faster supply resources, can provide customers with alternatives such as make to stock, make to order and finish to order. Conversely, from the inward supply side, effective cooperative planning may relate to zero defects, on-time delivery, shared products and information exchanges relating to such matters as shared specifications, design support, multi-year commitments and technology exchange. Overall, both supply and customer can benefit from reduced costs of inventory, capacity, order

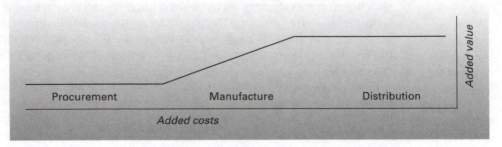

Figure 3.3 The added value aspect of logistics

handling and administration. Cooperative planning utilises, as appropriate, manu-facturing and scheduling techniques including:

Manufacturing
- Computer aided design (CAD)
- Computer integrated manufacture (CIM)
- Flexible manufacturing systems (FMS)
- Materials requirement planning (MRP)
- Manufacturing resources planning (MRP II)
- Optimised production technology (OPT)
- Strategic lead time management (STM)

Production
- Just-in-time (JIT)
- Materials requirement planning (MRP)
- Manufacturing resources planning (MRP II)

This can be explained by the cost–value curve shown in Figure 3.3.

1 The lowest cost value is at the procurement stage when supplies are purchased.
2 During transportation of supplies, value remains low because little capital is invested until raw materials and components enter production; the only costs incurred refer to acquisition and holding costs.
3 The curve becomes steeper as raw materials and components are gradually incorporated into the final product. This is because of accumulated manu-facturing costs and increasing interest costs that reflect the value of capital invested.
4 The curve becomes flatter at the end of the production process because no more manufacturing costs apply. At this stage the invested capital is at its highest value and the cost of stocking finished goods instead of selling them involves higher opportunity costs than holding the initial supplies. This shows why the logistician is, if anything, more concerned with PDM than MM, since the potential for cost reduction is the highest at this point of the total supply chain. Cost reduction by speeding flows of materials, work in

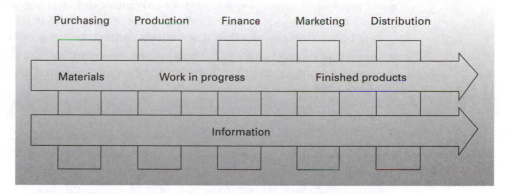

Figure 3.4   Material, product and information flows across an organisation

progress and finished products is not the only concern of the logistician. Logistics management involves two flows. The first, as stated above, is the flow of materials and work in progress across the organisation to the ultimate customer. The second, as shown in Figure 3.2, is a reverse flow of information in the form of orders or other indicators on which future demand forecasts can be based. Such forecasts, as Gattorna stated, can in turn 'trigger replenishment orders which produce inventories at distribution centres. These orders influence production schedules which, in turn, help to determine the timing and quantities with which raw materials are procured'.[6]

Logistics management should be regarded as a total system rather than as a function. In essence it is a way of thinking about, planning and synchronising related activities. Figure 3.4 also shows how logistics management crosses conventional functions.

3.3   Logistics management objectives

The whole purpose of logistics is to provide 'availability'. Everyone will be familiar with the cliché, 'the right product in the right place at the right time'. If one adds 'at least cost' then that is precisely the objective of logistics management.

Apart from reduced costs and increased availability, logistics management seeks to:

■ reduce conflict and promote cooperation and coordination between subsystems concerned with material and information flows, based on the recognition that their activities are interrelated and interdependent;

■ reduce the time spent at every stage of the chain from procurement to delivery to the customer, i.e. lead time, production time, transportation time;

■ ensure the highest possible level of customer service and satisfaction by achieving the right combination of product availability and dependability;

■ control and, where possible, reduce inventory of materials, work in progress and finished goods to provide stock levels at which the costs of stockholding are balanced by production requirements and customer service;

■ encourage a commitment to quality improvement so that both bought-out supplies and the products in which they are incorporated are right first time, every time.

3.4   Reverse logistics

Reverse logistics are the opposite of forward logistics and may be defined as:[7]

> **The process of planning, implementing and controlling the efficient, cost-effective flow of raw materials, in process inventory, finished goods and related information from the point of consumption to the point of origin for the purpose of recapturing value or proper disposal.**

The two principal drivers of interest in reverse logistics in waste disposal have been the increased importance attached to the environmental aspects of waste disposal and a recognition of the potential returns that can be obtained from the reuse of products, or parts or the recycling of materials. Reverse logistics may also apply to goods sent to distributors on a sale-or-return basis, unused materials to be returned to stores from contracts or from subcontractors. The main activities involved with reverse logistics are therefore as shown in Figure 3.5.

Figure 3.5 shows that the main reverse logistical activities include collection of returnable items, their inspection and separation and the application of a range of disposition options including repair, reconditioning, upgrading, remanufacture, demanufacture (parts reclamation) and recycling. Disposition-logic also includes

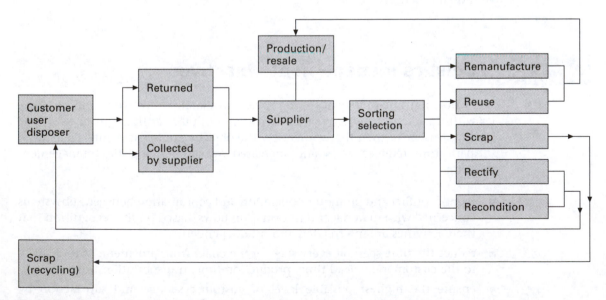

Figure 3.5   Reverse logistics network

channel or routing logic, i.e. the returned items and components can be sent back to the customer, routed to a warehouse or production or sold in secondary markets.

In the computer industry, for example, companies such as IBM are seeking ways of enabling customers to refurbish existing computers or to buy used parts. A number of software providers have devised programs to provide logistics solutions along the entire life cycle of a product including the options available at the end of its working life.

3.5 Logistics and supply chains

Comparison of the diagram of a simplistic internal supply chain shown in Figure 3.6 with Figures 3.2 and 3.4 relating to logistics management shows that the areas of coverage are virtually the same.

There are many definitions of the term 'supply chain', of which the following is typical:[8]

> **A supply chain is that network of organisations that are involved, through upstream and downstream linkages, in the different processes and activities that produce value in the form of products and services in the hands of the ultimate customer.**

Again, a comparison with the earlier definitions of logistics will indicate common ground. Such considerations have led writers such as Bowersox[9] to regard the issues of logistics and supply chain management as practically synonymous. Another writer, Greenwood[10] observes: 'If we analyse what the experts are calling supply chain management we find that they are really talking logistics but driven by the requirements of the decade'.

The UK Institute of Logistics and Transport[11] also relates the two approaches by stating that:

> **Logistics is the time-related positioning of resources or the strategic management of the total supply chain.**

An alternative definition is that supply chain management is:

> **The coordination of material, information and financial flows between and among all the participating enterprises.**

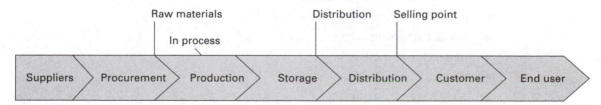

Figure 3.6 A simple supply chain

In this

- *information flows* relate to the demand forecasts, order transmissions and delivery status reports;
- *product flows* relate to the movement of products from supplier to customer and the reverse via product returns, servicing, recycling and disposal;
- *financial flows* relate to credit card information, credit terms, payment schedules, consignment and title ownership arrangements.

Other writers such as Cooper *et al.*,[12] however, distinguish between logistics and supply chain management, and regard the former as concerned with material and information flows and inventories in the chain. Supply chain management is the integrating of all business processes across the supply chain.

The elements in the framework of supply chain management as identified by Cooper *et al.* are shown in Figure. 3.6. Cooper states that supply chain business processes can cross intra- and inter-organisational boundaries independently of formal structure. They define a business process as:

A specific ordering of work activities across a time and place, with a beginning, an end and clearly identified inputs and outputs, a structure for action.

Cooper *et al.* note seven processes identified by the International Centre for Competitive Excellence:

- customer relationship management
- customer service management
- demand management
- order fulfilment
- manufacturing flow management
- procurement
- produce development and commercialisation.

From a review of the literature, Cooper *et al.* also identify 10 supply chain management components:

- planning and control
- work structure
- organisation structure
- product flow facility structure
- information flow facility structure
- product structure
- management methods
- power and leadership structure
- risk and reward structure
- culture and attitude.

Cooper *et al.* conclude that, to achieve the objective of integrated supply chain management most if not all management functions and business processes are involved. This integrated concept makes SCM more than logistics.

3.6   Supply chain networks

Most supply chains are actually networks. Although the word 'chain' is commonly used, the terms 'supply network' or 'supply web' are generally more technically accurate. Lamming[13] has defined a supply network as:

> A set of supply chains which together describe the flow of goods and services from their original sources to their end users. The term 'network' is intended to imply a more strategic concept in line with the idea that networks compete with networks, rather than simply firms with firms.

The typical network presentation of a supply chain is shown in Figure 3.7. The nodes represent activities or facilities that add value to the supply chain. The links to the nodes represent transportation lanes for the materials, components, semi-finished and finished products.

Research by Zheng *et al.*[14] identified nine different types of activity that companies can perform in coordinating and managing supply networks:

- partners
- risk and benefit sharing
- resource integration
- information processing
- knowledge capture
- social coordination
- decision making

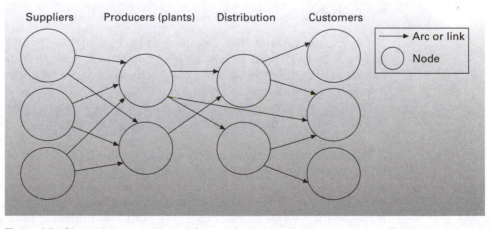

Figure 3.7   Network representation of a supply chain

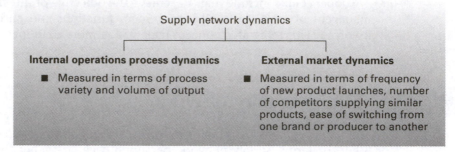

Figure 3.8 Supply network dynamics

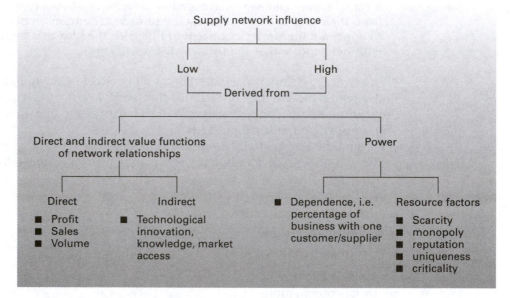

Figure 3.9 Supply network influence

- conflict resolution
- motivation.

The researchers found that a number of these activities tend to cluster together and be more associated with some networks than others. They also identified two factors as providing the basis of a classification of chain networks: supply network dynamics and supply network influence.

The *dynamics factor* shown in Figure 3.8 describes the internal process dynamics and the external market dynamics which jointly determine the difficulty of the supply process.

The *supply network influence* shown in Figure 3.9 is a measure of a particular organisation's ability to manage its supplier network. This factor was measured according to whether research respondents perceived their supplier as too large or too powerful for them to influence. Respondents with a high degree of influence *managed* their supply networks. Those with low influence only *coped* with their supply networks.

Zheng *et al*. concluded that the dimensions of the degree of supply network influence have a substantial impact on how firms attempt to manage within supply networks, i.e. their pattern of networking. A combination of the two dimensions also enables the identification of four types of supply network:

Type 1: Dynamic / Low degree of focal firm influence.

Type 2: Dynamic / High degree of focal firm influence.

Type 3: Routinised / Low degree of focal firm influence.

Type 4: Routinised / High degree of focal firm influence.

The characteristics of each of the above four supply networks are set out in Table 3.2.

The significance of the above research is that focusing on the relationships between types of supply network and network creation and operation enables managers to identify the type of network they are in and to apply networking activities in an appropriate manner according to their circumstances.

3.7 Value chains

Supply chains are linked to value chains. The concept of *value chain analysis* developed by Porter[15] views procurement as a support activity which contributes to the competitive advantage of a business by adding value. A value chain may be defined as:[16]

A linear map of the way in which value is added through a process from raw materials to finished delivered product (including continuing service after delivery).

An alternative definition is:

A strategic collaboration of organisations for the purpose of meeting specific market objectives over the long term and for the mutual benefit of all links of the chain.

Important models of value chains have been developed by Porter and Hines.

3.7.1 Porter's model

Porter's approach may be summarised as follows:

1 Within an industry many business units produce products or services that are similar if not identical to those of their competitors.

2 A business unit can obtain a competitive advantage over its rivals in two basic ways: cost leadership and differentiation. *Cost leadership* means that the business unit has a significant cost advantage over the competitors. *Differentiation* implies that the product or service offers something unmatched by its competitors that they value more than a lower price. An enterprise can obtain

Table 3.2 Characteristics of four supply networks

	Network type 1	Network type 2	Network type 3	Network type 4
Operating conditions	Dynamic	Dynamic	Stable	Stable
Factors influencing dynamic/stable operating conditions — Internal	■ High product variety ■ Low volumes of output		■ Low product variety ■ High volumes of output ■ Cost and quality as primary competitive priorities	
Factors influencing dynamic/stable operating conditions — External	■ Many competitors supplying similar products ■ High frequency of product launches ■ Demand therefore uncertain		■ Small number of competitors supplying similar products ■ Low frequency of new product launches ■ Mature industries with established supply chains	
Degrees of influence	Low	High	Low	High
Factors relating to degree of influence	■ Relatively small size of focal firm in volume terms compared with other customers/suppliers ■ Low profile of focal firm making it an unattractive business reference to other firms	■ Relatively large size in volume terms compared with other customers/suppliers ■ High profile of focal firm making it an attractive business reference to other firms ■ High profits contributed to other firms ■ Focal firm may be a 'bottleneck supplier' or market conduit providing access to other relationships	■ Due to factors similar to those in network type 1	■ Due to factors similar to those in network type 2
Organisational examples	Electronic suppliers dealing with large OEMs, e.g. Filtronics	Large telecommunications OEMs, e.g. Nokia, Motorola	Minor suppliers in processor textile industries, e.g. Bairdwear	Centrally positioned car assemblers or high volume food and drink manufacturers e.g. Toyota or Ikea
Significant activity clusters	■ Risk and benefit sharing ■ Knowledge capture ■ Human resource integration ■ Motivating	■ Partner selection (focal firms can select their partners) ■ Knowledge capture ■ Human resource integration ■ Decision making	■ Risk and benefit sharing ■ Equipment integration ■ Information processing ■ Motivation	■ Partner selection ■ Equipment integration ■ Information processing ■ Decision making
Management control over network	Coping largely outside management control	Managing network	Coping as type 1	Managing network

OEM original equipment manufacturer

Source: Zheng, J., Johnsen, T.E., Harland, C.M. and Lamming, R.C., *A Taxonomy of Supply Networks*, 10th International Annual IPSERA Conference, 2001

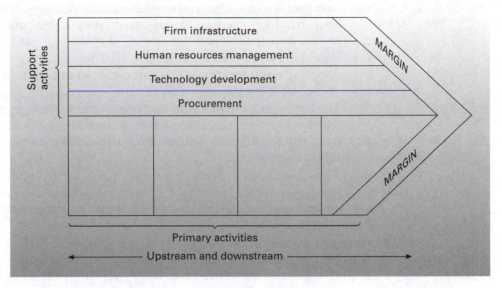

Figure 3.10 The value chain

competitive advantage by improving products, employing new procedures, implementing new technologies and in many similar ways.

3   The activities of a business unit can be classified into five primary and four support activities, each of which will contribute to the competitive advantage of the business these comprise the *value chain* (see Figure 3.10).

The five core activities are:

(a) *Inbound logistics* – all activities linked to receiving, handling and storing inputs into the production system including warehousing, transport and stock control.

(b) *Operations* – all activities involved in the transformation of inputs to outputs as the final product(s). In a manufacturing enterprise these would include production, assembly, quality control and packaging. In a service industry these include all activities involved in providing the service, e.g. advice, correspondence and preparation of documents by a legal firm.

(c) *Outbound logistics* – activities involved in moving the output from operations to the end user including finished goods warehousing, order processing, order picking and packing, shipping, transport, maintenance of a dealer or distribution network.

(d) *Marketing and sales* – activities involved in informing potential customers about the product, persuading them to buy and enabling them to do so, including advertising, promotion, market research and dealer/distributor support.

(e) *Service* – activities involved in the provision of services to buyers, offered as part of the purchase agreement, including installation, spare parts delivery, maintenance and repair, technical assistance, buyer enquiries and complaints.

The four support activities to the above primary activities are:

(a) *Firm infrastructure* or general administration, including activities, cost and assets relating to general management safety and security, management information systems and the formation of strategic alliances.

(b) *Human resources* – all activities involved in recruiting, hiring, training, developing and sanctioning the people in an organisation.

(c) *Technology development* activities relating to product design and improvement of production processes and resource utilisation, including research and development, process design improvement, computer software, computer aided design and engineering, and development of computerised support systems.

(d) *Procurement* – all activities involved in acquiring resource inputs to the primary activities including the purchase of fuel, energy, raw materials, components, sub-assemblies, merchandise and consumable items from external vendors.

4   Each activity within a value chain provides inputs which, after processing, constitute added value to the output received by the ultimate customer in the form of a product or service or as the aggregate of values at the end of the value chain. Value is what a company creates measured by the amount buyers are willing to pay for the product or service. The difference between value and cost determines the company's profitability. Competitive advantage comes from the company having a lower cost or higher value than its competitors.

5   *Linkages* are the means of joining the interdependent parts of the value chain. Such linkages take place when one element affects the costs or effectiveness of another in the value chain. Thus the installation of a computer system may reduce the cost of administration. E-procurement can lower the cost of obtaining resources. Linkages require coordination. Ensuring delivery on time requires the coordination of operations (production) outbound logistics and service activities.

6   Value chains differ. This is because activities in individual companies are affected by many variables, including ways of working, the size and financial resources of the enterprise, capacity for innovation, workforce skills and the degree of internal integration. The internal costs of a manufacturer that makes all of its own parts will normally be higher than those of a competitor who buys from external suppliers and only performs assembly operations.

7   *Value systems* reflect that a company value chain has both internal and external linkages. Thus a company can obtain competitive advantage by managing the links between itself and suppliers and customers. An example of such linkages is a just-in-time system where the close integration of a purchaser's operations with those of suppliers is essential.

A representation of a value system is given in Figure 3.11.

8   The procurement activity, which links both with the other eight internal core and support activities and with the external environment, has tremendous potential to contribute to the competitiveness of the business unit. This competitiveness is not limited to reducing the cost of purchased materials.

3.7.2   Hines' model

Writing in 1993, Peter Hines[17] both recognises and provides a critique of Porter's work and presents an alternative model. Hines' approach is summarised below.

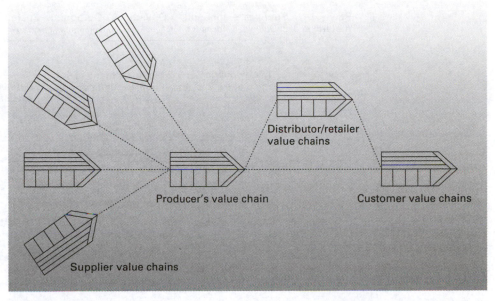

Figure 3.11   A value system

Source: adapted from Porter, M.E., *Competitive Advantage*, Free Press, 1985

The contribution of Porter

Hines recognises that Porter's work has made two major contributions to our understanding of value chain systems:

> Firstly, it has placed a major emphasis on the Materials Management value adding mechanism, raising the subject to a strategic level in the minds of senior executives.
> Secondly, it has placed the customer in an important position in the supply chain.

A critique of Porter

Three major problems are identified in relation to Porter's model.

- Neither Porter nor the firms discussed concede that consumer satisfaction and not company profit should be their primary objective. The focus of the Porter model is on the profit margin of each enterprise, not the consumer's satisfaction.

- Although Porter acknowledges the importance of integration, his model shows a rather divided network, both within the company and between the different organisations in the supply chain.

- Hines believes that the wrong functions are highlighted as important in both Porter's primary and secondary activities.

Hines suggests that the above three criticisms result from the fact that Porter's model is based solely on American cases 'without reference to more innovative

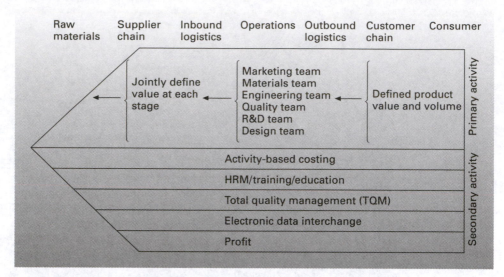

Figure 3.12 Hines' integrated materials value pipeline

Japanese enterprises'. Porter's conclusions may therefore 'prove inappropriate for companies facing the challenges of the 21st Century with the prospect of an array of more developed competitors. Indeed in some cases close adherence to Porter's methodology may prevent firms from further continual development'.

Alternative models

To correct the above problems, Hines offers two models: (i) a *micro* integrated materials value pipeline and (ii) a *macro* ten force partnership model. The integrated materials value pipeline is shown in Figure 3.12.

The main contrasts between the Porter and Hines models are summarised in Table 3.3.

Table 3.3 Porter's and Hines' models contrasted

	Porter	*Hines*
Principal objective	Profitability	Consumer satisfaction
Processes 1	Push system	Pull system
Structure and direction	Series of chains linking firms pointing from raw material source to customer	One large flow pointing from consumer to raw material source
Primary activities	Inbound logistics, operations, outbound logistics, marketing and sales service	Teams concerned with marketing, materials, engineering, quality, R&D and design
Secondary (support) activities	Firm infrastructure, HRM, technology development, procurement	Activity-based costing, HRM/training/education. TQM, EDI, profit

Important features of the Hines model are:

- The value chain points in the opposite direction from that in the Porter model, emphasising differences in both objectives and processes.
- Demand is determined by collective customer-defined price levels.
- Primary functions in each of the separate firms in the value chain must be integrated and 'traditional arm's length external barriers and internal divisions broken down'. An emphasis on collaboration rather than competition.
- Key primary functions and secondary activities differ as shown in Table 3.3. The significance of each of the secondary activities identified by Hines is, briefly:
  - Activity-based costing (ABC) enables the exact cost of products and the benefits of activities such as *Kaizen* or value analysis to be ascertained. By allocating costs to activities rather than functions we can identify the true costs involved in delivering the product. A simpler method of value chain analysis is to call the price charges to the customer at the end of the supply chain 100 per cent and, by working backwards, ascertain the cost of each supply activity. Activity-based costing is considered further in Chapter 18. It enables the most serious non-value-adding problems to be identified first and promptly addressed.
  - Human resources management (HRM), and especially employee training and education, facilitates effectiveness, efficiency and proactive thinking.
  - Total quality management (TQM) provides a culture for all network members.
  - Electronic data interchange (EDI) facilitates quick response to customer requirements and draws network members closer together.
  - Profit which should be roughly equalised between network members and result from reducing total production and consumption costs below what consumers are willing to pay for products meeting their specifications.

The macro ten force partnership model shown in Figure 3.13 widens the analysis from that of a company with a single supply source to the whole range of supply pipelines and identifies the forces that encourage rapid and sustained development. The whole network includes several tiers or layers of supplying companies.

Hines states that the ten forces identified in Figure 3.13 describe a variety of forces that encourage rapid and sustained continual development. It should be noted that the model as shown by Hines in Figure 3.13 relates to assembly-type production, thus the first of the ten forces is the creative tension developed between competing final assemblers or OEMs (original equipment manufacturers). This creative tension results from both cooperation and competition between OEMs. The cooperation derives from OEMs developing common suppliers. The competition is rivalry in attempting to meet consumer requirements. Cooperation is fostered through supplier associations referred to later in this book.

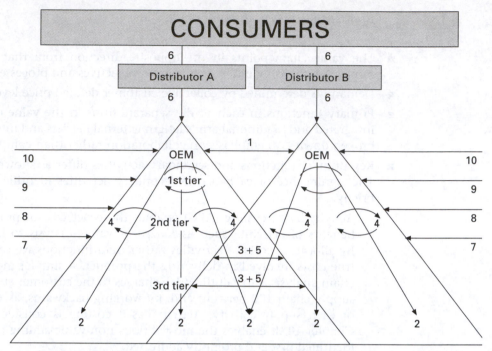

1. Creative tension between cooperation and competition, perhaps between different industrial sectors
2. Supply chain development and OEM (original equipment manufacturer) development by equitable profit feedback benefits
3. Cross-network benefit spread effect
4. *Kyoryoku Kai* internal subcontractor development
5. Inter-supplier rivalry to find a favoured network position
6. The consumers' changing needs and tastes
7. New entrants
8. Substitutes
9. Stable long-term cheap finance
10. Government agencies creating a developmental environment

Figure 3.13   Hines' ten force partnership model

3.8   Supply chain requirements and software

Essential supply chain requirements are connectivity, integration, visibility and responsiveness.

■ *Connectivity* is the capability of exchanging information with external supply chain partners in a timely, responsive and usable format which facilitates inter-organisational collaboration.

■ *Integration* is the process of combining or coordinating separate functions, processors or producers and enabling them to interact in a seamless manner.

■ *Visibility* is the ability to access or view pertinent data or information as it relates to logistics and the supply chain.

■ *Responsiveness* is the ability to react quickly to customer needs or specifications by delivering a product of the right quality, at the right time at the right place at the lowest possible cost.

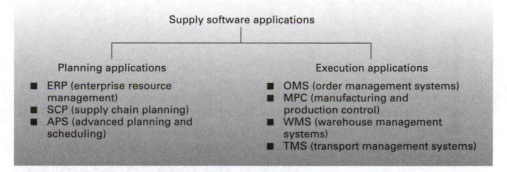

Figure 3.14   Supply software applications

Initially, software providers specialised in either management planning and execution applications, as shown in Figure 3.14. The current emphasis is on the creation of software that integrates each of the software types shown in Figure 3.14 and deals with the supply chain as a continuous process rather than as individual stages. The leading ERP (enterprise resource management) vendors have either purchased or partnered with an APS (advanced planning and scheduling) vendor and are swiftly developing internet versions of their supply chain offerings. Internet supply chains cause the walls between internal and external supply chains to break down. EAI (enterprise application integration) enables providers to convert their entire suites of enterprise applications into e-business applications and provide a framework that ties businesses electronically to their customers, suppliers, supply chains, electronic trading communities and business partners. Such suites offer several advantages:

■ An integrated suite presents a single view to the user from screen to screen. Information is stored in a single database and the rekeying of information from one system into another is eliminated.

■ A single database provides a tighter integration of business processes.

■ Maintenance is cheaper and upgrades easier when there is only one system to upgrade and one supplier to work with.

■ For the above reasons, connectivity, integration, visibility and responsiveness are the hallmarks of software systems now coming to market.

3.9   Lean and agile supply chains

3.9.1   Lean supply

As an aspect of lean production, lean supply is defined by Lamming[18] as:

> The state of business in which there is dynamic competition and collaboration of equals in the supply chain, aimed at adding value at minimum total cost, while maximising end customer service and product quality.

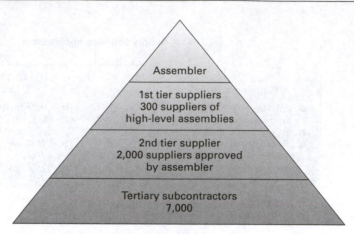

Figure 3.15 Typical Japanese supplier tier structure

The core concept of lean thinking is the Japanese term *muda*, exemplified in the practice of Japanese motor manufacturers as described in *The Machine that Changed the World* by Womack *et al.*[19] *Muda* means 'waste' or any human activity which absorbs resources but creates no value. Examples of *muda* are spoiled production, unnecessary processing steps, the purposeless movement of employees and goods, time wasted in waiting for materials, uneconomic inventories, and goods and services which fail to meet customers' requirements. Lean thinking is lean because it does more with less.

The main features of supply relationships between the car producers (termed assemblers) and their suppliers as described by Womack *et al.* are:

- Purchase of whole components or sub-assemblers, e.g. seats, rather than constituent parts of an assembly from first-tier supplies.
- First-tier suppliers are not selected on the basis of bids but on the basis of past relationships and a proven record of performance.
- First-tier suppliers usually have teams of second-tier suppliers – specialist independent manufacturers who may, in turn engage third- or even fourth-tier suppliers. Second- and other tier companies make individual parts to drawings supplied by the first-tier company. See Figure 3.15.
- Complex parts are provided by one supplier. Less complex parts are ordered from two or more suppliers.
- Target costing in which the car assembler establishes a target price for the vehicle. Assembler and suppliers then work backwards to ascertain how the car can be made for the price while allowing reasonable profit for both the assembler and suppliers.
- The use of value engineering, value analysis and learning curves to reduce initial and subsequent cost of suppliers.
- Use of teams of highly skilled workers and use of highly flexible automated machines.
- Just-in-time (JIT) deliveries to assembly lines.

- Zero defective parts. Where a supplier fails to meet quality or reliability requirements a cooperative effort is made to ascertain the cause. In the interim, part of the business is temporarily transferred to another supplier.

- Cooperation between assembler and first-tier suppliers effected through supplier associations which meet to share new findings on better ways to make parts. Some companies also have associations with their second-tier suppliers.

- Through negotiations the assembler and supplier agree on a cost-reduction curve over the four-year life of the product. Any supplier-derived cost savings beyond those agreed to go to the supplier.

- Relationships between assembler and supplier based on a 'basic contract' which expresses a long-term commitment to work together for mutual benefit. The contract also lays down rules relating to prices, quality assurance, ordering, delivery, proprietary rights and materials supply.

3.9.2 Agile supply

An agile enterprise has been defined as:[20]

> **A fast moving, adaptable and robust business capable of rapid adaptation in response to unexpected and unpredicted changes and events, market opportunities and customer requirements. Such a business is founded on processes and structures that facilitate speed adaptation and robustness and deliver a coordinated enterprise that is capable of achieving competitive performance in a highly dynamic and unpredictable business environment that is unsuited to current enterprise practices.**

Agile production is the latest stage of a movement away from the mass production of the 1970s, through the decentralised production of the 1980s and the lean production of the 1990s. The drivers for agile production include rapidly changing and unpredictable markets, the emphasis on mass customisation rather than mass production, the rapid rates of technological innovation and shorter product life cycles.

Sometimes lean and agile production are regarded as synonymous but there are significant differences that are reflected in lean and product supply chains. Harrison et al.[21] identify five major differences in emphasis between lean and agile systems. These differences, together with a comparison of efficient/functional and innovative/responsive supply chain processes derived from Fisher et al.[22] in which the former approximate to 'lean' and the latter to 'agile' mindsets, are set out in Table 3.4.

As Harrison et al.[23] states, there is 'no suggestion that agility should replace the concept of leanness. Rather agility is a better long term strategy for a supply chain to cope with turbulence in mass markets – here leanness should be viewed as an enabler to agility'.

3.9.3 Time compression

Time compression is an important facet of agile supply chains since it increases productivity and reduces risk while providing competitive advantage by rapid

Table 3.4   Comparison of lean and agile production systems

Factor	Lean production	Agile production
Primary purposes	■ Meeting predictable demand efficiently at the lowest possible cost ■ Elimination of waste from the supply chain	Rapid response to unpredictable demand to minimise stockouts, forced markdowns and obsolete inventory
Manufacturing focus	Maintenance of a high average utilisation unit	Deployment of excess buffer capacity
Inventory strategy	High stock turn and minimum inventory	Deployment of significant buffer stocks of parts to respond to demand
Lead time focus	Shorten lead time provided it does not increase cost	Invest aggressively in resources that will reduce lead times
Approach to supplier selection	Select for cost and quality	Select primarily for speed, flexibility and quality
Supply linkages	Emphasis on long-term supply chain partnerships that are consolidated over time	Emphasis on virtual supply chains where partnerships are reconfigured according to new market opportunities
Performance measurement	Emphasis on world class measures based on such criteria as quality and productivity	Emphasis on customer-facing metrics such as orders met on time in full
Work organisation	Emphasis on work standardisation, i.e. doing it the same way every time	Emphasis on self-management and ability to respond immediately to new opportunities from all involved in work processes
Work planning and control	Emphasis on the protection of operations core by a fixed period in the planning cycle to help balance resources, synchronise material movements and reduce waste	Emphasis on the need for immediate interpretation of customer demand and instantaneous responsl

response to customer requirements. Time compression, as Beesley[24] states, 'is all about the reduction of the time consumed by business through the elimination of non-value-adding process time'. Waste of time is more serious than waste of material since time cannot be replaced. While some processes produce very little added value and should be eliminated, the majority do add some value and should be subject to compression where time is used as a measure. Beesley claims that at least 95 per cent of the process time is accounted as non-value-adding. The time compression approach has applications to order processing inventory and costs. Thus, as Beesley shows, 'as a general rule, the volume of inventory held in a supply chain is proportional to the length of the chain expressed as the total time to customer'. If the supply chain is time compressed, work in progress, cycle and buffer stocks are reduced, with consequent lower overhead, capital and operating costs.

| 3.10 | **Supply chain optimisation** |

This may be defined as:

> the management of complex supply chains in their entirety with the objectives of synchronising all value adding production and distribution activities and the elimination of such activities that do not add value.

Cannon[25] points out that supply chain management is 'not about minimising the effectiveness and profitability of the individual units whether factories, warehouses or transport fleets' but 'optimising the whole to achieve better service at lower cost with less industry'. He instances five ways in which this can be done:

- Reducing waste and non-value-adding activities such as handling or excess inventory.
- Increasing customer service responsibilities, for example by reducing lead times.
- Improving supply chain communication especially with regard to forecasting.
- Reducing the time for new product development.
- Coordinating better the efforts of all component links in the supply chain.

| 3.11 | **Supply chains and purchasing** |

The supplier chain concept may affect traditional purchasing in several ways.

- Purchasing may no longer be regarded as a discrete function but as an activity within an integrated supply chain.
- The head of purchasing may report to a materials, logistics or supply chain manager rather than at a higher level. Figures 3.16 and 3.17 are based on a 1997 survey by the Bourton Consultancy Group.[26] Figure 3.16 shows that responsibility for supply chain issues is headed by a dedicated director in about 15 per cent of responding companies and by a specific manager in another 45 per cent. In a further 20 per cent, responsibility is with the operations or production director.

  Figure 3.17 indicates that the person running the supply chain reports to the managing director or chief exeartive officer in just under half of the responding companies. In the other half ultimate responsibility is mainly with directors and general managers or with operations or manufacturing directors. Reporting responsibility for the supply chain appears to be below director level in about 16 per cent of cases.
- The number of purchasing staff is likely to be reduced owing to some former purchasing activities being made redundant by IT or taken over by other teams, e.g. supplier selection, inventions control.

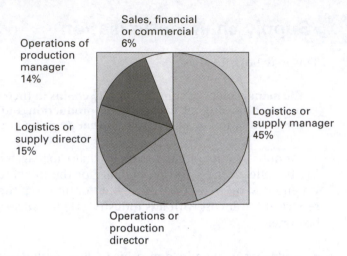

Figure 3.16 The people who run the supply chain in a sample of 344 companies

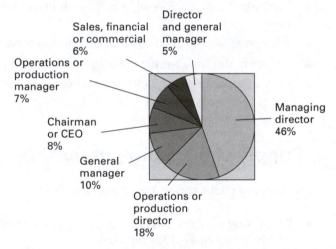

Figure 3.17 The reporting levels of people with supply chain responsibility in a sample of 344 companies

- Conversely there is a growing recognition that purchasing is more than a transaction activity in the supply chain. Since world class operations require world class suppliers, the emphasis of purchasing will be less on cost and more on supplier relationships and alliances and on contributing to the achievement of enterprise objectives along the entire supply chain.

- Purchasing staff will have to acquire competence in other supply chain activities and general management skills along with the capacity to think strategically rather than functionally and operationally. This gives further force to the observation of Lamming quoted in Chapter 1, that strategic purchasing requires a broad rather than a narrow knowledge base.

Supply chains are basically a series of suppliers and customers; every customer becomes in turn a supplier to the next downstream activity or function until the finished product reaches the consumer. As an upstream supply chain member, purchasing can undertake a number of significant activities including:

- Providing downstream customers with expert analysis of forecasting, servicing, delivery and supplies information throughout the supply chain.
- Providing critical information to strategic managers on material, prices, availability and supplier issues.
- Selecting and rationalising the number of first-tier suppliers.
- Ensuring that appropriate contractual mechanisms are employed.
- Ensuring that suppliers meet performance expectations.
- Forging effective relationships and long-term partnerships with key suppliers and resolving problems as they arise.
- Locating suppliers who can, where required, contribute agility to supply chains.
- Negotiating the best possible contracts and procedures for transportation and distribution.
- Providing suppliers with accurate forecasts of requirements and facilitating such approaches as just-in-time and vendor-managed inventory.
- Working as part of a consortium to obtain maximum possible value in respect of all supplies through the implementation of value engineering and value analysis.
- Advising on make-or-buy decisions, outsourcing, leasing and similar strategies.
- Involvement in the selection of appropriate supply chain packages and the implementation of e-procurement.
- Ensuring that staff receive appropriate training in general management, supply chain strategies and special aspects of purchasing.

? Discussion questions

3.1 Consider the activities listed under production and consumer logistics in Figure 3.1. In what ways will the execution of such activities differ in civilian as distinct from military situations?

3.2 In the nineteenth century the standard grain and hay ration for horses was about 25 pounds (11.4 kilograms) and the daily forage of a corps of 10,000 cavalry weighed as much (allowing for remounts) as the food for 60,000 men. Forage requirements also tended to be self-generating since the animals needed to transport it also had to be fed.

In World War II, without counting transoceanic shipment, fuel made up half the resupply and replacement needs of US forces in Europe, and the average ammunition requirements of western forces in combat zones was 12 per cent of total needs.

Consider some of the logistical implications of the above facts.

3.3 Under what conditions would you recommend a materials management approach as appropriate to the needs of an enterprise? What are some possible disadvantages of materials management?

3.4 In what ways, if any, can reverse logistics add value?

3.5 A frequent observation is that the traditional supply chain is on its way out, to be superseded by new models reliant on information flow and cooperation for supply chain success.

How may modern supply chains differ from older models in respect of the four characteristics of

■ connectivity

■ execution

■ creativity and innovation

■ speed?

3.6 Sovereign is a producer of chair lifts for use in homes, hospitals and hotels. The main elements of the chair lift are the electronics including the motor, the track, and the seat mechanism. The electronics and seal mechanisms are fairly standard and are purchased from outside suppliers. The track varies in length and shape according to the individual application and is ordered for a specific application. The chair lifts are distributed through hospitals and local authority social service departments as well as being sold directly to customers through advertising. It is necessary for either Sovereign or distributors to install and maintain the chair lifts and sometimes remove them from the premises of users when they are no longer required.

Draw a supply chain showing the acquisition of bought-out parts to the installation of the chair lift. What are the main logistical problems to be considered?

3.7 Flint[27] suggests five supply cost areas where specific ideas for cost savings can be made. These are shown below. Under each heading insert examples of possible cost savings.

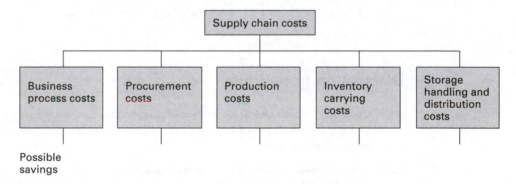

Possible
savings

3.8 From your own experience provide examples to support the following statement by Peter Drucker: 'The economy is changing structure. From being organised around a flow of things and the flow of money, it is becoming organised around the flow of information.'

3.9 Writing in the 1950s, W.H. Bower in *Some Ethical Problems of Management*, declared: 'The object of industry or commerce is not to make a profit and incidentally thereby to render a product or a service to the Community but rather the object of industry is to provide a needed product or service and thereby make a profit.'

Has this statement any relevance to the differing views of value chains of Porter and Hines?

3.10 What, if any, is the difference between a supply chain and a 'pipeline'. If there are differences, are there problems that could occur with pipelines and not supply chains and vice versa?

3.11 Womack, speaking to an aerospace conference, observed: 'The common snail travels at 0.007 miles per hour. This is more than ten times the average velocity of a part flowing through a typical fighter aircraft production system'.

What is the relevance of this statement to time compression? If you were a logistics manager in the aircraft factory what steps would you take to compress time?

3.12 In supply chains there is a danger that purchasing will be seen as an unimportant activity that can be outsourced. How can purchasing staff show that they are important contributors to supply chain effectiveness?

? Past examination questions

1 Explain the concept of *Lean Supply* and discuss how it affects the tactics and operation of the purchasing function?

(CIPS, Purchasing and Supply Chain Management II:
Tactics and Operations, May 1997)

2 The buyer of the future will probably need to be more clearly empowered and able to function effectively within a multifunctional team operating through the supply chain. Explain why this is likely to become necessary?

(CIPS, Purchasing and Supply Chain Management I: Strategy, November 1997)

3 What are the main areas of focus for the buyer when strategically planning requirements and capacity in supply chains?

(CIPS, Purchasing and Supply Chain Management I: Strategy, May 1998)

4 A strategically managed and efficient supply chain can be developed quickly. Explain the steps that need to be taken to achieve such a strategically managed supply chain.

(CIPS, Purchasing and Supply Chain Management I: Strategy, May 2000)

5 Discuss the contribution of 'Materials Management' to the strategic management of the supply chain.

(CIPS, Purchasing and Supply Chain Management I: Strategy, November 2000)

Notes

1. NATO, *Logistics Handbook*, 1997, paras 103–104
2. Knight Wendling, Logistics Report 1988 (published for private circulation)
3. Crompton, H.K. and Jessop, D.A., *Dictionary of Purchasing and Supply*, Liverpool Business Publishing, 2001, p.88
4. Council of Logistics Management USA

5. Institute of Logistics and Transport, *Glossary of Inventory and Materials Management Definitions*, 1998, p.10

6. Gattorna, J., 'Strategic issues in logistics', *Focus on Physical Distribution and Logistics Management*, Oct./Nov. 1986

7. Rogers, D.S. and Tibben-Lembke, R. Reverse Logistics Glossary on http://equinoxscs.unv.edu/homepage/rtl/reverse/glossary.html

8. Christopher, M., 'Supply chain strategy: its impact on shareholder value', *International Journal of Logistics Management*, Vol.10, No.1 (1999), p.3

9. Bowersox, D.J. and Closs, D.J., *Logistical Management: The Integrated Supply Chain Process*, McGraw-Hill, 1996

10. Greenwood, M.C., 'Continuous flow manufacturing in a quickened marketplace', *Logistics Focus*, March, 1997, pp.9–11

11. Institute of Logistics and Transport, as n.5 above.

12. Cooper, M.C., Lambert, D.M. and Pugh, J.D., 'Supply chain management – more than a new name for logistics', *International Journal of Logistics Management*, Vol.8, No.1 (1997), pp.1–4

13. Lamming, R., Johnsen, T., Zheng, J. and Harland, C.

14. Zheng, J., Johnsen, T.E., Harland, C.M. and Lamming, R.C., *A Taxonomy of Supply Networks*, 10th International Annual IPSERA Conference, 2001

15. Porter, M.E., *Competitive Advantage: Creating and Sustaining Superior Performance*, Free Press, 1985

16. Adapted from Stannock, P. and Jones, M., *The Death of Purchasing Procedures*, IPSERA, 1996

17. Hines, P., 'Integrated materials management: the value chain redefined', *International Journal of Logistics Management*, Vol.4, No.1 (1993), pp.13–22

18. Lamming, R., *Beyond Partnership – Strategies for Innovation and Lean Supply*, Prentice Hall, 1993, Ch.9, p.239

19. Womack, J.P., Jones, D.T. and Roos, D., *The Machine that Changed the World*, Maxwell Macmillan, 1990

20. Cheshire Henbury on http://www.CheshireHenbury.com (accessed 2001)

21. Harrison, A., Christopher, M. and Remko van Hock, *Creating the Agile Supply Chain*, School of Management, Cranfield University, Sept. 1999

22. Fisher, M.L., Hammond, J. and Obermeyer, W., 'Making supply meet demand in an uncertain world', *Harvard Business Review*, May/June 1994

23. Harrison *et al.*, as n.21 above, p.6

24. Beesley, A., 'Time compression – new source of competitiveness in the supply chain, *Logistics Focus*, June 1995, pp.24–5. For an excellent description of time compression see Beesley, A., 'Time compression in the supply chain', in Water, D. (ed.), *Global Logistics and Distribution*, Kogan Page, 1999, Ch.11, pp.180–92

25. Cannon, S., *Restructuring the Supply Chain* on www.cips.org.uk (accessed 2002)

26. Bourton Group, *Half Delivered – A Survey of Strategies and Tactics in Managing the Supply Chain in Manufacturing Businesses*, 1997, pp.26–7

27. Flint, C., *Logistics Focus*, November 1997, p.27

Purchasing and supply chain strategy

Learning goals

After reading this chapter you should be able to:

- Define the terms strategy, strategic planning and strategic decisions.
- Distinguish between alternative views of strategy.
- Differentiate between strategy and tactics.
- Distinguish between institutional, corporate, business, functional/operational and global strategies.
- State the characteristics of the four 'grand' strategies, i.e. growth, stability, combination and retrenchment.
- Identify the main growth strategies.
- Discuss the competitive and adaptive strategies of Porter, Miles and Snow.
- State the main stages in the strategic planning process.
- Distinguish between purchasing/procurement strategy at corporate/business and functional/operational levels.
- Describe the purposes and processes of environmental scanning.
- Classify material requirements from strategic perspectives.
- Discuss Porter's five forces model of industrial attractiveness.
- Prepare vision and mission statements relative to purchasing.
- Derive purchasing and supply chain objectives from mission statements.
- Relate purchasing objectives to supply objectives.
- Show how functional/operating decisions are derived from corporate strategy decisions.
- Distinguish between strategy formulation and implementation.
- Prepare purchasing policy statements.
- State some principles and policies of strategy evaluation and control.
- Identify the main strategic options.

The first part of this chapter aims to provide an understanding of strategy, the levels at which it operates and how strategy is formulated, implemented and evaluated. The second part applies such concepts to purchasing and supply chain management.

4.1 The vocabulary of strategy

4.1.1 Strategy

Mintzberg[1] points out that 'the word strategy has long been used implicitly in different ways even if it has traditionally been defined in only one'. He therefore offers five definitions of strategy as ploy, pattern, position and perspective and plan:

- As a *ploy*, strategy can be 'a specific "manoeuvre" intended to outwit an opponent or competitor'.
- As a *pattern*, strategy is a 'stream of actions (demonstrating) consistency in behaviour whether or not intended'.
- As a *position*, strategy is a 'means of locating an organisation in an "*environment*"'. By this definition strategy becomes the mediating force between the organisation and all the external forces – competitive, cooperative, economic, ethical, legal, political – with which it interacts.
- As a *perspective*, strategy is a concept or 'ingrained way of perceiving the world'. As Mintzberg observes: 'It is important to remember that no one has ever seen a strategy or touched one; Every strategy is an invention, a figment of someone's imagination, whether conceived of as intentions to regulate behaviour before it takes place or inferred as patterns to describe behaviour that has already occurred'.
- As a *plan*, an intended course of action.

4.1.2 Strategic management

Strategic management is concerned with: The formulation, implementation and evaluation of strategies designed to achieve the objectives of an enterprise and functions within that enterprise.

Mintzberg[2] states that strategy formulation can:

- be created entrepreneurially by a visionary leader who recognises the environmental opportunities and threats facing an organisation;
- emerge incrementally as managers through the organisation adopt corporate and functional strategies to meet environmental changes.

4.1.3 Strategic planning

Strategic planning is:[3]

The process aimed at achieving an enterprise's mission and objectives by reconciling its resources with opportunities and threats in the business environment.

4.1.4   Strategic decisions

Strategic decisions are:[4]

Those that determine the overall direction of an enterprise and its ultimate inability in the light of the predictable, the unpredictable and the unknowledgable changes that may occur in its most important surrounding environment.

4.1.5   Strategic business units

Strategic business units (SBUs) are single businesses or collections of single businesses that are independent and form their own strategies.

4.1.6   Strategy and tactics

Tactics are:[5]

short-term decisions made in response to changing circumstances so as to make the best use of existing resources, sometimes known as operational planning.

Strategic plans must be broken down into less generalised operating or tactical plans designed to implement the strategic plans of top management. *Tactical plans* relate to limited functional areas, e.g. finance, production, purchasing. They also encompass shorter timeframes than strategic plans.

4.2   Levels of strategy

Strategies are formulated, implemented and evaluated at five organisational levels: institutional, corporate, business, global, and functional and operational.

4.2.1   Institutional strategy

Institutional strategy involves making decisions and commitments that define the human and social standards by which the organisation operates. It asks that strategic question 'what kind of reputation, character or personality do we wish this enterprise to have?' Institutional strategy has therefore strong, ethical implications.

4.2.2   Corporate strategy

Corporate strategy involves making decisions that set and guide resource allocations for the total enterprise. It asks the strategic question 'what business or businesses should we be in?' Corporate strategy is concerned with decisions

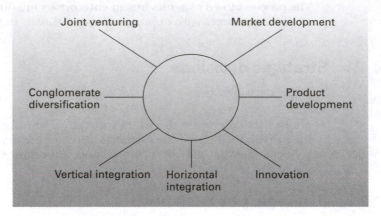

Figure 4.1 Some corporate growth strategies

relating to the four 'alternative' grand strategies: growth, stability, combination and retrenchment.

Growth strategy

This is adopted when an organisation seeks to expand its relative market share through increasing its level of operations as shown in Figure 4.1.

■ *Market development* focuses on finding new markets for existing products and services or achieving increased penetration by recruiting new customers in existing markets.

■ *Product development* focuses on the application of research and development to create new products or services in related areas or funding new applications for existing products/services.

■ *Innovation* focuses on creating entirely new products/services that make those of both the enterprise and its competitors obsolete so that customers will upgrade to the new products/services available.

■ *Horizontal integration* focuses on expanding operations by acquiring other enterprises operating in the same industry or merging with customers thereby reducing competition as shown in Figure 4.2.

From a purchasing and supply chain management standpoint, *backward* integration might be considered:

– when the volume of bought-out business is large enough to yield the same economies of scale that occur to suppliers;

– when suppliers' profit margins are high;

– when purchased items are major cost components;

– when suppliers' skills and expertise can be easily acquired;

– to reduce dependence on suppliers of critical components;

– to reduce vulnerability to price rises by key or powerful suppliers.

Forward integration can:

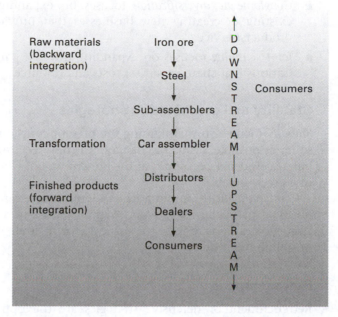

Figure 4.2   Vertical integration

–   avoid dependence on distributors who have no particular allegiance to a particular brand or product and tends to 'push' items that yield the highest profits;

–   provide production with stable, continuous and predictable demand requirements;

–   provide cost savings by eliminating intermediaries or distributors.

Some disadvantages of vertical integration include:

–   Difficulties in balancing capacity at each stage of the supply chain since the efficient scale of operation of each link in the supply chain can vary. When internal capacity is inadequate to supply the next stage it will be necessary to supply the deficiency by buying out. Conversely, excessive capacity gives rise to the need to dispose of the surplus.

–   High investment in technology and development may inhibit innovation and change owing to the need for redesign, retooling and retraining.

–   Backward or forward integration often calls for highly diversified skills and abilities, e.g. manufacturing, transport and distribution require different business capabilities.

For the above reasons many manufacturers, particularly in car and food manufacture, have vertical integration in favour of:

–   outsourcing;

–   long-term partnership agreements with suppliers;

–   *Keiretsu* strategies. *Keiretsu* is the Japanese word for 'affiliated chain'. Such chains comprise mutual alliances that extend across the entire supply chain of suppliers, manufacturers, assemblers, transporters and distributors;

–   The creation of virtual companies that use suppliers on an 'as needed' basis.

- *Conglomerate diversification* focuses on expanding operations by acquiring existing or creating new businesses that provide apparently disconnected products/service.
- *Joint venturing* focuses on expanding through partnerships with other organisations that share expertise, costs and resources.

Stability and combination strategies

Stability focuses on maintaining the present course of action and the avoidance, so far as possible, of major changes. It is not necessarily a 'do nothing' approach but a considered decision that the present way of working is the most appropriate in a given situation.

Combination is the simultaneous adoption of several strategies according to the needs of particular aspects of a business. Thus in a divisionalised organisation, strategic decisions may be to pursue a growth strategy in some divisions and one of stability in others.

Retrenchment

Retrenchment or defensive strategies are the opposite of those focusing on growth. Typical retrenchment strategies include:

- *Harvesting* – maximising short-term profits and cash flow while maintaining investment in a product flow.
- *Turnaround* – attempting to restructure operations to restore earlier performance levels.
- *Divestiture* – selling off one or more units of an enterprise to raise cash or concentrate on core activities.
- *Liquidation* – the decision to cease business and dispose of all assets.

4.2.3   Business strategy

Business strategy is the strategy for a single division or strategic business unit (SBU) that operated with some autonomy within a larger organisation. In a single business organisation, institutional and corporate strategy will also be the business strategy. Business strategy involves making decisions concerned with the achievement of competitive advantage by making the best use of the distinctive competences of the enterprise and integrating the various functional areas of the business. It seeks to answer the strategic question 'how are we going to compete in this particular business area?' Two well known approaches to sell strategic planning are:

- The *competitive strategy* of Michael Porter.[6] This identifies three strategies that can be used to give an SBU a competitive advantage. These strategies are:
  - *Cost leadership* – operating efficiencies so that an organisation is the low-cost producer in its industry.
  - *Differentiation* – attempting to develop products that are regarded industry-wide as unique.
  - *Focus* – concentration on a specific market segment.

■ The *adaptive strategy* of Miles and Snow[7] based on the premise that an organisation should formulate strategies that will allow each of its SBUs to adapt to its unique environmental challenges. Four major strategies are identified:

– *Defender* – this emphasises output of reliable products for steady customers and is appropriate for very stable environments.

– *Prospecto*r – this emphasises a continuous search for new market opportunities and innovation and is appropriate for dynamic environments with untapped opportunities.

– *Analyser* – this emphasises stability while responding selectively to opportunities for innovation and is appropriate for moderately stable environments.

– *Reactor* – this is really no strategy. Reactors respond to competitive pressures by crisis management.

4.2.4 Global strategies

A global strategy has been defined as:[8]

> **The search for competitive advantages outside an organisation's domestic borders.**

Jolly[9] suggests that the best way of judging global strategies is in terms of degrees of globalness. The more a company scores on each of the following five attributes the more it can be considered a global competitor:

■ Possession of a standard product (or core) that is marketed uniformly across the world.

■ Sourcing of all assets, not just production, on an optional basis.

■ Achievement of market access in line with the break-even volume of the needed infrastructure.

■ Ability to contest assets as much as products when circumstances require.

■ Provision of a global orientation to all functions or competences.

Jolly points out that:

> Sourcing products and components internationally based on comparative advantage and availability has long been a feature of international business. What is new is the possibility to source assets or capabilities related to any part of the value chain. Whether it is capital from Switzerland, software skills from Silicon Valley or electronic components from Taiwan, global companies now have a wider latitude in accessing resources from wherever they are available or cost competitive.

4.2.5 Functional and operational strategies

Functional strategies are concerned with the formulation of action plans relating to the six main areas that constitute a business, namely financial strategy, human resources strategy, technology strategy, purchasing strategy, production/manu-facturing strategy and marketing strategy. Responsibility for such strategies is normally delegated to the head of the particular function or activity unless the chief executive chooses to exert a strong influence. In any event, functional strategies are expected to integrate into the wider business strategy rather than achieve their own narrow objectives. Functional strategies are primarily concerned with:

■ ensuring that the skills and attributes of functional specialists are effectively utilised;
■ integrating activities within the functional area, e.g. purchasing, marketing;
■ ensuring that functional strategies mesh with SBU strategies.

Operational strategies are concerned with the even narrower strategic activities such as those concerned with the management of key operating units or tasks. Operating units might be a plant, office, warehouse or distribution centre. Tasks might be obtaining materials or components, inventory control and transport. Such responsibilities will be undertaken by front-line managers reporting to higher ranking executives. Often managers responsible for operations will be given targets to achieve and will need to devise appropriate action plans for their attainment.

It is sometimes difficult to distinguish between functional and operating strategies. Whether purchasing strategies are functional or operational will depend largely on the strategic importance of procurement within the supply chain.

4.3 The strategic planning process

Figure 4.3 provides an overview of the four planning stages involved in the strategic planning process, namely scanning the environment, strategy formulation, strategy implementation and strategy evaluation and control. It provides a background for a detailed consideration of purchasing strategy.

4.4 Purchasing strategy

As shown in Table 4.1, purchasing strategy at the functional or operational levels, derive from corporate or business strategies. For single businesses, corporate and business strategy is synonymous.

Information and advice provided by the purchasing function may also influence the framing or adjustment of corporate strategies. The extent to which this takes place will be largely determined by purchasing's contribution to competitive advantage as perceived by top management. The purchasing executive who reports directly to the chief executive is clearly in a stronger position to contribute to corporate strategy than one who is lower in the hierarchy and reports to a

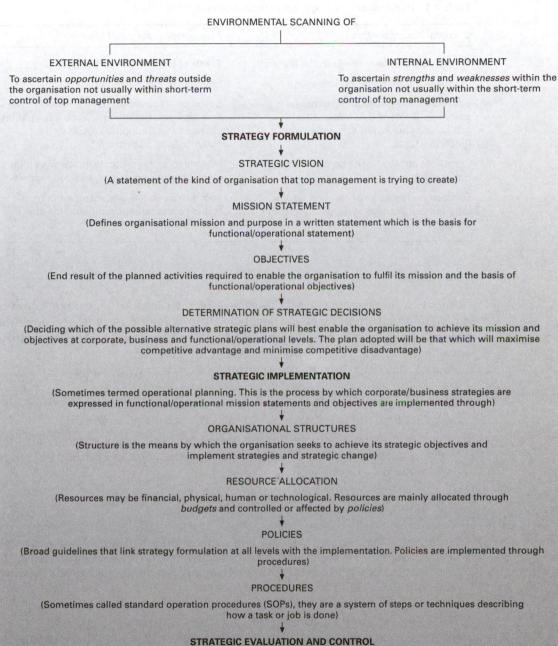

ENVIRONMENTAL SCANNING OF

EXTERNAL ENVIRONMENT

To ascertain *opportunities* and *threats* outside the organisation not usually within short-term control of top management

INTERNAL ENVIRONMENT

To ascertain *strengths* and *weaknesses* within the organisation not usually within the short-term control of top management

STRATEGY FORMULATION

STRATEGIC VISION

(A statement of the kind of organisation that top management is trying to create)

MISSION STATEMENT

(Defines organisational mission and purpose in a written statement which is the basis for functional/operational statement)

OBJECTIVES

(End result of the planned activities required to enable the organisation to fulfil its mission and the basis of functional/operational objectives)

DETERMINATION OF STRATEGIC DECISIONS

(Deciding which of the possible alternative strategic plans will best enable the organisation to achieve its mission and objectives at corporate, business and functional/operational levels. The plan adopted will be that which will maximise competitive advantage and minimise competitive disadvantage)

STRATEGIC IMPLEMENTATION

(Sometimes termed operational planning. This is the process by which corporate/business strategies are expressed in functional/operational mission statements and objectives are implemented through)

ORGANISATIONAL STRUCTURES

(Structure is the means by which the organisation seeks to achieve its strategic objectives and implement strategies and strategic change)

RESOURCE ALLOCATION

(Resources may be financial, physical, human or technological. Resources are mainly allocated through *budgets* and controlled or affected by *policies*)

POLICIES

(Broad guidelines that link strategy formulation at all levels with the implementation. Policies are implemented through procedures)

PROCEDURES

(Sometimes called standard operation procedures (SOPs), they are a system of steps or techniques describing how a task or job is done)

STRATEGIC EVALUATION AND CONTROL

(The process of comparing actual performance with desired results to enable managers at all levels to take corrective action and solve problems)

FEEDBACK

(For evalution and control to be effective, managers must obtain prompt and unbiased feedback from their subordinates at each stage of the above process)

Figure 4.3   The strategic planning process

Table 4.1 Procurement strategy at corporate and functional levels

Corporate/business level	Functional/operational level
Formulated at higher levels in the hierarchy	Taken at lower levels in the hierarchy
Emphasise purchasing effectiveness	Emphasise purchasing efficiency
Based on widespread environmental scanning. Some of this information will be communicated upwards from functional level	Based on information from a more limited environmental scanning. Some information obtained from suppliers etc. may be communicated upwards
Corporate strategy must be communicated downwards	Integrated with corporate strategies so far as these are communicated and understood
Focused on issues impacting on future long-term procurement requirements and problems	Focused on issues impacting on current tactical procurement requirements and problems

materials or logistics manager. Irrespective of their level of reporting, however, purchasing staff should seek to contribute to corporate strategy by the provision of intelligence on the basis of which decisions can be made, and by competitive advantage by improving the effectiveness of the function.

Kraljic[10] states that a company's need for a supply strategy depends on:

■ the strategic importance of purchasing in terms of the value added by the product line, the percentage of materials in total costs, and so on;

■ the complexity of the supply market gauged by supply scarcity, pace of technology and/or materials substitution, entry barriers, logistics cost or complexity, and monopoly or oligopoly condition.

Kraljic claims that:

By assessing the company's situation in terms of these two variables, top management and senior purchasing executives can determine the type of supply strategy the company needs both to exploit its purchasing power *vis-à-vis* important suppliers and reduce its risks to an acceptable minimum.

The application to purchasing of the four stages of the strategic planning process – environmental scanning, strategy formulation, implementation and evaluation – can now be considered.

4.5 Environmental scanning

Spekman[11] has identified two major components in environmental analysis: environmental monitoring and determination of strategic impacts.

4.5.1 Environmental monitoring

Environmental monitoring involves three stages:

- Searching the environment for signals that may portend significant changes, e.g. monetary trends, inflation, strikes, shortages, technological breakthroughs and industry overcapacity.
- Identification of commodities/materials which may be threatened or benefit from environmental changes such as sensitive commodities (see Chapter 12).
- Evolution of the possible consequences to the organisation of changes in supply conditions arising from such environmental changes and the probability of such changes occurring.

4.5.2 Determination of the strategic impact on profit and supply risk

Kraljic[12] states that the *profit impact* of a given supply item can be defined in terms of:

- volume purchased;
- percentage of total purchase cost;
- impact on product quality or business growth.

Supply risk is assessed in terms of:

- availability;
- number of suppliers;
- competitive demand;
- make or buy opportunities;
- storage risks;
- substitution opportunities.

Kraljic points out that on the basis of the above profit and supply risk criteria all purchase items can be assigned to one of the four categories shown in Table 4.2.

An evaluation of such impacts can enable managers at the appropriate level to prioritise what materials and allied supply considerations require immediate attention.

4.5.3 Other approaches to environmental scanning

PEST (political, economic, social and technology) analysis

PEST analysis focuses on the external factors that affect a business, as shown in Figure 4.4.

Other writers have extended the analysis to incorporate ecological and demographic classifications. All such factors are, however, interdependent and, in practice, the pattern of interrelationships may be difficult to interpret. PEST factors input into SWOT analysis.

Table 4.2 Classifying purchased materials requirements

Procurement focus	Main tasks	Required information	Decision level
Strategic items (high profit impact, high supply risk)	Accurate demand forecasting Detailed market research Development of long-term supply relationships Make-or-buy decisions Contract staggering Risk analysis Contingency planning Logistics, inventory and vendor control	Highly detailed market data Long-term supply and demand trend information Good competitive intelligence Industry cost curves	Top level (e.g. vice-president purchasing)
Bottleneck items (low profit impact, high supply risk)	Volume insurance (at cost premium if necessary) Control of vendors Security of inventories Backup plan	Medium-term supply demand forecasts Very good market data Inventory costs Maintenance plans	Higher level (e.g. department heads)
Leverage items (high profit impact, low supply risk)	Exploitation of full purchasing power Vendor selection Product substitution Targeted pricing strategies Negotiations Contract/spot purchasing mix Order volume optimisation	Good market data Short- to medium-term demand planning Accurate vendor data Price/transport rate forecasts	Medium level (e.g. chief buyer)
Non-critical items (low profit impact, low supply risk)	Product standardisation Order volume monitoring/optimisation Efficient processing Inventory optimisation	Good market overview Short-term demand forecast Economic order quantity inventory levels	Lower level (e.g. buyers)

POLITICAL	ECONOMIC
■ Legislation, e.g. ■ Employment law ■ Health and safety ■ Political pressures ■ Regulatory powers	■ State of national economy ■ State of industry ■ Sector decline/growth ■ International factors
SOCIAL	TECHNOLOGY
■ Consumer tastes ■ Pressure groups	■ Pace of technological change ■ New product developments

Figure 4.4 PEST analysis

SWOT (strengths, weaknesses, opportunities and threats) analysis

As shown in Figure 4.5, this analysis assesses internal strengths and weaknesses in relation to the external opportunities and threats in the organisation's environment.

Figure 4.6 indicates that SWOT analysis is the essential preliminary to the formulation of strategies at corporate, business and functional/operating levels.

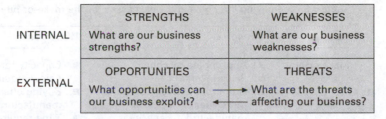

Figure 4.5 SWOT analysis

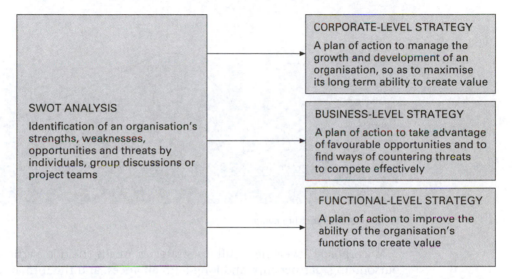

Figure 4.6 SWOT analysis at strategic levels

STRENGTHS	WEAKNESSES
■ Purchasing power ■ Regular demand ■ Purchasing probity and goodwill	■ Highly sensitive imported material
THREATS	OPPORTUNITIES
■ Competition for the material from competitors ■ Few suppliers ■ Exchange rates	■ Alternative materials ■ Possibility of vertical integration with a supplier ■ Outsourcing ■ Partnerships ■ Virtual company formation

Figure 4.7 SWOT analysis applied to a supplies situation

At each level SWOT analysis can be applied to a particular purchasing issue by appraising internal and external factors by means of a cruciform chart, as shown in Figure 4.7. This example relates to the identification of the fact that the organisation is under some threat owing to the reliance on a major product and highly sensitive material obtainable from a limited supply source.

Table 4.3 Identifying strengths and weaknesses for the make-or-buy decision

Issue	Strengths	Weaknesses
Make or buy	■ Appropriate machinery ■ Skilled workforce ■ On pure cost basis can make more cheaply if part of manufacturing capacity is dedicated to this purpose	■ Capacity for manufacture already below requirements ■ Buying effectively expands the manufacturing resource of enterprise ■ Time required for changeover ■ Added value greater by making

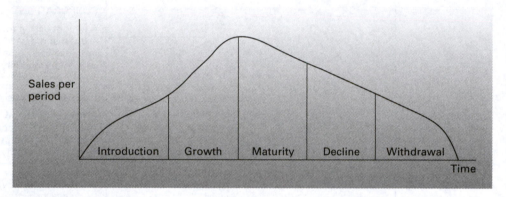

Figure 4.8 Product life cycle

At corporate level the resultant strategies might include vertical integration, outsourcing, partnerships and long-term alliances, and the formation of a virtual company. At the functional level there could be a search for alternative materials.

Evans[13] suggests that as a variation on SWOT analysis it is more useful to determine the strategic *issues* facing purchasing in the future:

■ effects of e-procurement;

■ difficulty in recruiting purchasing staff of the right calibre;

■ suppliers going out of business;

■ patents, leading to monopoly supply sources;

■ exchange rate fluctuations;

■ outsourcing possibilities.

For each issue relevant strengths and weaknesses can be identified as shown in Table 4.3.

Life cycle analysis

This is based on the concept that all products in their original, unmodified form, have a final lifespan as shown in Figure 4.8.

The product life cycle, or Gopertz curve, plots the actual or potential sales of a new product over time and show the stages of development: growth, maturity, decline and eventual withdrawal. Important aspects of product life cycles are:

- *Their length* – from development to withdrawal. This may be short with products subject to rapid technological advances.
- *Their shape* – not all products have the same shape to their curve. So-called high learning, low learning, fashion and fad products have different curves reflecting different marketing strategies.
- *The product* – this can vary depending on whether the product life cycle applies to a *class*, i.e. the entire product category or industry, to a *form*, i.e. variations within the class, or to a *brand*.

The life cycle approach has become increasingly important for the following reasons:

- *Environmental factors*, e.g. the relative environment performance of a product as in the case of purchasing of packaging and paper and the subsequent management of waste.
- *Durability factors*, e.g. competition between substitute commodity products such as aluminium and steel in the car industry.
- *Obsolescence* with regard to capital equipment which may be a factor in deciding to adopt an outsourcing strategy.
- *Changing demand*. This concept of the product life cycle helps marketing managers to recognise both that products may need continual changes to prevent sales decline and that there is a need to formulate marketing strategies to stimulate demand. This strategy may impact on purchasing strategies such as how far in advance to place orders for materials or components that are likely to change.

Scenario planning

Scenario planning consists in developing a conceptual forecast of the future based on given assumptions; thus by starting with different assumptions many different future scenarios can be presented. The assumptions can be based on the examination of trends relating to economic, political and social factors that may affect corporate objectives and supply and demand forecasts. Planning therefore involves deciding which scenario is most likely to occur and devising appropriate strategies. An example is examining how the price of sensitive commodities changes in the scenarios of glut and shortage.

System modelling

System modelling in which computer-based models are developed to simulate key aspects of a function, e.g. purchasing and its environment. Purchasing staff then proceed through a number of what-if? situations to determine the consequences of a particular strategy. Likely consequences can then be evaluated before the strategy is implemented.

Strategic issue management

Strategic issue management (SIM) involves the identification of one or a few key issues that are perceived as crucial to the function in achieving its performance objectives and evaluating the impact of such issues and their potential consequences, both positive and negative, for the function. An example would be the loss of a preferred supplier or an unacceptable rise in prices. Awareness of potential environmental changes allows purchasing a longer time in which to formulate alternative strategies.

Delphi method

This is a subjective approach to forecasting based on a systematised approach to reaching agreement among a group of forecasters. The forecasters do not initially communicate with each other but receive reports on each other's opinions. The various reports are then adjusted until opinion is reached.

4.5.4   Porter's five forces model

All the above approaches to environmental scanning tend to focus either on opportunities and threats within the general environment or on strengths and weaknesses of the particular organisation. Porter's concept of *value chain analysis* to which reference was made in Chapter 3 focuses on the position of an SBU *within the industry to which it belongs*. As shown in Figure 4.9, Porter identifies five competitive forces that determine the intensity of competition in an industry and the total value of profits or value generated in that particular industry.

Each of the five forces in Porter's analysis can be broken down into their constituent elements. As Mintzberg and Quinn[14] point out, they:

- highlight the critical strengths and weaknesses of the company;
- animate the positioning of the company in its industry;
- clarify the areas where strategic changes may yield the greatest pay-off;
- highlight the places where industry trends hold the greatest promise as either threats or opportunities.

Figure 4.9   Porter's five forces model of industrial attractiveness

Source: adapted from Porter M.E., *Competitive Advantage*, Free Press, 1985

New entrants[15]

The seriousness of the threat of entry depends on the barriers present and the likely reaction of existing competitors. *Barriers to entry* derive from six main sources:

- Economies of scale, e.g. high initial investment in production, research, marketing.
- Product differentiation, e.g. brand identification requires heavy advertising to overcome loyalty.
- Capital requirements, e.g. the need to invest large capital resources.
- Cost advantages independent of size, e.g. patents, know-how, access to best materials resources.
- Access to distribution channels, e.g. the more existing competitors have these tied up the tougher entry to the industry will be.
- Government policy, e.g. licence requirements and limits on access to raw materials

Reaction of existing customers can take such forms as:

- Resources to meet the threats posed by new entrants, e.g. financial strength, productive capacity, power to influence distributors and customers.
- Price-cutting to keep market share or because of excess capacity industrywide.
- Slow industry growth probably causing the financial performance of all competitors to decline.

Industry competitors

Jockeying for position among existing competitors uses such tactics as price competition, product introduction, comparative advertising. Factors relating to rivalry include:

- equality in size and power of competitors;
- slow industry growth precipitating fights for market shares;
- high fixed costs or perishable products with the temptation to cut prices if demand slackens;
- high exit costs;
- demand characteristics.

Substitute products

The more attractive the price–performance trade-off offered by substitute products, the firmer the lid placed on the industry's profit potential.

Suppliers and buyers

Suppliers can exert bargaining power by:

- raising prices;
- reducing the quality of purchased goods and services.

Customers too can

- force down prices;
- demand higher quality or more service;
- play competitors off against each other;

all at the expense of industry profits.

Porter[16] states that a *supplier* group is powerful if:

- it is dominated by few companies and is more concentrated than the industry to which it sells;
- its product is unique or at least differentiated or if it has built up switching costs. Switching costs are fixed costs buyers face in changing suppliers. These arise because, among other things, a buyer's product specifications tie it to particular suppliers, or it has invested heavily in specialised ancillary equipment, or in learning how to operate a supplier's equipment (as in computer software), or its production lines are connected to the supplier's manufacturing facilities (as in some manufacture of beverage containers).
- It is not obliged to contend with other products for sale to the industry. For instance, the competition between the steel companies and the aluminium companies to sell to the can industry checks the power of each supplier.
- It poses a credible threat of integrating forward into the industry's business. This provides a check against the industry's ability to improve the terms on which it purchases.
- The industry is not an important customer of the supplier group. If the industry is an important customer, the supplier's fortunes will be closely tied to the industry, and the supplier will want to protect the industry through reasonable pricing and assistance in activities like R&D and lobbying.

A buyer group is powerful if:

- It is concentrated on purchases in large volumes. Large volume buyers are particularly potent if heavy fixed costs characterise the industry so that it is important to keep capacity filled.
- The products it purchases from the industry are standard or undifferentiated. The buyers are sure that they can always find alternative suppliers, and may play one off against another.
- The product it purchases from the industry form a component of its product and represent a significant fraction of its cost. The buyers are likely to shop for a favourable price and purchase selectively. Where the product sold by the industry in question is a small fraction of the buyers' costs, buyers are usually much less sensitive.
- It earns low profit, which creates great incentive to lower its purchasing costs. Highly profitable buyers, however, are generally less price sensitive (where the price does not represent a large fraction of these costs).

■ The industry's product is unimportant to the quality of the buyers' products or services. Where the quality of the buyers' products is very much affected by the industry's products, buyers are generally less price sensitive. Industries in which this situation obtains include oil field equipment, where a malfunction can lead to large losses, and enclosures for electronic medical and test instruments where the quality of the enclosure can influence the user's impression about the quality of the equipment inside.

■ The industry's product does not save the buyer money. Where the industry's product or service can pay for itself many times over, buyers are rarely price sensitive; rather, they are interested in quality. This is true in services like investment banking and public accounting, where errors in judgement can be costly and embarrassing.

■ The buyers pose a credible threat of integrating backwards to make the industry's product. Sometimes an industry engenders a threat to buyers that its members may integrate forward.

4.5.5 A critique of Porter's five forces model

Porter's models such as the value chain and five forces diamond have had a lasting impact on strategic management. They are, however, subject to increasing criticism. Hines' alternative model of the value chain was discussed in Chapter 3. Other criticisms of the five forces model include the following:

■ *Changed economic conditions*. Porter's theories relate to the economic situation of the 1980s characterised by strong competition, inter-enterprise rivalry and relatively stable structures. They are less relevant in today's dynamic environment in which the internet and e-business applications have the power to transform entire industries.

■ *Identification of new forces*. Downes[17] has identified digitalisation, globalisation and deregulation as three new forces that influence strategy.

  – *Digitalisation*, i.e. putting data into digital form for use in a digital computer, has provided all players in a market with access to more information thus enabling even external players to change the basis of competition.

  – *Globalisation* enables businesses to buy, sell and compare prices globally. Competitive advantage can derive from cooperation, ability to develop strategic alliances and manage extensive global networks for the mutual advantage of buyers and sellers.

  – *Deregulation*, i.e. a much reduced involvement of central government in the control of such industries as airlines, banking and public utilities.

Downes states that the foremost differences between what he terms the 'Porter world' and 'the world of new forces' is information technology. The old economy used IT as a tool for implementing change. Today technology has become the most important driver for change.

The three forces of digitalisation, globalisation and deregulation have effectively removed the barriers to industrial entry and enabled new competitors and new ways of competing to develop at an accelerated speed.

4.6 Strategy formulation

As shown by Figure 4.3, strategy formulation at corporate, business and functional/operational levels relates to:

- the formulation of a vision statement;
- the preparation of a mission statement;
- the deriving of objectives;
- the determination of strategic decisions.

Each of these stages is considered from a purchasing perspective.

4.6.1 Formulation of a vision statement

A vision statement articulates a realistic, credible and positive projection of the future state of an organisation or functions or activities within an organisation.
A typical vision statement for the purchasing activity might be:

To develop procedures and personnel capable of providing all activities throughout the enterprise with the highest achievable standards of strategic sourcing, decision support and collaboration to ensure that through integrated effort competitive advantage is achieved through lowered purchasing costs, shortened supply cycles and enhanced cooperation with suppliers.

4.6.2 Preparation of a mission statement

Vision and mission statements are sometimes considered to be synonymous, but Campbell and Yeung[18] point out some differences:

- Vision refers to a future state, 'a condition that is better than now'. Thus British Airways aspires to become 'The World's Favourite Airline' and Microsoft to have a PC in every home. Mission statements refer to the 'here and now'.
- When a vision is achieved a new vision needs to be developed; but a mission can remain the same.
- A vision is more associated with a goal, whereas a mission is more associated with a way of behaving.

A mission is therefore a more timeless concept, more concerned with the way the organisation is managed today and its purpose. It is the sense of purpose provided by a mission statement that helps in both strategy formulation and maintaining the focus of strategic plans.
At the functional level, a mission statement should indicate:

- the overall aims of the function;
- how the aims will be achieved;
- the basis of internal and external relationships;
- the link with corporate strategies.

These four points are exemplified in Figure 4.10.

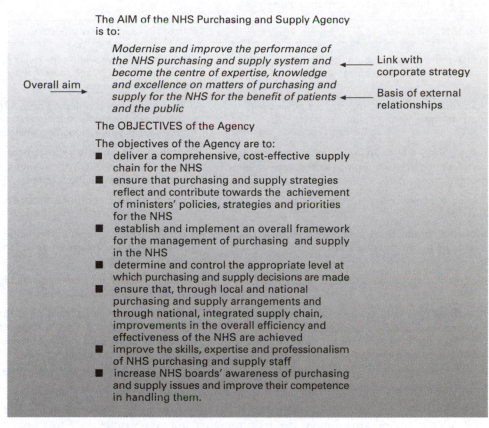

The AIM of the NHS Purchasing and Supply Agency is to:

Overall aim →

Modernise and improve the performance of the NHS purchasing and supply system and become the centre of expertise, knowledge and excellence on matters of purchasing and supply for the NHS for the benefit of patients and the public

← Link with corporate strategy

← Basis of external relationships

The OBJECTIVES of the Agency

The objectives of the Agency are to:

■ deliver a comprehensive, cost-effective supply chain for the NHS

■ ensure that purchasing and supply strategies reflect and contribute towards the achievement of ministers' policies, strategies and priorities for the NHS

■ establish and implement an overall framework for the management of purchasing and supply in the NHS

■ determine and control the appropriate level at which purchasing and supply decisions are made

■ ensure that, through local and national purchasing and supply arrangements and through national, integrated supply chain, improvements in the overall efficiency and effectiveness of the NHS are achieved

■ improve the skills, expertise and professionalism of NHS purchasing and supply staff

■ increase NHS boards' awareness of purchasing and supply issues and improve their competence in handling them.

Figure 4.10   Aims and objectives of NHS Purchasing and Supply Agency

4.6.3 Deriving objectives

Objectives can be corporate, business or functional. Corporate and business objectives are strategic, long-term and general, whereas functional objectives are tactical, short-term and specific.

The classic definition of the overall purchasing task is:

To obtain materials of the right *quality* in the right *quantity* from the right *source* delivering to the right *place* at the right *time* at the right *price*.

This definition is somewhat simplistic for the following reasons:

■ The term 'right' is situational: each company will define 'right' differently.

■ What is 'right' will change as the overall purchasing context and environment change.

■ The above rights must be consistent with corporate goals and objectives from which functional/operating goals and objectives are derived.

■ In practice some rights are irreconcilable, e.g. it may be possible to obtain the right quality but not at the right price – 'the best suppliers are often the busiest but also the dearest'.

Table 4.4 Purchasing and corporate objectives

Business objectives	Purchasing and supply objectives
A statement of the position the firm is aiming for in its markets, including market share	The objective of providing the quantity and quality of supplies required by the market share and market positioning objectives
A key objective of, say, moving out of speciality markets and entering volume markets	A key objective of developing new, larger suppliers and materials flow systems more geared to larger numbers of fewer parts while keeping total inventory volume low
A key objective to build new businesses which will generate positive cash flow as well as reasonable profits	Contribute to cash flow improvement through lower average inventory and by negotiating smaller delivery lots and/or longer payment terms
A plan to develop some specific new products or services	A plan to develop appropriate suppliers
An overall production/capacity plan, including an overall policy on make or buy	A plan to develop systems which integrate capacity planning and or purchase planning, together with the policy on make or buy
A plan to introduce a cost reduction programme	A plan to introduce supplies standardisation and supplier reduction programmes
A financial plan, setting out in broad terns how the proposed capital expenditure is to be financed; together with an outline timescale and an order in which the objectives need to be achieved	A financial plan, setting out broadly the profit contribution expected from purchasing and supply, together with the time in which it should be achieved and the priorities of the objectives

Purchasing objectives have therefore to be balanced according to overall corporate strategy and requirements at a given time.

An alternative definition of the key purpose for the purchasing and supply chain, devised for the UK Purchasing and Supply Lead Body for National Vocational Qualifications by the University of Ulster, is:

To provide the interface between customer and supplier in order to plan, obtain, store and distribute as necessary, supplies of materials, goods and services [m, g, s] to enable the organisation to satisfy its external and internal customers.

As shown in Table 4.4, purchasing objectives derive from corporate objectives. Short-term objectives are those set for a short period, e.g. one year, so that actual achievement can be measured against the original objectives distinguishing between factors relating to attainment or non-attainment for which the purchasing activity and its staff can be held accountable. The NHS Purchasing and Supply Agency, for example, is required to produce an annual business plan which details its planned activities for the year and how they relate to its overall objectives. For the year 2001/02 the Agency sought to achieve the following targets:

Target 1:   The value of the Agency's contracts will be increased from £2.3 billion to £2.6 billion and purchasing savings of at least £130 million will be achieved.

Target 2:   In conjunction with regional offices and the Audit Commission, key performance measures will be established and included in the quarterly reviews of trust performance undertaken by regions. Pilot exercises with NHS trusts will be undertaken and completed by 31 May 2001.

Target 3:   Existing supply management arrangements will be reviewed and agreement reached with the NHS on appropriate levels of purchasing activity (for example, national, consortium or local).

Target 4:   One hundred per cent commitment by the NHS to the Agency's contracts, where appropriate, will be secured on those contracts negotiated during 2001/02.

Target 5:   Seventy per cent of all Agency buyers and above will have, or will be working towards, an appropriate professional qualification.

Target 6:   E-commerce – contracts will be awarded for:

- an e-tendering and supplier information database module by February 2002 subject to availability of funds;
- a national e-trading and finance system, linked to the Shared Services Initiative, by February 2002, subject to the availability of funds.

Target 7:   The EFQM excellence model will be rolled out and a formal diagnostic review will be held in September 2001.

Target 8:   A strategy and action plan will be established jointly with the NHS Logistics Authority for delivering a modern, integrated, cost-effective supply chain for the NHS.

Target 9:   BS 7799 Information Management System accreditation will be achieved by 31 December 2001.

Target 10:   Investors in People award will be gained.

4.6.4 Determination of strategic decisions

Table 4.5 shows how functional operating decisions are derived from corporate strategical decision.

4.7   Strategy implementation

The principal distinctions between strategy formulation and strategy implementation are shown in Table 4.6.

Strategy implementation as shown in Figure 4.1 relates to: organisational structures, resource allocation, policies and procedures.

4.7.1 Organisational structures

Organisation structure relates a function or activity to all other activities in the organisation and in the supply chain. Purchasing organisation is considered in Chapter 5.

Table 4.5 Strategic procurement decisions at corporate and functional/operating level

Corporate/business level	Functional/operational level
'Grand' strategies relating to procurement, e.g. ■ forward and backward integration ■ reciprocal buying ■ outsourcing ■ co-makership ■ global sourcing ■ countertrade ■ partnerships and *Keiretsu* ■ the size of the supplier base ■ creation of virtual companies	Operational issues within the 'grand' strategies, e.g. ■ sourcing and supplier appraisal ■ negotiating ■ contracting and order placing ■ supplier improvement and development ■ supplier relations and building supplier goodwill ■ logistics issues – storage, transportation, delivery
General directives as to the supplier base Quality directives	■ supplier evaluation ■ reducing the supplier base ■ supplier relationships ■ specifications ■ value analysis and engineering ■ quality control processes ■ price/cost analysis ■ functional structure and allocation of functional duties and responsibilities ■ procurement systems including records
Organisation structures and positioning of procurement within the structure: ■ discrete function or integrated into materials or logistics management ■ centralised, decentralised or 'mixed' procurement ■ coordination of procurement activities	
Allocation of resources to procurement	Budgetary control and cost reduction
Approvals of materials and purchasing budgets	Decisions relating to revenue expenditure
Decision relating to large-scale capital expenditure	
Ethical aspects of procurement deriving from general ethical policies	Strategies and decisions to ensure purchasing conformity
Decisions relating to general staff training and development	Decisions relating to procurement, staff training and development

Table 4.6 Contrasts between strategy formulation and implementation

Strategy formulation	Strategy implementation
The positioning of forces before the action	Management of forces during the action
Focuses on effectiveness	Focuses on efficiency
Is primarily an intellectual process	Is primarily an operational process
Requires good initiative and analytical skills	Requires special motivation and leadership skills
Requires coordination among a few individuals	Requires coordination among many persons

4.7.2   Resource allocation

In most organisations the financial, physical, human and technological resources allocated to a function/activity will be reduced to quantitative terms and expressed in budgets or financial statements of the resources needed to achieve specific objectives or implement a formulated strategy.

4.7.3   Policies

Policies are instruments for strategy implementation. A policy is:

> **A body of principles, express or implied, laid down to direct an enterprise towards its objectives and guide executives in decision making.**

Policies are mandatory and must be adhered to by all persons and activities throughout the organisation.

It is useful to consider the advantages of policy and purchasing policies.

The advantages of policy

At corporate, functional and operational levels, policies have the following advantages:

- Corporate policies provide guidelines to executives in formulating functional and operating strategies.
- Policies provide authority based on principle and/or precedent for a given course of action.
- They provide a basis for management control, allow coordination across organisation units and reduce the time managers spend in making decisions.
- They provide management by exception by providing guidelines for routine actions; a new decision is required only in respect of exceptional circumstances.
- Policies lead to uniformity of procedures and consistency in thought and action.

Purchasing policies

These include the following:

- Policies relating to supply relationships, e.g.

    Our policy is to be selective about the types of relationships we establish with suppliers, but in all cases to treat them with professional respect and to hold our dealing with them as confidential to the parties concerned.

    We should aim to actively promote an image rather than let one form by default. We wish to be seen as fair, tough, totally professional and demonstrably operating according to the highest standards of business practice.

- Internal policies, e.g.

    Our policy is to support internal suppliers to the fullest extent and to develop product and service quality to the same high standards as those available in the external market. Employees may not use the Company's name or purchase leverage to obtain materials or services at preferential rates for their personal use, or for use by other parties in whom the 'buyer' has an interest.

■ Sourcing policies, e.g.

Only those suppliers who satisfy the requirements of the Company's supplier appraisal process and are able to meet their contractual obligations to the company in full should be used. Buyers should actively source from the world market where practical, taking into account corporate guidelines and statutory regulations.

Policy statements can be written in respect of virtually every aspect of purchasing activity. Other important areas to which policy statements may be prepared include:

■ Purchasing authority – who may purchase and limitations on authority
■ Use of purchasing cards
■ Purchase of capital equipment
■ Environmental policies
■ Disposal of waste and surplus
■ Purchasing from SMES and local purchasing
■ E-procurement
■ Ethical policies

The Federation of Economic Organisations[19] has, however, recommended that the procurement policies of individual organisations should conform to three basic principles:

■ Procurement policies should aim to select and procure in an economically rational manner the best possible goods and services available.
■ Suppliers worldwide should be eligible to participate in procurement transactions in open, fair and transparent principles and easy to understand, simple procedures.
■ Procurement transactions have an important contribution to society worldwide. For example, corporate purchasing practices should consider the effective preservation of natural resources and protection of the environment.

Purchasing policies are usually specified in a purchasing manual which is regularly revised. The policies may be varied to meet an exceptional situation, e.g. a breakdown in supplies, but this should only be done on the authority of the executive with ultimate responsibility for purchasing.

4.7.4 Procedure

Procedures are the formal arrangements through which policies are implemented. A cluster of related procedures each consisting of a number of operations which together provide information or guidance to managers and staff relating to an activity is termed a *system*. Purchasing procedures are referred to in Chapter 6.

4.8   Strategy evaluation and control

Strategy evaluation is undertaken at the formulation and post-implementation stages. At the formulation stage the aim is to evaluate which of several possible strategic options is likely to provide the greatest competitive advantage. At the post-implementation stage, evaluation is concerned with whether the chosen strategy has been successful and what changes are required to meet contemporary opportunities and threats.

4.8.1   Evaluation at the formulation stage

Rumelt[20] identifies four principles that can be applied to strategic evaluation:

- *Consistency* – the strategy must not present mutually inconsistent policies.
- *Consonance* – the strategy must represent an adaptive response to the external environment and to the critical changes occurring within it.
- *Advantage* – the strategy must provide for the creation and/or maintenance of a competitive advantage in the selected area of authority.
- *Feasibility* – the strategy must neither overtax available resources nor create insoluble problems.

An alternative set of criteria is that a given strategy should (i) meet the requirements of a given situation, (ii) provide sustainable competitive advantage and (iii) improve company performance.

4.8.2   Methods

There are a number of methods by which the suitability of a particular strategy can be evaluated. These include:

- *Return analysis*, i.e. the returns likely to accrue from the adoption of a particular strategy. This may be done on the basis of an analysis of profitability or cost/benefit.
- *Profitability analysis* includes measures such as: return on capital employed (ROCE), payback and discounted cash flow referred to in Chapter 18.
- *Risk analysis*, i.e. the risk attaching to each of the available strategies. Appropriate measures include break-even analysis and matters relating to liquidity and security, e.g. the risks entailed in sourcing abroad.
- *Resource deployment analysis*, i.e. the assessment of the likely effect on key resources of adopting a particular strategy. Thus, a decision whether or not to adopt an outsourcing strategy with regard to a support service will be preceded by an analysis of the effects on tangible and intangible resources including finance, equipment, human resources, competitive advantage and goodwill.

4.8.3 **Post-implementation evaluation, control and review**

This is concerned with verifying the degree to which implemented strategies are fulfilling the mission and objectives of the organisation. Evaluation differs from control. Post-implementation can apply the principles listed in section 4.8.1 above. Spekman[21] states that the objective of evaluation is to enable procurement managers to understand both the process and results of strategic planning and offers the following list of evaluation criteria:

- Internal consistency
  - Are the procurement strategies mutually achievable?
  - Do they address corporate/division objectives?
  - Do they reinforce each other? Is there synergy?
  - Do the strategies focus on crucial procurement issues?
- Environmental fit
  - Do the purchasing strategies exploit environmental opportunities?
  - Do they deal with external threats?
- Resource fit
  - Can the strategies be carried out in the light of resource constraints?
  - Is the timing consistent with the department's and/or business's ability to adapt to the change?
- Communication and implementation
  - Are the strategies understood by key implementers?
  - Is there organisational commitment?
  - Is there sufficient managerial capability to support effective procurement planning?

The control process involves four stages as shown in Figure 4.11. Setting standards is not easy owing to the multitude of possibilities.

Normally, specific performance standards can be grouped under four headings: (i) service to internal and external customers, (ii) contributors to the competitive

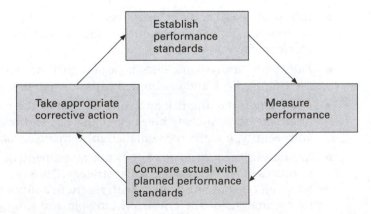

Figure 4.11 Steps in control process

advantage of other elements in the supply chain; (iii) staff effectiveness and efficiency; (iv) financial measures, i.e. cost reductions, conformity to budgets.

Appraisal of the performance of purchasing personnel is dealt with in Chapter 15. Performance measurement as applied to the purchasing function is considered in Chapter 18.

Johnson and Scholes[22] state that in reviewing strategic options it is important to distinguish between three interrelated aspects of any strategy (typical purchasing strategies/tactics or contributions for each of the three aspects of strategic development are shown in Table 4.7):

Table 4.7   Typical aspects of purchasing strategies, tactics or contributions to corporate development strategies

Aspect of strategic development	Typical purchasing strategies/tactics contributions
Generic strategy	
Cost leadership	Lower purchase costs through consolidation of purchases, single sourcing, global procurement. Reduction in costs of purchasing systems and administration. Value for money spent. Logistical contributions to competitive advantage. Buying of sub-assemblies in lieu of components etc.
Differentiation	Involvement of suppliers in product design and development, value analysis, total quality management, alternative materials. Stimulation of technological developments in one supplier market etc.
Focus	Location of specialist suppliers, make-or-buy decision for specialist components, subcontracting, outsourcing etc.
Alternative directions	
Do nothing	
Withdrawal	Running down/disposal of inventory. Negotiating of contract cancellations etc.
Consolidation	Moving to standard/generic materials/components to increase potential use. Negotiation of limited period contracts etc.
Market penetration	Provision of information regarding competitors, price volatility, unused capacity in the supplier market. Negotiation of contracts with options for increased supply or stocking of inventory at suppliers etc.
Product development	Liaison with design and production. Partnership sourcing; supplier appraisal. Negotiation re ownership of jigs and tools for bought out items. Timing of supply deliveries. MRP II. Value engineering etc.
Market development	Liaison with marketing. Partnership sourcing specifying packaging and shipping instructions. Identification of vital points in the supply/value chain
Diversification	Supply considerations, e.g. effect on set-up costs and production runs. Purchasing quantity considerations. Promotion of interchangeability of materials and components etc.
Alternative methods	
Internal development	Organisational aspects of purchasing. Recruitment or development of purchasing staff. Integration of purchasing into materials management or logistics
Acquisition	Corporate-level issues relating to: ■ Backward integration – activities concerned with securing inputs, e.g. raw materials by acquisition of supplies ■ Forward integration – activities concerned with securing outputs, e.g. acquisition of distribution channels, transport undertakings etc. ■ Horizontal integration – activities complementary to those currently undertaken, e.g. consortia, franchising, licensing or agency agreements

1 The *generic strategy* to be pursued, i.e. the basis on which the organisation will compete or sustain excellence, namely:

   (a) Cost leadership through:

      (i)   cost structure

      (ii)   lean purchasing

      (iii) product experience

      (iv) special skills, systems

      (v)   technologies

   (b) Differentiation which is recognised and valued by consumers/users, e.g.

      (i)   product life

      (ii)   reliability

      (iii) rapidity of delivery

      (iv) convenience

      (v)   economy

      (vi) after-sales service

      (vii) esteems value, etc.

   (c) Focus – a combination of cost leadership and differentiation directed at a particular target, e.g.

      (i)   a national/international market

      (ii)   a niche strategy directed at a very small part of the market secure from large organisations

      (iii) customer requirements.

2 *Alternative strategy directions* in which the organisation may choose to develop, e.g.

   (a) Do nothing

   (b) Withdrawal

   (c) Consolidation

   (d) Market penetration

   (e) Market development

   (f) Diversification

      (i)   related

      (ii) unrelated

3 *Alternative methods* by which any direction of development may be advanced, e.g.

   Internal development

   Acquisition

   Joint development

4.9   The CIPS purchasing and supply process model[23]

The CIPS model is shown in Figure 4.12 and should be related to the contents of this chapter so far. Thus, the model shows how organisational vision, mission and values and corporate strategy are derived from environmental factors such as the government, customers, competitors, stakeholders and other external influences and an evaluation of organisational competences.

The model also shows how purchasing strategies interface with and are related to other organisational functions/activities such as R&D, finance, marketing, human resources and technical/IT.

The analysis of procurement shown in the model are all related to appropriate sections of this book.

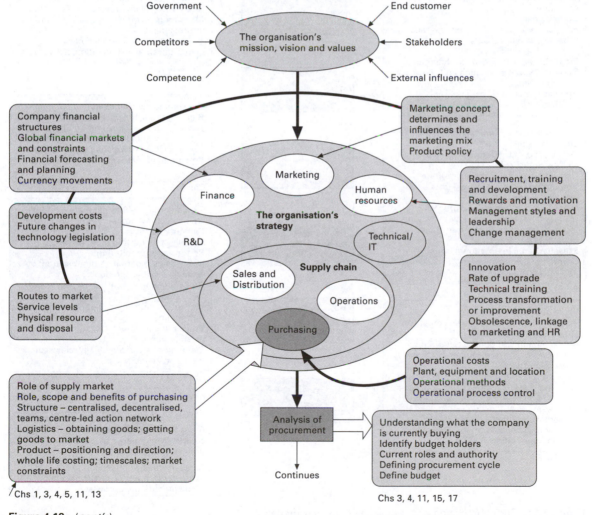

Figure 4.12   (cont's)

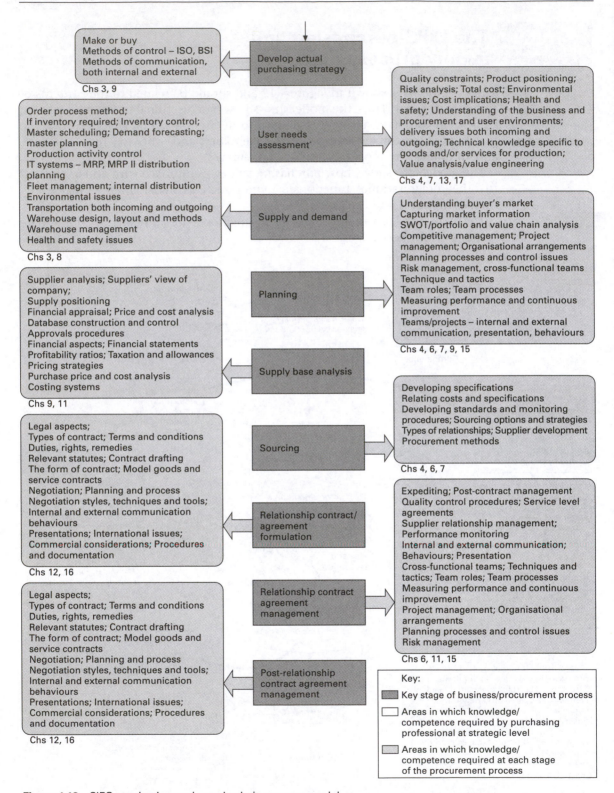

Make or buy
Methods of control – ISO, BSI
Methods of communication,
both internal and external

Chs 3, 9

Develop actual
purchasing strategy

Quality constraints; Product positioning;
Risk analysis; Total cost; Environmental
issues; Cost implications; Health and
safety; Understanding of the business and
procurement and user environments;
delivery issues both incoming and
outgoing; Technical knowledge specific to
goods and/or services for production;
Value analysis/value engineering

Chs 4, 7, 13, 17

Order process method;
If inventory required; Inventory control;
Master scheduling; Demand forecasting;
master planning
Production activity control
IT systems – MRP, MRP II distribution
planning
Fleet management; internal distribution
Environmental issues
Transportation both incoming and outgoing
Warehouse design, layout and methods
Warehouse management
Health and safety issues

Chs 3, 8

User needs
assessment

Supply and demand

Understanding buyer's market
Capturing market information
SWOT/portfolio and value chain analysis
Competitive management; Project
management; Organisational arrangements
Planning processes and control issues
Risk management, cross-functional teams
Technique and tactics
Team roles; Team processes
Measuring performance and continuous
improvement
Teams/projects – internal and external
communication, presentation, behaviours

Chs 4, 6, 7, 9, 15

Supplier analysis; Suppliers' view of
company;
Supply positioning
Financial appraisal; Price and cost analysis
Database construction and control
Approvals procedures
Financial aspects; Financial statements
Profitability ratios; Taxation and allowances
Pricing strategies
Purchase price and cost analysis
Costing systems

Chs 9, 11

Planning

Supply base analysis

Developing specifications
Relating costs and specifications
Developing standards and monitoring
procedures; Sourcing options and strategies
Types of relationships; Supplier development
Procurement methods

Chs 4, 6, 7

Legal aspects;
Types of contract; Terms and conditions
Duties, rights, remedies
Relevant statutes; Contract drafting
The form of contract; Model goods and
service contracts
Negotiation; Planning and process
Negotiation styles, techniques and tools;
Internal and external communication
behaviours
Presentations; International issues;
Commercial considerations; Procedures
and documentation

Chs 12, 16

Sourcing

Relationship contract/
agreement
formulation

Expediting; Post-contract management
Quality control procedures; Service level
agreements
Supplier relationship management;
Performance monitoring
Internal and external communication;
Behaviours; Presentation
Cross-functional teams; Techniques and
tactics; Team roles; Team processes
Measuring performance and continuous
improvement
Project management; Organisational
arrangements
Planning processes and control issues
Risk management

Chs 6, 11, 15

Legal aspects;
Types of contract; Terms and conditions
Duties, rights, remedies
Relevant statutes; Contract drafting
The form of contract; Model goods and
service contracts
Negotiation; Planning and process
Negotiation styles, techniques and tools;
Internal and external communication
behaviours
Presentations; International issues;
Commercial considerations; Procedures
and documentation

Chs 12, 16

Relationship contract
agreement
management

Post-relationship
contract agreement
management

Key:

Key stage of business/procurement process

Areas in which knowledge/
competence required by purchasing
professional at strategic level

Areas in which knowledge/
competence required at each stage
of the procurement process

Figure 4.12 CIPS purchasing and supply chain process model

4.10   Emerging strategic themes

Because of the importance of strategy to the organisation, strategy is a subject that has an immense body of knowledge. Due to size constraints in a book of this nature, it is possible to give only an overview of the essence of strategic planning and how it is applied to purchasing and supply chain management.

The complexity and volume of knowledge on the topic can perhaps be emphasised by Mintzberg *et al.*[24] who have identified ten schools of thought. These are:

- The Design School – a conceptual approach to strategy formation;
- The Planning School – a formal process to strategy formation;
- The Positioning School – an analytical approach;
- The Entrepreneurial School – strategy as a visionary process;
- The Cognitive School – strategy formation as a mental process;
- The Learning School – strategy as an emergent process;
- The Power School – strategy as a process of negotiation;
- The Cultural School – strategy as a collective process;
- The Environmental School – strategy as a reactive process;
- The configuration School – strategy formation as process of transformation.

The approach to strategy described in this book has been mostly that of the rational planning approach. In essence it reduces strategic planning to a series of stages, analysing the situation facing the firm, making choices based on this analysis, looking at the resources at its disposal and then implementing the strategy. Finally it involves comparing progress with the set objectives. While this is still carried out by countless organisations, it does have some major disadvantages. For instance, it has been suggested that it is very difficult to predict the future accurately, plans may not be able to be implemented as originally perceived, and that the adopted strategy is 'cast in stone', thus being difficult to change. In many respects it over simplifies what is a series of complex and interrelated decisions.

A different approach to this is that of emergent strategy (The Learning School). Lynch[25] states that this is derived from the fact that people are not always rational and logical as indicated by prescriptive approaches to strategy. Strategy emerges, adapting to needs of the individual and develops as the organisation learns. Mintzberg and Waters[26] identified intended strategies imposed by senior management. However, these strategies may not always work. They also identified that strategies can come from all levels of the organisation – emergent strategy. The advantages of the emergent approach include the fact that it takes into consideration the people of the organisation learning as the situation develops.

The final approach that is worthy of consideration is that of the resource based approach (The Cultural School). Haberberg and Rieple[27] trace the development of this approach over the last forty years, stating that the resource based view of the firm now represents the mainstream of orthodox strategic management theory. The resource based view moves away from the idea that competitive advantage is gained from market based approaches such as those advocated by Porter. Instead, its focus is on the internal resources of the firm, and therefore capabilities, as being the way to secure competitive advantage. It is necessary to identify the 'strategic resources' of the organisation. Barney[28] states that a strategic resource must:

- be rare within the industry – something that few in the industry has;
- be valuable – it must make a significant difference to costs or differentiation, or economy, effectiveness and efficiency;
- it must be inimitable – i.e. a high degree of difficulty for others to copy or obtain for themselves;
- be not capable of being substituted for.

Case study[29]

Occasions Expressed (OE) is a UK business, based in the North East of England. OE's core business is design, print and sales of birthday and Christmas cards. This is a family-run business with a total turnover of £80m. Mr Edward Joseph is the founder and managing director. He is also the sole designer. Mr Joseph is planning to retire at the end of this year due to ill health.

Mr Joseph's two sons, Edward junior and James, and his daughter Rebecca have recently joined the business after gaining qualifications in design and print.

The only other staff working in OE are three printers and a salesforce of five who have been employed by Mr Joseph senior over the last two years to cover the entire UK which has been divided into six regions. There has been a slow progression of the business over the past 30 years, with little investment in new technology.

Mr Edward Joseph senior currently funds any developments to the business from profits made in the previous year. He is cautious about business expansion and likes to oversee the printing and sales operation personally.

Edward Joseph junior, the eldest son of the family, has many ideas for the business as he prepares to take over from his father. His philosophy in business is very different from that of his father.

Edward junior has discussed his ideas with James and Rebecca and these are some of his initial thoughts:

- Expansion of the range of cards, e.g. christening, get well, congratulations etc.
- The introduction of new product lines, e.g. gift tags, banners, gift paper etc.
- An increase in sales throughout the UK.
- The development of marketing and publicity plans for the next five years.
- The introduction of new technology in both design and print.
- Recruitment of more staff to assist in the management of all operations, including procurement of materials, design, print and sales.
- The restructuring of the entire business with plans to open divisional offices in the five other districts in the UK.
- The expansion of the business into Europe.

Questions

1   Draft and justify a suitable mission statement for OE under the direction of Edward Joseph junior.

2   Identify environmental and organisational characteristics which are likely to affect future strategic decisions for this business and its supply chain.

3   If you were Mr Edward Joseph junior, explain whether you would plan for the strategy to expand and develop the business first, or whether you would restructure the business both in the UK and in Europe first?

   In your answer, you should refer to the information in the case study to explain what strategy you would adopt and the thinking behind why you feel it is appropriate.

? Discussion questions

4.1   Figure 4.1 indicates seven strategies for organisation growth. Complete the following table by identifying one example in respect of each strategy.

Strategy	Example
Joint venturing Market development Product development Innovation Horizontal development Vertical integration Conglomerate diversification	

4.2   Prepare simple diagrams of vertical integration in respect of

(a)   Food manufacture

(b)   Book publishing.

4.3   In respect of retrenchment strategies give examples of the following

Strategy	Example
Harvesting Turnaround Divestiture Liquidation	

4.4   Try to think of examples in each case of how an organisation may seek to obtain

(a)   A cost advantage or cost leadership

(b)   Differentiation

(c)   Focus.

4.5 In relation to the organisation in which you are employed list up to five items under each of the following headings:

Key strengths

Key weaknesses

Key opportunities

Key threats

4.6 Using the guidelines given in this chapter, write a mission statement for the purchasing function/activity in which you are engaged.

4.7 From the mission statement prepared in answer to question 4.6 derive some relevant objectives.

4.8 Identify some operational strategies relating to how you propose to achieve the objectives identified in question 4.7.

4.9 Value is created through innovation. In what ways is e-business innovative?

4.10 As shown below, Kraljic analysed the purchasing portfolio of an enterprise on the basis of two variables: (i) the importance of purchasing to the company and (ii) the supply risk.

Impact of purchasing on the financial results of the enterprise	Leverage supplies	Strategic supplies
	Routine supplies	Bottleneck supplies

Supply risk

Under which of the headings 'leverage', 'strategic', 'routine' and 'bottleneck' would you place the following items?

(a) Office supplies

(b) Bottling equipment for a brewery

(c) Steel plate

(d) Natural flavourings for food manufacture

(e) Cleaning materials

(f) Pigments for the paint industry

(g) Sub-assemblies

(h) Nuts and bolts

4.11 Prepare a policy statement relating to one of the following.

(a) Quantity required from suppliers

(b) Training of purchasing staff

(c) Payment of suppliers

(d) Purchases from local suppliers

? Past examination questions

All the questions below are taken from the CIPS Professional Stage papers, Purchasing and Supply Chain Management I: Strategy.

1   As the purchasing and supply activity develops so its role within the organisation is likely to become more strategic. Identify and explain which areas you would attempt to measure in accessing the strategic performance of purchasing and supply?

(May 1997)

2   What are the main areas of focus for the buyer when strategically planning requirements and capacity in supply chains?

(May 1998)

3   Define and discuss the major macro-environmental factors likely to affect purchasing and supply chain strategies?

(May 1998)

4   Explain what effort might be made by the purchasing function, in a proactive organisation, to make the supply chain more effective and efficient and what success might be achieved at a strategic level for such a proactive organisation.

(November 1998)

5   Explain what strategic role the purchasing and supply function has in planning the requirement of goods and services within the organisation.

(May 1999)

6   Describe what efforts a well developed purchasing and supply function could make to help the supply chain become more efficient and effective.

(May 1999)

7   At all strategic levels what do you consider to be the common areas of concern for the purchasing and supply function in respect of the management of the supply chain across various organisations and sectors of the economy.

(May 2000)

8   A strategically managed efficient and effective supply chain cannot be developed quickly. Explain the steps that need to be taken to achieve such a strategically managed supply chain.

(May 2000)

Notes

1.   Mintzberg, H., 'Five P's for strategy', in Mintzberg, H., Quinn, J.B. and Goshal, S. (eds), *The Strategy Process*, Prentice Hall, 1995, Ch.1, pp.13–21
2.   Mintzberg, H., 'Strategy making in three modes', *Californian Management Review*, Vol.16, No.2 (1973)
3.   Smit, P.J. and Cronje, G.J. (eds), *Management Principles*, Jula (South Africa), 1993, Ch.5, p.107
4.   Quinn, J.B., 'Strategies for change', in Mintzberg, H., Quinn, J.B. and Goshal, S. (eds), *The Strategy Process*, Prentice Hall, 1995, Ch.1, p.5
5.   Kempner, T. (ed.), *A Handbook of Management*, Penguin, 1976, p.384
6.   Porter, M.E., *Competitve Strategy: Techniques for Analysis Industries and Competitors*, Macmillan, 1980

7. Miles, R.E. and Snow, C.C., *Organisational Strategy Structure and Process*, McGraw-Hill, 1978

8. Quoted in Robbins, S.P., *Management*, 3rd edn, 1991, Prentice Hall, Ch.8, p.230

9. Jolly, V., 'Global strategies in the 1990s', in *Mastering Management*, Pitman, 1997, Module 18, p.573

10. Kraljic, P., 'Purchasing must become supply management', *Harvard Business Review*, Sept/Oct. 1983, p.110

11. Spekman, R.E., 'A strategic approach to procurement planning', *Journal of Purchasing and Supplies Management*, Winter 1981, pp.2–7

12. Kraljic, P., as n.10 above

13. Evans, E., 'Strategic planning in purchasing', *Purchasing and Supply Chain Management*, May 1994, p.36

14. Mintzberg, H. and Quinn, J.B., *The Strategic Process*, 2nd edn, Prentice Hall, 1991, Ch.4, p.63

15. The analysis of the five forces in Porter's description of competitive advantage is based on Porter M.E., 'How competitive forces shape strategy', *Harvard Business Review*, Mar./Apr. 1979, pp.137–45

16. Porter, M.E., as n.6 above

17. Downes, L., 'Beyond Porter', in *Context Magazine* available at http://www.contextmag. com/setFrameDirect.asp?src=/archives/199712/technosynthesis.asp

18. Campbell, A. and Yeung, S., 'Creating a sense of mission', in De-Wit, B. and Meyer, R., *Strategy, Process, Content, Context*, West Publishing, 1994, Ch.4, pp.153–4

19. Keidanien (The Federation of Economic Organisations) *Guidelines of Procurement Policies*, 24 April 1990

20. Rumelt, R.P., 'Evaluating business strategy', in Mintzberg, H. Quinn, J.B. and Goshal, S. (eds), *The Strategy Process*, Prentice Hall, 1995, Ch.3, p.94

21. Spekman, R.E., 'A strategic approach to procurement planning', *Journal of Purchasing and Supplies Management*, Spring 1989, pp.3–9

22. Johnson, G. and Scholes, K., *Exploring Corporate Strategy, Text and Cases*, Prentice Hall, 1998, Ch.6, pp.147–69

23. The authors gratefully acknowledge the permission of the CIPS to use this model

24. Mintzberg, H., Ahlstrad, B. and Lampel, J., *Strategy Safari*, Prentice Hall, 1998, p.5

25. Lynch, R., *Corporate Strategy*, Prentice Hall, 2000, pp.59–63

26. Mintzberg, H. and Waters, J., 'Of strategies, deliberate and emergent', *Strategic Management Journal*, July–September 1985, pp.257–72

27. Haberberg, A. and Rieple, A., *The Strategic Management of Organisations*, Prentice Hall, 2001, pp.217–22

28. Barney, J., 'Firm resources and sustained competitive advantage', *Journal of Management*, 1991, 17, pp.99–120

29. The authors gratefully acknowledge the permission of the CIPS and the case study author to use this case study which was set for the May 1998 examination in Purchasing and Supply Chain Management I: Strategy

Supply organisations and structures

After reading this chapter you should be able to:

- Define the term 'organising'.
- Distinguish between the structural and staffing aspects of organising.
- Contrast and compare mechanistic and organic structures.
- State the advantages and disadvantages of functional structures.
- Indicate the advantages and disadvantages of divisional structures.
- State the advantages and disadvantages of matrix structures.
- Describe the main characteristics of new type organisational structures.
- Describe the main characteristics of networks, lean, agile and virtual organisations.
- Identify differences between lean and agile organisations.
- State the main determinants of structure as identified by Mintzberg.
- Explain the relationship between structure and strategy.
- Explain the development of horizontal purchasing organisations.
- State some ways in which design, marketing and production activities interface with purchasing.
- Discuss the advantages and disadvantages of centralised purchasing.
- Indicate some factors influencing the trend to decentralised purchasing.
- Suggest how the internal organisation of purchasing might be structured.

This chapter falls into two broad parts. The first part provides an introduction to some concepts underlying organisational structure and design. The second part applies such concepts to the organisation of purchasing.

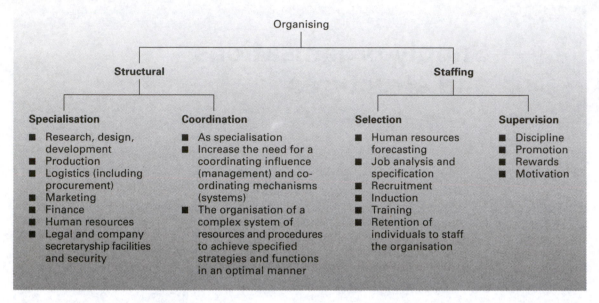

Figure 5.1 The elements of organising

5.1 Organising

Organising, along with planning, controlling and leading, is a key management function. Organising may be defined as:

The process of structuring tasks and working relationships into manageable components and coordinating human effort to achieve organisational goals.

The traditional approach to organising identifies two main activities – structural and staffing – each of which has two aspects as shown in Figure 5.1.

5.2 Organisational structures

Mintzberg[1] has defined the structure of an organisation as:

The sum total of the ways in which [the organisation] divides it's labour into distinct tasks and then achieves coordination among them.

5.2.1 Specialisation

Specialisation is an extension of the division of labour described by Adam Smith in *The Wealth of Nations* (1776). Smith showed that if a man set out to make pins by his unaided labour he could scarcely produce one pin a day. When, however, even a few people divide up the work of pin-making into measuring the wire, cutting it, polishing the material, putting on the points and pin heads, and packing the pins then it is possible to produce thousands of pins daily. Similarly the activities of an organisation are divided into many functions, occupations, jobs and tasks.

5.2.2 Coordination

Coordination has been described as the purpose of all organisation and the glue that holds organisations together. Mintzberg identifies five coordinating mechanisms

- *Mutual adjustment* which achieves the coordination of work by the simple process of informal communications.
- *Direct supervision* which achieves coordination by having one individual take responsibility for the work of others.
- *Standardisation of work processes*, e.g. by assembly lines, plans, instruction materials.
- *Standardisation of skills*. Skills (and knowledge) are standardised when the kind of training required to perform the work is specified. Training is more than the imparting of skills: it can also result in uniform action, e.g. the coordination of the response to a command by soldiers on a parade ground. Training can also result in a common ethos such as that for the professions of law and medicine.
- *Standardisation of norms*. Workers share a common set of beliefs and can achieve coordination based on it.

Two other important coordination mechanisms are policy and committees:

- Policy and the advantages of policy were considered in the previous chapter.
- Committees can promote coordination in three ways:
  - As *advisory* bodies which assist executives by bringing together the knowledge and experience of various other members of the organisation for the purpose of deliberating on problems of common interest such as a value analysis committee. Buying centres or teams are really committees of specialists who pool their knowledge to arrive at sourcing and purchasing decisions.
  - As *consultative bodies* that ensure that the view points of persons or functions related to the matters in hand are brought forward for consultation.
  - As coordinated channels of information to ensure that all interested persons receive the same information in the same form and at the same time.

Coordination is also a means of keeping harmony in development or similar activities and ensuring coordination of progress as well as of policy and action.

Increasingly the term 'coordination' is coming to mean integration, as with the coordination of all the activities in a supply chain. Information technology is an important influence in such integration.

5.2.3 Staffing

Staffing is concerned with those activities that help an organisation to attract and retain the quantity and quality of employees required to meet the current and future human resource requirements of the organisation. Since the 1980s, human resources management (HRM) has tended to supercede the earlier term 'personnel management'. This change reflects a broadening in the scope of the staffing activity. Some HRM aspects of purchasing are discussed in Chapter 15.

5.3 Organisational design

Organisational design may be defined as:

> **Managerial decision making concerned with the process of choosing and implementing structures that meet the needs of an organisation and subunits within the organisation.**

There are broadly two generic organisational design models, namely 'mechanistic' and 'organic' structures. These concepts originated with the work of Tom Burns, a former professor of sociology at Edinburgh University who collaborated with psychologist G.M. Stalker. Their major work, *The Management of Innovation*, appeared in 1968.

Burns identified two 'ideal' types of structure: *mechanistic* structures are adapted to stable conditions and *organic* to dynamic environments in which novel problems constantly arise. Mechanistic and organic systems are compared in Table 5.1.

5.4 Mechanistic structures

In mechanistic structures, work is divided up on either a functional or divisional basis.

5.4.1 Functions and departments

A function is:

> **A group of people who possess similar knowledge and skills or utilise similar tools or techniques to do their jobs.**

As shown in Figure 5.2, such functions are usually grouped into departments and the sub-units or sections within the department, e.g. research and development, procurement, and human resources.

Functional structures are based on the *inputs* required to perform the *primary* tasks of the organisation. As shown in Figure 5.2, these inputs are specialisms such as research and development, production, purchasing, marketing, finance and human resources management. Such functions or specialisms are grouped

Table 5.1   A comparison of mechanistic and organic structures

Mechanistic	Organic
1. Tasks highly fractionalised and specialised, little regard paid to clarifying relationships between tasks and organisational objectives	1. Tasks are more interdependent; emphasis on the relationship between tasks and organisational objectives
2. Tasks are rigidly defined unless altered formally by top management	2. Tasks are continually adjusted and redefined through the interaction of organisational members
3. Specific role definition (rights, obligations and technical methods are prescribed for each member)	3. Generalised role definition; members accept responsibility for task accomplishment beyond the individual role definition
4. Hierarchical structure of control, authority and communication. Sanctions derive from the employment contract between the employee and the organisation	4. Network structure of control, authority and communication. Sanctions derive more from a community of interest than contractual relationships
5. Information relevant to the situation and operations of the organisation formally assumed to rest with the chief executive	5. Leader not assumed to be omniscient; knowledge centres identified where located through the organisation
6. Communication is purely vertical between superior and subordinate	6. Communication is both vertical and horizontal, depending upon where information resides
7. Communications primarily take the form of instructions and decisions issued by supervisors information and requests for decisions supplied by inferiors	7. Communications primarily take the form of information and advice
8. Insistence on loyalty to the organisation and obedience to superiors	8. Commitment to organisation's tasks and goals more highly valued than loyalty or obedience
9. Importance and prestige attached to identification with the organisation and its members	9. Importance and prestige attached to affiliations and expertise in the external environment

Source: derived from Burns, T. and Stalker, G.M., *The Management of Innovation*, Taivistock Publications, 1968

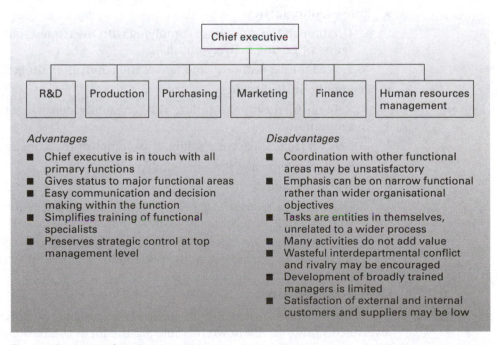

Figure 5.2 caption and diagram:

Chief executive
— R&D — Production — Purchasing — Marketing — Finance — Human resources management

Advantages
- Chief executive is in touch with all primary functions
- Gives status to major functional areas
- Easy communication and decision making within the function
- Simplifies training of functional specialists
- Preserves strategic control at top management level

Disadvantages
- Coordination with other functional areas may be unsatisfactory
- Emphasis can be on narrow functional rather than wider organisational objectives
- Tasks are entities in themselves, unrelated to a wider process
- Many activities do not add value
- Wasteful interdepartmental conflict and rivalry may be encouraged
- Development of broadly trained managers is limited
- Satisfaction of external and internal customers and suppliers may be low

Figure 5.2   A basic functional structure

into departments, each controlled by a manager with defined authority and responsibility.

Purchasing will not report to the chief executive unless it is a primary activity of strategic importance to the undertaking.

An example of functional parochialism as evidenced by attempts to extend the authority and status of the purchasing function is provided by Strauss.[2] Strauss interviewed a number of purchasing agents employed in manufacturing companies. He observed that most of those interviewed did not play a major role in purchasing decisions and he sought to ascertain whether or not they had tried to enhance their status and, if so, the approaches they had used. Strauss found that not only had they made concerted attempts to extend their influence but they had also used specific techniques. Strauss termed these techniques 'tactics of lateral relationships' because they were frequently directed at those in functional areas or departments at approximately the same level in the organisational hierarchy.

The following tactics are described by Strauss as applying to a situation in which the purchasing department is attempting to counteract a requisition from the scheduling department for immediate delivery of an externally purchased item.

- **Rule-oriented tactics**
  - Appeal to some common authority to direct that this requisition be revised or withdrawn.
  - Refer to some rule (assuming one exists) that provides for longer lead times.
  - Require the scheduling department to state in writing why quick delivery is required.
  - Require the requisitioning department to consent to having its budget charged with extra costs (such as air freight) required to get quick delivery.
- **Rule-evading tactics**
  - Go through the motions of complying with the request, but with no expectation of getting delivery on time.
  - Exceed formal authority and ignore the requisition altogether.
- **Personal-political tactics**
  - Rely on friendships to induce the scheduling department to modify the requisition.
  - Rely on factors, past and future, to accomplish the same result.
  - Work via political allies in other departments.
- **Educational tactics**
  - Use direct persuasion, that is try to persuade the scheduling department that its requisition is unreasonable.
  - Use what might be called indirect persuasion to help the scheduling department see the problem from the purchasing department's point of view.

5.4.2 Divisionalisation

Divisional structures are usually adopted by large complex organisations pursuing diversified strategies. As shown in Table 5.2 the focus of divisionalisation can be product or service, geographic or customer.

Table 5.2   The basis of divisional structures

Type	Focus	Example
Product or service	Product or service Produced or provided	ICI Paints Division, Rentokil Pest Control
Geographical	Location of activity	UK division, European division
Customer	Customer or client served	UK Government contracts Consumer division

Each division is a collection of functions, departments or processes serving different customers or locations. In large organisation a central office provides services such as legal and financial assistance to the divisions which otherwise operate as autonomous units under a chief executive who is accountable for the results. At some level a divisionalised structure will be split into functionally based departments each responsible for a group of activities.

5.4.3   Divisional structures

Divisional structures are based on the *outputs* of the organisation, i.e. products or services. Other bases for divisionalisation include geographical areas or processes. Divisionalisation is usually the organisational pattern for large, highly diversified organisations, often operating in several regions or countries. As shown in Figure 5.3, a divisionalised structure will usually be split into functionally based departments each responsible for a particular function or process. Certain key functions such as policy making may be centralised.

The present trend, however, is towards decentralisation for the following reasons:

- The need for decisions to be made as closely as possible to the problems to be solved.

- General trends towards independent profit centres with decentralised responsibility.

- Normally, decentralisation facilitates closer relationships with customers, suppliers and local communities.

- The trend away from functional specialisation for integrated problem solving.

5.5   Organic or flexible structures

5.5.1   The nature of organic structures

Mintzberg[3] defines organic structures as those characterised by 'the absence of standardisation in the organisation'. In a rapidly changing environment,

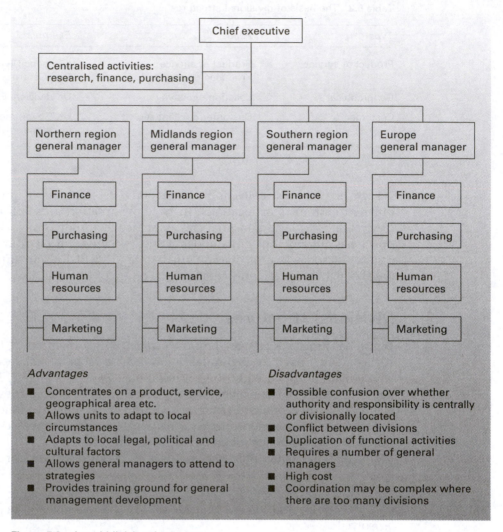

Figure 5.3 A multidivisional structure

continual readjustment and redefinition of individual tasks is essential. Dynamic conditions require more frequent changes of position and roles than mechanistic structures, less hierarchical structures and greater interaction between the various functions in an organisation. Problems arise which require the application of technical expertise for their resolution rather than the application of bureaucratic rules. Flexible structures aim to respond more rapidly to environmental and customer needs. The term 'customer' in this context refers to the users of a product or service provided by an organisation or sub-unit of that organisation. Thus, 'customers' are not only those who buy products of a manufacturing or retail enterprise but also the patients of a hospital or the pupils of a school. An organisation may also have internal customers. Production and other functions may be regarded as customers of the design, purchasing and human resources functions who provide them with drawings, materials and personnel, respectively.

Table 5.3 Some characteristics of mechanistic and organic organisation structures

Characteristic	Mechanistic (rigid)	Organic (flexible)
Number of hierarchical levels	Many	Few
Tall or flat structure	Tall	Flat
Degree of centralisation of decision making	High	Low
Degree of empowerment	Low	High
Quantity of formal rules	High	Low
Specifically of aims and objectives	High	Low
Span of control	Narrow	Wide
Content and flow of communications	Orders and instructions; vertical through the official channels	Advice; lateral, by cooperation
Job specification	Rigid	Flexible
Knowledge-based authority	Low	High
Position-based authority	High	Low

A summary of the main differences between mechanistic and organic structures is provided by Table 5.3 as an alternative to the comparison by Burns and Stalker in Table 5.1.

5.5.2 Matrix structures

Matrix structures are based on two forms of departmentalisation. Firstly, functional departmentalisation, and secondly on departmentalisation according to project and product. Members of matrix organisations are therefore simultaneously members of a specific function, e.g. purchasing, and of a project team. These structures are therefore characterised by two intersecting lines of authority. As shown by Figure 5.4, the easiest way to visualise a matrix structure is to impose project-based departments or teams onto an existing functional structure but at right angles. Attachment to a team is for the duration of the project.

Grinnel and Apple[4] state that matrix structures should be considered only for the following situations:

- When complex, short-run products are the principal products of an organisation, e.g. aerospace construction products.
- When a complicated product design calls for both innovation and timely completion.

Matrix structures are generally applicable when the following factors obtain:

- High uncertainty
- Complicated technology
- Medium/long project duration
- Medium/long internal dependence
- High differentiation

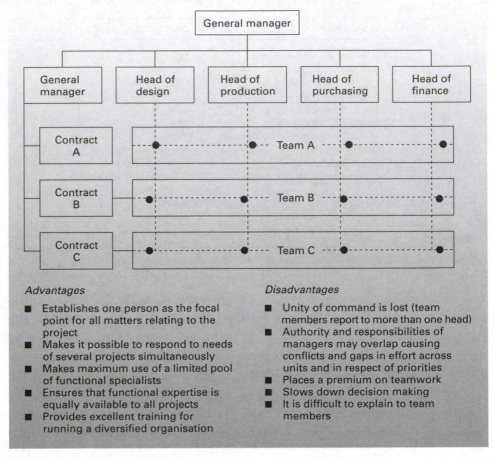

Advantages

- Establishes one person as the focal point for all matters relating to the project
- Makes it possible to respond to needs of several projects simultaneously
- Makes maximum use of a limited pool of functional specialists
- Ensures that functional expertise is equally available to all projects
- Provides excellent training for running a diversified organisation

Disadvantages

- Unity of command is lost (team members report to more than one head)
- Authority and responsibilities of managers may overlap causing conflicts and gaps in effort across units and in respect of priorities
- Places a premium on teamwork
- Slows down decision making
- It is difficult to explain to team members

Figure 5.4   A matrix organisational structure

5.6   New type organisations

The neat and tidy relationships shown on conventional 'family tree' mechanistic organisation charts are too rigid, too slow and insufficiently innovative to meet the requirements of organic enterprises in which working and working relationships have been transformed by such factors as information technology and the search for competitive advantage.

5.6.1   Characteristics of new type structures

Hastings[5] has identified seven characteristics of new type organisations, all of which have implications for PSM.

- *Radical decentralisation*. This, combined with a belief that 'small is beautiful' splits the organisation into many small autonomous units the smallest of which is the individual who, when 'empowered', is given considerable autonomy with consequent responsibility and accountability.

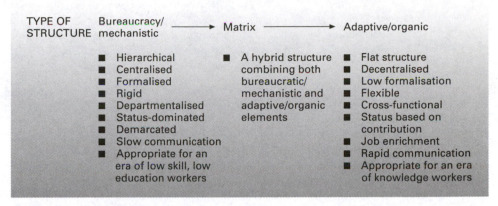

Figure 5.5 The development of the new type structure

- *Intense interdependence.* This emphasises interdependence and multidisciplinary approaches and is implemented by assembling teams and coalitions to pursue common objectives. Both individuals and the organisation itself realise that in order to compete they have to cooperate.

- *Demanding expectations.* Organisations and the individual comprising them have a clear sense of the goals they are expected to achieve. Individuals are demanding of others and expect their cooperation as of right.

- *Transparent performance standards.* Demanding performance standards and performance measures are set and communicated in a transparent fashion so that all are aware of how they are doing in relation to others. The emphasis is on improvement, not winners and losers.

- *Distributed leadership.* Leadership is not confined to senior management but is distributed among people who are required to display maturity and responsibility.

- *Boundary busting.* To achieve adaptability and flexibility, physical personal, hierarchical, functional, cultural, psychological and practical barriers to cooperation and communication are identified and systematically eliminated.

- *Networking and reciprocity.* Direct relationships and communication between individuals irrespective of their roles, status, functions, culture or location are encouraged and facilitated by the abandonment of conventional rigid organisation structures so that a pervasive culture of reciprocity and exchange mediates all relationships.

The movement from traditional bureaucratic/mechanistic to modern adaptive/organic structures is depicted in Figure 5.5.

Examples of new type organic structures emphasising empowerment, functional redundancy and the facilitation of communication between employee 'teams' and external 'parties' are networks, lean, agile and virtual organisations.

5.6.2 Networks

Networks from the perspective of supply chains were referred to in Chapter 3. It is, however, useful to reconsider them from the standpoint of organisation structure. A network structure may be defined as:[6]

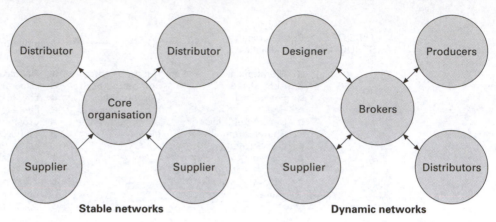

Figure 5.6   Stable and dynamic networks

A series of strategic alliances that an organisation creates with suppliers, manufacturers and distributors to produce and market a product.

Networks may be stable or dynamic. In *stable networks* a core organisation,
departmentalised by function or product contracts out some functions to selected
partners thus enabling it to concentrate on those things it does best. *Dynamic
networks* are those in which a 'broker' organisation builds a network in which a
large proportion of the work is done be other network partners who may change
over time and projects. Stable and dynamic network structures are depicted in
Figure 5.6.

Miles and Snow[7] identify four fundamental design characteristics of dynamic
networks:

- *Vertical disaggregation.* In a network such functions as product design, marketing and some aspects of production are undertaken by independent
  organisations tied together in a network.
- *Brokers.* The broker links together the various functions through subcontracting,
  licensing or joint venture agreements. The broker therefore coordinates, controls and supervises the achievement of a given objective, project or contract.
- *Market mechanisms.* Market forces rather than formalised structure are the
  means by which the parties to a network are bonded together. Thus contracts
  and payments are based on performance. Where performance falls below the
  required standard the broker may discontinue the arrangement and form a
  new alliance.
- *Full disclosure information systems.* Elaborate information systems are the
  means by which the various network participants are linked together so that
  their individual (value added) contributions can be mutually and instan-
  taneously verified.

The advantages and disadvantages of dynamic networks are summarised in
Table 5.4.

Table 5.4 Some advantages and disadvantages of networks

Advantages	Disadvantages
Networks allow organisations to specialise in what they do best and thus develop distinctive competences	Network structures have less control over operations. Even slight misunderstandings can result in product misspecifications
Networks can display the technical specialisation of functional structures, the market responsiveness of divisions and the balanced orientation of matrix structures	Network organisations are vulnerable to competition from their manufacturing contractors
	If a network partner fails or goes out of business the entire network can break down
Synergy (i.e. the whole is greater that the sum of its parts) results from the cooperation of the network partners	It is difficult to guard innovations developed, designed and manufactured by network partners
	Dynamic organisations lose their organic advantage when they become legalistic, secretive and too binding of the other partners

5.6.3 Lean and agile organisations

Lean, agile and virtual organisations are all developments of the network concept. Lean and agile organisations were discussed in some detail in Chapter 3.

Lean production

Lean thinking is 'lean' because it does more with less compared with traditional mass production.

> Half the human effort in the factory, half the manufacturing space, half the invest-ment in tools, half the engineering hours to develop new products in half the time. Also it requires less than half the needed inventory on site, results in fewer defects and produces a greater than ever variety of products.[8]

A report by research teams from the Universities of Bath and Warwick[9] on the 'people' implications of lean organisations identifies three phases of lean devel-opment and their associated production and human resources approaches. These are shown in Table 5.5.

The advantages claimed for lean organisations include greater flexibility, reduced waste, quicker response to customer demands, shorter throughput time, lower supervision costs, lower stock levels and improved quality as feedback on problems is quicker.

Agile production

Harrison *et al.*[10] state that:

> Strategic agility focuses on a more flexible manufacturing process which pervades every level of an organisation. It involves the coordination of the marketing, manu-facturing and R&D functions within the organisation.

Table 5.5 The three phases of lean development

Phase	Concerned with	Approaches
1. Leanness as transition	Efforts made by the organisation to become lean	Delayering, i.e. flattening the organisation Downsizing, i.e. a deliberated reduction in the workforce Outsourcing, i.e. focusing on core activities and subcontracting non-core activities to outside providers
2. Leanness as an outcome	Assumed structural flexibility following a period of delayering, downsizing and outsourcing	Business process re-engineering (BPR). The fundamental rethinking and radical redesign of business processes to achieve dramatic improvements in critical contemporary measures of performance, e.g. cost, quality, service, speed. Lean production characterised by: ■ elimination of waste in terms of both material and human resources ■ low inventories ■ zero defects – prevention rather than rectification of faults ■ integrated production chains ■ teamworking ■ involvement of all employees and suppliers in a continuous process to improve products and job design
3. Leanness as a process	Focuses attention on the attributes of those organisations that can respond to environmentally produced change	Total quality management (TQM). Management philosophy and company practices that aim to harness the human and material resources of the organisation in the most effective way to achieve the objectives of the organisation Just-in-time (JIT). An inventory control philosophy whose goal is to maintain just enough material in just the right place at just the right time to make just the right amount of product

An important concept in agile production is that of *postponement*, defined as holding a product in its lowest common denominator until the customer places an order for it.

Agility therefore involves making the supply chain fast and flexible so that manufacturers can postpone final design and production decisions as far down the supply chain as is feasible or at least until the requirements of the customer are accurately known thereby reducing the variety of components and processes within the system.

Virtual organisations

A virtual organisation has been defined as:

> **A temporary network of independent organisations linked by information technology to share skills and costs in pursuit of a common goal.**

Thus, a virtual organisation is a cluster of units or an organisation associated for a single project which disbands after the project is complete. The structure has been compared to that of an orchestra with a conductor and many specialised musicians all playing from the same score. The idea of the virtual organisation derives from the Japanese concepts of *Keiretsu* and *Kaizen*. The former is an organisational collective based on cooperation and mutual shareholding among a group of manufacturers, suppliers and trading and finance companies. Virtual organisations can, however, choose their memberships from a wider base and are therefore potentially more powerful and flexible than Japanese collectives. The second concept, *Kaizen*, is based on the ongoing search for improvement in which all members of the organisation are continuously encouraged to identify and implement new ideas.

The main characteristics of virtual organisations are:

- *Cooperation facilitated by the use of telecommunications technologies.* Virtual organisations tend to operate in 'cyberspace', a term coined by the writer William Gibson who, in his novel *Neuromancer* refers to the electronic environment within which information is shared.

- *Cooperation based on trust.* Trust is important because there is a sharing of previously unshared, confidential information.

- *Cooperation based on equality and a shared vision.* Although the partners in a virtual organisation may differ in size, all are regarded as peers who recognise their interdependence and who each contributes practices and products which they regard as the best. Members have a common sense of identity and purpose based on a shared vision of where the organisation is going and how it will get there.

- *Cooperation based on core competences.* Competitiveness requires an organisation to analyse what it can do better than others. This enables the organisation to identify its core competences. The concept of core competences looks at the organisation not as a portfolio of products and services but as a system of activities some of which may be more critical than others.

5.7 The determinants of structure

What is known as the contingent approach emphasises that there is no one ideal structure. Mintzberg[11] has identified four such contingency or situational factors, namely age and size, technical systems, power, and the environment. He advances a number of hypotheses under each of the four headings.

5.7.1 Age and size

Mintzberg suggests that the older and larger an organisation the more formalised or standardised will be its behaviour and the more specialised and standardised will be its policies, procedures and practices. Because of these factors, changes in design and practices are often difficult to implement in older, larger organisations.

5.7.2 Technical systems

Mintzberg holds that the more a technical system controls the work of the operators the more standardised will be the operating system and the more bureaucratic the organisation structure. Conversely, automation of an operational structure may transform a bureaucratic administrative structure into a more flexible one.

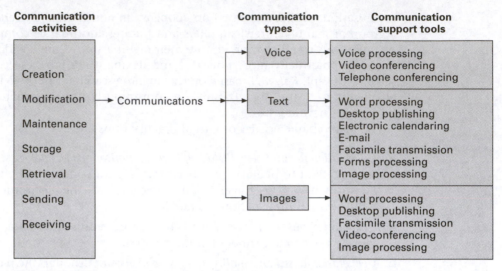

Figure 5.7 Office automation and communication

At present, and increasingly in the future technology is, and will be, associated with automation and information technology.

Automation **is a technological change that replaces people with machines.**

Information technology **is the acquisition, processing, storage and dissemination of vocal, pictorial, textual and numerical information by a microelectronic-based combination of computing and telecommunication.**[12]

One of the most visible examples of information technology in the administrative context is office automation or the application of computers and telecommunications in the office environment. Office activities include the management of data, documents, decisions, projects, and individual and group schedules. Other office activities are basically concerned with the creation, modification, maintenance, storage, retrieval and sending of communications. Such communications are basically of three types: voice, text and image communication. All modern office support tools are designed to facilitate these three types of communication. The relationship between communication devices, types and support tools is shown in Figure 5.7.

The application of information and computer technologies leads to fundamental changes in organisational structures, the nature of managerial work, job design and working practices.

5.7.3 Power

Mintzberg[13] points out that the design of organisational structures is influenced not only by age, size and technical systems but also by power factors. Power may be defined as the capacity of an individual to influence decisions. Five sources of power are identified by French and Raven[14] under the classifications shown in Figure 5.8.

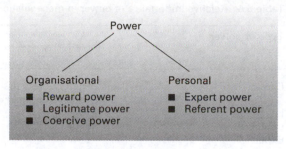

Figure 5.8   The sources of power

- *Reward power* is based on individual or group perceptions that another individual or group has the ability to provide varying amounts and types of rewards.

- *Legitimate power* is based on the values held by an individual or the formation of particular values through socialisation. It exists when an individual or group accepts that it is legitimate for another individual or group to influence their actions.

- *Coercive power* is based on individual or group perceptions that another individual or group has the ability to administer penalties.

- *Expert power* is based on individual or group perceptions that another person or group has greater knowledge or expertise and is thus worth following.

- *Referent power* is based on the desire of an individual or group to identify with or be like another person or group.

There are significant differences between organisational and personal power. Organisational power is conferred and dependent on the position of the individual or group in the organisational hierarchy. Personal power is inherent and dependent on the personal characteristics of the holder. Personal power is therefore less removable from the holder than organisational power.

Other research[15] has shown that, in relation to departments, those most powerful in an organisation are those who (i) control important resources; (ii) have to cope effectively with uncertainty and (iii) have scarce expertise. This research implies that the most powerful departments are those concerned with uncertainty, e.g. marketing in highly competitive industries and purchasing where materials form a high proportion of the total cost particularly where the prices of the materials are unstable.

The relative importance of the sources of organisational and personal power in mechanistic and organic systems is shown in Table 5.6.

5.7.4 The environment

The importance of environmental scanning to the formulation of strategies was discussed in Chapter 3. The environment may be defined as 'all the factors external to an organisation'. Environments are both general and specific, both of which must be considered in relation to organisational structures and decision making.

Table 5.6 Relative importance of power in mechanistic and organic structures

Type of power	Organisation type	
	Mechanistic	*Organic*
Reward	High but less than in an organic organisation	High
Legitimate	High	Low
Coercive	High	Low
Expert	Low	High
Referent	Low	High

The general environment comprises the political, economic, legal, social and technological conditions within which all organisations operate at a given time. The specific environment comprises the persons, groups and organisations with whom a particular enterprise must interact. These include clients, customers, regulators, resource suppliers, trade unions and numerous others.

Both general and specific environments have special significance for organisations that operate internationally.

Mintzberg[16] states that environments can range from:

- *Stable to dynamic.* In stable environments more mechanistic designs will apply. The more dynamic the environment the more organic will be the design.

- *Simple to complex.* The more complex the environment the more decentralised will be the organisational design, and vice versa.

- *Integrated to diverse.* The more diversified the organisation's markets, the greater the propensity for it to split into market-based units (give favourable economics of scale).

- *Munificent (liberal and friendly) to hostile.* An extremely hostile environment will drive an organisation to centralise its structure at least temporarily.

5.8 Strategy and structure

5.8.1 Structure follows strategy

Mintzberg's analysis emphasises that different environments lead to different strategies. Different strategies require different structures. Thus as Chandler[17] concluded after a study of almost 100 large American companies, changes in corporate strategy precede and lead to changes in organisation structure, i.e. structure follows strategy. This environment–strategy–structure link is shown in Figure 5.9.

5.8.2 McKinsey's 7S model

McKinsey, as quoted by Waterman,[18] regarded the simple strategy–structure model of Chandler as inadequate and identified seven interrelated factors that organisa-

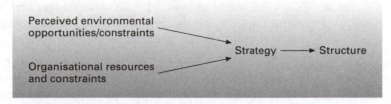

Figure 5.9 The environmental strategy link

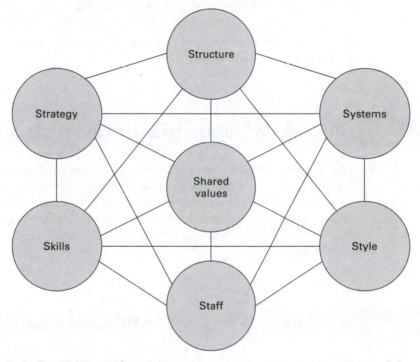

Figure 5.10 The McKinsey 7S model

tions wishing to become more customer oriented and outward-looking need to address. These factors are shown in Figure 5.10.

Figure 5.10 shows that shared values are at the core of the organisation. While formal structure is important the critical issue is not how activities are divided up but rather the ability to focus on those dimensions that are important to organisational development. From a purchasing standpoint these seven dimensions are:

- *Shared values.* The importance of purchasing sharing in the corporate culture or 'ways in which things are done around here'. The recognition by the organisation and purchasing that procurement is a contributor to the achievement of organisational objectives. The relating of all purchasing activities to the ethical and environmental policies of the organisation.

- *Structure.* The breaking down of functional barriers based on specialisation and the integration of purchasing into logistics and supply chain processes in a seamless manner.

- *Skills*. The development of staff knowledge and competences relative to purchasing and the sharing of such knowledge and competence with both internal customers and external suppliers.
- *Strategy*. In what ways can purchasing contribute to the achievement of marketing, alliance, growth, diversification, outsourcing and similar strategies?
- *Style*. The building of supplier goodwill and cooperation through good supplier relationships based on trust, courtesy, information sharing and adherence to ethical principles.
- *Staff*. Securing the right mix of purchasing and support staff to ensure that procurement contributes competitive advantages, training and rewarding staff.
- *Systems*. The development of procedures and information flows and the facilitation of e-procurement.

5.9 Purchasing and organisational structures

The position of purchasing within organisational structures was considered in Chapter 1 and purchasing as a supply chain activity in Chapter 3. Five other structural aspects relevant to purchasing are: purchasing within horizontal organisations; purchasing interfaces; purchasing in multi-plant organisations; purchasing as a decentralised departmentalised function; and the internal organisation of purchasing.

5.10 Purchasing in horizontal organisations

5.10.1 Factors for change

Stewart[19] mentions three factors that have influenced a change in many organisations from functional, hierarchical to horizontal structures:

- The high involvement the workplace based on the empowerment of employees, delayering and self-management teams.
- An emphasis on managing business processes rather than functional departments, e.g. materials or logistics management rather than purchasing.
- The rapid development of information technology enabling knowledge, accountability and performance to be distributed widely both internally and externally. Externally, for example, purchasing will increasingly operate as part of a loosely structured network of organisations each specialising in particular activities or services and cooperating through short- or long-term alliances. Internally there will be a breaking down of functional barriers to ensure that supply chain optimisation is achieved not as a series of sequential activities of which purchasing is one but rather as a series of parallel processes.

5.10.2 Characteristics of horizontal organisations

The characteristics of horizontal organisations have been identified by Osstreff and Smith[20] as:

- Performance objectives based on customer needs and satisfaction.
- Processes not tasks as the basis of organisations identifying the processes that meet customer needs. These processes then become the main organisational components.
- Flatter organisation structures through delayering and reduction in the size and scope of functional departments.
- Teams of multiskilled staff responsible for whole processes previously split between different departments.
- Processes and process performance entrusted to senior leaders.
- Combination of managerial and non-managerial activities whenever possible, e.g. delegation of operational purchasing teams.
- Team members required to develop several competences so that only a few specialists are required.
- Maximise supplier and customer contact with everyone in the organisation.
- Rewards focused on team rather than individual performance alone.

The above approach contains many of the concepts associated with lean and agile production and supply chain management.

5.11 Purchasing interfaces

The term 'interface' is used differently in physics and computing. In physics an interface is a surface forming a common boundary between two regions. The concept of a boundary implies a rigid demarcation between two functional activities. The greater the demarcation between functionally organised departments the greater is the need for coordinative mechanisms such as planning, standard operating procedures, a common manager and communications/human relations training.

In computing, however, an interface is an apparatus for connecting two pieces of equipment so that they can be jointly operated. It is in this sense of working together or interaction that the term is used in the present context.

5.11.1 The systems approach to management

Systems theory asserts that the parts of a whole interact with each other *and* with the larger world external to the whole. Many of the concepts of 'general systems theory' derive from the work of a German biologist, Ludwig von Bertalanffy, who defined a system as 'an organised or complex whole'. The word 'system' is now in common use, and we thus speak of computer and transport systems. Both cars and the human body are complex systems, each with a number of subsystems.

Thus, cars have cooling, steering and suspension subsystems. Similarly departments of an organisation, e.g. design, production, marketing, finance etc., can be considered as subsystems.

Systems theory distinguishes between closed and open systems. A *closed* system is isolated from and independent of its environment. An *open* system, such as business organisation, is in constant interaction with its environment receiving inputs such as labour, finance and materials, and through a series of activities transforms them into outputs such as information, services and products.

A system is healthy or 'in balance' when all the subsystems work together to achieve the corporate objectives of the organisation. Purchasing as a subsystem probably works most closely with the design and production activities. It also has close contacts with marketing and finance.

5.11.2 Specialist cooperation

Some issues on which interaction and cooperation may take place between purchasing and 'user' activities such as design and production or marketing, whether separately or as contributors to buying centres or purchasing teams, include the following:

Purchasing and design

- Preparation of specifications for purchased materials and components.
- Quality assurance or 'defect prevention'.
- Value engineering and value analysis.
- Information to design departments regarding availability of materials, suppliers and costs.
- Agreement of alternatives when specified materials are not available.
- Issues arising from the increasing importance of buying rather than making, i.e. reduction of vertical integration.
- Importance of buying complete systems rather than individual components.
- Evaluation of cheaper alternative materials.
- Building co-makership/designership relationships.
- Creation of a library of books, catalogues, journals and specifications for joint use by the design and purchasing departments.

Purchasing and marketing

- Provision of sales forecasts on which purchasing can base its forward planning of material, components etc.
- Ensuring that, by efficient buying, purchasing contributes to the maintenance of competitive prices.
- Obtaining materials on time to enable marketing and production to meet promised delivery dates.
- Exchange of information regarding customers and suppliers.
- Marketing implications of partnership sourcing.
- Liaison with respect to reciprocal trading.

Purchasing and production or 'user' departments

■ Preparation of material schedules to meet just-in-time requirements.

■ Ensuring that delivery schedules are maintained.

■ Control of inventory to meet production requirements.

■ Disposal of scrap and obsolete items.

■ Quality control or defect detection and correction.

■ Approval of 'first-off' samples.

■ Make-or-buy decisions.

■ Supplier development.

■ General involvement in such techniques and systems as optimised production technology, computer integrated technology, materials requirement planning (MRP) and manufacturing resource planning (MRP II).

5.11.3 Patterns of interaction

A useful model of the interaction between purchasing and 'user' departments is that of Cannon[21] who offers a market 'segmentation' model. In this model the market comprises all the orders/contracts which the organisation wishes to place. Each item purchased can be categorised according to four variables:

■ rapidity of technological change associated with the product;

■ total volume of spend;

■ number of orders placed annually;

■ number of suppliers.

Cannon suggests that, on the basis of such segmentation, interaction between purchasing and its internal customers can be related to three scenarios:

■ When the total value of spend is low, the internal customer should do the buying and the purchasing function should provide training in such areas as:
  – vendor appraisal;
  – preparation of invitations to tender;
  – the legal significance of contract terms and conditions;
  – tender procedures and evaluation;
  – negotiation;
  – contract administration;
  – claims resolution;
  – contracts close out.

  This arrangement has the advantages of reduced paperwork, e.g. the elimination of requisitions, of speed and lower costs.

■ When there is a high rate of technological change and the value of spend is high, user departments and the purchasing function should work jointly to procure the organisation's requirements. In this scenario purchasing will again provide training relating to the areas listed above. A service agreement will demarcate the respective areas of responsibility and the possibility of using targeted added value techniques to achieve savings should be investigated by both parties.

- When the value of spend is high but the rate of technological change is low, procurement should be the sole responsibility of purchasing which should offer its internal customers added value, service and expertise.

As stated earlier, the functional approach in which purchasing works independently of other departments, setting its own objectives and rules, may not coincide with the objectives of other functions or even those of the organisation. What purchasing perceives as the right quality, quantity, source, place and time may not coincide with wider strategic considerations or the objectives of other functions such as mentioned above. Materials and logistics management approaches attempt to bridge or eliminate such functions. Such functional divides provide synchronous management of all the activities in the supply chain.

5.12 Purchasing in multi-plant organisations

When an undertaking is located on a single site, purchasing will normally take place in one centralised office. Where the undertaking's activities are spread over many plants, the question arises as to where purchasing should be located. Findings from an investigation of 74 companies reported by Jonathan Lyles and Robert Payne of Market Research Focus Ltd[22] indicate three 'models' of centralised procurement:

- Coordinated devolved procurement
- Centralised procurement
- Consultative centralised procurement

These three models are shown in Figure 5.11.
 Lyles and Payne report:

- Most organisations that now have a centralised or consultative structure have evolved from a devolved model such as that shown in Figure 5.11.
- In 2000 the most common procurement model in the companies research was one of centralised control and devolved authorisation. Ninety-three per cent of the respondents considered that the *control* over the purchasing of products and services in their organisation was centralised, whereas only 5 per cent described this control as devolved. At the same time, 84 per cent stated that the authorisation of the expenditure is devolved against 14 per cent centralised. By deduction, around 9 per cent of the sample had centralised control *and* authorisation of expenditure.[23]

Purchasing will tend to be *completely centralised* where the items required at each plant are largely homogeneous. An example would be a confectionery

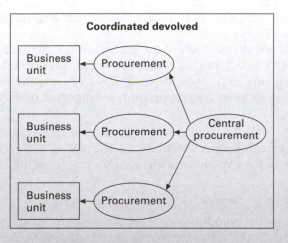

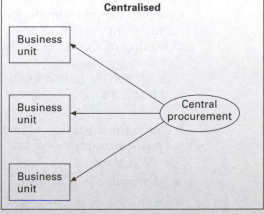

- Most procurement activities are carried out within the business units or operating divisions of the organisation, but they are coordinated by a centralised procurement function

- Procurement of products and services common to more than one area of the business is usually centralised

- Procurement strategy, policy, systems and standards are controlled centrally

- No independent procurement departments or staff exist within the business units or operating divisions of the organisation

- Procurement strategy, policy, systems and standards are controlled centrally and all procurement activities are carried out centrally

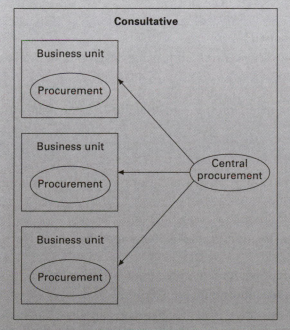

Procurement activities of both a strategic and an operational nature are carried out within the business units or operating divisions, but taking guidance and advice from a centralised procurement function

The overall control of procurement strategy, policy.

Figure 5.11   Models of centralised procurement

company with a large number of plants, each using large quantities of flour, sugar etc. In this case, orders would be placed centrally and deliveries made against the contract as required by the local plants.

Purchasing may be *coordinated and devolved* where the group is a conglomerate consisting of a number of plants each producing widely dissimilar products. In this case, purchasing is done at plant level since the materials and components used are specific to that location. Complete decentralisation is supported by such arguments as:

- Since the efficiency of purchasing influences profitability, the manager of each plant should have control over the expenditure incurred on materials for his or her plant.
- Centralised purchasing proliferates paperwork and leads to delays.
- Some plants are so large that the economies of scale referred to earlier are already present and there is an optimum after which diseconomies of scale set in.

One relevant objection to complete decentralisation is that the competition between plants may lead to a loss of group purpose.

As Lyles and Payne show, in most group undertakings there is a compromise, some purchasing activities being undertaken centrally and others at plant level. It is, therefore, necessary to determine:

- What activities shall be undertaken centrally?
- What activities shall be centralised?
- How shall coordination between central and plant level purchasing be achieved?

In each case the answers will depend on the undertaking but the following arrangements are typical:

Centralised activities

- Determination of major purchasing strategies and policies, e.g. organisation, single sourcing, reciprocal purchasing.
- Preparation of standard specifications for the whole undertaking.
- Negotiation of bulk contracts for homogeneous items used by a number of plants.
- Purchase of stationery and office equipment and computerised systems.
- Purchasing research into market conditions, suppliers etc.
- Rationalisation of the share of orders to be received by suppliers. This will apply particularly when purchasing controls a large section of the available orders or, for social reasons, needs to spread its purchasing power fairly among a number of dependent suppliers.
- Control of group inventory.
- Staff training and development.

Decentralised activities

■ Small orders and MRO (maintenance, repair and operating) items.

■ Items used only by that plant.

■ Emergency purchases, i.e. where local initiative may avoid an interruption of production.

■ Local buying to save transport costs.

■ Local purchasing undertaken for social reasons, i.e. plant is part of the community in which it is situated and can, by the exercise of the purchasing power, contribute to the prosperity of the locality.

■ Staff purchases.

Centralisation and decentralisation are considered further in the following section.

5.13 Purchasing as a departmental function

Although the supply chain approach regards purchasing as a process, many organisation structures still show purchasing as a separate rather than as an integrated activity. It is therefore useful to consider the advantages and disadvantages of centralising purchasing in a functional department.

The general advantages and disadvantages of departmentalisation have been listed in Figure 3.2. Applied specifically to purchasing, the advantages claimed for concentrating procurement in a strong central department responsible for coordinating purchasing across the organisation relate to economies of scale and the coordination and control of the purchasing activity.

5.13.1 Economies of scale

Centralised purchasing enables an organisation to use its purchasing power of leverage to the best effect since:

■ Consolidation of quantities can take place resulting in quantity discounts or rebates.

■ Suppliers dealing with a centralised purchasing department have an incentive to compete for the whole or a substantial proportion of an undertaking's requirements.

■ Cheaper prices by enabling suppliers to spread overheads over longer production runs.

■ Specialist staff can be employed for each of the major categories of purchase.

■ Specialist support staff may be employed, e.g. an export or import procedure where there is substantial global sourcing.

■ Lower administration costs, e.g. it is cheaper to place and process one order for £10,000 than ten each for £1,000.

5.13.2 Coordination of activity

- Uniform policies can be adopted, e.g. single sourcing, partnership sourcing.
- Uniform purchasing procedures can be followed.
- Competitive buying between departments within the organisation is eliminated.
- Standardisation is facilitated by the use of companywide specifications.
- The determination of order quantities and delivery dates is facilitated.
- Backup services, especially stock control and progressing, can be coordinated.
- Staff training and development can be undertaken on a systematic basis.
- Purchasing research into sources, qualities and supplier performance is facilitated.
- Suppliers find it more convenient to approach one central purchasing department than a number of individuals or plants.

5.13.3 Control of activity

- The purchasing department may become either a separate cost centre, i.e. a location within the organisation in relation to which costs may be ascertained, or a profit centre, i.e. a unit of the organisation which is responsible for revenues and profits as well as expenditure. This is dealt with in Chapter 18.
- Budgetary control may be applied both to the purchasing department and to the total expenditure on supplies.
- Uniformity of purchase prices obtained by centralising purchasing assists standard costing.
- Inventories can be controlled, reducing obsolescence and loss of interest on capital locked up in excessive stocks.
- Approaches such as just-in-time and MRP II can be implemented.
- Purchasing department performance can be monitored by setting objectives and comparing actual results with predetermined standards.

Many of the above claimed advantages are, however, not restricted to a functional departmental approach and apply equally when purchasing is a group within an integrated supply chain structure. There are also a number of disadvantages of centralised purchasing as set out below.

5.13.4 Disadvantages of departmentalisation

The disadvantages, all of which have implications for purchasing, include:

- Coordination among related functional areas is more difficult, hence the move to materials management and logistics approaches.
- Departmentalisation can foster a parochial emphasis on functional objectives with a minimum appreciation of or concern for overall organisational goals.
- Employee identification with a specialist group or function can make it difficult to implement change.

- Training of managers with broad perspectives and wide understanding of business may be inhibited.

- Interdepartmental rivalry and conflict may be encouraged as in the example of functional parochialism given by Strauss earlier in this chapter.

- Where buyers lack technical knowledge time is often saved if design or user departments deal directly with suppliers.

- User departments will resort to informal procedures if formal purchasing procedures are too slow, unreliable or otherwise unsatisfactory.

- Departmentalisation tends to look inwards whereas in today's competitive environment the emphasis is on the customer and how the enterprise can respond quickly to his or her requirements.

- Departmentalisation can result in many activities that involve expenditure and time without adding value.

The best ways of meeting these objectives are for purchasing to take the initiative in setting up consultative procedures through which users can express their views and preferences and to offer such a standard of service to production and other functions that the need to circumvent purchasing does not arise.

When purchasing is regarded as a separate function within the organisation structure wasteful conflict between purchasing and other functions can arise from such reasons as the following:

- Competition between purchasing and other functions involving the allocation of scarce resources, e.g. budget conflicts.

- Role conflict arising from differing perspectives of organisational behaviour. For example, the purchasing department may assume that its role is to buy at the right price, time, quality etc. which may entail buying from sources different from those prescribed by production, which assumes that its role includes the prerogative of specifying supply sources with purchasing providing only a servicing function. This can be an example of role ambiguity.

- Differences between the objectives and priorities of purchasing and other functions, e.g. engineers are primarily concerned with quality and reliability and place less emphasis on such purchasing objectives as price and delivery.

- Pressure from competing non-purchasing functions to adjudicate between them, e.g. where marketing seeks to reduce price at the expense of quality. This adjudication expectancy arises from the centrality of the purchasing manager in the buying communication network.

- Pressure from other functions for purchasing to deviate from standard policy and procedures to meet their needs, e.g. favouring a particular supplier.

The overall trend is, however, as stated in section 5.6 to *decentralisation*. Wikstrom and Normann[24] refer to the paradox of integration. Vertical disintegration refers to the trend towards the break-up of large, monolithic companies with everything under one roof. This process is, however, offset by the fact that information technology makes greater cohesion possible even for loosely scattered units whether these are externally or internally located. Other reasons adduced in favour of decentralisation include:

- The need for purchasing decisions to be made as closely as possible to the problems to be solved.
- General trends towards independent profit centres with decentralised responsibility. The view is sometimes expressed that if purchasing costs account for more than half of the total costs, then each profit centre should be given the right to make its own decisions regarding purchasing and suppliers.
- Normally, decentralisation facilitates closer relationships with suppliers.
- The trend away from functional specialisation towards integrated problem solving.
- Benchmarking with other locations is possible.
- Support of local suppliers with consequent lower transportation costs.

5.14 The internal organisation of purchasing

Whether a departmentalised function or a process within a supply chain, purchasing will be under the control of a specialised manager or executive. Two important considerations will be the division of responsibility for purchasing activities and the organisation of support services.

5.14.1 Division of purchasing responsibilities

In a large organisation where purchasing is of high strategic importance, purchasing may be under the control of a director of procurement responsible for a number of managers some of whom are specialist buyers and others responsible for important support services. Such an arrangement is shown in Figure 5.12.

In designing departmental structures, it should be remembered that the greater the number of levels, e.g. purchasing director/manager, senior buyers, assistant buyers, the smaller will be the amount of delegated authority exercised by junior staff, with consequent demotivation.

Among the bases on which purchasing may be subdivided are:

- by major groups of purchased items;
- by the products for which purchased items are to be used, e.g. conveyors, cranes, buildings in an engineering company;
- by stage of manufacture, e.g. raw materials, partly finished components, finished components;
- by plant location, e.g. plant buyers in Sheffield, Middlesbrough and Stoke;
- by customer, e.g. where an undertaking has a few major customers such as government departments.

5.14.2 Support services

Supporting services can be organised on a vertical or horizontal basis. In the vertical systems, supporting services such as stock control, progressing and work

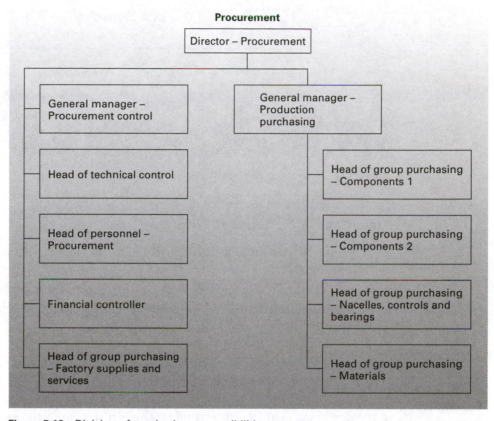

Figure 5.12　Division of purchasing responsibilities

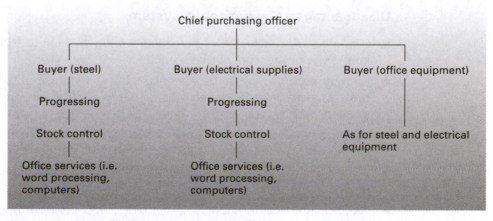

Figure 5.13　Supporting services (vertical structure)

processing are completely covered in each section and form a vertical line as in Figure 5.13. In the horizontal system services are distinct activities as shown in Figure 5.14.

The advantages of one system are largely the disadvantages of the other.

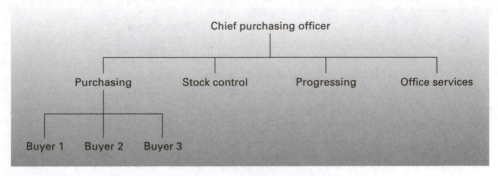

Figure 5.14 Supporting services (horizontal structure)

Advantages of a horizontal system

■ Staff concentrate on a specific activity, such as stock control, in which they become specialist.

■ A specialised function such as stock control or progressing will be better able to assess the needs of the organisation as a whole and to adjudicate between pressure from different buyers.

■ Easier staff training programme.

■ Preparation of departmental statistical and other statements, e.g. disposal of scrap, is facilitated when such activities are the responsibility of a specialised section.

■ Possible increased job satisfaction for support staff since they report directly to the chief purchasing officer and not to a buyer.

Disadvantages of a horizontal system

■ Support staff attached to a particular section of buying will have a better knowledge of the work of that section.

■ Communication may be slower since a buyer requiring information on the progress of an order has to refer the matter to another section head instead of someone in his or her own section.

■ Staff in an integrated section obtain a better grasp of how their function relates to the work of the whole section.

■ Irritation may be caused to suppliers when they deal with different sections for purchasing, progressing etc.

■ People employed in supporting activities, e.g. progressing, may have less opportunity of becoming buyers than if they were attached to a vertically integrated section.

Information technology has expedited or made redundant many support activities by eliminating procedures or providing real-time information on which decisions and actions can be based.

Case study

Electrical Industries is a large manufacturer of electrical products. Initially it concentrated on the production of consumer products including washing machines, refrigerators and smaller items such as irons, toasters and hairdryers. Later, as a result of the acquisition of other companies, it diversified into the manufacture of industrial items including electric motors and electric components including ignition systems for the motor industry. It currently manufactures consumer products at its works at Barchester where the head office is situated. It also has works in Galliford and Prescote which are mainly but not solely concerned with industrial products. About 60 per cent of the turnover is derived from industrial products.

Notwithstanding the shift in emphasis from consumer to industrial products, the company's organisational structure at head office has remained unchanged and is depicted in the partial organisation chart shown below.

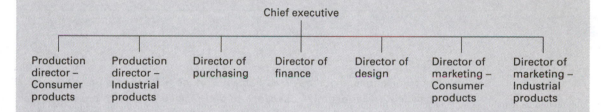

All purchasing, irrespective of the value or strategic importance of the item, is done at head office. Similarly, all orders from customers are routed through head office where decisions regarding the works at which they are to be manufactured are taken.

Recently a significant number of complaints have been made, both internally and externally, with respect to production and purchasing efficiency and consumer service. These complaints have mainly concerned product defects, delay in receiving supplies that have resulted in production delays and breakdowns, and poor customer service. Internally, control of operations has been unsatisfactory even though the majority of Electrical Industries' managers, most of whom have spent the whole of their working lives in the company and have risen through the ranks, are highly dedicated. One middle manager observed, 'we are simply not responsive enough to modern demands'.

Questions

1 Identify some of the current organisational problems at Electrical Industries.

2 Suggest, with reasons, how such problems might be solved.

3 Do you think that the problems experienced by Electrical Industries are typical in firms that have had a rapid expansion of product lines? Why or why not?

? Discussion questions

5.1   As a logistics manager, what devices or procedures might you use to achieve the coordination or integration of all the activities in the supply chain?

5.2   List six organisational committees of which a purchasing executive might be a member and in each case specify two areas on which he or she might contribute specialist knowledge.

5.3   Consider the comparison of mechanistic or organic systems in Table 5.1. In respect of the nine factors listed, decide whether the organisation in which you work can be described as mechanistic or organic. From an examination of your decisions state whether, on balance, the system under which you work is mechanistic or organic. It might be useful to tabulate your results as follows:

Factor	Mechanistic		Organic		Reasons
	Yes	No	Yes	No	
1					
2					
Etc.					

5.4   Many organisations, e.g. the Armed Forces, work on a functional basis because a commanding officer can give directions to and receive advice from line and staff officers who can then translate those orders into the language and contexts of the different areas for which they are responsible. This allows for tight control at the top and accountability upwards. Why might a system that works well in say the Army, be less successful in a civilian context?

5.5   Either individually or as a group exercise, provide examples of functional parochialism in a purchasing context under each of the following headings:

(a)   rule-oriented tactics

(b)   rule evading tactics

(c)   personal-political tactics

(d)   educational tactics

5.6   (a)   Draw simple diagrams to illustrate the following types of divisionalisation:

(i)   product organisation; (ii) a geographic organisation; (iii) a customer organisation.

(b)   Explain, with examples, the following statement:

The more divisionalised the organisation, the more centralised the staff functions used by all the divisions.

The more divisionalised the organisation, the better the intradivisional rivalry.

(Khandwalla, P.N., *The Design of Organisations*, Harcourt Brace Jovanovich, 1977, p.49)

5.7   Use Table 5.3 in the same way as Table 5.1 (see question 5.3 above) to determine whether, on balance, your organisation may be described as mechanistic or organic.

5.8 Under which type of structure would you prefer to work: (i) departmental or (ii) matrix? Give reasons for your choice.

5.9 The three key characteristics of networks have been identified as:

(a) Transactional – what is exchanged between network numbers.

(b) The nature of links – the strengths and qualitative nature of the network relationships, e.g. the degree to which members honour their network obligations or agree about the appropriate behaviour in their relationships.

(c) Structural characteristics – how members are linked, the roles played by individuals within the network.

With reference to suppliers with whom you network, identify examples to illustrate each of the above characteristics.

5.10 From your own experience try to identify examples of the advantages and disadvantages of networks listed in Table 5.4.

5.11 The Toyota Production System identified seven commonly accepted wastes:

(a) Overproduction

(b) Waiting

(c) Transportation

(d) Inappropriate planning

(e) Unnecessary inventory

(f) Unnecessary motion

(g) Defects

In respect of each of the above suggest how waste might be reduced or eliminated.

5.12 What are the sources of power that may be exploited by a purchasing executive?

5.13 You are the purchasing manager reporting to the managing director in a company organised on a functional basis. Write a one-page memo to the managing director outlining the benefits of regular meetings between the heads of design, marketing, production and yourself.

5.14 Write another memo setting out the advantages and disadvantages of allowing internal customers to place their own orders for low value, low risk supplies. What safeguards would you recommend to prevent 'maverick' buying?

5.15 Consider the comparison between lean and agile systems set out in Table 3.4.

(a) What aspects of your own organisation incorporate aspects of (i) Lean production; (ii) agile production?

(b) To what extent is it true that lean production is more likely to be associated with large, and agile productions with smaller, organisations?

(c) How might you improve agility within your organisation?

5.16 You have been appointed the purchasing manager to a company with a remit of making the purchasing function more effective, efficient and responsive to organisational needs. To what extent might a knowledge of McKinsey's 7S model assist you in determining your priorities?

5.17 What are the implications for supply chain management of centralised and decentralised purchasing?

5.18   The following simple organisation chart refers to two ways in which a company departmentalises the manufacture of a product comprising four components A, B, C and D that are made in-house.

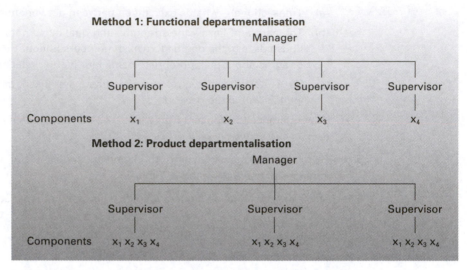

(a)   In which structure is the job of supervisor most demanding?

(b)   In which structure will supervisors be better qualified to progress to the post of manager?

(c)   In which structure is there likely to be the greater conflict?

(d)   Which structure enables the performance of supervisors to be best appraised?

(e)   Which structure facilitates a temporary shut down due to a shortage of orders?

(f)   What lessons learned from this simple example can be applied to the grouping of purchasing support services as described in Figures 5.13 and 5.14?

? Past examination questions

1   A centralised purchasing system is often viewed as 'outdated'. Explain why many organisations believe that devolving purchasing is the most effective approach.

(CIPS, Introduction to Purchasing and Supply Chain Management, May 1998)

2   Explain what you mean by the term *purchasing and supply interface* and discuss the effect on the strategic management of the supply chain of poor information flow within the context of this term.

(CIPS, Purchasing and Supply Management I: Strategy, May 1998)

3   Discuss the relationship between purchasing and the following functions:

(a)   Design

(b)   Finance

(CIPS, Introduction to Purchasing and Supply Chain Management, November 1998)

4 Discuss what you understand by the terms *centralised* and *decentralised* in the context of purchasing organisational structures. Explain the advantages of both types of structure.

(CIPS, Purchasing and Supply Management I: Strategy, November 1998)

5 Describe three different types of purchasing and supply structure and discuss the advantages and disadvantages of these in the context of their ability to meet the strategic objectives of the purchasing and supply function.

(CIPS, Purchasing and Supply Management I: Strategy, May 1998)

6 Centralisation refers to an organisational approach in which decision about staffing, investment, budgets etc. are primarily taken by a central head office function. In a decentralised organisational approach the authority to take such decisions is delegated down the line to local management.

Discuss these types of organisational approach in the context of the factors involved in a decision to totally centralise or decentralise the purchasing function in an organisation.

(CIPS, Purchasing and Supply Management I: Strategy, November 1999)

7 Explain the importance of internal interfaces within an organisation in the strategic management of the supply chain.

(CIPS, Purchasing and Supply Chain Management I: Strategy, November 2000)

8 Decisions concerning strategy and structure are interrelated. Discuss this statement in the context of a new strategy, developing your answer with examples.

(CIPS, Purchasing and Supply Chain Management I: Strategy, November 2000)

Notes

1. Mintzberg, H., *The Structure of Organisations*, Prentice Hall, 1979, Ch.1, p.2
2. Strauss, G., 'Tactics of lateral relationships: the purchasing agent', *Administrative Science Quarterly*, Vol.7, No.2 (1962), pp.161–86
3. Mintzberg, H., as n.1 above. Ch.5, p.87
4. Grinnel, S.K. and Apple, H.P., 'When two bosses are better than one', *Machine Design*, 9, Jan. 1975, p.86
5. Hastings, C., *The New Organisation*, McGraw-Hill, 1993, Ch.1, pp.7–8
6. Jones, George J. and Hill, C., *Contemporary Management*, McGraw-Hill, 1998, Glossary, p.625
7. Miles, R.E. and Snow, C.C., 'Organisations: new concepts of new forms', *California Management Review*, 28, Spring 1986
8. Womack, J.P., Jones, D.T. and Roos, D., *The Machine that Changed the World*, Maxwell Macmillan, 1990, p.13
9. See 'People management: applications of leaner ways of working', Institute of Personnel and Development, Working Paper No.13. The authors are indebted to the CIPD for permission to use this table
10. Harrison, A., Christopher, M. and Remko van Hock, *Creating the Agile Supply Chain*, Cranfield University, September 1999, p.18

11. Mintzberg, H., as n.1 above, Ch.15
12. Longley, D. and Shain, M., *Dictionary of Information Technology*, Macmillan, 1982, p.165
13. Mintzberg, H., as n.1 above, Ch.16
14. French, P., Jr and Raven, B., 'The basis of social power', in Cartwright, D. (ed.), *Studies in Social Power*, Michigan Institute for Social Research, 1959
15. Hickson, D. *et al.*, 'A strategic contingencies theory of organisational power', *Administrative Science Quarterly*, No.16 (1971), pp.216–19
16. Mintzberg, H., as n.1 above, Ch.15
17. Chandler, A.D., *Strategy and Structure: Chapters in the History of Industrial Enterprise*, MIT Press, 1962
18. Waterman, R., 'The seven elements of strategic fit', *Journal of Business Strategy*, No.3 (1982), pp.68–72
19. Stewart, T.A., 'The search for the organisation of tomorrow', *Fortune*, 18 May 1992, pp.67–72
20. Osstreff, F. and Smith, D., 'The search for the organisation of tomorrow', as n.19 above
21. Cannon, S., 'Purchasing's segmented market', *Purchasing and Supply Chain Management*, November 1994, pp.35–9
22. Market Research Focus Ltd, *Strategic Purchasing Review*, 2001, p.7. The authors are grateful to Jonathan Lyles and Robert Payne of Market Research Focus Ltd for permission to include this material
23. Market Research Focus Ltd, *Strategic Purchasing Review*, 2000, p.4
24. Wikstrom, S. and Normann, R., *Knowledge and Value*, Routledge, 1994, p.30

Purchasing procedures

Learning goals

After reading this chapter you should be able to:

- Outline the three stages of traditional purchasing procedures.
- State the inefficiencies of traditional procedures.
- Distinguish between MRO (maintenance, repair and operating) purchases and the purchase of more complex supplies and services.
- Describe e-procurement procedures for MRO supplies.
- Differentiate between e-hubs, exchanges and marketplaces.
- Distinguish between vertical, horizontal, supplier/purchaser and neutral marketplaces.
- Define the term 'e-catalogue'.
- Discuss the advantages and types of e-catalogue.
- Define the term e-auction.
- Explain some types of auction bidding.
- Describe the concept of reverse auctions and when to use them.
- Indicate guidelines for the successful operation of reverse auctions.
- Discuss the advantages and disadvantages of reverse auctions.
- Indicate some low cost procedures for the efficient handling of low value purchases.
- Suggest what purchasing records should be maintained and for how long such records should be kept.
- Describe the advantages, disadvantages, contents and distribution of purchasing manuals.
- State the essential requirements of a valid contract.
- Explain what is meant by 'the battle of the forms'.
- State why a knowledge of mercantile law is important for purchasing professionals.

6.1   What are procedures?

In Figure 4.3 it is stated that procedures are a system of sequential steps of techniques describing how a task or job is done. Procedures are also the formal arrangements through which policies linking strategy formulation at all levels are implemented. A cluster of reliable procedures each consisting of a number of operations which, together, provide information enabling staff to execute, or managers to control an activity, is called a system.

6.2   Traditional purchasing procedures

Apart from pre-purchase activities such as a participation in the preparation of specification and budget decisions, purchasing has traditionally involved three main phases, each involving specific documents and considerable clerical activity.

6.2.1   Identification phase

Notification of the need to purchase by either:

■ a requisition issued by the stores or stock control, or
■ a bill of materials issued by the drawing office or production control department.

6.2.2   Ordering phase

On receipt, the requisition or bill of materials will be checked by the buyer for accuracy, conformity to specifications and purchase records to ensure whether the purchase is a 're-buy' or a 'new-buy' request. If the item is a standard re-buy request for an item that has been previously purchased from a satisfactory supplier at an acceptable price a repeat order may be issued. If, however, the item is a 'new-buy', the following steps will be involved:

1 *Enquiries or requests for quotation (RFQs)* will be sent to possible suppliers accompanied by additional documents, e.g. drawings, specifications, etc. which will enable them to quote.
2 *Quotations* will be received in response to the enquiries and compared with respect to price, quality, delivery, tool costs, etc. and terms of business.
3 When quantities are substantial and quality and/or delivery of great importance, further *negotiation* with suppliers, including an evaluation of their capacity to undertake the order, may be required.
4 A *purchase order* will be issued to the vendor whose quotation, amended where necessary by subsequent negotiation, is most acceptable. A copy of the order will be retained in the purchasing department. (Sometimes two copies

are retained for filing both alphabetically and numerically.) Further copies of the order may be provided for:

    the department originating requisition

    progress section

    stores

    production control

    computer section

    accounts

    inspection

5   An *order acknowledgement* should be required from the vendor. On receipt, the acknowledgement should be examined to ensure that the order has been accepted on the terms and conditions agreed, and filed.

6.2.3 Post-ordering phase

1   It may be necessary to progress the order to ensure that delivery dates are met or to expedite delivery of overdue orders.

2   An *advice note*, notifying that the goods have been dispatched or are ready for collection, will be issued by the supplier. Copies of the advice note may be sent to relevant departments, e.g. progress and stores.

3   On receipt, the goods will be checked for quantity by the stores. Where matters of quality or specification are involved they will be examined by the inspection department. If satisfactory, a *goods received note* will be completed and copies sent to the purchasing department. If not satisfactory, the purchasing department will be notified so that the complaint can be taken up with the supplier.

4   An *invoice* for the value of the goods will be received from the supplier. This will be compared with the purchase order and goods received note. Usually prices will be checked by the purchasing department, paying special attention to the legitimacy of any variations from the quoted price. If satisfactory, the invoice will be passed to the accounts department for payment.

5   On completion the order will be transferred to a completed orders file.

6.3   Inefficiencies of traditional procedures

The inefficiencies of traditional procedures include:

■   A sequence of non-value-adding clerical activities.

■   Excessive documentation – for a new-buy purchase a minimum of seven different documents (requisition, enquiry quotation, order acknowledgement, advice note, goods received note and invoice) will be involved with expensive copying for purchase department records and information to other departments.

- Excessive time in processing orders both internally and externally.
- Excessive cost on purely clerical work.

It is because of such inefficiencies that many organisations have recognised that:[1]

> In many organisations administrative paperwork often serves merely to document a chain of events or to provide a logistical trail. Leading edge purchasing organisations need to transform this administrative function into a value-added process by reducing, eliminating or combining steps whenever possible.

Analysts have projected that by the end of 2003 the total value of transactions flowing through e-procurement systems will be in excess of $2 trillion.[2]

All organisations are therefore being forced to consider the strategic implications of e-procurement. E-procurement has many applications. Cox *et al.*[3] use the generic term 'e-supply strategy' to refer to any initiative in which an organisation adopts an internet software application to assist with the management of procurement, logistics or supply chain activities, whether such initiatives apply to many applications or to just one.

6.4   What is e-procurement?

6.4.1   Definitions

E-procurement has been defined by the CIPS[4] as:

> **The combined use of information and communication technology through electronic means to enhance external and internal purchasing and supply management processes. These tools and solutions deliver a range of options that will facilitate improved purchasing and supply management.**

An alternative, shorter definition is:[5]

> **E-procurement is the business-to-business purchase and sale of supplies and services over the internet.**

The key enabler of e-procurement is the ability for systems to communicate across organisational boundaries. While the technology for e-procurement provides the basic means, the main benefits derive from the resultant changes in business procedures, processes and perspectives. E-procurement is made possible by the open standard of XML (extensible markup language), a structured language that allows easy identification of data types in multiple formats and can be understood across all standard internet technologies. Adoption of XML will help organisations to integrate applications seamlessly and exchange information with trading partners.

As shown in Figure 6.1, e-procurement may be related to two broad purchasing situations.

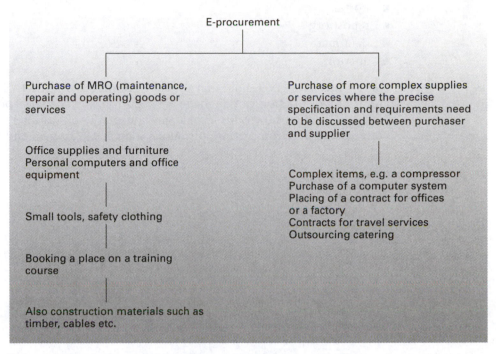

Figure 6.1   Purchasing situations from an e-procurement perspective

6.5   E-procurement procedures for MRO supplies

It has been estimated that MRO (maintenance, repair and operating) items account for some 20–30 per cent of overall business expenditure. Automating paper-based processes can effect substantial savings in cost and time and enable purchasing staff to focus on strategic supplier relationships. The step-by-step example shown in Figure 6.2 illustrates how an organisation and its employees can use e-procurement systems to order supplies more easily and cost effectively.[6]

6.6   E-hubs, exchanges and marketplaces

6.6.1   Terminology

There is some confusion regarding the semantics of e-marketplaces and writers and organisations often use different terminology to refer to the same thing. Among the terms used, each prefixed by 'e' or 'i' to show that the word is being used in an internet context, are the following:

- exchange
- hub
- marketplace

- portal
- repository
- data mart
- auction

Some writers, however, hold that the above terms are not strictly interchangeable and that a distinction can be made between hubs, exchanges and marketplaces. Figure 6.3[7] shows how hubs, exchanges and marketplaces interrelate in context with existing electronic communications such as EDI, e-mail and fax.

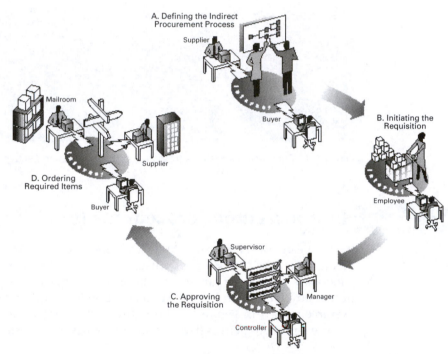

A.   Defining the Indirect Procurement Process

1.   Buyers set up purchase agreements with qualified suppliers for corporate purchases. Besides strategic negotiations, procurement establishes rules for updating electronic catalogs, electronic communication flow, payment methods, delivery and all other operational facets of mediating business.

2.   Procurement leverages functionality embedded in its portal to make product catalogs available. All employees can now search the catalog for specific items and information, such as prices, quantity breaks and delivery times.

3.   Procurement sets up the workflow rules for approval of purchases. A graphic representation of the workflow allows users to see the complete approval path for any item.

4.   Buyers manage all aspects of supplier relationships, including account status, performance history and all other data required by the procurement function.

B. Initiating the Requisition

1. Employees in need of an item search a broad range of electronic catalogs, which provide ready access to all data required to make an educated decision. The shopping cart is filled as the employee selects items.
2. Alternatively, the employee can select from a set of pre-defined or personalized shopping carts.
3. If an item is not found, an employee can add ad-hoc items to the requisition.

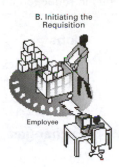

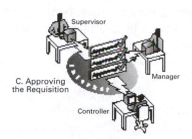

C. Approving the Requisition

1. The requisition is saved and forwarded for approval according to workflow rules.
2. Requisition approvers are notified via e-mail that they have requisitions to approve. They click on a link to the approval screen from the e-mail or go directly to the approval page.
3. Comments can be added, and if a requisition is not approved, it can be rerouted or returned to the originating employee.

D. Ordering Required Items

1. An automated fulfillment process begins immediately upon the completion of the approval process.
2. If an item is available in-house, the stock person is notified electronically to issue to the employee.
3. If an item is not available in-house, and the item is a catalog purchase with a purchase agreement, a purchase order release is generated, consolidated and communicated to the supplier via e-mail or XML document for fulfillment.
4. If the item is neither available in-house nor a catalog purchase with a purchase agreement, the requisition is forwarded to a buyer for sourcing.

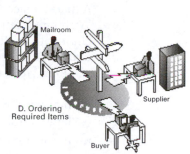

Figure 6.2 A step-by-step look at indirect procurement

Source: Epicor Software Corporation, *A Strategy for Success in the New Global Economy*, October 2001, pp.28–9, with permission

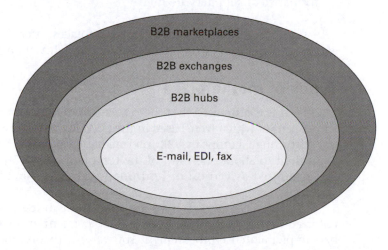

Figure 6.3 Hubs, exchanges and marketplaces in context

Hubs

In the context of internet technology a hub is a device that connects several networks together. As used in e-business a 'hub' generally refers to a central repository or private exchange such as the star network shown in Chapter 2.

Exchanges

An exchange is a B2B (business-to-business) website where purchases and suppliers meet to transact business. A distinction may be made between private and public exchanges. The former is usually operated by a single organisation and available by invitation only to the organisation's suppliers and trading partners. Such private exchanges are frequently used for collaborative business procedures such as real-time supply chain management and logistics. The latter means an independent exchange open to all organisations willing to pay a subscription to become a member. Public exchanges are often used for auctions and reverse auctions.

Marketplaces

A marketplace is a website that enables purchasers to select from many suppliers. With e-marketplaces the buyer is in control since open marketplaces enable purchasers to evaluate all potential suppliers for a particular product or service and make informed decisions regarding what and where to buy.

E-marketplaces are particularly applicable where:

- markets are large and the search costs to find suppliers are high because of the large number of potential suppliers;
- product specifications and information are subject to rapid change;
- buyers have difficulty in comparing similar products from different vendors because of an excess of features and characteristics that may not be clearly indicated;
- internal costs of such processes as locating, appraising and evaluating the performance of suppliers are high.

In summary it may be said that marketplaces offer greater functionality than exchanges which, in turn, offer more functionality than hubs.

6.6.2 Types of marketplace

In 2000 it was estimated that there were around 1,000 marketplaces in existence, 75 per cent of which were based in the USA. By 2004, however, goods and services traded through European B2B intermediaries are expected to total $408 billion, equivalent to about one-third of the total European B2B market.[8] E-markets may be categorised as vertical or horizontal and either supplier/purchaser-owned or neutral.

Other sources, however, have presented a much less rosy picture. Bradley *et al.*[9] reported that up to 2001 only about 8–10 per cent of the Global 5,000 companies had implemented e-procurement software, with disappointing results and that almost every company had experienced one or more of the following issues:

- difficulty in implementing and integrating e-procurement software into existing legacy systems;
- catalogue management had been more difficult and costly that anticipated;
- slow 'adoption' of new e-procurement systems by users;
- difficulty in implementing cross-functional process changes with a consequent slowdown in output;
- failure of software to live up to its promise;
- adoption of different solutions by different divisions thus creating an 'e-patchwork' that quelled any hope of integrating procurement data companywide;
- over sanguine forecasts on the part of e-procurement suppliers, i.e. that their technology would save 10–15 per cent across the company's entire spend base even though promises of double-digit savings on external spend in industries where supplier net margins average no more than 5–8 per cent were suspect from the start.

Four types of marketplaces have been identified:

- *Vertical e-marketplaces* provide goods or services to a specific industry. Examples include Chemdex.com in life sciences; buzzsaw.com in construction; and utilyse, a European e-commerce procurement company offering an online marketplace for the purchasing of electricity, gas, water and telecommunications.
- *Horizontale-marketplaces* provide goods and services to a range of organisations in different market segments rather than to specific industries. Thus horizontal markets can be created for payment and banking services, logistics and office supplies. A typical example is World Crest for MRO supplies.
- *Supplier/purchaser marketplaces*, as the name implies, are those controlled by groups of suppliers. Thus the four leading European steel producers, Corus, Thyssen Krupp, Usinor and Arbed decided to collaborate on the launch of two B2B marketplaces, the first, Steel, 24–7.com focusing on marketing steel products; the second, BuyingforMetals.com serving a more horizontal market concerned with the purchasing of related goods and services. An example of a purchasing hub is Covisint, a coalition of Ford, General Motors and Daimler/Chrysler.
- *Neutral marketplaces*. A typical example is MRO.com which is horizontal rather than vertical and facilitates the transaction of a variety of MRO items.

6.7　E-catalogues

Printed catalogues or product lists provide specifications, prices and frequently illustrations of the items that suppliers can provide. The disadvantages of hard copy catalogues is that they may be obsolete even before they are published and are too slow to provide information in a dynamic marketplace.

6.7.1 Definition

At their simplest, B2B marketplaces are just online catalogues. An e-catalogue may be defined as:

A web page that provides information on products and services offered and sold by a vendor and supports online ordering and payment capabilities.

6.7.2 Advantages of e-catalogues

E-catalogues benefit both purchasers and suppliers in that they:

- facilitate real-time two-way communication between buyers and sellers;
- allow for the development of closer purchaser/supplier relationships through improved vendor services and informing purchasers of products of which they might otherwise be unaware;
- enable suppliers to respond quickly to market conditions and requirements by adjusting prices and repackaging.
- the virtual elimination of the time lag between the generation of a requisition by a catalogue user and the issue of the purchase order since:
  - authorisation, where required, can be done online and notified and confirmed by e-mail;
  - where users are authorised to generate their own purchases (subject to value and item constraints), the order can be automatically generated without the intervention of the purchasing department;
- 'maverick' or 'off-contract' purchasing is reduced because it is simpler and quicker to purchase from contracted suppliers than to go outside the official system.

6.7.3 Types of e-catalogue

Sell-side catalogues

These provide potential purchasers with access to the online catalogues of a particular supplier who provides an online purchasing facility.

Sell-side catalogues provide many benefits to suppliers including ease of keeping the contents up-to-date, savings on advertising costs and the costs of processing sales. The benefits to potential purchasers include 24 hour, 7 day access to information and ease of ordering.

Sell-side catalogues have, however, several disadvantages, including:

- Insufficient time for purchasers to surf all the available supplier websites.
- Buyers may become overdependent on particular suppliers since training in the use of new software may be required if suppliers are changed.
- Where the price of a product differs from one purchaser to another the use of personalised, restricted, pre-negotiated catalogues or encrypted catalogues may be necessary.

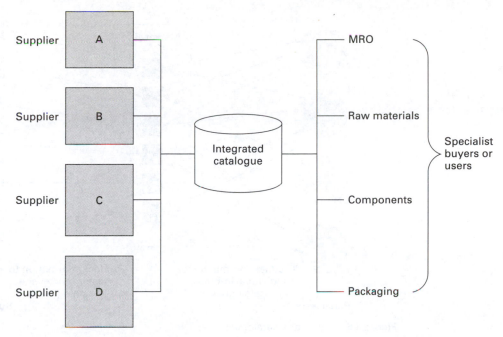

Figure 6.4   Buy-side catalogue operation

Buy-side catalogues

These are catalogues created by purchasing organisations. Normally such catalogues are confined to goods covered by pre-negotiated prices, specifications and terms and run by a program that is integrated into the purchasing organisation's intranet. An example of the operation of buy-side catalogues is shown in Figure 6.4.

The benefits to purchasers include:

- reduced communication costs;
- increased security;
- many catalogues can be accessed via the same intranet application.

The compilation and updating of buy-side catalogues does, however, require a large investment in clerical resources that will be uneconomical for all but the largest organisations. Suppliers wishing to be included in the catalogue will also be required to provide their content in a standard format. For suppliers dealing with a large number of purchasers the workload of providing information in the form required by each online catalogue will be unsustainable.

Third-party catalogues

The disadvantages of sell- and buy-side catalogues can be minimised by outsourcing the process to an electronic marketplace or buying consortium. This can

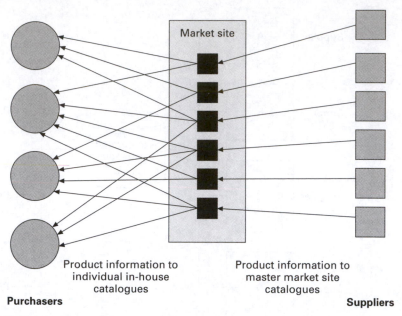

Figure 6.5 Third-party catalogues

be done by linking the in-house e-procurement catalogue to a master catalogue administered by the marketplace as shown in Figure 6.5.[10]

The system works as follows:

■ Standard information for inclusion in the 'market site' or 'master catalogue' is provided by the suppliers. This information is then made available to the in-house catalogues of individual purchasing organisations.

■ Product information from suppliers can either reside in the in-house catalogue or be hosted in the master catalogue.

■ The responsibility of managing and updating product and other information rests with the suppliers.

Advantages of this system include:

■ Suppliers have a greater incentive to provide information in the specified standard format since the master catalogue will be available to a large number of purchasing organisations.

■ The in-house procurement catalogues draw product and other information from the master catalogue and purchasers or users can pass electronic orders to suppliers via the master site.

■ Product information can be divided into two parts: (i) public and (ii) encrypted. Public information will include a basic product description and specification often accompanied by an illustration or diagram. Encrypted information will provide details of prices, discounts and similar matters applicable to specific purchasers which cannot be accessed by unauthorised users.

6.8   E-auctions

One step up from e-catalogues are e-auctions. An e-auction may be defined as:[11]

> **An electronic market, which can exist in both business-to-business and business-to-consumer contexts. Sellers offer goods or services to buyers through a website with a structured process for price setting and fulfilment.**

Web auctions may follow English, Dutch, sealed-bid and reverse-bid processes.

- *English bid process*. In this process bids are replaced by higher bids to obtain the highest price for a given item.
- *Dutch bid process*. The English process is unsuitable for selling thousands of items to a number of different buyers. This can, however, be easily and quickly done through the 'Dutch auction' developed in seventeenth century Amsterdam for the sale of flowers. In the Dutch auction the auctioneer starts at a high price and then descends by steps until a bid is received. The successful bidder then decides whether to buy the whole or a proportion of the items on offer at that price. The auctioneer increases the offer price for any items remaining in the current lot and then again descends by steps and continues in this manner until either the whole of the items comprising the lot are sold or a reserve price is reached.
- *Sealed-bid process*. This process is broadly similar to tendering. A potential purchaser issues a request for bids to be submitted by a prescribed date and time under a sealed format. At the specified date and time the purchaser's representatives will evaluate and compare the bids according to a rating grid. The winning bid is the bid that achieves the maximum score. Should several bids obtain the same score the bid offering the best price is the winner.

6.9   Reverse auctions

6.9.1   What is a reverse auction?

In a reverse auction, buying organisations post the item(s) they wish to buy and the price they are willing to pay while suppliers compete to offer the best price for the item(s) over a prescribed time period. For example, a buying organisation is interested in purchasing 1,000 castings to a published specification at the lowest possible price. It therefore creates a reverse auction, stating the dimensions, quality, performance and delivery requirements and, often bid decrements. Suppliers enter the marketplace and bid on the auction. Winners are declared according to the agreed auction rules.

At the conclusion of the auction both purchaser and supplier are bound by the sale. If a reserve price is set but not met the buying organisation decides the winning bid. Suppliers can bid more than once in the prescribed time. Apart from the names of the suppliers and reverse sealed-bid auctions, all the bids are available for everyone to see. Most online auction sites use automatic bidding agents or 'proxy bidders' that automatically place bids on the suppliers' behalf.

Example 6.1   Reverse auction 1

Bids are solicited for 100 items of product X. The opening bid is £25 per product with bid decrements of £5.

Supplier A bids £25 each for 100 items

Supplier B bids £20 each for 50 items

Supplier C bids £15 each for 50 items

The result of the auction is that:

Supplier A is unsuccessful

Supplier B sells 50 items for £20

Supplier C sells 50 items for £15

There are several variations of the bidding process. In what is known as the reverse English manual system, the buying organisation specifies the opening bid and the suppliers bid higher. At the conclusion of the auction the purchaser selects the winners manually. Each winning bidder sells at the bid price made. The criteria for the winning bid may not be disclosed.

Example 6.2   Reverse auction 2

Bids are selected for 100 items of product X. The opening bid is £10.

Supplier A bids £10 per item for 100 items

Supplier B bids £20 per item for 100 items

Supplier C bids £20 per item for 100 items

The result of the auction is that:

Supplier A is unsuccessful

Supplier C sells 100 items for £20

because of closer geographical proximity to the purchaser than supplier B.

6.9.2   When to use reverse auctions

Most reverse auctions are used for spot buying and eliminate the time-consuming offline process of selecting suppliers, requesting quotations and comparing quotes received. Marketplaces with many suppliers can offer purchasers a compiled list of suppliers. Purchasing organisations conducting reverse auctions on their own sites must invite prospective suppliers in advance if they wish such suppliers to participate. Reverse auctions are particularly useful in the following circumstances:

■ When there is uncertainty in the size of the market and the willingness of sellers to supply a product.

■ For the purchase of large quantities of items for which clear specifications are possible.

- For the sale of surplus assets.

- For some services, e.g. car rentals, freight services, hotel accommodation.

In general, lowest price reverse auction processes should be used only where there is little concern about production specifications or the suppliers selected. They are not appropriate for complex products or projects requiring collaboration or considerable negotiation.

6.9.3 Reverse auction guidelines

The following guidelines relating to reverse auctions have been compiled by the US Federal Technology Service.[12]

(i) **The acquisition process changes little when using a reverse auction to determine price.** The requirements of the procurement process do not change with the use of reverse auctions which are simply a different way of arriving at a fair and reasonable price.

(ii) **Reverse auctions are not appropriate for all acquisitions and it is important to know when to use them.**

(iii) **Evaluate the capabilities of several enablers before choosing one.** Many contractors can provide the enabling technology to conduct a reverse auction. Each will offer different levels of service and pricing. The right vendor is the one that provides the right level of service at a reasonable price.

(iv) **Be aware that different levels of service can be obtained.** These include researching the market for additional bidders or having foreign language interpreters if bidders are located internationally. Extra services entail extra fees and consideration should be given to whether such extras are required.

(v) **When selecting a contractor to provide the auction enabling technology be aware that different fee structures exist.** E.g. a share in savings based on the difference between the initial and final price, or fees based on licensing agreements.

(vi) **The bigger the spend the greater the time compression and the greater the savings.** Greater price compression will be attained if the quantities and their estimated value are significant.

(vii) **Greater savings can be gained through the use of reverse auctions if there is competition.**

(viii) **Bidders must be present (online), fully prepared and qualified.**

(ix) **Bidders should receive training from the enabler who will be hosting the auction.** The training should be simple and conducted as close to the actual time of the auction as possible. Mock auctions are helpful. An open phone can be used during auctions to alleviate fears that bidders and the contracting office may have.

(x) **The contracting officer must be in charge of the entire process.** The contracting officer is the key to a successful auction and should be present throughout the bidding.

(xi) **Ensure that the specification is 'bullet-proof'.** Specifications should be as detailed as possible so that bidders can compete fairly in the online bidding process. Details of sale and delivery should be clearly stated.

(xii) **Consider breaking the specifications into lots or logical groupings of items to be acquired.** A contract for the furnishing of an office can be on an 'all or one' basis or broken down into various categories of furniture and equipment.

(xiii) **Ensure that the documentation received from the auction enabler at the close of the auction is appropriate for the contract file.** Minimum requirements are a list of the bidders identities, aliases, number of bids, amount of bid, time of bid, and whether connection was sustained throughout the auction.

(xiv) **The contracting officer must establish the rules of the auction prior to the auction event.** Once rules have been established it is important that these are strictly enforced by the contracting officer.

(xv) **Use language in the solicitation that permits the purchase of additional quantities of 10 per cent to 20 per cent at the final auction price.** At the end of an auction purchasers will often have surplus funds due to the savings achieved from the auction. The successful bidder is not, however, obliged to sell other than the specified quantity at the auction price. By reserving the right to purchase an extra 10 per cent or 20 per cent at the final bid price surplus funds can be used to purchase extra quantities that can be processed under one order.

(xvi) **Reverse auctions are merely pricing mechanisms and do not preclude the use of the best value criteria for the contract award.** Consider also such factors as the bidder's technical management and past performance.

(xvii) **Consider inviting only small businesses to participate.** Small businesses appreciate opportunities they would not normally receive under the 'three quotes' rule.

6.9.4 Advantages of reverse auctions

Reverse auctions provide benefits for both buyers and sellers. The benefits for buyers include:

■ Savings over and above those obtained from normal negotiation as a result of competition. On average the auction process drives down supplier prices by 11 per cent, with savings ranging from 4 to 40 per cent.[13]

■ Reduction in acquisition lead times.

■ Access to a wider range of suppliers.

■ A global supply base can be achieved relatively quickly.

■ Sources of market information are enhanced.

■ More efficient administration of requests for quotations (RFQs) and proposals.

■ Auctions conducted on the internet generally provide total anonymity so that time is not wasted on seeing supplier representatives.

The benefits for suppliers include:

■ An opportunity to enter previously closed markets. This is particularly import-ant for smaller companies.

■ Reduced negotiation timescales.

- Auctions provide a good source of market pricing information.
- Auctions give clear indications of what must be done to win the business.

6.9.5   Disadvantages of reverse auctions

Some objections to reverse auctions include:

- Reverse auctions are based on a win–lose approach:

    The seller is trying to get the most money while the buyer is after the best deal. The goal is to screw your opponent to 'win' either a good deal or a profitable sale at the other person's expense. The logical progression is always towards cheating. Thus, such a system can't be sustained without burdensome watch-dogs and regulators.[14]

- Reverse auctions can cause an adverse shift in buyer/seller relationships since the suppliers may feel exploited and become less trustful of purchasers.
- Possible long-term adverse effects on the economic performance of both suppliers and purchasers since:
    - some suppliers may not be able to sustain sharp price reductions over the long term;
    - suppliers who cannot compete at the lower price levels may be removed, or asked to be removed, from the purchaser's approved supplier list so that purchasers eventually have reduced supplier bases.
- In order to ensure that the exact goods and services required are obtained considerable time may be taken in completing detailed specification sheets.

6.10   E-procurement: an appraisal

6.10.1   Benefits

Recent surveys[15] indicate that the main benefits of e-procurement are:

- *Improved information flow and service* through real-time market intelligence and information. Such information includes finding the best price and quality points across a large range of suppliers through the use of marketplaces; order status and tracking; reduced inventory levels; better demand forecasting.
- *Reduced transaction costs* through the automation of requisitioning, purchase order management and accounting processes by the use of internet technology including online ordering, empowered users (direct order entry), XML integration (common standards). Analysis by a purchasing manager in a UK-based chemical company has shown that the average cost of processing a paper-based purchasing transaction from receipt of a requisition to payment of the supplier is about £60. With a fully automated process that figure falls to around £8.[16]

- *Reduction of 'maverick' purchasing*, i.e. purchases made outside the organisations contractual arrangements.
- *Increased speed and efficiency.*
- The *ability to aggregate purchasing* across multiple departments or divisions without taking away any needed individual control or introducing time-wasting authorisation routines.

The perceived benefits of e-procurement do, however, vary across industries. Speed and efficiency appear to be seen as most beneficial by retail undertakings; reduced transaction costs in manufacturing and improved relationships in engineering. While the adoption of e-procurement is expected to increase rapidly the *E-business Report 2001* states that 'the claims made for the Internet to transform all aspects of supply chain management appear to be overblown. Only 23 per cent of the organisations surveyed are currently using the Internet to improve aspects of their supply management activities'.[17] The principal reason for the lack of e-supply strategy appears to be a failure to develop an e-business strategy for the organisation as a whole. Other reasons include the lack of suitable infrastructure both internally and on the part of suppliers and lack of internal IT expertise. The CIPS[18] also points out that:

> E-procurement will change the dynamics of the purchasing and supply management profession as for example, there will be a greater emphasis on knowledge management. It is suggested that e-procurement will change the culture of purchasing and supply management in an organisation and may lead to a greater emphasis on cost and prices. E-procurement will also facilitate purchasing from global sources.

6.10.2 Implementation issues

The CIPS[19] has provided the following list of issues to be overcome when implementing e-procurement:

- Ensuring that by deploying e-procurement, organisations are not simply passing costs or process inefficiencies onto another part of the organisation or onto suppliers.
- Competition issues, e.g. in exchanges using collaborative purchasing.
- Possible negative perception from suppliers, e.g. their margins reduced further from e-auctions.
- Website and information control lost to exchange administrators.
- Negotiated procurement benefits may be shared with other exchange users who may be competitors.
- Creation of catalogues can be a long process and costly to suppliers.
- Catalogue management can be costly.
- Product coding and classification can also be costly.
- The cost of changing suppliers once they have invested in catalogue production may inhibit competition and lead to inertia.
- Culture profile within organisations, e.g. resistance to change.

6.11 Small value purchases

A 1997 enquiry by the National Audit Office into low value purchases by the Ministry of Defence found that procurement costs, i.e. requisitioning, obtaining quotes and issuing a purchase order for a padlock costing 80p, amounted to £90. Low value orders increase costs and hamper purchasing and accounting productivity. Low cost procedures for the efficient handling of low value purchases include:

- *Placement of own orders*. Users can place orders to specified limits and with approved suppliers over the internet. Such procedures have been referred to earlier in this chapter.

- *Procurement cards*. These are similar to consumer credit cards and involve a provider such as Mastercard, Visa, American Express and, usually, an issuing bank. When used for low value purchases they enable any user e.g. a foreman on a building site, to make purchases and provide payments to suppliers. Such cards eliminate the need for purchase orders. Limitations on the value of purchases and other rules for the use of such cards will need to be specified.

- *Telephone orders*. Requirements are telephoned to the supplier who is provided with an order number. The agreed price is recorded on the order form but no order is sent. The goods are invoiced by the supplier against the order form.

- *Petty cash purchases*. Items obtained directly from local suppliers on presentation of an authorised requisition and paid for at once from petty cash. The main problem is that of controlling the number and size of purchases. This can be done by providing potential users with a petty cash imprest out of which such payments are made.

- *Standing orders*. All orders for a range of items, e.g. electrical fittings, fasteners, are placed with one supplier for a period of, say, 12 months. A special discount is often negotiated and quantities specified. Required items are called off by users who transmit releases directly from the supplier in a fax, telephone or computer interface. The amount due is summarised by the supplier, either electronically or tabulated as a single invoice, and segregated by user's cost centres for easier coding by the accounts function.

- *Self-billing*. This also uses electronic data interchange (EDI). Pugsley[20] reports that when the Rover Group, which trades electronically, receives goods from a supplier, it checks that the goods were ordered and then simply pays. The supplier does not need to raise an invoice. Self-billing enables both customer and supplier to make savings.

- *Blank-cheque orders*. A system devised in the USA in which a cheque form with a specified liability is attached to the order form. On forwarding the goods the supplier fills in the cheque which he deposits in his own bank. The cheque can only be deposited and not cashed. The need for invoicing and forwarding of payment is thus avoided.

- *Stockless buying*. This is virtually the same as blanket ordering but the supplier agrees to maintain stocks of specified items.

6.12 Purchasing records

Purchasing records are concerned with the storage of information. With manual systems this information will be entered on card indexes or filed in appropriate systems. Computerisation using master files or databases not only enables vast amounts of information to be stored but also obviates duplication and ensures the efficient retrieval of data. It would be impracticable to reproduce rulings or purchase records in this book. Apart from files of requisitions, purchase orders and other original documents, purchase records may include:

- supplier index giving details of addresses, telephone, staff and items supplied;
- supplier rating giving details of supplier performance relating to price, quality, delivery etc.;
- supplier visits giving details of visits paid to suppliers to inspect their facilities;
- record of items purchased giving details of standard descriptions of bought-out items and particulars of suppliers and the orders placed;
- price trends of 'sensitive' commodities – graphs of the trend of prices;
- records of material issued to subcontractors;
- jigs, tools and patterns owned by the purchaser, whether in the possession of suppliers or otherwise;
- contract records, i.e. contracts for the supply of materials or components over a period of time and quantities called off against them;
- order registers providing a record of all orders placed each day to:
  - facilitate reference to orders placed and filed alphabetically, numerically or by project;
  - provide information regarding the number of orders placed during a given period;
  - facilitate checking actual against budgeted purchasing expenditure.

The question is sometimes raised regarding the period for which records providing evidence relating to contracts (e.g. order forms, acknowledgements and related correspondence) should be retained. Contractual obligations are not enforceable for ever. The Limitations Act 1980 specifies that the general periods within an action may be brought are as follows:

- Actions based on a *simple* contract will be barred after 6 years from the date when the cause or action accrued.
- Actions based on a contract made by *deed* can be brought up to 12 years from the date when the cause or action accrued.

Provided the above periods have not expired, the time limit may be extended where the party in breach either acknowledges liability in a written form signed by him or his agent or makes a part-payment in respect of his claim or debt. The period of 6 or 12 years will begin to run afresh from the time of acknowledgement or payment.

In general, therefore, the period for the retention of evidence should be based on such considerations as the assize of the possible payment and the possibility, however remote, of legal action. For small amounts, records need to be kept for no longer than the expiry period of the contract. For substantial contracts, made in simple form, it is prudent to retain evidence for a minimum of six years.

6.13   Purchasing manuals

6.13.1   What is a purchasing manual?

A purchasing manual is in essence a medium for communicating information regarding purchasing policies, procedures, instructions and regulations.

■ *Policies* may be general or consequential. *General* policies state in broad terms the objectives and responsibilities of the purchasing function. *Consequential* policies state, in expanded form, how general policies are applied in specific activities and situations, e.g. the selection of suppliers.

■ *Procedures* prescribe the sequence of actions by which policies are implemented, e.g. the receipt of bought-out goods.

■ *Instructions* give detailed knowledge or guidance to those responsible for carrying out the policies or procedures, e.g. the number of copies of a purchase order required and their distribution.

■ *Regulations* are detailed rules regarding the conduct of purchasing and ancillary staff in the various situations arising in the course of their duties, e.g. concerning the receipt of gifts from suppliers.

When drafting a purchasing manual it is useful to keep these distinctions clearly in mind.

6.13.2   Advantages of purchasing manuals

The advantages claimed for purchasing manuals include the following:

■ Writing helps precision and clarity.

■ The preparation of a manual provides an opportunity for consultation between purchasing and other departments, to look critically at existing policies and procedures and, where necessary, to change them.

■ Procedures are prescribed in respect of activities undertaken or controlled by purchasing, thus promoting consistency and reducing the need for detailed supervision of routine tasks.

■ A manual is a useful aid in training and guiding staff.

■ A manual can help the annual audit.

■ A manual coordinates policies and procedures and helps to ensure uniformity and continuity of purchasing principles and practice. It also provides a point of reference against which such principles and practice can be evaluated.

- A manual may help to enhance the status of purchasing by showing that top management attaches importance to the procurement function.
- Computerisation, which needs detailed and well-documented systems, has given further impetus to the preparation of purchasing manuals.

6.13.3 Disadvantages of purchasing manuals

The disadvantages urged against manuals are as follows:

- Manuals are costly to prepare.
- Manuals tend to foster red tape and bureaucracy and to stifle initiative.
- Manuals must be continually updated to show changes in procedures and policy.

6.13.4 Format of purchasing manuals

A manual should be:

- Normally of A4 size.
- Loose-leaf, to permit the issue of sections to separate parts of the organisation and insertion of amendments.
- Simply written and illustrated by relevant flowcharts, etc.
- Well produced, easily handled, durable and clearly printed.

The main factors to be considered when deciding on the format are:

- durability of content
- ease of storage
- ease of reference
- legibility
- portability
- ease of updating by user
- ease of updating by author
- compactness
- cost

6.13.5 Contents of purchasing manuals

A purchasing manual may consist of three main sections dealing respectively with organisation, policy and procedures.

Organisation

- Charts showing the place of purchasing within the undertaking and how it is organised both centrally and locally.

- Job descriptions for all posts within the purchasing function, including, where applicable, limitations of authority to commit the undertaking.
- Administrative information for staff, e.g. absences, hours of work, travelling expenses etc.

Policy

- Statements of policy setting out the objectives, responsibilities and authority of the purchasing function.
- Statements, which can be expanded, of general principle relating to price, quality etc.
- Terms and conditions of purchase.
- Relationships with suppliers, especially regarding gifts, entertainment etc.
- Supplier selection.
- Employee purchases.
- Reports to management.

Procedures

- Descriptions, accompanied by flowcharts, of procedures relating to requisitioning, ordering, expediting, receiving, inspecting, storing and payment of goods.
- Procedures relating to the rejection and return of goods.
- Procedures in respect of the disposal of scrap and obsolete or surplus items.
- Illustrations of all documents used in connection with purchasing and ancillary activities, with instructions for their use and circulation.
- Reference to purchase records and their maintenance.

6.13.6 Distribution of purchasing manuals

Complete copies of the manual should be sent to:

- the board of directors or similar body;
- the chief executive of the undertaking;
- heads of functions or teams with whom purchasing has contacts;
- members of the purchasing staff both centrally and locally.

6.14 Legal aspects of purchasing

Although purchasing procedures may have changed from manual to electronic methods, all commercial transactions must conform to the requirements of a valid contract.

6.14.1 The essentials of a contract

A valid contract is a promise or agreement that the law will enforce. To be legally enforceable a contract must satisfy the following essentials:

1 *Intention*. Both parties must intend to enter into a legal relationship.

2 *Agreement*. In a dispute the courts must be satisfied that the contracting parties had reached a firm agreement and were not still negotiating. Agreement will usually be shown by the unconditional acceptance of an offer. It is important to determine by whom the offer is made, whether the offer is valid and if it has been accepted.

3 *Consideration*. The English law of contract is concerned with *bargains* not mere promises. Thus, if A promises to give something to B, B will have no remedy if A breaks his promise. If, however, B has undertaken to do something in return so that A's promise is dependent on B's, the mutual exchange of promises turns the arrangement into a contract. The consideration must also exist and have some ascertainable value, however slight, otherwise there is no contract.

4 *Form*. Certain exceptional types of agreement are valid only if made in a particular way, e.g. in writing, thus conveyances of lands and leases for over three years must be by deed. The absence of written evidence, while not affecting the validity of a contract, may make it unenforceable in the courts. This evidence may be from correspondence or any other documentation created at the time the contract was made or subsequently. Such written evidence must clearly identify the parties against whom the evidence is to be used or by his authorised agent.

5 *Definite terms*. There will be no contract if it is not possible to determine what has been agreed between the parties. Where essential terms have yet to be decided the parties are still in the stage of negotiation. An agreement to agree in future is not a contract.

6 *Legality*. Some agreements, such as contracts to defraud the Inland Revenue, or immoral contracts such as agreements to fix prices or regulate supplies, while not illegal are void under the Competition Acts unless the parties can prove to the Restrictive Practices Court that their agreement is beneficial and in the public interest.

6.14.2 The 'battle of the forms'

One of the essential elements of a valid contract (i.e. a contract that can be enforced) is an unconditional acceptance by the offeree (i.e. the party to whom the offer is made) of an offer made by the other party known as the offerer. If the acceptance seeks to vary the terms of the offer in any way there is a counter-offer and the original offer lapses. Thus, in the case of *Hyde v Wrench* (1840), Wrench (W) offered to sell a farm to Hyde (H) for £1,000. H replied offering £950 which W refused and without informing H of his intention sold the farm elsewhere. Hyde later wrote accepting the original price of £1,000 and, on finding the farm sold, sued W for breach of contract. The court held that the counter-offer of £950 rejected the original offer which could only be revived by W.

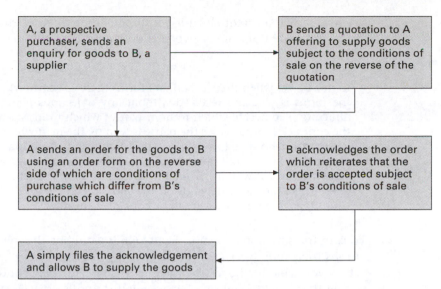

Figure 6.6   In the event of a dispute between A and B, which conditions prevail?

Quotations, order forms and acknowledgements often contain, on their reverse side, or make reference to, standard conditions of sale or purchase. The situation that can arise is shown in Figure 6.6.

The term 'battle of the forms' was coined by Lord Denning in the case of *Butler Machine Tool Co. Ltd v Ex-Cell-O Corporation (England) Ltd* (1979) which arose from differing sets of standard conditions. Butler Machine Tool, the seller, made a quotation offering to sell a machine tool to Ex-Cell-O, the buyer, for £75,000. The offer was stated to be subject to terms and conditions which 'shall prevail over any terms and conditions in the Buyer's order'. These included a price variation clause for the goods to be charged at the price ruling on the date of delivery. The buyer ordered the machine, its order being subject to terms and conditions materially different from those of the seller and containing no price variation clause. At the foot of the buyer's order was a tear-off acknowledgement of receipt of the order stating: 'We accept your order on the Terms and Conditions stated hereon'. The acknowledgement was completed by the seller and returned to the buyer with a letter stating that the buyer's order was being entered in accordance with the seller's quotation.

On delivery, the seller claimed a price increase of £2,892 which the buyer refused to pay. The seller brought an action claiming that the variation clause entitled them to increase the price. Although the buyer contended that the contract had been concluded on its terms and was therefore a fixed price contract, the judge found for the seller on the grounds that the contract had been concluded on the basis that the seller's terms were to prevail since price variation was stipulated in the opening offer and this applied to subsequent negotiations.

This verdict was, however, reversed on appeal on the grounds that the seller, by completing and returning the buyer's terms, could not claim to increase the price under the price variation clause contained in its offer. The seller's letter referring to the quotation was irrelevant since it referred only to the price and identity of the machine and did not incorporate the seller's terms into the contract.

The case is important since it emphasises that whether the buyer's or seller's terms and conditions apply depends on the facts of the case. As Lord Denning stated:

> In most cases when there is battle of forms there is a contract as soon as the last of the forms is sent and received without any objections being taken to it . . . The difficulty is to decide which form or part of which form is a term or condition of the contract. In some cases the battle is won by the man who fires the last shot. He is the man who puts forward the latest terms and conditions and if they are not objected to by the other party, he may be taken to have agreed to them. In some cases the battle is won by the man who gets his blow in first . . . There are yet other cases where the battle depends on the shots fired by both sides . . . The terms and conditions of both parties are to be construed together.

Thus in the situation shown in Figure 6.6 it would be the seller's terms and conditions that would prevail.

It is advisable for buyers to include a clause in their conditions of purchase stating that liability will only be accepted for orders placed subject to the terms and conditions stated on their order forms which the seller accepts by signing and returning an acknowledgement form referring to those conditions within a stipulated time, e.g. 14 days.

6.14.3 Law and the buyer

Commercial or mercantile law includes agency agreements, contracts for the sale of goods and services, insurance, negotiable instruments and carriage by land, sea and air. Clearly all such legislation together with that relating to electronic trading (see Chapter 2) and European procurement is applicable to purchasing. There are at least three good reasons why all purchasing professionals should have a working knowledge of commercial law. Firstly, the principle of *ignorantia juris non excusat* (ignorance of the law does not excuse) means that a company (which in law is a legal person) and its servants such as purchasing specialists, are presumed to know the law. Secondly, all purchasing staff should have an awareness of the possible legal consequences of their actions. Thirdly, 'a little knowledge is a dangerous thing' and a knowledge of the law should indicate when it is advisable for buyers to seek professional advice.

General structure of a contract

■ *The agreement*. This names the parties to the contract. In a standard contract it is necessary only to change the names and any other relevant details. If the parties sign on the front page this saves leafing through the whole, but there should be a statement that the parties have read and understood all the terms and conditions appertaining to the contract.

■ *The terms and conditions*. These comprise:

– *Definitions*. These are inserted to avoid ambiguity and avoid the repetition of long sentences. When, in the text a capital letter is used for a word it indicates that the word has been defined in the definitions section.

- *General terms.* These comprise the general agreements clause, a changes, alterations and variations clause, a 'notice' clause stating how and by what method any notice relating to the contract is to be sent and a clause stating that the headings and definitions are for information only.

- *Commercial provisions.* These set out the rights and obligations of the supplier and, in a separate clause, the rights and obligations of the purchaser. A separate clause will specify payment terms.

- *Secondary commercial provisions.* These deal with such matters as conditions, warranties, confidentiality, intellectual property, indemnity and termination.

- *Boilerplate clauses.* These are standard clauses which appear in almost all contracts, e.g.

  - *Severability* – the right of a court to remove a term or condition that is invalid, void or unenforceable without prejudice to the rest of the contract.

  - *Waiver* – a statement that failure to enforce a 'right' at a given time will not prevent the exercise of that right later.

  - *Force majeure* – applicable where a 'major force' such as an act of God, war, riots, floods, tempests etc. prevents or delays the performance of the contract.

  - *Law and jurisdiction* – the law that governs the contract. The *Principles of International Contracts* produced by UNIDROIT (International Institute for the Unifications of Private Law) in 1994 aim to 'establish a balanced set of rules designed for use throughout the world, irrespective of the legal traditions and the economic and political conditions of the countries in which they are to be applied'. These principles have no legal force and depend for their acceptance on their perceived authority. When, however, the parties agree, they can become legally binding.

Interpretation of contracts

It is useful for purchasing staff to know something of the general principles of interpretation and the rules of evidence including how the courts will construe the words used, resolve ambiguities, take account of trade usages, vary written terms and 'fill the gaps' in respect of issues not covered in the contract.

Case study

Rollers plc assembles about 10,000 conveyor rollers weekly. The rollers comprise a mild steel outer cover, two die-cast roller ends, a spindle and two ball bearings. The rollers are filled with oil and sealed with two seals held in place by circlips. An illustration of a typical roller is given below.

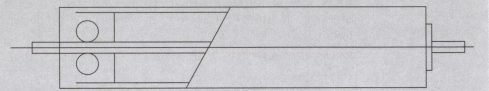

The die-cast roller ends are ordered in quantities of 500,000 and delivered on a JIT basis. Rollers plc had the option of purchasing the moulds from the foundry Arena Diecastings at an extra cost or allowing the moulds to remain in the possession of the die-casters. They opted for the latter alternative. Because of the relatively small number of standard components, most purchasing is done by Ray Harrison the designer draughtsman. Tom Unsworth, the managing director, has read of the savings reported in respect of bids received from potential suppliers at reverse auctions. He therefore instructs Ray to invite reverse auction bids from possible alternative suppliers, pointing out that a penny reduction per item on a contract for 500,000 die-castings would provide a saving of £5,000. Arena Diecastings and four other die-casters selected at random from a directory are asked to submit bids.

One bidder, Supercastings, offers a saving of 5p over the lowest bid from Arena and offers to supply the moulds, which will remain the property of the die-caster, free of charge. Arena states that it cannot match the bid but points out that during the four years it has been supplying Rollers plc not one faulty casting has been returned and they have not been late with a delivery. Tom, however, points out that a saving of 10p per roller cannot be missed in what is a highly competitive business. The first batch of 20,000 castings supplied by Supercastings is faulty in that the diameter is slightly undersize so that a tight fit in the roller end is not achieved. It takes three weeks to rectify this fault since new moulds are required. Although Rollers plc had a buffer stock of one week's supply, this problem meant that for two weeks no rollers were assembled and some of Roller's customers had to seek alternative suppliers. Supercastings also had two strikes, each of one week's duration and each of which disrupted assemblies. Tom contacted Arena to see if they could help but they had filled the capacity reserved for Roller plc with orders from other sources. Complaints are also being received from customers that the roller-ends provided by Supercastings easily break and allow oil to escape.

Questions

1 What mistakes did Tom and Ray make?
2 What should be done to rectify the situation?

❓ Discussion questions

6.1   (a)   Prepare a flowchart of a traditional, paper-based purchasing system from the receipt of a requisition to the payment of the supplier.

(b)   Estimate the time taken and, the cost of each stage in the above process.

(c)   Prepare a flowchart showing how the same activities would be done under e-procurement.

(d)   Estimate the savings in time and cost by e-procurement.

6.2   Why, in many organisations, is e-procurement limited to MRO items?

6.3   Does your organisation

(a)   currently use e-procurement?

(b)   plan to use e-procurement?

(c)   not plan to use e-procurement?

If the answer is (c), state why.

6.4   A consultancy undertook research into the most significant benefits that a sample of 200 major UK companies derived from e-procurement and those aspects that the companies regarded as 'not at all significant'. Arrange the following into two lists: (a) those that you would consider 'very significant' and (b) those you would consider 'not at all significant'. Give reasons for your rankings.

(i)   Savings from enterprise-wide contracts

(ii)   Improved supplier relationships

(iii)   Increase in purchases under approved contracts

(iv)   Improved management information

(v)   Reduce requisition to payment time

(vi)   Reduced cost per transaction

6.5   A survey (2001) reported that: 'Despite the current growth in the number of e-marketplaces there appears to be uncertainty regarding their use. A number of correspondents do not know when, or if, they will use them'.

Suggest some reasons for this uncertainty.

6.6   There is evidence that purchasers of fine art are reluctant to take place in online auctions provided by companies such as Sothebys. To what factors would you attribute such reluctance?

6.7   You have several items of production plant that are now surplus to requirements. What benefits might be obtained from offering them for sale through a reverse auction?

6.8   Is it possible to use reverse auctions and also build long-time supplier relationships?

6.9   It is suggested the e-procurement will change the culture of purchasing and supply management in an organisation.

(a)   What is meant by the term 'culture'?

(b)   What differences would you expect to find in companies with mechanistic and organic structures?

    (c)   How may the introduction of e-procurement change the cultural outlook of an individual employed in purchasing with regard to (i) working practices; (ii) relationships with suppliers; and (iii) relationships with internal customers?

6.10 Draft rules and guidelines for the information for staff to whom procurement cards have been issued.

6.11 Do we need hard-copy purchasing manuals when intranet facilities are available?

6.12 The following legal terms are not referred to in the text. From your knowledge of the law how many can you define or explain?

(a)	Accord and satisfaction	(m)	Implied conditions
(b)	Anticipatory breach	(n)	Impossibility of performance
(c)	Agent	(o)	Liquidated damages
(d)	Assumpsit	(p)	Misrepresentation
(e)	Caveat emptor	(q)	Mistake
(f)	Condition	(r)	*Quantum meruit*
(g)	Disclosure	(s)	Rescission
(h)	Duress	(t)	Restraint of trade
(i)	Estoppel	(u)	Specific performance
(j)	Express terms	(v)	*Uberrima fides*
(k)	Frustration	(w)	Vicarious performance
(l)	Fundamental breach	(x)	Warranty

Past examination questions

1 Research shows that low value orders create costs out of all proportion to their individual value. Critically examine procedures and techniques which can be implemented in order to minimise such costs and improve purchasing efficiency.

(CIPS, Purchasing, May 1998)

2 Explain the importance of an organisation's having agreed terms and conditions in place when purchasing from suppliers.

(CIPS, Introduction to Purchasing and Supply Chain Management, November 1998)

3 The problem of low value orders and purchasing's time dealing with them needs to be efficiently resolved if the purchasing activity is to develop a higher profile. Explain

(a) the implications of this statement

(b) the methods of dealing with low value orders

(CIPS, Purchasing, May 1999)

4 Discuss the similarities and differences in the procedures used by a buyer of metal components in selecting a supplier, and by a buyer obtaining the services of a caterer.

(CIPS, Introduction to Purchasing and Supply Chain Management, May 1999)

5 For several months on the back of CIPS magazine *Supply Chain Management* there has been an advertisement for a bank that issues Visa purchasing cards. The advertisement shows a paperclip with a price ticket of £50. In the text it states, 'while the humble paperclip itself only costs 1.18p buying it costs a relative fortune'. Explain the reasons for this and how the costs involved in buying low value materials can be reduced.

(CIPS, Introduction to Purchasing and Supply Chain
Management, November 1999)

6 The use of e-commerce is likely to have a major impact on the way in which buyers conduct business in the future with suppliers. Using an example of your choice identify the likely scope and benefits of this relatively new development.

(CIPS, Purchasing, May 2000)

7 How and in what ways could a buyer deal with the problem of low value orders?

(CIPS, Purchasing, May 2000)

8 (a) Explain why low value items have recently been referred to as 'the enemy of lean supply' and suggest ways in which the problems of low value items can be overcome.

(b) Briefly discuss how their changes impact upon the role of purchasing.

(CIPS, Purchasing and Supply Chain Management II:
Tactics and Operations, November 2000)

9 Explain how small value items can be efficiently controlled.

(CIPS, Introduction to Purchasing and Supply Chain
Management, November 2000)

Notes

1. Killen, K.H. and Kamauft J.W., *Managing Purchasing*, National Association of Purchasing Management (USA), 1995, Ch.2, pp.17–18
2. *E-procurement: The Transformation of Corporate Purchasing*, PricewaterhouseCoopers, 2001
3. Cox, A., Chicksand, L., Ireland, P. and Day, M., *The E-Business Report 2001*, Centre for Business Strategy and Procurement, University of Birmingham 2001, p.246
4. CIPS, *Policy Statement on Procurement*
5. Hewlett Packard, 2001
6. The authors are grateful to Paul Farell of the Epicor Software Corporation for permission to reproduce this extract from *A Strategy for Success in the New Global Economy*, October 2001, pp.28–9
7. http://www.mysupplychain.co.uk.B2B/b2b_introduction.htm (accessed 2001)
8. *E-Procurement. Vol. I: Concept Report*, The Butler Group, 2000, p.78
9. Bradley, S., Griffiths, S. and Mahler, D., *Rediscovering the Promise of E-Procurement in Global Purchasing and Supply Chain Strategies*, International Federation of Purchasing and Materials Management (IFPMN), 2001
10. The authors are indebted to the ACTIVE Secretariat, 20 Eastbourne Terrace, London W2 6LE for permission to use this figure taken from the *E-Business Opportunities Study*, 2000, p.20

11. Epicor 2000, *The Strategy*, Glossary, p.91
12. Federal Technology Service, Buyers.gov on http://www.buyers.gov/GuideToBestProducts.pdf (accessed 2001)
13. Lascelles, D., *Managing the Supply Chain*, Business Intelligence Ltd, 2001, Ch.2, p.44
14. Duorak, J., *What's Wrong With Auction*, http://www.zdnet.com products (accessed 5 July 2001)
15. These include *E-Procurement* published by the Butler Group, Aug. 2000; *E-Procurement in the UK* published by Business Intelligence, 2001, and the *E-Business Report* published by Birmingham Business School, 2001
16. Quoted in the *E-Business Opportunities Study* published by the ACTIVE Secretariat (see n.9 above), p.19
17. See n.3 above, Section D, p.313
18. CIPS, as n.4 above
19. Ibid.
20. Pugsley, W., 'EDI implementation – who is in the driving seat?', *Purchasing and Supply Management*, May 1994, pp.22–3

PART TWO

Strategy, tactics and operations (1): purchasing factors

Specifying and managing quality

Learning goals

After reading this chapter you should be able to:

- Provide alternative definitions of quality.
- State the main dimensions of quality.
- Distinguish between quality and reliability.
- Define the term 'total quality management' (TQM) and state the main TQM principles.
- Name the main quality gurus and outline their contributions to quality philosophy.
- Discuss the contributions to quality philosophy of Deming and Taguchi.
- Describe the main steps in the design process.
- Indicate some differences in orientation between purchasing and design professionals.
- Outline the contributions of Wynstra and Calvi to supplier and purchasing involvement in product development.
- Give reasons why purchasing professionals should have a knowledge of specifications.
- Distinguish between specifications and standards.
- Differentiate between types of specification.
- Identify the main contents of a typical specification.
- State some principles of specification preparation.
- Indicate some alternatives to individual specifications.
- Discuss the subject matter, purpose and range of applications of 'standards'.
- Show the advantages of standardisation to purchases.
- Define the terms 'value analysis' and 'value engineering'.
- Describe the implementation and procedures of value analysis.
- Distinguish between quality control and quality assurance.
- Define the term 'quality system'.

- Outline the requirements of BS EN ISO 9000:2000.
- Indicate some sources of independent quality assurance and certification.
- Describe some tools for quality and reliability.
- Explain failure mode and effects analysis (FMEA) and its implementation.
- Define and describe the operation of quality circles.
- Categorise the main cost of quality.
- Indicate how effective purchasing can contribute to quality.

7.1 What is quality?

7.1.1 Definitions

There are numerous definitions of quality. ISO 8402 defines quality as:

> **The totality of features and characteristics of a product that bears on the ability to satisfy stated or implied needs.**

In this definition, 'features and characteristic of product' implies the ability to identify what quality aspects can be measured, or controlled, or constitute an acceptable quality level (AQL), and 'ability to satisfy given needs' relates to the value of the product or service to the customer including economic value as well as safety, reliability, maintainability and other relevant features.

Crosby[1] defines quality as 'conformity to requirements not goodness'. He also stresses that the definition of quality can never make any sense unless it is based on what the customer wants, i.e. a product is a quality product only when it conforms to the customer's requirements.

Juran[2] defines quality as 'fitness for use'. This definition implies quality of design, quality of conformance, availability and adequate field service. There is, however, no universal definition of quality. Garvin, for example, has identified five approaches to defining quality[3] and eight dimensions of quality.[4] The five approaches are:

1 *The transcendent approach* – quality is absolute and universally recognisable. This concept is loosely related to a comparison of product attributes and characteristics.
2 *The product-based approach* – quality is a precise and measurable variable. In this approach differences in quality reflect differences in the quantity of some product characteristics.
3 *The use-based approach* – quality is defined in terms of fitness for use, or how well the product fulfils its intended functions.
4 *The manufacturing-based approach* – quality is 'conformance to specifications', i.e. targets and tolerances determined by product designers.

5   *The value-based approach* – quality is defined in terms of cost and prices. Here, a quality product is one that provides performance at an acceptable price or conformance at an acceptable cost.

These alternative definitions of quality often overlap and may conflict. Perspectives of quality may also change as a product moves from the design to the marketing stage. For these reasons it is essential to consider each of the above perspectives when framing an overall quality philosophy.

Garvin's eight dimensions of quality are:

1   *Performance* – the product's operating characteristics.

2   *Reliability* – the probability of a product surviving over a specified period of time under stated conditions of use.

3   *Serviceability* – the speed, accessibility and ease of repairing the item or having it repaired.

4   *Conformance* – the degree to which delivered products meet the predetermined standards.

5   *Durability* – measures the projected use available from the product over its intended operating cycle before it deteriorates.

6   *Features* – 'the bells and whistles' or secondary characteristics which supplement the product's basic functioning.

7   *Aesthetics* – personal judgements of how a product looks, feels, sounds, tastes or smells.

8   *Perceived quality* – closely identified with the reputation of the producer. Like aesthetics, it is a personal evaluation.

While the relative importance attached to any of the above characteristics will depend on the particular item, the most important factors in commercial or industrial purchasing decisions will probably be performance, reliability, conformance, availability and serviceability.

Other factors that determine 'the right quality' for a particular application include:

■   *Price*, since the competitive selling price of the product in which the item is to be incorporated will determine the prices paid for bought-out items.

■   *Customer specifications* or those laid down by statutory or similar organisations.

■   *Durability* also influences quality specifications for components, e.g. if the expected life of the final product is only three years there is little point in incorporating a component with a life of five years where cheaper alternatives are available. The reputation of the product must, however, be of paramount consideration.

Quality is therefore determined by balancing technical considerations such as fitness for use, performance, safety and reliability against economic factors including price and availability. It is therefore the *optimum quality* for the application that should be sought rather than the highest quality.

As the British Standards Institution (BSI) has stated, in drafting quality specifications, the aim should 'always be the minimum statement of optimum (not the highest) quality in order not to increase cost unnecessarily, not to restrict processes of manufacture, not to limit the use of possible alternatives'.

7.1.2 Reliability

As shown above, reliability is an attribute of quality. It is, however, so important that the terms 'quality' and 'reliability' are often used together. Reliability has been defined as:[5]

> **A measure of the ability of a product to function successfully when required, for the period required, under specified conditions.**

Reliability is usually expressed in terms of mathematical probability ranging from 0 (complete unreliability) to 100 per cent (or complete reliability). Failure mode and effect analysis (FMEA) is performed to evaluate the effect upon the overall design of a failure in any one of the identifiable failure modes of the design components and to evaluate how critically the failure will affect performance is referred to below.

7.2 The importance of TQM

7.2.1 Definitions

Total quality management (TQM) has been defined as:[6]

> **A way of managing an organisation so that every job, every process, is carried out right, first time and every time.**

This means that each stage of manufacture or service is 100 per cent correct before it proceeds. An alternative definition is:[7]

> **An integrative management concept of continually improving the quality of delivered goods and services through the participation of all levels and functions of the organisation.**

7.2.2 TQM principles

TQM is based on three important tenets:

1 *A focus on product improvement from the customer's viewpoint.* The key words in this principle are 'product improvement' and 'customer product improvement'. Juran emphasised the importance of achieving annual improvements in quality and reductions in quality-related costs. Any improvement that

takes an organisation to levels of quality performance previously unachieved is termed a 'breakthrough'. Breakthroughs are focused on improving or eliminating chronic losses or, in Deming's terminology, 'common causes of variation'. All breakthroughs follow a common sequence of discovery, organisation, diagnosis, corrective action and control.

The term 'customer' in this context is associated with the concept of quality chains which emphasise the linkages of suppliers and customers. Quality chains are both internal and external, thus internally, purchasing is the customer of design and the supplier of production. Staff within a function or activity are also suppliers and customers. Like all chains, the quality chain is no stronger that the weakest link. Without strong supplier–customer links both internally and externally, TQM is doomed to failure. Quality chains are one way of avoiding the functional conflict and power tactics referred to in Chapter 5. The first step in implementing an internal quality chain approach is for each activity to determine answers to the following questions relating to customers and suppliers:[8]

Customers

- Who are my internal customers?

- What are their true requirements?

- How do, or can, I find out what the requirements are?

- How can I measure my ability to meet the requirements?

- Do I have the necessary capability to meet the requirements? (If not then what must change to improve the capability?)

- Do I continually meet the requirements? (If not then what prevents this from happening when the capability exist?)

- How do I monitor changes in the requirements?

Suppliers

- Who are my internal suppliers?

- What are my true requirements?

- How do I communicate my requirements?

- Do my suppliers have the capability to measure and meet the requirements?

- How do I inform them of changes in the requirements?

The second step, based on answers to questions such as the above, is to determine the level of service which a function, e.g. purchasing, will provide. Cannon[9] has identified four factors affecting decisions about service types and levels: (i) what the customer wants; (ii) what the function can provide; (iii) close collaboration to solve disagreements; (iv) redefining both type and level of service at regular intervals. It is also important to determine the technical expertise of purchasing, 'since it is this expertise which enables the function to add value to the procurement activity beyond that which the internal customer can perform without the function's assistance'.

The questions posed earlier in this section can also be reframed by substituting the word 'external' for 'internal' so that external quality chains can be considered from both supply and customer angles. In the capacity of customers, purchasing organisations expect suppliers to compete in terms of quality, delivery and price. Zaire[10] states that the best approach to managing suppliers is based on JIT which from its inception has the objective of obtaining and sustaining superior performance. The other important aspect of external customer supplier value chains refers to the management of customer processes since the purpose of TQM is customer enlightenment and long-term partnerships.

2 *A recognition that personnel at all levels share responsibility for product quality.* The Japanese concept of *Kaizen,* or ongoing improvement, affects everyone in an organisation at all levels. It is therefore based on team rather than individual performance. Thus, while top management provides leadership, continuous improvement is also understood and implemented at shopfloor level. Some consequences of this principle include:

(a) provision of leadership from the top;

(b) creation of a 'quality culture' dedicated to continuous improvement;

(c) teamwork, i.e. quality improvement teams and quality cycles;

(d) adequate resource allocation;

(e) quality training of employees;

(f) measurement and use of statistical concepts;

(g) quality feedback;

(h) employee recognition.

Zaire[11] states: 'Once a culture of common beliefs, principles, objectives and concerns has been established, people will manage their own tasks and will take voluntary responsibility to improve processes they own'.

3 *Recognition of the importance of implementing a system to provide information to managers about quality processes which enable them to plan, control and evaluate performance.*

Most of this chapter is concerned with various aspects of quality implementation.

7.2.3 Factors that have contributed to the development of TQM

■ *Global competition* for sales, profits, jobs and funds in both the private and public sectors leading to the concept of world class manufacturing with the emphasis of using manufacturing to gain a competitive edge through improving customer service.

■ *Just-in-time* (JIT) and similar strategies based on the philosophy of zero defects, i.e. that it is cheaper to design and build quality into a product than to attempt to ensure quality through inspection alone.

■ *Japanese quality procedures* such as *Kaizen* (unending improvement) and *Poka-Yoke* (foolproofing) and a quality culture implemented in European manufacturing units, e.g. Toyota and Nissan.

■ *Quality philosophies* associated with internationally respected experts.

Table 7.1 Four quality gurus

Name	Principal book	Important principles
Philip B. CROSBY	*Quality is Free* (McGraw-Hill, 1983)	■ Five absolutes of quality management: (1) 'Quality means conformity to requirements – not elegance'; (2) 'There is no such thing as a quality problem although there may be an engineering machine problem'; (3) 'It is always cheaper to do the job right first time'; (4) 'The only performance indicator is the cost of quality'; (5) 'The only performance standard is zero defects' ■ The 14-step quality improvement programme
Armand V. FEIGENBAUM	*Total Quality Control* (McGraw-Hill, 1983)	■ 'The underlying principle of the total quality view . . . is that . . . control must start with identification of customer quality requirements and end only when the product has been placed in the hands of a customer who remains satisfied. Total Quality Control guides the coordinated actions of people, machines and information to achieve this goal. The first principle is to recognise that quality is everybody's job'
Kaoru ISHIKAWA	*What is Total Quality Control The Japanese Way* (Prentice Hall, 1985)	■ The first to introduce the concept of quality control circles ■ Originator of Fishbone or Ishikawa diagrams now used worldwide in continuous improvement to represent cause–effect analysis ■ Argues that 90–95 per cent of quality problems can be solved by simple statistical techniques not requiring specialist knowledge
Joseph M. JURAN	*Quality Control Handbook 1988* (McGraw-Hill, 1988)	■ Quality is 'fitness for use' which can be broken down into quality of design, quality of conformance, availability and field service ■ Companies must reduce the cost of quality ■ Quality should be aimed at controlling (1) sporadic problems or avoidable costs; (2) unavoidable cost. The latter requires the introduction of a new culture intended to change attitudes and increase companywide knowledge

7.3 The quality gurus

7.3.1 Some quality gurus

A guru is a guide, mentor or knowledge resource for others. A brief outline of four such gurus – Crosby, Feigenbaum, Ishikawa and Juran – is given in Table 7.1. Two others, Deming and Taguchi, are considered in greater detail.

7.3.2 Deming

Dr W. Edwards Deming (1900–93) was known as 'the father of the Japanese post-war industrial revival' and considered by many to be the leading US quality guru. He believed that '85 per cent of industrial problems are caused by management and only management can fix them'. His '14 points for management' as set out in *Out of Crisis*[12] were revised in 1990.

The following three 'principles' are especially relevant to purchasing:

(3)   Cease dependence on inspection to achieve quality. Eliminate the need for inspection on a mass basis by building quality into the product in the first place.

(4)   End the practice of awarding business on the basis of price tag. Instead, minimise the total cost. Move towards a single supplier for any one item, on a long term relationship of loyalty and trust.

. . .

(9)   Break down barriers between departments. People in research, design, sales and production must work as a team, to foresee problems of production and in use that may be encountered with the product or service.

7.3.3   Taguchi

Dr Genichi Taguchi (b. 1924), a Japanese statistician, became the director of the Japanese Academy of Quality and an advisor to the Japanese Standards Association. In 1982, Taguchi was invited to provide seminars to executives of the Ford Motor Company and the following year became executive director of the Ford Supplier Institute, later renamed the American Supplier Institute.

Taguchi defines quality as the avoidance of the '*loss a product causes to society after being shipped*'. This includes loss due to failure to meet customer expectations, failure to meet performance requirements and harmful side-effects caused by the product such as noise and pollution which may lead to social costs such as medical claims. By relating loss expressed in money terms to quantifiable product characteristics, Taguchi makes the transition from engineering to management perspectives.

Taguchi's methods are applicable to all aspects of product, service and process quality and relate to both on-line and off-line quality control. *On-line control* concentrates on the manufacturing process. Taguchi, however, states that no amount of on-line inspection can improve a product, quality must be designed into a product off-line. In other words the bugs should be removed *before* not after manufacture. Taguchi's approach is therefore that quality loss must be measured on a life cycle basis (loss to society) not just as the internal costs of non-conformance or defect detection at the time of shipment. Two important Taguchi concepts are the continuous loss function and robust design.

Continuous loss function

Loss function derives from the concept that deviation from a specific target value increases the loss to society through scrap and warranty costs including other waste factors. The aim should therefore be to make products that minimise waste thus reducing the loss, expressed in money terms to society. As shown in Figure 7.1, losses accompanied by reduced consumer dissatisfaction increase (as a quadratic, U-shaped function) with deviations from a target specification. Loss or cost is at a minimum and consumer satisfaction at a maximum when the product or service is at the target value.

Figure 7.1 shows the warranty costs of two firms, A and B. Significantly lower warranty costs are incurred by A whose tolerances deviate less from the target or nominal specification than B who has wider variations from the target. The

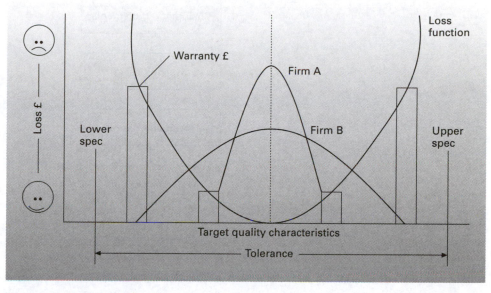

Figure 7.1   Taguchi loss function

Source: adapted from Devor, R.E., Chang, T.S. and Sutherland, J.W., *Statistical Quality Design and Control*, Macmillan, 1992, p.50

farther away from the target the higher the loss incurred through warranty repairs. The Taguchi loss function can be calculated by the formula

$$L(x) = R(x - T)^2$$

where x is any value of the quality characteristic, T is the target value and R is some constant.

Example 7.1   Taguchi loss function

Assume a product with tolerances of 0.500 ± 0.20. Further assume that if the deviation from the target exceeds 0.20 on either side that product will fail during the warranty period. From records, the cost of repairing the product under warranty will be £50. Then:

$$50 = R(0.20)^2$$

$$R = \frac{50}{0.0004} = 125,000$$

Therefore the loss function is:

$$L(x) = 125,000(x - T)^2$$

Thus if the deviation is only 0.10 the estimated loss will be:

$$L(0.010) = 125,000(0.010)^2$$
$$= 125,000(0.0001)$$
$$= £12.50$$

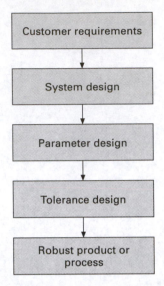

Figure 7.2   Taguchi's approach to product design

The Taguchi loss function can be applied to any non-conformance cost such as complaint handling, inspection and testing, rework of defective parts, scrap and warranty repairs. All such costs arise from not doing the work right first time. By improving quality such costs can be reduced. Thus the cost of quality is a misnomer since quality can actually produce a profit.

Robust design

Taguchi's approach to product design is shown in Figure 7.2.

- *Customer requirements* are what the customer assumes will be received from the product.
- *Systems design* is the phase at which overall conceptual design takes place and requires an understanding of both customer needs and the environment in which the product will operate. In the design of a product it is necessary to consider functional, technological and economic factors.
- *Functional factors* include size, weight, appearance, safety, serviceability and maintenance considerations.
- *Technological factors* include the selection of the materials and production methods.
- *Economic factors* relate to the specific consumer market for which a product is intended. Thus in designing a product for a mass consumer market, costs of material and production must be kept low so that the price charged may be correspondingly low.
- *Parameter design* involves determining the target specification settings or limits for the product or process and reducing variability due to manufacturing and environmental factors. As shown in Figure 7.3, Taguchi distinguishes between controllable and non-controllable factors or 'noise'.

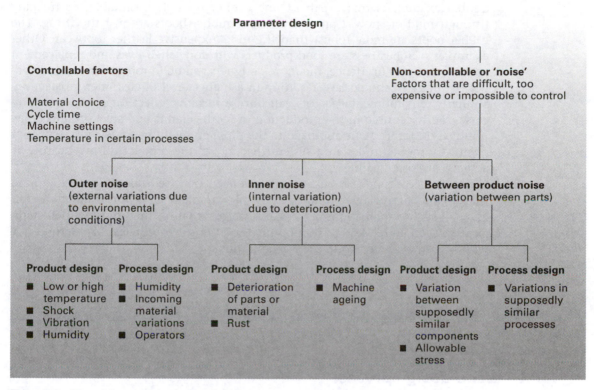

Figure 7.3   Taguchi's concept of controllable and non-controllable factors

Noise factors are primarily responsible for causing performance of a product to deviate from its target value. Hence by analytical methods or carefully planned experiments, parameter design seeks to identify settings of the control factors which make the product more robust, i.e. less sensitive to variations in the noise factors. Taguchi states that many designers consider only system and tolerance factors. He maintains, however, that without parameter design it is almost impossible to produce a high quality product.

Tolerance design is concerned with how much variation of the design and noise factors is permissible. Engineers tend to associate quality with narrow tolerances. Narrow tolerances enhance interchangeability, product performance and product life but increase costs. Conversely, wide tolerances increase material utilisation and machine and labour productivity and reduce costs while having a negative effect on interchangeability, product performance and life. Taguchi's parameter design approach allows for improving the quality without requiring better parts or materials and aims to improve quality while maintaining or reducing cost.

Robust products and processes

A robust product is the outcome of robust design which is the purpose of the parameter design stage. Some products are designed to perform only within a narrow range of conditions whereas others have greater applicability. A frequently quoted example is that a pair of fine leather boots is unsuitable for trekking through mud or snow. Conversely, heavy rubber boots are just the thing. The rubber boots are more robust than the more expensive leather footwear. Other examples of robustness are food products with long shelf-lives and replacement parts that always fit. Hence, the more designers can build robustness into a product the better it should last, resulting in a higher level of customer satisfaction. Similarly, environmental factors can have a negative effect on production processes. Furnaces used in the production of food, ceramic and steel products may not heat uniformly. One approach to the problem might be to develop a superior oven. Another is to design a system that moves the product during heating to achieve uniform heating.

Taguchi's concept of robust design has been criticised mainly on the ground that because of the large number of possible parameters it is impossible to investigate all such combinations. Critics also suggest that his methods are inefficient, expensive and often lead to non-optimal solutions. Nevertheless his methods are widely used by many world class organisations.

7.4 Further aspects of product and process design and redesign

7.4.1 The design process

As Taguchi emphasised, the ultimate performance, value, reliability and saleability of a product are determined at the design stage. As shown by Figures 7.2 and 7.4, the process of design or redesign involved several sub-stages.

The actual design will be prepared by a specialised function responsible for ensuring that all relevant design input requirements are correctly translated into specifications, drawings, procedures and written instructions. This function is also responsible for ensuring that designs comply with legal requirements relating to such issues as safety and the environment together with all matters relating to patents.

7.4.2 Collaboration in design

Product design is a team enterprise in which the marketing, management accounting, production and purchasing functions together with suppliers are all involved in such ways as the following.

Marketing

The marketing function will ask such questions as: What are the characteristics that customers are looking for in the product, e.g. appearance, ease of operation and installation, reliability and durability, exclusiveness, etc.? What features are required to ensure that the product provides and advantage over those of competitors? What is the present and anticipated market penetration? How and through what channels will the product be marketed? Marketing will also be involved in piloting.

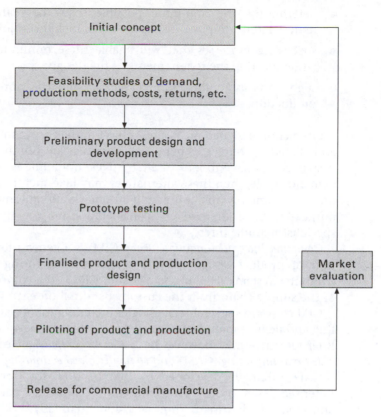

Figure 7.4 The design process

Management accounting

Traditionally, western manufacturers have determined costs and set a selling price based on the costs involved. In contrast, Japan introduced the concept of *target costing*. Target costing uses market research to estimate what the market will pay for a product with specific characteristics.

Subtracting an acceptable profit margin from the estimated selling price leaves an implied maximum per unit product target cost which is compared with an estimated product cost. If the estimated cost is higher than the target cost the manufacturer involves all members of the planning team (design, engineering, production, purchasing, suppliers, marketing and management accounting) in value analysis, value engineering and production design exercises to determine how costs can be reduced to meet the desired target. If such reduction cannot be achieved, either a lower profit may be accepted or the manufacturer may decide not to enter the market.

Production

Production designers are initially responsible for determining production methods and minimum product cost. They are concerned with:

- determining the minimum possible costs that can be obtained through material and component specifications, tolerances, joining of parts, etc.;
- specifying processes that will enable these minimum costs to be achieved while meeting the requirements of the design;
- such costs as tooling, indirect labour and the non-manufacturing cost of production.

Production designers are always subject to the constraints of available machinery and skilled operatives. Where such resources are not available then production designers will have to look at alternatives. If volume is large and the design and demand stable, then these alternatives may take such forms as buying in special-process technology including semi-automatic and automatic processes or special-purpose layouts. Alternatively, consideration may be given to subcontracting to specialist manufacturers.

Computer integrated manufacturing (CIM) is a general term for the total integration of product design, planning and manufacturing by means of complex computer systems. The ultimate goal of CIM is the computerisation of all phases of the supply chain from the customer's initial order to its ultimate delivery.

CIM comprises several technologies including robots, automated material handling and flexible manufacturing systems which are beyond the scope of this book. Brief reference may however be made to *computer aided design* (CAD), *computer aided manufacturing* (CAM) and *computer aided estimating* (CAE).

CAD, originally developed by IBM in 1960 for General Motors, is a computerised design process for creating new products or parts, altering existing ones and replacing drafting traditionally done manually. With CAD the designer uses a powerful desktop computer and computes graphics to manipulate geometric shapes. The programs provide:

- a three-dimensional projection of any part on the screen;
- calculations of area, volume, weight and stress;
- a databank of existing product or part designs as what is required may only be a variation on what is already available;
- simulation of strength and stress tests without the need for a prototype;
- analysis of manufacturing considerations relating to the production of an item;
- several alternative design solutions for consideration by the designer;
- the translation of the approved design into two-dimensional drawings for use in manufacturing;
- bills of materials (BOM) parts lists or bills of quantities (for architectural work).

CAM utilises computers to design production processes and materials flow. CAM is therefore linked to CAD by the production of manufacturing instructions that will produce the finalised design. The integration of the two systems is known as a CAD/CAM system. Such a system is the first step towards a paperless factory.

CAE refers to computerised systems for the estimation of costs, including those relating to design, manufacture and distribution. CAE programs enable an estimator to draw on a databank of cost elements, perform calculations and produce a product selling price for customer quotation purposes.

CAD, CAM and CAE have numerous advantages, including:

- greatly reduced time in the production of designs, estimates and products with consequent improved utilisation of the services of skilled designers, estimators and production personnel;
- through electronic data interchange (EDI) designers and estimators can communicate directly with customers' CAD/CAM systems thereby facilitating collaboration in design and production;
- rapid response to the request of potential customers for quotations;
- efficient updating of parts and products with the elimination of inconsistencies between specification and drawings and finished products;
- the timeframe from product conception to production can be substantially reduced;
- simplified control.

7.4.3 Purchasing and design

Some contributions of purchasing to design have already been mentioned in section 5.11 of chapter 5. Dowlatshahi[13] has drawn attention to the differences in orientation that may arise between purchasing and design:

Purchasing orientation	*Design orientation*
■ Minimum acceptable margin of quality, safety and performance	■ Wide margins of quality, safety and performance
■ Use of adequate materials	■ Use of ideal materials
■ Lowest ultimate cost	■ Limited concern for cost
■ High regard for availability	■ Limited regard for availability
■ Practical and economical parameters, specification, features and tolerances	■ Close or near perfect parameters, specifications, features and tolerances
■ General view of product	■ Conceptual abstraction of product quality
■ Cost elimination of materials	■ Selection of materials
■ Concern for JIT delivery and supplier relationship	■ Concern for overall product design

Dowlatshahi states that the reconciliation of these differing views is possible only in a concurrent engineering environment which he defines as:

The consideration and inclusion of product design attributes such as manufacturability, procurability, reliability, maintainability, schedularability, marketability and the like in the early stages of product design.

7.5 Supplier and purchasing involvement in development

Early supplier involvement (ESI) and *early buyer involvement* (EBI) in product innovation and development are closely related. ESI recognises that supplier involvement can be beneficial in terms of costs, quality and innovation. Purchasing as part of a cross-functional design team can play an important role in supplier selection and supplier management.

7.5.1 The increasing involvement of purchasing in product development

The increasing involvement of purchasing in product development is attributed by Wynstra *et al.*[14] to two main factors:

- Increasing awareness of the purchasing function's possible contribution to the strategic position of an organisation.
- The growing importance of innovation and product development in creating competitive advantage. In this context writers such as Womack *et al.*[15] and Lamming[16] have pointed out that by relying on the specialised skills, competence and knowledge of suppliers Japanese car manufacturers had been able to turn out new cars at a faster pace, with more innovative features and less effort in terms of development hours or the number of engineers involved.

7.5.2 Areas of purchasing involvement

Wynstra *et al.*[17] also identify four areas of purchasing involvement in product development, each of which has a different time horizon and each involving different activities. These four areas and the activities associated with them are set out in Table 7.2.

Wynstra *et al.*[18] also points out that 'activities relating to purchasing involvement in product development appear to be performed at different organisational levels as shown in Figure 7.5.

7.5.3 Development responsibility and risk

Wynstra and ten Pierick[19] identified two important variables relating to the management of supplier involvement: (i) the degree of responsibility for product development contracted out to the supplier and (ii) development risk.

Development responsibility

This is the level of responsibility delegated to the supplier in the development of a building block or component. Calvi *et al.*[20] states that this responsibility or 'supplier autonomy' is a function of the supplier's know-how and of the importance of intellectual property rights owned.

The degree of supplier responsibility to be contracted out is determined by the manufacturer after deciding such questions as the following:

Table 7.2 Areas of purchasing involvement in product development

Area of involvement	Associated activities
1. Development management The higher the level of availability and stability and the lower the level of dependence, the greater possibilities to 'buy' the technology and leave the development to suppliers	Determining which technologies to keep/develop in-house and which to outsource Policy formulation for supplier involvement Policy formulation for purchasing-related activities of internal departments Internal and external communication of policies
2. Suppler interface management Proactive, continuous research with the aim of identifying suppliers or technologies that may be relevant for the development of new products	Monitoring supplier markets for technological developments Pre-selecting suppliers for product development collaboration Motivating suppliers to build up/maintain specific knowledge or develop certain products Exploiting the technological capabilities of suppliers Evaluating suppliers' development performance
3. Project management Involves two sub-areas: project planning and project execution	Project planning activities are primarily carried out during or before initial development and include: ■ Determining specific develop-or-buy solutions ■ Selecting suppliers for involvement in the development project ■ Determining the extent of supplier involvement Project execution involves activities during the project and include: ■ Coordinating development activities between suppliers and manufacturer ■ Coordinating development activities between different first-tier suppliers ■ Coordinating development activities between first- and second-tier suppliers ■ Ordering and chasing prototypes
4. Product management Directly contributing to the specifications of the new product	Activities can be divided into two categories: ■ Extending activities – those aimed at increasing the number of alternatives including: – providing information on new products and technologies already available or in course of development – suggesting alternative suppliers, products and technologies that can yield higher quality ■ Restrictive activities – those aimed at limiting the number of alternative specifications: – evaluating product designs in terms of part availability, manufacturability, lead time, quality and costs – promoting standardisation and simplification

Source: derived from Wynstra, F., van Weele, A. and Axelsson, B., 'Purchasing involvement in product development', *European Journal of Purchasing*, Vol.5 (1999), pp.129–41

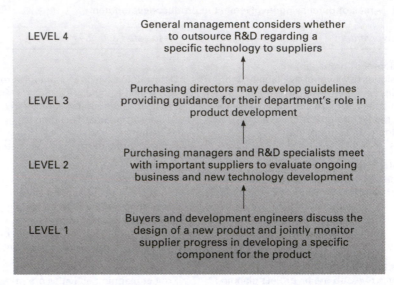

Figure 7.5 Organisational levels which purchasing may be involved in product development

- Considering the organisation's core technological competences, into how much detail should it go in developing specifications?
- Are there suppliers whose relevant product or production knowledge in relation to the component is greater than that of the manufacturer?
- Are there suppliers that can do the development work more efficiently than the manufacturer?
- To what extent does the manufacturer need development capacity (person-hours) of suppliers to meet the project targets?

Calvi *et al.* point out that deciding the level of responsibility to assign is a strategic decision because it involves a consideration of the manufacturer's competences. It also involves a make-or-buy decision by a cross-functional team.

Development risk

Calvi *et al.*[21] identify six categories of risk that can be ascertained by asking the following questions:

- What is the link between the building block or component and the performance of the final product?
- What is the level of newness and differentiation brought by the building block or component?
- What is the position of the building block on the critical path, i.e. what is the reliability of the supplier's resources, e.g. capacity, workforce, in meeting delivery schedules?
- What is the newness of the production technologies involved?

	Low	High
High	Arm's length development	Strategic development
Low	Routine development	Critical development

Figure 7.6   The supplier involvement portfolio of Wynstra

- What is the weighted cost of the building block or component in relation to the cost of the final product?
- What is the internal complexity, i.e. how many different technologies are used in the building block/component? A number of different technologies may produce difficulties in coordination among different suppliers.

The higher the development risk the sooner collaboration between the manufacturer and supplier should start and the greater the importance of shared information and regular and rapid communication between manufacturer and supplier.

7.5.4 The supplier involvement portfolio

On the basis of the above two variables both Wynstra and colleagues and Calvi *et al.* develop supplier involvement portfolios which distinguish, respectively, between four and five types of supplier involvement as set out in Table 7.3.

The two variables can be shown on a matrix as in Figure 7.6. For simplicity, only the Wynstra model is shown.

The normal approach to 'filling' the portfolio is:

1 (a) Decide the degree of supplier responsibility for the development.

    (b) Decide the degree of development risk.

2 Position the supplier-component in the portfolio.

3 Reflect on the distribution of the various supplier/component combinations across the portfolio and reposition if necessary.

7.6 Specifications

7.6.1 Specifications and purchasing

Lysons[22] has suggested the following reasons why purchasing staff should be knowledgeable about specifications:

- The primary purpose of purchasing is to contribute to the profitability of an undertaking by obtaining the best quality products or services in terms of fitness for use at the least possible total cost.

Table 7.3 Wynstra and Calvi approaches to supplier involvement

| Terminology | | Purchaser–supplier collaboration | | Development risk and supplier responsibility | | Functional disciplines | Content of communication |
Wynstra	Calvi	Wynstra	Calvi	Risk	Supplier responsibility		
Strategic development	Strategic co-development	Close cooperation in design of requirements as 'sparring partners' or 'joint developers'	'CO' indicates close cooperation to clarify needs and their evolution in supplier development	High	High	Diverse	Technical/commercial
Critical development	Critical co-development		Deep collaboration since there is uncertainty by both parties regarding what is required and who should make it	High	Shared	Diverse	Technical/commercial
	Coordinates development of technical specifications	Design of manufacturer's requirements on basis of manufacturer's specifications by suppliers	Manufacturer notifies supplier of design changes to meet evolving specifications	High	Low	Purchasing/sales and development	Market and technical
Arm's-length development	Global development based on functional specifications	Independent development of manufacturer's specifications by supplier	Product designed by supplier on basis of manufacturer's performance specifications	Low	High	Development and purchasing/sales	Technical and status
Routine development	Classic subcontracting based on technical specifications	Manufacturers/suppliers inform each other about specification changes	Manufacturer prepares specification and asks supplier to suggest improvements	Low	Low	Purchasing/sales	Status

- Purchasing staff are the intermediaries between the user and the supplier. They are therefore responsible for checking the completeness of product or service specifications. When negotiating with suppliers purchasing staff must know what they are negotiating about.

- The satisfaction of user requirements depends on obtaining reliable suppliers.

- Purchasing staff should be expert in the application of value analysis and the provision at the design or specification stage of innovative suggestions aimed at achieving cost reduction without detriment to the required performance, reliability, quality and maintainability.

- Purchasing staff should be able to advise on whether any of the requirements stated in the specification are liable to cause commercial, environmental or legal problems.

7.6.2 Definitions

Specifications must be distinguished from standards and codes of practice. A *specification* has been defined in the following ways:

> A statement of the attributes of a product or service.[23]

> A statement of requirements.[24]

> A statement of needs to be satisfied by the procurement of external resources.[25]

A standard is a *'specification intended for recurrent use'*. Standards differ from specifications in that whereas every standard is a specification not every specification is a standard. The guiding principle of standardisation considered later in this chapter is the elimination of unnecessary variety.

Codes of practice are less specific than formal standards and provide guidance on the best accepted practice in relation to engineering and construction and for operations such as installations, maintenance and service provision.

7.6.3 The purpose of specifications

Both specifications and standards aim to:

- *indicate fitness for purpose or use* – as indicated in Table 7.1 'fitness for purpose or use' was the definition of quality given by Juran. Juran stated that quality is linked to product satisfaction and dissatisfaction: satisfaction relates to superior performance or features; dissatisfaction to deficiencies or defects in a product or service;

- *communicate* the requirements of a user or purchaser to the supplier;

- *compare* what is actually supplied with the requirements of purpose, quality and performance stated in the specification;

- *provide evidence* in the event of dispute of what the purchaser required and what the supplier agreed to provide.

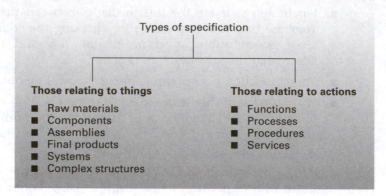

Figure 7.7 Types of specification

7.6.4 Types of specification

As shown in Figure 7.7, specifications can broadly be divided into two types: those relating to things and those relating to actions.

Several of the above elements may be combined in one specification. Thus, a specification for a component (a thing) may also state how it shall be made (a process) and how it shall be tested (a procedure). The specification may also state what the component is intended to do (function) and what a product or service should achieve under given conditions (performance).

7.6.5 Request for quotation (RFQ)

Requests for quotation are specifications on the basis of which a potential purchaser communicates his or her requirements to a potential supplier so that the latter has sufficient information to prepare a quotation or tender.

7.6.6 Contents of a specification

The contents of a specification will vary according to whether the specification is written from the standpoint of the user, designer, manufacturer or seller. The specification will also vary according to the material or item concerned. For a simple item the specification may be a brief description, whereas in the case of a complex assembly it will be a comprehensive document, perhaps running to many pages. The following order of presentation for a specification relating to a product, process or service is adapted from BS 7373 (now BS 7373,2:2001):

1 Identification – title, designation, number, authority.
2 Issue number – publication history and state of issue, earlier related specifications.
3 Contents list – guide to layout.
4 Foreword – the reason for writing the specification.
5 Introduction – describes content in general and technical aspects of objectives.
6 Scope – range of objectives/content.

7   Definitions – terms used with meanings special to the text.

8   Requirements/guidance/methods/elements – the main body of the specification.

9   Index – cross-references.

10 References – to national, European and international standards or other internal company specifications.

The requirements specified may relate to the following:

- Conditions in which the item or material is to be installed, used, manufactured or stored.
- Characteristics – these may be shown by:
  - design, samples, drawings, models, preliminary tests or investigations;
  - properties, e.g. strength, dimensions, weight, safety, etc. with tolerances where applicable;
  - interchangeability (functional, dimensional);
  - materials and their properties (including permissible variability), approved or excluded materials;
  - requirements for a manufacturing process, e.g. heat treatment (this should be specified only when critical to design considerations);
  - appearance, texture, finish, including colour, protection, etc.;
  - identification marks, operating symbols on controls, weight of items, safety indications, etc.;
  - method of marking.
- Performance:
  - performance under specified conditions;
  - test methods and equipment for assessing performance; where, how and by whom carried out; reference to correlation with behaviour in operation;
  - criteria for passing tests, including accuracy and interpretations of results;
  - acceptance conditions;
  - certification and/or reporting, i.e. reports, test schedules or certificates required.
- Life.
- Reliability, i.e. under stipulated conditions and tests and control procedures required.
- Control of quality checking for compliance with specification:
  - method of checking compliance;
  - production tests on raw materials, components, sub-assemblies, and assemblies;
  - assurance of compliance, e.g. by suppliers' certificates or independent manufacturer/supplier;
  - instructions regarding reject material or items;

- instructions with regard to modification of process;
- applicability of quality control to subcontractors, etc.
■ Packing and protection:
  - specifications of packaging, including any special conditions in transit;
  - condition in which the item is to be supplied, e.g. protected, lubricant free, etc.;
  - period of storage;
  - marking of packaging.
■ Information from the supplier to the user, e.g. instructions and advice on installation, operation and maintenance.

7.6.7 Some principles of specification writing

Purdy[26] has identified four principles that should be observed by all specification writers. These and other principles are as follows:

■ *If something is not specified it is unlikely to be provided*. The corollary is that all requirements should be stated in the specification before awarding the purchase order. Suppliers will normally charge as 'extras' requirements added subsequently.

■ *Every requirement increases the price*. All specifications should therefore be submitted to rigorous value analysis. Value analysis is considered later in this chapter.

■ *The shorter the specification the less time it takes to prepare it*. The expenditure in staff time devoted to the preparation of a specification can be high. This expenditure can be significantly lower when the length of a specification is reduced.

■ *The specification is equally binding on both the purchaser and the vendor*. Omissions, incorrect information or imprecision in a specification can be cited by the vendor on any dispute with the purchaser. A rule of evidence is that words are construed against the party who wrote them. Where there is uncertainty about the meaning of a specification the court will generally interpret them in the vendor's favour.

■ *Specifications, should, so far as possible, be presented in performance terms rather than as a detailed design*. This is particularly applicable to items about which the purchaser has little expert knowledge. By section 14(3) of the Sale of Goods Act 1979 (SGA) as amended by the Supply and Sale of Goods Act 1994 (SSGA), where the seller sells goods in the course of a business and the buyer, expressly or by implication, makes known to the seller any particular purpose for which the goods are being bought there is an implied 'term' that the goods supplied under the contract are of satisfactory quality. For the purpose of the SSGA, goods are of satisfactory quality if 'they meet the standard that a reasonable person would regard as satisfactory, taking account of any description of the goods, the price (if relevant) and all other relevant circumstances'.

■ *Specifications, should, whenever possible be 'open' and not closed*. Open specifications are written so that the stated requirements can be met by more than one supplier. By making the requirements sufficiently flexible to be met by several suppliers, competition is encouraged and prices reduced.

■ *Specifications must not conflict with national or international standards or health, safety or environmental laws and regulations.* National and international specifications should be incorporated into individual specifications and identified by their numbers and titles.

7.7   Alternatives to individual specifications

7.7.1   Existing specifications

It should only be necessary to write a specification in respect of non-standard requirements. For most standard industrial and consumer products it is usually sufficient to use:

■ manufacturers' standards as stated in catalogues or other promotional literature;
■ national or international standards.

All products or services, will, however, require materials, components or other elements for which existing standards will be available. An essential first step for designers or specification writers is to ascertain what relevant standards exist. Searching for such standards is facilitated by consulting reference publications, especially the British Standards Catalogue (available in most large libraries), or by the use of databases. Especially useful are the services provided by Technical Indexes Ltd (tel. 01344 426311) which offers comprehensive, reliable, full-text databases of manufacturers' technical catalogues, national and international standards and legislative material, delivered online through the internet on an annual subscription basis. The Technical Indexes information services cover more than 90 per cent of the world's most commonly used standards including:

■ British Standards Online – a complete collection of over 35,000 British Standards;
■ Worldwide standards on the internet;
■ UK and US defence standards;
■ US government specifications service.

7.7.2   Adapting existing specifications

Adaptation of existing specifications is often the most economical approach for construction projects or computer systems where architects or suppliers may be able to amend the specifications to meet a new application.

7.7.3   Alternative methods of specifying

Alternative methods of specifying include the use of brand or trade name and specifications by sample.

7.7.4 The use of a brand or trade name

England[27] lists the following circumstances in which descriptions by brand may be not only desirable but also necessary:

- When the manufacturing process is secret or covered by a patent.
- When the manufacturing process of the vendor call for a high degree of workmanship or skill that cannot be exactly defined in a specification.
- When only small quantities are bought so that the preparation of specifications by the buyer is impracticable.
- When testing by the buyer is impracticable.
- When the item is a component so effectively advertised as to create a preference or even a demand for its incorporation into the finished product on the part of the ultimate purchaser.
- When there is a strong preference for the branded item on the part of the design staff.

The main disadvantages of specifying branded items are:

- The cost of a branded item may be higher than an unbranded substitute.
- The naming of a brand effectively results in what Haslam[28] refers to as a 'closed specification'. Closed specifications, which can take the form of naming a particular brand, manufacturer or supplier, do not permit the use of alternatives. Closed specifications are most applicable when the need for duplication of an existing product is important or where it is desirable to maintain a low spares range. Closed specifications inhibit competition but also cut out fringe suppliers who may be unable to meet quality requirements.

7.7.5 Specification by sample

The sample can be branded by either the buyer or the seller and is a useful method of specification in relation to products such as printing or materials, e.g. cloth. When, orders are placed by products specified by reference to a sample previously submitted by a supplier it is important that the samples on which the contract is based should be (i) identified, (ii) labelled and (iii) retained by both purchaser and supplier.

By section 15 SGA and section 15 of the Supply of Goods and Services Act 1982 (SGSA) as amended by SSGA there is an implied 'term' (later defined as 'condition') that where goods are sold by sample:

- the bulk must correspond to the sample in quality;
- the buyer must have a reasonable opportunity of comparing the bulk with the sample;
- the goods must be free from any defect making 'their quality satisfactory' (not unmerchantable), which a reasonable examination of the sample would not reveal.

7.7.6   Specification by a user or performance specification

Here, the purchaser informs the supplier of the use to which the purchased item is to be put. This method is particularly applicable to the purchase of items about which the buyer has little technical knowledge.

By section 14(3) SGA and section 4 (sections 4 and 5 Supply of Goods and Services Act 1982, or SGSA) as amended by the SSGA, where the seller sells goods in the course of a business and the buyer, expressly or by implication, makes known to the seller any particular purpose for which the goods are being bought there is an implied 'term' that the goods supplied under the contract are of satisfactory quality. For the purpose of the SSGA, goods are satisfactory if 'they meet the standard that a reasonable person would regard as satisfactory, taking account of any description of the goods, the price (if relevant) and all the other relevant circumstances'. By section 2B SSGA the quality of the goods include their state and condition, and the following (among others) are, in appropriate cases, aspects of the quality of goods:

- fitness for all purposes for which goods of the kind in question are commonly supplied;
- appearance and finish;
- freedom from minor defects;
- safety;
- durability.

By section 2C SSGA the 'term' does not extend to any matter making the quality of goods unsatisfactory:

- which is specifically drawn to the buyer's attention before the contract is made
- where the buyer examines the goods before the contract is made which that examination ought to reveal, or
- in the case of a contract of sale by sample, which would have been apparent on a reasonable examination of the sample.

Section 4 SSGA provides that, when the seller can prove that the deviation from the specification is only slight that it would be unreasonable for the buyer to reject the goods, the buyer may not treat the breach of contract as a condition entitling him to reject the goods but only as a warranty giving a right to damages arising from the breach.

Section 4 SSGA also makes a distinction between commercial buyers and consumers. If the buyer is a consumer, the right to reject the goods on the grounds that the quality of the goods is unsatisfactory is not affected.

Section 3(2) SSGA states that the section applies unless a contrary intention appears in or is to be implied from the contract. As Woodroffe[29] observes: 'This time buyers must look to their own ts and cs, for a well drafted clause will enable a buyer to terminate a contract for any breach of Section 13–15 whether slight or not'.

7.8 Standardisation

Standards may be distinguished according to their subject matter, purpose and range of applications.

7.8.1 Subject matter

The subject matter of a standard may relate to an area of economic activity, e.g. engineering, and to items used in that field, e.g. fasteners. Each item may be further subdivided into suitable subjects for standards. Thus 'fasteners' may lead to standards for screw threads, bolts and nuts, washers, etc.

7.8.2 Purpose

Standards may relate to one or more aspects of product quality. These aspects include:

- *Dimensions*, thus encouraging interchangeability and variety reduction. BS 308 is a British Standard which lays down technical drawing principles and conventions which are widely accepted in the UK and will be easily understood worldwide.
- *Performance requirements* for a given purpose, e.g. BS 1515 covers all stressing and constructional features of fusion-welded pressure vessels necessary for a design to meet statutory requirements and those of manufacturers, users and insurers.
- *Environmental requirements* relating to such maters as pollution, waste disposal on land, noise and environmental nuisance. Environmental performance objectives and targets are covered by BS 7750 and ISO 14000.

In addition to the above, standards may also cover codes of practice, methods of test and glossaries. *Codes of practice* give guidance on the best accepted practice in relation to engineering and construction techniques and for operations such as installation, maintenance and provision of services. *Methods of test* are required for measuring the values of product characteristics and behaviour standards. *Glossaries* help to ensure unambiguous technical communication by providing standard definitions of the terms, conventions, units and symbols used in science and industry.

7.8.3 Range of application

The range of application relates to the domain in which a particular standard is applicable.

- *Individual standards*. These are standards laid down by the individual user.
- *Company standards*. These are prepared by agreement between various functions to guide design, purchasing, manufacturing and marketing operations. Ashton[30] has drawn attention to the importance of keeping registers or

data-bases of bought-out parts and company standards which can be referred to by codes listed in a codes register as a means of reducing variety and obviating variations in tolerances, finishes, performance and quality.

- *Association or trade standards*. These are prepared by a group of related interests in a given industry, trade or profession, e.g. the Society of Motor Manufacturers and Traders.

- *National standards*. British Standard specifications of particular importance are BS 4778 *Quality Vocabulary*, BS 6143 *Guide to the Economics of Quality*, BS 7850 *Total Quality Management* and BS EN ISO 9000:2000 *Quality Management Systems*.

- *International standards*. The two principal organisations producing worldwide standards are the International Electrotechnical Commission (IEC) and the International Standards Organisation (ISO). The former, established in 1906, concentrates on standards relating to the electrical and electronic fields. The latter, founded in 1947, is concerned with non-electrical standards. Both organisations are located in Geneva. In western Europe, progress is being made for the development of standards that will be acceptable both as European and as international standards. This work is being done through the European Committee for Standardisation (CEN) formed by west European standards organisations. The demarcation of European standardisation mirrors the international arrangement, with CEN covering non-electrical aspects and the European Committee for Electrotechnical Standardisation (CENELEC) and the European Telecommunications Standards Institute (ETSI) being responsible for the others.

Different standards and specifications can often be used in conjunction.

7.8.4 Purchasing and standardisation

Purchasing staff should be aware of the major trade, national and international standards applicable to their industry and the items bought. They should also appreciate the advantages that standardisation offers to the buyer:

- Clear specifications and the removal of any uncertainty as to what is required on the part of both buyer and supplier.

- Standardisation helps to achieve reliability and to reduce costs.

- Saving of time and money by eliminating the need to prepare company specifications and reducing the need for explanatory letters, telephone calls, etc.

- The saving of design time may also reduce the time for production of the finished product.

- Accurate comparison of quotations, since all prospective suppliers are quoting for the same thing.

- Less dependence on specialist suppliers and greater scope for negotiation.

- Reduction in error and conflict thus increasing supplier goodwill.

- Facilitation of international sourcing by reference to ISO standards.

- Saving in inventory and cost through variety reduction (see Chapter 8). By a coordinated effort between purchasing, design and production, one company reduced 30 different paints to 15; 120 different cutting fluids to 10; 50 different tools steel to 6; and 12 different aluminium casting alloys to 3. Standardisation and coding of items also discovered 36 different terms in use for a simple washer.

- Reduced investment in spares for capital equipment.

- Reduced cost of materials handling when standardisation is used.

- Elimination of the need to purchase costly brand names.

- Irregular purchases of non-standard equipment supplies are revealed.

7.9 Value analysis and engineering

7.9.1 Background and definitions

Value analysis (VA) was developed by the General Electric Company (USA) at the end of World War II. One of the pioneers on this approach to cost reduction was Lawrence D. Miles, whose book *Techniques of Value Analysis and Engineering* (McGraw-Hill, 1972) is still the classic on the subject. The term 'value engineering' (VE) was adopted by the US Navy Bureau of Ships in respect of a programme of cost reduction at the design stage, aimed at achieving economies without affecting the needed performance, reliability, quality and maintainability. Miles described value analysis as:

> a philosophy implemented by the use of a specific set of techniques, a body of knowledge, and a group of learned skills. It is an organised, creative approach which has for its purpose the efficient identification of unnecessary cost, i.e. cost which provides neither quality nor use nor life, nor appearance nor customer features.

Value analysis results in the orderly utilisation of alternative materials newer processes, and abilities of specialist suppliers. It focuses engineering, manufacturing and purchasing attention on one objective: equivalent performance at lower cost. Having this focus, it provides step-by-step procedures for accomplishing its objective efficiently and with assurance.

Although the terms VA and VE are often used synonymously, they may be defined as follows:

> *Value analysis* is a systematic procedure aimed at ensuring that necessary functions are achieved at minimum cost without detriment to quality, reliability, performance and delivery. This is normally a post-production activity.

> *Value engineering* is the application of value analysis at the pre-production or development stage.

This distinction may be summarised by the statement that VA is concerned with cost correction, VE with cost avoidance. Since VA includes VE, the former term will be used.

The keywords for an understanding of VA are 'function' and 'value'. The function of anything is that which it is designed to do, and should normally be capable of being expressed in two words, a verb and noun; thus the function of a pen is to 'make marks'. 'Value' is variously defined. The most important distinction is between use value, i.e. that which enables an item to fulfil its stated function, and esteem value, i.e. factors that increase the desirability of an item. The function of a gold-plated pencil and a ballpoint pen costing £70.00 and 50p, respectively, is in both cases to 'make marks'. The difference of £69.50 in the price of the former over the latter represents esteem value.

7.9.2   Implementation of value analysis

The necessary implementation of VA depends on choosing the right people and the right projects.

The right people

Value analysis may be carried out by the following:

- A team comprising representatives from such departments as cost accounting, design, marketing, manufacturing, purchasing, quality control research and work study.
- A specialist VA engineer, where the turnover warrants such an appointment. A VA engineer often has the responsibility of coordinating a VA team. Such a person should have:
  - experience of design and manufacturing related to the product(s);
  - understanding of a wide range of materials, their potentials and limitations;
  - a clear concept of the meaning and importance of value;
  - creative imagination and flair for innovation;
  - knowledge of specialist manufacturers and the assistance they can provide;
  - the capacity to work with others and a knowledge of how to motivate, control and coordinate.

Just-in-time (JIT) approaches emphasise the importance of consultation with suppliers and their co-option to VA teams.

The right project

In selecting possible projects, the VA team or engineer should consider the following:

- What project shows the greatest potential for savings: the greater the total cost the larger the potential savings. Consider two examples, A and B:

	A	*B*
Present cost each	10p	100p
Possible savings (10%)	1p	10p
Annual usage	100,000	1,000
Projected annual savings	£1,000	£100

Component A offers the greatest potential return from the application of VA.

■ What products have a high total cost in relation to the functions performed, i.e. is it possible to substitute a cheaper alternative?

■ What suggestions for projects emanate from design, production staff and suppliers?

■ Are there drawings or designs that have been unchanged in the last five years?

■ Is manufacturing equipment installed more than, say, five years ago now obsolete?

■ What inspection and test requirements have not been changed over the last five years?

■ Do single-source orders where the original order was placed more than, say, two years ago offer possibilities for savings?

Some areas of VA investigation include the following:

■ Product performance, i.e. what does it do?

■ Product reliability, i.e. reducing or eliminating product failure or breakdown.

■ Product maintenance, i.e. reducing costs of routine maintenance such as cleaning, lubrication, etc. and emergency repairs and replacement.

■ Product adaptability, i.e. adding an additional function or expanding the original use.

■ Product packaging, i.e. improving the saleability or protection of the product.

■ Product safety, i.e. eliminating possible hazards, e.g. sharp edges, inflammability.

■ Product styling, i.e. specifying lighter, stronger or more flexible materials or simplifying instructions.

■ Product distribution, i.e. making it easier to distribute, e.g. by reducing weight or by better transportation.

■ Product security, i.e. making the product less liable to theft or vandalism, e.g. better locks, imprinting the customer's name on easily moveable equipment.

7.9.3 Value analysis procedure

The 'job plan' for a VA project comprises the following stages:

1 *Project selection* (see above).
2 *Information stage.*

(a)   Obtain all essential information relating to the item under consideration, i.e. cost of materials and components, machining and assembly times, methods and costs, quality requirements, inspection procedures, etc.

(b)   Define the functions of the product, especially in relation to the cost of providing them.

3   *Speculation stage.* Have a brainstorming session in which as many ideas as possible are put forward for achieving the desired function, reducing costs or improving the product. Some questions that may promote suggestions at this stage include:

(a)   What additional or alternative uses can we suggest for the item?

(b)   How can the item be adapted, i.e. what other ideas does the item suggest?

(c)   Can the item be modified, especially with regard to changes in form, shape, material, colour, motion, sound, odour?

(d)   Can the item be augmented, i.e. made stronger, higher, longer, thicker, developed to provide an extra value, etc.

(e)   Can the item be reduced, i.e. made stronger, smaller, condensed, lighter, or features omitted?

(f)   Can the item be substituted, i.e. other materials, components, ingredients, processes, manufacturing methods, packaging?

(g)   Can we rearrange the item, i.e. change the layout or design, alter the sequence of operations, interchange components?

(h)   Can the item or aspects of the item be reversed, i.e. reversing roles or functions or positions, turned upside-down or front to back?

(i)   Which aspects of the product can be combined, i.e. functions, purposes, units, other parts, etc?

4   *Investigation stage.* Select the best ideas produced at the speculation stage and evaluate their feasibility. When VA is organised on a team basis, each specialist will approach the project from his or her own standpoint and report back.

5   *Proposal stage.* Recommendations will be presented to that level of management able to authorise the suggested changes. The proposals will state:

(a)   what changes or modifications are suggested;

(b)   information relating to the cost of making the suggested changes, the projected savings, the period(s) over which the savings are likely to accrue.

6   *Implementation stage.* When approved by the responsible executive the agreed recommendations will be progressed through the normal production, purchasing or other procedures.

VA checklist

The following checklist which every material component or operation must pass was prepared by the purchasing department of the General Electric Company.

1   Does its use contribute value?

2   Is its cost proportionate to its usefulness?

3 Does it need all its features?

4 Is there anything better for the intended use?

5 Can a usable part be made by a lower cost method?

6 Can a standard product be found which will be usable?

7 Is it made on proper tooling – considering the quantities used?

8 Are the specified tolerances and finishes really necessary?

9 Do material, reasonable labour, overhead and profit total its cost?

10 Can another dependable supplier provide it for less?

11 Is anyone buying it for less?

7.9.4 Purchasing and value analysis

Purchasing should be the most cost-conscious of all departments. Where no VA team exists, all buyers should be encouraged to understand and apply the approach. As a member of a VA team, purchasing can make the following contributions:

- *Provision of information* concerning:
  - materials and components, e.g. alternative materials such as plastics instead of metals;
  - costs, e.g. material cost of bought-out components;
  - standards, e.g. use of a supplier's standard part instead of a special.
- *Suggestions for buying economies*:
  - economic order quantities;
  - reduction in costs of packing, handling and transportation;
  - purchase of assemblies other than components;
  - alternative reliable suppliers.
- *Encouraging supplier participation.* This involves examining, with the suppliers, the function of the item being analysed and seeking their specialist advice as to how the cost can be reduced. Usually specialist suppliers will provide advice free in the interest of good business relationships. It may, however, be sensible to provide the supplier with some financial incentive to collaborate with VA.

7.10 Quality control and quality assurance

Quality control (QC) has been defined as:[31]

> **The operational techniques and activities that are used to fulfil requirements for quality.**

Quality assurance (QA) differs from quality control and is defined as:[32]

> All those planned and systematic activities implemented within the quality system and demonstrated as needed to provide adequate confidence that an entity will fulfil requirements for quality.

Quality control is concerned with defect *detection* and *correction* and relates to such activities as determining where, how and at what intervals inspection should take place, the collection and analysis of data relating to defects and determining what corrective action should be taken. Since defects are detected through post-production inspection and are not prevented, Schonberger[33] has referred to QC as the 'death certificate' approach.

Quality assurance is concerned with defect *prevention* and has become synonymous with the quality systems BS 5750 and its international counterpart ISO 9000.

7.11   Quality systems

7.11.1   What is a quality system?

A quality system is defined as:[34]

> The organisational structure, responsibilities, procedures, processes and resources for implementing quality management.

A quality system typically applies to, and interacts with, all activities pertinent to the quality of a product or service. As shown in Figure 7.8 it involves all phases from initial identification to final satisfaction of requirements and customer expectations.

All organisations have a quality management system. This may, however, be informal and insufficiently documented. The advantages of a properly documented system such as that required by BS EN 9001:2000 are that it:

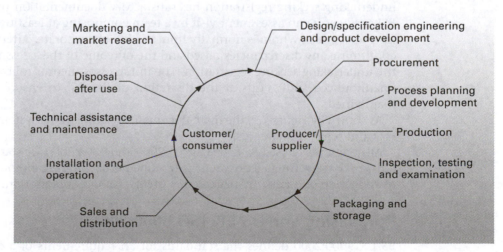

Figure 7.8   The quality loop

Source: British Standards Institution; reproduced by permission

- ensures that all aspects of quality are controlled;
- ensures consistent and efficient work practices;
- indicates best practice;
- provides objective evidence for determining and correcting the causes of poor quality;
- increases customer confidence;
- gives competitive advantage.

7.11.2   BS EN ISO 9000:2000

The British Standards Institution (BSI) was established in 1901 as the Engineering Standards Committee and, after the grant of a Royal Charter in 1929, changed to the present name in 1931.

The CEN (European Committee for Standardisation) and CENELEC (European Committee for Electrotechnical Standardisation) were created in the late 1960s, the former to 'promote technical harmonisation in Europe in conjunction with world wide bodies and its partners in Europe'.

The ISO (International Standards Organisation) was founded in 1947, since the existence of non-harmonised standards for similar technologies can constitute technical barriers to international trade. ISO 9000, as worldwide derivative of BSI's BS 5750 *Quality Management Systems* launched in 1979, appeared in 1987. ISO standards, now adopted by over 140 countries, are revised every five years.

The current BS EN ISO 9000:2000 series, published in December 2000, provides the principles which are put into practice by the BSI system for the registration of firms assessed capability. To be registered, an undertaking is required to have a documented quality system which complies with the appropriate parts of BS/EN 9000 and with a quality assessment schedule (QAS) which defines in precise terms the scope and special requirements relating to a specific group of products, processes or service. QASs are developed by BSI in cooperation with a particular industry after consultation with purchasing and associated interests. When an undertaking seeking registration has satisfactory documentation procedures, the BSI arranges for an assessment visit by a team comprising at least two experienced assessors, one of whom is normally from the BSI inspectorate. Afterwards a report confirming any discrepancies raised and the outcome of the assessment is sent to the undertaking seeking registration. The initial assessment is followed by regular unannounced audit visits at the discretion of the BSI to ensure standards are maintained.

As shown by Figure 7.9, the main documents relating to the system are a vocabulary and separate standards.

Although the revised BS EN ISO 9001:2000 and 9004:2000 are standalone standards, they constitute a 'consistent pair' aimed at facilitating a more user-friendly introduction of quality management systems into an organisation.

7.11.3   Purchasing and BS EN ISO 9000:2000

BS EN 9000:2000 defines the standards for an requirements of a quality system under four main sections: (i) management responsibility; (ii) resource management; (iii) product realisation and (iv) measurement, analysis and improvement.

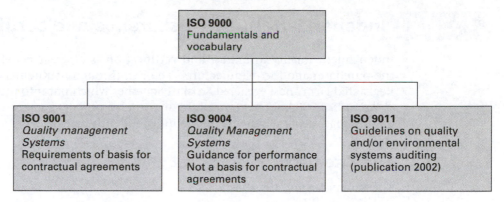

Figure 7.9 The main documents relating to ISO 9000:2000 standards

Purchasing is referred to under 'resource management' in clause 7.4. In this context the word 'organisation' refers to the undertaking that is seeking conformity with the standard, i.e. 'us'. The term 'supplier' refers to 'our' suppliers. An 'interested party' is a person or group having an interest in the performance or success of an organisation.

Section 7.4 contains provisions relating to the purchasing process (7.4.1), purchasing information (7.4.2) and verification of purchased produce (7.4.3). These sections should, however, be read in conjunction with BS EN ISO 9004:2000 which specifies the activities that should be included in a quality system for purchasing. Subsection 7.4.2, for example, provides examples of ways in which an organisation can ensure that suppliers have the potential capability to provide required products 'effectively, efficiently and within schedule', such as:

■ evaluation of relevant supplier experience;

■ performance of suppliers against competitors;

■ review of purchase product quality, price, delivery performance and response to problems;

■ audits of supplier management systems.

Cognisance should also be taken of the ISO 14000 series. This supersedes BS 7750 which was the world's first standard for environmental management systems.

7.11.4 Directories of ISO 9000 certified companies or organisations

There is no complete database of ISO certified organisations but reference may be made to the following:

■ *ISO 9000 Web Directory*

■ *ISO Register*

■ *QSU Online ISO 9000 Registered Company Directory*

■ *Quality Digest – International ISO Database*

■ *The International Quality Systems Directory*

7.12 Independent quality assurance and certification

Independent quality assurance and certification is of great benefit to the user, the purchaser and the manufacturer. The BSI, through its Kitemark, Safety Mark, Registered Firm and Registered Stockist Schemes which put into practice the principles of ISO 9000, set out procedures by which a product's safety and a supplier's quality management systems can be independently assessed.

7.12.1 The Kitemark

The Kitemark indicates that:

1 BSI has tested samples of the product against the appropriate British Standard and confirmed that the requirements of the Standard have been met;

2 BSI has assessed the manufacturer's quality management system against BS EN ISO 9000;

3 both company and product are subject to continual surveillance by BSI.

7.12.2 The Safety Mark

This indicates compliance with a British or International Standard specifically concerned with safety or with the safety requirements of a standard covering additional product characteristics. As with the Kitemark scheme, the Safety Mark Scheme includes the testing of samples and assessment of the manufacturer's quality system, followed by continual surveillance by BSI. There is also the European Safety Mark which does not claim to be a mark of safety or compliance with standards.

7.12.3 Registered Firm Scheme

Reference to this scheme is made in 7.11.2 above.

7.12.4 Registered Stockist Scheme

This scheme provides for the registration with the BSI of stockists of electronic components, chemicals, metal fasteners, plastics, etc. that have a quality management system in accordance with the scheme and applicable to all items stocked. Buyers have an assurance that all items supplied by a registered stockist will emanate from a quality-assured source. Details of approved products and licensed manufacturers are given in *The Buyers' Guide* published annually by the BSI.

7.12.5 Testing houses

About 30 third-party certification bodies are members of the Association of British Certification Bodies (ABCB). A number are set up by trade associations such as the Manchester Chamber of Commerce Testing House for the Cotton Trade, the Bradford Chamber of Commerce for the Wool Trade, the Shirley Institute,

Manchester, and the London Textile Trading House. Certification bodies assessed by the National Accreditation Council for Certification Bodies (NACCB) are entitled to use the NACCB National Quality 'Tick'.

7.13 Tools for quality and reliability

It would not be practical in this book to attempt even an outline of quality control assurance and reliability techniques. In this section brief reference is made to inspection, seven simple quality control tools, benchmarking, statistical process control, failure mode and effects analysis (FMEA) and quality circles. Buyers requiring further information should consult one of the specialised quality texts and, in particular, the relevant parts of BS EN ISO 9000:2000 especially 9001:2000 and 9004:2000.

7.13.1 Inspection

Although, as stated below, inspection is now regarded as a non-value-adding activity, reference may be made to incoming inspection, source inspection and source control.

Incoming inspection

Items are inspected on delivery according to a specified acceptable quality level (AQL). The results of incoming inspections are tabulated by the quality control department and this information will be provided to purchasing so that appropriate action can be taken. Items that pass inspection will be received into the store. Rejected items may be dealt with in one of the following ways:

- Returned to the supplier at the supplier's expense for correction or replacement.
- Parts may be corrected by the purchaser and the supplier charged with the cost. This may interfere with production schedules and shop loadings.
- Where the rejected items are usable, although not strictly in accordance with the specification, the buyer may negotiate a price reduction.

One major disadvantage of incoming inspection is that a tendency may emerge for some suppliers to rely on the purchaser's inspection.

Source inspection

The purchaser has either resident inspectors at the vendor's plant or arranges for the inspectors to visit the vendor at regular intervals.

Advantages
- Reduction in the time-period for rejection, return, reworking and redelivery.
- Inspectors become experts in dealing with the supplier's products.
- The supplier's specialised inspection and test equipment can be utilised.

Disadvantages

■ Source inspection is usually more costly than incoming inspection
■ The supplier's responsibility for meeting quality requirements may be reduced, i.e. responsibility is transferred to the purchaser rather than retained by the supplier.

While inspection can ensure 'conformance to specification', it has, as Saunders[35] points out, 'a major limitation because it does not permit questions to be asked with regard to the correctness or appropriateness of the specification'.

Source control

The emphasis is now on the reduction or elimination of inspection by the purchaser of goods received by making the supplier wholly responsible for supplying a product in accordance with a given specification and reporting inspection results to the purchaser by a test certificate or by one of the procedures specified in BS EN ISO 9004. In many industries, e.g. the automotive industry, suppliers are required to set up quality systems to provide for the control of incoming quality, the prevention of in-process discrepancies, timely and corrective action where required and the prevention of shipment of non-conforming products.

7.13.2 Seven simple quality control tools

The traditional tools to help organisations to understand their processes with a view to improving their quality techniques are stated below.

Checksheets

A checksheet is used to collect data relating to quality so that the information collected can be interpreted directly from the form without further processing. By including data such as specification limits, for example, the number of non-conforming items can be seen at a glance.

Cause and effect diagrams

These are also known as Ishikawa or 'fishbone' diagrams after Kaoru Ishikawa, a Japanese engineer, who invented the chart. As shown in Figure 7.10, such a chart

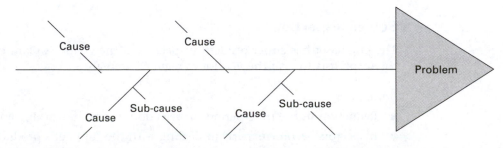

Figure 7.10 Fishbone cause and effect diagram

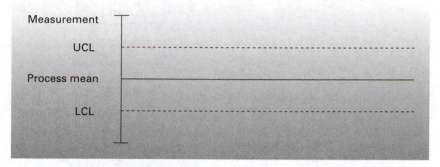

Figure 7.11 The structure of a control chart

resembles a fish skeleton in which the problem forms the head from which the spine extends. From the spine are other bones representing possible causes with, possibly, other bones representing sub-causes of the larger cause. This approach is useful in brainstorming sessions designed to locate and identify the causes of organisational problems.

Control charts

Developed in the 1920s by Dr Walker Shewart of the Bell Telephone Company, control charts are the most technically sophisticated statistical quality management (SQM) tool. A typical control chart as shown in Figure 7.11 is a graphical display of a quality characteristic that has been computed from a sample. The chart comprises two horizontal lines known as upper (UCL) and lower (LCL) control limits and a centre line that represents the average value of the quality characteristic measure on the vertical axis. The limits are chosen so that there is a high probability (generally greater than 0.90) that, if the process is in control, sample values plotted on the control chart will fall within the limits.

Control charts are based on the principle of exception, i.e. they focus attention on items or results which fall outside the control limits. The causes of exceptions can be either *random* or *special*.

Random causes affect everyone associated with the process and tend to act on the process in a predictable manner, e.g. overtime, temperature changes.

Special causes do not affect everyone and only arise because of specific circumstances and are therefore assignable causes, e.g. material variation, operator performance, tool wear.

Information flow diagrams

These are a form of flowchart which provides a graphical representation of the steps in a process as shown in Figure 7.12.

Histograms

Histograms indicate the shape of a data distribution. They are also known as column diagrams or bar charts in which the horizontal axis is used for class intervals and vertical axis for frequencies.

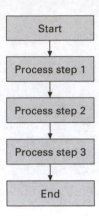

Figure 7.12   A flowchart

Pareto charts

These charts are graphical tools used for ranking causes from the most to the least significant. Pareto charts are referred to again in Chapter 8.

Scatter diagrams

These analyse the relationship between two variables, typically causes and effects such as training and performance, education and income, cost and reliability. The scatter diagram in Figure 7.13 shows that there is a high correlation between income and education in the sample of men interviewed.

The above seven tools have been expanded by such approaches as benchmarking, statistical quality control and approaches relating to reliability such as failure mode and effects analysis (see below).

7.13.3 Benchmarking

Benchmarking is an approach in which an organisation measures its performance against industry leaders in areas such as quality control and procedures. The four basic types of benchmarking are:

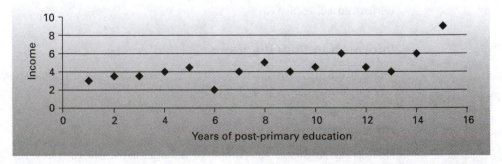

Figure 7.13   Years of post primary education sample of 17 men aged 40 showing income in relation to post-primary education

- *Internal* – comparison of internal operations or activities.

- *Competitive* – comparison of the costs, output, procedures or other aspects of products or functions relative to those of one or more competitors.

- *Functional* – comparison of similar functions within the same industry or those of industry leaders.

- *Generic* – comparison of similar business processes irrespective of the particular industry.

Benchmarking is considered later in Chapter 18.

7.13.4 Statistical process control

This is the application of statistical techniques to control a process. It uses control charts (see above) to determine if a process is in or out of control. The calculation of the mean and standard deviation and the concept of the normal curve which are the basis of control charts have many other applications, including forecasting the probability of stockouts, and are therefore dealt with as an aspect of inventory control in Chapter 8.

7.14 Failure mode and effects analysis (FMEA)

7.14.1 What is FMEA?

FMEA, which originated in the USA aerospace industry, is an important reliability engineering technique which has the following main objectives:

- To identify all the ways in which failure can occur.

- To estimate the effect and seriousness of the failure.

- To recommend corrective design actions.

FMEA has been defined as:[36]

> **A systematic approach that applies a tabular method to aid the thought process used by engineers to identify potential failure modes and their effects.**

7.14.2 Types of FMEA

The analyses take three forms:[37]

- *Systems FMEA* is used to analyse systems and subsystems in the early concept and design stages. System function is the design or purpose(s) of the system and is derived from customer wants. It can also include safety requirements, government regulations and constraints.

- *Design FMEA* is used to analyse products before they are released to production.

■ *Process FMEA* is used to analyse products before they are released to the customer.

7.14.3 The preparation of an FMEA

The Ford Motor Company, which was the first of the UK motor manufacturers to request suppliers to use FMEA in their advance quality planning, recommends a team approach led by the responsible system, product or manufacturing/assembly engineer who is expected to involve representatives from all affected activities. Team members may be drawn from design, manufacturing, assembly, quality, reliability, service, purchasing. Testing, supplier and other subject experts as appropriate. The team leader is also responsible for keeping the FMEA updated.

For proprietary designs, the preparation and updating of FMEAs is the responsibility of the suppliers.

With a design FMEA, for example, the team is initially concerned with identifying how a part may fail to meet its intended function The seriousness of the effect of a potential failure is rated on a ten-point scale as shown in Figure 7.14.

Starting with the failure modes with the highest severity ratings, the design FMEA team then ascertains the possible causes of failure based on two assumptions:

■ that the part is manufactured/assembled within engineering specifications;
■ that the part design may include a deficiency that may cause an unacceptable variation in the manufacturing or assembling process.

The team then proceeds to ascertain:

■ the cumulative number of failures that could occur over the life of the part;
■ design evaluation techniques that can be used to detect the identified failure causes;
■ what design actions are recommended to reduce the severity, occurrence and detection ratings.

The completed design FMEA in respect of a lighting switch subsystem is shown in Figure 7.15. The technique is further described in BS 5750.

7.14.4 Advantages of the FMEA approach

The advantages of FMEA are listed by Ford as:

■ Improved quality, reliability and safety of Ford products
■ Improved Ford image and competitiveness
■ Increased customer satisfaction
■ Reduction in product development timing and cost
■ Documentation and tracking of actions to reduce risk.

Effect	Rating	Criteria
No effect	1	No effect.
Very slight effect	2	Very slight effect on vehicle performance. Customer not annoyed. Non-vital fault noticed sometimes.
Slight effect	3	Slight effect on vehicle performance. Customer slightly annoyed. Non-vital fault noticed most of the time.
Minor effect	4	Minor effect on vehicle performance. Fault does not require repair. Customer will notice minor effect on vehicle or system performance. Non-vital fault always noted.
Moderate effect	5	Moderate effect on vehicle performance. Customer experiences some dissatisfaction. Fault on non-vital part requires repair.
Significant effect	6	Vehicle performance degraded, but operable and safe. Customer experiences discomfort. Non-vital part inoperable.
Major effect	7	Vehicle performance severely affected, but drivable and safe. Customer dissatisfied. Subsystems inoperable.
Extreme effect	8	Vehicle inoperable but safe. Customer very dissatisfied. System inoperable.
Serious effect	9	Potentially hazardous effect. Able to stop vehicle without mishap – gradual failure. Compliance with government regulation in jeopardy.
Hazardous effect	10	Hazardous effect. Safety related – sudden failure. Non-compliance with government regulation
		Severity is a rating corresponding to the seriousness of the effect(s) of a potential failure mode. Severity applies only to the effect of a failure mode

Figure 7.14   Severity rating table for design (FMEA)

7.14.5   Some disadvantages of the FMEA approach

A study undertaken by UMIST[38] concluded that engineers still view FMEA as a hard slog; more use should be made of computerised aids to reduce the effort of preparing and updating the FMEA. The main difficulties are related to time constraints and lack of understanding of the importance of FMEA, training and commitment.

7.15 Quality circles and task teams

7.15.1 Definition of quality circles

A quality circle (QC) may be defined as:

> A small group of volunteers, usually from the same work area, meeting regularly under the leadership of their immediate superior to analyse and solve problems relating to their responsibilities and, where appropriate, themselves implement solutions agreed with management.

This definition may be analysed as follows:

POTENTIAL FAILURE MODE AND EFFECTS ANALYSIS (DESIGN FMEA)

Subsystem/Name <u>17.05.01/Lighting Switches Subsystem</u>   Supplies and plants affected _____

Design responsibility <u>Lighting Department</u> _____   Model year/Vehicle(s) _____

Other areas involved <u>TBD</u> _____   Engineering release date _____

Part name and number Part function	Potential failure mode	Potential effect(s) of failure	s e v	△	Potential cause(s) of failure	o c c u r
(9) Electric Switch (F9DB-999-AB)/ Pass current to headlamp filament	(10) Switch fails to pass current (Row 1)	(11) System: Primary function will not be provided (S = 8) Other effects: see note in text explanation	8		(14) (1.0) Crystal fails to pass current when pressed	7
Electric switch crystal material/ Generate signal when pressed	(1.0) Crystal fails to pass current when pressed (Row 2)	Switch fails to pass current (S = 7) Other effects: Same as row 1 above	8		(1.1) Electric crystal material cracked (1.2) 0 degree vertical orientation not maintained (see row 5)	7
Electric switch crystal material/ Generate signal when pressed	(1.1) Electric crystal material cracked (Row 3)	Same as row 2 above	8		(1.1A) Surface area supporting crystal is too small	3
					(1.1B) Crystal material is too brittle at −10 deg C (Row 4)	3
	(1.2) 0 degree vertical orientation not maintained Row 5	Same as row 2 above	8		Improper design allows switch to be improperly installed (i.e. 0 degree vertical orientation not maintained)	7

Electric Company							Page 1		Rows 1		through 5	
1999/Electric Vehicle							Prepared By					
98-07-93							FMEA date (Orig.) 93-05-14 (Rev.) 92 04-01					

Design evaluation technique	Detec	RPN	Recommended action(s)	Area/ Individual responsible and completion date	Action results				
					Action taken	Sev	Occ	Det	RPN
(16) Vehicle Durability Test (D = 8) Laboratory Accelerated Life Test (D = 5)	5	280	(19) (Transfer cause 1.0 to failure mode in row 2)	(20)	(21)				
Buck/Assembly Test (D = 3) Installation drawing (D = 5)	3	168	(Determine root causes of 1.1 – see rows 3 and 4 below)						
Computer program (Calculate bending stresses)	5	120	Increase crystal support structure area to distribute load evenly over crystal surface (P)		Supporting surface area increased from 3 to 6 sq. mm. Rev-DD added to drawing on 93-06-18	8	2	5	80
(16) Vehicle Durability Test (D = 8) Laboratory Accelerated Life Test (D = 5)	5	120	Add lab Test to support structure mode when crystal is subjected to design load at −40 deg C (D)		Lab test added to vehicle durability Test program on 93-06-18	8	3	3	72
Buck Assembly Test (D = 3) Installation drawing (D = 5)	3	168	Add tab to switch housing to prevent misorientation during assembly (P)		Tab added to switch housing. Rev-DE added to dwg on 93-06-17	8	1	3	24

Figure 7.15 Completed design FMEA in respect of a lighting switch subsystem

- *'A small group'.* Normally a QC comprises between 3 and 12 persons. Membership must be large enough to generate ideas and cater for absenteeism but not too large for genuine participation.

- *'Volunteers'.* Employee participation is voluntary.

- *'From the same work area'.* Unlike a value analysis team, which is made up of representatives from several departments, a QC usually consists of persons from the same work area. This gives the circle its identity. Exceptionally a QC may have members sharing the same problems but drawn from different departments.

- *'Meeting regularly'.* Meetings take place fortnightly, monthly or more frequently as required.

- *'Their immediate superior'*. One benefit of a QC is that the leader's role is enhanced. Circle leaders should therefore be of at least supervisory level.

- *'To analyse and solve problems'*. Projects may be either identified by the QC or referred to it by management.

- *'Themselves implement solutions agreed by management'*. All proposed solutions must be submitted to management for evaluation and approval before they are implemented.

7.15.2 The establishment of quality circles

The earliest QCs, comprising mainly shopfloor employees, were developed in Japan in the 1960s by Kaoru Ishikawa as part of a national quality drive. QCs are now concerned with projects relating to matters other than quality, such as cost reduction, safety, communications and energy conservation. The main steps in setting up QCs are as follows:

1 Obtain the commitment of senior management to the QC concept.
2 Inform the trade unions of the intention to establish QCs and obtain their cooperation.
3 Form a steering committee chaired by a senior manager to provide guidance, direction and resources, to monitor the progress of QCs and to support the facilitator.
4 Appoint a facilitator responsible for initiating, coordinating and directing QC activities in the organisation.
5 Provide training for QC leaders. In addition to group dynamics the content of this training may include such all-purpose techniques as the application of statistical techniques, lateral thinking and Pareto analysis.
6 Form the QCs. This should be done after considering what areas of the organisation might benefit from their introduction.

7.15.3 Objectives of quality circles

Objectives may include:

- Reduction of errors and enhancement of quality.
- Problem prevention rather than detection and correction.
- Reduction in product or service costs.
- Improved productivity.
- Increased employee involvement, motivation, job satisfaction and commitment.
- Improved teamwork and working relationships.
- Development of employee problem-solving ability.

7.15.4 Task teams

Task teams are a variant of QCs since they are formed to undertake a specific task or solve a specific problem. Unlike quality circles which usually comprise people from a single functional area who meet on a continuing basis, task teams involve specialists from several functions and disband when the specific task is completed. The *self-managed* team is a development of the task team approach. This moves the focus from a management-initiated drive for quality and improvement to a self-directed work team concept. A self-managed team is defined as:[39]

> **A highly trained group of employees, from 6 to 18 on average, fully respons-ible for turning out a well defined segment of finished work. The segment could be a final product like a refrigerator or a service like a fully processed insurance claim. It could also be a complete but intermediate product or ser-vice like a finished refrigerator motor, an aircraft fuselage or the circuit plans for a television set.**

7.15.5   Work cells

Work cells are typified by Walker's[40] description of the development by Rover Cars. Work cells comprise about 80 persons controlled by a production manager rather than a supervisor. The production manager's responsibilities extend to employee welfare, training and education in addition to technology and produc-tion. Cell members are encouraged to suggest production and product quality improvements. While each team takes on enhanced quality responsibilities (the concept was introduced as a consequence of JIT and minimal inventory control systems), cell autonomy is restricted by such factors as the flow-time rate and orders received.

7.15.6   Purchasing, quality circles and task teams

There is nothing to prevent the establishment of a purchasing QC. Purchasing, however, is more likely to be involved as a member of a task or self-managed team. Virtually any problem that can be considered by a value analysis team is also suitable for the attention of a task team.

7.16   Quality function deployment

Quality function deployment (QFD) is a complex technique, developed in Japan. Because the matrix that is used resembles a house, the alternative name for this technique is the 'House of Quality' (Figure 7.16).

QFD is a cross-functional team approach and incorporates the needs of the customer (the whats), which have been prioritised, hence QFD is also known as the voice of the customer. These whats are recorded on the left of the matrix. The hows are the ways that the team identify how the whats can be satisfied. The rela-tionship between the whats and the hows are recorded in the centre block of the matrix, the strength of the relationship being recorded by a designated symbol. The roof of the matrix records the relationship between the various hows that have been identified. These can be strongly or weakly positive or negative, and this again is recorded by some assigned symbol.

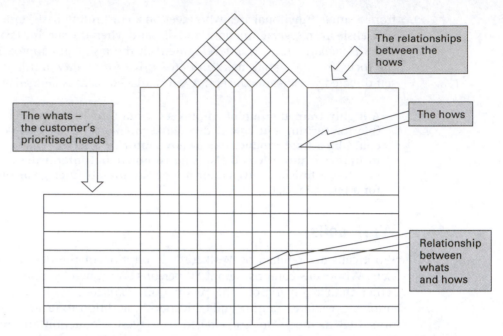

Figure 7.16 Simplified QFD matrix

The benefits of QFD are said to be a better designed product with fewer design changes needed, giving a quicker time to market and ultimately a satisfied and loyal customer.

7.17 The cost of quality

7.17.1 Definitions

The cost of quality may be defined as the costs of conformance plus the costs of non-conformance or the cost of doing things wrong.

Cost of conformance (COC) is defined by BS 6143 as:

> The cost of operating the process as specified in a 100 per cent effective manner. This does not imply that it is efficient or even a necessary process but rather that the process when operated with the specified procedures cannot be achieved at a lower cost.

Cost of non-conformance (CONC) is defined as:

> The cost of inefficiency with the specified process i.e. over resourcing of excess cost of people, materials and equipment arising from unsatisfactory inputs, errors made, rejected outputs and various other sources of waste. These are regarded as non-essential process costs.

Cost elements associated with the process can be categorised under one of the following headings:

- People
- Equipment
- Material
- Environments

The main costs of quality are set out in Table 7.4.

Table 7.4 The costs of quality

Costs of conformance	
Prevention costs	*Appraisal costs*
(Costs of any action taken to investigate, prevent or reduce defects and failures including:)	(Cost of assessing the quality achieved)
	■ Laboratory acceptance testing
■ Quality engineering (or quality management, department or planning)	■ Inspection tests (including 'goods inward')
■ Quality control/engineering including design/ specification review and reliability engineering	■ Product quality audits
■ Process control/engineering	■ Set-up for inspection and test
■ Design and development of quality measurement and control equipment	■ Inspection and test material
■ Quality planning by other functions	■ Product quality audit
■ Calibration and maintenance of production equipment used to evaluate quality	■ Review of test and inspection data
■ Maintenance and calibration of test and inspection equipment	■ Field (on-site) performance testing
■ Supplier assurance including supplier surveys, audits and ratings, identifying new sources of supply, design evaluation and testing of alternative products, purchase order review before placement	■ Internal testing and release
	■ Evaluation of field stock and spare parts
■ Quality training	■ Data processing inspection and test reports
■ Administration, audit and improvement	

Costs of non-conformance	
Internal failure	*External failure*
(Cost arising within the manufacturing organisation before transfer of ownerships to the customer)	(After transfer of ownership to the customer)
	■ Complaints
■ Scrap	■ Product or customer service, product liability
■ Rework and repair	■ Products rejected and returned, recall reject
■ Trouble shooting or defect/failure analysis	■ Returned materials repair
■ Reinspect, retest	■ Warranty costs and costs associated with replacement
■ Scrap and rework, fault of vendor, downtime	
■ Modification permits and concessions	
■ Downgrading, i.e. losses for quality reasons resulting from a lower selling price	

7.17.2 Data collection

Quality costs become absorbed and hidden in various overheads unless they are recorded separately and collected. Collection of data usually involves obtaining information from a number of sources and charging expenditures against a quality or budget centre using appropriate codes. Activity-based costing (see Chapter 18) is one way of charging quality costs to products. Sources of cost data relating to quality include:

- payroll analysis
- manufacturing expense reports
- scrap reports
- rework or rectification authorisation/reports
- travel expense claims
- product cost information
- field repair, replacement and warranty cost reports
- inspection and 'test' records
- material review records

7.17.3 Quality cost formulae or records

The collating and reporting of quality costs is stated by BS 6143 to be a shared activity between the quality and accounting functions. BS 6143 should be consulted by readers wishing for more information on quality costing systems. Briefly, this involves allocating quality costs to accountable cost centres by the use of account codes under appropriate headings. When accumulated, it is possible to build up a typical quality cost element comparison as shown in Table 7.5.

BS 6143 points out that 'quality costs alone do not provide sufficient information for management to put them into perspective with other operating costs or to identify critical areas in need of attention'. To establish the significance of quality costs it is necessary to use ratios showing the relationships between total quality costs and the costs of prevention, appraisal and failure. Typical ratios include:

Table 7.5 Typical example of quality cost element comparison

Segment	Element	Percentage of total quality cost
Failure	Scrap	35
	Rework	11
	Reinspection	9
	Additional operation	8
	Warranty	5
	Downgrading	2
	Others	2
	Total failure cost	72
Appraisal	Inspection and test	26
Prevention	Control of prevention activities	2
Grand total		100

$$\frac{\text{Prevention cost}}{\text{Total cost}}$$

$$\frac{\text{Cost of supplier assessment}}{\text{Prevention cost}}$$

$$\frac{\text{Cost of incoming test and inspection}}{\text{Value of purchased parts}}$$

7.18   Purchasing and quality

Purchasing contributions to design have already been mentioned in Chapter 5, section 5.11. References to purchasing and standardisation value analysis and BS EN ISO 9000 are made earlier in this chapter. It may, however, be useful to summarise the numerous ways in which effective purchasing can contribute to specifying and assuring the quality of supplies.

General

■ Contributing to the competitive advantage of the undertaking by participating in the procurement of bought-out items at the most economical cost.

■ Ensuring that quality is not confused with price and grade.

■ Providing a high level of expertise with regard to quality to both internal and external customers of the purchasing function.

■ Ensuring that purchasing's responsibilities in relation to quality meet with the requirements of BS EN ISO 9000.

■ Determining the level of quality risk attached to the purchase of a particular item, i.e. the chance of something going wrong with a consequential adverse impact on the achievement of customer satisfaction. Factors to be considered in assessing the level of risk include:

– Design *process complexity*, i.e. the difficulty of carrying out design development work.

– *Design maturity*, i.e. what percentage of the design is known and proven.

– *Manufacturing complexity*, e.g. close tolerances, strength, resistance to corrosion abrasion and creep, number of moving parts, etc., all have quality implications.

– *Safety*, i.e. the probability and consequences of product of service failure

– *Economics*, i.e. the total costs of conformance and non-conformance referred to earlier.

Purchasing staff should seek the advice of experts when unsure about any of the above factors.

As a support service to design and production

■ Serving as a member of teams concerned with concurrent design, value engineering and value analysis, and special projects/problems.

- Advocating, where appropriate, the involvement of suppliers in design, value analysis, etc. teams.
- Advising on costs in relation to fitness for purpose, e.g. lower priced alternative materials such as aluminium rather than zinc or pressure rather than gravity manufacture for die-castings.
- Suggesting more economic forms of procurement, e.g. assemblies rather than components.
- Providing information on the availability of items of a specified quality.
- Assisting, from the standpoint of quality, in drafting company specifications.
- Emphasising the quality advantages of using standard specifications.
- Ensuring that items of the right quality are purchased when no formal specifications exist.
- Advising on the availability of alternatives of the same quality but at a cheaper price than brand names.

At the pre-ordering stage

It is suggested that the purchasing staff should take as a guide the requirements of BS EN ISO 9004–1 relating to the following:

- selection of acceptable suppliers;
- agreement on quality assurance;
- agreement on verification methods;
- receiving inspection and planning and control.

At the ordering stage

- The above BS EN ISO 9004–1 requirement relating to specifications, drawings and purchase documents.
- Including in the terms and conditions of purchase appropriate terms relating to quality including provision of the settlement of quality disputes.

At the post-ordering stage

- Vendor rating with respect to quality.
- Feedback to suppliers, with regard to quality improvement.
- Maintenance of quality records with respect of purchased items.
- Negotiations with suppliers in respect of items rejected as unsatisfactory.

Training

To carry out the above responsibilities purchasing staff should have appropriate training in the following areas:

- An appreciation of design and production processes.
- Quality control and assurance procedures and methods.

- Procedures relating to reliability, e.g. FMEA.
- The provisions of BS EN ISO 9000:2000.
- Quality assurance and risk.

Case study

Acme is a large assembler of domestic electrical appliances. In keeping with a policy of substantially reducing its supplier base, Acme had only one supplier of component 149 used in the manufacture of a domestic cleaner. The home and export sales amount to over 10,000 products. Component 149 is relatively cheap but has a high safety risk factor, one requirement being that the component should be adequately insulated to obviate any possibility of users receiving an electrical shock.

Component 149 is supplied by Elston Electrical Industries plc. Elston was selected by Acme some six years ago from a shortlist of five potential suppliers. The selection criterion was that Elston was considerably cheaper in price than the nearest of its competitors. Additionally Elston had relevant BS EN ISO certification, and a thorough independent review of its quality system had been carried out by Acme's design and purchasing staff. Elston delivers 750 items of component 149 to Acme at two-day intervals towards an estimated monthly usage of 15,000. Elston's works are 60 miles distant from those of Acme. Acme keeps a small buffer stock of two days' supply. A condition of the contract is that there is no need for Acme to carry out any independent inward inspection of component 149.

Until recently there has been no record of any failure in the quality of components supplied by Elston. Acme has therefore regularly renewed the contract on a yearly basis subject only to agreed price increases. Confidence in the quality of the component supplied has resulted in no audit by Acme of Elston's quality systems since the placing of the original order.

Acme has recently started to receive complaints from retailers who have been approached by users of the cleaner who have had slight shocks. More seriously, a letter from a solicitor has threatened court action because it is claimed that the death of a user with a weak heart is attributable to the shock received. Adverse publicity regarding the cleaner has also appeared in the national press and there has been a fall-off in sales.

Investigation shows that the shocks are due to component 149. Further investigation reveals that Elston, without notifying Acme, had decided a cheaper insulation might be used for component 149 thereby enabling Elston to maintain its price differential by reducing their costs.

Acme had decided to call in some 35,000 cleaners sold during the last four months. Elston has also been instructed that the insulation must revert to the original standards, but Elston states that it will be at least 14 days before its own supplier can meet this requirement and that a price increase will also be necessary. In the meantime, assembly at Acme will be at a standstill.

Questions

1 How might Acme have improved its quality assurance requirements?
2 What legal issues arise in respect of:
   (a) Claims by users against Acme
   (b) Claims by Acme against Elston?
3 Tabulate the costs that Acme is likely to incur as a result of the quality failure.
4 What constructive action should Acme take to:
   (a) restore the reputation of its product
   (b) obviate such happenings in the future?

? Discussion questions

7.1 Take two similar products, e.g. two different makes of car intended for the same consumer group or two washing machines, and compare them against Garvin's eight dimensions of quality. On the basis of your comparison recommend which of the two you consider gives the best value for money? What other factors apart from the eight stated might you have to consider when making your recommendation?

7.2 'Without strong supplier–customer links both internally and externally, TQM is doomed to failure.'
   (a) Can you think of four arguments to support this statement?
   (b) As managing director, what steps would you take to forge such links (i) internally, (ii) externally?

7.3 An important aspect of *Kaizen* is the creation of a quality 'culture'. One definition of culture is:

   The system of shared values, beliefs and habits within an organisation that interacts with the formal structure to produce behavioural norms.

   (a) How would you go about creating a 'quality culture'?
   (b) How may a quality culture sometimes clash with production and marketing cultures?

7.4 Deming advocated 'moving towards a single supplier for any one item'. Can you list three advantages and three disadvantages of such a policy?

7.5 Assume a product with tolerances of 0.500 ± 0.10. Further assume that if the deviation from the target exceeds 0.10 on either side the product will fail during the warranty period. From records, the cost of repairing the product under warranty is £100. Calculate the loss according to the Taguchi loss function formula.

7.6 Explain why the cost of detecting quality problems increases dramatically with the distance from the source of the problem.

7.7 Noriaki Kano identified three classes of consumer need:

(i) Dissatisfiers – those features that the product or service is *expected* to provide.

(ii) Satisfiers – the features that customers say they want

(iii) Exciters/delighters – new or innovative features that customers would not expect but which they like.

(a) In respect of a car, give two examples of each of these consumer needs?

(b) Why is it important that designers are aware of these three categories of need?

7.8 The quality of the picture on a TV varies according to the room temperature. How would Taguchi describe the TV set?

7.9 Why is it desirable for purchasing professional to have an outline knowledge of CAD and CIM?

7.10 BS 7373 categorises the typical elements relating to performance that may be included in a specification under three headings: (i) function, (ii) material and (iii) dependability. Two such elements are shown under each heading below. In each case can you identify a further *five* elements?

	Function	Material	Dependability
Examples	Capacity Efficiency Effectiveness	Elasticity Strength	Maintainability Reliability

7.11 'Every requirement increases the price.'

'If something is not specified it is unlikely to be provided.'

Why is it often difficult to reconcile these two principles that should be observed by specification writers?

7.12 Value analysis and 'creative thinking' are closely related. State, in each case, how you would counter the barriers to creative thinking quoted below:

(a) 'We always do it this way.'

(b) 'It won't work.'

(c) 'Why change it?'

(d) 'We tried that ten years ago.'

(e) 'We know more about this than anyone.'

(f) 'There is no better material.'

(g) 'We can get it anywhere else.'

(h) 'The customers like it this way.'

(i) 'We'll try it next year.'

(j) 'We don't want to upset the staff/workers/suppliers/customers/etc.'

(k) 'It may work in theory but not in practice.'

(l) 'Lower costs mean lower quality.'

7.13 Take a simple everyday product, e.g. a pen, watch, lamp, etc., and carry out a value analysis exercise.

7.14 What are the possible additional costs arising from the following:

(a) A rough casting is overspecified in respect of wall thickness.

(b) A component is specified with unnecessarily close tolerances.

7.15 For what reasons might a company seek BS or ISO registration?

7.16 Imagine that you have been unemployed for six months during which time you have failed to secure an employment interview. Attempt a cause and effect diagram relating to your problem.

7.17 Failure in respect of a certain machine has occurred after the following number of hours:

11, 6, 16, 18, 9, 22, 29, 10, 13, 20, 5, 14, 8, 12, 15, 12, 17, 11, 4, 19, 7

Prepare a histogram and state any conclusions reached.

7.18 The number of defects found in 30 samples of an assembly taken on a daily basis over one month is given below. Plot the data on a control chart and work out the average value.

6, 1, 5, 5, 3, 4, 2, 2, 6, 4, 1, 2, 1, 3, 4, 1, 4, 5, 6, 1, 12, 15, 3, 6, 3, 4, 3, 3, 5, 2, 4, 7

7.19 An alternative classification of 'effects' to those indicated in Figure 7.14 in the text is:

Category 1 – catastrophic

Category 2 – critical

Category 3 – marginal

Category 4 – minor

Attempt definitions of each category and, in respect of a motor vehicle, provide examples of each category.

7.20 The structure for quality circles has been depicted as shown below. Identify the functions that you would expect to be undertaken at each level.

Past examination questions

1 Explain the work of some of the *Quality Management* pioneers, and its relevance to the field of commercial relationships.

(CIPS, Commercial Relationships, November 1997)

2 Describe the work of three influential thinkers in relation to quality assurance.

(CIPS, Commercial Relationships, November 1998)

3 In the management of quality, the concept of zero defects is no longer considered to be a sufficiently tight creation and the trend is to move away from control and inspection towards the critical appraisal of designs and the early involvement of suppliers. Discuss some of the techniques which can be utilised in this new approach to quality management and identify the role of purchasing within the approach.

(CIPS, Purchasing and Supply Chain Management II: Tactics and Operations, November 1998)

4 Value analysis cannot be successfully implemented without the involvement of the buyer. Discuss this statement.

(CIPS, Introduction to Purchasing and Supply Chain Management, May 1999)

5 Involving the supplier at the outset of the product development cycle is referred to as Early Supplier Involvement (ESI). Explain why ESI may be desirable and identify the possible benefits of such involvement. Suggest some of the possible disadvantages of embarking upon ESI.

(CIPS, Purchasing and Supply Chain Management II: Tactics and Operations, May 1999)

6 To what extent do you consider that quality is a legitimate purchasing responsibility when specifications are devised by the design or engineering functions and manufacturing standards maintained by operations management? Assuming purchasing does have some responsibility, discuss the contributions purchasing can make towards the continuous improvement of quality and some of the means by which it can make this contribution.

(CIPS, Purchasing and Supply Chain Management II: Tactics and Operations, May 1998)

7 Explain the term *'cost of quality'* and indicate why, with reference to relevant techniques, off-line controls over quality have a greater impact on the costs of quality than on-line controls.

(CIPS, Purchasing and Supply Chain Management II: Tactics and Operations, November 1999)

8 Describe and explain the contribution purchasing can make to quality issues within an organisation.

(CIPS, Introduction to Purchasing and Supply Chain Management, May 2000)

9 There is an old saying in management which says 'if you can't measure it you can't manage it'. Discuss, with reference to relevant techniques, how this saying applies to the management of quality at the tactical and operational level.

(CIPS, Purchasing and Supply Chain Management II:
Tactics and Operations, November 2000)

Notes

1. Crosby, P.B., *Quality is Free*, Mentor Books, 1980, Ch.2, p.15
2. Juran, J.M., *Quality Control Handbook,* 3rd edn, McGraw-Hill, 1974, sec.2, p.27
3. Garvin, D.A., 'What does product quality really mean?', *Sloan Management Review*, Fall 1984, pp.25–38
4. Garvin, D.A., 'Competing in eight dimensions of quality', *Harvard Business Review*, Nov./Dec. 1987, No.6, p.101
5. Logothetis, N., *Managing Total Quality*, Prentice Hall, 1991, Ch.8, pp.216–17
6. DTI, *Total Quality Management and Effective Leadership*, 1991, p.8
7. Evans J.R., *Applied Production and Operations Management*, 4th edn, 1993, p.837
8. DTI, as n.6 above, p.10
9. Cannon, S., 'Supplying the service to the internal customer', *Purchasing and Supply Management*, April 1995, pp.32–5
10. Zaire, M., *Total Quality Management for Engineers*, Woodhead Publishing, 1991, Ch.9, p.193
11. Ibid, p.216
12. Deming, W.E., *Out of Crisis*, MIT Centre for Advanced Engineering Study, 1986, Ch.2.
13. Dowlatshahi, S., 'Purchasing's role in a concurrent engineering environment', *International Journal of Purchasing and Materials Management*, Winter 1992, pp.21–5
14. Wynstra, F., Van Weele, A. and Axelsson, B. Purchasing Involvement in Product Development, *European Journal of Purchasing*, vol.5, 1999, pp.129–41
15. Womack, J.P., Jones, D.T. and Roos, D., *The Machine that Changed the World*, Maxwell Macmillan, 1990
16. Lamming, Beyond Partnerships – Strategies for Innovation and Lean Supply, Prentice Hall 1993
17. Wynstra *et al.*, as n.14 above
18. Wynstra *et al.*, ibid.
19. Wynstra, F. and ten Pierick, E. 'Management supplier involvement in new product development', *European Journal of Purchasing and Supply Management*, vol.6, 2000, pp.49–57
20. Calvi, R., Le-Dain M.A., Harbis and Bonotta, M.V., 'How to manage early supplier involvement (ESI) into the new product development process (HPDP)', *Proceedings of the 10th International Annual IPSERA Conference*, 2001, pp.158–62
21. Ibid.
22. Lysons, K., *How to Write Specifications*, CIPS, 2001
23. British Standards Specification (BS) 7373
24. Purdy, D.C., *A Guide to Writing Successful Engineering Specifications*, McGraw-Hill, 1991
25. Central Unit on Purchasing, *Specification Writing*, CUP Guidance Note 30, 1991
26. Purdy, n.24 above

27. England, W.B., *Modern Procurement*, 5th edn. Richard D. Irwin, 1970, Ch.4, p.306
28. Haslam, J.M., *Writing Engineering Specifications*, Spon, 1988, Ch.2, p.31
29. Woodroffe, G., 'So farewell then market overt', *Purchasing and Supply Management*, February 1995, pp.16–17
30. Ashton, T.C., 'National and international standards', in Lock, D. (ed.), *Gower Handbook of Quality Management*, 2nd edn, Gower, 1994, Ch.10, pp.144–5
31. BS EN ISO 8402, 1995, p.25, sec.3.4
32. BS EN ISO 8402, 1995, pp.25–26, sec.3.5
33. Schonberger, R.J., *Building a Chain of Customers*, Free Press, 1990
34. Ibid.
35. Saunders, M., *Strategic Purchasing and Supply Chain Management*, Pitman, 1994, Ch.6, p.154
36. Ford Motor Co Ltd, *Failure Mode and Effects Analysis Handbook*, 1992, p.22
37. Ibid.
38. Dale, B.G. and Shaw, P., 'Failure mode and effects analysis: a study of the use in the motor industry', Occasional Paper 8904, University of Manchester, Institute of Science and Technology, 1990
39. Osborn, J.D., Horan, L., Musselwhile, E. and Zenger, J.N., *Self-directed Work Teams*, Business One/Irwin, 1990, Ch.1, p.8
40. Walker, D., 'Creative employment at Rover', in Henry, J. and Walker, D. (eds), *Managing Innovation*, Sage, 1991

Matching supply with demand

After reading this chapter you should be able to:

- Define the terms 'inventory' and 'inventory control'.
- State some inventory classifications.
- Compute the rate of stock-turn and define aggregate inventory value.
- List the aims of inventory management.
- Identify the factors comprising the 'right quality'.
- Distinguish between dependent and independent demand.
- Explain acquisition, holding costs and cost of stockouts.
- Describe the concept and application of ABC analysis.
- Demonstrate an understanding of variety reduction.
- Calculate economic order quantities (EOQs).
- Define the term 'lead time'.
- Forecast demand using moving and exponentially weighted averages.
- Distinguish between fixed order and periodic review stock control systems.
- List the advantages and disadvantages of fixed and periodic review systems.
- Define materials requirement planning (MRP) and the main terms used.
- Compare fixed order point and MRP systems.
- State the aims and applications of MRP.
- Define and explain manufacturing resource planning (MRP II).
- Define and explain the advantages and disadvantages of enterprise resource planning (ERP).
- Define and explain distribution requirements planning (DRP).
- Define and explain just-in-time (JIT) purchasing.
- List the benefits and possible disadvantages of JIT.
- Compare the concepts of JIT and MRP.
- Explain optimised production technology (OPT).

- Define, and describe the aims, implementation, advantages and disadvantages of, vendor-managed inventory.
- Distinguish between static and dynamic lot sizing.
- Calculate service and safety stock levels.
- Indicate some special factors relating to inventory.

The development and maturing of MRP, MRP II, JIT and VMI approaches, described in this chapter, together with the emphasis on partnership sourcing, shorter lead times and the elimination or reduction in stock levels have brought about dramatic changes in inventory management. Nevertheless every organisation has inventories of some kind and the economics and techniques of inventory management and control are still relevant.

8.1   Definitions

Inventory is an American accounting term for the value or quantity of raw materials, components, assemblies, consumables, work in progress (WIP) and finished stock that are kept or stored for use as the need arises. The term is also applied to:

- a detailed list of goods or articles in a given place, or
- a stocktaking.

Inventory (or stock) control refers to the techniques used to ensure that stocks of raw materials or other supplies, WIP and finished goods are kept at levels which provide maximum service levels at minimum costs.

8.2   Inventory classifications

The term 'supplies' has been defined as:[1]

> All the materials, goods and services used in the enterprise regardless of whether they are purchased outside, transferred from another branch of the company or manufactured in house.

The classification of supplies for inventory purposes will vary according to the particular undertaking. In a manufacturing enterprise, for example, inventory might be classified as:

- *Raw materials* – e.g. steel, timber, cloth, etc. in an unprocessed state awaiting conversion into a product.

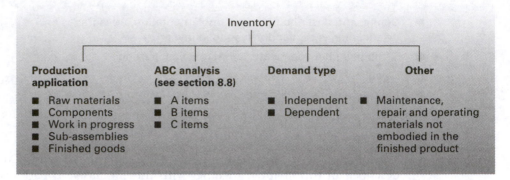

Figure 8.1 Inventory classification

- *Components and sub-assemblies* – e.g. ball bearings, gearboxes, to be incorporated into an end product.
- *Consumables* – all suppliers in an undertaking which are classified as indirect and which do not form part of a saleable product. Consumables may be sub-classified into (i) production, e.g. detergents; (ii) maintenance, e.g. lubricating oil; (iii) office, e.g. stationary; (iv) welfare, e.g. first-aid supplies, etc. These are often referred to as maintenance, repair and operating (MRO) items.
- *Finished goods* – products manufactured for resale which are ready for dispatch.

Following supply chain usage, inventory may also be classified into:

- *Primary inventory*, i.e. raw materials, components and sub-assemblies, work in progress and finished goods.
- *Support inventories*, i.e. MRO consumables of various categories.

A third classification is shown in Figure 8.1.

8.3   Inventory measures

Two important measures are (i) aggregate inventory value and (ii) rate of stock-turn.

Aggregate inventory value

Aggregate inventory value is the total value of all items of all raw materials, components, MRO, WIP and finished goods held by an organisation at a given date at cost or current market price, whichever is the less.

As an example, suppose A is a raw material that is transformed into a sub-assembly B, which after further operations becomes a finished product C. One unit of A may have a relatively small value; B will, however, be worth considerably more because of the value-adding operations expended on A. C again will have a higher value than B. If the inventory comprised only items A, B and C, the aggregate inventory value would be:

[(Number of items of item A) × (Value of each unit of A at cost)] +

[(Number of items of item B) × (Value of each unit of B at cost)] +

[(Number of items of item C) × (Value of each unit of C at cost)]

The aggregate inventory value is required to ascertain the opening and closing stocks of the annual trading or manufacturing account of a business. It also informs managers of what proportion of an organisation's current assets is tied up in inventory. If this is excessive the organisation may be short of working capital. Manufacturing organisations typically have between 20 and 30 per cent of their assets in inventory. The corresponding figure for wholesalers and retailers averages about 75 per cent.

Rate of stock-turn

Rate of stock-turn is obtained by dividing annual turnover (sales) at cost by the annual average aggregate inventory value, i.e.

$$\frac{\text{Cost of goods sold}}{1/2(\text{Value of inventory (cost) at start} + \text{Value of inventory (cost) at end})}$$

Example 8.1   Rate of stock-turn

Annual turnover = £72,000, beginning inventory = £12,000, ending inventory = £10,000. Then,

$$\text{Rate of stock turn} = \frac{£72,000}{1/2(£12,000 + £10,000)}$$

$$= \frac{£72,000}{£11,000}$$

$$= 6.5 \text{ stock turns per year}$$

What is considered a 'good stock turn' varies by the product and industry. Turnover of supermarket breakfast foods is 20–25 times that of pet foods. For a car showroom a stock-turn of 6 means that the average stock on the car changes every two months.

8.4   Aims of inventory management

The three main aims of inventory management are:

- To provide both internal and external customers with the required service levels in terms of quantity and order rate fill.

- To ascertain present and future requirements for all types of inventory to avoid both overstocking and bottlenecks in production.

- To keep costs to a minimum by variety reduction, economical lot sizes and analysis of costs incurred in obtaining and carrying inventories.

8.5 The right quantity

In manufacturing or assembly-type organisations, the most important factors that determine the right quality are as follows:

- The demand for the final product into which the bought-out materials and components are incorporated.
- The inventory policy of the undertaking.
- Whether job, batch, assembly or process production methods are applicable.
- Whether demand for the item is independent or dependent (see section 8.6 below).
- The service level, i.e. the incidence of availability required. The service level required for an item may be set at 100 per cent for items where a stockout would result in great expense through production delays or, as with some hospital supplies, where lack of supplies may endanger life. For less crucial supplies, the service level might be fixed at a lower level, e.g. 95 per cent. The actual service level attained in a given period can be computed by the formula:

$$\frac{\text{Number of times the item is provided on demand}}{\text{Number of times an item has been demanded}}$$

- Market conditions, e.g. financial, political and other considerations that determine whether requirements shall be purchased on a 'hand-to-mouth' or 'forward' basis.
- Factors determining economic order quantities (see section 8.10 below). In individual undertakings the quantity of an item to be purchased over a period may be notified to the purchasing department in several ways, as shown in Table 8.1.

8.6 Demand

Demand may be either independent or dependent. *Independent demand* for an item is influenced by market conditions and not related to production decisions for any other item held in stock. In manufacturing, only end items, i.e. the final product sold to the customer, have exclusively independent demand. *Dependent demand* for an item derives from the product decisions for its 'parents'. The term 'parent' is an item manufactured from one or more *component* items. A table, for example, is a parent made from a top, legs and fasteners. A component is one item that goes through one or more operations to be transformed into a parent.

Independent demand can only be estimated. Although fluctuating with random market influences, independent demand usually demonstrates a continuous and definable pattern. Dependent demand, on the other hand (see Figure 8.2), derives from production decisions for its parents and can therefore be forecast. Owing to the practice of scheduling manufacturing in lots, dependent demand is usually discontinuous and 'lumpy'. Entirely different production and inventory control systems are utilised according to whether demand is being forecast or dependent (derived).

Table 8.1   Purchasing and quantities

Type of purchase	Quantities indicated by
Materials or components required for a specific order or application, e.g. steel sections not normally stocked	■ Materials specifications or bill of materials for the job or contract
Standard items kept in stock for regular production, whether job, batch or continuous flow	■ Materials budgets derived from production budgets based on sales/output target for a specified period. ■ 'One-off' materials specifications or bills of materials showing quantities of each item needed to make one unit of finished product. These are then multiplied by the number of products to be manufactured ■ Materials requisitions raised by storekeeping or stock control ■ Computerised reports provided at specified intervals, e.g. daily or weekly, relating to part usage, stocks on hand, on order and committed. With some programs reordering can be carried out automatically
Consumable materials used in production, plant, maintenance or office administration, e.g. oil, paint, stationery and packing materials	■ Requisitions from stores or stock control or computerised inventory reports as above. These may be ordered directly by users against previously negotiated contracts or from purchasing consortia arrangements
Spares – these may be kept to maintain production machinery or they may be bought-out components for resale to customers who have bought the product in which the component is incorporated	■ Requisitions from sales department ■ Computerised inventory reports as above

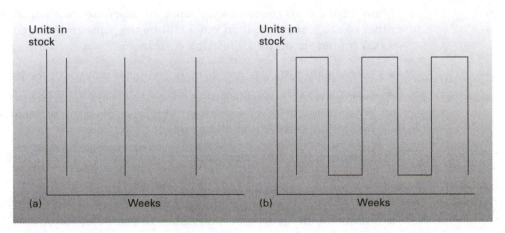

Figure 8.2   Contrast between (a) independent, continuous and (b) dependent, 'lumpy' demand (usage) patterns

Independent demand is associated with:

■ company customers
■ finished goods
■ forecast and booked customer orders
■ fixed order quantities
■ continuous and periodic review systems
■ ABC analysis
■ Economic order quantities (EOQs)

Dependent demand is associated with:

■ Parent items
■ WIP and raw materials
■ Calculated requirements
■ Materials requirement planning (MRP)
■ Distribution requirements planning (DRP)
■ Optimised production technology (OPT)

8.7 The economics of stock management

The economics of stock control are determined by an analysis of the costs incurred in obtaining and carrying inventories under the headings of acquisition costs, holding costs and costs of stockouts.

8.7.1 Acquisition costs

Many of the costs incurred in placing an order are incurred irrespective of the order size, e.g. the cost of an order will be the same irrespective of whether 1 or 1,000 tonnes are ordered. Ordering costs include:

■ preliminary costs, e.g. preparing the requisition, vendor selection, negotiation;
■ placement costs, e.g. order preparation, stationery, postage, etc.;
■ post-placement costs, e.g. progressing, receipt of goods, materials, handling, inspection, certification and payment of invoices.

In practice, it is difficult to obtain more than an approximate idea of ordering costs since these vary with:

■ the complexity of the order and the seniority of staff involved;
■ whether order preparation is manual or computerised;
■ whether repeat orders cost less than initial orders.

Sometimes the total cost of a purchasing department or function over a given period is divided by the number of orders placed in that time. This gives a completely fallacious figure since the average cost per order reduces as the number of orders placed increases, which may be indicative of inefficiency rather than the contrary.

8.7.2   Holding costs

There are two types of holding cost:

- Cost proportional to the value of the inventory, e.g.:
  - financial costs, e.g. interest on capital tied up in inventory. This may be bank rate or, more realistically, the target return on capital required by the enterprise;
  - cost of insurance;
  - losses in value through deterioration, obsolescence and pilfering.
- Cost proportional to the physical characteristics of inventory, e.g.:
  - storage costs, e.g. storage space, stores rates, light, heat and power;
  - labour costs relating to handling and inspection;
  - clerical costs relating to stores records and documentation.

8.7.3   Cost of stockouts

The costs of stockouts, e.g. the costs of being out of inventory, comprise:

- loss of production output;
- costs of idle time and of fixed overheads spread over a reduced output;
- costs of action taken to deal with the stockout, e.g. buying from a stockist at an increased price, switching production, obtaining substitute materials;
- loss of customer goodwill because of inability to supply or late delivery. Often, costs of stockouts are hidden in overhead costs. Where the costs of individual stockouts are computed these should be expressed in annual figures to ensure compatibility with acquisition and holding costs. Costs of stockouts are difficult to estimate or incorporate into inventory models.

8.8   ABC analysis

A household will buy many different items in the course of a year. The weekly shopping will include a number of basic food items such as bread, milk, vegetables, etc. These basic food items may account for the bulk of the annual expenditure in shops. Because these items are so important in the household budget it is worthwhile taking care to choose a shop that gives good value. Information about the prices charged elsewhere can be obtained from advertisements and visits to other supermarkets. In ABC analysis these basic items are known as class A items. These items merit close day-to-day control because of their budgetary importance.

Other items such as replacement rubber washers for water taps may be needed occasionally. A packet of washers costs very little – less than one pound. Spending hours comparing the price from different suppliers does not make economic sense. The possible saving is at most a few pence, and a year or more may elapse before another packet is needed. Items like this that account for only a small proportion of spending are known as class C items.

Table 8.2 ABC analysis

	Percentage of items	Percentage value of annual usage	
Class A items	About 20%	About 80%	Close day to day control
Class B items	About 30%	About 15%	Regular review
Class C items	About 50%	About 5%	Infrequent review

Class B is the set of items that is intermediate between class A and class C. They should be regularly reviewed but are not as closely controlled as class A items.

The Italian statistician Vilfredo Pareto (1848–1923) discovered a common statistical effect. About 20 per cent of the population owns 80 per cent of the nation's wealth. About 20 per cent of employees cause 80 per cent of problems. About 20 per cent of items account for 80 per cent of a firm's expenditure. The terms 'Pareto analysis' and 'ABC analysis' are used interchangeably.

Table 8.2 summarises the main points of ABC analysis. In the table the term 'usage' means the value in money terms of the stock items consumed.

Example 8.2 illustrates how items may be divided into classes A, B or C.

Example 8.2   ABC analysis

A purchasing department surveyed the ten most commonly used components last year.

Item number	101	102	103	104	105	106	107	108	109	110
Unit cost (pence)	5	11	15	8	7	16	20	4	9	12
Annual demand	48,000	2,000	300	800	4,800	1,200	18,000	300	5,000	500

Step 1   Calculate the annual usage in £ and the usage of each item as a percentage of total cost (Table 8.3).

Table 8.3   Calculation for step 1

Item number	Unit cost (pence)	Annual demand	Usage (£) $\dfrac{(Demand \times Cost)}{100}$	Usage as % of total $= \dfrac{Usage \times 100}{Total}$
101	5	48,000	2,400	32.5
102	11	2,000	220	3.0
103	15	300	45	0.6
104	8	800	64	0.9
105	7	4,800	336	4.6
106	16	1,200	192	2.6
107	20	18,000	3,600	48.8
108	4	300	12	0.2
109	9	5,000	450	6.1
110	12	500	60	0.8
Total usage			**7,379**	

Step 2 Sort the items by usage as percentage of total. Calculate the cumulative percentage and classify the items (Table 8.4).

Table 8.4 Calculation for step 2

Item number	Cumulative % of items	Unit cost (p)	Annual demand	Usage (£)	% of total	Cumulative % of total	Classification
107	10	20	18,000	36,700	48.8	48.8	A
101	20	5	48,000	2,400	32.5	81.3	A
109	30	9	5,000	450	6.1	87.4	B
105	40	7	4,800	336	4.6	92.0	B
102	50	11	2,000	220	3.0	94.9	B
106	60	16	1,200	192	2.6	97.5	B
104	70	8	800	64	0.9	98.4	C
110	80	12	500	60	0.8	99.2	C
103	90	15	300	45	0.6	99.8	C
108	100	4	300	12	0.2	100.0	C

There are 10 items, thus each item accounts for 10/100 = 10% of usage

Step 3 Report your findings (Table 8.5).

Table 8.5 Results of calculations (step 3)

Items	Percentage of items	Percentage usage	Action (%)	
A	107, 101	20	81.6	Close control
B	109, 105, 102, 106	40	16.2	Regular review
C	104, 100, 103, 108	40	2.5	Infrequent review

Step 4 Illustrate your report with a diagram if required (see Figure 8.3). The diagram is a percentage ogive and is called a Pareto diagram. This is done by plotting cumulative percentage usage against cumulative percentage items. The data needed has been extracted to Table 8.6.

Table 8.6 Data for Pareto diagram (step 4)

Item number	107	101	109	105	102	106	104	110	103	108
Cumulative % items	10%	20.0%	30.0%	40.0%	50.0%	60.0%	70.0%	80.0%	90.0%	100.0%
Cumulative % usage	48.8%	81.3%	87.4%	92.0%	94.9%	97.5%	98.4%	99.2%	99.8%	100.0%
Classification	A	A	B	B	B	B	C	C	C	C

In a real firm there may be hundreds of items used each year. A computer package may be used to determine the percentage of annual usage for which each item accounts. The package can be used to sort the items into order.

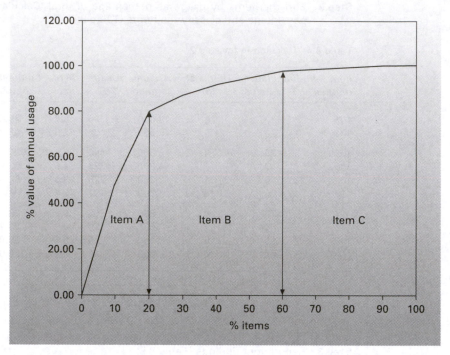

Figure 8.3   Pareto curve

The boundary between class A and class B might not be as sharply defined as in Example 8.2. The purchasing manager may need to use judgement in deciding where the class boundaries should be drawn.

The purpose of this classification is to ensure that purchasing staff use resources to maximum efficiency by concentrating on those items that have the greatest potential savings. Selective control will be more effective than an approach that treats all items identically.

8.9   Variety reduction

Variety reduction can make substantial savings in inventory by standardising and rationalising the range of materials, parts and consumables kept in stock. Variety reduction can be proactive or reactive.

Proactive variety reduction can be achieved by using, so far as possible, standardised components and sub-assemblies to make end products that are dissimilar in appearance and performance so that a variety of final products use only a few basic components. Proactive approaches to variety reduction can also apply when considering capital purchases. By ensuring compatibility with existing machinery the range of spares carried to insure against breakdowns can be substantially reduced.

Reactive variety reduction can be undertaken periodically by a special project team comprising all interested parties who examine a range of stock items to determine:

- the use for which each item of stock is intended;
- how many stock items serve the same purpose;
- the extent to which items having the same purpose can be given a standard description;
- what range of sizes is essential;
- how frequently each item in the range is used;
- what items can be eliminated;
- to what extent can sizes, dimensions, quality and other characteristics of an item be standardised;
- what items of stock are now obsolete and unlikely to be required in the future.

The advantages of variety reduction include:

- reduction of stock holding costs;
- release of money tied up in stocks;
- easier specifications when ordering;
- narrower range of inventory;
- a reduced supplier base.

8.10 Economic order quantity

8.10.1 Definition

The economic order quantity (EOQ) is the optimal ordering quantity for an item of stock that minimises cost.

To calculate the EOQ a mathematical model of reality must be constructed. All mathematical models make assumptions that simplify reality. The model is valid only when the assumptions are true or nearly true. When an assumption is modified or deleted, a new model must be constructed.

8.10.2 Basic model

The basic (or simple) model makes the following assumptions:

1 Demand is uniform, i.e. certain, constant and continuous over time.
2 The lead time is constant and certain.
3 There is no limit on order size due either to stores capacity or to other constraints.
4 The cost of placing an order is independent of size of order. The delivery charge is also independent of the quantity ordered.
5 The cost of holding a unit of stock does not depend on the quantity in stock.
6 All prices are constant and certain. There are no bulk purchase discounts.
7 Exactly the same quantity is ordered each time that a purchase is made.

Example 8.3 Economic order quantity

An undertaking has an annual requirement of 6,000 units of component. Each component cost £2.00. Ordering costs £15.00 per order. The cost of holding one unit for a year is £0.10. There are no bulk discounts and the price of the item is constant. Because of this, price is not included in the analysis.

The undertaking currently places two orders per year. Calculate the total cost of placing orders and holding stock.

Solution
The cost of placing orders is 2 × £15.00 = £30.00.
The holding costs are the average number of units in stock × £0.10.

Since the demand is uniform, a graph of the stock level against time can be drawn.

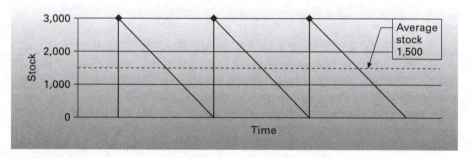

The graph shows that, in this ideal case, stock levels fall from a maximum of 3,000 immediately after a delivery to a minimum of zero immediately before the next delivery. This is only possible because the lead time is certain and mathematically precise.

The average stock is 1,500 or half the maximum stock level 3,000.
The holding costs are thus 1,500 × £0.10 = £150.00.

The total cost of ordering and holding this item is thus

£30.00 + £150.00 = £180.00

8.10.3 Optimum order quantity

To determine the optimum order quantity a number of other possible order quantities should be tried. This is shown in the Table 8.7 for the data given in Example 8.3.

The calculations shown in Table 8.7 indicate that the EOQ is between 1,500 and 1,200 units. A more precise estimate may be found by drawing a graph as in Figure 8.4. The graph shows that the minimum total cost occurs when holding and ordering costs are equal. The graph also shows that the EOQ is just under 1,400.

8.10.4 Algebraic formula for EOQ

The 'trial and error' and graphical methods used above involve a lot of work. An algebraic formula can be used which makes calculating the EOQ much easier:

Table 8.7 Economic order quantities

Number of orders per year	Quantity ordered (units)	Average stock (units)	Cost of ordering (£)	Holding cost (£)	Total cost (£)
1	6,000	3,000	15.00	300.00	315.00
2	3,000	1,500	30.00	150.00	180.00
3	2,000	1,000	45.00	100.00	145.00
4	1,500	750	60.00	75.00	135.00
5	1,200	600	75.00	60.00	135.00
6	1,000	500	90.00	50.00	140.00
7	857	428	105.00	42.80	147.80
8	750	375	120.00	27.50	157.50
9	667	333	135.00	33.30	168.30
10	600	300	150.00	30.00	180.00

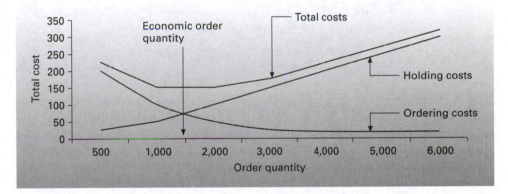

Figure 8.4 Ordering and holding costs

$$EOQ = \sqrt{\frac{2ca}{h}}$$

where:

  c = acquisition cost per order

  a = annual usage in units

  h = holding cost per unit per year

In examination questions, the holding cost is sometimes given as a percentage of the price of a unit. For example, if the holding cost is 5 per cent and the price of a unit is £8.00 then

$$h = \frac{£8.00}{100} \times 5 = £0.40$$

The derivation of the formula for EOQ is shown next. This may be omitted if you are not preparing for a mathematical examination.

1   *Ordering costs*

The number of orders placed each year is expressed as:

$$\frac{\text{Annual usage in units}}{\text{Order quantity in units}} = \frac{a}{q}$$

The ordering costs are:

$$\text{Cost of placing an order} \times \text{Number of orders} = c\left(\frac{a}{q}\right) = \frac{ac}{q}$$

2   *Holding costs*

The average stock level is half the order quantity, i.e. $q/2$.
   The holding costs are:

$$\text{Average stock level} \times \text{Holding cost} = \left(\frac{q}{2}\right)h = \frac{hq}{2}$$

3   *Total cost*

Total cost = Holding cost + Ordering costs

$$\Rightarrow T = \frac{hq}{2} + \frac{ac}{2}$$

4   *Minimum cost*

T will be maximised or minimised when $\partial T/\partial q = 0$.

$$\frac{\partial T}{\partial q} = \frac{h}{2} - \frac{ac}{q^2}$$

$$\frac{\partial T}{\partial q} = 0 \Rightarrow \frac{h}{2} - \frac{ac}{q^2} = 0$$

$$\Rightarrow hq^2 = -2ac \text{ on cross-multiplying}$$

$$\Rightarrow q^2 = -\frac{2ac}{h}$$

$$\Rightarrow q^2 = \sqrt{\frac{-2ac}{h}}$$

Since q cannot be negative only the positive square root is used. The second derivative is positive at a minimum and negative at a maximum.

$$\frac{\partial^2 T}{\partial q^2} = 0 = \frac{2ac}{q^3}$$

This is a positive since q, a and c are all positive. Thus the total cost is a minimum when:

$$\text{EOQ} = q = \sqrt{\frac{2ca}{h}}$$

To check that this formula works, apply it to the problem solved by 'trial and error' and by graph. In this problem $a = 6{,}000$, $c = 15$, $h = 0.10$. Hence:

$$EOQ = q = \sqrt{\frac{2ca}{h}}$$

$$= \sqrt{\frac{(2)(15)(6,000)}{0.01}}$$

$$= \sqrt{\frac{180,000}{0.1}}$$

$$= \sqrt{1,800,000} = 1,342$$

This agrees with the previous estimates of between 1,200 and 1,500 by trial and error and also with a value of under 1,400 by graph.

8.11   Quantity discount model

A quantity discount is simply a reduced price (p) for the item that is purchased in larger quantities.

Example 8.4   Quantity discount model

Assume an annual usage a of 10,000 units. The price per unit is shown in the table below. The holding cost h is 20 per cent of the price of a unit. Delivery and ordering costs are £50.00 per order. What is the optimum order quantity?

Quantities	Discount price per item (£)
0–999	10.00
1,000–1,999	9.80
2,000 or more	9.75

Solution
Two assumptions of the basic model are no longer valid.

- All prices are not constant and certain. There are bulk purchase discounts.
- The cost of holding a unit of stock depends on the quantity in stock. There is indirect dependence since the holding cost depends on price, price depends on order quantity, and order quantity affects stock levels.

The basic EOQ model needs to be modified. The quantity to be minimised is

Total cost = Purchase costs + Holding costs + Ordering costs

A graphical approach is shown in Figure 8.5. It is evident from the graph that the total cost drops from about £101,500 to about £99,500 when the order quantity is 1,000 and this is the lowest total cost.
    To check that an order quantity of 1,000 minimises total cost, solve the problem algebraically. This is shown in Table 8.7.

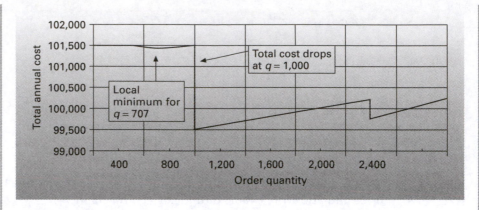

Figure 8.5　Total cost

Table 8.7　Calculation of order quantity

Order quantity, q	Price	Holding cost per unit, h	Optimum order quantity	Annual cost (£)	
Under 999	10.00	2.00	$EOQ = \sqrt{2ca/h}$ $= \sqrt{\dfrac{2 \times 50 \times 10{,}000}{2.00}}$ $= 707$	Holding Ordering Purchase **Total**	707.00 707.21 100,000.00 **101,414.21**
				Order quantity 707	
			$EOQ = \sqrt{2ca/h}$ $= \sqrt{\dfrac{2 \times 50 \times 10{,}000}{1.96}}$ $= 714$	Holding Ordering Purchase **Total**	980.00 500.00 98,000.00 **99,480.00**
1,000–1,999	9.80	1.96	■ This is outside the range of allowed order quantities at this price ■ Choose the order quantity nearest to the EOQ and within the allowed range, i.e. 1,000	Order quantity 1,000	
			$EOQ = \sqrt{2ca/h}$ $= \sqrt{\dfrac{2 \times 50 \times 10{,}000}{1.95}}$ $= 716$	Holding Ordering Purchase **Total**	1,950.00 250.00 97,500.00 **99,700.00**
Over 2,000	9.75	1.95	■ This is outside the range of allowed order quantities at this price ■ Choose the order quantity nearest to the EOQ and within the allowed range, i.e. 2,000	Order quantity 2,000	

The figures in the annual cost column of Table 8.7 are calculated as follows:

Holding $= \frac{1}{2}qh$ e.g. $\frac{1}{2}(707)(2.0) = 707.0$

Ordering $= \frac{ca}{h}$ e.g. $\frac{(50,000)(10,000)}{707} = 707.21$

Purchase = Price × a   e.g. $10.00 \times 10,000 = 100,000.00$

The minimum annual cost is £99,480.00. This is obtained when the order quantity is 1,000 and the price £9.80.

8.12   Lead time

Lead time is the period taken to obtain a requirement from the time the need is ascertained to its fulfilment. It comprises the following operations:

1   preparation of requisitions
2   forwarding of requisition to purchasing
3   processing by purchasing from enquiry to preparation of the order
4   transmission of order to supplier
5   execution of order by supplier
6   transportation of order
7   receipt, inspection and storage
8   issue to production or sales

Not all delays are attributable to suppliers since lead time is longer than delivery time. Steps 1, 2, 3 and 7 are controllable by the purchaser and can be improved by efficient clerical or computerised procedures, including electronic data interchange (EDI), vendor appraisal and specification of the most rapid method of transport.

It is important to recognise that consistency of lead time is more important than its actual length. Even with MRP and JIT techniques, events such as stoppage of delivery dates or receipt of defective materials require constant scrutiny to ensure that suppliers maintain consistency. In uncertain conditions it may be necessary to maintain safety stocks.

8.13   Forecasting demand

Before an effective system of inventory control can be implemented it is essential to analyse from records of usage what has been the trend of demand for a given item of stock over an approximate period of time with a view to forecasting future requirements. The two most common approaches are the use of moving averages and of exponentially weighted averages. These methods can be used in respect of any type of purchase and are not necessarily confined to stock.

8.13.1 Moving averages

A moving average is an artificially constructed time series in which each annual (or monthly, daily etc.) figure is replaced by the average or mean of itself and values corresponding to a number of preceding and succeeding periods.

Example 8.5   Moving averages

The usage of a stock item for six successive periods was 90, 84, 100, 108, 116 and 127. If a five-period moving average is required, the first term will be:

$$\frac{90 + 84 + 100 + 108 + 116}{5} = 99.6$$

The average for the second term is:

$$\frac{84 + 100 + 108 + 116 + 127}{5} = 107$$

At each step, one term of the original series is dropped and another introduced. The averages, as calculated for each period, will then be plotted on a graph. There is no precise rule about the number of periods to use when calculating a moving average. The most suitable, obtained by trial and error, is that which best smooths out fluctuations. A useful guide is to assess the number of periods between consecutive peaks and troughs and use this.

8.13.2 Exponentially weighted average method (EWAM)

The moving average method has been largely discarded for inventory applications since it has a number of disadvantages:

- It requires a large number of separate calculations.
- A true forecast cannot be made until the required number of time periods have lapsed.
- All data are equally weighted, but in practice, the older the demand data, the less relevant it becomes in forecasting future requirements.
- The sensitivity of a moving average is inversely proportional to the number of data values included in the average.

These difficulties are overcome by using a series of weights with decreasing values which converge at infinity to produce a total sum of 1. Such series, known as an exponential series, take the form of:

$$a + a(1 - a) + a(1 - a)^2 + a(1 - a)^3 + \ldots = 1$$

where a is a constant between 0 and 1.

In practice, the values of 0.1 and 0.2 are most frequently used. Where a small value such as 0.1 is chosen as the constant, the response, based on the average of a considerable number of past periods, will be slow and gradual. A high value, i.e. $a = 0.5$, will result in 'nervous' estimates responding quickly to actual changes. With exponential smoothing all that is necessary is to adjust the previous forecast by a fraction of the difference between the old forecast and the actual demand for the pervious period, i.e. the new average forecast is:

a(Actual demand) + $(1 - a)$(Previous average forecast)

Example 8.6   Exponentially weighted average

The actual demand for a stock item during the month of January was 300 against a forecast of 280. Assuming a weighting of 0.2, what will be the average demand forecast for February?

Solution

$$0.2(300) + (1 - 0.2)(280) = 60 + 224$$

Forecast for February = 284. By subtracting the average computed for the previous month from that calculated for the current month we obtain the trend of demand.

8.14   Fixed order point and period review systems

Most methods of stock control fall into two main categories: fixed order point systems and periodic review (reorder cycle) systems.

8.14.1   Fixed order point system

This is also known as *continuous review system* or *reorder point system*. It is also termed a two-bin system owing to the fact that this approach provided a simple, non-mathematical approach to checking inventory. Under the two-bin system the stock of a particular item is segregated into two bins. Stock is initially taken from the first bin. The reorder level, when the storekeeper issues a requisition for new supplies, is when that bin becomes empty. The purchase order is therefore a fixed quantity (which can be based on EOQ).

In practice, reviews are made frequently, i.e. on a daily basis rather than upon each withdrawal.

Example 8.7 illustrates how the most important control levels are calculated.

In practice it may also be necessary to take into account items already allocated to back orders and scheduled receipts from orders already placed but not yet

Example 8.7 Calculation of control levels

We have the following data:

Normal usage:	120 items per day
Minimum usage:	60 items per day
Maximum usage:	150 items per day
Lead time:	25/20 days
EOQ (already calculated)	5,500 items

The control levels are calculated as:

1 *Reorder level*

$$\text{Reorder level} = \text{Maximum usage} \times \text{Maximum lead time}$$
$$= 150 \times 30$$
$$= 4,500 \text{ items}$$

2 *Safety or buffer level*

$$\text{Safety level} = \text{Reorder level} - \text{Average use in maximum lead time}$$
$$= 4,500 - (120 \times 30)$$
$$= 900 \text{ items}$$

3 *Minimum level*

$$\text{Minimum level} = \text{Reorder level} - \text{Average use for average lead time}$$
$$= 4,500 - (120 \times 27.5)$$
$$= 4,500 - 300$$
$$= 1,200 \text{ items}$$

4 *Maximum level*

$$\text{Maximum level} = \text{Reorder level} + \text{EOQ} - \text{Minimum anticipated usage in lead time}$$
$$= 4,500 + 5,500 - (60 \times 25)$$
$$= 10,000 - 1,500$$
$$= 8,500 \text{ items}$$

Example 8.8 Calculation of inventory position

Given the following information:

Inventory on hand OH = 20 units
Reorder point R = 200 units
There are no back orders BO = 0

There is one open order for 400 units

should a new order be placed?

Solution

$$\text{IP} = \text{OH} + \text{SR} - \text{BO}$$
$$= 20 + 400 - 0$$
$$= 420$$

As IP *exceeds* R (420 vs 200), it is not necessary to reorder.

delivered. The inventory position (IP), i.e. the item's ability to satisfy future demand relying only on future receipts, can be calculated by the formula:

$$IP = OH + SR - BO$$

where: IP = the inventory position of the item (in units)

OH = the number of units in on-hand inventory

SR = scheduled receipts (open orders)

BO = number of units either back ordered or allocated

8.14.2   Periodic review system

As the name implies, in this system an item's inventory position is reviewed periodically rather than at a fixed order point. The periods or intervals at which stock levels are reviewed will depend on the importance of the stock item and the costs of holding that item. A variable quantity will be ordered at each review to bring the stock level back to maximum (hence the system is sometimes called the topping-up system).

Maximum stock can be determined by adding one review period to the lead time, multiplying the sum by the average rate of usage and adding any safety stock. This can be expressed as:

$$M - W(T + L) + S$$

where: M = predetermined stock level

W = average rate of stock usage

T = review period

L = lead time

S = safety stock

Safety stock may be calculated in a similar manner to that indicated for the fixed order-point system.

Example 8.9   Periodic review system

Assume an average rate of usage 120 items per day.

Review period:	4 weeks (say, 20 days)
Lead time:	25/30 days
Safety stock:	900 items

$$M = 120(20 + 30) + 900 = 6,900 \text{ items}$$

If, at the first review period, the stock was 400 items, an order would be placed for 2,900 items, i.e. 6,900 maximum stock minus actual stock at the review date.

8.14.3   Advantages and disadvantages of fixed order point and periodic review systems

Fixed order point

Advantages

■ On average, stocks are lower than with the periodic review system.

■ EOQs are applicable.

- Enhanced responsiveness to demand fluctuations.
- Replenishment orders are automatically generated at the appropriate time by comparison of actual stock levels against reorder levels.
- Appropriate for widely differing inventory categories.

Disadvantages

- The reordering system may become overloaded if many items of inventory reach reorder level simultaneously.
- Random reordering pattern due to items coming up for replenishment at different times.

Periodic review

Advantages

- Greater chance of elimination of obsolete items owing to periodic review of stock.
- The purchasing load may be spread more evenly with possible economies in placing of orders.
- Large quantity discounts may be negotiated when a range of stock items are ordered from the same supplier at the same time.
- Production economies due to more efficient production planning and lower set-up costs may result from orders always being in the same sequence.

Disadvantages

- On average, larger stocks are required than with fixed order point systems since reorder quantities must provide for the period between reviews as well as between lead times.
- Reorder quantities are not based on EOQs.
- If the usage rate changes shortly after a review period, a stockout may occur before the next review date.
- Difficulties in determining appropriate review period unless demands are reasonably consistent.

8.14.4 Choice of systems

- A fixed order point system is more appropriate if a stock item is used regularly and does not conform to the conditions below.
- A periodic review system is most likely to be appropriate if orders are placed with and delivered from suppliers at regular intervals (e.g. daily, monthly) or a number of different items are ordered items from and delivered by the same supplier at the same time.

8.15 Materials requirement planning

8.15.1 Definition

Materials requirement planning (MRP) is a product-oriented computerised technique aimed at minimising inventory and maintaining delivery schedules. It relates the dependent requirements for the materials and components comprising an end product to time periods known as 'buckets' over a planned horizon (typically of one year) on the basis of forecasts provided by marketing and sales and other input information.

8.15.2 Comparison of fixed order point and MRP systems

A comparison of the two systems is made in Table 8.9.

8.15.3 MRP terminology

- *Bills of materials* or BOM contain information on all materials, components and sub-assemblies required to produce each end item.
- An *end item* or master scheduled item is, as stated in section 8.6, the final product sold to the customer. Inventory for end items from the accounting standpoint will either be work in progress or finished goods.

Table 8.9 Comparison of fixed order point and MRP systems

Stock replenishment systems	MRP systems
1. Assumes that demand for an item is independent, i.e. unrelated to other inventory items	Based on the recognition that demand for an item may be dependent, i.e. related to the demand for other inventory items
2. Deriving from 1 above, the emphasis is on the individual part	Deriving from 1 above, the emphasis is on the end product into which related parts are incorporated
3. Assumes average usage rates with gradual depletion of inventory until it is replenished by the next delivery	Recognises that usage rates may be erratic or 'lumpy' depending on demand for the end product.
4. Quantities required are specified on the basis of historical demand	Quantities required are specified on the basis of future demand
5. Demand for inventory items is forecast	Demand for inventory items is not forecast but precisely determined from the master production schedule for the end product
6. Orders placed when triggered by a reorder point signal using data relating to the costs of ordering and stocking	Orders for items placed when triggered by a time-based signal. Time phasing uses a lead time information and need dates
7. Safety stocks are maintained for all inventory items	Safety stocks are in theory maintained only in respect of the end product. Factors such as stoppage of delivery dates or defective material may, in practice, necessitate safety stocks in some cases

- A *parent*, also referred to in section 8.6, is an item manufactured from one or more component items.
- A *component item* is an item that goes through one or more operations to be transformed into a parent.
- An *intermediate item* is one that has at least one parent and one component. Intermediate items are classified as work in progress.
- A *sub-assembly* since it is 'put together', as distinct from other means of transformation, is a special case of intermediate item.
- A *purchased item* is one that has no components because it comes from a supplier but has one or more parents. For accounting purposes, inventory of purchased items is regarded as raw materials.
- *Part commonality* is the extent to which a component (part) has one or more parents. This concept is related to standardisation. Thus a standard ball bearing may have numerous parents.
- *Usage quantity* relates to the number of units of a component required to make one unit of its parent.
- A *bucket* is a time period to which MRP relates, e.g. one week.

8.15.4 Applications of MRP

While having elements common to all inventory situations, MRP is most applicable where:

- the demand for items is dependent;
- the demand is discontinuous, i.e. 'lumpy' and non-uniform;
- in job, batch and assembly or flow production, or where all three manufacturing methods are used.

8.15.5 The aims of MRP

- To synchronise ordering and delivery of materials and components with production requirements.
- To achieve planned and controlled inventories and ensure that required items are available at the time of usage or not much earlier.
- To promote planning between the purchaser and the supplier to the advantage of each. The forward projection of orders, for example, can assist suppliers to reduce lead time and production costs and minimise the inventory costs of the purchaser.
- To enable rapid action to be taken to overcome material or component shortages due to emergencies, late delivery, etc.

A simple example of the synchronising aims of MRP may be given. Suppose an end product X is assembled from four components, A, B, C, D, which are requisitioned on a reorder-point system using safety stocks on the basis of providing a 90 per cent 'off-the-shelf' service level. Product X clearly cannot be assembled without all four components being available. Each component will be available

90 per cent of the time, but not the same 90 per cent. The probability of all four items being available simultaneously is:

$$0.9 \times 0.9 \times 0.9 \times 0.9 = (0.9)^4 = 66\%$$

In other words, for 34 per cent of the time there will be a shortage. Items of inventory will, therefore, be in stock which have to be paid for and incur loss of interest and possibly losses through pilferage, etc. To raise the service level we would have to have a heavier investment in safety stocks.

MRP aims to ensure that items are available when wanted and not before, and in this way to minimise inventory and maintain delivery schedules.

8.15.6 MRP inputs and outputs

The inputs and outputs of an MRP system are shown in Figure 8.6.

Figure 8.6 may be explained as follows:

1 *Forecasts* of demand for the end product will be provided by the marketing function. The overall demand for the materials or components comprising the end product will be augmented by orders for spares and other orders not related to the regular production plan which will have to be treated as additions to the forecast production requirements.

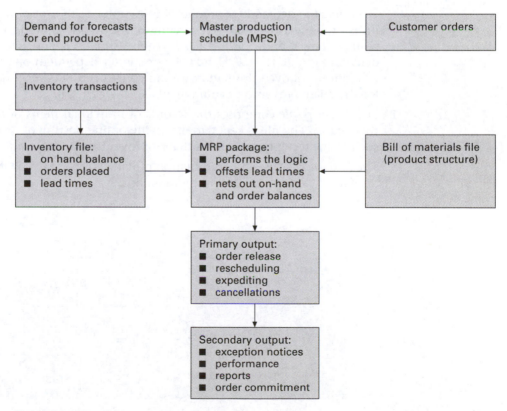

Figure 8.6 Materials requirement planning

Week	1	2	3	4	5	6	
Product X	30		14		10	8	Time buckets
Product Y		38	13	30	13	13	Time horizon

Figure 8.7 Master production schedule

2 The *master production schedule(s)* (MPS) uses the inputs from marketing and sales to forecast demand for quantities of the final product over a planned time horizon subdivided into periods known as 'time buckets' (see Figure 8.7). These buckets are not necessarily of equal duration. Without the MPS(s), MRP cannot generate requirements for any item.

3 The *bill of materials file* (BOM), also known as the product structure, lists all the items that comprise each assembly and sub-assembly that make up the final product or end item. Each BOM is given a level code according to the following logic:

Level 0 The final product or end item not used as a component of any other product

Level 1 Direct component of a level 0 item

Level 2 Direct component of a level 1 item

Level n Direct component of a level $(n-1)$ item

Assume the demand for product X is 30 units. Each unit of X requires three units of A and two of B. Each A requires one C, one D, and three Es. Each B requires one E and one F. Each F requires three Gs and two Cs. Thus the demand for A, B, C, D, E, F and G is completely dependent on the demand for X. From the above information we can construct a BOM or product structure for the related inventory requirements as in Figure 8.8.

4 The *inventory file* comprises the records of individual items of inventory and their status. The file is kept current by the online posting of inventory events such as the receipt and issue of items of inventory or their return to store.

5 The *MRP package* uses the information provided by the MPS, BOM and inventory files to perform the following functions:

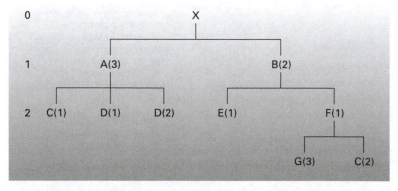

Figure 8.8 Product structure for X

(a) Explode or cascade the end product into its various assemblies, sub-assemblies or components at various levels. Thus the number of units of each item needed to produce 30 units of product X would be:

Part A = 3 × no. of Xs	(3)(30)	= 90
Part B = 2 × no. of Xs	(2)(30)	= 60
Part C = 1 × no. of As + 2 × no. of Fs	(1)(90)+(2)(60)	= 210
Part D = 1 × no. of As	(1)(90)	= 90
Part E = 3 × no. of As + 1 × no. of Bs	(3)(90)+(1)(60)	= 330
Part F = 1 × no. of Bs	(1)(60)	= 60
Part G = 3 × no. of Fs	(3)(60)	= 180

Thus to produce 30 units of X we shall need 90 units of A, 60 units of B, 210 units of C, 90 units of D, 330 units of E, 60 units of F and 180 units of G.

(b) Offset for lead time. Lead times for each item must be fed into the system. Subtracting the lead time from the date of the net requirement so as to position the planned order release date in advance of the timing of the net requirement it covers is called 'offsetting the lead time'.

(c) Net out on-hand and on-order balances using the following equation:

$$\text{Net requirements} = \underbrace{\text{Gross requirements}}_{\text{Total requirements}} - \underbrace{\text{Inventory on hand} + \text{Units on order}}_{\text{Available inventory}}$$

In an MRP system net requirement quantities are always related to some date or period, i.e. they are time phased (as shown by Figure 8.7). The primary outputs of the MRP system are:

(a) Order release instructions for the placement of planned (i.e. future) production or purchasing orders.

(b) Rescheduling instructions notifying the need to advance or postpone open orders to adjust inventory coverage to net requirements.

(c) Expediting instructions in respect of overdue orders.

(d) Cancellation or suspension instructions in respect of open orders.

MRP systems have also the capacity to produce much secondary data.

8.15.7 Manufacturing resource planning (MRP II)

What is known as MRP II has wider implications than materials planning outlined in the above description of MRP. MRP II is concerned with virtually any resource entering into production, including manpower, machines and money in addition to materials. For this reason the word 'resource' is usually substituted for 'requirement' when referring to MRP II.

MRP II is a *closed loop* system. In a closed loop system there is automatic feedback from the manufacturing or production functions to the ultimate production plan or master production schedule, followed by the automatic adjustment of the input to correct or modify the system.

Manufacturing resource planning has been defined by the American Production and Inventory Control Society as:

A system built around materials requirements planning and also including the additional planning functions of production planning, master production scheduling and capacity requirements planning.

Further, once the planning phase is complete and the plans have been accepted as attainable, the execution functions come into play. These include the shopfloor control functions of input/output measurements, detailing scheduling and dispatching, plus anticipated delay reports from both the shop and the vendors, purchasing, follow-up and control, etc. The term 'closed loop' implies not only that each of these elements is included in the overall system but also that there is feedback from the execution functions so that the planning can be kept valid at all times.

Both MRP and MRP II have many detailed aspects which cannot be covered in this book. Readers seeking further information should refer to specialist texts.

8.16   Enterprise resource planning

8.16.1   What is ERP?

Enterprise resource planning (ERP) is the latest and possibly the most significant development of MRP and MRPII. While MRP allowed manufacturers to track supplies, work in progress and the output of finished goods to meet sales orders, ERP is applicable to all organisations and allows managers from all functions or departments to have a consolidated view of what is, or is not taking place throughout the enterprise. Most ERP systems are designed around a number of modules each of which can be stand-alone or combined with others.

- *Finance*. This module tracks financial information such as accounts receivable and payable, pay role and other financial and management accounting information throughout the enterprise.
- *Logistics*. This module is often further broken down into sub-modules covering inventory and warehouse management, and transportation.
- *Manufacturing*. This module tracks the flow of orders or products including MRP and the progress and coordination of manufacturing.
- *Supplier Management*. This module tracks the purchasing process from requisitioning to the payment of suppliers and monitors delivery of supplies and supplier performance.
- *Human resources*. This module covers many human resource management activities including planning, training and job allocation.

ERP can be defined as:

A business management system that, supported by multi-module application software integrates all the departments of functions of an enterprise.

Initially ERP systems were enterprise-centric. The development of the Internet and e-business has, however, made the sharing of accurate real time information

Table 8.10   Differences between ERP and ERPII

Factor	ERP	ERPII
Role	Concerned with optimising within an enterprise	Concerned with optimising across the whole supply chain through collaboration with business partners
Domain	Focused on manufacturing and distribution	Cross all sectors and segments of business including service industries, government and asset-based industries such as mining
Function	General applications	Designed to meet the needs of specific industries thereby providing steep functionality for users
Process	Internally focused	Externally focused, especially on connecting trading partners irrespective of location
Architecture	Monolithic and closed	Web-based and open to integrate and inter-operate with other systems. Built round modules or components that allow users to choose the functionality they require
Data	Information on ERP systems is generated and consumed within the enterprise	Information available across the whole supply chain to authorised participants

across the whole supply chain essential to business success. Gartner, the consultancy that coined the term ERP, now uses ERPII to refer to systems that facilitate collaborative commerce or c-commerce in which a key requirement is the sharing of information outside the enterprise. Some differences between ERP and ERPII are shown in Table 8.10.[2]

8.16.2   The advantages of ERP

These are summarised by Kampf:[3]

- *Faster inventory turnover*. Manufacturers and distributors may increase inventory turns by tenfold and reduce inventory costs by 10 per cent to 40 per cent.

- *Improved customer service*. In many cases an ERP system can increase fill rates to 80 per cent or 90 per cent by providing the right product in the right place at the right time thus increasing customer satisfaction.

- *Better inventory accuracy, fewer audits*. An ERP system can increase inventory accuracy to more than 90 per cent while reducing the need for fewer physical inventory audits.

- *Reduced set up times*. ERP can reduce set up time by 25 per cent to 80 per cent by grouping similar production jobs together ensuring coordination of people, tools and machinery together with the efficient use of equipment and minimising downtime through efficient maintenance.

- *Higher quality work*. ERP software with a strong manufacturing component proactively pinpoints quality issues providing the information required to increase production efficiency and reduce or eliminate re-work.

■ *Timely revenue collection and improved cash flow.* ERP gives manufacturers the power to proactively examine accounts receivable before problems occur instead of just reacting. This improves cash-flow.

8.16.3 The disadvantages of ERP

■ *ERP implementation is difficult.* This is because implementation involves a fundamental change from a functional to a process approach to business.

■ *ERP systems are expensive.* This is especially so when the customisation of standard modules to accommodate different business processes is involved. It has been estimated that some 50 per cent of ERP implementations fail to deliver the anticipated benefits. The cost is often prohibitive for small enterprises.

■ *Cost of training employees to use ERP systems can be high.*

■ *There may be a number of unintended consequences* such as employee stress, and resistance to change and the sharing of information that was closely guarded by departments or functions.

■ *ERP systems tend to focus on operational decisions* and have relatively weak analytical capabilities. This topic is briefly dealt with below.

8.16.4 Supply chain management systems

While ERP systems can provide a great deal of planning capability the various material, capacity and demand constraints are all considered separately in relative isolation from each other. Further ERP systems have many tasks to fulfil. Analytical Supply Chain Management systems, however, can consider all relevant factors simultaneously and perform real time adjustments in the relevant constraints. Thus while getting decisions or information from an overloaded ERP system can take hours a separate SCM may provide the required answers in minutes. SCM systems such as 1.2 Technologies and Manugistics usually span all the supply chain stages and have the analytical capabilities to produce planning solutions and strategic level conditions. Analytical systems do, however, rely on legacy systems or ERP systems to provide the information on which the analysis is based. Because of this there is currently a rapid convergence between ERP and SCM software.

8.17 Distribution requirements planning

8.17.1 Definitions

Distribution requirements planning (DRP) is an inventory control and scheduling technique that applies MRP principles to distribution inventories. It may also be regarded as a method of handling stock replenishment in a multi-echelon environment. An echelon is defined by *Chamber's Dictionary* as: 'A stepwise arrangement of troops, ships, planes, etc.' Applied to distribution the term 'multi-echelon' means that instead of independent control of the same item at different distribution points using EOQ formulae, the dependent demand at a higher

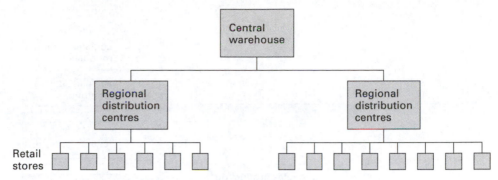

Figure 8.9 A supermarket multi-echelon distribution system

echelon (e.g. a central warehouse) is derived from the requirements of lower echelons (e.g. regional warehouses). DRP is useful for both manufacturing organisations, such as car manufacturers that sell their cars through several distribution points, e.g. regional and local distributors, and purely merchandising organisations, e.g. supermarkets (see Figure 8.9).

All levels in a DRP multi-echelon structure are dependent except for the level that serves the customer, i.e. the retailers in the above illustration.

8.17.2 DRP and MRP

DRP has been described as the mirror image of MRP. Some of the contrasts between the two approaches are set out in Table 8.11.

MRP and DRP approaches have, however many common aspects:

- As planning systems, neither uses a fixed or periodic review approach.
- Both are computerised systems.
- Just as MRP has been expanded into MRP II so DRP has been expanded into DRP II (distribution resource planning).
- DRP utilises record formats and processing logic consistent with MRP.

The last point is the most important since it provides the basis for integrating the database throughout the whole supply chain from purchasing through to distribution. Both MRP and DRP therefore contribute to a logistics system as shown in Figure 8.10.

Table 8.11 Comparison of MRP and DRP

MRP	DRP
■ Bills of materials apply time-phased logic to components and sub-assemblies to products in the management of materials (MOM) network	■ Bills of distribution (the network) use time-phased order point logic to determine network replenishment requirements
■ An 'explosion' process from a master production schedule to the detailed scheduling of component replenishments	■ An 'implosion' process for the lowest levels of the network to the central distribution centre
■ Goods in course of manufacture	■ Finished goods

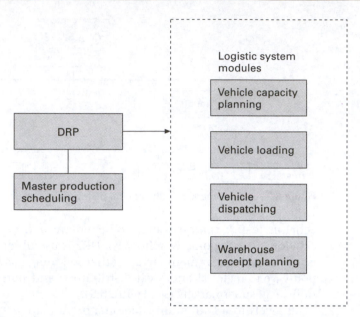

Figure 8.10 Distribution requirements planning and logistics

Source: adapted from Vollman, T.E., Berry, W.L. and Whybark, C.D., *Manufacturing Control Systems*, 2nd edition, Irwin, 1988, Ch.19, p.798

Thus as Vollman *et al.* observe:[4]

> Distribution requirements planning serves a central role in co-ordinating the flow of goods inside the factory with the system modules that place the goods in the hands of the customers. It provides the basis for integrating the Manufacturing Planning and Control (MRP) system from the firm to the field.

8.17.3 DRP planning

The fundamental document used in distribution planning is the DRP display. This document time phases across the planning horizon which is typically divided into weeks. A hypothetical example of a DRP display is shown in Figure 8.11.

It is assumed:

Time horizon:	10 weeks
Balance on hand at start:	175 items
Safety stock:	50 items
Lead time:	2 weeks
Order quantity:	250 items

The above records, gathered from a number of distribution points will be passed to the next higher stage in the echelon. The aggregates of the regional echelons will be passed to the central warehouse and from there, in a full logistics system, to the factory. This process is referred to as an 'implosion'. This is different from the MRP manufacturing concept of 'explosion' where a finished product is broken down into its components. The process, however, is the same but reversed.

	Balance	Period (weeks)									
	Week	1	2	3	4	5	6	7	8	9	10
Gross requirements		60	60	80	75	70	60	80	70	90	95
Schedule receipts				250			250			250	
Balance (projected on hand quantity)	175	115	55	225	150	80	270	190	120	280	185
Planned orders		250			250			250			

Figure 8.11 DRP display or record

From the example in Figure 8.11 it can be seen that:

- The emphasis in DRP is on scheduling rather than on ordering.
- This is a time-phased order point (TPOP) system. (Time phasing is 'the scheduling of inventory requirements and replenishments by need date over a specified time horizon'.[5]
- For a given period, net requirements = (gross requirements + safety stock) – (scheduled receipts + projected on hand for the previous period).
- Replacement stock is ordered one lead time prior to the period in which the gross requirements will eat into the safety stock.
- The projected on-hand quantity is revised at the end of each quarter. For a given period, projected quantity on hand = projected on hand of the prior period + scheduled receipts – gross requirements.
- The planned order quantity becomes a gross requirement on the same time period for the parent supply centre at the next level.

8.18 Just-in-time purchasing

Just-in-time (JIT) is a lean production system used mainly in repetitive manufacturing.

8.18.1 Definitions

Just-in-time purchasing has been defined by Lee White as:[6]

> An inventory control philosophy whose goal is to maintain just enough material in just the right place at just the right time to make just the right amount of product.

More concisely, JIT is:

> The exact adjustment of production to quantity and time held.

8.18.2 **The development of JIT**

The JIT concept originated in Japan in the 1950s when the Toyota Motor Company developed a system known as *Kanban* to meet customer demand for various vehicle models with minimum delivery delays. *Kanban* in Japanese means 'ticket' and refers to an information system in which instructions relating to the type and quality of items to be withdrawn from the preceding manufacturing process are conveyed by a card affixed to a container. Each container holds a predetermined quantity. JIT is a 'demand pull' system in which manufacturing planning begins with the final assembly line and works backwards, not only through the various manufacturing processes, but also to the vendors and subcontractors supplying materials and components. The exact quantity to replace the items withdrawn to meet the requirements of one manufacturing stage are provided by the preceding process. The aim is that by limiting production and assembly to what is actually needed, both materials and work-in-progress inventories can be eliminated or significantly reduced.

The number of *Kanban* cards required can be computed by the formula:

$$N = \frac{UT(1 + x)}{C}$$

where: N = the number of containers

U = planned usage rate for work centre

T = average waiting time for replenishment of parts plus average production time for a container of parts

x = policy variable set by management that reflects the possible inefficiency in the system (the closer to zero, the more efficient the system)

C = capacity of a standard container (should be no more than 10 per cent of daily usage of the part)

Note that U and T must use the same time units (e.g. minutes, days).

Example 8.10   A JIT system

Usage at a work centre is 600 parts per day and a standard container holds 50 parts. The average for a container to complete a circuit from the attachment of the *Kanban* card to the return of the empty container is 0.24 compute the number of *Kanban* cards required if $x = 0.20$.

$$N = \frac{(600)(0.24)(1 + 0.20)}{50} = 3.456$$

The answer of 3.456 can be rounded up or down. Rounding up will cause the system to be looser; rounding down will cause it to be tighter. Normally rounding up is used.

JIT has several versions known by such names as ZIPS (zero inventory production systems), MAN (materials as needed), DOPS (daily overhead and perfect supply) and NOT (nick-of-time). In all such cases the essential requirement is that supplies must be delivered frequently, in relatively small quantities, 'just in time' for use.

8.18.3   JIT and purchasing

For JIT to work, two things must happen:

1   All parts must arrive where they are needed, when they are needed and in the exact quantity needed.

2   All parts that arrive must be usable parts.

Where these requirements are not achieved, JIT may easily become 'just too late'. In achieving these requirements, purchasing has the following responsibilities:

- *Liaison with the design function.* The emphasis should be on performance rather than design specifications. Looser specifications enable suppliers to be more cost effective by being more innovative with regard to the quality/function aspect of supplies. In JIT purchasing, value analysis is an integral part of the system and should include suppliers.

- *Liaison with suppliers* to ensure that they understand thoroughly the importance of consistently maintaining lead times and a high level of quality.

- *Investigation of the potential of suppliers* within reasonable proximity of the purchaser to increase certainty of delivery and reduction of lead time.

- *Establishing strong, long-term relationships with suppliers* in a mutual effort to reduce costs and share savings. This will be achieved by the purchaser's efforts to meet the supplier's expectations with respect to:
  - continuity of custom;
  - a fair price and profit margin;
  - agreed adjustments to price when necessary;
  - accurate forecasts of demand;
  - firm and reasonably stable specifications;
  - minimising order changes;
  - smoothly timed order releases;
  - involvement in design specifications;
  - prompt payment.

- *Establishment of an effective supplier certification programme* which ensures that quality specifications are met before components leave the supplier so that receiving inspections are eliminated.

- *Evaluation of supplier performance* and the solving of difficulties as an exercise in cooperation.

8.18.4   Benefits of JIT

The potential benefits of JIT to an organisation, and its purchasing function in particular, have been summarised by Schonberger and Ansari as follows:[7]

- *Part costs* – low scrap costs; low inventory carrying costs.
- *Quality* – fast detection and correction of unsatisfactory quality and ultimately higher quality in purchased parts.
- *Design* – fast response to engineering change requirements.
- *Administrative efficiency* – fewer suppliers; minimal expediting and order release work; simplified communications and receiving activities.
- *Productivity* – reduced rework; reduced inspection; reduced parts-related delays.
- *Capital requirements* – reduced inventories of purchased parts, raw materials, work in progress and finished goods.

8.18.5 Possible disadvantages of JIT

Some organisations have experienced problems with JIT for the following reasons:

- Faulty forecasting of demand and inability of suppliers to move quickly to changes in demand.
- JIT required the provision of the necessary systems and methods of communication between purchasers and suppliers ranging from vehicle telephones to EDI. Problems will arise if there is inadequate communication both internally, i.e. from production to purchasing, and externally from purchasing to suppliers and vice versa.
- Organisations with, ideally, no safety stocks are highly vulnerable to supply failures.
- Purely stockless buying is a fallacy; lack of low-cost class C items can halt a production line as easily as a failure in the delivery of highly priced class A items
- The advantages of buying in bulk at lower prices may outweigh the savings negotiated for JIT contracts, since suppliers may increase their prices to cover costs of delivery, paperwork and storage.
- JIT is not generally suitable for bought-out items having a short life cycle and subject to rapid design change.
- JIT is more suitable for flow than batch production and may require a change from batch to flow methods with consequent changes in systems required to support the new methods.
- Even mass production manufacturers produce a substantial percentage of components by number, if not value, on batches as well as a small number of high value components on dedicated flow lines.
- Apart from suppliers, JIT requires a total involvement of people from all disciplines and the breaking down of traditional barriers between functions within an organisation. This may involve a substantial investment in organisational development training.
- Rhys *et al.*[8] have drawn attention to Japanese transport factors arising from some relocating of suppliers at greater distances from purchasers (although these are normally still nearer to users than in Europe), road congestion and lighter vehicles, i.e. for every one vehicle required in Europe, two or three are

required in Japan. In consequence, JIT in Japan is now 'neither lean nor green'. Nieuwenhuis[9] makes the following comparison of Japanese and European approaches in terms of vehicle use for a given road.

Japan	*Europe*
More journeys	Fewer journeys
More journey time	Less journey time
More traffic congestion	Less traffic congestion
Greater fuel use	More fuel efficient
More vehicles needed	Fewer vehicles needed
More air pollution and road damage	Less air pollution and road damage
Shorter distances	Longer distances

A consideration of these factors leads Nieuwenhuis to conclude that:

– There will be a far-reaching restructuring of Japanese supply systems, whereby some features of JIT will be retained. Overall, however, JIT as we have come to know and admire it will die.

– Rather than the wholesale adoption of pure JIT in Europe, we are more likely to see a convergence taking place of the Japanese and European approaches to supply systems, whereby the Europeans should see some benefits from the greater adoption of JIT principles in terms of reduced costs and greater integration of the supply network. The Japanese manufacturers, on the other hand, will be forced to adopt more European systems of supply, with a possible increase in costs.

The conclusion must be that careful appraisal of all factors involved including transport costs and environmental issues, should precede a decision to implement JIT.

8.18.6 JIT and MRP

■ JIT serves production line manufacturing industry where the product range is small, often with a high element of common parts, and with an assembly programme fixed for several months ahead. MRP serves a batch or job production environment where the aim is to translate customer's orders into a master production schedule consistent with stock in hand and suppliers' lead times and the explosion of a bill of materials, so that scheduling can be built around critical items in terms of lead times.

■ JIT tends to be used for higher usage items. Lower usage, large, expensive items tend to be controlled by MRP.

■ JIT is 'demand pull' system. MRP is a system in which material is *pushed* through the production line.

■ JIT and MRP are often complementary and can be made to work together. It is sometimes stated that MRP is a good planning but a poor execution system, while JIT has limited planning capability but is an excellent execution tool. The combined effect of operating an MRP system and a simplified JIT environment often provides the best solution.

8.19   Optimised production technology

Developed in Israel, optimised production technology (OPT) claims, like JIT, to minimise inventories of materials and work in progress and manufacturing lead times, particularly with regard to batch or continuous production.

■ The aim of OPT is to increase profitability by simultaneously increasing throughput and reducing inventory. (Throughput is not the same as output, but is the revenue from sales.) A basic tenet is that if an item cannot be sold it should not be manufactured.

■ Market forecasts are scheduled backwards from the required delivery dates.

■ Based in utilisation, manufacturing resources are classified as critical or non-critical, known respectively as bottlenecks and non-bottlenecks. A bottleneck is the slowest machine or resource in the manufacturing chain. Time lost at a bottleneck is time lost to the whole system. Time saved at a bottleneck has no real significance, i.e. when a bottleneck feeds a non-bottleneck the output of the second machine is governed by the number of components that reach it from the first machine. Conversely, where the non-bottleneck feeds the bottleneck, the first machine is limited only by its own capacity and so produces an output that simply accumulates in front of the bottleneck.

■ OPT computerised programs, therefore, simultaneously program for continuous production while regulating the output of non-bottlenecks just in time to keep the bottlenecks supplied. While bottlenecks are, therefore, the key to increasing throughput, non-bottlenecks are the key to reducing inventory.

■ The aim is, therefore, to relieve and remove bottlenecks until the whole production line is 'balanced'.

■ It is claimed that OPT is easier and less disruptive to implement than JIT, since attention can be directed to remedying bottlenecks rather than to the wholesale introduction of a new system.

8.20   Vendor-managed inventory

Vendor-managed inventory (VMI) is a JIT technique in which inventory replacement decisions are centralised with upstream manufacturers or distributors. Acronyms for VMI include

■ Continuous replenishment programs (CRP)

■ Supplier assisted inventory management (SAIM)

■ Supplier assisted inventory replenishment (SAIR)

■ Efficient consumer response (ECR)

VMI may also be considered as an extension of distribution requirements planning (DRP).

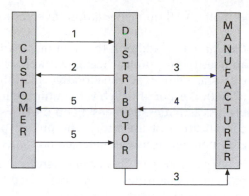

Figure 8.12 A simple VMI model

The aim of VMI is to enable manufacturers or distributors to eliminate the need for customers to reorder, reduce or exclude inventory and obviate stockouts. With VMI, customers no longer 'pull' inventory from suppliers. Rather, inventory is automatically 'pushed' to customers as suppliers check customers' inventories and respond to previously agreed stock levels. VMI is particularly applicable to retail distribution. VMI can also relieve the customer of much of the expense of ordering and stocking low-value MRO items.

8.20.1 Implementation of VMI

A simple model of VMI is shown in Figure 8.12.

The model is based on the assumption that the customer has entered into a collaborative or partnership agreement with a distributor under which the latter agrees to stock a specified range of items and meet specified service levels. In return the customer undertakes to buy the specified items solely from the distributor and no longer keeps the items in stock. There must therefore be a high level of trust between the customer and the distributor.

The various steps in Figure 8.12 may be explained as follows:

Step 1 The customer sends information on items sold to the distributor. This information may be collected by bar-coding and scanning technology and transmitted to the distributor by EDI or the internet.

Step 2 The distributor processes the information and forwards an acknowledgement to the customer giving details of the quantities and descriptions of the products to be delivered, the delivery date and destination, and releases the goods.

Step 3 The distributor collects details of all customer orders which are consolidated and sent daily to the manufacturers via EDI or the internet.

Step 4 The manufacturer replenishes the distributor's stock.

Step 5 The distributor invoices the customer who remits payment. Very large customers may transmit their requirements directly to the manufacturer from whom they receive direct deliveries.

Normally, VMI implementation involves four stages:

1 *Preparation.* In addition to initial negotiations between customer and supplier and setting up project teams with clearly defined roles and responsibilities, this stage involves collaborative planning, forecasting and replenishment (CPFR), the aim of which is to minimise inventories and focus on value-added process activities. By focusing on the flow of supply to consumers without the complication of inventory, the project participants' can often discover and eliminate previously undetected bottlenecks in the flow.

2 *Pre-implementation.* This is an extension of CPFR involving the determination of forecast quantities, safety stocks, lead time, service levels, key performance indicators and ownerships issues.

3 *Implementation.*

4 *Refinement.* Improvements that may be made in the light of experience, including the resolution of technical difficulties encountered subsequent to implementation.

8.20.2 Advantages of VMI

VMI is advantageous to both suppliers and customers. *Supplier advantages* include:

■ *Demand smoothing.* VMI information improves forecasts of customer requirements thereby enabling manufacturers to plan production to meet customer demand.

■ *Long-term customer relationships* owing to the high cost to the customer of switching to an alternative supplier.

■ *Enhanced operational flexibility* enabling production times and quantities to be adjusted to suit the supplier.

Customer advantages include:

■ *Reduced administrative costs* owing to the elimination of the need to monitor inventory levels, paper to computer entries and reduced reordering costs.

■ *Enhanced working capital* owing to reduced inventory levels and obsolescence and enhanced stock-turn with improved cash flow.

■ *Reduced lead times* with enhanced sales and a reduction of list sales through stockouts.

8.20.3 Disadvantages of VMI

These also apply to both suppliers and customers. *Supplier disadvantages* include:

■ *Transfers of customer costs to the supplier.* These costs include those relating to administration and the cost of carrying increased inventory to meet customer demand.

■ *Reduced working capital* owing to the enhanced inventory and administration costs stated above.

Customer disadvantages include:

- *Increased risk* resulting from dependence on the manufacturer or distributor.

- *Disclosure of potentially sensitive information to the supplier.* The possession of such information will put the supplier in a strong position when a contract is renegotiated.

- *Customers may be better positioned than suppliers to make replenishment decisions.* Chopra and Meindl[10] point out that:

  > One drawback to VMI arises because retailers often sell products from competing manufacturers that are substitutes in the customer's mind. For example, a customer may substitute detergent manufactured by Procter and Gamble with detergent manufactured by Lever Brothers. If the retailer has a VMI agreement with both manufacturers, each will ignore the impact of substitution when making its inventory decisions. As a result, inventories at the retailer will be higher than optimal.

8.21   Lot sizing

Manufacturers or distributors must decide what quantity or lot size of an item to produce or purchase. Lot sizing may be static or dynamic. Fixed order sized or EOQ systems are static, i.e. the same quantity is maintained each time an order is issued. Planned order release systems, as with MRP and DRP which provide for a different quantity each time an order is issued, are dynamic. A comparison of the two systems was given in Table 8.9.

Dynamic lot sizes can be determined in the following ways:

- By a *lot-for-lot-rule*, i.e. the lot size covers the gross requirements for a single order or period; there is, thus, no forward buying beyond these parameters. Tersine[11] states that this approach:

  - minimises inventory holding costs;

  - is suitable for very expensive items or items with a highly discontinuous demand where a high level of inventory control must be exercised;

  - is well suited to high volume, continuous assembly production.

  It does, however, ignore order placement or set-up costs.

- By the *periodic order quantity rule* in which when an order is placed its lot size must be enough to cover the requirements for X weeks. The lot size or periodic order quantity (POQ) is determined by the formula:

  $$POQ = GR + SS - B$$

  where: GR = gross requirement for X weeks beginning with the week of placement

  SS = any desired safety stock

  B = projected balance from previous week

8.22 Safety stock and service levels

8.22.1 Definitions

Safety stock is needed to cover shortages due to the agreed lead time being exceeded or the actual demand being greater than that anticipated.

A *service level* is the ability to meet the demands of customers from stock. It is expressed as:

$$\frac{\text{Number of times an item is provided on demand}}{\text{Number of times an item is demanded}}$$

8.22.2 The relationship between service levels and safety stock

Figure 8.13 shows that the service levels and safety stock are related. Thus by increasing the investment on inventory, service levels can be increased.

For single items an extra investment in inventory (higher safety stock) will always increase customer service levels. Conversely higher service levels imply larger safety stocks and an increased investment in inventory.

It is not possible to achieve 100 per cent service levels for the total inventory. High safety stocks for all items would be uneconomical and the costs would be prohibitive.

JIT implies a low or zero inventory. This is achieved by removing uncertainty regarding supply. Safety stock is a cost-adding factor and, as such, should be eliminated.

If the uncertainty regarding supply cannot be eliminated, safety stocks are required. High service levels for all items would be uneconomical since the investment in inventory this would require is prohibitive.

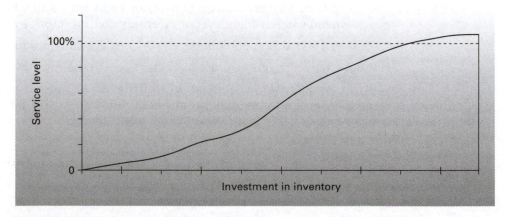

Figure 8.13 Service level inventory trade-off curve

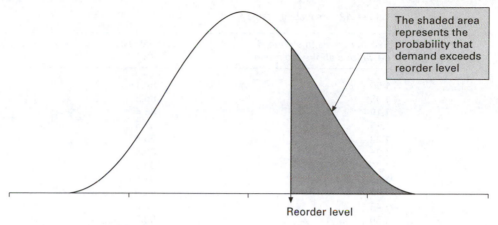

Figure 8.14   The normal distribution curve

- The items that have high stockout costs can be identified by ABC analysis.
- An acceptable risk of stockout should be determined for these items.
- Statistical theory provides methods of calculating the order quantities and safety stocks needed to ensure that the chances of a stockout do not exceed the acceptable level of risk. A brief introduction of the relevant parts of statistics is given below.

8.22.3   Normal distribution

The probability that demand exceeds a particular inventory level during the lead time can be found from the normal distribution (see Figure 8.14).

Tables of this distribution are given in most statistics textbooks. To use these tables we need to know two facts about the demand during the lead time: its mean and its standard deviation. These can be found as follows:

1. From records, randomly select a sample of orders sent to the supplier of the item. This should be a reasonably sized sample, about 30 orders.

2. For each order find the date on which the order was placed and the date of delivery. From stores records calculate the demand between these dates.

3. Find the mean or arithmetic average demand during the lead time as follows:

$$\text{Mean} = \frac{\text{Sum of the demands}}{\text{Number of lead times}} = \sum \frac{x}{n}$$

4. Calculate the standard deviation of demand from the following formula:

$$\text{Standard deviation} = \sqrt{\left(\frac{n}{n-1}\right)\left(\frac{x^2}{n} - \left(\frac{x}{n}\right)^2\right)}$$

or by using the statistical functions on your calculator or spreadsheet. The reorder level required can then be found from Table 8.12.

Table 8.12 Probability table

Reorder levels in standard deviations above the mean	Service level (%)	Probability of a stockout (%)
1.00	84.1	15.9
1.05	85.3	14.7
1.10	86.4	13.6
1.15	87.5	12.5
1.20	88.5	11.5
1.25	89.4	10.6
1.30	90.3	9.7
1.35	91.1	8.9
1.40	91.9	8.1
1.45	92.6	7.4
1.50	93.3	6.7
1.55	93.9	6.1
1.60	94.5	5.5
1.65	95.1	4.9
1.70	95.5	4.5
1.75	96.0	4.0
1.80	96.4	3.6
1.85	96.8	3.2
1.90	97.5	2.5
1.95	97.4	2.6
2.00	97.7	6.1
2.05	98.0	5.5
2.10	98.2	4.9
2.15	98.4	4.5
2.20	98.6	4.0
2.25	98.8	3.6
2.30	98.9	3.2
2.35	99.1	2.5
2.40	99.2	2.6
2.45	99.3	2.3
2.50	99.4	2.0
2.55	99.5	1.8
2.60	99.5	1.6
2.65	99.6	1.4
2.70	99.7	1.2
2.75	99.7	1.1
2.80	99.7	0.9
2.85	99.8	0.8
2.90	99.8	0.7
3.00	99.9	0.6

Example 8.11 Calculating the reorder level from the normal distribution

The average (mean) demand is 10. A 99 per cent service level is required, i.e. the probability of a stockout is 1 per cent or less.

Table 8.12 shows that for a service level of 99 per cent the reorder level should be 2.35 standard deviations above the mean. Thus the reorder level is:

$$140 + 2.35 \times 10 = 163.5 \simeq 164$$

8.23   Special inventory factors

The emphasis of this chapter has been on minimising stock levels consistent with a given level of customer service and the avoidance of production disruption. There are, however, special circumstances in which it may be desirable to allow stocks to rise or fall above previously determined maximum or minimum levels.

Particularly with sensitive commodities, anticipated world shortages owing to natural factors, e.g. a poor wheat harvest, industrial action, or political uncertainty may cause companies to maximise their stocks particularly of 'bottleneck' materials which, if unavailable, would disrupt production.

Stocks may also be increased or reduced in anticipation of a rise in prices or a fall in the value of money due to inflation. Here the total costs associated with holding stocks may be less than the anticipated rise in raw material prices.

Such decisions cannot be made by the application of formulae but require decision making based on environmental information and the exercise of sound procurement judgement.

Case study 1[12]

It is early autumn, and the new CIPS classes at Oldport College are just getting under way. The group of students who are undertaking the Stores and Inventory Management syllabus are coming towards the end of their first session, and their tutor, Nick Finley, has spent most of the session going through the syllabus with them. During the last few minutes, a fairly lively discussion has developed, instigated of course by Nick. What is happening is that each of the students, who are from a wide range of manufacturing, commercial, and service sector backgrounds, is claiming that the matching of supply with demand in his or her particular organisation is especially difficult, and that there are special characteristics in each of their organisations which make the mainstream textbook and study material to some extent irrelevant to their particular world. They good-naturedly accept that the basics are well covered in the generalist literature, but insist that the reality of their organisations is such that there are particular challenges, calling for rather special skills and techniques. Nick, two minutes before the teaching session is scheduled to end has said, with the intention of raising controversy, 'It can't be that difficult, all you need to do is look at your operating plans, see what materials are likely to be needed, and get them in good time'. He is, of course, not surprised to hear the noisy protests of his students. 'It's time to end the class, and I can't hear anybody clearly with all this noise, so this is what I want you to do,' he says. 'For homework, each of you bring a few notes explaining why matching supply with demand is especially difficult in your organisation and the techniques you employ to help you in making this match'.

Nick now has to prepare his own notes for the next session; he needs to anticipate what the students will say about their problems and techniques so he can lead a further class discussion.

Four of the students who have been particularly keen to promote their own problems as being especially difficult are:

Said Hussain works as a buyer for Tessway Stores, a major multiple outlet grocery concern. His commodity group is soft drinks, fruit juices and other non-alcoholic drinks, and he is challenged by the need to attempt to have neither too much nor too little of any particular item.

Joanne Greeves works as a stock analyst for a major oil company and her responsibilities include the provision of spare parts from standby stocks for the maintenance and repair of oil industry facilities, with two major areas of responsibility being offshore production platforms, and refinery maintenance. Some of the maintenance is done on a planned basis, but the majority of supplies looked after by Joanne are required rapidly in response to operational problems. Joanne is responsible for both inventory levels and physical storage of her group of materials.

Keith McIvor works for International Electric, and is a buyer of production materials, in particular electronic items for the company's range of mass produced domestic appliances. His company operates on a JIT basis.

Kim Dutton works for Farm Nutrition, an animal feed company, and she cooperates with the buyers in accommodating the large quantities of raw materials which are bought in anticipation of need, and often available unexpectedly in large lots at attractively low prices.

Question

Assuming the role of Nick Finley, prepare summaries of the particular problems and associated techniques you would expect each of the four students to come up with.

Case study 2[13]

James Johnson (JJ) is an organisation involved in the manufacture, distribution and after-sales service of lawn mowers and related powered garden products. It has a sales turnover of £150 million (1999–2000) with the majority of its sales derived from the UK.

JJ is a traditional organisation in terms of its attitudes towards working practices, management studies and functional approaches towards running the business. Its profits have been falling steadily over the last few years. The last set of published accounts showed profits had fallen to £3 million. This led to the resignation of the managing director and the appointment of a new one. John Smith, the new MD, commissioned a group of management consultants to investigate each functional area and identify where improvements might be achieved.

For stores and inventory management the following observations were made:

1   Stores and inventory department reports to the production manager.

2   Stock levels currently stand at £80 million, which seems high compared with rival organisations' stock levels. While it is necessary to hold stock for spare part requirements, it is felt that a separate system of control is required for production items;

3   Stock turnover is considered to be low compared with comparative organisations.

4   Staff have little or no training and are poorly paid. The production manager's approach to staffing is to have more storekeepers but at low wages. He also encourages ex-production staff to work in stores when they are no longer able to give of their best in the production areas.

5   The rest of the organisation generally believes that stores is a 'necessary evil' and complain regularly about stockouts, damaged stock and failure to get stock to where it is required. Generally the interface is bad with other parts of the organisation.

6   The MRP system used at JJ constantly fails to achieve what is expected of it. Stores and inventory control gets most of the blame because of its inability to give accurate stock figures.

7   All stock is delivered to one set delivery point, this leads to numerous hold-ups in production.

8   The stores itself operates on a fixed location system for all stock, even though space is at a premium. There does not seem to be any clear zoning system. The majority of stock is stored in non-adjustable racking. Racking height in most cases never exceeds three metres. The use of mechanical handling equipment is limited to three basic forklift trucks that are constantly breaking down. There is no automation of stock.

9   Security of stock is a major issue with high rates of pilferage of 'attractive items'. It is also agreed that obsolete and redundant stock is a major problem that must be resolved quickly.

10 Apart from the MRP system, computer systems within the stores and inventory are non-existent. There is no bar coding and regular inputting errors occur in the MRP system.

Question

You have recently been appointed as the stores and inventory control manager. Produce a report to the new managing director in which you suggest short- and long-term solutions to the problems listed. The report should explain clearly the rationale and methodology you would use to achieve solutions to the problems.

? Discussion questions

8.1 Calculate the rate of stock-turn using the following information:

Turnover at *selling* price	= £125,000
Mark up	= 25%
Opening stock at *selling* price	= £60,000
Closing stock at *selling* price	= £70,000

8.2 Calculate the rate of stock-turn using the following information:

Turnover at cost price	= £100,000
Opening stock at cost price	= £48,000
Closing stock at cost price	= £56,000

8.3 How may the cost of ordering MRO items be reduced?

8.4 What information does an operations manager require to make effective use of dependent demand inventory models?

8.5 What are the implications for management of the following statements?

(a) The cost of carrying inventory has been estimated by leading logistics experts at between 18 and 75 per cent per year depending on the type of products and the business.

(b) The standard rule of thumb for inventory carrying costs is 25 per cent of the value of inventory on hand.

8.6 The total inventory cost of item 423 is estimated at 25 per cent. What percentage of the total inventory cost might be allocated to each of the following constituents?

(a) Cost of money, i.e. interest on capital tied up in stock

(b) Rates

(c) Warehouse expenses

(d) Physical handling

(e) Clerical and stores control

(f) Obsolescence

(g) Deterioration and pilferage

8.7 You have been asked to suggest four ways by which inventory costs might be reduced. What would you suggest?

8.8 A company categorises its inventory into three classes according to their usage value. Calculate the usage values of the following items and classify them along Pareto lines into A, B and C items.

Item no.	Annual quantity used	Unit value (£)
1	75	80.00
2	150,000	0.90
3	500	3.00
4	18,000	0.20
5	3,000	0.30
6	20,000	0.10
7	10,000	0.04

8.9   Carry out an ABC analysis on the basis of the following figures

Item no.	Annual usage	Unit cost (£)
1	2,500	0.20
2	1,500	5.00
3	1,250	0.16
4	6,450	20.00
5	8,200	15.00
6	5,000	45.00
7	1,470	100.00
8	200	12.50
9	675	200.00
10	20,000	35.00
11	800	15.00
12	84	250.00
13	2,900	10.00
14	800	80.00
15	9,000	0.50
16	300	5.00
17	3,250	125.00
18	10,000	35.00
19	5,000	25.00
20	2,000	65.00

8.10   A company discovered that its stock of the following item was greatly in excess of its requirements.

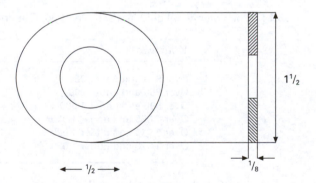

It ascertained that the cause of overstocking was because the item had 10 different designations in the stores vocabulary.

(a)   How many such designations can you suggest?

(b)   What steps would you take to ensure that only one standard designation is used throughout the organisation?

8.11   Calculate the EOQ where:

Annual quantity required = 600,000

Cost of ordering   = £11 per order

Cost of carrying   = £20 per unit

8.12   A supermarket divides large blocks of cheese into pieces of approximately 500g before displaying these for sale. A sample of the pieces cut by one shop assistant has the following distribution:

Grammes	Number of blocks
450 but under 470	15
470 but under 490	20
490 but under 510	35
510 but under 530	18
530 but under 550	12

(a) Calculate the mean and standard deviation of this sample.

(b) Calculate the median of this sample.

8.13 The delivery times for the most recent 50 orders from a supplier are tabulated below:

Delivery time in days	Number of deliveries
5 and under 9	6
9 and under 13	12
13 and under 17	17
17 and under 21	10
21 and under 25	5

(a) Calculate the mean and standard deviation of this sample of delivery times. Give your answers correct to one decimal place.

(b) Calculate the median delivery time.

8.14 The volume of liquid in a sample of 60 containers is shown below:

Volume (ml)	Number of containers
Over 970 and under 980	5
Over 980 and under 990	10
Over 990 and under 1,000	14
Over 1,000 and under 1,010	15
Over 1,010 and under 1,020	12
Over 1,020 and under 1,030	4

(a) Calculate the median of this sample.

(b) Calculate the mean and standard deviation of this sample.

8.15 An engineering company used the EOQ model to decide that it should buy item 500 which is in constant use in quantities of 1,920. The EOQ recommendation was based on the following information:

Annual demand for component 500	= 48,000 items
Cost per item	= £24.00
Inventory holding charge	= £36.00
Order cost	= £76.00

The combined inventory and ordering costs for component 500 is £3,974.

The manufacturer of component 500 offers the following quantity discount schedule:

Order size	Discount	Unit cost
0–7,999	0	£24.00
8,000–23,999	3%	£23.28
24,000 and over	5%	£22.80

Calculate:

(a) The optimal ordering quantity

(b) Annual inventory holding cost

(c) Annual ordering cost

(d) Annual purchase cost

8.16 A product is assembled from five components B, C, D, E and F. A BOM of X is as follows:

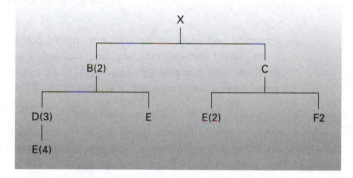

(a) Use the above information to compute the quantities of each component B, C, D, E, and F to assemble one X.

(b) What quantities of each component will be required to manufacture 100 Xs?

8.17 Attempt a BOM for: (a) a simple bicycle and (b) a table lamp.

8.18 Consider the following DRP display:

	Period						
	1	2	3	4	5	6	7
Gross requirements	30	30	30	30	30	30	30
Balance projected (in-hand quantity) 44	14	64	34	84	54	24	74
Planned orders							

Safety stock = 20, order quantity = 80, lead time = 1.

In what periods would the reorder points fall for the situation depicted above?

8.19 Compute the number of containers required for a work centre that uses 200 parts per hour if the cycle time (move, wait, empty, return, fill) is 60 minutes and a standard container holds 80 parts. An efficiency factor of 0.10 has been adopted.

? Past examination questions

1 Your finance director is concerned that over the last year the value of stock held has increased by 30 per cent while sales have remained static. As procurement manager, explain how you intend to reduce the value of stock held over the next six months.

(CIPS, Introduction to Purchasing and Supply Chain Management, May 1997)

2 Orlicky (1975) identified a set of requirements for successful materials requirements planning (MRP). These include data integrity and known lead times. In view of these requirements identify how the following would impact on successful MRP operations
   (a) Low levels of inventory record accuracy
   (b) Inaccuracy in the bill of materials
   (c) Unreliable supplier delivery performance

(CIPS, Purchasing and Supply Chain Management II: Tactics and Operations, May 1997)

3 Compare and contrast the problems posed by the need to manage dependent and independent demand supplies, and explain in detail one appropriate approach for each of these two classes of demand. Illustrate your answer by means of examples either from your experience or your studies of your chosen approaches.

(CIPS, Stores and Inventory Management, May 1997)

4 Explain the main features of an MRP system, and explain the circumstances in which such a system would, and would not, be appropriate in the determination of requirements.

(CIPS, Stores and Inventory Management, November 1997)

5 In order to reduce the cost of holding stock many organisations operate JIT.
   (a) Provide an explanation of the item JIT.
   (b) Discuss the information required to ensure the effective implementation of JIT.

(CIPS, Introduction to Purchasing and Supply Chain Management, May 1998)

6 Where demand is independent, the EOQ approach provides many organisations with a useful approximation when determining *how much* to order, but it is not helpful when deciding *when* to order. Say whether or not you agree with this statement, and explain how a stock controller might make decisions on the timing of orders. (NB Do not spend time explaining the EOQ formula; the examiner will assume you know this.)

(CIPS, Stores and Inventory Management, May 1998)

7 Compare and contrast, using examples, 'push' and 'pull' in the supply of materials and explain a system or technique associated with each.

(CIPS, Stores Inventory Management, November 1998)

8 The cost of acquiring stock and holding stock in a warehouse is a drain on an organisation's resources. Summarise the costs incurred and how these costs can be controlled.

(CIPS, Introduction to Purchasing and Supply Chain Management, May 1998)

9   Identify and explain how the different elements of cost incurred in keeping stock can be minimised.

(CIPS, Introduction to Purchasing and Supply
Chain Management, November 1999)

10 Vendor-managed inventory (VMI) refers to arrangements whereby the supplier manages inventory on the buyer's behalf and according to Professor D Jessop, 'a well designed and developed approach can lead not only to reduction in inventory levels in the supply chain but also to secondary savings arising from the simplification of procedures' (Jessop, D., *Supply Management*, Feb. 1999). Discuss this statement showing clearly how savings in the supply chain may be achieved, and describe how such a system may be operated, suggesting areas of inventory where the technique may be appropriate.

(CIPS, Purchasing and Supply Chain Management II:
Tactics and Operations, November 1999)

11 Two common approaches to the assessment of supply system performance are *service level* and *stock turn*. Achievement of good figures for each criteria alone is relatively easy but to excel against both criteria is problematic.
    (a)   Explain the meaning of each term, and the tension between them.
    (b)   Suggest how this tension might be accommodated in a performance assessment scheme.

(CIPS, Stores and Inventory Management, November 1999)

12 Compare and contrast dependent and independent demand and indicate appropriate approaches to inventory management for each class of demand.

(CIPS, Stores and Inventory Management, November 1999)

13 Describe how MRP might be employed to determine ordering times and quantities, and explain the benefits, the problems and the limitations of MRP techniques.

(CIPS, Stores and Inventory Management, May 2000)

14 Define the terms MRP II and DRP and explain the benefits to be gained through their use.

(CIPS, Introduction to Purchasing and Supply
Chain Management, November 2000)

Notes

1. Compton, H.K. and Jessop, D., *Dictionary of Purchasing and Supply Management*, Pitman, 1989, p.135
2. The writers are indebted to an analysis in Kampf, R., *ERP Systems, Situations and Future Development* on http://www.ebz.beratungszentrum.de/pps-seiten/sonstige8/erp-engl.htm
3. As n.2 above
4. Adapted (with permission) from Vollman, T.E., Berry, W.L. and Whybark, C.D., *Manufacturing Control Systems*, 2nd edn, Irwin, 1988, Ch.19, p.798

5. Tersine, R.J., *Principles of Inventory Management*, 3rd edn, Elsevier Science, 1988, Ch.10, p.430

6. White, L., 'JIT – What is it and how does it affect DP?', *Computer World*, June 1985, pp.41–2

7. Schonberger, R.J. and Ansari, A., 'Just-in-time purchasing can improve quality', *Journal of Purchasing and Materials Management*, Spring 1984

8. Rhys, D.G., McNabb, J. and Nieuwenhuis, P., 'Japan hits the limits of just-in-time EIU', *Japanese Motor Business*, December 1992, pp.81–9

9. Nieuwenhuis, P., 'Environmental implications of just-in-time supply in Japan – lessons in Europe', *Logistics Focus*, Vol.2, No.3 (1994), pp.2–4

10. Chopra, S. and Meindl, P., *Supply Chain Management*, Prentice Hall, 2001, Ch.9, p.247

11. Tersine, R.J., *Principles of Inventory Management*, 3rd edn, Elsevier Science, 1988, Ch.10, p.63

12. The authors gratefully acknowledge the permission of the CIPS to use this case study from May 1999 Stores and Inventory Management examination

13. The authors gratefully acknowledge the permission of the CIPS to use this case study from the December 2000 Stores and Inventory examination

Sourcing and supplier information

Learning goals

After reading this chapter you should be able to:

- Distinguish between strategic, tactical and operational sourcing levels.
- Show the importance to purchasing of an analysis of market conditions.
- State and discuss important sources of information relating to market conditions.
- Differentiate between European, central and local government and company procurement directives and explain their importance.
- State and discuss the main sources of information relating to potential suppliers.
- Indicate the applicability and scope of supplier appraisal.
- Prepare a checklist for visits to suppliers.
- Evaluate and rate potential suppliers.
- State and discuss the Ten Cs of effective supplier evaluation.
- Explain the concepts of the supplier base and supplier base optimisation.
- Distinguish between strategic and tactical make-or-buy decisions and some factors involved in such decisions.
- Define outsourcing and compare the advantages and disadvantages of outsourcing.
- List the stages involved in implementing outsourcing.
- Discuss the feasibility of outsourcing purchasing.
- Define subcontracting and discuss factors relevant to the selection and control of subcontractors.
- Explain the reasons for and possible consequences of tiering and the responsibilities of first-tier suppliers.
- List the aims and objectives, benefits and disadvantages of supplier associations.
- Indicate the objectives of partnering.
- Distinguish between traditional and partnership supplier relationships.

- Identify the types of relationship most suitable for partnering and the advantages and problems of partnering.
- Implement partnership sourcing.
- Provide reasons derived from research relating to partnering failure.
- Analyse the concept of relationship as applied to relationship purchasing and purchasing relationships.
- Classify some forms of purchasing relationships.
- Define the terms 'co-destiny' and 'co-makership' and discuss the factors relating to their successful implementation.
- Differentiate between open book and cost transparency.
- Discuss aspects of reciprocal trade.
- Discuss the advantages and disadvantages of local, large and small suppliers and purchasing consortia.
- Classify factors that influence industrial buying decisions.
- Indicate some general, strategic and product considerations in deciding the source from which to buy.

9.1   Sourcing levels

Sourcing of suppliers is undertaken at the strategic and tactical/operational levels of an undertaking.

9.1.1   Strategic sourcing

Strategic sourcing is concerned with top-level, longer-term decisions relating to high profit/high supply risk strategic items and low profit/high supply risk bottleneck items (see Table 4.2). It is also concerned with the formulation of long-term purchasing policies relating to core competences, strategic make-or-buy decisions, thin supplier base, partnership sourcing, reciprocal and intra-company trading, globalisation and counter trade, the purchase of capital equipment and ethical issues.

9.1.2   Tactical and operational sourcing

Tactical and operational sourcing is concerned with lower level decisions relating to high profit/low risk non-critical items. It is also concerned with short-term adaptive decisions as to how and from where specific supplier requirements are to be met. Thus, suggestions may be made to top management regarding temporary tactical deviations from strategic decisions. Although strategically it may have been decided to buy rather than to make a certain component, this decision may be tactically reversed in conditions of manufacturing for stock work or supplier failure.

Strategic sourcing has been defined as:[1]

The process of creating a value adding (or optional mix) of supply relationships to provide a competitive advantage.

It is important, however, that purchasing staff at tactical and operational levels are also aware of their roles in providing value-adding support services to sourcing and thereby contributing to the competitive advantage of their enterprise.

Sourcing information can be considered under three headings:

- sourcing information (sections 9.2–9.9)
- sourcing strategies and tactics (sections 9.10–9.12)
- sourcing decisions (sections 9.23–9.24)

9.2   Sourcing information

Sourcing information can be divided into the following areas:

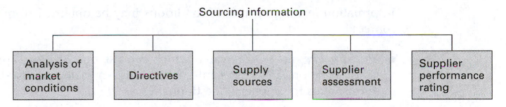

Sourcing information

| Analysis of market conditions | Directives | Supply sources | Supplier assessment | Supplier performance rating |

9.3   Analysis of market conditions

9.3.1   What is a market?

The term 'market' can mean:

- A place where goods and services are bought and sold. For example, the European Economic Community is a market created by agreement between the participating countries to reduce barriers to the internal movement of labour and capital.
- Large groups of buyers and sellers of wide classes of goods, e.g. the consumer goods market, the capital market.
- Demand and supply of a single class of commodity, e.g. the steel market, the cotton market.
- The general economic conditions relating to the supply of goods and services applying at a particular time. Of special importance to purchasing is the distinction between a buyer's and a seller's market.

9.3.2   Why is the analysis of market conditions important to sourcing?

Analysis of market conditions is useful for the following reasons:

- It helps in forecasting the long-term demand for the product of which bought-out materials, components, assemblies, etc. are part. It has therefore an identity of interest with market research.
- It assists in forecasting the price trends of bought-out items and how material costs are likely to affect production costs and selling prices. The need for cheaper prices may influence sourcing decisions.
- It indicates what alternative goods and supply sources are available, e.g. might it be more economical to source abroad?
- It gives guidance on the security of supply sources. This is particularly important with sensitive commodities sourced abroad.

Table 4.2 indicates the importance of long-, medium- and short-term market data in relation to such sourcing issues as make-or-buy decisions, volume insurance, vendor selection and product standardisation.

9.3.3 What sources of information relating to market conditions are available?

Information relating to market conditions may be obtained from the following sources:

- *Primary data*, i.e. field research which can use one or more approaches such as observation, analysis of internal records, e.g. sales trends and order book levels, visits to suppliers, questionnaires.
- *Secondary data*, i.e. statistics and reports issued by external organisations.
  - *International sources*. For the researcher in the UK a good starting point is the Export Market Information Centre, 66–74 Victoria Street, London SW16 6RB. This library contains all the major international statistical sources.
  - *Government sources*. Full details of publications can be obtained from HMSO. The most important sources include:
    - *Abstracts of Statistics* (published annually and monthly)
    - *Economic Trends*
    - *Census of Production*
    - *Department of Employment Gazette*
    - *British Business* (published weekly by the Department of Trade and Industry)
    - *Business Monitors* (the P series covers a wide sector of industrial activities)
    - *Bank of England Reports*
  - *Non-government sources*. These include:
    - The Economist Intelligence Unit
    - Chambers of commerce
    - Professional associations. Of particular importance to procurement staff is *Supply Management*, the journal of the Chartered Institute of Purchasing and Supply.

- The press, e.g. *The Economist*, *Financial Times* and the 'quality' daily and Sunday newspapers.

- Economic forecasters, e.g. the Confederation of British Industries publishes *Economic Situation Report*. Oxford Economic Forecasting has a range of publications including *UK Economic Prospects*; *World Economic Prospects*; *UK Industrial Prospects*; *European Economic Prospects*.

- The internet. Surf under such headings as 'business information', 'UK economic statistics' and 'Treasury statistics'.

9.4   Directives

A directive is a general instruction. Typical directives relating to sourcing include those issued by the EU, central and local government offices, and companies.

9.4.1   EU directives

Background

All organisations which receive public funding are likely to be affected by European procurement legislation. Such organisations include central government departments, local authorities, NHS trusts, universities and utility companies. The legislation covers most contracts for supplies (i.e. goods), work and services and aims to ensure:

- *Equality of treatment*, i.e. public authorities must take all measures necessary to ensure that all tenderers are treated in an equal manner. This requires that contracting authorities ensure that all applicants have advance information relating to the tender rules and apply the rules impartially.

- *Transparency*, i.e. contracting authorities must make public their intention to award a contract.

- *Proportionality*, i.e. any requirements set by the contracting authority in relation to such matters as performance and technical specifications are both necessary and appropriate and are not excessive or disproportionate to the subject of the contract.

- *Mutual recognition*, i.e. a member state must accept the products and services supplied by economic operators in other EU countries if the products and services are sufficient to meet, in the same manner, the objectives of the contracting authority.

The aim is to enforce such principles by:

- the establishment of common procedures;
- competition;
- compliance with procurement legislation by all member states.

European directives take precedence over national law irrespective of when the domestic law was enacted. The political aim is to create a single market for public procurement so that European companies may, in principle, have access to contracts without any kind of discrimination.

Breach of the EU public procurement rules may have significant legal consequences. Under the Remedies Directive and implementing regulations, for example, the High Courts of England and Wales, and Northern Ireland, and the Court of Session in Scotland have power to review the award of a contract and apply a number of remedies including (i) declaring the contract void, (ii) varying the contract, and (iii) an award of damages to an injured party.

The directives

The main 'elements' of EU directives are:

- The *thresholds*, below which it is not necessary to follow the EU rules.
- The *time limits*, which are laid down to make sure that potential bidders particularly those from other member states have enough time to respond to the public invitations to tender.
- The *criteria for selection of bidders* and the award of contractors, which have to be made explicit in the advertisements and cannot afterwards be changed. The main directives are shown in Table 9.1.

Thresholds are calculated according to special drawing rights expressed in euros net of value added tax and in national currency; they are adjusted in 1 January in even years (i.e. 2000, 2002 etc.). The current (2002) values of these thresholds, which can be obtained from the EU *Official journal of the European Communities* (*OJEC*) in euros and sterling, are shown in Table 9.2.

Table 9.1 Main EU procurement directives

Legislation	Directive	Official Journal reference
Public sector		
Works	93/37/EEC	L199 9/8/93
Supplies	93/36/EEC	L199 9/8/93
Services	92/50/EEC	L209 24/7/92
Remedies	89/665/EEC	L395 30/12/89
GPA directive	97/52/EC	L328 28/11/97
Utilities		
Works	93/38/EEC	L199 9/8/93
Supplies	93/38/EEC	L199 9/8/93
Supplies (Telecoms)	93/38/EEC	L199 9/8/93
Services	93/38/EEC	L199 9/8/93
Services (Telecoms)	93/38/EEC	L199 9/8/93
Remedies	92/13/EEC	L76 23/3/92
GPA directive	98/4/EC	L101 1/4/98

Table 9.2   Threshold values in euros and sterling by which public contracts must be published in *OJEC*, 1 January 2002 to 31 December 2002

Supplies
General threshold
€200,000 = £123,740 not including VAT

Annual indicative notices (budget forecasts)
€750,000 = £464,024 not including VAT

Central government bodies
€162,293 = £100,410 not including VAT
€249,681 = £154,477 not including VAT

Works
General threshold
€5,000,000 = £3,093,491 not including VAT

Central government bodies
€6,242,028 = £3,861,932 not including VAT

Small lots
€1,000,000 = £618,698 not including VAT

Services
General threshold
€200,000 = £123,740 not including VAT

Annual indicative notices (budget forecasts)
€750,000 = £464,024 not including VAT

Small lots
€80,000 = £49,496 not including VAT

Central government bodies
€162,293 = £100,410 not including VAT
€249,681 = £154,477 not including VAT

Utilities
Supplies and services, general
€400,000 = £247,479 not including VAT

Supplies and services, telecommunications
€600,000 = £371,219 not including VAT

Works
€5,000,000 = £3,093,491 not including VAT

Small lots (works)
€1,000,000 = £618,698 not including VAT

Annual indicative notices (budget forecasts), supplies and services
€750,000 = £464,024 not including VAT

Central Government bodies, supplies and services
€499,362 = £308,955 not including VAT

Central Government bodies, works
€6,242,028 = £3,861,932 not including VAT

Table 9.3 Open, restricted and negotiated procedures

Procedure	Characteristics	Deadline for requests to participate	Deadline for receipt of tenders
Open	Any company can submit a tender		Not less than 52 days[a]
Restricted	Each company must prove suitability to the contracting authority before being invited to submit a tender	Not less than 37 days	Not less than 40 days
Negotiated[b]	The contacting authority negotiates the terms of a contract directly with one or several companies	Not less than 37 days	

[a] These deadlines may be reduced if an indicative notice has been published
[b] As with the open and restricted procedures, contracts should be advertised on Tenders Electronic Daily (TED) and a minimum of three companies selected to ensure competition. However, in very exceptional circumstances a single company may be selected without a call for competition

Procedures

As shown by Table 9.3, there are currently three types of procedures: open, restricted and negotiated.

Open procedures mean those national procedures whereby all interested parties may submit a tender. Contracts are generally advertised using open procedures when the most important consideration in purchasing a product is the price.

Restricted procedures mean those whereby only providers invited by the potential purchaser may submit a tender. This is the most commonly used procedure as it enables the bidding process to be restricted to suitably qualified providers.

Negotiated procedures are those in which the contracting authority is able to invite a shortlist of companies from those expressing interest to bid for the contract. Terms and conditions are then negotiated with the selected party/parties.

Timescales relate to the prescribed minimum period from the date of dispatch of the contract notice allowed to tenderers to return the completed tender documents. The purpose of the timescales is to offer equal opportunities to any potential provider to submit a bid. As shown in Figures 9.1 and 9.2, the timescale varies according to the procedure adopted by the contracting authority. Before the actual tender procedure, public authorities may issue prior information relating to a specific project or a variety of supplies of services to be procured throughout the following year. For open and negotiated procedures the timescales can be reduced if such notice has been given.

Evaluation criteria

The procedure for the award of contracts and the debriefing of successful tenderers is shown in Figure 9.3.

Contracts may be awarded on the basis of either the lowest price or the most economically advantageous tender. The latter allows factors other than price, e.g. quality, delivery and after-sales service, to be considered.

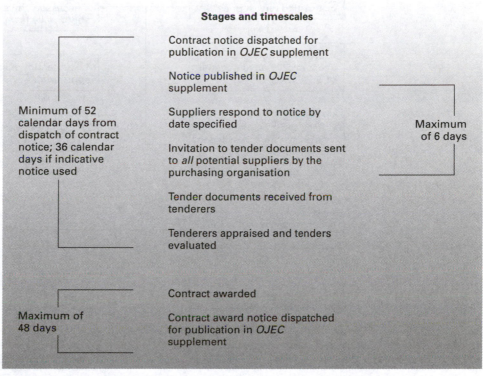

Figure 9.1 Open procedure for the procurement of supplies and services

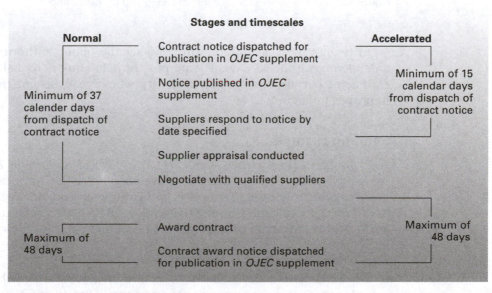

Figure 9.2 Negotiated procedure for the procurement of supplies or services *with* prior publication of a negotiated procedure notice

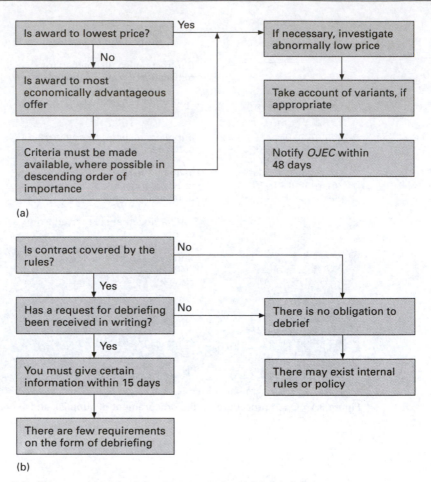

Figure 9.3 EU procedures for (a) contract award and (b) debriefing

On request from an unsuccessful tenderer the public authority must provide a debriefing within 15 days. The purpose of debriefing is to assist not only the contractor but also the issuing authority which may benefit from potentially improved future bids.

Pending changes

Following responses to the Green Paper *Public Procurement in the European Union: Exploring the Way Forward* issued in November 1996, the European Commission has recognised the need to simplify the legal framework and adapt it to the new electronic age while maintaining the stability of its basic structure. The proposed amendments to the directive are grouped into two parts as follows:

Simplification of the directive

- On 19 January 2002, MEPs approved a draft directive on public supply that will consolidate the three 'classic directives' (Directives 92/50/EEC, Directive 93/36/EEC and Directive 93/38/EEC) into a simplified and combined single text.

- The European Parliament also laid down that local authorities must give greater prominence to social and economic factors when awarding contracts.
- The thresholds that determine the application of the new instruments are also to be simplified and will be expressed in euros instead of special drawing rights.

Substantive amendments

The Commission also identified seven areas for substantive amendments as follows:

- The introduction of electronic purchasing mechanisms and their consequences in terms of reducing the length of an award procedure.
- The introduction of a new case for the use of the negotiated procedure which, for particularly complex contracts, permits a 'dialogue' between the contracting authority and the different candidates, while ensuring that there is competition and compliance with the principle of equality of treatment.
- The possibility for public procurement of concluding so called framework agreements not all of whose conditions are fixed, and on the basis of which contracts can be awarded without applying all the obligations of the directive to each one.
- Clarification of provisions relating to 'technical specifications', thus encouraging effective competition through the participation of the greatest possible number of tenderers and, in particular, innovative businesses.
- A strengthening of the provision relating to award and selection criteria.
- A simplification of the thresholds.
- The introduction of a common procurement vocabulary.

9.4.2   Central and local government guidelines

Guidance rather than directives relating to government purchasing is provided by the Procurement Policy Guidelines issued by the Office of Government Commerce in 1998 which replaced earlier Consolidated Guidelines published in 1987 and the Central Unit on Procurement (CUP) established in 1986 to obtain value for money improvements in non-war-like purchasing of goods and services.

The Procurement Policy Guidelines lay down general principles such as:

- Purchasers should base all procurement of goods and services on value for money, i.e. quality (or fitness for purpose) and delivery against price. Value for money should be judged on whole-life costs, not simply initial costs.
- Goods and services should be acquired by competition unless there are good reasons to the contrary.
- Government departments are responsible for ensuring that they comply appropriately with their legal obligations under the EC procurement rules and other international agreements.
- The rules and responsibilities of staff should be clearly defined and there should be adequate separation of duties.

CUP Guidance Notes have in some cases been superseded by the Government Construction Procurement Guidance Series. There are currently (2002) some

61 CUP Guidance Notes. (These are obtained from the Public Enquiries Unit HM Treasury or can be viewed on http://www.ogc.gov.uk/ogc/procurement.nsf/textpages/CUPGuidance.html)

Purchasing by local authorities is subject to mandatory competitive tender. This principle, when embodied in local authority orders, has the force of a directive. Regulations and guidance to local authorities may also be given in statutory instruments issued by the government.

Thus, following the publication in 1998 of the White Paper *Modernising Local Government*, the Department of the Environment, Transport and the Regions (DETR) has issued a number of new regulations to amend the framework for compulsory competitive tendering in respect of local authority services. In September 1999, for example, the DETR issued Circular 16/97 which aimed to make tendering more flexible and encourage local authorities to move towards an approach to service delivery more consistent with the concept of best delivery.

The guidelines emphasise the importance of:

- Transparency in the tender process, e.g. the need for the competition process to be undertaken and seen to be undertaken, in an open and transparent manner.
- Consultation with service users and providers.
- Ensuring that local authorities secure economically effective and efficient services, in which considerations of price and quality are properly balanced.
- Ensuring that all competing bids are objectively balanced and that tender evaluation processes are fair, auditable and in accordance with the authorities' legal and fudiciary duties.
- The need to act fairly between competitors and making sure that tendering practice does not advantage any one potential supplier or suppliers.

9.4.3 Company directives

Company directives may be issued by the top management of an organisation instructing that, for reasons of strategy or in pursuance of agreements, particular supplies must be obtained from a specific source, e.g. directives relating to intra-company or reciprocal trading.

9.5 Early buyer and supplier involvement

The importance of such involvement has been referred to in Chapter 7, section 7.5.

9.6 Sources of supply information

Three main issues may be considered under this heading: (i) who can supply, (ii) supplier assessment and (iii) supplier rating.

Sources of information relating to potential suppliers include the following:

- Catalogues. The value of printed catalogues depends on:
  - the information they contain, e.g. some provide valuable technical information;
  - the ease with which the information in them can be found;
  - the format of the catalogue. One survey reported that users would rather have one thick catalogue than several thin catalogues each devoted to a single product line.

  Electronic catalogues have many advantages over hard-copy documents. E-catalogues are dealt with in Chapter 6, section 6.7.

- Trade directories, e.g. *Kompass, Rylands, Buyer's Guide* etc. These are useful for new product requirements, unusual or occasional requirements and emergency items.

  Many trade directories are on databases (see below).

- Yellow Pages.

- Databases (see Chapter 2, section 2.9). Databases can provide up-to-date information and may be space-saving substitutes for large reference collections. Some important databases relevant to purchasing include: *Directory of Databases, Vol.1 On-line Databases, Reuters, Metal Service, 3T Telecom Gold and Prestel, Kompass On-line, Pergamon Infoline*. Details of how database access may be obtained to various databases can be obtained from the Director of On-line Databases Britline, Directory of British Databases (EPID Ltd).

  A number of government agencies, Business Links and Training and Enterprise Councils in addition to individual suppliers and agencies such as Chambers of Commerce have developed databases accessible over the internet. Access to such databases may be free and unrestricted or subscriber-only. Thompson and Homer[2] point out that:

  > In all cases the aim is the same, to provide a method whereby a company can search the various databases in order to satisfy their need for supplier information. For example, a company manufacturing forged components for vehicle steering systems might access such databases in order to identify and locate a company who has the capability to heat-treat their high molybdenum content forged components. In this example, the databases are being used to procure new suppliers (or sometimes, customers).

  Thompson and Homer also highlight several problems that limit the value of these online searchable databases:

  - The effort and time required to access several databases to find an answer to a query.
  - The quality of data content as reflected in differences in the method, terminology or units used to express quantitative data which reduces the value of any internet searches based on the data, resulting in the search excluding potentially useful companies simply because the format or units in which the data is held for a crucial field search to be inappropriate.
  - Duplication of data, e.g. the same organisation being listed differently within the same database, e.g. Small Parts Ltd, Small Engineering Ltd.

 - Timeliness of data content. Databases may contain information regarding organisations that have ceased trading or show wrong addresses, telephone numbers etc.
 - The power and flexibility of available search methods. Several online searchable databases investigated by the researchers revealed a considerable divergence in the search methods available to users ranging from rudimentary, e.g. a mere list of suppliers, to more sophisticated methods allowing for an increasing identification of supplier capabilities.

Thompson and Homer have developed a working model to avoid many of the above shortcomings.

■ Salespersons. The usefulness of salespersons is related to their knowledge of the product they are seeking to promote. Sales staff are often able to provide useful service information regarding suppliers, e.g. items other than those manufactured by their own undertaking.

■ Exhibitions. These provide an opportunity for comparing competing products, meeting representatives of suppliers and attending presentations by exhibitors. Exhibition catalogues and other literature usually provide details of the main suppliers in a particular field and should be retained for reference purposes.

■ Trade journals. These journals provide the buyer not only with information regarding new products, substitute materials, etc., but also with trade gossip which keeps the buyer informed of changes in the policies of suppliers and in their personnel.

■ Trade associations. The Trade Association Forum[3] maintains a website aimed at assisting buyers, government departments, researchers and the public to access information about UK trade associations and business sectors.

■ Informal exchange of information between purchasing professionals.

■ Invitations to tender. See also the section on internet auctions in Chapter 6, section 6.8.

■ Internet exchanges and marketplaces. See Chapter 6, section 6.6.

■ Information provided by prospective suppliers in response to a questionnaire designed to elicit further information from undertakings wishing to be placed on a database.

9.7 Supplier appraisal and assessment

9.7.1 When to appraise

Supplier appraisal may arise when a prospective vendor applies to be placed on the buyer's approved list or in the course of negotiation when the buyer wishes to assure him/herself that a supplier can meet requirements reliably.

Supplier appraisal can be a time consuming and costly activity. It should therefore be selective. Lysons[4] states that there are certain situations in which appraisal is essential. These include:

- where potential suppliers do not hold BS EN ISO 9000:2000;
- purchase of strategic high profit, high risk items;
- purchase of non-standard items;
- placing of construction and similar contracts;
- expenditure on capital items, including plant, machinery and computer systems;
- for purposes of supplier development, i.e. what needs to be done to bridge the gap between the present resources and competences of a supplier or potential supplier and the standard required by the purchaser;
- when entering into JIT arrangements;
- when contemplating a supplier association. A supplier association has been defined by Hines[5] as 'a group of companies linked together on a regular basis to share knowledge and experience in an open and co-operative manner';
- when engaging in global sourcing;
- when establishing e-procurement arrangements with long-term strategic suppliers;
- when negotiating total quality management (TQM) and quality in respect of high profit or high risk items;
- when negotiating outsourcing contracts;
- before agreeing subcontracting by a main supplier in respect of important companies;
- when negotiating service level agreements.

9.7.2   What should be appraised?

Supplier appraisal is situational. What to appraise is related to the requirements of the particular purchaser. All appraisals should, however, evaluate potential suppliers from seven perspectives:

- finance
- production capacity and facilities
- human resources
- quality
- performance
- environmental and ethical considerations
- information technology

Such information may be obtained from questionnaires sent to prospective suppliers who have applied to be added to the purchaser's list of approved suppliers, or may be obtained prior to a supplier visit.

Finance

The DTI[6] points out that financial appraisal should reduce, but not eliminate, the risk of placing business with a company whose financial viability is in doubt. It does, however, provide information enabling considered decisions to be made either when sourcing suppliers or when evaluating tenders. The checks recommended are:

- The assessed turnover of the enterprise over three years.
- The profitability and the relationship between gross and net profits of the enterprise over three years.
- The value of capital assets and return on capital assets and return on capital employed.
- The scale of borrowings, and the ratio of debts to assets.
- Whether the firm has a financial backer or guarantor of some sort.
- The possibility of takeover or merger affecting ability to supply.
- Whether the firm is tied to a small number of major customers, so that if one or more withdrew their businesses it might cause the firm financial difficulties.

Such enquiries are advisable for SME (small and medium enterprises) in respect of one-off or annual contracts in excess of, say, £15,000. Often the appraisal can be undertaken internally by accounting staff from a study of the supplier's annual report and accounts over the past three or four years.

Credit reports may also be obtained from bankers of credit references and credit reports provided by such agencies as Dun and Bradstreet. Important information provided by Dun and Bradstreet Supplier Evaluation Reports include:

- *Sales* – gives a picture of the firms financial size in terms of sales/revenue volume.
- *Financial profile* – evaluates how the enterprise is doing financially compared with its industry. To understand the profitability and solvency of a supplier, five key financial ratios are calculated which provide industry benchmarks against a peer group of suppliers.
- *Supplier risk score* – an evaluation of the risk involved in dealing with a supplier. This presents an at-a-glance 1–9 rating based on financial, public records and operational information with 1 being the lowest and 9 the highest risk. This predictive score helps purchasing to understand the general financial status of a supplier and benchmark the supplier against others.

Production capacity

Capacity has been defined as:[7]

> **The limiting capability of a productive unit to produce within a stated time period, normally expressed in terms of output units per unit of time.**

Capacity is an elusive concept because it must be related to the extent that a facility is used, e.g. it may be the policy to utilise production capacity five days weekly, one shift daily or to produce a maximum of 2,000 units monthly. Plant capacity can normally be increased by overtime and adding new facilities, and suppliers' attention should be given to the following considerations:

- The maximum productive capacity in a normal working period.
- The extent to which capacity is currently over- or undercommitted. A full order book may raise doubts about the supplier's capacity to take on further work. Why is a substantial amount of capacity underutilised?
- How existing capacity might be expanded to meet future increased demand.
- The percentage of available capacity utilised by existing major customers.
- What percentage of capacity would be utilised if the potential supplier were awarded the business of the purchaser. This can also be assessed in terms of annual turnover. Care should be taken to avoid making the supplier over-dependent on one or two customers.
- What systems are used for capacity planning?

Production facilities

Appraisal of production facilities depends on the purpose of appraisal. Appraisal of machinery, for example, depends on what is to be produced. In general, attention should be given to such aspects as:

- Has the supplier a full range of machinery to make the required product?
- How would any shortage of machinery be overcome?
- Are machines modern and well maintained? (Machine breakdown will affect delivery.)
- Is plant layout satisfactory?
- Is there evidence of 'good housekeeping'?
- Has the supplier adopted such approaches as computer aided design (CAD), computer aided manufacture (CAM) or flexible manufacturing systems (FMS)?
- Are health and safety provisions satisfactory?

Human resources

No organisation is better than the people who comprise it. Information should be obtained regarding:

- Number of persons employed in manufacturing and administration.
- Use of human resources – whether economical, with everyone busy, or extravagant, with excess people doing little or nothing.
- Names, titles, qualifications and experience of managerial staff.
- Training schemes for supervisory and executive staff.
- Encouragement of teamwork and empowerment.
- Worker representation and recognised trade unions.
- Days lost through industrial disputes in each of the past five years.
- Turnover in respect of managerial and operative staff.
- Worker attitudes to the organisation and concern for meeting customer requirement.

Quality

In respect of suppliers not included in the BSI Register of Firms of Assessed Quality, appraisal may require satisfactory answers to such questions as:

- Has the supplier met the criteria for other BSI schemes such as Kitemark, Safety Mark and scheme for registered stockists?
- Has the supplier met the quality approval criteria of other organisations, e.g. Ford Quality Awards, the Ministry of Defence, British Gas etc?
- To what extent does the supplier know about and implement the concept of total quality management?
- What procedures are in place for the inspection and testing of purchased materials?
- What relevant test and inspection does the supplier process?
- What statistical controls are applied in respect of quality?
- Does quality control cover evaluation of subcontractors?
- Can the supplier guarantee that the purchaser can safely eliminate incoming inspection? This is especially important in respect of JIT deliveries.

Performance

Particularly when appraising suppliers of non-standard products such as construction projects or the installation of computer systems, questions should be asked regarding:

- What similar projects the supplier has already undertaken.
- What current projects are in hand.
- What are/were the distinctive features of such projects.
- What innovations might be introduced.
- What customers can the supplier cite as referees.

Environmental and ethical factors

ISO 14001 provides guidelines on environmental policies and, where applicable, suppliers should be expected to have an environmental policy and procedures for the implementation of such a policy. A wide number of EU directives have also been issued relating to air, water, chemicals, packaging and waste.

Apart from reference to ISO 14001 and EU directives, suitable questions include:

- Has responsibility for environmental management been allocated to a particular person?
- Are materials obtained, so far as possible, from sustainable sources, e.g. timber?
- What is the life cycle cost of the suppliers' product?
- What facilities has the supplier for waste minimisation, disposal and recycling?
- What energy savings, if any, do the supplier's product provide?

- What arrangements are in place for the control of dangerous substances and nuisance?

Ethical questions may include:

- Has the supplier an ethical policy relating to the sale and purchase of items?
- Who is responsible for enforcement of such a policy?
- What guidelines and procedures are provided relating to the confidentiality of information provided by a customer?
- What guidelines apply to the receipt of gifts and hospitality?
- What principles apply in respect of conflicts of interest?

Information technology

Recent research indicates that more than one-third of buyers use the internet to conduct transactions and such usage us likely to increase dramatically. Additionally, the web also supports a variety of activities such as: identifying new sources of supply; finding product information including products, prices and delivery; tracking orders; and receiving technical advice and after-sales service.

It is useful to ask mainly open-ended questions under this heading since the replies will indicate the extent to which the supplier is exploiting the possibilities of e-business. Typical questions might be:

- Does your organisation have a website?
- What information does the website provide?
- What business activities does your organisation process electronically?
- In what ways does your organisation:
  - reduce or eliminate paper transactions?
  - shorten order cycles?
  - reduce inventory?
  - provide real-time information on product availability and inventory?
  - provide collaborative planning?
  - integrate its supply chain?

9.7.3 Visits to suppliers

Supplier visits should always be undertaken by a cross-functional team including a senior member of purchasing and experts on quality and production engineering. Each member of the team is able to evaluate the supplier from a specialist viewpoint and ensures shared responsibility for the decision to approve or reject a supplier. The purposes of a supplier visit include:

- The confirmation of information provided by the supplier in a preliminary questionnaire.
- To discuss the products and services offered by a potential supplier and ways in which the supplier can contribute to the requirements of the visiting organisation.

- To resolve uncertainties, problems or conflicts.
- To establish personal relationships between key personnel of both the purchasing and selling organisations.

When visiting suppliers, desk research should always precede field research. If the team has 'done its homework' it can, from previous desk research using published or unpublished data, e.g. company reports, balance sheets, references, strike records etc., establish the veracity of the answers received in the course of the visit. Where visits are undertaken regularly, a standard 'supplier appraisal rating form' can be prepared. This ensures that no important questions are overlooked and provides a permanent record of the visit and the reasons for the decision reached.

9.7.4 Checklist for supplier visits

The following checklist indicates areas which warrant particular attention by procurement staff when making appraisal visits to potential suppliers:

- *Personal attitudes.* An observant visitor can sense the attitudes of the supplier's employees towards their work and this provides an indication of the likely quality of their output and service dependability. The state of morale will be evident from:
  - an atmosphere of harmony or dissatisfaction among the production workers;
  - the degree of interest in customer service on the part of supervisory staff;
  - the degree of energy displayed and the interest in getting things done;
  - the use of manpower – whether economical, with everyone usually busy, or extravagant and costly, with excess people doing little or nothing.
- *Adequacy and care of production equipment.* Close observation of the equipment in a plant will indicate whether it is:
  - modern or antiquated;
  - accurately maintained or obviously worn;
  - well cared for by operators or dirty and neglected;
  - of proper size or type to produce the buyer's requirements;
  - of sufficient capacity to produce the quantities desired.

The presence or absence of ingenious self-developed mechanical devices for performing unusual operations will be indicative of the plant's manufacturing and engineering expertise.

- *Technological know-how of supervisory personnel.* Conversations with supervisors, shop superintendents and others will indicate their technical knowledge and their ability to control and improve the operations of processes under their supervision.
- *Means of controlling quality.* Observation of the inspection methods will indicate their adequacy to ensure the specified quality of the product. Attention should be given to:

- whether the materials are chemically analysed and physically checked;
- frequency of inspection during the production cycle;
- employment of such techniques as statistical quality control;
- availability of statistical quality control.

■ *Housekeeping.* A plant which is orderly and clean in its general appearance indicates careful planning and control by management. Such plant inspires confidence that its products will be produced with the same care and pride in their quality. The dangers of breakdown, fire or other disasters will also be minimised, with a consequent increased assurance of continuity of supply.

■ *Competence of technical staff.* Conversations with design, research and laboratory staff indicate their knowledge of the latest materials, tools and processes relating to their products and on anticipated developments in their industry.

■ *Competence of management.* All the above areas are, in essence, a reflection of management and therefore indicate its quality. Particularly in the case of a new supplier, an accurate appraisal of executive personnel is of paramount importance.

9.8   Supplier performance rating

9.8.1   Purpose

The purpose of a supplier appraisal is to evaluate the performance in respect of one or more of the factors, price, quality, delivery and service, of an actual supplier. It will:

■ provide the buyer with objective information on which judgements relating to source selection can be based;

■ enable the buyer to provide the supplier with an indication of his or her performance rating and of where improvements, if any, are required.

9.8.2   Subjective rating

All buyers make subjective appraisals of supplier performance. Such appraisals may be adequate for low cost, routine items although they have the following deficiencies:

■ They are 'in the head' of the individual buyer and are lost should the buyer leave.

■ They often have a 'halo' effect, i.e. a tendency to be biased in favour of a supplier by some quite irrelevant impression or estimate (good or bad) of that supplier.

9.8.3   Quantitative ratings

The aim of quantitative ratings is to remedy the deficiencies of subjective ratings. The disadvantages of such procedures are as follows:

- The high cost of collecting data on which ratings are based. With quality rating, for example, this data may relate to the costs of defect prevention, detection and correction, involving considerable sub-analysis of what is involved under each heading. (The introduction of computers has, however, made the collection of data easier. In any event, such ratings should only be attempted in respect of critical or high cost items using the Pareto approach.)

- Ratings may give the impression of scientific accuracy whereas in fact they are no more accurate than the assumptions on which they are based.

- Supplier performance is often affected by circumstances outside the control of the vendor.

9.8.4 Vendor rating forms

Rating forms can be used to assess the overall competence of a supplier with a view to determining whether:

- to grant preferred supplier status;
- to work with the supplier to develop and improve performance;
- to abandon the vendor as a source of supply.

Extracts from the Guide to the Supplier Performance and Review System of a leading engineering enterprise are shown below.

- As indicated by Figure 9.4, suppliers are assessed under four measurement dimensions (i) quality; (ii) cost; (iii) delivery and (iv) partnership. The four dimensions are equally important (equally weighted) and are examined together to give a fuller picture of performance in that dimension.

- As shown in Table 9.4, each measurement dimension consists of several elements each of which may have different weightings and combine to reflect performance in that dimension. The performance of a measurement dimension is the total actual scores of each measure expressed as a percentage of its maximum possible score.

- Performance is classified by reference to look-up tables based upon the performance potential of a company. The tables award points either automatically through the company's computer system or manually as calculated by the persons conducting the measure.

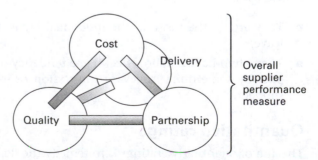

Figure 9.4 Supplier performance measurement dimensions

Table 9.4   Performance measurement dimensions

Dimension		Measure	Description
Quality	Q1	Delivered quality (PPM)	Number of defective parts in a period including parts returned or renewed
	Q2	Quality concessions (PPM)	Number of parts declared upon concessions raised with the period
	Q3	Delivered quality (incidence)	Number of incidents of discovery of defective parts in the period
	Q4	Quality concessions (incidence)	Number of concessions raised in the period
	Q5	Customer complaints	Number of vendor-liable customer complaints in the period, i.e. customer complaints from external to XYZ plc and complaints from other suppliers
	Q6	Critical action	Severity of action required in the period as a result of defectives
	Q7	Problem resolution (quality)	The highest level the supplier has escalated to on one of three levels of problem resolution within the measurement period
	Q8	Quality and environmental management systems	The level of formal certification and management systems possessed by the supplier
Cost	C1	Total acquisition cost	This measure is still under development. The supplier's score will be unaffected
	C2	Quality of service	The responsiveness and flexibility in response to commercial issues
Delivery	D1	Adherence	Number of batches delivered on time, in full, expressed as a percentage of total order requirement
	D2	Scan	Number of part numbers delivered expressed as a percentage of total order requirement
	D3	Problem resolution (delivery)	The highest level to be achieved on one of three levels, within the measurement period with respect to delivery problems
Partnership	P1	Design and development assessment	The quality of research, design and development
	P2	Project management	Project management performance in achieving gateway requirements
	P3	Management assessment	Comparison of the supplier's operations against preferred management methods
	P4	Responsiveness (logistics)	Level of responsiveness, flexibility and effort with regard to logistics

■ Points are awarded for each measure based on the performance classification achieved by the supplier. For each measure the score will be:

Class-leading	100 points
Standard	66 points
Substandard	33 points
Unsatisfactory	1 point
Not applicable	0 points

All suppliers are expected to achieve at least standard performance.

■ Weightings are applied to each measure within a dimension reflecting their relative importance.

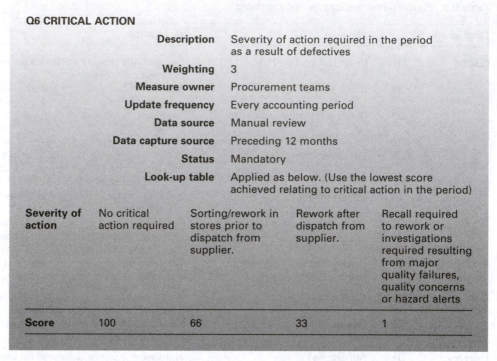

Figure 9.5 Method of scoring in an example of a Vendor Rating Scheme

Two examples of the scoring method are given in Figures 9.5 and 9.6.

The advantages of the system include the following:

- Feedback on performance is provided to suppliers. The importance of such communication is highlighted by Egan:[8]

   When in 1980, Jaguar started to knobble component suppliers for poor performance of their product, they (component suppliers) were often surprised because until that time no one had bothered to give them feedback of this kind and they, therefore, could be partly forgiven for believing that everything in the garden was rosy. I say partly because component suppliers did very little to find out how their products performed in service.

- The assessment provides a framework for discussion between purchaser and supplier and can be used to the benefit of each in achieving improvements.

- The scores of competing suppliers within a defined family group of parts can be used to rank individual vendors.

- The headings in the scheme can be used to appraise potential as well as to rank the performance of actual suppliers.

9.9 The Ten Cs of effective supplier evaluation

Many of the aspects of supplier appraisal are neatly summarised by Carter[9] as the 'Seven Cs of Supplier Evaluation':

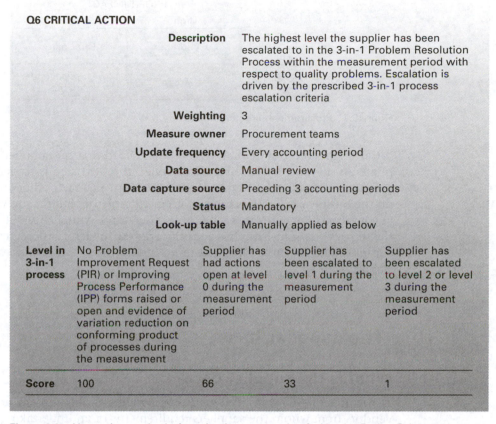

Q6 CRITICAL ACTION

Description	The highest level the supplier has been escalated to in the 3-in-1 Problem Resolution Process within the measurement period with respect to quality problems. Escalation is driven by the prescribed 3-in-1 process escalation criteria
Weighting	3
Measure owner	Procurement teams
Update frequency	Every accounting period
Data source	Manual review
Data capture source	Preceding 3 accounting periods
Status	Mandatory
Look-up table	Manually applied as below

Level in 3-in-1 process	No Problem Improvement Request (PIR) or Improving Process Performance (IPP) forms raised or open and evidence of variation reduction on conforming product of processes during the measurement	Supplier has had actions open at level 0 during the measurement period	Supplier has been escalated to level 1 during the measurement period	Supplier has been escalated to level 2 or level 3 during the measurement period
Score	100	66	33	1

Figure 9.6 Alternative method of scoring in an example of a Vendor Rating Scheme

1 *Competence* of the supplier to undertake the tasks required.

2 *Capacity* of the supplier to meet the purchaser's total needs.

3 *Commitment* of the supplier to the customer in terms of quality, cost driving and service.

4 *Control systems* in respect of inventory, costs, budgets, people and information.

5 *Cash resources and financial stability* ensuring that the selected supplier is financially sound and is able to continue in business into the foreseeable future.

6 *Cost* – commensurate with quality and service.

7 *Consistency* – the ability of the supplier to deliver consistently and, where possible, to improve levels of quality and service.

Three further Cs not identified by Carter are:

8 *Culture* – suppliers and purchasers should share similar values.

9 *Clean* – suppliers and products should satisfy legislative and other environmental requirements.

10 *Communication* – can the supplier communicate and receive information electronically?

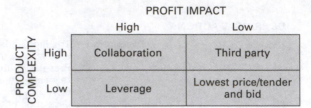

Figure 9.7 Procurement targeting matrix

Carter goes on to state that, having established that the supplier has the appropriate attributes to be an effective supplier, the next step is to define some contingent system of weighting the Seven Cs relative to each other and their impact on the business, and offers the procurement targeting matrix shown in Figure 9.7 as a method of prioritising each C according to the complexity of the product and the impact on profit. Thus, for a specification such factors as cost, consistency and commitment might be weighted more highly than cash resources and financial stability.

9.10 The supplier base

9.10.1 What is the supplier base?

The supplier base relates to the number, range location and characteristics of the vendors from whom the suppliers requirements of an undertaking are obtained.

Supplier bases may be described as broad, lean, narrow, single-sourced, local, national, international, diversified or specialised. They can relate to a 'family' of related supplies and suppliers or to the totality of vendors with whom a purchaser does business.

Factors influencing the supply base of an enterprise include:

- the core competences of the enterprise;
- make, buy, outsourcing and subcontracting decisions;
- single, multiple and partnership decisions;
- tiering;
- international and global sourcing;
- countertrade, inter-company trading and reciprocal trade;
- risk aspects especially ensuring continuity of supply;
- miscellaneous factors such as the social responsibilities of a large company to local industry or the support of small companies.

9.10.2 Supplier base optimisation

Supplier base optimisation or supplier base rationalisation is concerned with determining the approximate number of suppliers with whom the purchaser will do business. The need for such rationalisation derives from:

■ the need to control cost and procurement processes. A large number of suppliers will entail higher administrative costs. Electronic procurement will usually lead to a rationalisation of supplier bases by integrating business processes and data with key suppliers and facilitating collaborative relationships;

■ the need to eliminate suppliers incapable of meeting the purchaser's performance requirements or from whom few purchases are made.

The aim of supplier base optimisation is therefore to leverage the buying power of an organisation with the smallest number of suppliers consistent with security of supplies and the need for high quality goods and services at competitive prices.

Supplier base optimisation will therefore start with an analysis of the existing supply base and the evaluation of suppliers on criteria such as performance, cost, service, quality and the amount of business transacted during a specified period. Such an analysis may result in supplier base consolidation through such approaches as:

■ An approved or preferred supplier list.

■ Selection of a single supplier with whom to develop partnership or other collaborative arrangements.

The advantages of supplier base rationalisation include:

■ Savings in administrative costs.

■ Up to 80 per cent of supplies met by selected vendors.

■ The development of long-term partnerships and supplier associations.

■ Improved standardisation.

■ Elimination or reduction in maverick purchases.

■ Lower total production costs.

9.10.3 Possible risks of a reduced supplier base

■ Overdependence on a single supplier.

■ Danger of supply disruption due to strikes, production breakdowns, floods or similar natural disasters, disruption of suppliers' supplies.

■ Loss of supplier goodwill.

■ Reduced competition.

■ Failure to seek new or more competitive suppliers.

9.10.4 Core competences

Core competences are concerned with identifying the particular strengths that give an organisation an advantage over its competitors and areas of particular weakness, which are to be avoided. Core competence – 'ascertaining what we do best' and entrusting to others needed goods and services that *they* do best – is the key aspect of strategic and tactical decisions relating to whether to make, buy, outsource or subcontract.

9.11   Make-or-buy strategies and tactics

Make-or-buy decisions compare the cost of producing a component or providing a service internally with the cost of purchasing the component or service from an external supplier. Probert[10] identifies three levels of make-or-buy decision – strategic, tactical and component – all of which are linked to overall organisation strategy.

9.11.1   Strategic make-or-buy decisions

Strategic make-or-buy decisions determine the shape and capability of the organisation's manufacturing operation by influencing:

- what products to make;
- what investment to make in machines and labour to make the products;
- ability to develop new products and processes since the knowledge and skill gained by manufacturing in-house may be critical for future applications;
- the selection of suppliers since they may need to be involved in design and production processes;
- conversely, inappropriate allocation of work to suppliers may damage an enterprise by developing a new competitor or damaging product quality or performance;
- profitability, risk and flexibility.

They also provide the framework for shorter-term tactical and component decisions. Reference should also be made to Figure 9.8 on page 351.

9.11.2   Tactical make-or-buy decisions

Tactical make-or-buy decisions deal with the issue of temporary imbalance of manufacturing capacity:

- Changes in demand may make it impossible to make everything in-house even though this is the preferred option.
- Conversely, a fall in demand may cause the enterprise to bring in-house work previously bought out if this can be done without damaging supplier relationships.

In such situations, managers require criteria for choosing between the available options. Such criteria may be quantitative, qualitative or both.

9.11.3   Component make-or-buy decisions

Component make-or-buy decisions are made, ideally, at the design stage and relate to whether a particular component of the product should be made in-house or bought in.

9.11.4   Cost factors in make-or-buy decisions

Although such decisions are normally made on the basis of calculations provided by the management accountant, purchasing staff should understand the principles involved. Accurate make-or-buy decisions often require the application of marginal costing and break-even analysis.

Marginal costing

Marginal costing is defined as:[11]

> A [costing] principle whereby variable costs are charged to cost units, and the fixed cost attributable to the relevant period is written off in full against the contribution for that period.

The term 'contribution' in the above definition is the difference between the selling (or purchase) price and the variable cost per unit.

The marginal cost approach is shown by Examples 9.1 and 9.2.

Example 9.1   Marginal costing

	£
Direct material	60
Direct wages	30
Direct expenses	10
Prime cost	100
Works overhead (100% on direct wages)	30
Works cost	130
Office overhead (20% on works cost)	26
	156
Selling overheads £14 per item	14
Cost of sales	170
Net profit	30
Normal selling price	200

Assume:

1 that works overheads are 60 per cent fixed and 40 per cent variable;
2 that office overheads are constant;
3 that selling expenses are 50 per cent fixed and 50 per cent variable.

Then the *marginal* cost would be:

	£	
Direct materials	60	
Direct wages	30	
Direct expenses	10	
	100	
Works overhead	12	(i.e. 40% of £30)
Selling overheads £14 per item	13	(i.e. 50% of £26)
	125	

Any price over £125 represents a *contribution* to fixed overheads. If fixed overheads totalled £75,000, a selling price of £200 would represent a contribution of £75 per item to fixed overheads and it would be necessary to sell 1,000 items before the undertaking would break even. If, however, the selling price were reduced to £150 it would be necessary to sell 3,000 units before reaching the break-even point since the contribution per item would be only £25.

In make-or-buy decisions it is necessary to compare the vendor's price with the marginal cost of making, plus the loss of contributions of work displaced.

Example 9.2   Marginal costing

A company manufacturers an assembly, JMA 423, the normal annual usage of which is 10,000 units. The current costs are:

	£
Materials	90
Labour	40
Variable overheads	10
Fixed overheads	20
	180

The component could be purchased for £156 but the capacity used for its production would then be idle. Only 30 per cent of the fixed costs are recoverable if the component is bought.

Assuming there are no other relevant factors, should component JMA 423 be made or bought?

Solution
A superficial comparison suggests that the item should be bought rather than made. The correct comparison, however, is between the marginal cost of making and the buying price:

	Make	Buy	Difference
Variable costs (£90 + £40 + £10)	£140	£156	£16
Variable costs × Volume	£1,400,000	£1,560,000	
Fixed costs	£60,000	£60,000	
(30% of £20 × 10,000 units)	£1,460,000	£1,620,000	£160,000

The above figures indicate that it is more profitable to make than to buy. This is because the fixed costs of £60,000 would be likely to continue and, since the capacity would be unused, the fixed overheads would not be absorbed into production. In consequence, by buying instead of making, profits would be reduced by £160,000.

Opportunity cost

This is the potential benefit that is forgone because one course of action has been chosen over another, i.e. if the production facilities used in making had been applied to some alternative purpose.

Break-even point

The break-even point is:

The level of activity in units or value at which the total revenues equal total costs.

Estimated production quotas and actual usage may differ.

Example 9.3   Opportunity cost

An undertaking manufacturers 100,000 of item X at a total cost of £120,000 and a marginal cost of £100,000. Item X could be bought out for £1.50 each. The decision whether to make or buy depends on the cost of forgoing the opportunity to make something else. If the production capacity could be used to make an item with a contribution of £0.75 each, then the position would be:

Making	Buying but production capacity not used	Buying less opportunity cost
£100,000	£150,000	£150,000
		−£75,000
		£75,000

In this case it would be more profitable to buy the item.

Example 9.4   Break-even analysis

Using the data in Example 9.2, at what volume will the company be indifferent between buying and making component JMA 423?

Solution
This is found by the formula:

$$\frac{F}{(P-V)}$$

where: F = fixed costs
P = purchase price
V = variable cost per unit

In this case:

$$\frac{£60,000}{£156 - £140} = \frac{£60,000}{16} = 3,750 \text{ units}$$

If only 3,750 units are required there will be no effect on profits from making or buying. If fewer than 3,750 units are required, buying is the more profitable alternative. If more than 3,750 units are required, making is the better alternative.

Learning curves

Learning curves are dealt with in Chapter 17. When components are bought from a specialist manufacturer there may be little opportunity for learning. When the items are new, however, the costs of both making and buying may have to be adjusted for a learning factor. In comparing made-in and bought-out prices, therefore, learning is a factor that must, where applicable, be considered.

9.11.5   Other considerations in make-or-buy decisions

Apart from those mentioned above, a number of other quantitative and qualitative factors must be considered in deciding whether to make or buy.

Quantitative factors in favour of *making* include:

- Chance to use up idle capacity and resources.
- Potential lead time reduction.
- Possibility of scrap utilisation.
- Greater purchasing power with larger orders of a particular material.
- Large overhead recovery base.
- Exchange rate risks.
- Cost of work is known in advance.

Quantitative factors in favour of *buying* include:

- Quantities required too small for economic production.
- Avoidance of costs of specialist machinery or labour.
- Reduction in inventory.

Qualitative factors in favour of *making* include:

- Ability to manage resources.
- Commercial and contractual advantages.
- Worries are eliminated regarding such matters as the stability and continuing viability of suppliers or possible repercussions of changes in supplier ownership.
- Maintaining secrecy.

Qualitative factors in favour of *buying* include:

- Spread of financial risk between purchaser and vendor.
- Ability to control quality when purchased from outside.
- Availability of vendor's specialist expertise, machinery and/or patents.
- Buying, in effect, augments the manufacturing capacity of the purchaser.

9.11.6 Making the make-or-buy decision

From the above it is clear that, irrespective of whether they relate to the strategic, tactical or component levels, many quantitative and qualitative factors have to be considered when arriving at make-or-buy decisions. A simple procedure designed to answer the question 'are we competitive?' is shown in Figure 9.8.

9.12   Outsourcing

9.12.1 What is outsourcing?

'Outsourcing' is possibly a wider term than make-or- buy, although the two terms are often used synonymously. Outsourcing is:[12]

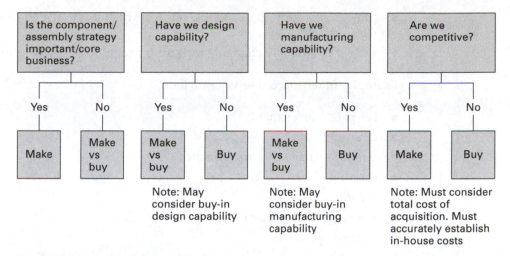

Figure 9.8   Decision processes for make or buy

Source: by permission of the Society of British Aerospace Companies

> The strategic use of resources to perform activities traditionally handled by internal staff and their resources . . . [It is a] management strategy by which an organisation outsources major non-core functions to specialised, efficient service providers.

Central to outsourcing are:

■ Make-or-buy decisions. 'Making' in this context also applies to the provision of services.

■ Partnerships between purchasers and suppliers. Since outsourcing relationships are often unequal it has been suggested that such arrangements should be termed 'co-sourcing'.

9.12.2   What to outsource

Outsourcing has developed as a reaction to the overdiversification that took place in the 1970s and early 1980s. This has led many enterprises to review their core activities and to concentrate on their core competences. Many organisations, it was argued, had little or no expertise in carrying out many ancillary or professional services or knowledge of the market rate for such activities. Therefore these activities should be put out to tender to ascertain their true market cost. Other things being equal, the enterprise should outsource these activities to specialists and concentrate its energies on core products or services.

The functions most easily outsourced according to the British government market testing programme (1993) are those which are:

■ resource intensive – especially with high labour or capital costs;

■ relatively discrete areas;

■ specialist and other areas;

■ characterised by fluctuating work patterns in loading and throughput;

- subject to quickly changing markets for which it is costly to recruit, train and retain staff;
- subject to a rapidly changing technology requiring expensive investment.

Examples of outsourced services include:

- car park management
- cleaning
- building repairs and maintenance
- catering
- security
- transport management
- waste disposal
- reception
- library
- medical/welfare
- travel administration
- pest control
- training centre management
- computers and information technology

9.12.3 What not to outsource

Rothery and Robinson[13] state that none of the following should be outsourced without careful consideration:

- management of strategic planning;
- management of finances;
- management of management consultancy;
- control of supplies;
- quality and environmental management;
- the supervision of the meeting of regulatory requirements such as: product liability, misleading advertising, quality, environmental regulations, staff health and safety, public safety, product/service safety.

9.12.4 Types of outsourcing

In relation to information technology (IT), Lacity and Hirscheim[14] provide a taxonomy of outsourcing options categorised as body shop, project management and total outsourcing.

- *Body shop outsourcing* refers to a situation where management uses outsourcing as a means of meeting short-term requirements, e.g. a shortage of in-house skills to meet a temporary demand.

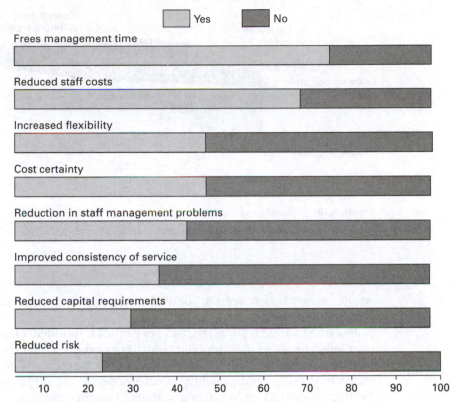

Figure 9.9   Main benefits of outsourcing

Source: taken from Carrington, L., 'Outside chances', *Personnel Today*, 8 February 1994, p.34

- *Project management outsourcing* is employed for all or part of a particular project, e.g. developing a new IT project, training in new skills, management consultancy.

- *Total outsourcing* is where the outsourcing supplier is given full responsibility for a selected area, e.g. catering, security.

9.12.5   Benefits of outsourcing

The main benefits identified by organisations that have adopted outsourcing is the freeing of management time to concentrate on core business operations. Other benefits are shown in Figure 9.9. Additional reasons for outsourcing other than those shown include:

- to gain access to world class capabilities;
- to improve organisational focus;
- to make capital funds available.

9.12.6   Problems of outsourcing

Outsourcing is not, however, without its problems and it can be up to two years before an organisation begins to benefit from any savings, and in some cases the

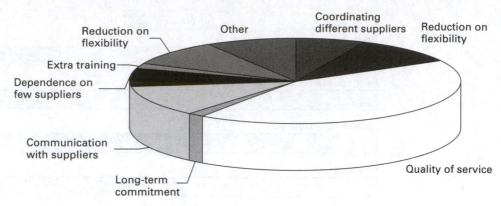

Figure 9.10 Problems of sourcing

Source: taken from Carrington, L., 'Outside chances', *Personnel Today*, 8 February 1994, p.34

whole process is cost neutral. Some of the problems of outsourcing are shown in Figure 9.10.

Research in 1993 reported that 46 per cent of respondents reported problems of overdependence on their supplier, and 40 per cent reported cost escalation and a lack of supplier flexibility.[15] The problems of outsourcing were described as: cost escalation, maintaining quality, overdependence on suppliers, lack of supplier flexibility, and lack of management skills to control supplier.

Reilly and Tamkin[16] mention that a principal objection to outsourcing is the possible loss of competitive advantage, particularly in the loss of skills and expertise of staff, insufficient internal investment and the passing of knowledge and expertise to the supplier who may be able to seize the initiative.

Lacity and Hirscheim[17] also point out that outsourcing does not seem to work well in the following areas:

- Where a specific or unique knowledge of the business is required.
- Where all services are custom.
- Where the employee culture is too fragmented or hostile for the organisation to come back together.

Problems reported in relation to outsourced supplies include:

- High staff turnover
- Poor project management skills
- Lack of commitment to the client or industry
- Shallow expertise
- Insufficient documentation
- Lack of control over larger suppliers
- Poor staff training
- Complacency over time

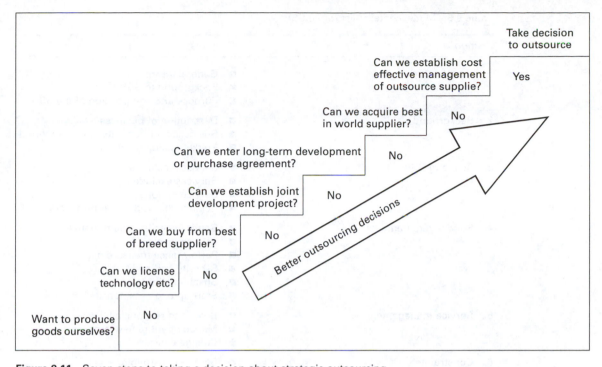

Figure 9.11   Seven steps to taking a decision about strategic outsourcing

Source: adapted by kind permission from Batram, P., *The Competitive Network*, Policy Publications, 1996, p.74

9.12.7 Implementing outsourcing

Implementation involves the following stages:

1 Consider the alternatives. These are shown in Figure 9.11.
2 Set up a working party to consider:
  (a) what to outsource;
  (b) why (strategy reasons);
  (c) cost comparisons of internal and external provision;
  (d) anticipated benefits and problems;
  (e) possible effects on staff, capital, finance and competitiveness.
3 Prepare as appropriate a technical performance or technical specification. An example of a statement of source requirements (SSR) prepared by the Central Computer and Telecommunications Agency (CCTA)[18] for market testing in respect of IS/IT services is shown in Table 9.5.
    The SSR describes the job needing to done, not the means for achieving it, and is not an invitation to tender. An SSR should be divided into three sections which:
  (a) set the source (sections 1, 2 and 3);
  (b) specify the requirements (sections 4, 5 and 6);
  (c) provide rules for those responding to the SSR (section 7).

Table 9.5 Model contents list for an SSR

Section	Contents
1. Introduction	■ General information ■ Background to SSR ■ Purpose and composition of the SSR
2. Background	■ Description of business ■ Business requirements to be supported ■ Market testing objectives
3. Scope of SSR	■ Services included ■ Services excluded ■ Service options ■ Relationship with other providers
4. Service requirements	■ Service specific requirements ■ Service levels ■ Performance measurement ■ Security and audit ■ Sustainability ■ Start-up and acceptance
5. Service management	■ Roles and responsibilities ■ Management review process ■ Change control
6. Constraints	■ Service constraints ■ Standards, methods and best practice ■ Contractual matters
7. Instructions to providers	■ Timetable for procurement ■ Format for proposals ■ Terms and conditions for submission of proposals ■ Evaluation approach ■ Further information

Supporting annexes	■ Business facts and figures
	■ Current IS/IT details:
	  – organisation
	  – costs and contractual commitments
	  – technical environment
	■ Mandatory requirements
	■ Desirable requirements

4 Consider possible suppliers.

5 Invite tenders against the specification.

6 Evaluate tenders against predetermined evaluation criteria.

7 Post-tender negotiation. Lacity and Hirscheim[19] provide the following advice relating to outsourcing contract negotiations:

(a) discard the vendor's standard contract;

(b) do not sign incomplete contracts;

(c)   hire outsourcing experts;

(d)   measure everything in the baseline period;

(e)   develop service level measures;

(f)   develop service level reports;

(g)   specify escalation procedures;

(h)   include penalties for non-performance;

(i)   determine growth;

(j)   adjust charges to changes in business volume;

(k)   select your account manager;

(l)   include a termination clause;

(m)   beware of 'change in character' clauses;

(n)   take care of your people.

8   Award contract.

9   Set up management control and monitoring processes.

Washington[20] suggests the following performance measures as applicable to the outsourcing of IT functions. Such measures may, however, be adapted to other outsourcing.

■ *Response time* – an average or specific response time for the maintenance of critical equipment.

■ *Availability* – what is to be provided on a daily shift or application basis.

■ *Downtime* – equipment shall not be available for less than a specified amount of time.

■ *Turnaround time or schedule of performance* – specify either a specific time on repairs to equipment or a particular performance time for services.

■ *Performance reports* – specify general performance criteria considered important to the outsourcing effort.

■ *Penalties for non-performance* – to emphasise the importance of meeting specific performance requirements.

■ *Satisfactory performance statement* – state the organisation's expectations of the vendor. These expectations need to be clearly specified.

■ *Subcontractor approval rights* – these should be built into the contract to aid in specifying what aspects of the work are to be handled only by the primary vendor.

Cost comparisons between those of the contractor and those of other providers should be undertaken at regular intervals. These comparisons can, for example, be made monthly on the basis of cost reports submitted by contractors. When compared with agreed target costs they can be the basis of incentive payments for improving on target costs or penalties for exceeding such standards or may provide a basis for negotiation.

9.13 Outsourcing purchasing

Organisations may consider outsourcing purchasing in the following circumstances:

- Where purchasing is a peripheral rather than a core activity. The characteristics of peripheral work as identified by Atkinson and Meager[21] are that it has:
  - low or generalised skill requirements;
  - internally focused responsibilities;
  - well defined or limited tasks;
  - jobs which are easily separated from other work;
  - no supply restrictions.

  These are also the characteristics of low-level operational purchasing. Beauchamp[22] also identified the following items as suitable for outsourcing consideration:
  - purchase orders, one-off and repeat needs;
  - locally and nationally procured needs (international sourcing and procurement may be rather specialised for outsourcing);
  - low value or low value/high order acquisitions;
  - brand name requirements;
  - call-offs against internally approved agreements;
  - set-up of commodity or service-based contracts;
  - obtaining goods for batch or volume manufacturing;
  - stocking and profiling for private/public sector needs;
  - finessing computerised purchasing or software-based manufacturing procurement;
  - all administration and paperwork associated with purchasing needs;
  - supply of stores staff at varying levels of skill;
  - multidimensional and multidepartmental sourcing.

- Where the supply base is small and based on proven cooperation, and there are no supply restrictions, the following may be outsourced:
  - well-defined or limited tasks;
  - jobs which are easily separated from other work.

  The above characteristics also apply to low-level operational purchasing.

- Where there is a small supplier base providing non-strategic, non-critical, low cost/low risk items. In such cases purchasing may be outsourced to:
  - specialist purchasing and suppliers' organisations;
  - buying consortia.

  Such organisations provide the advantage of:
  - bulk purchasing, giving them a strong negotiating position over a wide range of products;

  – wide-ranging product expertise;
  – clearly identified costs.

Before outsourcing purchasing, however, it is important to consider the potential problems as outlined in section 9.14.5 below.

9.14   Subcontracting

9.14.1   What is subcontracting?

Subcontracting may be distinguished from outsourcing in that the latter involves the total restructuring of an enterprise around core competences and outside relationships. Whatever the degree of outsourcing, enterprises must retain certain core capabilities. Outsourcing is a strategic long-term decision. Subcontracting is a tactical, short-term approach.

> If you want the most beautiful lawn in the neighbourhood and you hire someone to take responsibility for every aspect of lawn care, including cutting the grass, weed control, watering and fertilising, it's strategic sourcing. But hiring someone to only cut your lawn is subcontracting.[23]

9.14.2   Reasons for subcontracting

The buyer encounters problems of subcontracting in two main areas:

- Where the buyer's organisation is the employer or client entrusting work to a main contractor who, in turn, subcontracts part of the work. This is the case with most construction contracts.

- Where the buyer's organisation is the main contractor and subcontractor work for such reasons as:
  - overloading of machinery or labour;
  - to ensure completion of work on time;
  - lack of specialist machinery or specialist know-how;
  - to avoid acquiring long-term capacity when future demand is uncertain;
  - subcontracting is cheaper than manufacturing internally.

9.14.3   Organisation for subcontracting

- When subcontracting is a regular and significant part of the activity of an undertaking it may be desirable to set up a special subcontracting section either within or external to the purchasing department.

- Arrangements must be made for adequate liaison between all departments connected with subcontracting, i.e. design, production control, erection and site staff, inspection, finance etc.

■ Friction over who should negotiate with the selected suppliers sometimes develops between purchasing and design or technical departments. This can be avoided by a proper demarcation of authority and responsibility, purchasing having a power of commercial veto, and design, etc., a technical veto.

9.14.4 Selection of subcontractors

It may be necessary to check whether external approval of the selected subcontractor is necessary, as in government contracts or where a specific subcontractor has been specified by the client. Certain construction contracts may provide that subcontractors must not be selected on the basis of Dutch auctions.

9.14.5 Liaison with subcontractors

Matters to be considered include the following:

■ Planning, to ensure that the subcontractor can complete by the required date. Techniques such as Program Evaluation and Review Technique (PERT) are of assistance.

■ Ensuring that the subcontractor is supplied with the most recent copies of all necessary documentation including drawings, standards and planning instructions.

■ Arranging with the subcontractor for the supply by the main contractor of materials, tooling, specialist equipment etc., and the basis on which this shall be charged.

■ Control of equipment and materials in the possession of subcontractors.

■ Arrangements for returns at stocktaking of free-issue material in the possession of the subcontractor.

■ Arrangements for visits to the premises of the subcontractor by progress and inspection staff employed by the main contractor.

■ Arrangements for transportation, especially where items produced by the subcontractor require special protection, e.g. components with a highly finished surface.

■ Payment for any ancillary work to be performed by the subcontractor, e.g. painting on of part numbers.

9.14.6 Legal factors

These will depend on the circumstances of the specific contract. All major contracts for subcontracting should be vetted by the legal department of the main contractor. Where the buyer's undertaking is the client entrusting work to a main contractor, it is useful to remember the following generic principles.

Unless the contract has been placed on the basis, express or implied, that the work will be wholly performed by the main contractor, the client will have no authority to prevent the subcontracting of part of the work (this will not apply to contracts for personal service). If, therefore, the client wishes to specify particular subcontractors or to limit the right of the main contractor to subcontract, these matters must be negotiated when the order is placed. With construction and defence contracts, tenderers are often required to state what parts of the work will be subcontracted. In particular it is useful to include clauses stating that it is the duty of the main contractor to use reasonable care in the selection of subcontractors and that responsibility for the performance of subcontractors shall be with the main contractor exclusively.

9.15   Tiering

Tiering, as an aspect of lean supply was briefly mentioned in Chapter 3. The dissemination of knowledge relating to the significance of tiering owes much to the seminal work of Lamming, especially his book *Beyond Partnership: Strategies for Innovation and Supply*.[24]

9.15.1   Tiering levels

Lamming points out that the terms 'first' and 'second' tiers are 'used to indicate the degree of influence the supplier exerts in the supply chain rather than some fixed position in a hierarchy', and offers the following definitions:

> *First-tier suppliers* are those that integrate for direct supply to the assembler or who have a significant technical influence on the assembly while supplying indirectly.

> *Second-tier suppliers* are those that supply components to first-tier firms for integration into systems or provide some support service, such as metal finishing etc.

9.15.2   Reasons for tiering

Lamming shows that tiers may form for three reasons:

- Because the assembler may require first-tier suppliers to integrate diverse technologies not possessed by one organisation
- Where components required for systems will be very specialised and thus made by a small number of (large) firms, in large quantities (e.g. electronic parts), it is sensible for first-tier suppliers to buy these from specialist makers.
- The third level of subcontracted work is 'simple, low-value-added items required by first- and second-tier suppliers', e.g. presswork, fasteners.

9.15.3   Responsibilities of first-tier suppliers

First-tier suppliers are direct suppliers usually making high-cost, complex assemblies. They are empowered to relay the assembler's standards to second-tier or indirect suppliers and are responsible for large numbers of second-tier suppliers.

The responsibilities of first-tier suppliers, as identified by Lamming, include:

■ Research and development especially relating to technologies which are being applied to the assembler's product for the first time.
■ Management of subcontractors, including coordination previously undertaken by the assembler, e.g. sourcing, quality, delivery, payment.
■ True JIT supply.
■ Customer-dedicated staff who work in association with the design and production departments of the assembler.
■ Responsibility for warranty and end customer claims.

9.15.4 Some consequences of tiering

■ The key word at all tiering levels is collaboration since 'much of the competitive advantage required for lean production comes from the ability to deal as collaborators with subcontractors'.
■ Where tiering is carried out for either of the first or second reasons stated in section 9.15.1 above 'the relationship between the two suppliers becomes more akin to a strategic joint-venture than to a purchasing link. The product technology resides in both firms: the first tier supplier would find it just as difficult to replace the specialist second tier supplier as vice-versa. In this situation the suppliers . . . may even set up special companies to conduct business as joint-ventures'.
■ Apart from special companies coordination of activities and sharing of knowledge and experience between assemblers and first and second tier suppliers may be affected through Supplier Associations.

9.16 Supplier associations

9.16.1 What is a supplier association?

The supplier association or *Kyoryoku Kai* has been a feature of Japanese manufacturing since the 1950s. Assisted by *Kyoryoku Kai*, large Japanese manufacturers such as Toyota have been able both to coordinate and to develop their subcontractors in such ways as the dissemination of best practice, provision of technical assistance and, in some instances, training. Supplier associations also help to develop a climate of trust between the parties involved.

Hines[25] initially defined a supplier association as:

A mutually benefiting group of company's most important subcontractors, brought together on a regular basis for the purpose of co-ordination and co-operation as well as to assist all the members to benefit from the type of development associated with large Japanese assemblers such as Kaizen, Just-in-time, U-cell production and the achievement of zero defects.

A later definition is:[26]

> **A group of companies linked together on a regular basis to share knowledge and experience in an open and co-operative manner.**

The first UK organisation of this kind, Calsonic Llanelli Radiators Supplier Association, was instituted by the Welsh Development Agency in 1991. By April 1997 there were 35 such associations.[27]

Assemblers and sometimes their first-tier suppliers use supplier associations to develop suppliers and coordinate their efforts by such means as seminars and workshops for engineers and other staff of participating organisations; annual or biannual strategic meetings for senior staff from both customers and suppliers; and by sharing of knowledge and practice through interchange visits.

9.16.2 Aims and objectives of the *Kyoryoku Kai*

The aims and objectives of *Kyoryoku Kai* have been summarised by Hines[28] as:

- To improve the abilities and skills of suppliers, particularly in terms of JIT, TQM, statistical process control (SPC), value analysis, value engineering (VA/VE), CAD/CAM, management flexibility and cost reduction.
- To produce a uniform supply system using the same types of techniques.
- To facilitate the flow of information and strategy formulation to and from and within supplier networks.
- To increase trust between buyer and supplier allowing for closer business relationships.
- To keep suppliers and customers in touch with market developments and hence aid the translation of 'the voice of customers'.
- To enhance the reputation of the customer as someone suppliers should try to do (and increase) business with.
- To help smaller suppliers lacking specialist trainers.
- To increase length of relations.
- To allow development benefits to be shared.
- To provide an example to subcontractors of how to coordinate and develop their own suppliers.

9.16.3 Perceived benefits and disadvantages of supplier associations

In a study of eight Welsh supplier associations, Izushi and Morgan[29] reported that:

- A majority of the firms surveyed thought that their supplier associations helped them to form good relationships with other suppliers and build mutual trust between the participants.
- The majority also considered that their association gave then a better understanding of the customer firm and build mutual trust. This understanding derived from improved communication and 'stable orders' for goods from the

customer, early announcement of the customer's development plans and a less than arm's length approach on the customer's part to problem solving in scheduling and delivery.

■ A majority of the firms found their associations useful in assessing their competitive positions and learning general principles of best practice.

There were, however, a number of reservations. There was significant, if minority, support for the following statements:

■ 'A supplier association is no more than a gesture to show loyalty to a customer firm'.

■ 'A customer firm uses a supplier association to gain more control of its suppliers'.

In addition, supplier associations were criticised on the following grounds:

■ Associations may become 'talking shops' about general techniques which the customer leaves to suppliers to implement themselves.

■ Generalised presentations of techniques often pose difficulties in implementation because of supplier idiosyncrasies and problems.

■ The 'implement it yourself' approach may inhibit the development of mutual trust between customers and suppliers, e.g. when a customer asks suppliers to introduce techniques but refuses to disclose the results of implementation in its own organisation.

■ There may be difficulty in keeping momentum going between meetings.

Izushi and Morgan suggest that such shortcomings might be overcome by:

■ customer leadership in putting techniques into action and disclosing to customers how it implements them at its site;

■ making the best use of expertise possessed by member suppliers;

■ use of measurable goals and regular checking of achievements;

■ selection of member-suppliers who are conducive to collaboration and focusing on particular products or processes;

■ provision of training for the staff of supplier development teams to enable them to communicate with suppliers as partners.

9.17 Partnering

9.17.1 Definition and objectives

Partnering has been defined by Partnership Sourcing Ltd (PSL) as:[30]

A commitment to both customers and suppliers, regardless of size, to a long-term relationship based on clear, mutually agreed objectives to strive for world class capability.

Table 9.6 Comparison of traditional and partnering supplier relationships

Traditional	Partnership
Emphasises competitiveness and self-interest on the part of both purchaser and supplier	Emphasises cooperation and a community of interest between purchaser and supplier
Emphasis on 'unit price' with lowest price usually the most important buyer consideration	Emphasis on total acquisition costs (TAC) including indirect and hidden costs, e.g. production hold-ups and loss of customer goodwill through late delivery of material and components. Lowest price is never the sole buyer consideration
Emphasis is on short-term business relationships	Emphasis on long-term business relationships with involvement of supplier at the earliest possible stage to discuss how buyer requirements can be met
Emphasis on quality checks with inspection of incoming supplies	Emphasis on quality assurance based on TQM and zero defects
Emphasis on multiple sourcing	Emphasis on single sourcing although it is not, of necessity, confined to single sourcing. It will, however, reduce the supplier base
Emphasis on uncertainty regarding supplier performance and integrity	Emphasis on mutual trust between purchaser and supplier

Partnering marks a shift from traditional pressures exerted by larger customers on small/medium suppliers in which the latter were regarded as subordinates. Partnering aims to transform short-term adversarial customer/supplier relationships focused on the use of purchasing power to secure lower prices and improved delivery into long-term cooperation based on mutual trust in which quality, innovation and shared values complement price-competitiveness.

Some comparisons between traditional and partnering relationships are shown in Table 9.6.

Objectives

Griffiths[31] states that the reasons for seeking partnerships can include improvements in:

- design
- quality
- delivery and completion times
- production costs
- operating costs
- stock levels
- cash flow

The CIPS[32] has identified the following key drivers for establishing partnership relationships:

- drive for LAC (lower acquisition costs)
- reduced supplier base
- shorter product life cycles
- concentration on core business
- pressures towards lean supply

PSL has published a number of case studies of partnering in action (see the PSL website http://www.pslcbi.com).

9.17.2 What types of relationship are suitable for partnering?

PSL[33] has identified seven types of relationship that may be suitable for partnership:

- *High spend* – 'the vital few'.
- *High risk* – items and services which are vital irrespective of their monetary value.
- *High hassle* – vital supplies which are technically complex to arrange and take a lot of time, effort and resource to manage.
- *New services* – new products or services which may involve possible partners.
- *Technically complex* – involving technically advanced or innovative supplies where the cost of switching would be prohibitive.
- *Fast changing* – areas where knowing future technology or trends or legislation is critical.
- *Restricted markets* – markets which have few reliable or competent suppliers and where closer links with existing or new suppliers might improve supply security.

9.17.3 Advantages of partnering

The advantages of partnering are set out in Table 9.7.

9.17.4 Implementing partnership sourcing

Implementation should proceed through the following stages:

1 Identify purchased items potentially suitable for partnership sourcing:
    (a) high spend items and suppliers – Pareto analysis may show that a small number of suppliers account for a high proportion of total spend;
    (b) critical items where the cost of supplier failure would be high;
    (c) complex items involving technical and innovative supplies where the cost of switching sources would be prohibitive;
    (d) 'new buy' items where supplier involvement in design and production methods is desirable from the outset.

Table 9.7 Advantages of partnering

To the purchaser	To the supplier
Purchasing advantage through: quality assurance; reduced supplier base; assured supplies through long-term agreements; ability to plan long-term improvement rather than negotiating for short-term advantage; delivery on time (JIT); improved quality	*Marketing advantage* through: stability through long-term agreements; larger share of orders placed; ability to plan ahead and invest; ability to work with key customers on product and/or service; scope to increase sales without increasing procurement overheads
Lower costs through: cooperative cost reduction programmes, e.g. EDI; supplier participation in new designs; lower inventory through better production availability; improved logistics; reduced handling; reduced number of outstanding orders	*Lower costs* through: cooperative cost reduction programmes; participation in customer design; lower inventory through better customer planning; improved logistics; simplification or elimination of processes; payment on time
Strategic advantage through: access to supplier's technology; a supplier who invests; shared problem solving and management	*Strategic advantage* through: access to customer's technology; a customer who recognises the need to invest; shared problem solving and management

2 Sell the philosophy of partnership sourcing to:

    (a)   top management – demonstrating how partnership sourcing can improve quality; service and total costs throughout the organisation;

    (b)   other functions likely to be involved, e.g. accounting (will need to make prompt payments); design (will need to involve suppliers from the outset); production (will need to schedule supply requirements and changes);

    (c)   stress the advantages in section 9.17.3 above.

3 Define standards that potential suppliers will be required to meet. These will include:

    (a)   a commitment to TQM;

    (b)   ISO 9000 certification or equivalent;

    (c)   existing implementation or willingness to implement appropriate techniques, e.g. JIT, EDI, etc.;

    (d)   in-house design capability;

    (e)   ability to supply locally or worldwide as required;

    (f)   consistent performance standards with respect to quality and delivery;

    (g)   willingness to innovate;

    (h)   willingness to change, flexibility in management and workforce attitudes.

Partnership Sourcing Ltd states:[34]

> Remember that people are key. It is people who build trust and make relationships work. Are the people right? Is the chemistry right?
>
> Partnership is two-way: if one of your customers was evaluating your business on the same criteria that you are using on suppliers, would you qualify? If not, perhaps you should think again about your minimum entry standards.

Example 9.5   Benefits of partnering

A survey conducted by PSL in 1995 reported the following benefits (percentages are of those undertakings responding to the survey):

	%
Reduced cost	75.5
Reduced inventory	72.9
Increased quality	70.3
Enhanced security of supply	69.4
Reduced product development times	58.4

PSL[35] mentions the following important issues:

■ Ascertain your most important supplies by spend and criticality or customers by turnover and profit

■ Whether potential partner is much bigger or much smaller than the enterprise initiating the partnership is relatively important. Small undertakings are more responsive and flexible. Larger ones may have better systems

■ A potential partner may already have some experience of building partnership relationships and is therefore worth targeting

■ Do potential partners recognise that:
  – the business of the enterprise seeking to initiate the partnership is important to them?
  – there is scope for improvement in the product or service received, in short that partnering offers potential rewards?

4 Select one or a few suppliers as potential suppliers. Do not attempt to launch too many partnerships at once. A by-product of partnering is that a customer will be giving more attention to fewer suppliers, focusing available time where it will most benefit some issues.

5 Sell the idea of partnering to the selected suppliers. Stress the advantages in section 9.17.3 above.

6 If a commitment to partnership sourcing is achieved, determine through joint consultation what both parties want from the partnership and:

(a)   decide common objectives such as:

   (i)   reduction in total costs;

   (ii)   adoption of total quality management;

   (iii)   zero defects;

   (iv)   on-time payment;

   (v)   JIT or on-time deliveries;

   (vi)   joint research and development;

   (vii)   implementation of EDI;

   (viii)   reduction or elimination of stocks;

(b)   agree performance criteria for measuring progress towards objectives, e.g.:

   (i)   failure in production or with end users;

   (ii)   service response time;

      (iii)   on-time deliveries;

      (iv)   stock value;

      (v)   lead time and stability;

      (vi)   service levels;

  (c)   agree administrative procedures:

      (i)   set up a steering group to review progress and ensure development;

      (ii)   set up problem-solving teams to tackle particular issues;

      (iii)   arrange regular meetings at all levels with senior management steering the process;

  (d)   formalise the partnership. This should be on the basis of:

      (i)   a simple agreement;

      (ii)   letter of intent;

      (iii)   a simplified legal contract.

7 Review and audit the pilot project:

  (a)   review against objectives;

  (b)   quantify the gains to the business as a whole;

  (c)   report back to senior management on what has been achieved.

8 Extend the existing partnership:

  (a)   extend existing agreements;

  (b)   commit to longer agreements;

  (c)   get involved in joint strategic planning.

9 Develop new partners for the future.

9.17.5 Problems of partnership sourcing

- *Termination of relationships* – the aim should be to part amicably, preferably over a period of time through an agreed separation plan.

- *Business shares*, e.g. possible domination by the customer because of the supplier's overdependence on the customer. These issues need to be explored by joint consultation.

- *Confidentiality* – where prospective partners are also suppliers to competitors.

- *Complacency* – avoidance requires regular review of competitiveness through meetings of a multifunctional buying team.

- *Attitudes* – traditionally adversarial buyers and salespeople will require retraining to adjust to the new philosophy and environment.

- *Contractual* – where, for reasons of falling sales, recession etc., forecasts have to be modified. 'Agreements' should therefore be letters of intent and the forecasts should be updated regularly.

- *Public sector* – the CIPS[36] points out that it is less easy to establish partnership relations in the public sector due to government/EU procurement directive rules. In general, partnership relationships in the public sector should not exceed 3–5 years, after which retendering should be required.

9.18 Forming successful partnerships

Research at UMIST[37] concludes that to form successful partnerships, undertakings must take into account the commercial realities of their trading relationships and act consistently at all levels of the organisation.

The realities of a trading relationship are:

■ Objectives in critical areas will almost always be in conflict at the highest level, no two companies' strategies can be identical for long – that is why they are separate companies.

■ Cooperation endures only as long as there is mutual competitive advantage.

■ An effective relationship is less likely where there is an imbalance of power.

Successful partnership depends on consistency throughout the organisation. 'Unless the company is aligned to support supply chain development, it is all too easy for one part of the organisation to subvert the good intentions of another'.

The UMIST report observes that a company cannot leap straight to high-level strategic intervention and that the level at which it is capable of forming links depends on its degree of internal readiness. A four-part stages of excellence model is offered:

■ At stage I a company has entrepreneurial energy but lacks management control and consistency which must be achieved to pass to stage II.

■ Stage III companies have moved beyond control which eventually becomes stifling, to focus on quality and customer satisfaction.

■ At stage IV the company 'breaks down functional barriers to become a process-based organisation externally focused on providing value to the customer'.

Matching up the two dimensions of levels and integration as shown in Figure 9.12 defines a range of integration options:

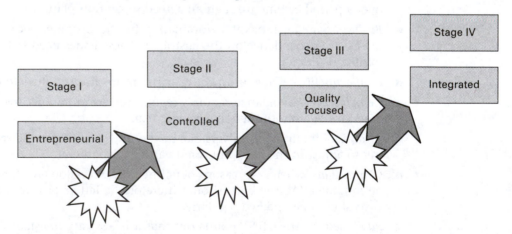

Figure 9.12   Stages of excellence

Source: A.T. Kerney Ltd. *Partnership and Power Plays*, UMIST, 1994. Reproduced by kind permission of A.T. Kerney Ltd.

- 'Companies with a sound functional foundation have a basis for integration at *transaction* level, providing efficiency improvements through, e.g., EDI.'

- Firms which have well-developed cross-functional processes internally may have scope for integration at *process* level, i.e. the re-engineering of linking processes across companies to eliminate duplicated activities. Examples include automatic stock replacement, invoiceless payment based on consumption, and direct delivery to the assembly line.

- Those firms that have mastered functional and process integration can choose to integrate at *strategic* level, forming an extended enterprise to secure competitive advantage for the supply chain as a whole rather than the individual parts. The UMIST research observes that this stage 'most closely resembles conventional ideas of partnership, but firms should recognise that the relationship may have a finite life span as external factors or changes in corporate interests cause supply chain strategies to diverge'.

- Supplier development. This is concerned with assisting actual and potential suppliers to meet the requirements of the purchasing organisation. One important aspect is that of extending the resources of a larger company to a smaller vendor which has demonstrated a willingness to meet the buying requirements of the purchaser. Such support, which can be either individual or through supplier associations, can take several forms, including:
  - financial, e.g. loans for purchase of equipment or special payment arrangements;
  - management support, e.g. advice on production control;
  - shared facilities, e.g. design, logistics;
  - purchasing assistance, e.g. placing the purchasing facilities of the buyer at the disposal of the supplier.

  Supplier development may be considered as a special aspect of partnership sourcing and subcontracting.

9.19 Why partnerships fail

Research by Ellram[38] covering 80 'pairs' of US buying firms and their chosen suppliers used 19 factors identified by previous studies as contributing to partnership failure. These factors, in the order of their ranking of importance by buyers, were:

1 poor communication;
2 lack of top management support;
3 lack of trust;
4 lack of total quality commitment by supplier;
5 poor up-front planning;
6 lack of distinctive supplier value-added benefit;
7 lack of strategic direction to the relationship;
8 lack of shared goals;

Table 9.8 Top factors contributing to partnerships that have not worked out or have been resolved

Factor	Buyer ranking	Supplier ranking
Poor communication	1	1
Lack of top management support	2	10
Lack of trust	3	4
Lack of total quality commitment by supplier	4	18
Poor up-front planning	5	5
Lack of strategic direction for the relationship	7	3
Lack of shared goals	8	2

9   ineffective mechanism for cost revision;

10   lack of benefit/risk sharing;

11   agreement not supportive of a partnering philosophy;

12   lack of partner firm's top management support;

13   changes in the market;

14   too many suppliers for customers to deal with effectively;

15   corporate culture differences;

16   top management differences;

17   lack of central coordination of purchasing;

18   low status of customer's purchasing function;

19   distance barriers.

As shown in Table 9.8, five of the top seven factors were common to both buying and supplying organisations.

There were also strong differences. Suppliers ranked 'central coordination of the buyer's purchasing function' as 12 compared with a ranking of 17 by buyers. Similarly the 'low status of the customer's purchasing function', 'lack of strategic direction' and 'lack of shared goals' were ranked significantly higher by suppliers than buyers.

Ellram's findings broadly agree with earlier research although Ellram's sample regarded corporate culture and top management differences as relatively unimportant.

9.20   Supplier relationships

9.20.1   Relationship purchasing and purchasing relationships

A relationship is *inter alia* defined as 'a connection or association'.[39] Relationships apply when individuals, organisations and groups within an organisation interact. Apart from the field of industrial sociology concerned with the study of group interaction within a workplace environment, the application of the study of relationships to business began with the concept of relationship marketing. As currently used, relationship marketing describes a long-term marketing strategy in which the emphasis is on building and maintaining long-term relationships with customers rather than on 'one sale at a time' approaches. On a business-to-business level, relationship marketing applies to the management of a range of purchasing–supplier relationships in the context of a broader network of inter-connected purchaser, supplier and competitor organisations.

Since purchasing is the mirror image of marketing, relationship purchasing aims to achieve strong, lasting relationships with suppliers with a view to secur-ing mutual benefits, added value or competitive advantages for both parties. There is, however, a difference between relationship purchasing and purchasing relationships. Not all purchasing relationships are concerned with long-term purchasing supplier associations. Purchasing relationships may be considered from two aspects: relationship formation and relationship forms.

9.20.2 Relationship formation

The process of relationship formation is well described by Holmlund.[40] As shown by Figure 9.13, Holmlund analyses interactions between two or more firms as tak-ing place at five aggregational levels: actions, episodes, sequences, relationships and partner base. At each level, interactions comprise processes and outcomes, i.e. what is done and the consequences of what is done. Thus interactions at a lower level are able to affect interactions at a higher level in the relationship, and vice versa. By focusing on either the process or the outcome, a different perspective on a particular relationship can be obtained.

- *Actions* are 'individual by focal firms' such as a telephone call or a supplier visit and may relate to products, information, money or social contracts.

- *Episodes* are groups of interrelated actions such as a negotiation or a shipping process comprising a number of actions.

- *Sequences* are larger and more extensive entities of interactions, e.g. a contract, product campaign or project. Holmlund further points out that:

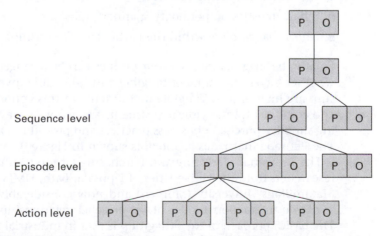

Figure 9.13 Processes and outcomes on different interaction levels

- – a sequence may also be related to the presence of a significant human actor in either of the organisations. A sequence may end if such a person is replaced in either business;

- – the completion of a sequence is a vulnerable time in which the relationship is evaluated by both parties and, possibly leads to the termination of the relationship.

■ *Relationships* comprise all the sequences which in turn comprise all related episodes and actions involved in one particular relationship between two firms.

■ The *partner base* refers to the relationship portfolio of a particular firm.

The formation of long-term relationships between individuals generally develop through the same stages. Thus a meeting (action level) may develop into friendship (episode level), courtship (sequential level) and marriage (relationship level). Each level is normally of a longer and more permanent duration than that preceding.

9.20.3 Some forms of supplier relationships

Supplier relationships may be classified in several ways, such as competitive/collaborative, adversarial/allied, tactical/strategic, short/long.

Bensaou,[41] in a study of 11 Japanese and 3 US automobile manufacturers suggests four buyer–supplier relationship profiles:

■ market exchange;
■ captive buyer;
■ captive supplier;
■ strategic partnership

For each profile he identifies distinguishing product, market and supplier characteristics. Bensaou also states three management variables for each category, namely:

■ information-sharing practices;
■ characteristics of 'boundary spanner's jobs';
■ the social climate within the particular relationship.

Finally, he suggests that the four profiles can be arranged in a matrix to indicate whether buyer and supplier tangible and intangible investments in the relationship are high or low. Tangible investments in this context are buildings, tooling and equipment. Intangible investments are people, time and effort spent in learning supplier–purchaser business practices and procedures and information sharing. The Bensaou matrix, as adapted, is shown in Figure 9.14.

The Industrial Marketing and Purchasing Group (IMP) formed in the 1970s by researchers from the Universities of Uppsala, Bath, UMIST, ESC Lyon and Ludwig Maximilians University (Munich) and now considerably extended, developed a dynamic interaction model of buyer–seller relationships in industrial markets. The basic approach of the IMP group is that in industrial markets buying and selling cannot be understood as a series of disembedded and serially independent

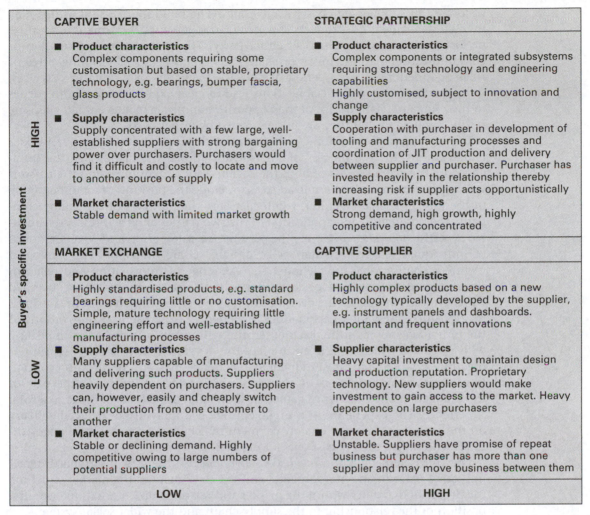

Figure 9.14   Bensaou's supplier profile matrix

Source: adapted from Bensaou, M., 'Portfolios of buyer–supplier relationships', *Sloan Management Review*, Summer 1999, pp.35–44

transactions but rather as a series of episodes in frequently long-standing, complex relationships between suppliers and purchasers which when studied over a long period are dynamic rather than stable.[42]

In the IMP model the marketing and purchasing of industrial goods is seen as an interaction process between two parties within a specific environment. The model analyses industrial marketing and purchasing under the four basic elements each of which are subdivided.

First is the *interaction process*. This involves the analysis of two factors: episodes and relationships. An *episode*, as stated earlier, is *a group of inter-related actions involved in a process* such as placing an order. In an industrial market relationship episodes involve the exchange of products or services, information, money and social attitudes or values, e.g. mutual trust between suppliers and purchasers. Episodes, especially social exchange episodes, are critical in the establishment of long-term supplier–purchaser *relationships*. The building of relationships may involve *adaptations* to products' financial arrangements, information routines or social relations on the part of either party. The exchange of information or communication may also involve *contact patterns* between persons filling different roles or functions. Over a period of time the exchange of products or services, money information and social relations lead to clear expectations in both parties in the roles and relationships of their opposite numbers which eventually become *institutionalised* so that they are unquestioned by either party.

The second element comprises the *interacting parties*. In addition to episodes and relationships the process of inter-organisational interaction will be influenced by the *characteristics* of both the organisations themselves and the persons who represent them. *Organisational factors* include the position of an undertaking in the market as manufacturer, wholesaler etc., the products of the selling company, the production and application of the two parties and their respective relative expertise. *Individual factors* are the persons, e.g. salesperson and buyer or groups of individuals (e.g. representatives of design, selling, transport etc.), involved in inter-organisational interactions. The exchange of information and relationships lead to the creation of social bonds between the individuals concerned which, in turn, influence the decisions of each enterprise involved in the business relationship. The varied personalities, experience, expertise and motivations of the individuals representing each enterprise will result in varied ways in dealing with episodes, which will, in turn affect the development of a long term inter-organisational relationships. Individual experience may also result in preconceptions concerning customers or suppliers which affect attitudes on the part of those affected. The experience gained in individual episodes aggregates to a total experience. The experience of a single episode e.g. incivility or delayed delivery on the part of the supplier or slow payment by a buyer can radically change attitudes which may then persist over a long period.

The third element is the *interaction environment*. Inter-organisational interaction takes place in an environmental context that includes the market structure, the degree of dynamics within the market and relationship, internationalism, the position of the relationship in the supply chain and the wider social system.

The fourth element, *the atmosphere*, relates to the power dependence which exists between suppliers and purchasers and such relationship variables as conflict, cooperation, closeness or distance and also the mutual expectations of the respective parties. This closer interaction between suppliers and purchasers will result in reduced costs or higher profits for one or both organisations. Another aspect of atmosphere is the ability of either party to control the other which derives from the perception of the power exercised by the other party in the relationship.

The IMP interaction model can be conceptualised as shown in Figure 9.15. From the model in Figure 9.15 we can see:

- The short- and long-term aspects of the 'interaction process' between supplier and purchasing organisation. Short-term 'exchange episodes' involve products or services, information, money and social exchange. Longer-term processes are those of 'adaptations' and 'institutionalisation'.

- The two circles (A and B) indicate that both the short- and long-term aspects of the interaction are influenced by the characteristics of the respective organisations and the individuals involved.

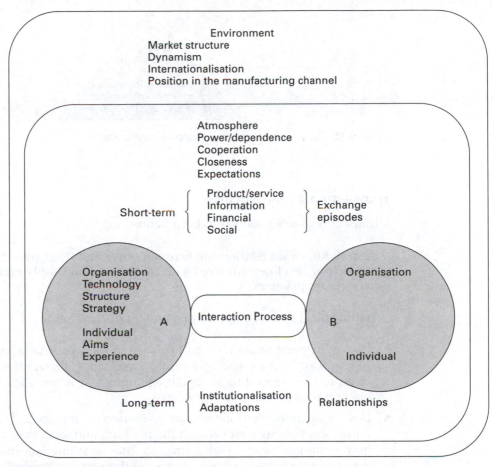

Figure 9.15 An illustration of the interaction model

Source: IMP Group, 'An interaction approach', *International Marketing and Purchasing of Industrial Goods*, Winter 1982, pp.10–27

■ Additionally, interaction takes place within an 'environment' consisting of the vertical and horizontal market structure and general social influences.

■ Finally as inter-organisational relationships develop so their perceptions of their relative power and the resultant 'atmosphere' of cooperation/conflict or cooperation/dependence will change.

The importance of the interaction model is that it can provide both marketing and purchasing practitioners with the ability to identify and solve problems, which might otherwise be neglected.

From the purchasing perspective, the key problems are the development of an appropriate supplier structure and the efficient management of supplier–purchaser relationships. Suppliers, for example, may be regarded as an external resource complementing the resources of the purchasing organisation in such ways as designing and producing a special product or supplying a standardised product at a low cost.

An alternative classification of purchasing relationships is shown in Figure 9.16.

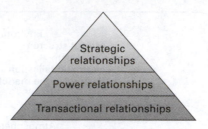

Figure 9.16   A Pyramid of purchaser–supplier relationships

Transactional relationships

A transactional relationship has been defined as:[43]

> **A straightforward relationship between buyer and seller whereby the two parties do not get closely involved with each other, but simply exchange goods or services for payment.**

Transactional relationships may be one-off or continuing.

- *One-off transactions* are for a particular item for a particular purpose which is not, at least in the foreseeable future, expected to be repeated, e.g. purchase of an item of second-hand capital equipment. It is not always the case that long-term relationships are profitable.
- *Continuing transactions* are similar to Bensaou's 'market exchange' category. Purchasers who are satisfied with the products and services of a given supplier may continue to use that source so that a strong informal relationship develops that enhances both supplier and purchaser goodwill. Goodwill was defined by Lord Eldon[44] as 'the probability that the old customers will resort to the old place'. A regular purchaser can build up supplier goodwill which may result in the latter making special efforts to meet the requirements of the former, particularly in critical circumstances.

Power relationships

Power relationships are those which give one party a bargaining advantage over the other. Power relationships can derive from such factors as size, volume of business, environmental conditions (e.g. buyers' or sellers' market) and the possession by one party of some asset not available to the other. Bensaou's captive buyer and captive supplier relationships fall into this category.

Strategic relationships

Strategic relationships in the present context may be non-partnership, partnership and supra-partnership.

- *Non-partnership strategic relationships* are those derived from long-term decisions based on expediency rather than a desire to enter into a closer association.

Examples include reciprocal trading, some global purchasing, and buying from local suppliers purely for logistical considerations.

- *Partnership relationships* are those in which two or more organisations link together on a regular basis to share knowledge and experience in an open and cooperative manner.

- *Supra-partnerships* are those in which there is more than a sharing of knowledge and experience. Such partnerships extend the concept of collaboration to mutual investment and risk taking. Thus, in Bensaou's model, buyer and supplier investments are represented by the vertical and horizontal axes respectively. Conversely, market exchange relationships involve only a low investment by both parties. Co-destiny and co-makership (described below) are examples of supra-partnerships.

9.21 Co-destiny and co-makership

9.21.1 Definitions

Co-destiny is where:

> The future of all the participating organisations depends to a greater or lesser extent on the success of a partnership relationship in which each organisation has made an investment.

Co-makership is often distinguished from co-development.
Co-makership may be defined as:

> Close cooperation between buyer and seller organisations in respect of product development, manufacture or supply.

An alternative definition is:

> Working together so that each party benefits more from collaboration than working independently.

Co-development is:[45]

> The ability of a customer to design competitive products in collaboration with their first tier suppliers.

The concept of co-development is thus closely related to early supplier involvement and concurrent engineering.

9.21.2 Factors in co-destiny and co-makership

Some of the most important factors can be summarised as the six Ts, namely top management vision, trust, transparency, technology utilisation, teams and training.

1 Top management vision

Top management vision plays a critical role in creating the climate in which the concepts of co-destiny and co-makership are understood and implemented. Often this involved a reorientation from competitive to collaborative attitudes and cultures.

2 Trust

Trust has been defined as:[46]

Stakeholder expectations of how a business will behave in the future.

Such expectations generally derive from stakeholders' experience of an organisation and, in new relationships, will develop over time. Since the future is uncertain, trust implies that both parties will:

■ keep their commitments (both implicit and explicit);
■ resort to neither exploitation nor coercion;
■ communicate openly and in a timely manner.

Trust requires that partners perceive each other to be trustworthy with regard to character, motives, competence and judgement.

3 Transparency

Transparency implies 'accessibility of information, responsiveness, realistic time scale for consultation and freedom from built-in bias',[47] and is both an aim and a consequence of information sharing. The information shared may be strategic or tactical and vary from information about logistical activities to that concerning customers and general market conditions. While operational partners such as manufacturers and retailers may share only information regarding stocks and product requirements, strategic partners will also share design, cost and market knowledge. Open book costing and cost transparency considered below are important aspects of information sharing.

4 Technology utilisation

Mentzer[48] points out that strategic partnership success is often based on improving supply chain performance through IT applications such as EDI, bar coding, scanning, advance shipment notices and sales forecasting. It may also lead to a greater reliance on time-based strategies along with more transparent logistics, organisational structures and an increased emphasis on performance measurement.

Technology utilisation may also extend to shared production technology where one partner is better equipped to manufacture components for final assembly. Thus, as stated earlier, the relationship between the final assembler and a first-tier supplier may become more akin to a strategic joint venture than to a purchasing link, especially where the assembler requires first-tier suppliers to integrate diverse technologies not possessed by one organisation.

5 Teams

Strategic decisions in co-destiny or co-ownership relationships will almost always require a team approach since one organisation is so dependent on the partnership that it cannot consider developing strategy without the other. Co-destiny and co-ownership will therefore require each partner to participate in inter-firm strategic teams.

6 Training

Joint inter-firm internal training, possibly through supplier associations, will normally be required in order to develop an understanding by both parties of strategic and tactical issues relating to co-destiny and co-ownership relationships.

9.22   Open book costing and cost transparency

9.22.1   Open book costing

Open book costing is a one-way, competitive process in which customers exert pressure on actual or potential suppliers to disclose cost information relating to their products and services. Government contracts, especially in respect of expensive military contracts, are often placed on a cost-plus basis in which an agreed percentage is added to the contractor's costs that may be subject to verification.

Open book costing may also be used as a basis for *incentivisation*, defined as:[49]

> A process by which a provider is motivated by achieve extra 'value-added' services over those specified originally and which are of material benefit to the user. These should be accessible against pre-determined criteria. The process should benefit both parties.

Incentivisation requires that the buyer should ascertain the total cost (i.e. direct cost plus overheads) of an existing service to the user organisation and also the make up of the supplier's costs.

As CUP Guidance Note 58 states:[50]

> Having established these costs, open book accounting will ensure that the supplier accepts the basis of the costings and that any subsequent changes to costs and/or practices are fully understood.

9.22.2   Cost transparency

Unlike open book costing, cost transparency is a two-way collaborative exchange of information aimed at enhancing the competitive advantage of both parties.

Lamming[51] regards cost transparency as an essential element in lean supply and defines the concept as:

> The sharing of costing information between customer and supplier, including data which would traditionally be kept secret by each party, for use in negotiations. The purpose of this is to make it possible for customer and supplier to work together to reduce costs (and improve other factors).

Lamming stresses that 'cost transparency is of no value . . . unless it is two way'.

Lamming *et al.*[52] state that the prime advantage of cost transparency is its ability to form the basis of successful supply chain optimisation. Facilitated by cost transparency, successful supply chain management can provide the following benefits:

- enhanced competitiveness;
- increased profitability;
- cost minimisation;
- more effective new product development;
- improved customer–supplier relationships;
- reduced expenditure of time and cost in negotiation;
- reduced conflict between the negotiating parties;
- the stimulation of cross-functional processes and management initiatives between supply chain associates.

Based on research relating to the views of purchasing and sales managers, Lamming *et al.* classified the inhibitors of cost transparency under structural and operational headings. *Structural inhibitors* are a consequence of either an aspect of a company's internal operation or its commercial relationships with external organisations. They tend to be permanent. Structural inhibitors include:

- Cultural factors, e.g. that cost transparency is a contravention of sensible business practice and alien to a company philosophy based on secrecy and adversarial relationships.
- Perceived risks in exposing sensitive information and revealing strategic plant which might lead to a loss of competitive advantage, or particularly for suppliers, loss of independence. Such perceived risks often derive from experiences of the misuse of sensitive information by trading associations.
- Lack of interorganisational dependence or a genuine community of interest between companies that would provide a climate for the introduction of cost transparency.
- Management instability which raised doubts regarding whether a commitment to cost transparency would continue with a change in senior management.

Operational inhibitors result from tactical deficiencies in a company's activities or its relationships with external organisations. They tend to be transient. Operational inhibitors include:

- Difficulties in desegregating cost data to make it meaningful to a single supply relationship.
- Difficulties in creating supply chain structures capable of using the cost information for process improvements.
- Lack of interorganisational trust between individuals within the organisations.

The large majority of respondents to Lamming *et al.*'s survey considered the negative potential of cost transparency to outweigh the positive. The researchers concluded that the essential 'first step' for the successful implementation of cost transparency is to address deficiencies in organisational relationships caused by many years of operating under a traditional secretive and adversarial culture. Failure to overcome structural inhibitors may signify that full and genuine cost transparency may not be appropriate for the immediate future. A failure to overcome operational inhibitors, given the required commitment, may preclude cost transparency only over the short to medium term.

9.23   Reciprocal trade

9.23.1   Definition

Reciprocity is defined by the *Shorter Oxford English Dictionary* as:

> **Mutual or correspondent concession of advantages or privileges, as forming a basis for commercial relations.**

Reciprocity is often referred to as a 'selling through the order book' when a policy is adopted of giving preference to those suppliers who are also customers of the buying undertaking.

9.23.2   Types of reciprocity

- *External*, i.e. suppliers have no relationship with the buying undertaking.
- *Internal*, i.e. supplier and buyer are both members of the same group.
- *Two-way reciprocity*, i.e. A agrees to buy B's product on condition that B buys from A.
- *Multi-reciprocity*, e.g. A is a large foundry seeking to sell castings to B, a manufacturer of mechanical handling equipment. B agrees to buy from A on condition that the latter buys from C, a mining and quarrying company which is a substantial customer of B.

9.23.3   Factors in reciprocity

Reciprocity is influenced by:

- *Economic climate* – pressures for reciprocal agreements increase in times of depression.
- *Type of product* – reciprocal dealing is greater where both supplier and buyer are producers of standard, highly competitive products. It does not arise where a buyer has no alternative but to buy from a given supplier.

9.23.4   Advantages of reciprocity

- Both supplier and buyer may benefit from the exchange of orders.
- Both supplier and buyer may obtain a greater understanding of mutual problems, thus increasing goodwill.

■ More direct communication between suppliers and buyers may eliminate or reduce the need for intermediaries and the cost of marketing or procurement operations.

9.23.5   Disadvantages of reciprocity

Where price, delivery and quality are at least equivalent to that offered by other suppliers then it is common sense for the buyer to give preference to customers of his or her undertaking. These conditions apply infrequently, and in practice reciprocity may have the following consequences:

■ Costs may increase owing to the reduced competitive position of the buyer without compensating benefits.

■ Sales must increase substantially to provide an equivalent saving on purchases (see section 1.7 in Chapter 1).

■ Selling through the order book uses purchasing to perform a market function. Credit may accrue to marketing while the performance of purchasing may be adversely affected.

■ Marketing effort may become slack.

■ Disputes may arise where the respective values of purchases and sales become substantially different.

■ The opportunity to buy cheaper, better quality alternatives may be denied to the buyer who is tied by a reciprocal agreement.

■ Business may be taken from satisfactory suppliers.

■ Difficulties may arise in finding alternative suppliers in an emergency.

■ In practice it is often difficult to terminate reciprocal relationships without friction.

■ The morale of the buying staff may be adversely affected.

Reciprocity in the final analysis is a top management decision. The buyer should respond to pressures to enter into such relationships by setting out in writing the advantages and disadvantages of any proposals made.

9.24   Intra-company trading

Intra-company trading applies to large enterprise and conglomerates where the possibility arises of buying certain materials from a member of the group. This policy may be justified on the grounds that it ensures the utilisation and profitability of the supplying undertaking and the profitability of the group as whole. It may also be resorted to in times of recession to help supplying subsidiaries to cover their fixed costs.

Policy statements should give general and specific guidance to the procurement function regarding the basis on which intra-company trading should be conducted. General guidance may be expressed in a policy statement such as the following: 'Company policy is to support internal suppliers to the fullest extent and to develop product and service quality to the same high standards as those available in the external market'. Specific guidance may direct buyers to:

- purchase specified items exclusively from group members regardless of price;
- obtain quotations from group members which are evaluated against those from external suppliers with the order being placed with the most competitive source whether internal or external.

Difficulties can arise where intra-company trading involves import or export considerations.

9.25 Local suppliers

What is local must be determined bearing in mind such factors as ease of transport and communication. The advantages of using local rather than distant suppliers include the following:

- Closer cooperation is facilitated between buyers and suppliers based on personal relationships.
- Social responsibility is shown by 'supporting local industries' and thus contributing to the prosperity of the area.
- Reduced transportation costs.
- Improved availability in emergency situations, e.g. road transport can be used to collect urgently needed items. The potential importance of localised confidence in the maintenance of lead times increases where a JIT system is adopted.
- The development of subsidiary industries situated close to the main industry and catering for its needs is encouraged.

The main principle in deciding where to place orders must, however, be what is best for the buying undertaking.

9.26 Small or large suppliers

9.26.1 Advantages claimed for small suppliers

Advantages claimed for small supplier include:

- Closer attention to buyer's requirements – many large suppliers, however, recognise that smaller accounts often grow.
- Relationships, especially at executive level, are more personal.
- Response to requests for special assistance from the buyer can be more rapid than with a large undertaking.

It is government policy to encourage the development of small firms and to improve the access of such undertakings to public sector business, not, however, by favouring small firms at the expense of competitiveness. The CIPS has issued *A Guide to Practice*[53] when buying from small suppliers. This recommends, *inter alia*, that larger organisations should:

- facilitate access by small firms by publishing the names of the larger organisation's purchasing staff and details of its organisation structure;
- confirm orders in sufficient time to allow small firms to meet completion dates;
- provide assistance to small suppliers, especially by means of:
  - prompt payment, thereby easing liquidity problems;
  - secondment of staff to deal with such problems as quality control, design and specification;
  - supply of materials either as a free issue or at a price which the small firm would not have been able to negotiate.

  If a large organisation merely wants to tender for price comparison purposes, the small company should be informed and in certain circumstances the cost of tendering should be paid;
- limit overdependence by a small supplier on them by setting a ceiling to the percentage of sales taken which, exceptional circumstances apart, should not be exceeded;
- through a written purchasing policy, state its policy towards small suppliers;
- be aware of and consider ameliorating the harmful impact which centralised purchasing may have on small, local suppliers.

9.26.2 Advantages claimed for large suppliers

These include:

- Reserve capacity to undertake extra work and cope with emergencies is usually greater.
- Special facilities and knowledge can be made available to the buyer.
- There is less danger of the supplier becoming too reliant on the buyer's business.

9.27 Purchasing consortia

9.27.1 Definition and scope

Purchasing consortia may be defined as:

> A collaborative arrangement under which two or more organisations combine their requirements for a specified range of goods and services to gain price, design, supply availability and assurance benefits resulting from higher volume purchases.

In public purchasing, for example, several separate authorities may establish a central purchasing organisation to provide three basic supply services to its constituent members, namely: delivery from stores, direct purchasing of non-stock items for users in constituent authorities and the negotiation of call-off or 'standing offer' contracts. Such an organisation is usually self-financed through a mark-up on the items supplied from store and through volume rebates received from suppliers which the consortium negotiates.

Purchasing consortia exist in a wide range of industries and cover for-profit and non-profit organisations, including universities and libraries.

Example 9.6   The Yorkshire Purchasing Organisation

A typical example of a purchasing consortium is the Yorkshire Purchasing Organisation (YPO) serving schools and local authorities mainly in Yorkshire, Greater Manchester and Merseyside. Originally selling mainly to 12 constituent authorities, new autonomy, especially in education, means that YPO is now selling to over 30,000 small customers whose orders have an average line value of under £10. Customers order by post or an EDI system devised by YPO using mail order catalogues covering over 15,000 lines ranging from alphabet pasta to xylophones. The consortium aims to meet a 97 per cent availability target.

9.27.2 Advantages of purchasing consortia

- The use of a consortium allows the constituent members to benefit from the economics of larger-scale purchasing than they could undertake themselves.
- Members can utilise the relevant professional purchasing skills of the consortia staff who can develop wide-ranging product expertise.
- Saving of time in searching for and ordering standard items.
- Bulk purchasing enables the consortium to have strong buying leverage over a wide range of supplies.
- Costs are clearly identified.

9.27.3 Disadvantages of consortia

- A consortium cannot insist on compliance by individual members who may treat the consortium as only one of a number of suppliers. This may secure nominal price savings but is unlikely to affect the administrative costs of appraising the consortium against alternative sources. It also weakens the strength of the consortium.
- When using a consortium it may be more difficult to agree standard specifications.
- Significant areas of spend are not covered by what consortia can provide.
- Some forms of consortia may be prohibited under EEC provisions. Thus Article 85(1) of the EEC Treaty provides that:

  All agreements, decision and concerted practices (hereafter referred to as agreements) which have as their object or effect the prevention, restriction or distortion of competition within the common market are prohibited as incompatible with the common market . . . [This] applies, however, only if such agreements affect trade between Member States.

In general, however, the Commission 'welcomes co-operation among small and medium sized enterprises where such co-operation enables them to work more efficiently and increase their productivity and competitiveness on a larger market'.[54]

9.28 Sourcing decisions

Sourcing decisions involve a consideration of: (i) factors influencing the organisational buying decision; (ii) factors in deciding where to buy; (iii) buying centres or teams; and (iv) buying situations.

9.28.1 Factors in deciding where to buy

Webster and Wind[55] classify factors influencing industrial buying decision into four main groups, as shown in Table 9.9.

It is of interest that Webster and Wind, writing in 1972, make no references to the linkage between purchasing and overall strategies and procurement decisions aimed at enhancing the competitive advantage of the buying organisation, such as the decision to source abroad.

9.28.2 Buying centres and procurement teams

The buying centre is the buying decision-making unit of an organisation and is defined by Webster and Wind as 'all those individuals and groups who participate in the purchasing decision process and who share some common goals and the risks arising from the decisions'.[56] The buying centre is a temporary, often informal group, which can change in composition and which functions from purchase to purchase.

More permanent units responsible for the sourcing and evaluating of suppliers and decision-makers in relation to a specified range of items such as food, drink,

Table 9.9 Factors in industrial buying decisions

Environmental	Organisational	Interpersonal	Individual
These are normally outside the buyer's control and include: ■ the level of demand ■ the economic outlook ■ interest rates ■ technological change ■ political factors ■ government regulations ■ competitive development	Buying decisions are affected by the organisation's system of reward, authority, status and communication, including organisational: ■ objectives ■ policies ■ procedures ■ structures	Involving the interaction of several persons of different status, authority, empathy and persuasiveness who comprise the *buying centre*	Buying decisions are related to how individual participants in the buying process form their preferences for products and suppliers, involving the person's age, professional identification, personality and attitude towards the risks involved in their buying behaviour

capital equipment etc. are often referred to as *procurement teams*. Such teams may also be responsible for framing of policies and procedures applicable to tendering and contracts. Both buying centres and teams should have a designated chairperson and clearly defined terms of reference.

The composition of the buying centre or team can be analysed as follows:

- By individual participants or job holders, e.g. the managing director, chief purchasing officer, engineer, accountant, etc.
- By organisational units, e.g. departments or even individual organisations, as when a group of hospitals decides to standardise on equipment.
- The buying centre or team comprises all members of the organisation (varying from 3 to 12) who play any of the five roles in the purchasing decision process, namely:
  - *users*, who will use the product or service and often initiate the purchase and specify what is bought;
  - *influencers*, such as technical staff who may directly or indirectly influence the buying decision in such ways as defining specifications or providing information on which alternatives may be evaluated;
  - *buyers*, who have formal authority to select suppliers and arrange terms of purchase. Buyers may help to determine specifications but their main role is to select vendors and negotiate within purchase constraints;
  - *deciders*, who have either formal or informal authority to select the ultimate suppliers. In routine purchasing of standard items the deciders are often the buyers. In more complex purchasing the deciders are often other officers of the organisation;
  - *gatekeepers*, who control the flow of information to others, e.g. buyers may prevent salespersons from seeing users or deciders.

9.28.3 The buying situation

Robinson *et al.*[57] identify three major types of organisational buying situation: straight re-buy, modified re-buy and new task.

Straight re-buy

Straight re-buy situations apply where:

- the item or commodity bought in is continuous or recurrent demand;
- suppliers are already known;
- the item is dealt with routinely by current purchasing arrangements;
- experience has established a reliable supply pattern.

Subject to value and item constraints, straight re-buy requirements can be placed with approved suppliers by users using e-procurement without the intervention of the purchasing function. Buyers take a leading role in the initial contract provided no technical differentiation is present.

Modified re-buy

Modified re-buy situations apply where:

- the demand for the item is continuous or recurrent but at expanded or reduced levels;
- minor changes have been made to the product specification;
- a significant change in specification is necessary owing to some unforeseen event, e.g. a shortage of material, the emergence of cheaper materials or as the result of a value analysis exercise;
- it is necessary to seek for cost reductions, better service or quality;
- for some reason a change in supplier is desirable;
- a potential new supplier suggests possible economies resulting from the conversion of a straight re-buy into a modified re-buy.

Buyers, along with product design, take a leading role in modified re-buy situations both as initiators of the change and as arbiters of the final purchase decision.

New task

New task situations apply where:

- the product or specification is new or unfamiliar;
- the purchase is of infrequent occurrence;
- a considerable expenditure on supplier sourcing and appraisal may be required since buyers may have little or no experience on which to draw;
- make-or-buy or outsourcing decisions may be required.

Buyers may not be involved in the early stages of new purchase decisions because it is generally accepted that the technical problems associated with new purchases must be solved before detailed commercial considerations of where to buy can be made.

Increasingly, however, important sourcing decision are being made on a team or buying centre basis owing to:

- the increased involvement of procurement in strategic as well as tactical and operational decision making;
- the integration of purchasing into materials management and logistics functions;
- the movement towards single and partnership sourcing;
- the increasing complexity of purchasing including global sourcing where many factors including political, currency and similar considerations enter into the purchasing decision;
- the desirability of spreading responsibility of high-risk purchasing decisions;
- the need to evaluate the risks and potential contribution to profitability of new materials, products technology and suppliers.

9.29   Factors in deciding where to buy

Assuming that the decision is taken that a product should be bought out rather than made in, many factors determine where the order is placed and by whom the decision is made. Such considerations include:

9.29.1   General considerations

■ How shall the item be categorised, i.e. capital investment, manufacturing material or parts, operating, supply or MRO item?

■ What are our current and projected levels of business for the item?

■ Is the item a one-off or a continuing requirement?

■ Is the item unique to us or in general use?

■ Are we currently buying the item or have we bought it before?

■ If it is being bought, or has been bought before, from what source was it obtained?

■ Is/was the present/previous supplier satisfactory from the standpoints of price, quality and delivery?

■ With regard to the value of the order to be placed, is the cost of searching for an alternative supply source justified?

■ What internal customers may wish to be consulted on the sourcing of the item?

■ Within what timescale is the item required?

9.29.2   Strategic considerations

■ What supply source will offer the greatest competitive advantage from the standpoints of:
  – price;
  – differentiation of product;
  – security of supplies and reliability of delivery;
  – quality;
  – added value through specialisation, production facilities, packaging, transportation, after-sales services etc.?

■ Is the source one with whom we would like to:
  – single source;
  – share a proportion of our requirements for the required item;
  – built up a long-term partnerships relationship;
  – discuss the possibilities of supplier development;
  – subcontract?

■ Does the supply source offer any possibilities for:
  – joint product development;
  – reciprocal or countertrade?

- What relationships has the supplier with our competitors?

- Is it desirable that, at least part of, our requirements should be sourced locally for political, social responsibility or logistical reasons.

- What risk factors attach to the purchase? Is the product (i) high profit impact/high supply risk; (ii) low profit impact/high supply risk; (iii) high profit impact/low supply risk; (iv) low profit impact/low supply risk?

9.29.3 Product factors

- What critical factors influence the choice of suppliers? Chisnall[58] reports a research finding that seven critical factors were found to influence buyers in the British valve and pump industry in the choice of their suppliers of raw materials: delivery reliability, technical advice, test facilities, replacement guarantee, prompt quotation, ease of contact, and willingness to supply range. These attributes helped to reduce the risk element to purchase decisions.

- What special tooling is required? Is such tooling the property of the existing supplier or the vendor?

- To what extent are learning curves applicable to the product? Are these allowed for in the present and future prices?

- Is the product special or is it standardised?

- In what lot sizes is the product manufactured?

- What is the estimated product life cycle cost?

- Is the product one that can be leased as an alternative to buying?

9.29.4 Supplier factors

Such factors are those normally covered by supplier appraisal and vendor rating exercises.

9.29.5 Personal factors

Personal factors relate to the psychological and behavioural aspects of those involved in making organisational buying decisions. Sheth[59] identified three principal components that combine to explain a purchasing decision outcome: expectations of the individual decision participants; the number of individuals involved; and approaches to conflict resolution.

Factors that determine participant expectations about the ability of suppliers and products to meet requirements include:

- Background of individuals, e.g. education, job orientation, lifestyles.

- Active information, search information, e.g. sources and amount available.

- Information distortion owing to the goals, values and differing experiences of individual buying centre members.

- Satisfaction with past purchases.

Factors that determine the number of individuals involved include:

Product factors
- Time pressure
- Perceived risk
- Type of purchase

Company factors
- Orientation
- Size
- Degree of centralisation

Approaches to conflict resolution among those involved include:

- Problem solving
- Persuasion
- Bargaining
- Politicking

Sheth also recognises that situation factors such as strikes at the supplier's factory, mergers and a sudden glut or shortage in the global supply of a critical commodity can influence purchasing decisions.

Case study 1[60]

You are purchasing director of Diversified Holdings, a company that has just taken over a smaller firm known as Office Products (OP). OP was, some years ago, an important manufacturer of office equipment and filing systems, employing about 1,000 people, and supplying customers in Britain and overseas in all sectors of the economy. Over the past 20 years, OP has decreased in size, and has transformed itself into a merchant and manufacturing distributor, with a very small design team. All products are now purchased, the last manufacturing operations were closed down about three years ago. OP currently employs 35 staff and has an annual turnover of some £4 million.

Although the management of OP has made claims to pursue a 'strategic downsizing' policy, a neutral observer might justifiably claim that the changes have been forced upon the company, which has changed reactively in order to survive. Nevertheless, the company has survived and is presently enjoying a modest growth in terms of both volumes of business and profitability. Demand for OP's equipment is buoyant, reflecting the present high level of activity in the economy generally.

OP has retained a good name for the supply of desk items, such as staplers, punches and small card index systems and concentrates on these lines. The capital investment required to produce similar goods is not great; the technology employed is not advanced, and nowadays the great majority of supplies are sourced in countries where labour costs are low. A great deal of attention has always been paid to quality control, and OP equipment retains its very good name with its corporate customers. The OP brand is not strong in the retail market where customers seem to buy according to price, quality being assessed, so far as this is possible, at the point of sale by means of a physical reaction.

Sally Hughes is the purchasing director of OP, and she has been with the company for four years, a period that coincides with the reversal of the organisation's profitability from decline to modest growth. She was brought in as part of a new management team appointed to turn the company around, and brought with her a reputation for being a tough, no nonsense executive. Naturally, Sally is inclined to take some of the credit for the company's improved fortunes, and she had the opportunity at the recent annual general meeting to explain her purchasing philosophy and her perceptions of the contribution she has made to the recent successes.

You have been conversing with Sally for the past hour or two and she made the following main points:

1 Procurement is a critical factor in the success or failure of any organisation. A penny saved in negotiation is a penny profit. I need to be tough with our suppliers. If they can't give me exactly what I want, when I want it, then I go elsewhere.

2 There is plenty of competition between suppliers in our market. I will make full use of this competition by seeking bids from a large number of suppliers whenever I wish to place a large contract. It doesn't take long to sort out the more attractive vendors, and competition keeps everybody on their toes.

3 The present volatility in the currency markets means that I have to watch those products that are sourced overseas very carefully. It doesn't take much of a shift in the exchange rate to make formerly attractive foreign suppliers no longer viable. I am keen to take advantage of overseas opportunities but I avoid long-term commitment as this takes away flexibility.

4 Clear specifications are important. I seek suppliers who will manufacture exactly to our designs and specifications. Sometimes suppliers will suggest 'improvements' to our designs or, worse still, complain about the difficulty of manufacturing exactly what we want. I am not sympathetic. In my view suppliers want to change specifications for one reason, to make the product easier to manufacture so that they can make more profit.

5 Of course, finding the cheapest supplier who can meet our needs is not the end of the story. Suppliers are not usually to be trusted. We have to expedite, to make sure that they meet their contractual obligations and, of course, we inspect all incoming goods carefully to ensure that they are not passing defective goods to us. We do find that the quality of some of our suppliers, both domestic and overseas, repays careful watching.

6 Business is essentially simple. Design products that you think will sell well (if you can make them at low cost), if not, contract with a supplier. Manage suppliers carefully, ensuring that they always meet their obligations under the contract.

You are currently assessing the contribution being made by the senior executives of OP. You have some misgivings about the appropriateness of Sally's views.

Question

Taking the six key ideas outlined by Sally in turn, produce notes summarising how, despite the benefits indicated by Sally, each might be detrimental to the long-term success of OP.

Case study 2

Painter's Products Ltd (PP) is a private company which has grown from small beginnings over the past 20 years to become a major supplier of chemicals, thinners, solvents and similar products to the painting and decorating trade. Its products are well liked by professional painters, and the company enjoys a good share of the market. PP has not, until recently, contemplated the supply of products to the retail market, but enquiries from a major national multiple store led to the supply of samples and the testing of PP's materials against the competing products, and discussions have now moved to the possibility of PP becoming a regular supplier. It is envisaged that products will be shipped in large quantities to the retailer's regional distribution centres, branded as the retailer's own product.

The management team of PP are attracted to this idea. It would enable them to expand their production and sales without the need to spend any money on marketing, and without the need to worry about setting up a distribution system. If the product is successful, it might lead to the launch of the PP brand through the retail trade, and possibly also to contracts with other major retailers for own-brand products.

PP has been having discussions with Vision packaging, its present supplier of plastics containers. These are five litres capacity, to a standard design, and are supplied in plain white. PP itself applies the label for its small range of trade products. Vision too is excited by the possible new business that PP's diversification will bring. It will be very happy to invest in the necessary tooling to produce blow moulded containers in large quantities to a design specified by PP and its retail customer. However, problems are emerging. Vision's plant is 200 miles from PP's, and shipping large quantities of containers is tantamount to shipping large volumes of fresh air. The cost of packaging is a large proportion of the cost of producing small retail packs of product. There is another local supplier who could supply at a lower and feasible cost, but PP has never dealt with them, and in any case has a sense of loyalty to Vision. It looks as if Vision may lose this business though.

After a brainstorming session, the management of PP have come up with the following possibilities. They have not, as yet, paid any attention to the feasibility or appropriateness of any of them.

1   Re-source the containers, saying 'thank you but good-bye' to Vision.

2   Invest in moulding machinery, hire the appropriate expertise, and integrate container production with their filling line, i.e. become a container maker.

3   Invite Vision to set up a small plant nearby.

4   Suggest a joint venture with Vision, sharing resources, investment, profits, worry and everything else.

5   Request the assistance of the retailer in managing this particular part of its supply chain.

This is not a complete set of possibilities, and some of the ideas on the list are not necessarily mutually exclusive.

Question

From a commercial relationships point of view, suggest and explain which of the above ideas (on the basis of the rather superficial information supplied) might be worth pursuing. Explain the implications for PP's supplier and customer relationships. Discuss any other possibilities you would propose for further study.

? Discussion questions

9.1.   'It is important, however, that purchasing staff at tactical and operational levels are also aware of their roles in providing value-adding support services to sourcing and thereby contributing to the competitive advantage of their enterprise.'

As a logistics manager responsible for the purchasing processes, how would you seek to ensure that tactical and operational purchasing staff are aware of their roles and responsibilities as described above?

9.2   Situation analysis is concerned with taking stock of where an organisation or activity within an organisation has been recently, where it is now and where it is likely to end up using present policies, plans and procedures. As the executive in charge of the purchasing of production materials and components you are asked to effect procurement economies without prejudicing final product quality. How might an analysis of market conditions help you to make constructive recommendations?

9.3   You purchase a 'sensitive commodity' such as zinc, copper or rubber. From what sources can you obtain information relevant to market conditions that might help you to decide whether to stockpile the commodity?

9.4   As the supplies manager for a municipal authority you are approached by a councillor who says that a small enterprise owned by his nephew can undercut any of the tenders recently considered by the committee of which the councillor is a member. How would you deal with the situation?

9.5   What problems, if any, have you experienced in using the internet to source potential suppliers?

9.6 How would you answer a manager who refuses to approve your visit to a trade exhibition on the grounds that such exhibitions are 'only an excuse for a day out'?

9.7 Draft a questionnaire designed to enable you to make a preliminary assessment of a supplier who asks to be considered for inclusion on your approved supplier list.

9.8 When evaluating the production capacity of a potential supplier it is useful to distinguish between:

(a) Design capacity, i.e. the maximum output that can possibly be achieved

(b) Effective capacity, i.e. the maximum possible outputs given a product mix, scheduling difficulties, machine maintenance, quality factors etc.

(c) Actual output, i.e. the rate of output actually achieved which is often less than effective capacity due to breakdowns, material shortages etc.

Two useful measures are *efficiency* (the ratio of actual output to effective capacity) and utilisation (the ratio of actual output to design capacity). Compare, in purchasing terms, the efficiency and utilisation of a potential supplier given the following figures:

Design capacity:	500 items weekly
Effective capacity:	400 units weekly
Actual output:	360 units weekly

9.9 Your management recognises that plant visits are one way in which purchasing personnel can learn about the capabilities of potential suppliers. Such visits, must however, be controlled. Prepare a set of brief guidelines informing purchasing staff of the procedure for obtaining authorisation to make such visits and how such visits should be conducted.

9.10 The cost of measuring the performance of suppliers can be high.

(a) What arguments would you use to justify the expenditure of measuring performance?

(b) What steps might you take to minimise such expenditure?

9.11 Suggest one way in which you might evaluate the performance of a supplier against each of the Ten Cs listed in section 9.9 of this chapter.

9.12 'Although supply bases may be drastically reduced many companies have found that, over time, they tend to grow again.'

(a) Is this true in your experience?

(b) Why might such renewed growth take place?

(c) What steps might you take to ensure that your supply base remains reasonably constant?

9.13 On the basis of the following figures you have been asked whether a certain component should be made in or bought out. You decide to base your decision on a marginal cost approach, i.e. Total cost = Fixed cost + Volume × Variable cost.

	Make	*Buy*
Annual fixed costs	£300,000	None
Variable cost per unit	£120	£160
Annual volume (units)	24,000	24,000

What is your recommendation? Would your recommendation be different if the annual volume in terms of units is 12,000?

9.14 In section 9.12.6 of this chapter a number of problems associated with outsourcing are reported, e.g. high staff turnover, poor project management skills etc. How, prior to entering into an outsourcing contract, would you attempt to minimise the likelihood of such problems arising?

9.15 On what grounds would you advise your management against outsourcing purchasing?

9.16 Because of overloading in your machine shop you have been asked to find a subcontractor able to produce spindles to close limits from 0.5 inch diameter mild steel round bars. You arrange for the steel bars to be delivered directly to the subcontractor by the steel producer. What controls might you devise over the use and security of the bars by the subcontractor?

9.17 Why may it be important for first-tier suppliers to be located nearer to the assembler than second-tier suppliers?

9.18 Rich and Hines[61] state:

> From the 1980s, three distinct themes of supplier collaboration have emerged. The first emphasises the development of long term partnerships and trust such that the benefits of the trading relationship can be shared. [The second emphasises] the development of a structured process of information exchange between the organisation and its supply chain such that inventory can be substituted with information in order to increase performance of suppliers throughout the chain. The third approach originates from the empirical study of Japanese exemplar manufacturing organisations. The latter includes tiering and supply associations.

Consider what the three types of supplier collaboration have in common and in what ways they differ.

9.19 What problems may arise in respect of reciprocal trading agreements when, owing to a change in demand, the quantity and value of goods bought by A from B falls substantially below the quantity and value of goods bought by B from A?

9.20 The main manufacturing base of your company is located in a small town. Over the years, a number of smaller undertakings have developed which rely mainly on your company for their business and survival. In some cases, for social responsibility reasons, you are paying local suppliers more than you would pay to non-local suppliers. Because of enhanced competition you do not consider that this practice can continue. What steps might you take to improve the competitiveness of the local suppliers?

9.21 A construction company has drawing offices in Glasgow and London. Staff from Glasgow often visit London for technical consultations with customers and colleagues, and vice versa. Such visits may extend over two or three days and entail high hotel costs. Your directors have decided to establish a team to source and negotiate with hotel groups in both centres with a view to offering special rates for accommodation and meals in return for exclusive business. Draft the terms of reference of the team.

9.22   Consider the following definition:[62]

> Company politics is the by-play that occurs when people want to advance them-
> selves or their ideas regardless of whether or not these ideas would help the
> company.

How may company politics influence sourcing decisions?

? Past examination questions

1   You spend £5 million a year on a range of products and 20 companies have written
to you stating they can supply this range. Explain how you would appraise these companies with the aim of establishing a list of five to whom you send an enquiry for the
supply of the range.

   (CIPS, Introduction to Purchasing and Supply Chain Management, May 1997)

2   How can the development of partnerships with key suppliers reduce strategic acquisition costs?

   (CIPS, Purchasing and Supply Chain Management I: Strategy, May 1997)

3   Much has been written about the benefits of outsourcing non-core activities of a business. Against this background discuss the potential benefits and possible dangers of
outsourcing the purchasing function of an organisation with which you are familiar,
clearly showing the safeguards and procedures which would need to be in place.

   (CIPS, Purchasing, May 1997)

4   (a)   The prevailing tendency is to concentrate on core activities and to outsource
those activities which are considered to be non-core. It is important, however,
that these outsourced activities are provided completely and meet the required
standards of performance. Select *one* of the following and discuss how you
would select a suitable supplier.

   (i)   Catering services

   (ii)   Warehousing and transport

   (iii)   Security

   (b)   Having selected a supplier, how would you ensure compliance with standards
and their maintenance in the longer term?

   (CIPS, Purchasing and Supply Chain Management II:
Tactics and Operations, November 1997)

5   Compare and contrast the role of first-tier supplies with that of suppliers in the second tier.

   (CIPS, Commercial Relationships, May 1998)

6   Explain, compare and contrast approaches which might be taken to:

   Vendor rating

   Supplier assessment

   Relationship assessment

   (CIPS, Commercial Relationships, November 1998)

7 Discuss the similarities and differences in the procedures used by a buyer of metal components in selecting a supplier, and by a buyer obtaining the services of a caterer.

(CIPS, Introduction to Purchasing and Supply Chain Management, May 1999)

8 'The problem with outsourcing is that while a series of incremental outsourcing decisions, taken individually make economic sense, collectively they represent the surrender of the business competitive advantage' (Zeng, G.J.).

(a) Explain the principles which lie behind the concept of outsourcing and why, as the quotation suggests, if it is not properly conducted it may actually surrender the firm's competitive advantage.

(b) With reference to a relevant example, show how the buyer can avoid these disadvantages.

(CIPS, Purchasing and Supply Chain Management II: Tactics and Operations, May 1999)

9 Outsourcing has become popular in recent years. Explain why this is the case and suggest ways in dealing with problems that may arise from its use.

(CIPS, Purchasing, November 1999)

10 Both transactional and long-term mutual relationships between buyer and seller may be appropriate in the right circumstances. Discuss the circumstances in which you would consider:
(a) The transactional approach to be appropriate
(b) A long-term relationship to be appropriate

(CIPS, Commercial Relationships, May 2000)

Notes

1. Killen, K.H. and Kamauff, J., *Managing Purchasing*, Irwin Publishing, 1995, Ch.1, p.7
2. Thompson, D.M. and Homer, G.R., 'Internet-searchable supplier database in the automotive supply chain – a critique of current practice', *Proceedings of 10th Annual IPSERA Conference*, 2001, pp.815–825
3. The Trade Association Forum, Centre Point, 103 New Oxford Street, London WC1A (020 7395 8284)
4. Lysons, C.K., *Supplier Appraisal*, CIPS 'How to' Series 2002
5. Hines, P., 'Integrated materials management: the value chain redefined', *International Journal of Logistics Management*, Vol.4, No.1 (1993), pp.13–22
6. DTI, *Sourcing and Supplier Appraisal*, Document E5
7. Buffa, E.S. and Kakesh, K.S., *Modern Production/Operations Management*, 5th edn, John Wiley, 1987, Ch.17, p.548
8. Egan, J., 'Benefits of total quality – a vehicle manufacturer's view', quoted in Lascelles, D.M. and Dale, B.G., 'The buyer–supplier relationship in total quality management', *Journal of Purchasing and Supply Management*, Summer 1989, pp.10–19
9. Carter, R., 'The Seven Cs of effective supplier evaluation', *Purchasing and Supply Chain Management*, April 1995, pp.44–5

10. Probert, D.R., *Make or Buy – Your Route to Improved Manufacture Performance*, DTI, 1995
11. ICMA, 'Management accounting', *Official Terminology*, 1996
12. Taken from *Outsourcing Interactive*, an online resource of the Outsourcing Institute on http://www.outsourcing.com
13. Rothery, B. and Robinson, I., *The Truth about Outsourcing*, Gower, 1995, Ch.5, p.66
14. Lacity, M.C. and Hirscheim, R., *Information Systems Outsourcing*, Wiley, 1995
15. P.A. Consulting, *UK IT Outsourcing Survey*, 1993
16. Reilly, P. and Tamkin, P. *Outsourcing – A Flexibility Option for the Future*, Institute of Employment Studies, 1996, Ch.4, pp.32–3
17. Lacity and Hirscheim, as n.14 above
18. CCTA, *Producing a SSR*, July 1993. The same model is reproduced in *Producing a Statement of Service Requirements*, CCTA (now part of the Office of Government Commerce), 1993
19. Lacity and Hirscheim, as n.14 above
20. Washington, W.N., 'Subcontracting as a solution, not a problem in outsourcing', *Application Review Quarterly*, Winter 1999, pp.79–86
21. Atkinson, J. and Meager, N., *New Forms of Work Organisation*, IMS Report 121, 1986
22. Beauchamp, M., 'Outsourcing everything else? Why not purchasing?', *Purchasing and Supply Management*, July 1994, pp.16–19
23. http://www.banta.com/tech/brief/199712/strat.htm/ (accessed 2001)
24. Lamming R., *Beyond Partnership: Strategies for Innovation and Supply*, Prentice Hall, 1998, Ch.6, p.17. The authors are especially indebted to Ch.7, pp.186–90 of the 1993 edition for most of this section
25. Hines, P., *Creating World Class Suppliers*, Pitman, 1994, Ch.5, p.143
26. Hines, P., Lamming, R., Jones, D., Cousins, P. and Rice, N., *Value Stream Management*, Prentice Hall, 2000, Ch.13, p.326
27. Rich, N. and Hines, P., 'Supply chain management and time based competition', *International Journal of Physical and Logistics Management*, Vol.27 (1997), pp.211–25
28. Hines, as n.25 above
29. Izushi, H. and Morgan, K., 'Management of supplier associations: observations from Wales', *International Journal of Logistics Research and Applications*, Vol.1 (1998), pp.75–91
30. Partnership Sourcing Ltd, *Making Partnership Sourcing Happen*, p.4
31. Griffiths, F., 'Alliance partnership sourcing – a major tool for strategic procurement', *Purchasing and Supply Management*, May 1992, pp.35–40
32. CIPS, *Partnership Sourcing*, p.3
33. PSL, *Creating Service Partnerships*, 1993, p.7
34. PSL, as n.30 above
35. CIPS, as n.32 above
36. PSL, as n.30 above, pp.5–6
37. A.T. Kerney Ltd and the University of Manchester Institute of Science and Technology, *Partnership Power Plays*, UMIST Occasional Paper, 1994, p.18. This research was undertaken by Drs S. New and S. Young
38. Ellram Lisa M., 'Partnering pitfalls and success factors', *International Journal of Purchasing and Materials Management*, Spring 1995, pp.36–44
39. *Concise Oxford English Dictionary*
40. Holmlund Maria, 'Perception configurations in business relationships', *Management Decision*, Vol.37, No.9 (1999), pp.686–96
41. Bensaou, M., 'Portfolios of buyer–supplier relationships', *Sloan Management Review*, Summer 1999, pp.35–44

42. For a full account of the IMP transactions model see Harkansson (ed.), *International Marketing and Purchasing of Industrial Goods: An Interaction Approach*, Wiley, 1982; Turnball, P.W. and Valla, J.P., *Strategies for International Industrial Marketing*, Croom Helm, 1986; and a good account is found in Ford, D. (ed.) *Understanding Business Marketing and Purchasing*, 3rd edn, Thomson Learning, 2002

43. Compton, H.K. and Jessop, D.A., *Dictionary of Purchasing and Supply*, Liverpool Business Purchasing, 2001, p.168

44. Judge Lord Eldon in *Crutwell v Lye* 1910

45. Littler, D., *et al.*, 'Factors affecting the process of collaborative product development', *Journal of Product Innovation Management*, Vol.12 (1995)

46. MacMillan, K. *et al.*, 'Successful business relationships', *Journal of General Management*, Vol.26, No.1 (2000), p.73

47. Compton and Jessop, as n.42 above, p.169

48. Mentzer *et al.*, 'Supply chain management', *Journal of Retailing*, Vol.76, No.4 (2000), pp.549–68

49. HM Treasury, *Incentivisation*, CUP Guidance Note 58

50. Ibid.

51. Lamming, as n.24 above, Ch.8, p.214

52. Lamming, R., Jones, O. and Nicol, D., 'Transparency in the value stream: from open book negotiation to cost transparency', in D. Hines, R. Lamming, D. Jones, P. Cousins and N. Rich (eds) *Value Stream Management*, Prentice Hall, 2000, pp.297–8

53. CIPS, *Guide to Practice on Use of Small Suppliers*, undated, available from CIPS

54. *Official Journal of the European Communities*, No.84 (28 August 1968)

55. Webster, F.E. and Wind, Y.J., *Organisational Buying Behaviour*, Prentice Hall, 1972, pp.33–7

56. Ibid.

57. Robinson, P.J., Farris, C.W. and Wind, Y.J., *Industrial Buying and Creative Marketing*, Allyn & Baron, 1967, p.14

58. Chisnall, P.M., *Strategic Industrial Marketing*, 2nd edn, Prentice Hall, 1989, Ch.3, pp.82–3

59. Sheth, J.H., 'A model of industrial buyer behaviour', *Journal of Marketing*, October 1978, pp.50–6

60. The authors gratefully acknowledge the permission of the CIPS to reproduce the two case studies used in this chapter

61. Rich, N. and Hines, P., 'Supply chain management and time-based competition: the role of the supplier association', *International Journal of Physical Distribution and Logistics Management*, Vol.22, Nos3/4 (1997)

62. Hegarty, E., *How to Succeed in Company Politics*, McGraw-Hill, 1976

Buying at the right price

After reading this chapter you should be able to:

- Define 'price'.
- Distinguish between elastic and inelastic demand.
- Calculate price elasticity of demand.
- State the conditions for perfect competition.
- Distinguish between imperfect competition and monopoly.
- Identify the main authorities responsible for UK competition policy.
- Outline the provisions of the Competition Act 1998 in respect of anti-competition agreements and abuse of a dominant position.
- Discuss the main factors considered by suppliers and purchasers in respect of pricing agreements.
- Distinguish between form and cost price agreements.
- Describe some characteristics and applications of variations to firm and cost price agreements.
- Define the term 'price analysis'.
- State some bases and advantages of price analysis.
- Indicate why prices may vary between suppliers and at different times.
- Calculate simple and weighted price index numbers.
- Outline some applications of index numbers.
- Explain the use of price adjustment formulae.
- Show the difference between price and value.
- List some ways in which purchasing techniques may be used to obtain value for money.

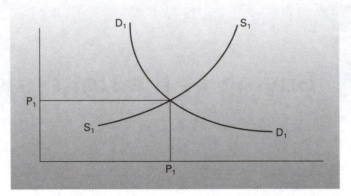

Figure 10.1 Equilibrium curve

10.1 Price

Price can be defined as the value of a commodity or service measured in terms of the standard monetary unit. In comparing two quotations, price enables us to appraise the relative value offered by each supplier.

Economic theory shows that demand and supply are balanced by the influence of price, the equilibrium price indicating the point at which demand and supply are equal. The equilibrium price can be represented diagrammatically as in Figure 10.1 in which D_1–D_1 is the demand curve indicating quantities demanded at various prices, S_1–S_1 is the supply curve indicating quantities demanded at various prices, and P_1 is the equilibrium price where demand and supply will be balanced.

At a particular moment in time the market price may differ from the equilibrium price because the effect of temporary influences may not have had the chance to work themselves out. When these factors have stabilised, however, a normal, i.e. equilibrium, price will apply. In the above analysis the shape of the demand and supply curves will be influenced by 'elasticity' or the degree of responsiveness of demand to supply to changes in price. Where a slight change in price will cause a substantial change in demand, then demand is said to be *elastic*. Demand is *inelastic* where a substantial change in price makes little difference to the amount demanded.

$$\text{Price elasticity of demand} = \frac{\% \text{ change in quantity demanded}}{\% \text{ change in price}}$$

Demand is likely to be less elastic where the following conditions obtain:

- There are few or no substitutes or competitors.
- There is 'buyer inertia', i.e. buyers are slow to change their buying habits and search for alternative sources or lower prices.
- Buyers do not notice or fail to challenge the higher price.

If demand is elastic, suppliers will consider reducing their price since a lower price will result in enhanced revenue.

$$\text{Price elasticity of supply} = \frac{\%\ \text{change in quantity supplied}}{\%\ \text{change in price}}$$

10.2   Conditions for perfect competition

The above theory is based on the concept of 'perfect' competition. For perfect competition to exist, the following five conditions must apply:

1 The item dealt in must be homogeneous so that buyers are indifferent regarding the sellers from whom they make their purchases, e.g. there must be an absence of trade or proprietary names.

2 The item must be easily transportable.

3 There must be many buyers and sellers so that the former cannot artificially restrict demand or the latter supply.

4 There should be an absence of preferential treatment of or discrimination against any buyer or seller.

5 Easy communication must exist between buyers and sellers so that they are immediately aware of what is happening anywhere in the market.

Under perfect competition there is only one price at which the entire quantity available can be sold.

10.3   Imperfect competition and monopoly

While perfect competition applies in the commodity markets as outlined in Chapter 11, most buyers operate under conditions of imperfect competition. Under imperfect competition there is no single selling price for an item.

Imperfect competition may take several forms according to the number of suppliers and the ease with which additional suppliers may enter the market. The most common forms of imperfect competition are shown in Table 10.1.

It would be impractical to deal with the effect of each of these conditions on demand, supply and price, and, in any case, a full treatment is contained in any standard textbook of economics. Buyers should remember that even a monopolistic supplier is not all-powerful. He or she can control the price or quantity sold but not both, and is thus subject to the 'sovereignty' of the consumer. If the

Table 10.1 Forms of imperfect competition

Type	No. of suppliers	Entry of suppliers into the market
Monopoly	One	No entry
Oligopoly	Few	Limited entry
Monopolistic competition	Many	Competition between suppliers

supplier overexploits his or her monopoly power, buyers will be provoked into searching for alternative products. Monopolies and restrictive trading may also give rise to intervention by central government.

10.4 Competition legislation

10.4.1 The UK framework

Overall responsibility for competition policy in the UK is vested in the secretary of state for trade and industry who is advised by the director-general of fair trading (DGFT) and the Competition Policy Directorate. The DGFT has strong powers to impose penalties on companies that breach the Competition Act 1998 and has responsibility for monitoring UK, EC and international monopolies, mergers, restrictive agreements and anti-competitive practices. In addition to advising the secretary of state, the Competition Policy Directorate of the Department of Trade and Industry (DTI) aims to develop, maintain and apply a clear, fair, proportionate framework of competitive legislation.

The secretary of state has discretionary powers to refer monopoly and other competition issues to the Competition Commission for investigation. If, as a result of such an investigation, the Commission finds that an anti-competition situation exists and is detrimental to the public interest, the secretary of state may exercise wide-ranging powers to make orders for companies or association of companies to reduce their prices or otherwise implement the Commission's recommendations. Recent investigations have resulted in orders directing car manufacturers and dealers to reduce their prices and amend their trading practices and for supermarkets to regulate relationships between themselves and their suppliers.

10.4.2 The Competition Act 1998

The Competition Act 1998 replaces the Restrictive Trade Practices Act 1976, the Resale Prices Act 1976 the majority of the Competition Act 1980 and other legislation concerned with competition. It also incorporates the prohibitions against anti-competitive agreements and the abuse of dominant powers contained in Articles 85 and 86 of the EC Treaty of Rome (now Articles 81 and 82 of the Treaty of Amsterdam). The 1998 Act does not, however, repeal the monopoly and merger provisions contained in the Fair Trading Act 1973. Under the 1998 Act, the UK regulatory authorities have power to investigate undertakings believed to be involved in anti-competitive activities and, where appropriate, to impose financial penalties. Third parties may be able to claim for damages in the courts.

Prohibition of anti-competitive agreements

Chapter 1 of the Competition Act 1998 applies to both formal and informal anti-competitive agreements. An 'agreement' refers to understandings or contracts between undertakings or associations of undertakings whether in writing or otherwise. Examples of such agreements include:

- Agreeing to fix purchase or selling prices or other trading conditions.
- Agreeing to limit or control production, markets, technical developments of investment.
- Agreeing to share markets or supply sources.
- Agreeing to apply different trading conditions to equivalent transactions, thereby placing some parties at a competitive advantage.

An agreement is, however, considered to be unlikely to have an appreciable effect where the combined market share of the parties involved does not exceed 25 per cent, although agreements to fix price, impose minimum resale prices or share markets may be regarded as having an appreciable effect even when the parties' combined market share is below 25 per cent.

Prohibition of abuse of a dominant position

Chapter 2 of the Competition Act 1998 covers the abuse by one or more undertakings of a dominant position in the market as determined by two criteria:

- The first criterion is that the undertaking must be in a dominant position. This will be decided by the Office of Fair Trading according to the undertaking's market share. In general, an undertaking is unlikely to be regarded as dominant if it has a market share of less than 40 per cent, although a lower market share may be considered dominant if the market structure enables the undertaking to act independently of its competitors. This should be contrasted with the scale and complex monopoly provisions of the Fair Trading Act 1973 in which the former related to the control by one undertaking of at least 25 per cent of the market and the latter where two or more undertakings together account for 25 per cent of a market and engage in similar conduct.
- The second criterion is that the undertakings concerned must be abusing its dominant market position in such ways as:
  - imposing unfair purchase or selling prices;
  - limiting production, markets or technical development to the prejudice of customers;
  - applying different trading conditions to equivalent transactions and thereby placing certain parties at a competitive advantage;
  - attaching unrelated supplementary conditions to a contract.

Exemptions and penalties

The Competition Act provides for certain individual, block and 'parallel' exemptions from Chapter 1. There are no exemptions from Chapter 2 prohibitions.

The Act also specifies three main consequences deriving from a breach of its provisions:

- Financial penalties of up to a maximum of the undertaking's UK turnover. Certain immunity from such penalties is given in respect of 'small agreements' on the grounds that the penalties might be 'unduly burdensome' to a small undertaking. Such immunities do not, however, extend to price-fixing agreements.

- The relevant agreement is void and unenforceable in the courts.
- Third parties who have sustained loss may have a claim for damages.

10.4.3 Mergers

UK mergers are considered by the three UK Competition authorities (the Office of Fair Trading, the Competition Commission and the secretary of state for trade and industry) under the Fair Trading Act 1973. Larger mergers are looked at by the European Commission under the EU merger rules.

In general, mergers can be considered by the UK authorities only if the assets taken over are more than £70 million or the merger creates or increases a 25 per cent share in a market for goods or services in the UK or a substantial part of it.

10.5 Pricing agreements

An important aspect of purchasing is the negotiation of the price to be paid to the supplier. Negotiation is the subject of Chapter 16 but it is useful to look at some factors that both suppliers and purchasers will consider when arriving at selling and buying prices respectively.

Suppliers will consider the following:

- Their position in the market, ranging from a monopoly position in which there is no product differentiation and the *seller* (subject to government control) sets the price, to pure competition in which the *market* sets the price.
- The nature of demand for the product, i.e. is it elastic as will be the case where there are substitutes, or inelastic where demand is not affected by the price.
- What the market or a particular purchaser will pay, i.e. charging what the market will bear.
- Prices charged by competitors in general. Higher prices can only be charged where it can be shown that the higher price is justified by product differentiation or other added value.
- The supplier's need for the business.
- The potential long-term value of the purchaser to the supplier in terms of continuity of orders, promptness of payment, etc.
- Is the product standard or a special.
- The order volume – long production runs make lower prices possible.
- The stage of the product in its life cycle. In general, the earlier a product is in its life cycle, the higher will be the price.

Purchasers will consider:

- The risk attached to the purchase and the method of pricing.
- The position of the purchaser in the market. Where the supplier is in a monopoly position the purchaser must exploit the fact that, except for products with an inelastic demand, the monopolist can control either the price or the quantity demanded, but not both.

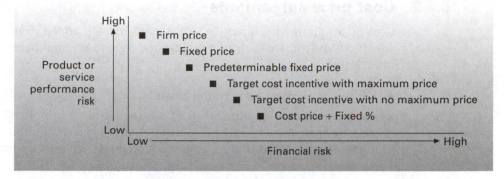

Figure 10.2   Risks of different pricing arrangements to the purchaser

Source: adapted from Behan, P., *Purchasing in Government*, Longman, 1994, p. 57

- The number of suppliers in the market and the possibility of alternative products.
- Prices paid by competitors. This information may be difficult to obtain.
- Whether learning curve factors are applicable to the product.
- The relationship between price and value in terms of competitive advantage.
- The period for which the price is to be agreed.
- What is a reasonable price based on a price analysis.
- What quantities are likely to be involved over what period.
- What may be considered a fair price from both the purchaser's and supplier's viewpoints.

All the above factors influence the selling or purchase price of a product. In practice, price agreements are basically of two types: firm and cost type. As shown in Figure 10.2, firm and cost agreements are at opposite ends of a continuum with a number of intermediate pricing arrangements aimed at reducing the risks to the purchaser.

10.5.1   Firm price agreements

Firm price agreements are not subject to any provision for variation. Such agreements are more advantageous to purchasers for the following reasons:

- All risks are borne by the supplier and the purchaser knows from the start what is to be paid.
- Suppliers have the maximum incentive to produce efficiently and complete the work on time. All cost savings *below* the price are kept by the supplier. All cost incurred *above* the price are met by the supplier.
- A minimum of administration is involved, e.g. auditing of costs.

The only possible disadvantage is that an unscrupulous supplier or contractor may attempt to enhance profits or reduce losses by 'taking it out of the job' to the long-term detriment of the product.

10.5.2 Cost price agreements

Cost price agreements, in which a fixed percentage is added to the production or construction cost, are the more disadvantageous to the purchaser for the following reasons:

■ All financial risks accrue to the buyer.
■ Such agreements are difficult to administer since the suppliers' cost schedules require to be checked by financial and management accountants and possible other specialist staff such as engineers, architects, quantity surveyors, etc.

10.6 Variations in firm and cost price agreements

In practice, factors such as the escalation in material costs, through inflation or wage rises during the period of a contract, the need to provide incentives or the difficulty of measuring the work to be done make it desirable to reduce the risks to both purchaser and supplier by incorporating variations into both firm and cost type contracts.

Some possible variations to firm and cost type agreements are shown in Table 10.2.

Example 10.1   Target cost with maximum price

Target price = £11 including £1 profit. Ceiling price = £12 with no profit. Cost savings shared in the ratio 80/20 between supplier and purchaser.

Cost (£)	Profit (£)	Price (£)
11.00	–	11.00
10.00	1.00	10.80
9.00	2.00	10.60
8.00	3.00	10.40

Example 10.2   Target cost without maximum price

Target cost per item = £10.00 with a profit of £1.00. Increases or decreases above or below this target cost shared equally between supplier and purchaser.

Cost (£)	Profit (£)	Price (£)
10.00 (target)	1.00	11.00
11.00	1.00	11.50
9.50	1.50	10.75

Table 10.2   Variations to firm and cost price agreements

Type of agreement	Characteristics	Application
Firm agreements		
Fixed price	Once determined price remains fixed until completion of the contract apart from changes in the scope of the contract	Standard items from stock or for short-term production
Firm fixed price with economic price adjustment	Provides for upward or downward revision of the fixed price on the occurrence of specified contingencies. The adjustments may be: ■ based on the fixed or contract price ■ based on actual increases/decreases in labour or material costs ■ based on specially mentioned indexes relating to labour or material	When the stability of market or labour conditions during the period of the contract is uncertain Contingencies that might occur can be identified and covered separately in the contract
Fixed price incentive contracts	Provides for an adjustment of profit and a final price based on a formula relating final negotiated total cost to a total target cost. The final price is subject to a maximum negotiated at the outset	Where a firm fixed price contract is unsuitable Where it is desirable to give the contractor a positive incentive to control cost To provide incentives to the contractor for technical performance or delivery on time.
Fixed price contracts with prospective price redetermination	A firm fixed price applies for an initial specified period after which price will be renegotiated or amended at stated times during the contract	Where it is possible to agree on a fair and reasonable fixed price for an initial period but not for subsequent periods of contract performance Where a learning element is involved as in prices subject to learning curves
Fixed price contracts with retroactive price redetermination	A fixed ceiling price is agreed subject to price redetermination within the ceiling after the contract is completed	Appropriate for research and development contracts where a firm and reasonable fixed price cannot be negotiated due to cost uncertainties
Firm fixed price, level of effort term contracts	Requires the contractor to provide a specified level of effort over an agreed period on work that can only be specified in general terms in return for a fixed amount	For research and development contracts Where payment is for effort expended rather than results achieved
Cost type agreements		
Target cost with maximum price	This is the same as the fixed price incentive contract described above. The maximum price is fixed including an agreed profit any reductions are shared on an agreed percentage basis between purchaser and supplier	Where target cost can be fixed with reasonable certainty but exact costs cannot be determined when the contract is placed.
Target costs without maximum price	No maximum price is fixed. Excess or reduced costs over target price are shared between supplier and purchaser in agreed proportions	Contracts extending over any period of time during which the supplier may require to be compensated for costs incurred over target or rewarded for cost savings

10.7   Price analysis

10.7.1   Definition

Price analysis is:

> The breaking down of a quoted price into its constituent elements for the purpose of determining the reasonableness, or otherwise, of the proposed charge.

The reasonableness of the proposed charge is an analysis of the quoted price to ensure that it covers the costs of an efficient producer and allows a fair profit commensurate with the risks involved in undertaking the work. An analysis of price can be based on:

- cost experience of the buyer's undertaking, e.g. when subcontracting items previously manufactured;
- cost estimates prepared by the estimating or cost department of the buyer's undertaking;
- cost information provided by the vendor.

It can also be undertaken as a joint exercise by the purchaser in association with the supplier.

10.7.2   Advantages of price analysis

Price analysis has the following advantages:

- It provides the buyer with a guide as to what he or she ought to pay.
- It highlights possible mistakes in quoting on the part of the vendor, i.e. where the price is exceptionally low or high.
- It provides a basis for subsequent negotiation that can benefit both vendor and buyer, i.e. cost reduction leading to price reduction.
- Management accounting provides a number of approaches that can be applied to price analysis including life cycle costing, target costing, absorption costing, activity-based costing and standard costing. These approaches are discussed in Chapter 17. Marginal costing and its application to make or buy decision is dealt with in chapter 9.

10.8   Price variation and adjustment

10.8.1   Price variation

Prices may vary between suppliers and at different times owing to the following factors:

- *Quantity considerations.* Quantity discounts are often given as an incentive to the buyer to give the vendor a larger share of the available business. The vendor may also pass on to the buyer a proportion of savings accruing from large quantities such as reductions in production, selling, transport and administration costs.

- *Payment considerations.* Cash discounts are given as an incentive to prompt payment, enabling the vendor to reduce borrowing and the risk of bad debts. Buyers do not always appreciate the true value of cash discounts. It would be necessary for the bank rate to exceed 36.1 per cent before it would pay an undertaking to forgo a cash discount of 2.5 per cent monthly account. Cash discounts also offer scope for negotiation. A cash discount of 3.5 per cent for 7 days is preferable to 2.5 per cent monthly.

- *Time considerations.* Vendors may sometimes offer discounts to encourage buying in slack trading periods or for buying out of season.

- *Quality considerations.* These reflect the cost of producing from more expensive materials, to higher standards of accuracy or from a brand name.

- *Distribution considerations.* Trade discounts are given to compensate suppliers or buyers for undertaking distributive functions. Manufacturers of original equipment give trade discounts since their market is widened both by the initial sale and the subsequent business in spares.

- *Transport considerations.* The meaning of such terms as CIF (cost, insurance, freight), FOB (free on board) and DDP (delivered duty paid) should be known and understood.

10.9   Price index numbers

A price index number is a measure designed to show average changes in the price of an item or group of items over a period of time.

10.9.1   Simple and weighted index numbers

Simple index numbers calculate price changes over time in respect of a simple item, e.g. coal or oil imports or population changes, and is calculated by the formula:

$$\text{Price index} = \frac{P_1}{P_0} \times 100$$

where P_0 is the price in a base year and P_1 the year to be compared.

10.9.2   Weighted index numbers

Where more than one item is involved, as in the index of retail prices (IRP), usually referred to as the 'cost of living index', the calculation of an index is more

---

Example 10.3   Price index calculation

The average price of an item for the years shown is as follows:

	1998	1999	2000	2001	2002
Price (£)	85	90	95	102	105

Assume P_0 the base year to be 1998, i.e. £85. The calculations will be:

Year	Price	Base price	Price relative calculation	Price relative	Index number
1998	85	85	85/85	1×100	100
1999	90	85	90/85	1.06×100	106
2000	95	85	95/85	1.12×100	112
2001	102	85	102/85	1.2×100	120
2002	105	85	105/85	1.23×100	123

Thus the price of the item is 23% higher in 2002 than it was in 1998.

---

complex. In the cost of living index, for example, which involves the prices of some 650 items in 14 categories and the collection of about 150,000 separate price quotations there are the differences that:

- some prices will fall and others will rise;
- prices will vary for different weights and quantities of the same item;
- some items are of greater importance to the cost of living than others;
- households spend their money in different ways.

Weighted index numbers attempt to make prices directly comparable. The weights used reflect the relative importance of a particular item.

The two most popular weighted indexes are those of Laspeyres and Paasche. The *Laspeyres index* uses base-year quantities and weights and indicates how much the cost of buying base-year quantities at current-year prices is compared with base-year costs. Different years can be compared with each other. The Laspeyres formula is:

$$\frac{\sum p_1 q_0}{\sum p_1 q_0}$$

where p_0 and p_1 are the base-year and current-year prices and q_0 the base-year quantity.

The *Paasche index* uses current-year quantities and weights and indicates how much current-year costs are related to the cost of buying current-year quantities at base-year prices. The different years can be compared only with the base-year and not with each other. The Paasche formula is:

$$\frac{\Sigma p_1 q_1}{\Sigma p_0 q_1}$$

The IRP may be defined as:

An average measure of change in the prices of goods and services bought for the purpose of consumption by the vast majority of households in the UK.

The IRP is based on the Laspeyres formula.

Example 10.4   Cost of living index calculation

Assume a family's budget is influenced by four main items, A, B, C, D. The weightings (w) of which are 3, 1, 2 and 4 respectively. The price per unit is shown for the years 2000 (p_0) and 2001 (p_1).

Commodity	Weighting	Price/unit 2000	Price/unit 2001
A	3	0.50	0.58
B	1	1.60	1.40
C	2	1.28	1.36
D	4	2.50	2.60

Using 2000 as base, the weighted price relative index will be:

$$\frac{\Sigma \frac{p_1}{p_0} w}{\Sigma w} \times 100 = \left(\left(\frac{0.58}{0.50} \right) \times 3 + \left(\frac{1.40}{1.60} \right) \times 1 + \left(\frac{1.36}{1.28} \right) \times 2 + \left(\frac{2.60}{2.50} \right) \times 4 \right) \times 100$$

$$= 1.064 \times 100 = 106.4$$

The cost of living is higher in 2001 by 6.4 per cent.

10.9.3   The use of index numbers

Index numbers can be used to:

- estimate current average product prices or costs using the prices or costs of similar items or groups of items at a previous base date;
- facilitate the analysis of a time series of prices and costs by eliminating the effects of inflation or deflation;
- estimate or negotiate future prices or costs allowing for changes in the value of a currency;
- identify and define price or cost changes as a basis for contract cost of price adjustments (see BEAMA example in the next section).

10.10 Price adjustment formulae

10.10.1 The BEAMA formula

Examples of methods of price variation have been given in section 10.6 above. Contract price adjustment (CPA) formulae have been developed for certain industries. The CPA formula originally developed by the British Electrical and Allied Manufacturers Association (BEAMA) was the prototype for similar formulae used by other trade associations, local and central government departments, etc.

The fundamental principle of the BEAMA formula is to calculate the variation of labour and material costs in relation to the incidence of expenditure and manufacture throughout the contract period. In the case of electrical machinery, the procedure is as follows:

1 Contract price is divided: 47.5 per cent labour, 47.5 per cent materials and 5 per cent fixed portion.

2 Materials costs are variated by reference to indices provided by the Office for National Statistics at two points in time, i.e. the tender date and the average of the indices between the two-fifths and four-fifths points of the contract period.

3 Labour costs are variated by reference to a labour index published by BEAMA and based on a Department of Employment figure of average earnings modified to include statutory payments made by the employer. Adjustments in labour costs are made by considering the labour index at the date of tender and the average of labour indices published for the last two-thirds of the contract period.

4 If the cost to the contractor of performing his or her obligations under the contract is increased or reduced by reason of any rise or fall in labour costs or in the cost of material, the amount of such increase or reduction is added to or deducted from the contract price as the case may be. No account is taken of any amount by which any cost incurred by the contractor has been increased by the default or negligence of the contractor.

5 Variations in the cost of materials and labour are calculated in accordance with the following formula:

$$P_1 = P_0\left(0.05 + 0.475\left(\frac{M_1}{M_0}\right) + 0.475\left(\frac{L_1}{L_0}\right)\right)$$

where: P_1 = final contract price

P_0 = contract price at date of tender

M_1 = average of producer price index figures of materials and fuel purchased for basic electrical equipment as provided by the Office for National Statistics commencing with the index last provided before the two-fifths point of the contract period and ending with the index last provided before the four-fifths of the contract period

M_0 = producer price index figure of materials and fuel purchased for basic electrical equipment last provided by the Office for National Statistics before the date of tender

L_1 = average of the BEAMA labour cost index figures for electrical engineering published for the last two-thirds of the contract period

L_0 = BEAMA labour cost index figure for electrical engineering published for the month in which the tender date falls

---

Example 10.5   BEAMA calculation

Basis of claim for contract price adjustment

A	Contract price	£20,000
B	Tender or cost basis date	20 January 1999
C	Date of order	14 February 1999
D	Date when ready for dispatch/taking over*	12 August 2000
E	Contract period between C and D (days)	545
F	Date at one-third of contract period	15 August 1999
G	Date at two-fifths of contract period	20 September 1999
H	Date at four-fifths of contract period	25 April 2000
I	Labour cost index at tender or cost basis date	464.9
J	Average of BEAMA labour cost indices for period F to D	499.0
K	BEAMA figures of materials for *basic electrical equipment/mechanical engineering last published before tender or cost basis date	91.0
L	Average of BEAMA index figures of materials commencing with the index last published before date at G and ending with the Index last published at H	92.2

M   Labour adjustment

$$47.5 \times \frac{J - L}{L} = \frac{34.1}{464.9} \times 47.5$$

$$= 3.4841\%$$

N   Material adjustment

$$47.5 \times \frac{L - K}{K} = \frac{1.2}{91} \times 47.5$$

$$= 0.6264\%$$

P   Total percentage adjustment for labour and materials   4.1105%

Assume contract price £20,000 × 4.1105%   = £822.10

10.10.2   Procedure for price adjustment

The procedure adopted for dealing with price increases should include the following:

- Adjustments should, wherever possible, be authorised by a single responsible official.
- Adjustments should be notified to all interested departments, e.g. design, estimating etc., or persons.
- Adjustments should be confirmed in writing.

- Where standard costing is in operation, a procedure for monitoring price adjustments and variances against standard material uses will be necessary.

- Where adjustments are calculated in accordance with an agreed formula, the base date of both the original contract and the circumstances giving rise to an adjustment should be clearly identified.

- Suppliers should be asked to provide data to justify price increase, e.g. an increase of 10 per cent on labour costs only justifies 1 per cent on the total price.

Where the vendor and the buyer cannot reconcile the request for a price adjustment, the latter may consider such strategies as:

- alternative suppliers;
- alternative materials;
- make or buy;
- value analysis;
- longer-term contracts requiring longer notification of adjustments;
- where the supplier is in a monopoly position the buyer may, as a last resort, take the matter to the Restrictive Practice Court.

10.11 Price and value

Both Oscar Wilde and John Ruskin recognised that price and value are not the same thing. Oscar Wilde[1] defined a cynic as 'A man who knows the price of everything and the value of nothing.' John Ruskin[2] is alleged to have declared:

> There is hardly anything in the world that some men can't make a little worse and sell a little cheaper, and the people who consider price only are this man's lawful prey.

Current public procurement policy is based largely on the White Paper *Setting New Standards: A Strategy for Government Procurement*.[3] A further White Paper, *Modernising Government*,[4] contains a commitment to procurement based on competition to secure best whole-life value, the use of partnerships to encourage innovation and continuous improvement and the Private Finance Initiative for capital projects.

The DTI[5] has defined value for money as 'taking into account the optimum combination of whole life cost and quality necessary to meet the customer's requirement'.

A number of purchasing techniques may be used to obtain the best value for money including:

- Value analysis, especially the elimination of non-essential features.
- Consolidation of demand, i.e. aggregating several orders to negotiate reduced prices or increased discounts.
- Negotiating contracts and prices centrally.

- Proactive sourcing – ensuring competition by challenging the repeated use of regular suppliers.
- Buying complete sub-assemblies rather than constituent components.
- Investigating the refurbishment or upgrading of existing or second-hand items rather than buying new.
- Encouraging standardisation thus reducing the cost of spares and maintenance.
- Adoption of a whole-life methodology rather than an initial price approach.
- Negotiation with existing or potential suppliers aimed at ensuring additional features or concessions.
- Application of learning curve analysis to negotiation.
- Post-tender negotiation.
- Elimination or reduction of inventory thereby avoiding unnecessary storage and holding costs.
- Applications of e-procurement.
- Global purchasing.

Case study

Progressive Applications plc is a company specialising in the development and production of machines with applications in the field of medical technology such as those used for kidney failure, cardiac surgery etc. The company has received substantial government backing to develop a revolutionary new machine that will facilitate the detection of incipient heart trouble. A condition of the grant is that two prototypes of the device must be ready for testing at leading teaching hospitals by a prescribed date.

The design involved the purchase of complex sub-assembly manufactured by one of a few specialist producers capable of very high precision engineering and working with specialist materials such as platinum and stainless steel. Time was also of the essence and the designers had only a rough idea of what the cost of manufacture would be. Cost, however, was a secondary factor to quality and delivery on time.

If the prototype was successful the demand for the sub-assembly would be high, but several specialist manufactures were unwilling to disrupt their existing production to make two prototype assemblies the success of which could not be guaranteed.

Gordon Ashton, head of purchasing at Progressive Applications, invited five small precision engineering organisations to a meeting at which he outlined the uncertainty and potential of the product for which the sub-assembly is required, the complexity of the item, the need to work to close tolerances and the paramount importance of delivery within 90 days of receiving the order. The sizes of the five companies as measured by the number of employees varied from 15 to 60. When convening the meeting Gordon emphasised that the purpose was to explain his company's precise requirements and obtain rough estimates but not firm prices which would require detailed consideration. Each company agreed to submit firm cost estimates within 10 days of the meeting.

In the event, two of the invited companies stated that they could not meet the deadline of 90 days and did not submit an estimate. The estimates received from the remaining three organisations were respectively £1,800, £3,500 and £6,000 per item.

The lowest estimate was from Birkett Engineering, a small private company specialising in precision work for the aircraft industry and headed by Robin Birkett. Gordon has placed previous orders with Birkett Engineering and has always been satisfied. He believes that, technically, Birkett's has the expertise to handle the order. Because of the other quotations and the complexity of the work, Gordon is worried that the cost estimate of £1,800 is far too low. He therefore convenes a further meeting between Robin Birkett, David Yates, chief design engineer at Progressive Applications and himself to analyse the estimate of £1,800 in detail. The analysis resulted in a revised cost estimate of £2,400 which all three persons agreed was a more realistic price.

After the meeting, Gordon is still undecided about the type of contract to offer to Birkett Engineering. He feels that a fixed price contract is inappropriate partly because of the higher prices received from equally reliable organisations and partly because the novelty of the work makes it virtually impossible to estimate costs accurately. Since delivery on time is essential, Gordon is also anxious to ensure that Birkett Engineering will not be unwilling to incur overtime costs should the need arise to enable the promised delivery date to be achieved.

Gordon also rejects the idea of placing a contract with a fixed price plus a ceiling with provision for a downward revision of prices. This is because he suspects that the agreed estimate of £2,400 might have too low a ceiling and could adversely affect delivery on time. Yet he did not think that a minimum price without a ceiling could be justified since Birkett Engineering had been selected on account of its low price.

Gordon next considered an incentive type contract with no ceiling or maximum. This, he reasoned, would both provide Birkett Engineering with an incentive to keep costs low and at the same time avoid the restrictions of a maximum price. He decided that a profit of 10 per cent on actual costs would be fair, so that Birkett would receive £240 profit if actual costs and target cost coincided. He also devised an 80/20 profit formula under which Birkett would receive an extra 20p profit for every £1 by which Birkett's actual costs were under target. Conversely, Birkett would receive a 20p profit reduction for every £1 by which actual costs exceeded target costs. This formula resulted in the set out in the table.

Birkett's actual cost per item (£)	Profit per item (£)	Price per item (£)
1,600	400	2,000
2,000	320	2,320
2,400	240	2,640
2,800	160	2,960
3,200	80	3,280
3,600	0	3,600

Gordon believes that in view of the uncertain costs, such a contract will encourage efficient low cost production with higher profits and at the same time allow Birkett Engineering to incur higher costs should it be necessary to do so to ensure delivery on time.

Questions

1 What are your views on the incentive contract devised by Gordon?

2 In respect of the given situation discuss the alternatives of (a) a fixed price contract, (b) a target price contract with a fixed ceiling and (c) a cost plus agreed profit contract.

Discussion questions

10.1 Which of the following statements are true?

Market prices

  (a) communicate information

  (b) determine supply

  (c) measure scarcity

  (d) provide incentives

10.2 Price elasticity of demand measures the responsiveness of demand to a given change in price

  (a) Give three examples each of household commodities for which demand is (i) elastic and (ii) inelastic.

  (b) Now give three examples each of the items purchased by a manufacturing organisation for which demand is (i) elastic and (ii) inelastic.

10.3 Complete the following table by indicating whether demand will be elastic or inelastic and why?

Characteristics	Elastic items	Inelastic items
Whether item is cheap or expensive		
Whether demand can or cannot be postponed		
Whether a rise in price will result in a large of smaller fall in demand		
Whether item is a luxury or necessity		
Whether or not there are substitutes		
Will the demand curve be steep of flat?		

10.4 'The most dramatic change about the internet revolution is that it is establishing something like the textbook condition across a wide range of activities'. What arguments would you use (a) to support or (b) to refute this statement?

10.5 A monopoly has been defined as a firm that is the *only* producer of a good or service for which there are *no close substitutes*.

Before privatisation, the UK gas, electricity, coal, steel, railways and postal services were all state monopolies.

Discuss the advantages and disadvantages of public utilities being state monopolies. What might be the consequences of nationalising the motor car industry?

10.6 Covisint is an electronic marketplace set up by six major automotive manufacturers – Ford, General Motors, Daimler, Renault, Nissan and Peugeot-Citroën – to serve procurement needs and those of their suppliers.

(a) What benefits did the members expect to derive from the establishment of Covisint?

(b) On what grounds might Covisint have been considered to violate completion and anti-trust legislation?

(c) On what grounds did the US Federal Trade Commission and the European Commission give regulatory approval for Covisint?

10.7 Draft policy statements suitable for inclusion in a purchasing manual

(a) stressing the importance of encouraging competition when sourcing;

(b) providing for an exception in the case of small local suppliers.

10.8 What types of pricing agreement would you recommend for the following situations?

(a) A pharmaceutical company wishes to commission the testing of a newly developed drug by a teaching hospital which will prepare a detailed report at the end of a fixed trial period.

(b) An engineering company wishes to place an order for the supply of a new component which will entail a lengthier learning period on the part of the supplier.

(c) A contract for the erection of a new school where there is some uncertainty regarding the depth to which foundations will be required.

(d) A contract for a bridge over a river.

(e) A contract extending over two years for the supply of a standard product to be delivered on a just-in-time basis.

(f) Where it is essential that a delivery date should not be exceeded and, if possible, should be improved upon.

10.9 The average purchase price (in pence per pound) of a raw material during the seven years 1995–2001 are shown below.

	1995	1996	1997	1998	1999	2000	2001
Average purchase price (p)	62.0	74.6	74.8	89.2	77	82.8	97.2

(a) Using 1995 as a base, find the price relatives corresponding to the years 1999 and 2001.

(b) Using 1997 as a base, find the price relatives corresponding to all the given years.

10.10   Using the following (imaginary) figures, compute the Laspeyres and Paasche index
numbers.

	1995	2000	1995	2000
Cotton	148.8	113.6	22.244	26.864
	(pence per pound)	(pence per pound)	(million sales)	(million sales)
Wheat	£7.82	£6.32	1,022.8	874.2
	(per bushel)	(per bushel)	(million sales)	(million sales)

1 bushel = 60 lb

10.11   Using the following figures calculate the total price adjustment using the BEAMA
formula.

A	Contract price	£40,000
B	Tender or cost basis date	16 July 2000
C	Date of order	16 July 2000
D	Date ready for dispatch	16 October 2001
E	Contract period between C and D dates	487 days
F	Date at third of contract period	27 November 2000
G	Date at two fifths of contract period	28 December 2000
H	Date at fourth fifths of contract period	11 July 2001
I	Labour cost index at tender/cost dates	390.2
J	Average of labour cost indices for period F–D	407.4
K	Office of National Statistics figures of materials for basic electrical equipment last published before tender date	113.4
L	Average of Office of National Statistics index figures of materials commencing with index last published before date of G and ending with index last published at H	114.6

? Past examination questions

1   When there is uncertainty regarding future costs, it may prove difficult for the buyer
to obtain fixed prices on long-term contracts. Explain why this is the case and assess,
utilising worked examples, two of the alternatives to fixed price contracts available to
the buyer in such situations.

(CIPS, Purchasing and Supply Management II: Provisioning, 1990)

2   Effective negotiation relies heavily on the planning stage and purchase price and cost
analyses are useful tools for the buyer to use in this context. Describe how they could
be used to plan a negotiation with the supplier of an important component who wants
to renew an existing 12 month contract with you but requires a 15 per cent increase
owing to increases in raw materials prices. How would you structure the resulting
information with your negotiations strategy.

(CIPS, Purchasing and Supply Chain Management II:
Tactics and Operations May 1998)

3 Compare and contrast the use of *contract price adjustment* and *incentives* clauses in commercial contracts, including in your example each type of clause.

(CIPS, Commercial Relationships, May 1998)

4 Explain the use of:

(a) incentive clauses, and

(b) contract adjustment clauses

Include in your answer an explanation of how these contract clauses might impact upon commercial relationships.

(CIPS, Commercial Relationships, November 1998)

5 Contract price adjustment clauses and incentive clauses have in common the fact that they allow the agreed contract price to be varied. However, the variation is allowed for different reasons. Explain the nature and purpose of each type of clause, giving a simple example of each.

(CIPS, Commercial Relationships, May 1999)

Notes

1. Wilde, Oscar, *Lady Windermere's Fan*, Act 3
2. Ruskin, J. (no date) (this statement is attributed to Ruskin but found in none of his writings)
3. Cmnd 2840 HMSO, 1995
4. Cm 4310, HMSO, March 1999
5. DTI, *Statement of General Procurement Principles*, HMSO, 2000, available at http://www.dti.gov.uk/about/procurement/procual15.html

PART THREE

Strategy, tactics and operations (2): buying situations

Contrasting approaches to supply

After reading this chapter you should be able to:

- Distinguish between consumer, industrial and resale products.
- Define the term 'capital equipment'.
- Identify six types of industrial equipment.
- State some characteristics of capital expenditure.
- List the main factors to be considered when buying capital equipment.
- Describe the advantages of buying used equipment and recognise some precautions to be taken.
- Evaluate the advantages and disadvantages of straight purchase, hire purchase and leasing in the context of capital equipment.
- Select and appraise suppliers of capital equipment.
- Evaluate capital investments using payback, average rate of return and discounting approaches.
- Indicate some contributions that buyers may make to the purchase of capital investment purchases.
- Classify production materials.
- Indicate the characteristics of raw materials and sensitive commodities.
- Know the main sources of information regarding market conditions affecting the purchase of raw materials.
- Distinguish between forward and futures dealing.
- Describe the main functions of commodity exchange.
- Define some terms used in futures contracts.
- Differentiate between fundamental and technical analysis as applied to material buying.
- Distinguish between time and £-cost averaging and the volume timing of purchases.
- Describe the purpose and types of bills of materials.
- Explain the meaning of operating supplies and characteristics of consumables.

- State some contributions made by purchasing to the acquisition of consumables.
- Explain how construction supplies differ from those purchased for manufacturing and service undertakings.
- Define and explain the purpose of bills of quantities.
- Define the terms 'merchandising enterprise', 'wholesale' and 'retailer'.
- Explain the main forms of retailing and the functions of retailers.
- Describe the buying process in a typical trade enterprise.

11.1 Introduction

The considerations that apply to the purchase of products, as distinct from services, can be contrasted according to the nature of the product, the types of production and the principal uses to which a purchased item will be put. We can also distinguish between purchasing of consumer, industrial and resale items.

- The term *'consumer products'* is used in this context to refer to goods purchased by individuals and households for personal consumption and are outside the scope of this book.
- *Industrial products* are purchased by organisations for use in the production of other products to make profits or achieve other objectives.
- *Resale products* are purchased by organisations in order to resell them at a profit.

This chapter is concerned with industrial products, consumables or maintenance, repair and operating (MRO) supplies and goods for resale.

11.2 Industrial products

These may be sub-divided into

- Capital equipment items
- Production materials.

11.3 Capital investment items

11.3.1 Definitions

Capital equipment has been defined by Aljian[1] as:

One of the subclasses of the fixed asset category and includes industrial and office machinery and tools, transportation equipment, furniture and fixtures and others. As such, these items are properly chargeable to a capital account rather than to expense.

Alternative terms include 'capital goods', 'capital assets' and 'capital expenditure', which can be defined as follows:

Capital goods – Capital in the form of fixed assets used to produce goods, such as plant, equipment, rolling stock.[2]

Capital assets – Assets used to generate revenues of cost savings by providing production, distribution or service capabilities for more than one year.[3]

Capital expenditure – An expenditure on acquisition of tangible productive assets which yield continuous service beyond the accounting period in which they are purchased.[4]

Of the above definitions, that for capital expenditure is the most useful, since it emphasises the three most important characteristics of capital equipment, namely:

- *Tangibility* – capital equipment can be physically touched or handled.
- *Productivity* – capital equipment is used to produce further goods or services.
- *Durability* – capital equipment has a life greater than one year.

From the marketing standpoint, Marrian[5] has distinguished six types of industrial equipment:

- *Buildings* – permanent constructions on a site to house or enclose equipment and personnel employed in industrial, institutional or commercial activities.
- *Installation equipment* – capital equipment, plant; essential plant, machinery or other major equipment used directly to produce the goods and services of producing organisations.
- *Accessory equipment* – durable major equipment used to facilitate the production of goods and services or to enhance the operations of organisations. Installation and accessory equipment often coincide but there is a distinction. Aircraft purchased by an airline, for example, would be installation equipment; aircraft purchased by a manufacturing organisation to facilitate the movement of executive personnel would be accessory equipment.
- *Operating equipment* – semi-durable minor equipment which is movable, used in, but not generally essential to, the production of goods and services, e.g. special footwear, goggles, brushes and brooms.
- *Tools and instruments* – semi-durable or durable portable minor equipment and instruments required for producing, measuring, calculating, etc., associated with the production of goods and services, e.g. word processors, all tools, surgical instruments, timing devices, cash registers, etc.
- *Furnishings and fittings* – all goods and materials employed to fit buildings for their organisational purposes but not that equipment used specifically in production, e.g. carpets, floor coverings, draperies, furniture, shelving, counters, benches, etc.

11.3.2 Capital expenditure

From the *accountancy* standpoint, expenditure on capital equipment results in the acquisition of fixed rather than current assets. One useful definition of capital equipment other than that already quoted is 'all expenditure which is expected to produce benefit to the firm over a period longer than the accounting period in which the expenditure was incurred'.

11.3.3 Characteristics of capital expenditure

Expenditure on capital equipment differs from that on materials and components in many ways including the following:

- The cost per item is usually greater.
- The items bought are used up gradually on facilitating production rather than as a part of the end product.
- Capital expenditure is financed from long-term capital or from appropriations of profit rather than from working capital or charges against profit.
- Tax considerations such as capital allowances and investment grants have an important bearing on whether to purchase capital equipment and the timing of such purchases.
- Government financial assistance towards the cost of capital equipment may be available, e.g. where a manufacturing organisation is located in a development area.
- The purchase of capital equipment is often postponable, at least in the short term.
- The decision to buy capital equipment often results in consequential decisions relating to sales, output and labour. In the latter case, consultations with the appropriate unions may be necessary.

The terms and conditions of purchase may have to be adapted to meet the circumstances arising from the acquisition of capital equipment.

The purchase of capital equipment is therefore usually a more complex procedure than that involved in the case of materials and components, a large proportion of which are repeat procedures.

11.3.4 Factors to be considered in buying capital equipment

Apart from the mode of purchase, finance and the return on the investment made, the factors to be considered include the following:

- *Purpose*. What is the prime purpose of the equipment?
- *Flexibility*. How versatile is the equipment? Can it be used for purposes other than those for which it was primarily acquired?
- *Standardisation*. Is the equipment compatible with any already installed, thus reducing the cost of holding spares?
- *Life*. This usually refers to the period before the equipment will have to be written off owing to depreciation or obsolescence. It is, however, not necessarily

linked to the total life span if it is intended to dispose of the asset before it is obsolete or unusable.

■ *Reliability*. Breakdowns mean higher costs, loss of goodwill through extended deliveries and possibly high investment in spares.

■ *Durability*. Is the equipment sufficiently robust for its intended use?

■ *Product quality*. Defective output proportionately increases the cost per unit of output.

■ *Cost of operation*. Costs of fuel, power and maintenance. Will special labour or additional labour costs be incurred? Is discussion with the unions advisable?

■ *Cost of installation*. Does the price include cost of installation, commissioning and training of operators?

■ *Cost of maintenance*. Can the equipment be maintained by own staff or will special agreements with the vendor be necessary? What estimates of mainten-ance costs can be provided before purchase? How reliable are these?

■ *Miscellaneous*. These include appearance, space requirements, quietness of operation, safety and aspects of ergonomics affecting the performance of the operator.

11.3.5 Life cycle costing

Life cycle costing (terotechnology) is an important aspect of capital expenditure. Life cycle costing is further considered in Chapter 17.

11.4   Buying used equipment

Used equipment available from dealers' auctions or direct purchase from a previ-ous owner may be an alternative to buying new.

11.4.1 Advantages of buying used equipment

■ Often cost is substantially lower than new.

■ Used equipment may be more readily available.

■ Used equipment, especially when reconditioned or rebuilt, may have a long life and be protected by guarantees or warranties.

■ It may be economical to buy low-priced used equipment when it would not pay to acquire new.

■ A used machine may be compatible with others already in use, thus reducing the costs of carrying spares.

■ It is often possible to inspect used equipment in use under actual working conditions.

11.4.2 Precautions

Although protection is given by the Sale of Goods, Trades Description and Misrepresentation Acts, the purchaser of used equipment should work on the principle of *caveat emptor* (let the buyer beware). Some questions that a prospective buyer of used equipment should ask include the following:

- Is a history of the equipment available?
- Is there any indication of age such as a serial number?
- How well has the equipment been maintained?
- Are spares readily available? Will they continue to be?
- How does the price asked for used equipment compare with the cost of buying new?
- Are the vendors well established? Have they a sound reputation?
- What special terms and conditions apply to the purchase?
- Do any guarantees or warranties supersede the protection given under the Sale of Goods Act?
- What trials, test or approval period will the vendor allow?
- Will the vendor permit an inspection by an independent assessor?
- What will be the cost, where appropriate, of dismantling, transporting and re-erecting/installing equipment?
- Is the equipment rebuilt or reconditioned? *Rebuilt equipment* will usually have been stripped down and built up again from base. Worn and broken parts will have been replaced and worn surfaces reground and realigned to meet the original tolerances. Rebuilt machines will also have been thoroughly tested and will come with a limited warranty. Such machines will cost between 50 and 70 per cent of a new counterpart. *Reconditioned machines* will not have been so thoroughly overhauled as rebuilt machines. They will, nevertheless, have been cleaned, have broken or worn parts replaced and repaired to look like new. The guarantee or warranty will, however, be less inclusive than for rebuilt machines. Reconditioned machines generally sell at between 40 and 50 per cent of new items.

11.5 Financing the acquisition of capital equipment

The acquisition of new or capital equipment may be financed by straight purchase, hire purchase or leasing.

11.5.1 Straight purchase

Advantages

- The total cost, particularly in comparison to rental is low.
- Equipment may have a residual or second-hand value.
- User has total control over the equipment (there may, however, be maintenance and software constraints).
- Capital allowances (normally 25 per cent annually on the reducing balance) may be set against tax.

Disadvantages

- Investment in fixed capital resources will reduce liquidity.
- Obsolescence or market changes may drastically reduce residual or second-hand market expectations.
- Long-term commitment to maintenance and software may be necessary to protect the capital equipment investment.
- Equipment may rapidly become obsolete and the costs of upgrading through sale, trade-in or leasing may be expensive.

The effect of a straight purchase is to increase fixed (equipment) and reduce current (cash) assets. The capital cost of acquisition and the revenue cost of maintenance may adversely affect the working capital of an enterprise and must, long term, be expected to have a positive return on the investment. Some assistance towards the purchase of capital equipment may be available from central or local government sources particularly if the company is located or prepared to locate in an 'assisted area'. Enquiries regarding help under the Enterprise Grant Scheme should be made to the regional office of the Department of Trade and Industry. Full information on capital allowances is given on the Inland Revenue website www.inlandrevenue.gov.uk/manuals/camanual/

Quotations for purchased capital equipment may be analysed with reference to the following factors:

	Supplier			
	A	B	C	
Factor	£	£	£	Notes
Ex works cost of equipment				
Delivery and handling costs				
Cost of insurance				
Addition costs for essential spares				
Installation costs for essential spares				
Installation costs payable to supplier				
Cost of extra work specified by purchaser				
Customer or other duties/tariffs in respect of imported equipment				
Price escalation charges computed by Reference to accepted formulae				
Terms of payment				
Warranty/guarantee payments				
Servicing, if any by supplier			————	
Less discounts:				
Trade-ins				
Other deductions				
Less capital allowances			————	
Final cost			————	

11.5.2 Hire purchase

Advantages

- Provides a compromise between straight purchase and leasing. Hire purchase agreements are easily negotiated and available.

- Subject to such factors as interest rates and the user's rate of return, hire purchase may be more financially effective than outright purchase or leasing.
- The most up-to-date technology may be hired and used to increase company productivity and efficiency.
- After all the payments have been made, the user becomes the owner of the equipment either automatically or on payment of an option to purchase fee.
- For tax purposes, the user is from the start regarded as the owner of the equipment and can claim capital allowance and VAT on the equipment.

Disadvantages

- Financing arrangements impose more restrictions than when equipment is purchased outright.
- Interest rates and the user's rate of return may make hire purchase a less financially effective method than outright purchase or leasing.
- There will, in general, be no opportunity to upgrade.
- The disadvantages of outright purchase stated above.

11.5.3 Leasing

Leasing is a contract between the leasing company the 'lessor', and the customer, the 'lessee'. Under a leasing contract, the lessor buys and owns the asset that the lessee requires. The lessee hires the asset from the lessor and pays rental over a predetermined period for the use of the asset.

As shown in Figure 11.1, there are two types of lease: finance leases and operating leases.

Leasing has the following advantages and disadvantages:

Advantages

- Certain costs are known in advance and cannot be amended without agreement once the lease is signed.

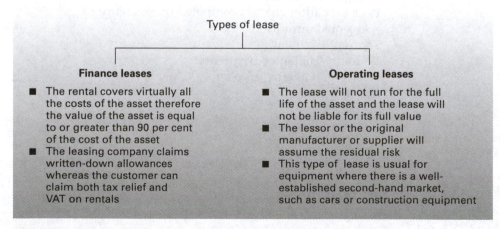

Figure 11.1 Types of lease

- Reduced need to tie up capital in fixed assets. Use of an asset can be obtained without capital outlay.

- Leasing is concerned only with rentals and not with grants, allowances, depreciation or other calculations.

- Leasing provides a hedge against the risk of obsolescence.

Disadvantages

- Fixed obligation to pay rental may create an embarrassment in depressed conditions.

- Does not provide the prestige or flexibility of ownership.

- Large organisations may be able to obtain capital or equal terms with lessors, and, because of a steady flow of taxable profit, be able to obtain the use of capital allowances for themselves.

- The flexibility to dispose of obsolete equipment before the end of the lease may be reduced.

Other advantages of leasing include easier replacement decisions. Ownership of an asset sometimes has the psychological effect of locking the owner into the use of an asset that should be replaced by a more efficient item of equipment. Leasing is also a hedge against inflation. The use of the asset is obtained immediately. The payments are met out of future earnings and are made in real money terms with the real costs falling over the years.

11.5.4   Leasing or buying

In practice, the decision to lease or buy is complex, depending on operating, legal and financial considerations.

- Operating factors relate to the advantages of a trial period before purchase, the immediate availability of cost-saving equipment, the period for which the assets are required and the hedges provided against obsolescence and inflation.

- Legal factors are important since the leasing agreements are one-sided in that most risks are transferred to the lessee. The lessee should therefore carefully examine the terms and conditions of the contract, especially with regard to such aspects as limitations on the use of the equipment and responsibilities for its insurance, maintenance, etc. Where possible, improved terms should be negotiated.

- Financial factors are usually crucial in deciding whether to lease or buy. These include:
  - the opportunity cost of capital, i.e. what the purchase price of the equipment would earn if used for other purposes or invested elsewhere;
  - the discounted cost of meeting the periodic rental payments over the term of the lease. Note that 'flat' interest rates, calculated on the initial amount owing rather than on the average amount owed, can be misleading.

Example 11.1   Lease or buy decision

Cash price of asset: £1,000
Leased cost, i.e. 20 payments of £75 per quarter over 5 years: £1,500
Excess cost of leasing over purchase: £500 or 50%
Annual flat rate of interest: 50%/5 = 10%

The true rate, however, is just over 20.4 per cent per annum, as can be seen from the table.

Quarterly periods	Balance brought forward (£)	Repayment in advance (£)	Interest 20.4064% compound (£)	Balance carried forward (£)
1	1,000.00	−75.00	43.95	968.95
2	968.95	−75.00	42.48	936.43
3	936.43	−75.00	40.94	902.37
4	902.37	−75.00	39.32	866.69
5	866.69	−75.00	37.62	829.31
6	829.31	−75.00	35.85	790.16
7	790.16	−75.00	33.98	749.14
8	749.14	−75.00	32.04	706.18
9	706.18	−75.00	29.99	661.17
10	661.17	−75.00	27.85	614.62
11	614.62	−75.00	25.62	564.64
12	564.64	−75.00	23.27	512.91
13	512.91	−75.00	20.81	458.72
14	458.72	−75.00	18.23	401.95
15	401.95	−75.00	15.54	342.49
16	342.49	−75.00	12.71	280.20
17	280.20	−75.00	9.75	214.95
18	214.95	−75.00	6.65	146.60
19	146.60	−75.00	3.40	75.00
20	75.00	−75.00	0.00	0.00
		−£1,500.00	£500.00	

Ignoring tax, the lessee will be indifferent on cost grounds whether to lease or buy if the opportunity cost of capital is about 20.4 per cent. If the cost of capital exceeds 20.4 per cent then leasing will be cheaper in net present value (NPV) terms. If less, then leasing will be the more expensive proposition.

Excluding such factors as the time value of money, capital allowances, and maintenance and other ownership costs, the simple lease versus buy break-even point can be calculated by the formula:

$$N = \frac{P}{L}$$

where: P = purchase cost of equipment

L = monthly leasing payment

N = the number of months needed to break even

If the equipment cost £5,000 and the leasing payment is £200 monthly, the simple break-even point is 25 months. This indicates that other considerations apart, owning is preferable to leasing if the equipment is used for more than 25 months.

Source: Sykes, A., *The Lease–Buy Decision*, BIM Management Survey Report, 1976

11.6   Selecting suppliers of capital items

A DTI Committee on Terotechnology provided the following checklist for purchasing personnel to use when selecting a supplier or before placing an order for capital equipment.[6]

Checklist when selecting a supplier

■ Check that the specification of the asset to be acquired is clear and unambiguous

■ Check that it covers all relevant aspects of life cycle performance.

■ Will it permit intending suppliers to prepare realistic estimates for costs and delivery?

■ Check that modifications to the specification (if any) proposed by intending suppliers have been fed back to the originators of the relevant part of the specification and actioned, if necessary, by amendment and reissue of the specification.

■ Have intending suppliers proposed any trade-offs between initial purchase price and estimated life cycle costs, e.g. will payment of a higher price permit a significant reduction in total outgoings?

■ Have they provided adequate information on forecast costs and availability of service and/or critical spare parts during the expected life of the asset?

Checklist before placing an order

■ Check that the information provided by intending suppliers is adequate for making or confirming the decision to acquire the asset in question (i.e. does it provide an adequate response to your enquiry); this applies equally to custom-built and catalogued items.

■ Check that your company's corporate plan includes the life cycle of an asset and makes financial provision for it.

■ Check that the purchase specification is a clear and complete statement of your requirements.

■ Check that the supplier's conditions of sale are not at variance with your short- and long-term requirements.

■ Check that the specification has been agreed by all those who will be connected with installation, commissioning, operation, maintenance and safety.

■ Have you consulted the quality department manager or engineer on quality aspects of the specification?

■ Check the vendor ratings of the intending suppliers.

■ Check the intending supplier's warranties and forecasts of availability of service and critical spare parts.

■ Check that the quantity and quality of the information supplied with the asset will be adequate for operation, overhaul and repair during the asset's expected life.

Checklist after delivery

■ Check that procedures and formalities concerned with acceptance of the asset have been completed correctly.

11.7 Evaluating capital investments

Although this is the province of the management accountant, buyers should have an awareness of the methods of appraising expenditure on capital items. Three highly simplified examples of these approaches (payback, average rate of return and two applications of discounted cash flow) are briefly considered.

11.7.1 Payback

Payback is the time required for cash returns to equal the initial cash expenditure.

Example 11.2   Payback

An enterprise buys two machines each costing £20,000. The net cash flows after operating costs and expenses but not allowing for depreciation are expected to be as shown in the table.

Year	Cash flow Machine A (£)	Cash flow Machine B (£)
1	5,000	4,500
2	5,000	4,500
3	5,000	4,500
4	5,000	4,500
5	5,000	4,500
6	–	4,500
7	–	4,500
	25,000	31,500

$$\text{Payback } \frac{£20,000}{5,000} = 4 \text{ years, or } \frac{£20,000}{4,500} = 4.4 \text{ years}$$

Example 11.2 shows the principle and fallacy of the payback approach. Machine A has the better payback since the initial cost is recovered in a shorter time. Machine B has an inferior payback but the return extends over two further years.

The payback method, because of its simplicity, is probably the most popular method of investment appraisal. With this approach the emphasis is on risk rather than profitability, i.e. the risk with machine B is somewhat greater because it has a longer payback period.

11.7.2 Average rate of return (prior to tax)

The average rate of return aims to assess the average annual net profit after depreciation and other cash outlays as a percentage of the original cost. Three simple calculations are required:

1 The annual rate of depreciation. This is calculated by the 'straight line' method, namely:

$$\frac{\text{Cost} - \text{Residual value}}{\text{Estimated value}}$$

Assuming that machines A and B in Example 11.2 each had an estimated residual value of £1,000, their annual depreciation rates would be:

$$\text{Machine A} = \frac{£20,000 - £1,000}{5} = £3,800$$

$$\text{Machine B} = \frac{£20,000 - £1,000}{7} = £2,174$$

2 Deduct depreciation from the average annual profit:

Machine A = £5,000 − £3,800 = £1,200

Machine B = £4,500 − £2,714 = £1,786

3 Express net annual profit after depreciation as a percentage of the initial cost:

$$\text{Machine A} = \frac{£1,200 \times 100}{£20,000} = 6\%$$

$$\text{Machine B} = \frac{£1,786 \times 100}{£20,000} = 8.93\%$$

An alternative formula is return on capital employed (ROCE):

$$\frac{\text{Average annual profit after depreciation}}{\text{Original capital invested}} \times 100\%$$

This method shows that the investment in machine B is the most profitable and allows comparison with the returns anticipated from alternative investments.

11.7.3 Discounting

Discounting is the opposite process to compounding. The latter shows the extent to which a sum of money invested now will grow over a period of years at a given rate of compound interest. Thus £100 invested now at 10 per cent compound interest will be worth £110 in one year's time and £121 at the end of two years.

Discounting shows the value at the present time of a sum of money payable or receivable at some future time. This present value can be obtained by dividing the amount now held by that to which it would have grown at a given rate of compound interest, i.e.

$$\frac{£100}{£110} = 0.9091, \text{ or } \frac{£100}{£110} = 0.8264, \text{ or } \frac{1}{(1 + r)^n}$$

Table 11.1 Present value of £1 at 10% and 12% discount rates

Years	10%	12%
1	£0.9091	£0.8923
2	£0.8264	£0.7972
3	£0.7513	£0.7118
4	£0.6830	£0.6355
5	£0.6209	£0.5674
6	£0.5645	£0.5066
7	£0.5132	£0.4523

where r is the rate of interest and n the number of years over which we are discounting.

These present values are *discount factors* and state that £100 at the end of one year at 10 per cent is now worth £0.9091, or £0.8264 if the discount period is two years. In practice, the discount factors would be obtained from present value tables. Table 11.1 shows the present values of £1 at 10 per cent and 12 per cent over a period.

Net present value and yield methods illustrate two of a number of approaches based on discounted cash flow.

11.7.4 Net present value

In the net present value (NPV) method the minimum required return on the capital investment is determined. The present value of anticipated future cash flows is that discounted at this rate. If the sum of these discounted cash flows exceeds the initial expenditure then the investment will be given a higher return than forecast. Using the figures given above and a minimum required rate of 10 per cent, the discounted cash flows for machines A and B are set out in Table 11.2.

Machine A has a total return less than the initial expenditure of £20,000, i.e. less than the 10 per cent required. In contrast, machine B will exceed the given figure. This approach is useful in evaluating which of two alternative investment proposals to adopt.

11.8 The buyer and capital investment purchases

Research findings indicate that:

- Capital equipment is more likely to be bought centrally than products of relatively continuous consumption such as materials and components parts.
- Purchasing decisions relating to capital items will be made by a buying centre, with the ultimate user, such as the production manager in the case of machinery, playing a dominant role.
- The greater the technical nature and complexity of an item the greater the influence of technical staff in the buying decision.

Table 11.2 Discounted cash flows for machines A and B

Year	Cash return (£)	10% factor (£)	Net present value (£)
Machine A			
1	5,000	0.909	4,545
2	5,000	0.826	4,130
3	5,000	0.751	3,755
4	5,000	0.683	3,415
5	5,000	0.621	3,105
6	–	–	–
7	–	–	–
	25,000	–	18,950
Machine B			
1	4,500	0.909	4,090
2	4,500	0.826	3,717
3	4,500	0.751	3,880
4	4,500	0.683	3,073
5	4,500	0.621	2,795
6	4,500	0.565	2,542
7	4,500	0.513	2,309
	31,500		22,406

A respected professional buyer can, however, do more than contribute a list of possible vendors to buying centre decisions. Other contributions may include:

- Emphasis on life cycle considerations relating to capital purchases.
- Countering prejudice of users in favour of one make of capital equipment which may exclude considerations of more innovative or competitive equipment available from other manufacturers.
- Provision of commercial, contractual and negotiating expertise.
- Identification of alternatives to the purchase of new machines, e.g. availability of second-hand items, leasing, subcontracting.

11.9   Production materials

Risley[7] has classified materials and parts for use in manufacture under three headings:

- *Raw materials* – these are primarily from agriculture and the various extractive industries: minerals, ores, timber, petroleum and scrap as well as dairy products, fruits and vegetables sold to a processor.
- *Semi-finished goods and processed materials* – goods and materials to which some work has been applied or value added. Such items are finished only in part or may have been formed into shapes and specifications to make them readily usable by the buyer. These products lose their identity when incorporated into

other products. Examples include: metal sections, rods, sheets, tubing, wires, castings, chemicals, cloth, leather, sugar, paper.

■ *Component parts and assemblies.* Completely finished products of one manufacturer which can be used as part of a more complex product by another manufacturer. These do not lose their original identity when incorporated into other products. Examples include: bearings, controls, gauges, gears, wheels, transistors, car engines and windscreens.

11.10 Raw materials

11.10.1 Characteristics

Raw materials are:

■ often 'sensitive' commodities;
■ frequently dealt with in recognised commodity markets;
■ safeguarded in many organisations by backward integration strategies.

11.10.2 Sensitive commodities

Sensitive commodities are raw materials (copper, cotton, lead, zinc, hides and rubber), the prices of which fluctuate daily. Here the buyer will aim to time purchases to obtain requirements at the most competitive prices. The main economic and political factors which influence market conditions are:

■ Interest rates, e.g. minimum lending rate.
■ Currency fluctuations, e.g. the strength of sterling.
■ Inflation, e.g. the effect of increased material and labour costs.
■ Government policies, e.g. import controls or stockpiling.
■ Glut or shortage supply factors, e.g. crop failure.
■ Relationships between the exporting and importing country, e.g. oil as a political weapon.

11.10.3 Information regarding market conditions

The main sources of information regarding present and future market conditions for a commodity such as copper are as follows:

■ *Government sources*, e.g. the Department of Trade and Industry.
■ *Documentary sources.* These may be 'general', e.g. *Financial Times*, or specialised, e.g. *World Metal Statistics* published by the World Bureau of Metal Statistics, or the *Metal Bulletin.*
■ *Federations*, e.g. the British Non-ferrous Metals Federation or the International Wrought Copper Council.

- *Exchanges*. These include independent research undertaken by brokers and dealers into metal resources and the short- and long-term prospects for the commodity and daily prices of commodities dealt with by the exchange.
- *Analysts*. These include economists and statisticians employed by undertakings to advise on corporate planning and purchasing policies and external units such as the Commodities Research Unit.
- *Databases*. These can provide up-to-date information and may be space-saving substitutes for large institutions.
- *Chambers of commerce*, e.g. the London Chamber of Commerce.

The task of the buyer is to evaluate information and recommendations from the above sources and put forward policies which fall broadly into two classes: hand-to-mouth and forward buying.

11.10.4 Hand-to-mouth buying

Hand-to-mouth buying is buying according to need rather than in quantities that are most economical. Circumstances in which this policy may be adopted are where prices are falling or where a change in design is imminent and it is desirable to avoid large stocks.

11.10.5 Forward buying

Forward buying applies to all purchases made for the purpose of increasing stocks beyond the minimum quantities required to meet normal production needs based on average delivery times. Forward buying may be undertaken:

- to obtain the benefit of economic order quantities;
- when savings made by buying in anticipation of a price increase will be greater than the interest lost on increased stocks or the cost of storage;
- to prevent breakdowns in production due to occurrences such as strikes or to stockpile to avoid shortages;
- to secure materials for future requirements when the opportunity arises, e.g. some steel sections are only rolled at infrequent intervals.

Forward buying can apply to any material or equipment. A particular aspect of forward buying applicable to commodities is dealing in futures.

11.11 Futures dealing

A commodity such as copper may be bought direct from the producer or on a commodity market. The latter provides the advantages of futures dealing. The London markets are divided into two main areas: metals and soft commodities. The six major primary non-ferrous metals dealt with on the London Metal Exchange (LME) are: primary high grade aluminium; 'A' grade copper; high grade zinc; primary nickel; standard lead, and tin. The LME also offers contracts for secondary aluminium and silver. The soft commodities markets dealing in cocoa, sugar, vegetable oils, wool and rubber are the concern of the Futures and Options Exchange. The International Petroleum Exchange covers crude oil, gas, gasoline, naphtha and heavy fuel oil.

11.11.1 Functions of exchanges

- To enable customers, merchants and dealers to obtain supplies readily and at the competitive market price. On the LME, for example, contracts traded are for delivery on any market day within the period of three months ahead, except for silver which can be dealt in up to seven months ahead.
- To smooth out price fluctuations due to changes in demand and supply.
- To provide insurance against price fluctuations through the procedure known as hedging (see below).
- To provide appropriately located storage facilities to enable participants to make or take physical delivery of approved brands of commodities.

11.11.2 Differences between forward and futures dealing

- Futures are always traded on a recognised exchange.
- Futures contracts have standardised terms (see section 11.11.4 below).
- Futures exchanges use clearing houses to ensure that futures contracts are fulfilled. The London Clearing House (LCH), for example, is a professional international clearing house owned by the six UK clearing banks. The responsibility for completing the execution of trade across the LME ring is transferred from the brokers to the LCH by what is called novation. The clearing house is thus the buyer and seller of last resort.
- Futures trading requires margins and daily settlement. A margin is a cash deposit paid by a trader to a broker who in effect lends money to enable the futures contract to be purchased. Traders hope to sell their futures contracts for more than the purchase price, enabling them to repay the broker's loan, have their margins returned and take their profits. No broker may margin a contract for less than the exchange minimum. Each trading day every futures contract is assessed for liquidity. If the margin drops below a certain level the trade must deposit an additional or 'maintenance margin'. Futures positions are easily closed since the trader has the option of taking physical delivery.

11.11.3 Purpose of and conditions for futures dealing

The purpose of futures dealing is to reduce uncertainty arising from price fluctuations due to supply and demand changes. This reduction in uncertainty benefits both producers and consumers. The producer can sell forward at a sure price; the consumer can buy forward and fix material costs in accordance with a predetermined price. Manufacturers of copper wire, for example, might be able to obtain an order based on the current price of copper. If they think the price of copper may rise before they can obtain their raw materials they can immediately cover their copper requirements by buying on the LME at the current price for delivery three months ahead, thus avoiding any risk of an increase in price.

For futures dealing to be undertaken, the following conditions must apply:

- The commodity must be capable of being stored without deterioration for a reasonable period.

- The commodity must be capable of being graded for the purpose of providing a basis for description in the contract.

- The commodity must be tradable in its raw or semi-raw state.

- Producers and consumers must approve the concept of futures dealing.

- There must be a free market in the commodity, with many buyers and sellers, making it impossible for a few traders to control the market and thus prevent perfect competition.

11.11.4   Some terms used in futures contracts

- *Arbitrage*. The (usually) simultaneous purchase of futures in one market against the sale of futures in a different market to profit from a difference in price.

- *Backwardation*. The backwardation situation exists when forward prices are less than current 'spot' ones.

- *Contango*. A contango situation exists when forward prices are greater than current 'spot' ones.

- *Force majeure*. The clause which absolves the seller or buyer from the contract due to events beyond his or her control, e.g. unavoidable export delays in producing countries owing to strikes at the supplier's plant. (There is now no *force majeure* clause in a London Metal Exchange contract. Customers affected by a *force majeure* declared by a producer or refiner can always turn to the LME as a source of supply. Equally, suppliers can deliver their metal to the LME if their customers declare *force majeure*.)

- *Futures*. Contracts for the purpose and sale of commodities for delivery some time in the future on an organised exchange and subject to all the terms and conditions included in the rules of that exchange.

- *Hedging*. Hedging is the use of futures contracts to insure against losses due to the effect of price fluctuations on the value of stocks of a commodity either held or to be acquired. Basically this is done by establishing a position in the futures market opposite to one's position in the physical commodity. The operations of hedging can be described by a simplified example.

- *Options*. An option gives the holder the right to buy or sell a specified futures contract at an agreed upon price before a specified expiration date.

- *Spot price*. The price for immediate cash payment.

- *Spot month*. The first deliverable month for which a quotation is available in the futures market.

- *Options contracts*. These relate to the sale or purchasing of commodities that will occur at a specified price on a specified future date but only if the prospective buyer or seller wishes to exercise the option to buy or sell at the predetermined 'strike' or exercise price. Options may be either 'call' or 'put'. Buyers of call options have limited risk since the most they can lose is the amount of the premium or the sum of money paid when the option is purchased. They have, however, an unlimited profit potential. Conversely, writers of options have unlimited risk but limited profit potential. Mathematically, however, the odds favour the option writer.

Example 11.3 Hedging

1 On 1 June, X (manufacturer) buys stocks of copper value £1,000 which she hopes to make into cable wire and sell on 1 August for £2,000, of which £750 represents manufacturing costs and £250 profit.

2 Price of copper falls by 1 August to £750 so that X sells at £1,750, i.e. she makes no profit.

3 To insure against the situation in (2), X, on 1 June, sells futures contracts in copper for £1,000.

4 In August if the price remains stable X will buy at this price thus making a profit of £250 on her futures contract, which will offset any loss on manufacturing.

If the price rises to £1,250, X will lose on her futures contract but this will be offset by gains on manufacturing. While trading refers to actual physical copper trading, a futures transaction is really dealing in price differences and the contract would be discharged by paying over or receiving the balance due.

11.11.5 Commodities at the right price

Buying commodities is the province of specialists who have access to current and relevant information. Such specialists use two approaches to determining the right price, namely fundamental analysis and technical analysis.

Fundamental analysis relies heavily on an assessment, both statistically and in other ways, of supply and demand. Statistics, in particular, indicate whether the trend of prices is up or down. In addition to trends, fundamental analysts take into account production, consumption and stocks. Thus an imbalance in production and consumption will affect prices. Prices will rise or fall according to whether less or more of a commodity is being produced than is consumed. Stock figures according to the mood of the market may be counted either way. In a 'bull' or rising market, stocks tend to be held by producers or merchants thus forcing consumers to bid higher for available stocks of the commodity. In a falling or 'bear' market consumers live off their stocks and buy less of the commodity than they are using while producers reduce prices to a level at which they can turn unsold stock into cash. Additionally, fundamental analysis pays attention to news items that make sensitive commodities sensitive such as wars, weather, natural disasters, political developments such as environmental legislation, labour unrest and macroeconomic statistics from major economies.

Technical analysis claims to be quicker and more comprehensive than fundamental analysis since the market is efficient and the current market price clears the market or brings it into equilibrium. If this is so then it is unnecessary to do more than look at the record of prices to read the future of prices. Technical analysis therefore make great use of chart formations such as can be obtained from plotting prices on two different timescales such as daily price movements and the one year rolling average (i.e. every day the latest day's price is added to the list of prices, the oldest price is dropped and a new average for the past year is calculated). Chartists have developed a language of their own for interpreting their charts, and terms include 'base formation', 'break out', 'overprofit' and 'oversold'.

The results of charting are offered to commodity market makers, often at a considerable charge. The basic concept is that of using the past to predict the future. Chartists, however, are no more able to forecast the effect of news than those who rely on fundamental analysis. In practice, a combination of the two approaches is often used. It has been rightly observed that 'the whole point of having an idea of the "right price" is to spot when the market price is wrong'. Companies have been forced into liquidation by making long-term forecasts on the assumption that today's price is right when in actuality it is wrong, and vice versa.

11.12   Methods of commodity dealing

Dealing in commodities is a highly complex activity involving the possibilities of heavy gains or losses. An undertaking buying large quantities of a commodity will

---

Example 11.4   £-cost averaging

Assume the monthly requirements for commodity X are 100 tonnes, the average price of which, from experience, is estimated at £100. We therefore budget to spend £100 × 100 = £10,000 monthly. The price fluctuates as shown in the table.

Date	Cost per tonne (£)	Amount spent (£)	Tonnes purchased
January	98	10,000	102.04
February	97	10,000	103.09
March	95	10,000	105.26
April	96	10,000	104.16
May	95	10,000	105.26
June	93	10,000	107.52
July	92	10,000	108.69
August	95	10,000	105.26
September	97	10,000	103.00
October	100	10,000	100.00
November	102	10,000	98.03
December	104	10,000	96.15
		120,000	1,238.46

$$\text{Average cost per tonne, total cycle} = \frac{£120,000}{1,238.46} = £96.89$$

Purchases over the total cycle exceed requirements by 38.46 tonnes. There is thus an average saving of £3.11 per tonne.

Example 11.5   Volume timing of purchases

Assume that the price of a commodity with a constant monthly requirement of 100 tonnes is between £100 and £120 per tonne. The buyer is authorised to purchase up to 3 months' supply.

In January, market intelligence is that the current price of £100 is likely to rise over the next three months to £120. An order is therefore placed for 300 tonnes at £100 per tonne.

In early March, intelligence is that over the next three months, April to June, the price of £120 will further rise to £135. A further 300 tonnes are ordered at £120 per tonne. In early June it is forecast that prices will fall. For July, August, September and October we therefore buy one month's supply at £130, £125, £120 and £110, respectively. In September the forecast is of a further rise to £125. We therefore place a forward order for three months at £110.

The savings from forward buying on the upswing and hand-to-mouth buying on the downswing are shown in the table.

Date	Quantity purchased (tonnes)	Price paid per tonne (£)	Market price per tonne (£)	Actual cost (£)	Market cost (£)
January	100	100	100	10,000	10,000
February	100	100	110	10,000	11,000
March	100	100	120	10,000	12,000
April	100	120	125	12,000	12,500
May	100	120	130	12,000	13,000
June	100	120	135	12,000	13,500
July	100	130	130	13,000	13,000
August	100	125	125	12,500	12,500
September	100	120	120	12,000	12,000
October	100	110	110	11,000	11,000
November	100	110	120	11,000	12,000
December	100	110	125	11,000	12,500
	1,200			136,500	145,000

$$\text{Average price paid per tonne over year} = \frac{£136,500}{1,200} = £113.75$$

$$\text{Average market price per tonne} = \frac{£145,000}{1,200} = £120.83$$

$$\text{Saving over total period} = \frac{\text{Average market price} - \text{Average price paid}}{\text{Average market price}}$$

$$= \frac{£120.83 - £113.75}{120.83} \times 100$$

$$= \frac{7.08}{120.83} \times 100$$

$$= 5.86\%$$

therefore employ a specialist buyer who has studied both the commodity and its markets. Often, commodity buying will be a separate department distinct from other purchasing operations. Where quantities or the undertaking are small, a broker may be retained to procure commodity requirements, in effect subcontracting this aspect of purchasing.

Other approaches are designed to enable non-specialists to undertake commodity buying with a minimum of risk. These are outlined below.

11.12.1 Time budgeting or averaging

Time budgeting is an application of hand-to-mouth buying, in which supplies of the commodity are bought as required and no stocks are held. As supplies are always bought at the ruling price, losses are divided, but, of course, the prospect of windfall gains are obviated. This policy cannot be applied if it is necessary to carry inventory.

11.12.2 Budgeting or £-cost averaging

The budgeting or £-cost averaging approach is based on spending a fixed amount of money in each period, e.g. monthly. The quantity purchased therefore increases when price falls and reduces when the price rises.

11.12.3 Volume timing of purchases

The volume timing approach is based on forward buying when prices are falling and hand-to-mouth buying when prices are rising. Its success depends on accurate forecasting of market trends.

11.13 Component parts and assemblies

Component parts and assemblies may be either standard, e.g. a ball bearing, or specific, e.g. a casting made to the design of a particular customer. Standard components are, generally, readily available and have the advantages listed in section 7.8 of Chapter 7.

Specific components:

- offer opportunities for liaison between design and purchasing regarding materials costs, suppliers and alternatives;
- may be jointly developed by purchaser and supplier;
- may involve detailed negotiation over such aspects as tooling costs, learning curves, etc.;
- should always be subject to value analysis;
- raise make-or-buy issues;
- can often be combined into sub-assemblies.

11.14 Production materials and bills of materials

11.14.1 Purpose of bills of materials

A bill of materials (BOM):

■ lists all the components, including the quantities of each required to produce one unit of the finished product;

■ enables a production schedule to be 'exploded' into a list of required items of all types, i.e. raw materials, components, assemblies, etc;

■ enables the total number of each item needed for a production order to be checked against inventory to enable purchasing to determine:

– what items are in stock;

– what items are not in stock and require to be purchased;

– what items and quantities need to be purchased to replenish stock;

– the net inventory, i.e. total inventory for each item minus the requirements of that item for a particular job.

11.14.2 Types of bills of materials

BOMs can be either *single-level* or *indented*. A single-level BOM comprises only those subordinate components that are immediately required, i.e. *not* the components of the components, e.g. five wheels for a car. An indented BOM is a listing of the components from the end item all the way down to each item comprising the component and the total components in the product. Thus, for a car an indented BOM would be:

> *Item: 30,122 Wheel (5 required)*
> 123 Wheel pressing   (1 × 5 required)
> 124 Tyres   (1 × 5 required)
> 082 Nuts   (4 × 5 required)
> 125 Cover   (1 × 5 required)

A fully indented BOM is often used by production engineers to determine how the product is to be physically assembled, and by management accountants for cost implosions.

A *bill of materials processor* is a computer software package that organises and maintains linkages in the BOM files. It is the BOM processor that is used in materials requirement planning to pass the planned orders for a parent part to gross requirements for its components.

11.15 Consumables

Consumables are subdivided by Risley[8] into operating supplies and maintenance, repair and overhaul items.

Operating supplies are defined as 'consumable items used in the operations of the business enterprise', for example stationery and office supplies, machine oil, fasteners, insecticides, fuels, small tools, packaging and wrapping materials. *Maintenance, repair and overhaul (MRO) items* are defined as 'items which are needed repeatedly or recurrently to maintain operational efficiency of the business', for example electrical supplies, caretaking requirements, lubricants, paint, plumbing and a wide range of repair parts or spares for plant and equipment.

11.15.1   Characteristics of consumables

Consumables and MRO items are, generally:

- low cost, low risk items (with the exception of 'critical' items, e.g. some spares);
- Pareto category items;
- revenue items, usually relating to one financial period in contrast to capital items relating to many financial periods;
- 'called off' by the actual consumers against orders negotiated with approved suppliers by the purchasing function;
- independent demand items suitable for fixed order and periodic stock control systems;
- purchased by one of the simplified procedures for small orders;
- linked to maintenance policies in the case of MRO items.

11.15.2   Maintenance and replacement policies

Breakdowns and repairs can never be totally avoided but regular, systematic and thorough maintenance will reduce their number and consequential costs such as lost production, idle time and hold-ups in respect of other production items. Pareto analysis can provide a useful guide as to where maintenance attention should be placed, i.e.

- Class A or critical items which are essential parts of the machine or system, whose failure would result in total breakdown with high repair and consequential costs.
- Class B or major components but where failure would not result in stoppage of the total system.
- Class C or minor components, the failure of which would not, in the short term, affect the overall process or system.

There are five approaches to planned maintenance aimed at keeping equipment or facilities in good operating condition:

- *Inspection.* By visual means on a regular, planned basis.
- *Breakdown (or corrective) maintenance.* This approach actually waits for the item to break down and it is then repaired.
- *Preventive maintenance.* This is an overall approach that combines inspection, repair and regular servicing based on a detailed plan.

■ *Planned replacement*. This policy sets fixed times or dates when components or machines will be replaced irrespective of their condition.

■ *Breakdown replacement*. This is a positive policy particularly appropriate for small items whose maintenance costs would be disproportionately high or for items that rapidly become obsolete.

11.15.3 Purchasing and consumables

Apart from negotiating the actual purchase of consumables and MRO items, the purchasing function can:

■ liaise with maintenance staff to ensure that information regarding the cost, availability and delivery times is available, especially in respect of 'critical' items;

■ advocate a policy of standardisation to avoid holding a variety of 'critical' spares;

■ suggest alternatives, e.g. outsourcing of catering and cleaning can obviate the need to hold stocks of food and cleaning materials;

■ minimise administrative and storage costs by the application of small-order procedures and direct requisitioning by users against call-off contracts, etc.;

■ analyse proposed maintenance contracts offered by suppliers and advise whether or not these should be accepted.

11.16 Construction supplies and bills of quantities

11.16.1 Construction supplies

Construction supplies differ in a number of respect from supplies purchased for manufacturing and service undertakings.

■ Construction supplies are purchased for use on a site which may be distant from the office from which orders are placed or even in another country altogether.

■ Many construction supplies have a high bulk relative to their value, e.g. bricks, steel. Because of the high cost of transport it is desirable that construction supplies are procured as near as possible to the site where they will be used.

■ With many construction schemes the purchasing department will probably be asked to negotiate agreements for electricity, gas and water supplies and, occasionally, for sewage or effluent disposal.

■ Specification of construction supplies will often be on the basis of:
  – instructions given by the client to an architect or civil engineer;
  – architect specifications.
These specifications are often stated in the Bill of Quantities.

- In the interests of security, it is important that purchased supplies should be delivered to site as closely as possible to the time they will be used.

- Because of the remoteness of the site from the contractor's office, procedures for recording of supplies received and issued will have to be agreed between the contractor's purchasing department and site engineer.

- Some construction supplies may be 'free issue' supplies, i.e. items provided by the client for use in connection with a construction project that is being undertaken on the client's behalf.

- Subcontracting is an important aspect of purchasing for construction contracts, e.g. contracts for foundations, drainage, air conditioning, lift installation, ventilation, structural steelwork, etc.

- Some construction supplies involve intra-company purchasing. Thus a construction company may also own stone, sand and gravel quarries which supply other companies within the group.

- Supplies may be transferred from one site or construction contract to another. It is therefore important to know what supplies are available at each site.

- Some discretion to arrange for the supply of materials and services must be allowed to the site engineer, e.g. discretion to hire plant for use in connection with a contract from a local plant hire undertaking. All such orders should be notified to the contractor's purchasing department to ensure that orders are placed and amounts due to suppliers duly paid.

11.16.2 Bills of quantities

Definitions

> Bills of quantities are documents, prepared by quantity surveyors from drawings and specifications prepared by architects or engineers, setting out as priceable items the detailed requirements of the work and the quantities involved.

Content of bills of quantities

Bills of quantities are usually formidable documents running to many pages and incorporating schedules of conditions of contract in addition to the specifications of labour and materials required for the particular construction project. A typical bill of quantities will fall into six categories:

- Section 1 Preliminary items and general conditions. This will set out the terms and conditions of the contract and responsibilities of the contractor, architect and other parties involved in the contract altogether with provision for the settlement of disputes arising from the contract.

- Section 2 Trade preambles. This sets out the general requirements relating to such aspects of a construction contract as:
  - excavation and earthwork
  - concrete work
  - brickwork and blockwork

- roofing
- woodwork
- structural steelwork
- metal work
- plumbing installation
- foul drainage above ground
- Holes/chases/covers/supports for services
- Electrical and heating installations
- Floor, wall and ceiling finishes
- Glazing
- Painting and decorating

■ Section 3 Demolition and spot items. Foundation work.
■ Section 4 General alteration and refurbishment work.
■ Section 5 Provisional sums and contingencies.
■ Section 6 Grand summary.

Sections 3 to 6 set out the quantities of work to be done. Typical extracts from sections 2 and 4 relating to plumbing installations are shown in Figures 11.2 and 11.3.

Purpose of bills of quantities

Bills of quantities:

■ enable tenderers to show against each item on the unpriced bill of quantities a price per unit covering labour, materials, overheads and profit. When totalled in the 'grand summary' the items will provide the tender price for the contract;
■ enable the quantity surveyor, on receipt of the successful tender, to ensure that the contractor has made no serious errors that could cause complications at a later date;
■ avoid the inclusion by the tenderer of a large amount for contingencies;
■ assist in verifying the valuation of variations due to changes in design requested or agreed by the client after the contract has been placed.

11.16.3 Purchasing and construction contracts

The purchasing function will be involved at both the tendering and implementation stages. At the tendering stages the purchasing function will provide estimators with prices for materials and subcontracted work on which the tender can be based. Since tendering is highly competitive the prices obtained by purchasing can determine whether a tender is competitive or otherwise. The following will be of particular importance:

■ Ensuring that transport costs for materials are kept low by purchasing built items from sources as near as possible to the point of use.

Clause	SECTION 2 Plumbing installation Trade Preambles
R1	**General** Before pricing the specification, contractors tendering are requested to visit the site, peruse the drawings and make themselves fully conversant with the nature of the works for which they are tendering **HOT AND COLD WATER** **GENERAL INFORMATION/REQUIREMENTS**
R2	**The installation** – Drawing references: See Architect's layout – Cold water: Mains fed – Hot water – direct system(s): Unvented direct water storage cylinder Heat source(s): Immersion heaters Control: Thermostat on immersion heater – Other requirements: Remove existing pipework Allow for general builders work
R3	ELECTRICAL WORK in connection with the installation is not included, and will be carried out by the electrical contractor. Provide all information necessary for the completion of such work.
R4	SERVICE CONNECTIONS are covered elsewhere by a provisional sum.
R5	FUEL FOR TESTING: Costs incurred in the provision of fuel for testing and commissioning the installation are to be included in clause B40 section 1. **GENERAL TECHNICAL REQUIREMENTS**
R6	PIPELINE SIZES: Calculate sizes to suit the probable simultaneous demand for the building and to ensure: – A water velocity of not more than 1.3 m/s for hot water and 2.0 m/s for cold water. – Suitable discharge rates at draw-off points. – A filling time for the cold water storage cistern of not more than 1 hour(s).
R7	INSTALLATION GENERALLY: – Install, test and commission the hot and cold water systems so that they comply with BS 6700, water supply bye-laws, and the requirements of this section to provide a system free from leaks and the audible effects of expansion, vibration and water hammer. – All installation work to be carried out by qualified operatives. – Store all equipment, components and accessories in original packaging in dry conditions. – Protect plastic pipework from prolonged exposure to sunlight. Wherever practicable retain protective wrappings until practical completion. – Securely fix equipment, components and accessories in specified/approved locations, parallel or perpendicular to the structure of the building unless specified otherwise, using fixing brackets/mountings etc. recommended for the purpose by the equipment manufacturer. – In locations where moisture is present or may occur, use corrosion resistant fittings/fixtures and avoid contact between dissimilar metals by use of suitable washers, gaskets, etc. – All equipment, pipework, components, valves etc., forming the installation to be fully accessible for maintenance, repair or replacement unless specified or shown otherwise.

Figure 11.2   Extract from a bill of quantities

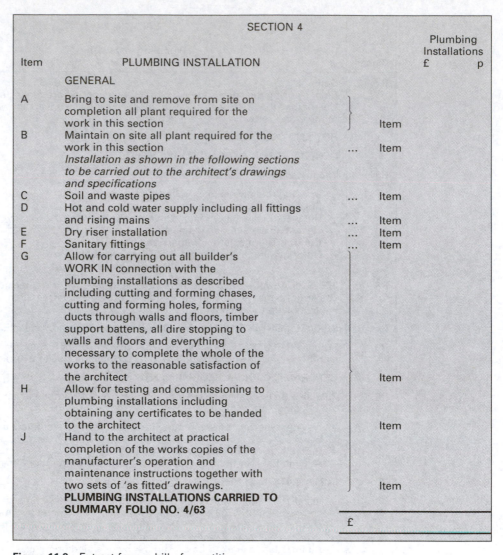

Figure 11.3 Extract from a bill of quantities

- Negotiating with subcontractors.
- Obtaining the best quality commensurate with the life of the item where the tenderer/contractor has discretion over what is bought.
- Effecting suitable delivery arrangements to ensure that supplies are delivered to site as near as possible on time to their use in the project.
- Negotiation of quantity and trade discounts.
- Control of all purchasing undertaken by site engineers etc.
- Control of surplus supplies and transfer to other contracts where it is economical to do so.

11.17 Goods for resale in wholesaling and retailing

11.17.1 Definitions

Merchandising enterprises are wholesalers or retailers that buy completed products for resale. They are therefore different from manufacturing enterprises that engage in activities involving the physical conversion or transformation of inputs into finished products.

Wholesalers sell to retailers, other wholesalers or to individual users but not in significant amounts to ultimate consumers.

Retailers are involved in selling, renting and providing products and services to ultimate consumers for personal, non-business use.

11.17.2 Forms of wholesaling

Wholesaling may be undertaken either by independent wholesaling intermediaries or by manufacturers who sell directly to retailers through sales branches, or depots or renting space in independently owned warehouses. Wholesalers may be:

- *General merchandisers* – carrying a broad assortment of goods.
- *Speciality merchandisers* – carrying an extensive assortment of goods within a specified range of products.
- *Rack jobbers* – who replenish display racks in retail stores with goods sold on a consignment or sale or return basis.
- *Cash and carry* – selling to buyers who visit the warehouse, pay cash for purchases and take away the goods bought.
- *Drop shippers* – soliciting orders from retailers which they arrange to be delivered directly from the manufacturer. These are strictly agents rather than wholesalers.

11.17.3 Wholesaling functions

Wholesalers carry out logistical, transactional and facilitating functions.

Logistical functions

- Breaking of bulk, i.e. buying in bulk from the manufacturers and selling in smaller quantities to retailers.
- Storing merchandise in convenient locations.
- Transportation of merchandise to retail outlets.

Transactional functions

- Buying goods, including importing.
- Sales calls on retailers.

Facilitating functions

- Provision of sales services to manufacturers.
- Provision of market information and research to retailers.

- Occasional preparation of goods for sale by grading, blending etc.
- Assisting the cash flow of both manufacturers and retailers by paying the former promptly and granting credit to the latter.

11.17.4 **Forms of retailing**

British retailers are usually grouped into three categories:[9]

- Independent retailers, including small chains with nine or fewer branches.
- Multiple retailers with ten or more branches but excluding retail cooperative societies.
- Retail cooperative societies.

Within these categories, retail outlets can be classified into store (brick and mortar establishments) and non-store retailers. *Store retailers* include:

- *Speciality stores* – carrying a wide assortment of a narrow range of products, e.g. books, pharmaceuticals, clothing.
- *Department stores* – carrying a wide variety of product lines each of which is operated as a separate department.
- *Supermarkets* – large, low cost, low margin, high volume, self-service stores carrying a wide variety of food and other household products.
- *Superstores and hypermarkets* – larger than supermarkets offering a wider range of goods including furniture, appliances, clothing. These offer discount prices and operate like warehouses.
- *Service businesses* – where the product line is actually a service, e.g. banks, restaurants, dry cleaners, travel agents.
- *Catalogue showrooms* – selling a wide selection of high mark-up, fast-moving goods at discount prices.

Non-store retailers include:

- *Direct mail* – send out letters, samples, offers etc. to people on their mailing list.
- *Mail order* – send out either general merchandise or speciality mail order catalogues to agents or customers.
- *Telemarketing* – the use of free call numbers to receive orders from television and radio advertisements or unsolicited telephone calls to prospective customers.
- *E-tailing* – the use of websites to sell goods direct to the public over the internet. Amazon.com, for example, uses the internet to sell books, music and other items at lower than traditional store prices.
- *Door-to-door retailing* – products such as Avon cosmetics.
- *Automatic vending* – cigarettes, beverages, etc.

11.17.5   Retailing functions

Retailing is the final link in the distributive chain and, as Barker[10] points out, is responsible for several important marketing functions, including:

- The physical movement and storage of goods.
- The transfer of title to goods.
- The provision of information to consumers concerning the nature and uses of goods.
- The standardisation, grading and final processing of goods.
- The provision of ready availability.
- The assumption of risk concerning the precise nature and extent of demands.
- The financing of inventory and extension of credit to customers.

11.17.6   Trade enterprises

Van Weele[11] uses the term 'trade companies' to refer to all types of wholesale and retail undertaking. Not all such undertakings are, however, companies. Accordingly the term 'trade enterprises' will be used for convenience for the remainder of this aspect of purchasing.

Buying in trade enterprises

Buying in trade organisations is similar in many respects to buying for industrial organisations. The standard purchasing definition of purchasing as 'buying the right quality in the right quantity at the right price from the right source' is, in fact, widely attributed to Gordon Selfridge, the founder of the famous London store.

Evans,[12] however, has drawn attention to some differences between industrial and retail buyers:

- Industrial buyers are generally told what to buy and in what quantities. Retail buying roles include merchandise selection and range building.
- Industrial buyers tend to analyse the supplier's material and labour costs and then negotiate with the supplier on an acceptable contribution to his or her fixed costs and profit. Retail buyers negotiate down to a cost price which provides an acceptable selling price and target margin.
- Industrial buyers in appropriate industries use JIT agreements as a means of improving return on capital employed. Retail buyers generally find JIT to be inappropriate and find a consignment stock approach of greater relevance. With the consignment stock approach the supplier retains ownership of the goods until they have been sold to the customer by the retailer. The supplier therefore receives payment only when the goods are sold, an arrangement which helps the retailer to try new lines without investing in stock.

Other special characteristics of buying in trade enterprises include:

- Purchasing and selling are closely integrated – 'goods well bought are half sold'.
- Owing to the extra responsibilities mentioned above, buying in trade enterprises is a high profile activity.

- Because of short lead times and stock turnover, the outcome of purchasing decisions in trade enterprises is easy to access. 'We know on Friday whether Monday's purchases were good or not.'

- Different buying considerations apply according to whether the goods to be purchased are 'staple', i.e. in regular demand, or 'fashion' in which case demand is subject to 'sales cycles'. The four stages of a sales cycle are: (i) *distinctiveness* when the product is custom made or produced in small quantities; (ii) *copying* when additional manufacturers produce larger quantities of the product; (iii) *mass fashion* when the concept has become very popular and manufacturers are geared up to mass production; (iv) *decline* when consumers start moving to other fashions. Some products are also seasonal.

- Merchandise inventories must be adequate to prevent loss of sales and customer goodwill through stockouts but small enough to reduce losses through excessive holding costs and the need for markdowns.

- Development such as bar coding and EPOS (electronic point of sale) (see Chapter 2) are helping to reduce stocks, improve service levels and integrate warehouse and branch inventory policy.

The aims of buying for trade enterprises

The aims include:

- To meet customer demands satisfactorily.
- To improve profits and improve returns on capital.
- To negotiate purchases on the most favourable terms and against predetermined profit margin targets.
- To 'bring some excitement into the store' by the introduction of new lines, sales promotion, etc.
- To manage stock positively by optimising investment in inventory, minimising slow-selling merchandise and keeping in mind the relationship between stocks and sales in achieving profit goals.

11.17.7 The qualities of a trade buyer

Evans[13] in a controversial statement declares that 'it is an undeniable fact that retail buyers are more entrepreneurial than their industrial counterparts', and states 'as a sweeping generalisation that they tend to be more creative, profit conscious and better negotiators'. Cox and Brittain[14] suggest that retail buyers should:

- be able to recognise customer needs, even though customers themselves are unaware of them;
- know thoroughly the merchandise they deal with, maintaining a balanced assessment;
- be good judges of quality;
- be good judges of resaleability;
- be able to recognise new and profitable lines ('flair' is required particularly in textiles, toys and other fashion goods);

- liaise effectively with suppliers, store management and other sections of the merchandising and marketing departments, e.g. advertising, sales promotion;
- plan effectively in numerate terms;
- for overseas buying, possess linguistic abilities and cultural awareness.

McGoldrick[15] states that because of the complexity of retail buying decisions, buyers need to be 'effectively able to assimilate large volumes of information, be highly competent in the mathematical appraisal of supplier's terms and also be effective communicators and negotiators'.

Trade buying is a subject area in its own right. For this reason and because of the many forms that trade enterprises can take, it is impracticable to do more than refer to three further aspects of purchasing in trade enterprises, namely: who buys, what to buy and how much to buy.

11.17.8 Who buys?

As with their industrial counterparts, purchasing in trading enterprises may be centralised or decentralised. The former is associated with buying for wholesalers and independent retailers, the latter with multiple stores and cooperative societies. Some enterprises also use the services of external buying organisations. Within such forms of organisation, buying may be undertaken by:

- *The owner* – as in small single trader enterprises.
- *Specialist individual buyers* – who possess the qualities outlined in section 11.17.7 above. Such buyers may be:
  - responsible for both the buying and selling and therefore the profit of a centre, branch, department, etc.;
  - responsible only for buying on the premise that it is desirable to separate the buying and selling functions.
- *A buying team* – this is similar in many ways to a buying centre in an industrial enterprise (see Chapter 9). At Marks and Spencer, for example, there are, as shown in Figure 11.4, five buying teams for clothing, each controlled by a category manager who reports to a business unit director. The business unit director reports to the UK board. Each category manager is able to call on the services of a central procurement function which provides expert purchasing assistance.

As shown in Figure 11.4, leading team roles are those of merchandisers, product developers and product technologists.

- *Merchandisers* are responsible for negotiating prices, estimating quantities and scheduling the production with manufacturers and suppliers. They constantly react to changing sales patterns to keep sales as high and stocks as low as possible.
- *Product developers* choose cloth, design and style and are responsible for offering an attractive choice to customers. They travel extensively, keeping abreast of the latest fashion trends, carry out comparative shopping to monitor

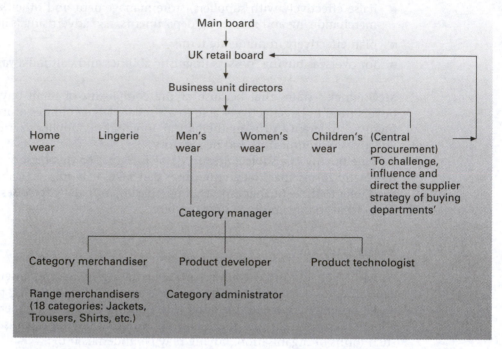

Figure 11.4 Clothing buying at Marks and Spencer (with special reference to menswear)

competitors and work closely with both manufacturers and the company's design departments.

- *Product technologists* develop and monitor specifications and quality control systems. They are technical advisors to the merchandisers and product developers and to manufacturers who may run into production problems.

Once a range is formulated within the department's budget the merchandiser decides which manufacturers will produce particular lines and styles. Merchandisers know how much each manufacturer can cope with or has the required skills. The merchandiser agrees a production programme with the manufacturer, detailing quantities required and delivery dates and contracts are signed.

11.17.9   What to buy

This is a complex subject. Decisions on what to buy tend to centre on the following considerations:

- The market to be served. This could be expensive, middle range or inexpensive merchandise, or a mixture of the three. Factors to be considered in deciding the quality of merchandise to carried include:
  - the market to be targeted, i.e. what quality is demanded;
  - competition in the market;
  - the store image and location;

- stock turnover required;
- profitability;
- whether the stock manufacturer's brands are supported by national advertising, deal brands or both;
- the need to employ skilled, knowledgeable sales staff if quality products are to be sold;
- customer-perceived goods and benefits, e.g. inexpensive merchandise tends to be bought primarily for its functional uses. High quality merchandise is bought for additional reasons such as prestige, style, exclusiveness, etc.

- Innovation, i.e. the extent to which new goods and lines should be marketed. Factors to be considered in deciding whether or not to stock new products include:
  - the market to be targeted, e.g. conservative or progressive;
  - potential for sales growth;
  - fashion trends and the stage at which a product has reached in the sales cycle;
  - effect of new goods on existing products. In general, old goods should be dropped when sales are low;
  - competition – whether the store should 'take the lead' or follow competitors;
  - store image – innovativeness should be consistent;
  - risk including investment costs, opportunity cost and supplier relations;
  - profitability – potential short- and long-term returns.

- The width and assortment of goods to be stocked. Assortment strategies may be:
  - wide and deep – many categories of goods and a large assortment in each category;
  - wide and shallow – as above but with a limited assortment in each category;
  - narrow and deep – few categories of goods but a large assortment in each category;
  - narrow and shallow – few categories of goods and a limited assortment in each category.

- Product knowledge of what goods are available and the extent to which stock requires replenishment. Such information can be obtained from:
  - information provided by manufacturers, wholesalers or agents through their representatives;
  - trade exhibitions and seminars;
  - trade journals;
  - observation of what is being sold by competitors;
  - customer enquiries;
  - historical data obtained from past experience or the analysis of statistical trends;
  - online information provided by EPOS technology.

11.17.10 Brands

A brand name is any word or device (design, shape, sound or colour) that is used to distinguish one company's products from a competitors.[16]
Branding aims to:

■ give a product a character or image, firstly through the name then through the packaging and thirdly through advertising;

■ create a monopoly or at least some form of imperfect competition so that the brand owner can obtain some of the benefits which accrue to a monopoly, particularly those related to decreased price competition.

Mercer[17] points out that the brand, 'whatever its derivation, is a very important investment for any organisation'. Rank Hovis McDougall, for example, values its international brands at anything up to 20 times its annual earnings.
Brands may be categorised as follows:

■ *Manufacturer brands*. These are produced and controlled by manufacturers and supported by manufacturer advertising.

■ *Dealer brands*. These have names designated by wholesalers or retailers. These are more profitable to retailers, and less expensive to customers and lead to retailers rather than manufacturer loyalty. Dealer brands are exclusive and cannot be sold by competing retailers. Where the retailer has a strong identity, this own brand may be able to compete against the strongest brand leaders.

■ *Generics*. These are unbranded goods which have little or no expensive advertising or packaging and are generally the least expensive to the customer. In the case of drugs, manufacturers' brands and generics may be identical in quality.

Trade buyers, especially in the retail sector, have to decide what mix of manufacturer and dealer brands and generics to stock.

11.17.11 How much to buy

Two important concepts are planned purchases and 'open to buy'.

Planned purchases

These may be calculated for a particular period by either of the following formulae:

Planned purchases = Planned sales + Planned reductions + Planned increase in stock, or – Planned decrease in stock

Planned purchase = Planned stock at end of period + Planned sales + Planned reductions – Stock in hand at beginning of period

To use either formula the buying team will have to have decided in money terms or value:

- anticipated sales for the period;
- stock in hand at the beginning of the period;
- desired stock in hand at the end of the period.
- planned reductions in the value of stock, i.e. 'markdowns' due to errors in buying, or stores promotional policies, e.g. 'sales to attract custom'.
- planned initial mark-ups.

Example 11.6   Planned purchases

Formula 1 – For October 200x

	£	£	£
Planned sales		20,000	
Planned reductions, i.e.		2,000	
Markdowns	1,800		
Shortages	200		
			22,000
Stock in hand 1 October		22,000	
Planned stock 31 October		44,000	
Planned increase in stock			4,000
Planned purchases			26,000
Formula 2 – Also for October			
Planned stock 31 October			44,000
Planned sales			20,000
Planned reductions			2,000
Total			66,000
Stock in hand 1 October			40,000
Planned purchases			26,000

Open to buy

Open to buy may be defined as:

> The amount or value of merchandise in terms of retail prices or at cost, which a buyer is open to receive into stock during a certain period on the basis of the formulated plans.

It may be regarded as the difference between planned purchases and purchase commitments already made by a buyer for a given time period, usually a month. It is therefore the amount that the buyer has left to spend during the period. Obviously the amount to buy balance is reduced whenever a purchase is made. Open to buy is always recorded at cost.

The open-to-buy approach has two significant strengths:

- It avoids under- or over-buying by establishing a specified relationship between stock in hand and planned sales.
- It helps a trader to adjust merchandise purchases to reflect changes in sales and markdowns.

On the downside, the open-to-buy figure must sometimes be exceeded when actual demand exceeds sales forecasts.

Example 11.7   Open to buy

Assume the planned purchases for October are £26,000 at *retail price*. Purchases already made amount to £18,000. The open-to-buy figure at retail value is therefore £8,000. To calculate the open-to-buy figure at cost price, the figure of £8,000 must be multiplied by the trader's merchandise costs (or cost of goods sold) as a percentage of selling price. If we assume these to be 60 per cent then:

$$\text{Open-to-buy at cost price} = £8,000 \times \frac{60}{100}$$

$$= £4,800$$

11.17.12   Automatic reordering systems

Buying for retailing has been revolutionised by the introduction of automatic reordering systems in which items in regular demand are reordered without frequent buyer intervention. This is similar to vendor managed inventory described in Chapter 8. Products such as food items that are regularly required have a predictable demand and the retailer's computer can be programmed to send an order when the predetermined items have fallen to a specified inventory level. Automatic reordering reduces routine work and enables buyers to spend time on more value adding activities. It is, however, necessary to examine sales periodically to ensure that required inventory levels are maintained and orders increased or reduced according to customer demand.

Case study

The Wiggleton Metropolitan Borough Council has its own print department that produces all printed documentation for the authority such as council minutes, brochures and publicity material. It also undertakes some work for external clients. The manager has 'head of department' status and reports to the council through the borough treasurer.

The manager has recently asked that one of his machines should be replaced by a more up-to-date model which would incorporate some additional non-standard cost saving improvements that the manager has designed. The council has approved the expenditure of up to £60,000 and has instructed the authority's purchasing department to seek tenders.

The council's policy is that departmental heads are responsible for the efficient operation of their departments and are expected to use their authority to ensure such efficiency. Interdepartmental conflicts are expected to be settled by discussion and negotiation between the heads concerned. There is, however, an arrangement, rarely used, for the convening of a sub-committee of non-involved heads under the chairmanship of the chief executive or his/her deputy who would reach a decision binding on both parties.

The authority's purchasing department handles over 90 per cent of both capital and revenue purchases. The purchasing department has the right to question any other department requesting or advocating the purchase of an item that it (purchasing) considers to be too dear, of inferior quality or in any way does not represent value for money. Standing orders direct that normally the cheapest tender shall be accepted, but this requirement may be waived where it can be shown that a dearer tender represents better value for money. There is also provision for the purchasing staff to engage in post-tender negotiations.

The purchasing department is regarded throughout the authority as a highly efficient unit. Capital equipment purchases are dealt with by a graduate mechanical engineer. There is seldom any conflict over the purchasing department's recommendations relating to capital equipment purchases. This is because purchasing recognises that the heads of user departments are entitled to a major part in any decision concerning from whom and at what price capital items should be bought.

Three tenders are received for the supply of the new printing machine. These are for £56,683 from Gog plc, £54,732 from Magog plc and £52,918 from Littlewoods plc. An additional tender has been sent in by Livermores, a used equipment company specialising in printing machinery, offering an almost new, reconditioned standard machine without the printing manager's additions for £38,740. The equipment buyer is confident that all three companies can provide a reliable machine to the authority's specification. He further ascertains that of the three tenders, £6,872, £7,000 and £6,742 respectively represent the cost of adding the print manager's required improvements. The equipment buyer therefore recommends either the acceptance of the Littlewoods tender or, alternatively, the purchase of the reconditioned, almost new machine and negotiating with the tenderers to add the improvements.

The head of printing is adamant, however, that the Gog's tender should be accepted on the grounds that (i) the company has a high reputation in the printing world; (ii) that the additions will be more reliable if incorporated into the machine during manufacture, and (iii) the engineers of Gog are probably better able to deal with any subsequent technical problems than those of the other two tenderers.

The suggestion of buying and adopting the almost new, reconditioned machine is rejected out of hand. The dispute is resolved to the sub-committee for a decision.

Questions

1 Do you consider the council's procedure for resolving disputes to be appropriate to the above situation?

2 As capital equipment buyer, state the grounds on which you would support your two alternative recommendations.

3 In respect of the reconditioned machine, what safeguards would you take before purchasing?

4 State, with reasons, whether you would

   (a) Support the print manager

   (b) Buy from Littlewoods

   (c) Buy and adapt the reconditioned machine

? Discussion questions

11.1 How many of the 'factors to be considered in buying capital equipment' listed in section 11.3.4 of this chapter do you take into account when purchasing (a) a new or secondhand car; (b) a new washing machine?

11.2 Explain the statement that it is necessary to classify capital equipment for the purposes of identification and control.

11.3 (a) Give an example of each of the following categories (i–iv) of capital equipment.

(b) How may acquisition policies and procedures differ in each case?

(c) At what management level may decisions be taken in respect of each of the following?

(i) Strategic new equipment

(ii) Replacement equipment

(iii) Vehicles and transportation

(iv) Administration

11.4 Draft a capital expenditure request form that can be used by senior managers seeking board approval for the acquisition of expensive capital equipment.

11.5 XYZ plc is deciding whether to lease or buy a machine. The machine will cost £2,000 and will have a life of three years, at the end of which it will have no scrap value. A loan for the purchase of the machine can be obtained for an annual rate of interest of 7 per cent payable at the end of each of the three years. The machine can also be leased from an equipment hire company in return for an annual payment of £762.10 payable at the end of each year.

Ignoring any taxation factors, which option will be the lowest cost solution? What factors might you take into account when making a decision?

11.6 Calculate the ROCE from the following figures:

Cost of machine:	£160,000
Expected life:	5 years
Estimated scrap value:	£20,000
Estimated profits before depreciation:	Year 1 £40,000
	Year 2 £80,000
	Year 3 £60,000
	Year 4 £30,000
	Year 5 £10,000

11.7 What would be the payback period for the machine in question 11.6?

11.8 Using the formula

$$\frac{1}{(1 + r)^n}$$

where r is the rate of interest and n the number of years, calculate the NPV of £100 for 1 and 5 years at 10 per cent compound interest.

11.9   Derivatives are financial products derived from some other existing product, thus rubber, copper, cocoa, zinc and currencies are all derivatives. In February 1995 the City of London's oldest merchant bank, Barings, collapsed as a result of losses in the derivatives market. What lessons can be learnt from this debacle in respect of commodity dealings?

11.10 Under what circumstances would you stockpile a sensitive commodity? What are the dangers of stockpiling?

11.11 Use the information below to do the following:

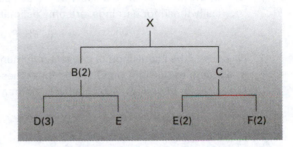

(a)   Calculate the quantities of B, C, D, E and F required to assemble one X.

(b)   Calculate the quantities of each company component that will be required to assemble 100Xs.

11.12 'Since tendering [for construction contracts] is highly competitive, the prices obtained by purchasing can determine whether a tender is competitive or otherwise.'

(a)   Why is the process of obtaining three quotes usually insufficient in the case of construction contracts?

(b)   What special knowledge do purchasing staff require to evaluate the competitiveness of prices quoted for material and subcontracted work?

11.13 How would you assess whether a particular applicant for a post as a deputy merchandiser has the potential to become a successful retail or wholesale buyer?

11.14 It is important for merchandisers to know why people are not purchasing a particular line of stock. As the merchandise manager responsible for women's wear you find that the range of outer wear you have commissioned is not attracting potential customers who are buying from your competitors. Suggest ten reasons why your range may not be selling.

11.15 You are responsible for buying all types of shoes for the footwear department of your store. Calculate your open-to-buy figure from the following details:

(i)   Opening stock of shoes for resale 1 July: £90,000

(ii)   Planned stock of shoes for 31 August: £120,000

(iii) Planned sales for the month with markdowns of £3,000: £42,000

(iv)   You have already placed orders for August of a retail value of £36,000

❓ Past examination questions

1   Your company is considering the purchase of a new item of plant, the capital cost of which is approximately £10,000. The item would be expected to have a useful life of 5 years and to produce an average income of £3,000 a year after deduction of operating and maintenance costs. Its residual value after 5 years would be nil.

   (a)   Describe the possible methods which you would use in order to evaluate whether or not your company should proceed with the investment.

   (b)   State which method you would recommend should be used, giving your reasons.

   (c)   Show how you would allow in the evaluation for the fact that the figures, especially those for earnings, are only estimates and could be wrong.

   (CIPS, Project and Contracts Management, 1994)

2   Faced with the acquisition of capital equipment, a purchaser has a number of options in addition to outright purchase. Identify these alternative approaches, and, using a specific item of your choice as a basis, compare their advantages and disadvantages with those of outright purchase.

   (CIPS, Purchasing, November 1997)

3   Explain the main features of an MRP system, and explain the circumstances in which such a system would, and would not, be appropriate for the determination of requirements.

   (CIPS, Stores and Inventory Management, November 1997)

4   Assess the ways in which a retail organisation can increase the rate of turnover of a particular retail outlet.

   (CIPS, Retail Merchandise Management, November 1997)

5   Good purchasing practices and systems found in the retail section could be usefully applied in other sections or purchasing. Identify these practices/systems that could, with suitable modifications, be of use to purchasing in other sections.

   (CIPS, Purchasing, May 1998)

6   Explain how the following buying or appraisal methods are used, giving appropriate examples:

   (a)   Hedging

   (b)   Capital investment

   (c)   Life cycle costing

   (CIPS, Purchasing, xxxx, 19xx)

7   Discuss the following:

   Traditionally the emphasis of retail advertising was to encourage immediate purchases, but now more and more of leading multiples are promoting the brand value of their name.

   (CIPS, Retail Merchandise Management, May 1999)

8   The purchase of capital equipment requires a team, each with their own specialised knowledge. What functions from within the organisation would you have represented in that team? Explain their roles.

   (CIPS, Introduction to Purchasing and Supply Chain Management, May 1999)

9   Discuss the factors which a buyer for a retail organisation should consider to determine the range of merchandise to be offered within a particular merchandise line.

(CIPS, Retail Merchandise Management, November 1999)

10 (a)   Explain the concept of DCF (discounted cash flow).

(b)   What are the recognised problems in the use of DCF?

(c)   What would it mean to you if you were told that the IRR of a project was 10 per cent? Explain whether the IRR would, alone, enable you to make a judgement as to whether the project should be undertaken or not?

(CIPS, Project and Contract Management, May 2000)

11 Explain the factors which need to be considered in selecting a pricing policy for a multiple retail organisation.

(CIPS, Retail Merchandise Management, May 2000)

12 Explain the value a buyer can add to an organisation that has a requirement for capital equipment.

(CIPS, Introduction to Purchasing and Supply Chain Management, May 2000)

13 The product structure for a child's yoyo is:

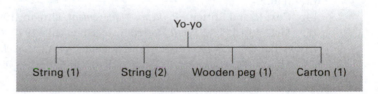

The current inventory and lead times (purchasing) are:

Part	Inventory	Lead time (weeks)
Wooden peg	100	1
String	500	1
Sides	200	5
Carton	Nil	1

Assembly time for 1,000 yo-yos is 1 week.

200 sides have already been ordered and are due to delivery in week 6.

1,000 yo-yos are required in week 10.

(a)   Do materials requirement planning (MRP) calculations that will show assembly and purchase schedules for all parts.

(b)   What further information and data files would be required to produce a 'closed loop' MRP schedule and what additional outcomes would result?

(CIPS, Operations Management, November 2000)

14 (a)   Identify and provide examples of the types of non-store retailing.

(b)   Explain the macroenvironmental factors that have facilitated the growth in non-store retailing.

(CIPS, Retail Merchandise Management, November 2000)

Notes

1. G.W. Aljian's *Purchasing Handbook*, National Association of Purchasing Management, USA, 1958, section 16.1
2. G.W. Aljian's *Dictionary of Business and Finance*, Van Nostrand, 1980
3. Barfield, J.T., Raibon, C.A. and Kinney, M.R., *Cost Accounting*, West Publishing, 1994, Ch.19, p.709
4. Definition provided by the Inland Revenue
5. Marrian, J., 'Marketing characteristics of industrial goods and buyers', in Wilson (ed.) *The Marketing of Industrial Products*, Hutchinson, 1965, Ch.2, pp.10–23
6. Department of Trade and Industry, *Terotechnology Check List No. 4 for Purchasing Personnel*, 1976 (now out of print)
7. Risley, G., *Modern Industrial Marketing*, McGraw-Hill, 1972, pp.24–5
8. Adapted from ibid.
9. Barker, M.J., *Marketing*, 4th edn, Macmillan, 1990, Ch.10, p.164
10. Ibid., p.158
11. Van Weele, A.J., *Purchasing Management*, Chapman & Hall, 1994, Ch.15, p.248
12. Evans, E., 'Retail buying,' *Journal of Retail and Distribution Management*, Sept./Oct. 1989, pp.15–16
13. Ibid.
14. Cox, R. and Brittain, P., *Retail Management*, Pitman, 1991, Ch.10, p.110
15. McGoldrick, P.J., *Retail Marketing*, McGraw-Hill, 1990, Ch.7, pp.189–90
16. Berkowitz, E.N., Kevin, R.A. and Rudelius, W.A., *Marketing*, Irwin, 1989, glossary p.687
17. Mercer, D., *Marketing*, Blackwell, 1993, Ch.6, pp.275–6

After reading this chapter you should be able to:

- Distinguish between international sourcing, multinational sourcing, foreign sourcing and strategic global sourcing.
- Identify the reasons for sourcing internationally.
- Identify the difficulties in buying abroad.
- Define the import transaction chain.
- Describe how to manage quality in a global sourcing context.
- Describe how to manage currency in a global purchasing context.
- Explain the use of documentary credits and bills of exchange.
- Identify cultural differences and how they affect negotiation when buying abroad.
- Have an appreciation of the international commercial world.
- Define the methods and explain the importance of countertrade.
- Explain the role of Customs and Excise and its operation.
- Define the key elements in successful global sourcing.

12.1 Terminology

Birou and Fawcett[1] distinguish between international sourcing, multinational sourcing, foreign sourcing and strategic global sourcing. They define the first three terms as 'buying outside the firm's country of manufacture in such a way that does not co-ordinate requirements among world-wide business units of a single firm'. Strategic global sourcing is defined as 'the co-ordination and integration of procurement requirements across world-wide business units, looking at common items, processes, technologies and suppliers'.

Stevens[2] highlights the fact that global sourcing involves integration in two respects: the internationalisation of purchasing and the adoption of a strategic orientation for all resource management. Global sourcing is, in fact, an international division of labour in which activities are performed in countries where they can be done well at the lowest cost and is common in the motor industry where components are manufactured or purchased in various parts of the world and then assembled by the final producer into the final product.

12.2 Reasons for sourcing internationally

It is important to understand why an organisation is sourcing abroad as this can affect the stance taken when negotiating. Reasons for international sourcing include (i) changes in the business environment and (ii) factors relating to the needs or competitiveness of the enterprise. In relation to the former, Carter and Narasimhan[3] identify such challenges as:

- Intense international competition.
- Pressure to reduce costs.
- Need for manufacturing flexibility.
- Shorter product development cycles.
- Stringent quality standards.
- Ever changing technology.

Factors relating to the needs or competitiveness of the enterprise include:

- Domestic non-availability, e.g. commodities, rubber, cotton, etc.
- Insufficient domestic capacity to meet demand.
- 'Insurance' reasons, buying abroad to maintain continuity of supplies owing to shortages or strikes.
- Competitiveness of overseas sources, e.g. lower prices, improved deliveries, better quality.
- Reciprocal trading and countertrade owing to policy reasons or government pressures owing to balance of payment considerations.
- Access to worldwide technology.
- To obtain penetration of a growth market, e.g. Toyota sources from the Pacific Rim not only to achieve lower costs but also to enter markets with restrictive quotas by increasing the local content component of the cars.

12.3 Difficulties in buying abroad

There is no magic formula that will guarantee success when buying abroad. For this reason, and because of the perceived difficulties, many buyers are reluctant to buy abroad unless absolutely necessary. Baily *et al.*[4] state that purchasing from a foreign source is not different in any fundamental way from purchasing from a domestic source. The same value for money objectives are pursued, and much the same range of methods and systems are employed in this pursuit. Difficulties that can arise are outlined below.

12.3.1 Contact with suppliers

Contact with suppliers is generally more difficult. This can be because of time zone differences, differences in the working week and physical methods of communication. The difficulties in time zones are perhaps dependent upon which part of the world you are dealing with. The further east you go from Great Britain then the greater the time difference. In reality, this reduces contact rather than eradicates it. In particular, it is not unusual to find that the Middle Eastern weekend is Thursday and Friday. The overall effect here is that the actual time for contact in a week is reduced to just three days if your weekend is Saturday and Sunday. Physical methods of contact such as telecommunications have greatly improved, aided by developments such as e-mail, faxes and mobile telecommunications.

12.3.2 Time required for negotiations

This is greatly increased compared with the time needed to negotiate with domestic suppliers. Time is also used as a tactic in negotiation in some cultures. This is explored later in the chapter.

12.3.3 Currency difficulties

Among matters to be resolved are:

- In what currency is the price quoted and payment to be made?
- What is the likely effect on currency of currency fluctuations?
- How is payment to be made?

The considerations are explored later in the chapter.

12.3.4 Legal difficulties

It is necessary to determine (*inter alia*) the following:

- What law shall govern the transaction, i.e. that of the importing or of the exporting nation. In general this will be the law of the country in which the contract is made. It is of course always possible to use the law of a third country selected by the parties to the agreement.
- Arrangements for arbitration. Arbitration is stated to be cheaper than litigation, quicker and is held in private thus avoiding bad publicity. Arbitrators may be chosen before the contract begins in conjunction with all parties. Arbitrators have technical, industry and market knowledge and are therefore likely to provide a more balanced decision than a member of the judiciary.

- Terms and conditions applicable to cancellation, deliveries and delays and the passing of property.
- Protection of buyer against infringements of patents.
- Protection of buyer against product liability.

12.3.5 Other difficulties

Other difficulties include:

- *Redress of complaints*, i.e. the return to the supplier of goods rejected or damaged in transit. The recovery of damages is awarded to the buyer by the courts or arbitration. (It is useful to ascertain what assets, if any, the supplier has in the buyer's country since these can be restrained by the courts in payment of damages due.)
- *Delays in delivery* due to weather, cargo transfer, dock strikes and customs action.
- *Transportation* including the terms of delivery. Incoterms 2000 are dealt with in Chapter 14.
- *Import duties, procedures and insurance.*
- *Documentation*, e.g. bills of lading, certificates of origin, and customs entry forms that are necessary in the home trade.
- *Price rises* due to increased costs incurred by the supplier and the basis on which these shall be calculated or allowed.
- *Specifications*, especially where there are differences in units of measurement. It is generally the view that clear and unambiguous specifications are essential and are a vital aid in the assurance that the right quality will be provided.
- *Quality*, especially how it is managed initially and in the long term.

12.4 International procurement cycle (import transaction chain)

Baily *et al.* have alluded to the fact (see section 12.3) that buying abroad does not differ substantially from buying nationally. At the heart of this statement is the fact that the basic processes and techniques of buying nationally are still used when buying abroad, but are often forgotten by buyers. This is illustrated in Figure 12.1.

Branch[5] states that, when buying abroad, there is the possibility of there being four contracts: the contract for finance, contract for transport, contract for insurance and finally the purchase order itself or sales contract. This perhaps exemplifies some of the factors that can make the act of buying abroad more complex. If we superimpose these and other factors on the basic procurement cycle, we can demonstrate in detail the import transaction chain (Figure 12.2). Some of these aspects are now examined in greater detail.

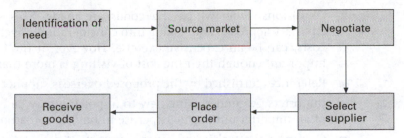

Figure 12.1 The basic procurement cycle

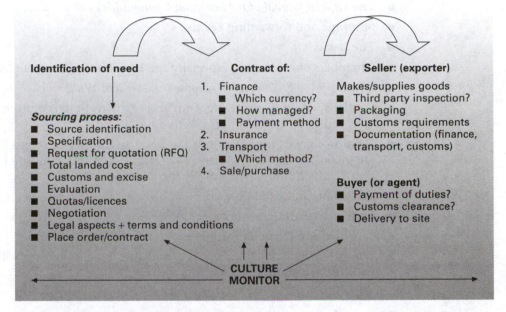

Figure 12.2 The import transaction chain
(Copyright Michael Gillingham)

12.4.1 Information regarding sourcing abroad

Because of the complexity of buying abroad, the buyer will have to acquire specialist knowledge regarding the following:

- The country from which it is intended to buy, i.e. its economic and political conditions and policies with regards to export subsidies.
- The supplier from whom it is intended to buy, i.e. capacity, financial position, reputation and reliability.
- The legal and commercial considerations and procedures involved in buying abroad, e.g. ordering, transportation and payment.

Such information may be obtained from the following sources:

- Visits to the proposed overseas supplier. It is only through visiting that the buyer will be able to see first-hand the site of the seller and ascertain the conditions under which the goods are made. This should be a multidisciplinary approach and, taking into consideration travel, subsistence and hotel costs, can be an expensive exercise. However, if the items to be bought are important enough then the cost of visiting is more than justified.

- References furnished by the proposed overseas supplier.
- Importers. An undertaking new to importing may be wise to use the services of an importer until some expertise in buying abroad has been established.
- Commercial attachés and other government departments of foreign nations.
- The Department of Trade and Industry.
- The *Official Journal of the European Communities*.
- Shipping and forwarding agents.
- The banks.
- Chambers of commerce, especially the London Chamber of Commerce.
- Directories, e.g. *Kompass, Thompson, Jaeger and Waldman*.
- Specialist enquiry agents, e.g. Dun and Bradstreet offers a product finding service and credit check on prospective suppliers.
- Details of goods imported into the UK, the country of origin and their value are given in the UK Trade and Navigation accounts published monthly, and also yearly in summary form, by the Stationery Office.
- Trade fairs and exhibitions.
- Professional and trade organisations.
- Customs and Excise departments.
- The internet, although there is always the possibility you will be swamped with information.

12.4.2 Managing quality

When buying abroad, in view of distance and time, delays due to quality problems need to be minimised or, more appropriately, eliminated. This is not helped by the fact that specifications may be translated into the language of the seller, that sizes and measurements may differ and there are in excess of one hundred standards-setting bodies in the world. Quality can be managed in the short term by:

- the use of specifications that are unambiguous and clear;
- thorough supplier appraisal visits prior to placing the order;
- visiting and testing during production or engaging a third party to carry this out on your behalf;
- the insistence on a quality or conformance certificate;
- the use of samples;
- pre-shipment inspection by a third party. Examples of third-party inspection organisations include Crown agents, Lloyds of London and Société Générale de Surveillance (SGS);
- the use of recognised standards e.g. International Standards.

In the long term, there is the need to use or develop a vendor rating system to monitor the performance of the supplier and to develop a closer relationship in order that an understanding of quality matters can be developed.

12.4.3 Request for quotation

When sourcing abroad, it is most likely that the buyer will include such items in the request for quotation (RFQ) as description of goods (or specification), quantity required, delivery requirements or lead time request, currency, method of payment, and unit of measurement. Careful thought at this stage can eliminate possible ambiguities (and therefore possible delays) in the future.

Caution should be exercised at the evaluation stage of RFQ's or tenders as, according to Beardon,[6] buyers may well dismiss opportunities because of different accounting conventions used in the country of the seller that may initially make a quotation seem unfavourable. Therefore there is the need for detailed analysis.

12.4.4 Managing currency

Currency management is an area requiring careful consideration when buying abroad. This is because there is always the risk that currencies will fluctuate and the buyer could end up paying more than originally envisaged. The degree of involvement of the buyer in the management of currency will vary between one organisation and another. Anecdotal evidence suggests that very few buyers in UK get involved in currency management. Large organisations such as multinationals usually have a corporate treasury department that manages currency transactions, as an organisation itself is at risk from currency movements in terms of transaction, translation and economic exposure. *Transaction exposure* is the extent to which short-term cash flows are affected by fluctuations in foreign exchange. *Translation exposure* is the effect that currency changes will have on the balance sheet of the organisation. *Economic exposure* is the effect that exchange rate fluctuations will have on the earning power of the organisation.

Techniques of managing currency available to the buyer include:

- Paying in own currency. A seller in a foreign country may well accept payment in the currency of the buyer. This is possibly owing to the fact that the currency of the buyer is attractive at that moment in time, or the seller also buys goods in the country of the buyer. The danger with this method is that the seller may well increase the price to protect against unfavourable currency movement.

- Paying in a mutually agreed currency that is not the currency of the country of the buyer or seller, e.g. US dollar, Swiss franc.

- Inserting a clause in the contract such as 'this contract is subject to an exchange rate of X plus or minus Y%'. If the exchange rate exceeds these parameters then the contract price is renegotiated.

- Inserting a clause in the contract that averages the sum of the exchange rates at the time of signing the contract and at the time of delivery.

- Entering into a futures contract to agree to buy a fixed amount of currency at a date in the future (i.e. the delivery date), at an agreed rate of exchange. The exchange rate used on this date is the rate agreed in the contract, not the rate for the currency that prevails on the day.

■ Buying the currency now and holding it until required. Although this ties up capital, it could earn interest, and the exchange rate is known from the outset.

■ Hedging. Just as it is possible to hedge with commodities, it is also possible to hedge with currency.

12.4.5 Methods of payment

When buying abroad there are a number of payment methods that can be used. What must be remembered is that, when buying abroad, the seller may not wish to release the goods until payment has been made, and similarly the buyer may not wish to pay until the goods have been received. Examples of payment methods include:

■ *Open account.* Even if you have not dealt with a supplier before, depending on the nature and value of the goods, it may be possible to pay by this method, i.e. usually 30 days after receipt of the goods.

■ *Payment in advance.* In effect the buyer is financing the transaction up-front and there is always the possibility that the seller will default.

■ *Stage or partial payments.* This method is usually associated with the purchase of capital equipment.

■ *Documentary credits – letter of credit.* This method of payment negates the worries that either the buyer or the seller may default in payment or the performance. The method of operation is outlined in Figure 12.3. At the heart of the transaction is a bundle of documents, usually agreed between the buyer and seller. It is these documents that will assure the buyer that what was ordered will be received. Similarly, the seller will know that if performance is to the required standard then payment will be guaranteed.

A *revocable letter of credit* is one that may have its terms altered by either party (or can even be cancelled) without reference to each other. This type is regarded as being less safe. An *irrevocable letter of credit* cannot be altered or cancelled without agreement by both parties. A confirmed letter of credit is one that guarantees payment to the seller and is used when there is some doubt as to the political or economic stability of the country of the buyer. Other forms of letter of credit include, standby, revolving, transferable and advanced payment. Letters of credit are expensive and should therefore not be used for low value amounts. It is worth keeping abreast of developments in the use of electronic documentary credits.

■ *Bills of exchange.* These have been in use in international trade for a considerable time and have been described as instruments that 'oil the wheels of commerce'. The alternative name for them is a draft. A bill of exchange has been defined as 'an unconditional order in writing, addressed by one person (the drawer) to another (the drawee), signed by the person giving it (the drawer), requiring the person to whom it is addressed, to pay on demand, or at a fixed or determinable future time, a certain sum in money to, or to the order of, a

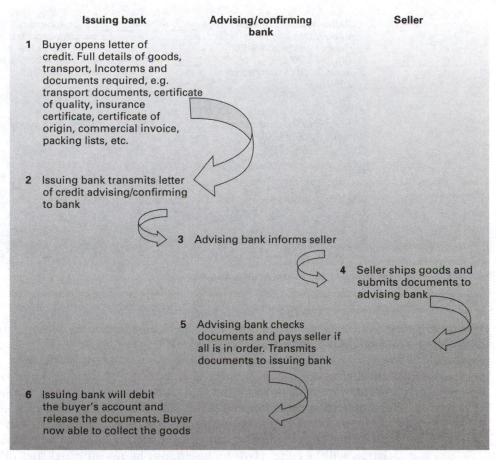

Issuing bank	Advising/confirming bank	Seller

1 Buyer opens letter of credit. Full details of goods, transport, Incoterms and documents required, e.g. transport documents, certificate of quality, insurance certificate, certificate of origin, commercial invoice, packing lists, etc.

2 Issuing bank transmits letter of credit advising/confirming to bank

3 Advising bank informs seller

4 Seller ships goods and submits documents to advising bank

5 Advising bank checks documents and pays seller if all is in order. Transmits documents to issuing bank

6 Issuing bank will debit the buyer's account and release the documents. Buyer now able to collect the goods

Figure 12.3 Letter of credit transaction

specified person or to the bearer (the payee). A bill of exchange can be in various forms such as being computer generated or even bought at a stationers. It may be either a sight draft or a usance draft. A usance draft usually has a set term (30, 60 or 90 days) before payment has to be made. It is possible for the seller to obtain his or her money for the goods virtually straight away by discounting the bill of exchange. The passage of a bill of exchange transaction is illustrated in Figure 12.4.

The value of the discounted bill to the seller can be calculated from:

$$\frac{\text{Value of bill} \times \text{Discount rate} \times \text{Number of days}}{365 \times 100}$$

Inserting values from the example used in Figure 12.4 gives:

$$\frac{\pounds100,000 \times 8 \times 90}{365 \times 100} = \pounds1,972.60$$

The seller would have received £98,027.40 and would no doubt have accounted for this in his or her quotation to the buyer.

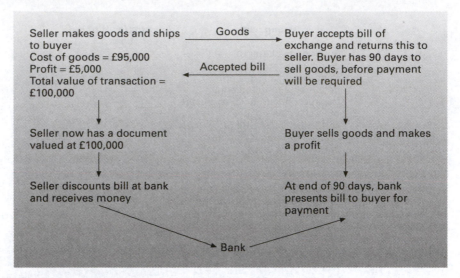

Figure 12.4 Bill of exchange transaction

12.5 Culture and negotiation

Hill[7] defines culture as 'the complex whole that includes knowledge, belief, art, morals, law, custom and other capabilities acquired by man as a member of society'. It involves people and it is complex, but when dealing with individuals from different cultures on a business basis, it is essential that the buyer has a sound understanding of culture. Culture will have a bearing on how business and negotiation will be conducted. It should also be remembered that different cultures may well have subcultures within them. Some individuals have the view that because of the concept of the 'global village', cultures are converging. This is based on the fact that the cost of travel has come down, transport is faster, people have access to videos, films, magazines, satellite television and the internet, and therefore exposure to other cultures will bring about greater understanding and less chance of making a cultural *faux pas*.

Bennett[8] states that managers need to know about cultural differences in order to communicate effectively with customers, suppliers etc., to conduct negotiations and understand the nuances of the bargaining postures of the other parties to a negotiation, to understand ethical standards and concepts of social responsibility.

12.5.1 Language

With more than three thousand languages in the world, it is hardly surprising that this is an area that could present problems, particularly in relation to translation. Language is a vital part of communication so it is essential that when negotiating abroad you express yourself clearly and without any risk of ambiguity, so that communication does not become a barrier to effective negotiation.

The situation is even more complex when dealing with high-context cultures such as Chinese, Japanese and Korean, where the message is derived from non-verbal signals, and verbal communication is of secondary importance. In low-context cultures, such as Germany, the UK and the USA, the message is clearly stated in written or spoken words. Non-verbal communication is used but is regarded as being of secondary importance.

12.5.2 Time

Attitude to time is another element influenced by culture. In northern Europe and the USA, we are driven by monochromic time, characterised by the need to stick to schedules and deadlines and the preference for doing one thing at a time. Delays and being kept waiting are anathema to these cultures. The opposite of monochronic time is polychronic time, where the attitude to time is flexible and there is a preference to perform more than one task or deal with several people at once. This is seen in some Middle East, Mediterranean and Latin American countries and can be a cause of conflict and irritation to those with a monochronic attitude to time.

12.5.3 Individualism versus collectivism

This is really about 'I' and 'we'. Negotiators from countries with a high degree of individualism, such as the USA, Canada and the UK, tend to make decisions individually, and accept responsibility for these decisions. Collectivism, on the other hand, involves much discussion and referral, and responsibility for the decision is a group affair. Countries with a high degree of collectivism include China, Japan and Singapore. With collectivism, it is usually the norm to see teams of negotiators and a lengthy decision-making process.

12.5.4 Role orderliness and conformity

Seen mostly in high context cultures, conformity means that great importance is attached to how things are done – the protocol, as opposed to the content. Relationships and behaviour are very important. This influences the tone of the negotiation, the formality and what is acceptable in terms of social discussion. Countries such as the USA and those of northern Europe do not have such rituals and formality. The focus is on the content and the need to conclude the deal.

12.5.5 Ethics

Ethics is basically a code of conduct which may be enforced on individuals by a written code of conduct (e.g. CIPS Ethical Code), or is enshrined in the cultural beliefs of a country. Ethical beliefs are going to influence such things as hospitality and the giving of gifts, and bribery and corruption. In some countries, lavish hospitality and the giving of expensive gifts is the norm and a reflection of esteem or value that the donor sees in the recipient. Not to accept could cause offence.

In some parts of the Middle East and Africa, it is not unknown for officials to expect some 'reward' for merely carrying out their official duties. Similarly, third parties may expect introduction fees to introduce a client to a principal. At the extreme end of the scale is the aspect of downright bribery and corruption where it is expected that everyone 'takes a cut of the action' and is rewarded.

12.5.6 Summary

It is therefore possible to summarise how negotiation will be affected by culture. Salacuse[9] identifies ten ways:

1 The negotiating goal: contract or relationship?
2 Negotiating attitude: win–win or win–lose?
3 Personal style: informal or formal?
4 Communication: direct or indirect?
5 Sensitivity to time: high or low?
6 Use of emotionalism: high or low?
7 Form of agreement: general or specific?
8 Building an agreement: bottom up or top down?
9 Team organisation: one leader or group consensus?
10 Risk taking: high or low?

Because of the influence of culture, when negotiating with suppliers from abroad it may be prudent at the evaluation stage to ascertain their commitment to ISO 14000 and SA 8000 (Social Accountability 8000). The former is a series of environmental management standards, the basis for an environmental management system. SA 8000, which is seeing growth in its acceptance, is a standard for workplace conditions, looking at areas such as use of child labour, forced labour, working hours, management systems etc. Organisations that source globally cannot be complacent about sources of supply that are suspect in terms of environmental management systems or social accountability. The damage to the image or reputation of the company could be costly.

12.6 The international commercial world

When engaged in global sourcing, the buyer will have to develop knowledge as regards economic groupings and the major institutions involved in international commerce. The main economic group classifications are:

■ *Free trade area.* In a free trade area the movement of goods and services between member countries should be free of tariffs. Additionally, non-tariff barriers, quotas and subsidies should also be absent. However, while there may be free movement of goods between member countries, each country is free to establish its own trade policies with non-member countries, including setting their own external tariffs.

■ *Customs union.* In a customs union, the countries forming it have removed tariffs on the movement of goods and services between them but have also established a common tariff and trade policy for dealing with non-member countries.

■ *Common market.* Like a customs union, members of a common market have a common external trade policy and there is free movement of goods and services among the member states. However, what characterises a common market is the additional development of the free movement of people and capital.

Some examples of the most important economic groups and other institutions involved in world trade are given below.

12.6.1   GATT / WTO

The General Agreement on Tariffs and Trade (GATT), the forerunner of the World Trade Organisation (WTO) came into existence in 1947 with the objectives of reducing tariffs and establishing multilateral trade. Traditionally, there had been a high degree of protectionism and high tariff rates that were a bar to the development of world trade. There were originally 23 signatories to the agreement; that number is now 144. The basic idea behind GATT was that of 'orderly marketing', where the fully industrialised countries would gradually open up their markets to imports from developing countries. The 'cement' of the GATT agreement was the 'most favoured nation principle', which basically decreed that whatever actions were put in place (such as restrictions or benefits) would be applied unconditionally to all members, i.e. trade without discrimination.

GATT developed through a series of trade rounds, and tariffs were gradually reduced. The most significant round of talks was the Uruguay round which lasted some eight years, and came into force in 1995. The outcomes of this round of talks were far-reaching and included such things as tariff cuts, bringing intellectual property rights into GATT, some progress on services and the agreement to set up the World Trade Organisation (WTO).

The demise of GATT was felt necessary as it had achieved as much as it could in its old form. Additionally, there was the need to establish a forum to settle trade disputes between nations and this was facilitated through the creation of the Dispute Settlement Body. The WTO did not displace GATT, but merely absorbed the principles of GATT into a more substantial body which had greater teeth and muscle. The main purpose of the WTO is to help free trade flow, serve as a forum for trade negotiations, and to be the organisation for settling trade disputes between member nations.

12.6.2   European Union

The foundations of the EU were created by the Schumann plan of 1950, by which France and Germany traded coal and steel between them. In 1951, these two were joined by Luxemburg, The Netherlands, Belgium and Italy to create the European Coal and Steel Community. It was this nucleus of countries that then went on, in 1956, to create the European Economic Community (EEC). Expansion ensued to the present number of 15 countries. Significant dates in the EU's history include:

1951   European Coal and Steel Treaty

1957   EEC Treaty signed

1968   Original six countries form a customs union

1973   UK, Denmark and Ireland join

1981   Greece joins

1986 Spain and Portugal join

1987 Single European Act

1990 Former East German state joins through unification of Germany

1991 EC and EFTA form the European Economic Area

1993 European single market

1995 Finland, Sweden and Austria join

1999 Eleven members launch the euro. European monetary union (EMU) launched

2002 The euro becomes legal tender and replaces the national currency of 12 EMU countries

The aims of the EU were originally the free movement of goods, services, money and people. For the buyer in UK, buying within the EU can be regarded as very much like buying nationally. Provided that goods are deemed to be in free circulation, then there are no tariffs to pay on goods brought in from EU countries. For the public sector buyer, there is the necessity to comply with the European procurement directives, which attempt to create a level playing field for public procurement.

12.6.3 North American Free Trade Agreement (NAFTA)

This is a free trade area formed in 1994 by the USA, Canada and Mexico. One of the principal features of NAFTA is to eliminate by 2004 the tariffs on virtually all goods traded between them. Similar goals also apply to services. Two of its members (USA and Canada) are two of the richest countries in the world. The population of NAFTA is in excess of 360 million. As a free trade area, Mexico has the lowest external tariffs for the import of goods.

12.6.4 Other examples

Other examples of economic groups, of which there are over thirty, include:

- ASEAN – Association of South East Asian Nations, a free trade area comprising Brunei, Indonesia, Malaysia, the Philippines, Singapore and Thailand.
- EFTA – European Free Trade Area, comprising Iceland, Norway, Switzerland and Liechtenstein.
- ECOWAS – Economic Community of West African States, consisting of 15 countries.
- MERCOSUR – a customs union comprising Argentina, Brazil, Paraguay and Uruguay.
- CARICOM – Caribbean Community and Common Market.

12.6.5 The World Bank

The correct title for this body is the International Bank for Reconstruction and Development (IBRD). Formed in 1944, its main purpose was to help developing countries. The IBRD lent money, and poorer countries merely paid an annual administrative charge. The role of this body has changed somewhat now from lending money to giving advice, owing mostly to the fact that there is a large amount of private funds available in the world for development work.

12.6.6 International Monetary Fund

The International Monetary Fund (IMF) was formed at the same time as the IBRD. The original aim was to establish fixed exchange rates for currency. Member countries deposit funds with the IMF, which, when they have balance of payment problems, gives them the right to draw against deposits. However, these 'loans' are paid in tranches and usually have economic conditions attached to them before further monies are released. These conditions have often been described as draconian, as the conditions usually cause severe hardship for individuals.

12.6.7 International Chamber of Commerce

The International Chamber of Commerce (ICC) was founded in 1919 and is a non-governmental organisation based in Paris. Its role is to promote trade and investment. It comprises businesses and business associations throughout the world. It has national committees in all continents which serve to give ICC views to governments and similarly to pass back to ICC in Paris relevant business concerns. Bodies of the ICC include the International Court of Arbitration, a leading body in the settlement of commercial trade disputes, and the International Maritime Arbitration Organisation. The ATA (admission temporaire/temporary admission) carnet system is also administered by the ICC.

12.7 Countertrade

12.7.1 Definition

Countertrade is a form of international reciprocal trading in which an order is placed by a purchaser with a supplier in another country on condition that goods to an equal or specified value are sold in the opposite direction. Because of the diversity in methods of countertrade it is a subject that is hard to define. Stevens[10] highlights the fact that there is no accepted definition of countertrade and terms may vary between country to country. He suggests a definition of:

> **A commercial transaction in which provisions are made, in one or a series of related contracts, for payment by deliveries of goods and/or services, in addition to or in place of financial settlement.**

Despite difficulty in definition and terminology, countertrade is of significance as today, approximately 25 per cent of all world trade is accounted for by countertrade. This is perhaps not too incredible given the number of countries in the world that have currencies that are non-convertible. Some countries have developed official countertrade policies.

12.7.2 Types of countertrade

Carter and Gagne[11] identify five types of countertrade:

- *Barter* – a one-off direct, simultaneous exchange of goods and services between trading partners, without a cash transaction. The duration is short, generally one contract, and only two parties involved.

- *Counterpurchase* occurs when a company in country X sells to country Y on the understanding that a set percentage of the sales proceeds will be spent on importing goods produced in country Y. Both trading partners agree to fulfil their obligations within a fixed time period and to pay for their respective purchases in cash.

- *Buy-back/compensation* occurs when the exporter agrees to accept, as full or partial payment, products manufactured by the original exported product, e.g. Occidental Petroleum negotiated a deal with the former USSR under which it would build several plants in the Soviet Union and receive partial payment in ammonia over a 20 year period. In general, buy-back deals tend to be for longer terms and larger amounts than other methods.

- *Switch trading* refers to the transfer of unused or unusable credit balances in one country to overcome an imbalance of money by trading partner in another country. Country X sells goods of a certain value to country Y. Country Y credits country X with the value of the goods which X can use to buy goods from Y. Country X, however, does not wish to buy goods from Y. X, therefore sells the credits to a third-party trading house at a discount. The trading house then locates a country or company wishing to buy goods from Y. In return for a small profit the trading house sells the credits to the country or company wishing to buy from Y.

- *Offset* (also referred to as industrial participation) is similar to counterpurchase. Offset is used by governments as an aid to reducing the cost of public sector purchases. Direct offset is where the selling country agrees to include materials, components, sub-assemblies obtained from the buying country.

A further method of countertrade is *tolling*. This operates when, for instance, a manufacturer is able to utilise only partial capacity (and therefore not supply its customers), due to the inability to buy raw materials. In tolling, a supplier in another country provides the raw materials and in turn is paid for them by a final customer after the raw material has been converted into the final goods.

12.7.3 Advantages and disadvantages of countertrade

The advantages and disadvantages of countertrade have been identified by Forker[12] as:

Advantages:
- Acceptance of goods or services as payment can:
  - avoid exchange controls;
  - promote trade with countries with inconvertible currencies;
  - reduce risks associated with unstable currency values.

- Overcoming the above financial obstacles enables countertrading enterprises to:
  - enter new or formerly closed markets;
  - expand business and sales volume;
  - reduce the impact of foreign protectionism on overseas business.
- Countertrade has enabled participants to:
  - make fuller use of plant capacity;
  - have longer production runs;
  - reduce unit expenses because of greater sales volume;
  - find valuable outlets for declining products.

Disadvantages:

- Countertrade negotiations tend to be longer and more complex than conventional sales negotiations and must sometimes be conducted with powerful government procurement agencies.
- There are additional expenses such as brokerage fees and other transaction costs that may reduce the profitability of countertrade deals.
- There may be difficulties with the quality, availability and disposal of goods taken as payback.
- Countertrade may give rise to pricing problems associated with the assignment of values to products/commodities received in exchange.
- Offset customers can later become competitors.
- Commodity prices can vary widely during the lengthy periods of countertrade negotiation and delivery.

12.7.4 Countertrade and purchasing

One advantage of countertrade not mentioned above is that a multinational company can use its purchasing power to forge strong supplier links as a means of exploiting sales opportunities in a foreign country. Thus, with what is termed 'reverse countertrade' an enterprise can present actual or potential trading partners with their current and future sourcing requirements. When the availability of these requirements has been established, the feasibility of selling its own goods abroad can be raised.

It should be remembered that the decision to enter countertrade is taken at a very senior level within the organisation, and the purchasing department may not become involved. Forker[13] states that fewer than 50 per cent of senior executives consult with procurement on the advisability of countertrade proposals. However, when they do, their opinions are given prime consideration in almost all cases.

12.7.5 Purchasing and countertrade

Purchasing can play a major part in countertrade by:

- identifying low-cost sources of supply that may be exploited on a countertrade basis;

- providing negotiating expertise when discussing countertrade arrangements with prospective foreign sources;

- ensuring that goods to be purchased under countertrade arrangements are of the right quality;

- finding internal uses for countertrade materials;

- developing long-term strategic countertrade partnerships;

- recognising that countertrade can be a major source of low-cost quality materials that will provide a competitive advantage over those to whom such sources are not available.

12.8 Customs and Excise

In a book of this nature, it is only possible to provide an overview of some of the operation of Her Majesty's Customs and Excise (HMCE), and the systems and procedures in use applicable to the import transaction chain. Apart from collecting duties and taxes on goods brought into the UK, HMCE is also responsible for collecting trade statistics, collecting value added tax and other levies such as landfill taxes. Preventive aspects of HMCE are primarily focused on the importation of prohibited goods and controlling goods subject to quarantine and health restrictions.

While systems and procedures can be described as complex, much has been done over the years to simplify or harmonise procedures within Europe and other parts of the world, particularly with the adoption of information technology. In the early 1990s, HMCE introduced a new computer system known as CHIEF (Customs Handling of Import Export Freight), which is capable of interfacing with the IT systems of the major trading countries of the world. Traditional views of UK Customs and Excise are perhaps that it is slow and bureaucratic. However, HMCE Charter lays down standards and performance that can be expected. Some of the more important aspects of HMCE of which buyers should be aware include the following:

- When bringing goods into the UK from outside of the EU, the goods must normally be declared. This is accomplished by the completion of Form C88, the Single Administrative Document (SAD). An alternative to this is to use what is known as direct trader input, where the declaration is made direct to HMCE by computer, for those authorised to do so. Goods from within the EU do not normally need to be declared.

- The *HM Customs and Excise Integrated Tariff of the United Kingdom* (*The Tariff*). This publication, which Butler[14] refers to as the importer's bible, is in three volumes and is published by the Stationery Office. As implied by Butler, the *Tariff* is the main source of information to the importer. It provides information on the classification of products, relief from duty, prohibited and restricted items, rates of duty, preferences, and customs procedures.

- Import charges, due when goods are imported into the UK, can be deferred by up to 30 days. However, an importer needs to be approved in order to do this. This is accomplished by an agreement to pay by direct debit or by providing an approved security.

  Customs charges can be calculated in two ways: ad valorem – by value (by percentage value of goods) – or by unit measurement – a specific amount per item. The *Tariff* lists all the customs duty rates on imported goods. The value for customs duty is calculated by using one of six ways or 'methods', although Method One is the first method that must be tried and is based on the transaction value. It is the stated method used for 90 per cent of imports.

  Some goods brought into the UK may be free of duty or have a reduced rate of duty. This is through such schemes as preference and tariff quota arrangements. Duty relief may also be obtained through such schemes as inward and outward processing relief. Inward processing relief is applicable where an importer in the UK processes its imports and then exports the finished item, i.e. exports the import. Outward processing relief is applicable when a seller exports materials to another country and then reimports them after the goods have been processed or finished, i.e. imports the export.

- Classification of goods is required in order to establish the commodity code for goods. This is necessary in order to prevent paying too much duty and VAT and to help maintain accurate trade statistics. The responsibility for classifying goods remains with the importer, and penalties may be applied if the wrong code is used. In order to classify goods, a full description of the goods is required and a copy of the *Tariff*. The *Tariff* is based on the Combined Nomenclature of the EU, which is based on the Harmonised Commodity Description and Coding System, which is used worldwide. As an example, *Tariff* notice 16/00, issued on 11 October 2000, classified foot propelled scooters under commodity code 8716 8000 00.

- Under Customs Freight Simplified Procedures (CFSP), authorised traders are eligible to use a range of electronic declaration procedures to clear imported goods. The benefits of such procedures include quicker release of goods, as well as better cash flows.

- EU legislation allows for six types of customs warehouse, of which there are only four types in UK. Warehousing allows certain advantages, including suspension and deferment of charges.

- Free zones have been around since the beginning of trade in ancient times, but only since 1984 in UK. UK examples of free zones include Tilbury, Liverpool, Southampton and Birmingham. Goods moved into a free zone do not incur import charges until the goods are moved into the hinterland. During their stay in the free zone, goods may be subjected to a range of prescribed minor processing. The advantages of using a free zone include, regulating cash flows, lower insurance, and flexibility in the supply chain.

- Provided goods are sealed in a container or other means such as a road vehicle, goods can be cleared at an approved inland clearance depot (ICD).

- Although not strictly the domain of HMCE, all goods imported into the UK require an import licence. In UK, this falls under the remit of the Department of Trade and Industry. Licences are needed to protect certain industries, prevent injurious products or materials entering the country, and for surveill-ance purposes. The basis of the licensing system is the open general import licence (OGIL). Goods that are covered therefore do not physically require a licence, it is the legislation that is the licence. Obviously, licences are required for items such as nuclear materials and firearms/ammunition.

12.9 Key elements in successful sourcing abroad

Birou and Fawcett,[15] on the basis of information obtained from 149 purchasing and management executives affiliated to the USA National Association of Pur-chasing Management, state that the key factors in international sourcing which participants considered most important are:

- top management support;
- developing communication skills;
- establishing long-term relationships;
- developing the skills unique to international sourcing.

Four other factors rated as being above average in importance are:

- understanding of international opportunities;
- knowledge of foreign business practices;
- foreign supplier certification/qualification;
- planning for international sourcing.

To these might now be added the following:

- The importance of worldwide information systems. Of particular importance is obtaining expert assistance in the development of an international sourcing strategy. Approaches to obtaining such expertise include:
  - training of in-house staff;
  - finding experts familiar with purchasing in specific geographical areas;
  - establishment of overseas buying offices;
  - use of international subsidiaries;
  - employment of an import broker or merchant.
- The need for purchasing department development and structure.

This latter point is highlighted by Moncza and Trent[16] who identified four stages that a firm goes through as it moves from domestic procurement to a global pur-chasing strategy:

- Phase 1 – domestic purchasing only
- Phase 2 – foreign buying based on need

- Phase 3 – foreign buying as part of procurement strategy
- Phase 4 – integration of global procurement strategy

Phases 1 and 2 are reactive, whereas phases 3 and 4 are reactive.

Moncza and Trent further identified five strategies firms went through in the development of a global strategy:

- Strategy 1 – domestic buyers designated by the business unit for international purchasing.
- Strategy 2 – business units use subsidiaries or other corporate units for international sourcing assistance. This recognises that foreign-based subsidiaries are familiar with the territory and therefore speak the language, have local supplier knowledge and understand the way that business is conducted.
- Strategy 3 – international purchasing offices (IPOs) established throughout the world. If staffed with foreign nationals they offer much the same benefits as strategy 2 but can also be responsible for expediting, negotiating supply contracts, managing quality, etc.
- Strategy 4 – assign design, build and sourcing responsibility to a specific business unit somewhere in the world, i.e. the exploitation of the comparative advantage of that business unit.
- Strategy 5 – integration and coordination of worldwide global sourcing strategy. This involves integration and coordination of procurement requirements and the maximisation of buying leverage on a global basis.

In addition to the above, Schniederjans[17] states that areas that can be considered as critical success factors in global supply management include understanding foreign culture, legal issues, economic issues, procurement channels and supplier selection issues. The first three of these critical success factors are self-explanatory. Schniederjans defines a procurement channel as the order-placing linkage between the purchaser and the supplier. These include:

- The direct channel route – directly from the purchasing organisation to the foreign supplier.
- The home country subsidiary channel – a subsidiary in the home country may have the expertise to deal with foreign suppliers that is absent from the head office.
- The host country subsidiary channel – this allows a global organisation to utilise the expertise of the host country subsidiary, i.e. it acts as an IPO.
- The home country third-party agent channel or host country third-party agent channel – brokers, independent of the global organisation, carry out duties very similar to those of an IPO.

He further suggests that selecting a supplier in a global context should be carried out very thoroughly, perhaps screening potential suppliers against perceived critical success factors.

CJ Engineering (CJE), the brainchild of CJ Henderson the founder, is based in the south of England. It has been in existence for some sixty years. From very humble beginnings, the company has grown and flourished and is now a well established engineering and construction group, operating on an international basis in order to meet the needs of its clients.

CJ Henderson is no longer head of the company. Having held the reins for over fifty years, the company passed on his retirement four years ago to his only child Agnes. Agnes is a graduate in media studies and has a career in television production. Despite the wishes of her father, Agnes installed a managing director (D.M. Bierbaum) to run the company on a day-to-day basis, while she oversaw things as chief executive. The reality of the situation is that Bierbaum runs the company with little interference from Agnes.

The company continues to prosper, particularly as a result of continued operations in the international arena. Bierbaum has recently successfully negotiated for the company to take part in a joint venture along with four other companies from France, America, Switzerland and Taiwan, to design, construct and equip a pulp mill in Catvia, a former State Trading Nation. This will be one of Europe's biggest pulp mills with an annual capacity of 650,000 tonnes of softwood pulp.

In order to keep her appraised of the situation, Bierbaum has prepared a report for Agnes, the salient points being:

- The value of the overall contract is US$940 million, of which approximately US$240 million is the level of business for CJE.
- Catvia is a landlocked country in eastern Europe and the nearest port from the site is 1,200 kilometres away.
- The climate is hostile. During winter months, travel and movement are severely restricted.
- The contract states that local labour has to be used wherever possible.
- Procurement of the goods and services required have to be obtained nationally in Catvia where possible. However, the Catvian government has noted that technical equipment will most likely need to be imported.
- The internal infrastructure is poor.
- The national airline of Catvia has to be used for all air movements.
- Payment is to be made in 50 per cent US dollars, with the remainder being made in Catvian ethnic goods and paper.
- There has been some political instability in Catvia in the past two years, although this now seems to have subsided.
- The duration of the contract is envisaged to be 42 months.
- CJE is to be responsible for some aspects of the design and build and is to be the sole provider of the mill equipment. Some of the equipment is to be procured from South America and is highly technical.

■ Historically, the government of Catvia has been difficult to work with, being particularly rigorous and demanding.

■ Within Catvia, there is a high degree of corruption.

■ It is believed that legal appointments in Catvia are political appointments.

Question

As a consultant to Agnes, write a report addressing the problems likely to be encountered if CJE is to undertake this project, and suggest possible solutions.

 ## Discussion questions

12.1 What difficulties may be encountered when buying abroad? From your own experience, are these difficulties more perceived than real?

12.2 Company A (based in Teeland) has been offered 5,000 mobile phones from Company B (based in Veeland). The terms of the offer state that delivery is DDP (delivered duty paid). What factors will company A have to consider in order to determine whether this offer is acceptable, bearing in mind there is a small local manufacturer of mobile phones in Teeland?

12.3 It is suggested by numerous sources that students should read the business pages of the quality press on a regular basis. With particular reference to global sourcing/international purchasing, why do you think this is necessary and what information would likely be of use to the international buyer?

12.4 Devise a set of terms and conditions suitable for use when buying on an international basis.

12.5 What do you consider to be the main critical success factors when buying abroad?

12.6 You are the purchasing manager of a small but successful engineering company based in the south of England. Because of heavy competition, a number of your suppliers have gone out of business and you are experiencing problems getting adequate quantities of some items. What you can get is often delivered late and the unit price is rapidly rising. Additionally, what you can get is often of an inferior quality standard.

At a recent trade exhibition you attended, you have been lucky in identifying a new source of supply for some of your key items. The quality looks excellent and this potential supplier already supplies a prestigious list of customers. The only problem that you can see is that the company is based in the Far East and you know that your managing director hates the thought of exporting jobs from England. However, you feel that this is an opportunity that cannot be missed and decide to send a report to your managing director. What would you put in your report? What points would you emphasise?

12.7 Using the internet or library, identify some of the trade disputes currently ongoing. What are they about? Do some countries seem to be involved more than others? Do they have any impact for your organisation?

12.8 Discuss whether you think it is possible to have partnerships with suppliers in other countries.

12.9 What effect on purchasing will there be if the EU expands even more?

? Past examination questions

1 Discuss the latest developments with regard to international purchasing in *one* of the following: (a) WTO, or (b) the European Union.

(CIPS, International Purchasing, May 1994)

2 'There are so many potential difficulties in buying from abroad (language problems, currency fluctuations, differing legal systems, etc.), it's a wonder anyone bothers' might be the view of some businesspeople. Discuss the reasons for purchasing from overseas.

(CIPS, International Purchasing, November 1994)

3 It has been estimated by some authorities that up to 25 per cent of the world's trade is not paid purely by currency changing hands. Explain the ways in which these transactions can be carried out, illustrating your answer with examples.

(CIPS, International Purchasing, November 1995)

4 Discuss the factors which lead to international purchasing, and comment on the view that international purchasing is destined to become ever more popular in all parts of the world.

(CIPS, International Purchasing, May 1996)

5 A study made in Sweden in the early part of 1996, came to the conclusion that, with the average customs tariff in the developed world falling to around 3 per cent, it was no longer cost effective to collect customs duties.

What do you think of this view? If this role was to disappear, what other work could a department of customs do?

(CIPS, International Purchasing, May 1997)

6 Every management activity has its current vogue concept. In purchasing and supply chain management one of these is global sourcing.

Discuss the difference between global sourcing and international purchasing.

(CIPS, International Purchasing, May 1997)

7 Quality is an issue that should be in the mind of every purchasing and supply professional. Explain what specific steps you would take to ensure that goods or services bought from abroad would be to an appropriate level of quality.

(CIPS, International Purchasing, November 1997)

8 A Confucian saying states that human beings draw close to one another by their common nature, but habits and customs keep them apart. Discuss how habits and customs and culture can affect negotiation when buying abroad.

(CIPS, International Purchasing, November 1998)

9   The terms 'global sourcing' and 'buying agencies' are often mistakenly understood to mean the same. Identify and discuss the factors that differentiate global sourcing from merely buying abroad.

(CIPS, International Sourcing, May 1999)

10 Discuss why it is necessary for an international buyer to have an understanding of culture when negotiating abroad.

(CIPS, International Purchasing, November 1999)

11 When buying abroad, the buyer is faced by a mass of regulations regarding import and export. Explain how and why these regulations operate. Where possible, illustrate your answers with examples.

(CIPS, International Purchasing, May 2000)

Notes

1.   Birou, L.M. and Fawcett, S.E., 'International purchasing benefits, requirements and challenges', *International Journal of Purchasing and Supply*, Spring 1993, pp.28–37

2.   Stevens, J. 'Global Purchasing in the supply chain', *Purchasing and Supply Management*, January 1995, pp.22–5

3.   Carter, J.R. and Narasimhan, R., 'Purchasing in the international marketplace', *Journal of Purchasing and Materials Management*, September 1990, pp.2–11

4.   Baily, P., Farmer, D., Jessop, D. and Jones, D. *Purchasing Principles and Management*, 8th edn, Pitman, 1998, Ch.13, p.242

5.   Branch, A., *International Purchasing and Management*, Thomson, 2001, Ch.14, p.285

6.   Beardon, R., *Purchasing Management Handbook*, Farmer, P. (ed.) Gower, 1985, p.220

7.   Hill, C., 'International business', *Competing in the Global Market Place*, McGraw-Hill, 1997, p.606

8.   Bennett, R., *International Business*, Pitman Publishers, 1996, p.81.

9.   Salacuse, J., Making *Global Deals*, Houghton Mifflin, 1991, pp.58–70

10. Stevens, J., 'Global purchasing and the rise and rise of countertrade', *Purchasing and Supply Management*, September 1995, pp.28–31

11. Carter, J.R. and Gagne, J., 'The do's and don'ts of countertrade', *Sloan Management Review*, Spring 1988, pp.31–7

12. Forker, L.B., 'Purchasing's views on countertrade', *International Journal of Purchasing and Materials Management*, Spring 1992, pp.10–19

13. Ibid.

14. Butler, J., *The Importer's Handbook*, Woodhead Faulkner, 1994, p.89

15. Birou and Fawcett, as n.1 above

16. Moncza, R.M. and Trent, R.J., 'Global sourcing: a development approach', *International Journal of Purchasing and Materials Management*, Vol.27, No.2 (Spring 1991), pp.2–8

17. Schniederjans, M.J., *Operations Management in a Global Context*, Quorum Books, 1998, pp.71–9

18. The authors are indebted to the CIPS for permission to reproduce this case study set at the November 1999 examination in International Purchasing

PART FOUR

Strategy, tactics and operations (3): logistics

Storing supplies

Learning goals

After reading this chapter you should be able to:

- Define the terms 'storage', 'stocks', 'supplies' and 'customers'.
- Discuss the aims of storage or warehousing.
- List the main stores operations.
- Classify stores according to their location, purpose, operation and characteristics.
- Indicate the main storage methods.
- State the main methods of moving and storing material.
- Distinguish between manual, semi-automated and automated systems of materials handling.
- State the main principles of materials handling.
- List the advantages of automatic, storage and reordering systems.
- Assess storage requirements within a particular organisation.
- Discuss materials flow, materials identification and space utilisation as aspects of stores layout.
- Describe the advantages, characteristics and types of stores coding.
- Distinguish between scrap, obsolescence and waste.
- Analyse the main causes of surplus.
- Indicate ways of salvaging and disposing of surplus.
- Indicate the common law and statutory duties of employers and employees regarding health and safety at work.
- Prepare policy statements relating to health and safety.
- Outline the content of EC directives concerning health and safety.
- Outline the provisions of the Fire Precautions (Workplace) Regulations 1997.

13.1 Storage and supplies

13.1.1 Definition

Storage is the physical holding in stores of stocks or supplies awaiting issue or transport to customers.

In the above definition, the terms 'stocks', 'supplies' and 'customers' are used as follows. *Stocks* are defined by the Chartered Institute of Management Accountants (CIMA)[1] as 'goods of inventory held comprising':

- goods or other assets purchased for resale;
- consumable stores;
- raw materials and components purchased for incorporation into products for sale;
- products and services in intermediate stages of completion (work in progress);
- long-term contract balances;
- finished goods.

Supplies are defined by Compton and Jessop[2] as 'all the materials, goods and services used in an enterprise regardless of whether they are purchased outside, transferred from another branch or manufactured in-house'. The term is less frequently used as applying to 'non-productive stocks used to support productive administration of other functions e.g. maintenance and office supplies'. *Customers* is a term applied to internal (i.e. manufacturing departments) or external (i.e. purchasers) users of stocks or supplies.

13.1.2 The aims of storage

Formerly the emphasis of storage or warehousing was in the efficient *holding* of stocks to meet internal or external customer requirements and avoid losses through wastage, deterioration, theft and obsolescence. Current emphasis is on the *movement* of stocks. This change is due to the following factors:

- Recognition of the need to reduce expenditure on providing storage facilities and handling costs.
- The widespread use of computer-based inventory systems and stores automation.
- The value-based supply chain concept aimed at balancing or optimising such conflicting goals as high customer service, low inventory investment and low operating costs.
- Changes in manufacturing philosophy especially the Japanese *Kanban* (just-in-time) concept (see Chapter 8)
- The development of logistics systems designed to integrate purchasing, transportation, inventory management and warehouse activities to provide the most effective means of meeting the requirements of internal and external customers.

- The 'time compression' concept, which aims to reduce the time consumed by business processes through the elimination of non-value-adding processes. Time is accounted as non-value-adding.[3]

13.1.3 Stores operations

Stores operations comprise the following:

- *Receiving* of stores from outside suppliers or internal departments.
- *Inspection*.
- *Recording* – receipts and issues of supplies either manually or by computerised systems.
- *Security* – protecting stocks against loss through theft or misplacement.
- *Maintenance* – protecting stocks against loss through deterioration from fire, water, weather, vermin.
- *Stock control* – determining the range and quantities of stock or supplies to be held and their receipt and issue.
- *Stocktaking* – checking of stocks and verification of stock records against actual physical quantities held in stock and also those at the work-in-progress stage and finished goods on hand. Stocktaking may be continuous or cyclical, i.e. at regular intervals or at the end of the financial year.
- *Disposal of surplus*, i.e. scrap, components or equipment identified as no longer in use or usable, by donating, reuse, cannibalising or sale.
- *Implementation of health and safety regulations relating to stores and stores staff.*

13.2   Type, location and siting of storage facilities

13.2.1 Types and location

As shown in Figure 13.1, stores can be classified according to their location, purpose, operation and the characteristics of the stocks held.

Location

Outdoor stores (stockyards) are used to store such items as steel sections, tubes, large castings, timber, bricks, sand, gravel and some finished products, e.g. cars and, in general, items which do not incur short- or medium-term deterioration from outdoor exposure.

Indoor stores may be single- or multi-storey and either purpose-built or adapted. The relative advantages of single- and multi-storey buildings respectively include:

Single storey

- Building costs per cubic metre are lower.
- Extensions are easier and cheaper.
- Stores layout can be more flexible.

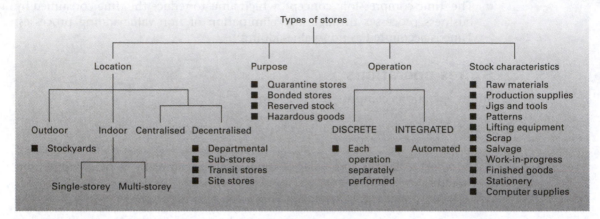

Figure 13.1 Types of stores

- Handling costs of materials are lower except when upper floors permit the use of gravity.
- Fire risks are reduced.

Multi-storey

- Storage capacity on a given site is greater.
- Restricted site space can be better utilised.
- Reduced heat loss since floors provide insulation.
- Gravity can be utilised for delivery of stores to lower levels.

Apart from architectural considerations that arise in relation to the siting and design of a new stores building, the siting of stores as a logistical issue – *centralised* or *decentralised* – can be approached from the standpoint of materials management or physical distribution management (see section 13.3.2 below).

Physical distribution management is concerned with the location of stores or warehouses to which consolidated stocks of finished goods can be delivered to decentralised regional depots for later distribution in smaller quantities to retailers or the point of use.

Materials management includes the issue of stock from stores to production. The perimeter of a works or factory stores may be centralised or decentralised on the principle that a store or stockyard should be sited as near as possible to the point of issue or greatest demand. In the materials management context, all stocks and supplies are received, stored and issued from one location. With decentralised stores, stocks and supplies may be issued by the main or centralised store to departmental or sub-stores to minimise handling and reduce time lost by operatives in visiting the stores – in practice, a combination of centralisation and decentralisation obtains.

13.2.2 **Purpose**

- *Quarantine stores* are used for items requiring inspection before acceptance or issue and should be located near to the point of receipt to avoid unnecessary handling.

- *Bonded stores* are used for items such as spirits and tobacco which are not subject to taxation until the stocks are released. The store is bonded by Customs and Excise to ensure payment on the release of the stock.
- *Reserve stores* are used for free issue materials supplied by customers or non-standard materials and components bought for a specific job or contract and stored separately until required for use.
- *Hazardous goods stores* are used for explosives, inflammable goods, dangerous chemicals, etc., which, for safety reasons, must have additional security and be located away from the main plant.

13.2.3 Operation

Stores operations may be regarded as discrete or integrated. Discrete operations, either manual or mechanical, are separately performed and necessarily related to those preceding or following as distinct from the integration provided by automated storage, handling and retrieval systems (see section 13.5 below).

- *Stock characteristics.* As indicated by the title, this categorisation refers to the different classes of stock kept within a particular stores location.
- *Siting of stores.* This matter can be approached from several aspects: external marketing, internal production, safety and architectural. Some general factors relating to siting include:
  - *Geographical* – the areas to be served having regard to the largest stores consuming units.
  - *Transport* – to facilitate both inward and outward movement of items. Especially important are good road access which should, if possible, be free from traffic congestion and where appropriate the possibility of rail sidings to enable direct loading and unloading.
  - *Essential services* – e.g. water, gas, electricity, sanitation.
  - *Space* – for current use and provision for future extension.

Other factors include availability of suitable land and availability of government or local authority grants.

13.3 Storage and materials handling equipment

Storage equipment can be categorised under three headings: storage methods, handling and picking.

13.3.1 Storage methods

As shown in Figures 13.2 and 13.3, storage, as distinct from handling equipment, is concerned with (i) storage methods and (ii) the forms in which material is moved and stored.

Two important items of storage equipment are pallets and racking.

Free stacking	Shelving and bins	Pallet racking	Drive-in or drive-through racking	Mobile racking	Live racking	Automatic retrieval systems	Automatic flow through racks
Bulk material Stacks of packages Stacks of units Intermediate bulk containers	Non-adjustable Semi-adjustable Readily adjustable Cantilever	Adjustable beam Tubular Cantilever		Mechanically assisted Manually operated Power operated	Gravity or incline Horizontal powered conveyor	Stacker crane Truck	Power driven with elevators and robot platform

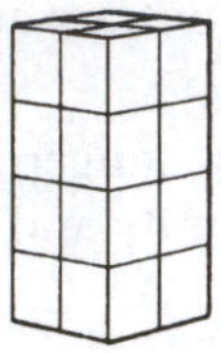

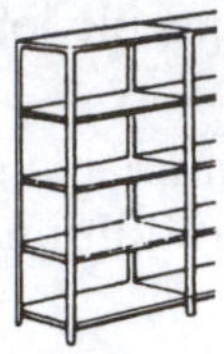

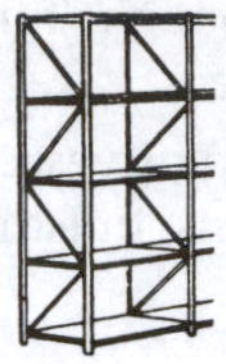

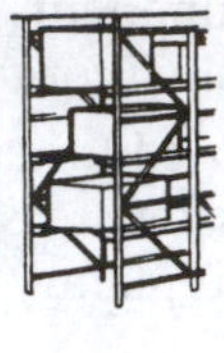

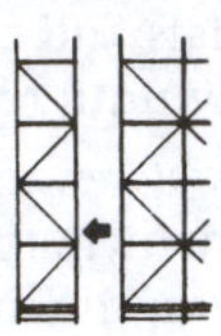

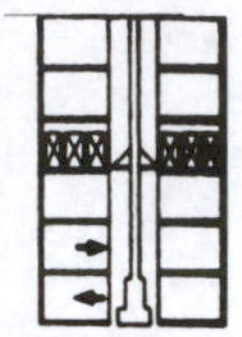

Figure 13.2 Storage methods

Bulk	Piece parts	Package	Unit load – supported	Unit load – without support	Intermediate bulk container	Container
Liquids Solids Pastes	Castings Forgings Components etc.	Bag/sack Drum Cask Cylinder	Pallets Stillages Post pallets Box pallets	Built-in units Shrink wrapped Stretch wrapped Strapped	Metal Plastic Other materials	End-loading Side-loading Top-loading

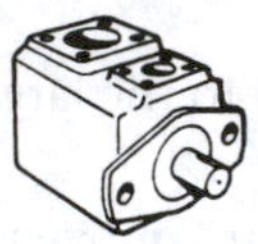

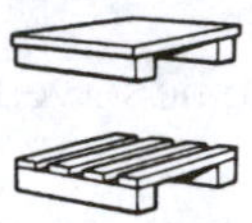

Figure 13.3 Forms in which material is moved and stored

Pallets

A pallet is defined by BS 2629 (BS ISO 6780) as:

> A load board with two decks separated by bearers, blocks or feet or a single deck supported by bearers, blocks or feet constructed with a view to transport and stacking, and with the overall height reduced to a minimum compatible with handling by fork-lift trucks and pallet trucks.

Pallets can be categorised by:

- form of entry, i.e. one-, two- or four-way entry;
- construction material, e.g. wood, corrugated metal, wire mesh, aluminium, expandable fibreboard;
- shape, e.g. basket, box pallets.

BS 2629 Part 1 provides standards for the dimensions, materials and marking of pallets for the unit load method of materials handling for through transport purposes. Part 2 makes recommendations for pallets for use as freight containers.

The principal benefits of palletisation are:

■ standardisation of loads moved by standardised equipment, transported in standardised vehicles;

■ better utilisation of storage space;

■ saving of time and labour in loading and unloading vehicles;

■ reducing damage to goods in transit;

■ delivery of supplies on pallets provided either by the supplier or purchaser to the supplier, enables the items to go straight into store plus minimises handling;

■ promotion of cleanliness, good housekeeping and, since goods are kept off the floor, easier handling.

Racks

Racks are frameworks designed to facilitate the storage of loads and usually comprise upright columns and horizontal members by supporting loads which are diagonally braced for security.

Pallet racks are simply shelves for pallets which makes it possible to remove the unit load at the bottom of the stack without disturbing those above it. Racks may be specially designed to stack, drums, containers, plates, sheets, bars, tubes, tyres, etc. Mobile racks are racks mounted onto rolling carriages and can be banked together in blocks requiring only one access aisle thus saving space.

13.3.2 Materials handling

Materials handling has three main aspects:

■ *Physical* – the movement, handling and storage of materials considered as materials flow into, through and away from an enterprise.

■ *Management* – the effective planning, control, review and improvement of the movement, handling and storage of materials and the associated management information.

■ *Technology* – the techniques of movement, handling and storage of materials and the associated management and information systems.

Main principles of materials handling

The main principles of materials handling are as follows:

■ *Planning principle* – all handling activities should be planned.

■ *Systems principle* – integrating as many handling activities as is possible and coordinating the full scope of operations covering supplier, receiving, storage, production, inspection packaging, warehousing, dispatch, transportation and customer.

- *Materials flow principle* – plan an operation sequence and equipment arrangement to optimise materials flow.
- *Simplification principle* – reduce, combine or eliminate unnecessary movements and equipment.
- *Gravity principle* – utilise gravity to move materials whenever possible.
- *Space utilisation principle* – make optimum use of building cubes.
- *Unit size principle* – increase quantity, size, weight of load handled. A unit load may be defined as:

  A number of items, or bulk material so arranged or restrained that the mass can be picked up and moved as a single project, too large for manual handling, and, upon being released, will retain its initial arrangement for subsequent movement.

- *Mechanisation selection principle* – use mechanised or automated handling equipment when practicable.
- *Equipment selection principle* – in selecting handling equipment, consider all aspects of the *material* to be handled, the *move* to be made and the *method(s)* to be utilised.
- *Standardisation principle* – standardise methods as well as types and sizes of handling equipment.
- *Adaptability principle* – use methods and equipment that can perform a variety of tasks and applications.
- *Dead-weight principle* – reduce the ratio of dead weight of mobile handling equipment to load carrier.
- *Utilisation principle* – reduce idle or unproductive time of both handling equipment and labour.
- *Maintenance principle* – plan for preventive maintenance and scheduled repair of all handling equipment.
- *Obsolescence principle* – replace obsolete handling methods and equipment when more efficient methods or equipment will improve operations.
- *Control principle* – use materials handling equipment to improve production control, inventory control and order handling.
- *Capacity principle* – use handling equipment to achieve full production capacity.
- *Performance principle* – determine efficiency of handling performance per unit.
- *Safety principle* – provide suitable methods and equipment for safe handling.

Types of materials handling system

Materials handling systems can take three main forms:

- *Manual systems* where items are stored, picked and issued by stores staff who will use powered equipment for heavier items.
- *Semi-automated systems* using a combination of human labour and computer-controlled machines.

■ *Automated systems* in which all the physical movement is carried out by computer controlled machinery.

Mechanical handling

Mechanical handling is the term applicable to the use of mechanical aids to handling ranging from hand to forklift trucks with or without the use of power. In general, mechanical handling is applicable when:

■ loads are in excess of 23 kg;

■ handling requires two or more persons;

■ travel time is greater than lifting and placing time;

■ space above floor level can be utilised.

As shown by Figures 13.4 and 13.5 there are in essence four categories of handling equipment: conveyors, lifting, mobile and stacking.

Equipment selection

Selecting the most appropriate type and size of equipment entails:

■ *handling* considerations, i.e. the product, quantities, frequency, distances, routes and utilisation of storage space;

■ *equipment* considerations, i.e. flexibility, adaptability, safety, availability of equipment and spares, estimated life;

■ *cost* considerations, i.e. fixed and variable costs directly and indirectly associated with the equipment acquisition and operation

Fixed costs include: interest in the investment, depreciation, capital allowances, insurance. Variable costs include: operatives' wages, fuel/power, maintenance and servicing.

Automated storage, handling and retrieval systems

Platts[4] states that an automated materials handling and retrieval system (AMHRS) can be understood as a materials handling system under the real-time control of a computer system. It can, in fact, be regarded as a computer system integrated with one or more materials handling components.

Types of AMHRS

Three categories of each equipment can be identified:

■ *Free path equipment*, which moves under the control of an on-board computer across normal floors following, but not physically connected to, some form of guide such as a wire in the floor emitting signals or a painted line. These use a horizontal transport vehicle, e.g. a forklift truck, usually termed an automated guided vehicle, to move a load from point to point.

Conveying equipment

Category	Type	Descriptor	Descriptor	Examples
Transporting	Towing mechanism			Overhead towline trolley conveyors, In-floor towline trolley conveyors, Robot tugs
	Powered conveyors – Continuous carrying			Flat belt; troughed; closed belt; carrier and chain conveyors
	Powered conveyors – Linked carriers			Bucket, *en masse*, apron and pan conveyors, crossbar conveyors
	Powered conveyors – Detachable carriers			Overhead trolley conveyors, Overhead chain conveyors
	Powered conveyors – Continuous carriers	Powered		Powered roller conveyors, Pneumatic conveyors, Air film conveyors
Conveying equipment	Free-rolling	Line	Unpowered	Roller, wheel and ball trucks
	Sliding	Unpowered	Intermittent	Chutes
	Propelling	Powered	Continuous	Screw conveyors, Spiral elevators
	Vibrating	Powered	Continuous	Vibratory feeders, screens, elevators

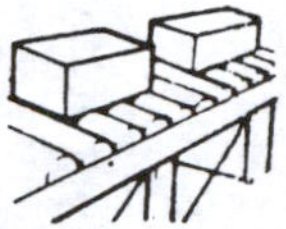

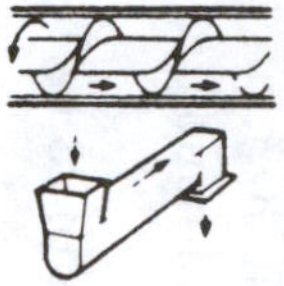

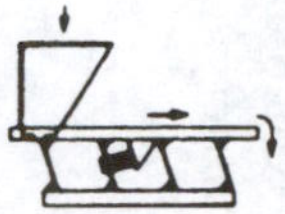

In conveyors of this type the transporting mechanism travels forward with the material conveyed

In conveyors of this type the transporting mechanism does not itself travel forward

Figure 13.4 Handling equipment: continuous movement

Lifting equipment

Vertical and horizontal positioning

		Point	Line		Area			
		Guided	Free	Straight	Curved	Angular	Circular	Angular and circular	Un-restricted
		Jacks, elevating tables	Capstans, winches	Girder trolleys Fixed girder	Overhead monorails	Travelling bridge and gantry cranes	Revolving cranes, jib cranes	Hinged jib loading cranes	Mobile cranes

Mobile equipment

	Horizontal movement		Lifting and horizontal movement
	Line	Area	Area
	Guided	Free	Free
	Rail vehicles	Powered and manual trucks and trolleys	Straddle trucks Stillage trucks

Stacking equipment

Horizontal and vertical movement

Un-restricted	Restricted
Fork lift trucks Reach trucks Stacking trucks	Narrow aisle trucks In-aisle stacker trucks

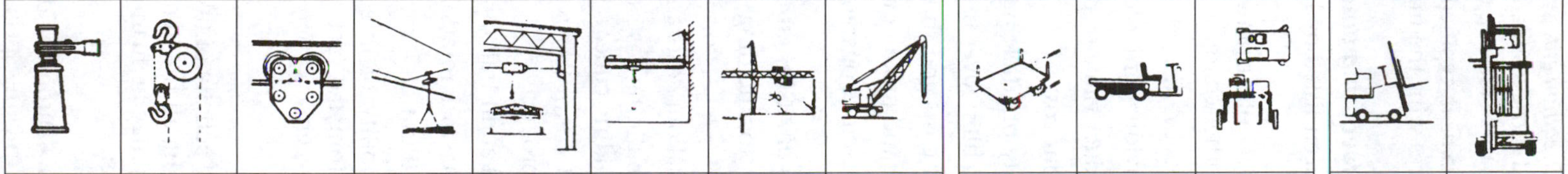

Figure 13.5 Handling equipment: discontinuous movement

- *Fixed path equipment*, which uses a vehicle running on a rail or rails which stores and retrieves loads on shelving or in racks. This is frequently known as an automated stacking crane.
- *Static equipment*, typified by a conveyor system which moves the load on moving surfaces with the unit itself remaining in place.

Conditions favouring automated storage and handling

These have been listed by Firth[5] as:

- A high level of sustained throughput without major fluctuations due to seasonal or other charges.
- Low product range.
- High individual order lots.
- High product value or profitability.
- High labour costs.
- Availability of article numbering systems.
- Market stability over time and particular product size stability.
- High unit costs and shortage of land.
- Unit load and product modularity.
- Round-the-clock operation.

Advantages of ASRS (automated storage and reordering systems)

- Reduced stockholding owing to improved stock location and reordering capability.
- Reduced labour costs and manning levels.
- Reduced building costs owing to higher storage densities and better utilisation of the building cube.
- Improved control of work in progress reducing the capital tied up in part-finished products.
- Improved audit trail owing to the automatic recording of stock movements.
- Automatic stock rotation (first in, first out).
- Greater utilisation – round-the-clock working if necessary.
- The possibility of integrating automated materials handling (AMH) into a single automated factory; AMH may reduce manufacturing labour costs by 25–35 per cent.

Picking

Picking is the activity of taking stock or supplies from bins, racks or other devices and assembling all the items specified on an issue note or other form of instruction. Picking may be manual or automated. Automated picking systems include the following:

- *'A' frames* – automatic dispensing of items onto a central conveyor collection belt at set picking speeds.

■ *Pick light systems* – picking is activated by the operator choosing an order number or scanning a bar code representing the item number. The computer sends a signal to a pick-face or read-out unit attached to the static flow rack which uses a flashing light to direct the operator to the item and to indicate the number of items to be picked.

■ *Radio frequency directed picking* – permits the interactive exchange of information including online enquiries and record and file updates between a host computer and an operator using a portable or mobile radio frequency (RF) terminal who is presented with pick directions. Can be used with any type of lift truck and storage rack.

■ *Robotic order selection* – the robot is a picking device usually fitted with a vacuum head selector mounted to a small automatic storage and retrieval arm or crane. The robotic selector's computer directs the crane to move into position along the rack to a particular storage location, place the required item into an onboard collecting basket and deliver the items to a waiting carton at the end of the aisle.

13.4   Assessment of storage requirements

Too much storage entails unnecessary expenditure on rent, rates, heating, water and maintenance (typically building and building services costs can be as high as 35–40 per cent of total annual storage costs). Too little storage results in inefficiency due to unsuitable storage locations, methods and material flow. Assessment of storage requirements entails consideration of both general stores objectives and specific factors relating to stocks and supplies within the particular organisation.

13.4.1   General stores objectives

■ Most efficient use of the space provided by the building cube.

■ Rapid and easy access to stock for input and output movements and verification.

■ Efficient and balanced patterns of traffic flow.

■ Mechanisation and automation as appropriate to stores operations.

■ Minimal travel distance of stock movements.

■ Positive location and identifications of stocks and supplies.

■ Grouping of products with similar storage characteristics and according to frequency of receipts and issues.

■ Maximum protection and security of stores items.

■ An orderly and efficient stores appearance.

13.4.2   Specific organisational factors

This involves obtaining data, usually by means of a storage analysis sheet, relating to the following:

- The estimated relative space requirements for each category of stocks – raw materials, components, sub-assemblies, maintenance items and special forms of storage.
- What stores are to be centralised or decentralised.
- Physical characteristics of stores at each location i.e. size, weight, shape, perishable, hazardous.
- Handling and flow of stores – frequency of handling, quantities handled at each location, distances, height, weight and bulk factors, turning requirements (for forklift trucks).
- Goods arrival factors – quantities, volume, frequency, packing, delivery, vehicles, whether items are subject to inspection or straight into store.
- Storage methods and equipment, e.g. pallets, racks, bins, containers.
- Goods dispatch factors, e.g. frequency and methods of issue, issue quantities, packaging.
- Inventory policy – just-in-time, buffer stocks, stockpiling.
- Security and safety – special arrangements for bonded stores, supplies awaiting inspection. Factory Act and other legislation relating to cleanliness, ventilation, lighting, lifting tackle, floor construction, fire precautions.
- Administration – office space and welfare amenities for stores staff and provision of stores records.

13.5 Stores layout

Stores layout can be considered from the aspects of (i) materials flow and (ii) materials identification and location and space utilisation. Two fundamental influences in stores layout are the shape of the stores building and the type of flow throughout the building. The Institute of Logistics' publication *Principles of Warehouse Design* identifies four types of layout deriving from the above two factors.[6] These are reproduced in Figures 13.6–13.9.

13.5.1 Inverted T warehouse flow

In the layout shown in Figure 13.6:

- goods in and goods out activities are on the same side of the building;
- shape allows the use of high, medium and low usage areas to minimise materials handling by locating high and low usage areas respectively nearest to and furthest from the goods received and goods outwards areas, thus minimising materials handling for high usage items.

Advantages claimed for this layout include the following:

- Better utilisation of receiving and issue areas and the associated mechanical handling equipment.

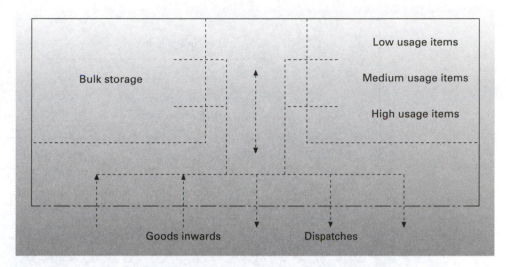

Figure 13.6 The inverted T warehouse flow

Source: Institute of Logistics, *Principles of Warehouse Design*, 1993. Reproduced with permission

- The total area required is less than where there are separate loading and unloading areas.
- Facility to extend the building (subject to site constraints) on one or more of three sides.
- Unified bay operations provide for better security control and easier surveillance.

The main disadvantage is that the centre aisle may become congested in high throughput situations.

13.5.2 Crossflow warehouse flow

The flow in this type of layout (see Figure 13.7) is a one-way system with an 'in-feed' aisle and a separate 'out-flow' from the other end of the racks. Front entry and dispatches uses a common yard area and the layout retains the benefits of the inverted T approach. Stock management benefits from the integration of bulk and picking stocks, but if bulk stocks are a large proportion of total stock this may not be practical.

13.5.3 Corner warehouse flow

In the corner warehouse flow, as shown in Figure 13.8, inward and outward flows are on adjacent but different sides of the building. This layout helps to reduce congestion of aisles in times of high throughput. The disadvantages are that expansion is possible only on the two sides without doors. As the activities in the yard and within the store are not visible from a single vantage point, there are potential problems in security and surveillance.

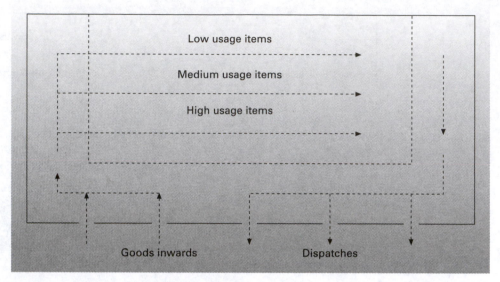

Figure 13.7 The crossflow warehouse flow

Source: Institute of Logistics, *Principles of Warehouse Design*, 1993. Reproduced with permission

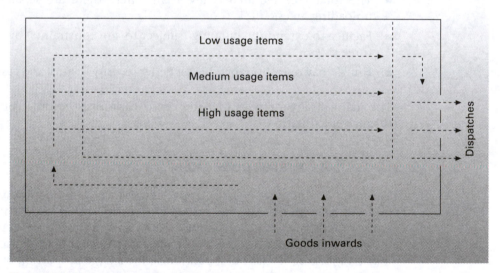

Figure 13.8 The corner warehouse flow

Source: Institute of Logistics, *Principles of Warehouse Design*, 1993. Reproduced with permission

13.5.4 Throughflow warehouse

In the throughflow warehouse, as shown in Figure 13.9, goods inwards and outwards are on opposite sides of the building. All items must therefore travel the full length of the store. The layout also requires separate goods in and dispatch management with dual yard access and doubles the internal bay areas.

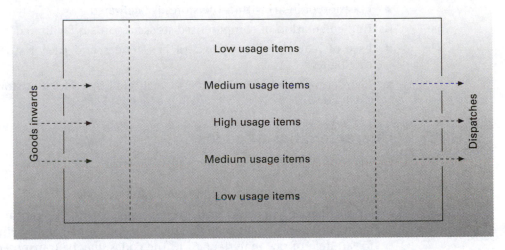

Figure 13.9 The throughflow warehouse

Source: Institute of Logistics, *Principles of Warehouse Design*, 1993. Reproduced with permission

The layout is useful where the goods in and out vehicle requirement is different, such as in their platform height, or where the nature of the unit load warrants the separation of the two facilities.

Disadvantages include the limitation of future extensions of the building.

13.6 Identification of stock items

Identification of a particular stock item and its location within the stores requires some form of code.

13.6.1 Definition

A code is defined by CIMA as:

> A system of symbols designed to be applied to a classified set of items, to give a brief accurate reference facilitating entry, collation and analysis.

13.6.2 Advantages of codes

These can be recalled by using the mnemonic SUPPLIER:

- Simplicity – avoidance of possible long and detailed item descriptions.
- Unique codes assist accurate identification and error avoidance.
- Promotion of standardisation, variety reduction and avoidance of duplication.
- Pricing and costing are simplified.

- Location of items within the stores is facilitated.
- Implementation of computerised stocks records is facilitated.
- Ease of requisitioning by use of brief codes and use of stores vocabulary/ catalogues.
- Reordering and purchasing is also facilitated by codes and stores vocabulary/ catalogues.

13.6.3 Characteristics of codes

Goods coding systems should have the following characteristics:

- *Uniqueness* – each item should have only one code.
- *Distinctiveness* – to avoid errors, codes representing different items should, so far as is possible, be distinctive. Thus, if a code for a component is 5.5513 and for an item of raw material 6.5513 the codes may be transposed even though they are unique.
- *Clarity* – codes should be entirely alphabetical or numerical. The latter are preferable for computer applications. Avoid the use of brackets, colons, dashes or strokes.
- *Brevity* – consistent with the requirements of the classification system, codes should be as brief as possible.
- *Expandable* – codes should be able to cope with new or additional items.
- *Unambiguous* – in alphabetical systems the letters I, O, Q, S and G should, where possible, be avoided because of their similarity to other letters.
- *Significant* – the code should signify something about the coded item, a code for a 165×13 tyre would include 165.
- *Mnemonic* – with alphabetical codes the code should, by letters or an acronym, to aid the memory e.g. MSJ for mild steel joists.

13.6.4 Types of code

Most codes fall into one of three categories, described below.

Alphabetic

Alphabetic codes have the advantage of a repertoire of 26 letters against 10 numbers and can have a mnemonic element, e.g. MSRD where the first two letters might refer to the materials, i.e. mild steel, the third to the shape, i.e. round, and the fouth to the dimension, e.g. 20 mm. They are, however, easily confused, unsuitable for computerisation and have limited application unless the range of stock is limited.

Alphanumeric

An alphanumeric system such as the National Supply Vocabulary has been used by the NHS since 1971 and by government departments since 1991. The coding system comprises three alpha characters, followed by four numerics. The first alpha character defines one of 26 sections A–Z. The second, the group, and the third the subgroup. (Each section can have as many as 26 groups, each of which contains up to 26 subgroups) the numerics are added subsequently and have no significance, for example:

R – Raw materials, tools, plant and equipment

RG – Materials – decorating

RJG – Paint – emulsion, masonry, oil, undercoat

RGJ0116 – Paint, aerosol, acrylic, 400 ml, gloss green

Numerical

Numerical codes use numbers only and are more frequently used. National/international numerical codes include the following

- *MESC.* The Materials and Equipment Standards and Code was developed by the Royal Dutch/Shell Group. The complete MESC number consists of ten numeric digits and allows for all commodities to be classified within 100 main groups, 100 subgroups and 200 sub-subgroups, e.g.:

Group 03	Drilling and production tools
Subgroup 32	Swivels and circulating heads
Sub-subgroup 59	Ideal type N. 24 swivels

- *NATO Codification System.* This is a set of rules on the subject of identifying and numbering millions of items stocked and provided for use by the armed forces of NATO countries. The code is always a 13 digit number comprising a 4 digit class code number, a 2 digit nation code and a 7 digit item number. For example:

NATO supply number	Class code	NATO nation code number	National identification number
Group 26	2610 Tyres and tubes	99 United Kingdom	809–3160 Denotes that the UK has identified the item and allocated this number
Class	Tyres and tubes, pneumatic except aircraft		which is non-significant in the sense that it cannot be translated to reveal the type of item to which it is allocated

- *BRISCH Classification and Coding.* The BRISCH organisation provides classification and coding especially created to meet the needs of a particular organisation. Each item is first allocated a classification which enables its accurate and unambiguous identification according to its permanent characteristics. Following classification, a code, wholly numerical and of constant length is designed which symbolises the classification categories and, at the same time, identifies every item by a unique set of digits appertaining to the particular item. For example:

Classification	25000	Jointings, tubes, pipes, pipe fittings for liquids and gases
Group	25600	Cocks, valves and their spares and accessories
Subgroup	25610	Cocks, valves, plug, type, cocks
Series	25613	Cocks, plug straight, squarehead
Nominal bore	404	WP 150 psi Steam without Gland ends screwed. BSP. Female ½"

The code 25613–404 would translate as copper alloy plug cock to 150 psi working pressure, without gland, ends screwed ½ inch BSP female.

- *Bar codes*. See section 2.6 in Chapter 2.

- *Colour codes*. These are simply colours painted or otherwise applied to the actual materials or components to provide a ready means of identification. Thus, possibly, red for steel, white for iron, blue for aluminium. A second colour can provide further information, e.g. red and green for mild steel, red and yellow for high carbon steel, red and blue for molybdenum.

- *Self-validating codes*. These aim to prevent common coding errors such as the transposition of digits or keying in wrong numbers. One verification system involves multiplying each digit in the code by a different number and using an agreed number (usually 11) as a divisor. If the code number is 423-275-552 this might be:

$$(4 \times 1) + (2 \times 2) + (3 \times 3) + (2 \times 4) + (7 \times 5) + (5 \times 6) + (5 \times 7) + (2 \times 8)$$

$$= 4 + 4 + 9 + 8 + 35 + 30 + 35 + 16$$

$$= \frac{121}{11}$$

$$= 11$$

The number 11 divides exactly into 121 indicating that there is no remainder. The check digit is therefore 0 and the code number becomes 423-275-552-0. If the code is wrongly keyed as 423-275-552, the final digit would be:

$$(4 \times 1) + (2 \times 2) + (4 \times 3) + (2 \times 4) + (7 \times 5) + (5 \times 6) + (5 \times 7) + (2 \times 8)$$

$$= 4 + 4 + 12 + 8 + 35 + 30 + 35 + 16$$

$$= \frac{144}{11}$$

$$= 13 + 1 \text{ remainder}$$

The figure 1 instead of 0 would indicate an error in coding.

13.7 Surplus

'Surplus' is an omnibus term covering materials or equipment that are in excess of requirements, no longer usable in their original form, or are superseded. Most such items can be categorised as 'scrap' or obsolete. *Scrap* is defined by the *Oxford Dictionary of Accountancy* as 'what is left of an asset at the end of its useful life which may have a salvage value. The waste from the production process which may have a salvage value'. *Obsolete* means that an item has gone out of use or has been superseded by equipment offering enhanced advantages such as speed, productivity, versatility or economy of operation. An obsolete item may, however, still be usable and have value. Various aspects of waste are considered in Chapters 5, 14 and 18.

The above definitions emphasise that surplus, whether scrap or obsolete items, may still have value and this should be realised as a contribution to the reduction of losses and an enhancement to profitability. Many undertakings have waste reduction programmes aimed at reducing losses due to scrap or obsolescence. Purchasing can play a major part in such programmes which normally involve the following activities.

13.7.1 Ascertaining surplus

A distinction can be made between *surplus* and *residue*, the latter term applying to no-value waste resulting from production operations. Such residue must be disposed of in the most efficient manner having regard to environmental directives and considerations designed to avoid pollution and other health hazards.

Although the amount of scrap can be reduced by careful purchasing, stores and production control, some scrap is inevitable. This scrap should, so far as possible, be collected in containers as near as possible to the point of origin and appropriately segregated, e.g. into ferrous or non-ferrous metals. Segregation can be facilitated by appropriate colour codings, e.g. red for mild steel, white for cast iron, blue for carbon steel, etc. Periodically, the contents of the containers will be transferred to centralised bins for disposal.

Surplus materials, components or equipment may remain in stock for long periods, occupying valuable storage space unless identified by an efficient stock control system. The algorithm for the identification of obsolete and slow-moving stock, shown in Figure 13.10, has been devised by Hollier and Cook.[7]

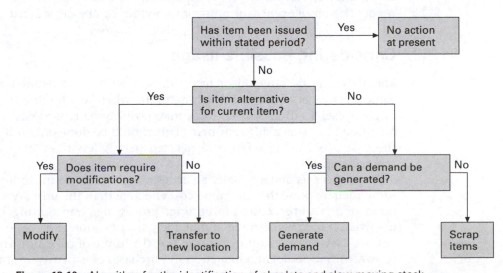

Figure 13.10   Algorithm for the identification of obsolete and slow-moving stock

13.7.2 Analysing causes

Having ascertained the quantities and varieties of scrap and obsolete or slow-moving material, components or equipment, the next step is to analyse the reasons why such surplus has arisen with a view to its future reduction or prevention. Such causes include:

- *Overbuying* – possibly to take advantage of favourable terms of discounts without regard to holding costs.

- *Overstocking* – to avoid production breakdowns or due to estimating demand.

- *Stockpiling* – in anticipation of price increases or material shortage.

- *Inefficient specification* – buying in sizes which result in excessive offcuts.

- *Inadequate stock control* – allowing surplus to simply remain in store thus incurring unnecessary holding costs. Overissues. Non-return of surplus.

- *Changes in design* – which may render stocks of materials and components surplus.

- *Duplication of description* – two names for the same item.

- *Production inefficiencies* – production should monitor scrap loss relative to operators, machines and operations to ascertain:

$$\text{Yield levels} = \frac{\text{Number of good units produced}}{\text{Total number of units produced}}$$

$$\text{Scrap rates} = \frac{\text{Number of units scrapped}}{\text{Number of good units produced}}$$

$$\text{Rework rate} = \frac{\text{Number of units reworked}}{\text{Number of good units produced}}$$

- *Breakages and deterioration* – through handling or inefficient stock preservation.

- *Incorrect procurement* – some equipment is better leased than purchased to obviate obsolescence, or non-core activities can be outsourced.

13.7.3 Considering possible usage

Materials may be salvaged or recycled. Salvage may be defined as the realistic value of an asset at the end of its useful life when it is no longer suitable for its original use. Scrap or spoiled work may possibly be reprocessed to enable it to be utilised to make a different item. This should be done only if it is certain that the cost of salvaging scrap or a rejected part is less than the expenditure on reprocessing.

Recycled, or secondary, materials are especially useful to the industries that consume them because they are more cost effective than the primary variety because none of the initial costs of running, processing, transporting or smelting is involved. It has been estimated that every tonne of metal recycled in Britain represents a saving of 1.5 tonnes of iron ore, 0.5 tonne of coke and when tin plate is recovered, a 3–5 kilogram reduction in purchases of expensive primary tin. There is also the environmental factor that when discarded products are allowed to stay out of the recycling system they may pollute air, land and water and disfigure the countryside.

With components and equipment, consideration should be given to:

- possible use elsewhere in the organisation;
- the salvaging or 'cannibalising' of useful parts prior to disposal;
- whether some renovating or repairing may increase the saleability of the equipment and enhance its value.

13.7.4 Disposal of surplus

Disposal of surplus is frequently entrusted to purchasing. A number of options are available. For scrap, whether metal, wood, paper or other materials the best course is disposal to a recognised broker. The term 'recognised' means a broker affiliated to an appropriate body such as the British Metals Federation.

Better prices may be negotiated if:

- the seller keeps abreast of the current scrap prices; the price of scrap is quoted daily on the London Metal Exchange;
- the scrap is segregated according to the buyer's requirements;
- scrap is suitably bailed.

Equipment or components may be disposed of:

- by sale through the trade press;
- by sale to a stockist or dealer;
- by auction or through trade auctions;
- return to the supplier – usually this will be at a discount but stock will have been turned into cash;
- sale to employees – especially cars, computers and office equipment;
- donations to charitable organisations.

13.8 Health and safety

13.8.1 The legal background

Health and safety at work is covered both by common law (i.e. law based on the decisions of judges) and Acts of Parliament termed statutes which comprise statute law. All Acts of Parliament are statutes; some statutes, however, such as orders in council are not Acts of Parliament. European Community law takes precedence over domestic law and it is now always necessary to consider not only domestic case law and statutes but also relevant EC Treaty law.

13.8.2 Duties of employers

Common law

The common law duties employers are to ensure:

- a safe place of work;
- safe plant and equipment;
- a safe system of work;
- reasonably competent fellow employees.

Statute law

The Health and Safety at Work Act 1974 (HSWA) (as amended by the Sex Dis-crimination Act 1986, Fire Safety of Places of Sport Act 1987 and the Employment Act 1989) remains law, but since 1 January 1993 has been supplemented by the Health and Safety at Work Regulations arising from European health and safety directives.

It is ultimately intended to replace all existing safety legislation with regula-tions and codes of practice under HSWA 1974. To facilitate this transfer of juris-diction, the Act absorbs the inspectorates created under the Factories Act 1961, Explosives Act 1875 and Mines and Quarries Act 1954 into a single Health and Safety Executive (HSE). The most important effects of the Act are the following.

General section 2 of the 1974 Act provides that it is the duty of every employer to ensure, so far as is 'reasonably practical', the health and safety at work of all its employees. There are four important aspects of this statement:

1 What is 'reasonably practical' involves an assessment by the employer of the risks to health and safety and the costs of safeguarding against them. If, for example, a risk is slight and the cost of safeguarding against it would be disproportionately high, the employer might be able to prove that it was not reasonably practical to take, or to have taken, the necessary protective meas-ures. The employer, must, however, be able to prove that he or she had assessed the risk and cost and show how this was done. In general, if something is prac-ticable, the courts are reluctant to rule it was not reasonably practical to do it. It is reasonably practical for employers to know changes in the law affecting their operations and to keep abreast of relevant HSE publications.

2 'Employers' for this purpose includes persons on government training schemes.

3 The matters to which the employers' duty extend include in particular:
   (a) the provision and maintenance of plant and systems of work that are, so far as is reasonably possible, safe and without risk to health;
   (b) arrangements for ensuring, so far as is reasonably practical, safety and absence of risks to health, in connection with the use, handling, storage and transport of articles and substances;
   (c) the provision of such information, instructions, training and supervision as is necessary to ensure, so far as is reasonably practical, the health and safety at work of employees;

(d) so far as is reasonably practical as regards any place of work under the employer's control, the maintenance of that place in a condition that is safe and without risks to health and the provision and maintenance of means of access and egress from it that are safe and without such risks.

4   The provision and maintenance of a working environment for employees, that is, so far as is reasonably practicable, safe without risks to health, and adequate as regards facilities and arrangements for their welfare at work.

13.8.3 Policy statements

Except where fewer than five people are employed, there is duty on employers to prepare and, as appropriate, revise, written statements relating to the health and safety of employees. These statements and their revisions must:

■ be brought to the notice of all employees;
■ give details of the organisation and arrangements that are in operation for the implementation of the policy;
■ be incorporated into appropriate procedures and rules.

Policy statements should be approved by the recognised trade unions before issue.

The HSE publication *Writing your Health and Safety Policy Statement* provides an outline policy statement in three sections.

Example 13.1   Outline health and safety policy statement

Section A
General statements of policy
Our policy is to provide and maintain safe and healthy working conditions, equipment and systems of work for all employees, and to provide such information, training and supervision as they need for this purpose. We also accept our responsibility for the health and safety of other people who may be affected by our activities.

The allocation of duties for safety matters and the particular arrangements which we will make to implement the policy are set out below:

The policy will be kept up to date, particularly as the business changes in nature and size. To ensure, the policy and the way in which it has operated will be reviewed every year.

There then follows:

■ The name and position of the person with overall and final responsibilities for health and safety in the undertaking.
■ The name and position of the person responsible for the policy being carried out on the premises.
■ The names of the supervisors responsible for safety in particular areas of the undertaking.
■ A general statement that all employees have a responsibility to cooperate with supervisors and managers to achieve a healthy and safe workplace and to take reasonable care of themselves and others.

- Arrangements for consultation on health and safety between management and employees.
- The names of other people (if any) responsible for:
  - safety training
  - carrying out safety inspections
  - investigating accidents
  - monitoring maintenance of plant and equipment

Section B
General arrangements relating to:

- *Accidents* – including the location of first aid boxes, names and locations of trained/qualified first aiders and the location of the accident record.
- *General fire safety* – detailed escape routes, locations of fire extinguishers, and fire alarms, the names and locations of persons responsible for checking equipment and the frequency of such checks.
- *Advice and consultation* – the name, address and telephone number of the local health and safety inspector and other sources of advice and support such as safety consultants and the works doctor and nurse.
- *Training* – the names and locations of persons responsible for health and safety training and details of special training for hazardous jobs.
- *Contracts and visitors* – house rules including arrangements for ensuring that such visitors are informed of, and accept, the health and safety rules of the undertaking.

Section C
Hazards relating to (as appropriate):

- *Housekeeping and premises* – with attached statements of rules relating to cleanliness, waste disposal, safe stacking and storage, marking and keeping clear exits and gangways, checking equipment, e.g. ladders, and special access to particular places.
- *Electrical equipment* – arrangements for regular checks on electrical equipment and installations including plugs and cables, and rules for the use of extension leads and portable equipment.
- *Machinery* – rules for the use of all machinery and equipment and for the regular checking and maintenance.
- *Dangerous substances* – rules designed to provide appropriate protection in handling, storage and other aspects, including the use of special protective equipment.
- *Fluids under pressure* – rules covering the operation, use and maintenance of compressed equipment, storage/labelling and use of compressed gases, precautions when using water under pressure.
- *Other important hazards* – rules relating to such matters as internal transport, use and care of protective equipment, noise, and maintenance of appliances.

13.8.4   Duties of employees

Every employee at work has a duty:

- to take reasonable care for his or her own and other persons' health and safety, e.g. to use the safety equipment provided, and

- to cooperate with his or her employer and any other person to enable them to perform their statutory duties.

The Robens Committee stressed the importance of securing the full cooperation and commitment of all employees with regard to safety and that participation in the making and monitoring of safety arrangements was prerequisite to the workforce accepting such responsibilities.

The Act, therefore, lays emphasis on:

- consultation with trade unions;
- the appointment of safety representatives and committees;
- the appointment of a designated safety officer;
- safety training and instruction;
- safety audits.

Employees who 'wilfully and without reasonable cause' do anything to endanger themselves or others or who interfere with and misuse safety appliances may be prosecuted and fined.

Employers have the right to dismiss employees who refuse to obey safety rules on the grounds of misconduct especially where the possibility of such dismissal is explicitly stated in the terms and conditions of employment.

13.8.5 Enforcement

Enforcement of HSWA 1974 and other statutory provisions is generally the responsibility of the HSE. Certain provisions, may, however, be enforced by local authority environmental officers.

If, upon an inspection visit, an inspector finds that the Act has been contravened, he or she can do any of the following:

- Inform the employer orally what is defective, instruct that it be put right and later ensure that this has been done.
- Serve the employer with either an improvement or a prohibition notice.
  - An *improvement notice* is a document stating that in the opinion of the inspector the employer is contravening one or more of the relevant Acts and requiring the matter to be put right within a period of not more than 21 days or such further period as the inspector specifies.
  - A *prohibition notice* is issued where an employer is carrying on activities which in the inspector's opinion involve or will involve the risk of serious personal injury. The notice will state that the activities must cease within the time stated in the notice and not be resumed until the specified matters have been remedied.
- Take proceedings in the magistrates court and allege that the employer has committed the offence.

Since most undertakings are limited companies, the Act makes provision for the individuals 'behind' the company to be individually liable where appropriate. Thus, where an offence by a body corporate:

is proved to have been committed with the consent or connivance of, or to have attributed to any neglect on the part of any director, manager, secretary or similar officer of the body corporate . . . he as well as the body corporate shall be guilty of that offence.

Claims against employers for compensation for injury or industrial disease arising out of other statutes, e.g. the Factories Act 1961, or for failing to observe the common law (e.g. the duty of care) have to be pursued separately in civil actions.

13.8.6 Management of Health and Safety at Work Regulations

Since 1 January 1993 the Management of Health and Safety at Work Regulations have incorporated into UK law the six major EC directives published in 1988. EC directives, as distinct from EC regulations, do not override national laws but rather set out objectives and requirements which all EC member countries are obliged to effect through their own laws. It is because, in general, EC directives add to rather than contradict UK laws on health and safety that they are implemented as regulations.

The Management of Health and Safety at Work Regulations implement a framework directive and five 'daughter' directives. The Regulations, available as statutory instruments (SIs) from HMSO, are described below.

Framework Directive (1992 SI 2061)

This directive is intended to provide a model setting out broad general duties on health and safety for all employers and employees in all sectors of work other than domestic service. In the UK the Health and Safety at Work Act 1974 remains law but since 1 January 1993, the Regulations have imposed additional obligations on employers relating to the following:

- Risk assessment, i.e. identification of risks likely to arise because of work activity.
- Arrangements for the planning, organisation, control, monitoring and review of protective and preventive measures.
- Appointment of 'competent persons' to assist employers in the development of protective and preventative measures.
- Procedures to be followed in the event of serious and imminent danger.
- Coordination of measures with other employees on recruitment and when risks change.
- Provision of information on which, by the Safety Representatives and Safety Committee Regulations 1977, the employer is required to consult safety representatives.

The Management of Health and Safety at Work Regulations also impose on employees duties additional to those laid down by the Health and Safety at Work Act 1974. These duties relate to:

- using machinery, equipment, dangerous substances, means of production and safety devices in accordance with instructions and training provided by their employers in accordance with their statutory duties;

- informing the employer or any employees given specific responsibility for health and safety, of any situation which might reasonably be considered to represent a serious and imminent danger to health and safety or to represent a shortcoming in the employer's protection arrangements for health and safety.

The daughter directives

The daughter directives also place additional obligations and duties on employers and employees but are concerned with specific work issues. There are five such directives:

- Workplace Directive
- Use of Work Equipment Directive
- Use of Personal Protective Equipment Directive
- Manual Handling of Goods Directive
- Display Screen Equipment (Visual Display Units) Directive

Workplace (Health, Safety and Welfare) Regulations 1992 (SI 3004)

These regulations cover *indoor* situations and, as such, include loading bays, stores and warehouses but exclude, for example, extractive industries and construction sites.

The Regulations place duties on employers or other persons who may be in control of a workplace in respect of five areas:

- *Safety of equipment*, including machinery, devices, systems, sanitary conveniences, emergency lighting, ventilation systems and escalators.
- The *working environment* – these replace, but retain much of the detail of, the Factories Act and Office Shops and Railway Premises Act provisions relating to ventilation, temperature, lighting and cleanliness.
- *Physical comfort*, including workspaces, workstations and seating.
- The *structure of buildings*, with reference to floors, falls or falling objects, windows, traffic routes, doors and gates, and escalators and moving walkways.
- The *provision of facilities* including sanitary and washing facilities, drinking water, clothing, rest and meal facilities including arrangements to protect non-smokers from discomfort and tobacco smoke, and rest facilities for pregnant women and nursing mothers.

Provision and Use of Equipment Regulations 1992 (SI 2932)

These regulations 'amplify and make more explicit the general duties on employers, the self employed and persons in control to provide safe plant and equipment'.

Work equipment means any machinery, appliance, apparatus or tool and any assembly of components which, in order to achieve a common end, are arranged and controlled so that they function as a whole. The definition covers tools provided by employers for their own use and lifts in non-domestic premises which are also workplaces.

Use in relation to work equipment means any activity involving work equipment and includes starting, stopping, programming, setting, transporting, repairing, modifying, maintaining, servicing and cleaning.

Duties of employers

- To ensure that work equipment is suitable for its purpose.
- To ensure that work equipment is maintained in efficient state.
- Where the use of work equipment is likely to involve a specific risk to health and safety, to ensure that its use and any repairs, modifications and servicing are restricted to adequately trained designated persons.
- To provide adequate information and, where appropriate, written instructions to operators and supervisors.
- To provide adequate training to operators and supervisors.

Personal Protective Equipment at Work Regulations 1992 (SI 2966)

These regulations revoke some pre Health and Safety at Work Act 1974 regulations and modify others which remain in force including the Control of Asbestos at Work Regulations 1987, the Noise at Work Regulations 1989 and the Construction (Head Protection) Regulations 1989.

Duties of employers

- To provide suitable personal protective equipment to employees who may be exposed to risk.
- To ensure that where, because of more than one risk, an employee has to wear more than one item of personal protective equipment, such equipment is compatible.
- To make an assessment to determine:
  - whether the risk could have been avoided by other means;
  - the characteristics the equipment must have in order to be effective, taking into account any risks which the equipment itself may create.
  - To review the assessment if there is reason to suspect that it is no longer valid or if there have been significant changes.
  - To ensure that personal protective equipment is maintained in an efficient state, in efficient working order and in good repair.
  - To provide adequate accommodation for personal protective equipment.
  - To ensure that employees are provided with adequate information, instruction and training in the use of maintenance of equipment.
  - To take all reasonable steps to ensure that personal protective equipment is properly used.

Duties of employees

- To use personal protective equipment in accordance with the training and instructions provided by the employer.

- To take all reasonable steps to ensure that equipment is returned to the accommodation provided for it after use.
- To report immediately to the employers any loss or obvious defect in the personal protective equipment.

Manual Handling Operations Regulations 1992 (SI 2793)

Manual handling operations are:

Any transporting or supporting of a load (including the lifting, putting down, pushing, pulling, carrying or moving thereof) by hand or by bodily force.

Duties of employers

- To avoid hazardous manual handling operations so far as is reasonably practical.
- To assess any hazardous manual handling operations that can be avoided.
- To reduce the risk of injury so far as is reasonably practical.

Duties of employees

In addition to those duties laid down under the Health and Safety at Work Act 1974 and the Management of Health and Safety at Work Regulations, employees have a duty to make full use of any system of work provided to them by their employer in compliance with the reputation relating to the reduction of risk.

Under the Lifting Operations and Lifting Equipment Regulations (LOLER) 1998, lifting equipment provided for use at work should be:

- strong and safe enough for its use;
- marked with its safe working load;
- installed and positioned to minimise risk;
- used safely;
- thoroughly examined and, where appropriate, inspected by a competent person on an ongoing basis.

Display Screen Equipment Regulations 1992 (SI 2792)

These regulations are the first legal provision relating to the health and safety of workers who use visual display units (VDUs).

Display screen equipment (DSE) is defined as:

Any alphanumeric or graphic display screen, regardless of the display process involved.

This definition extends not only to office VDUs but also microfiche and process control screens, although minimum workstation requirements are not necessarily applicable to the latter. Cash registers, calculators and window typewriters are also included.

A user is defined as an employee who habitually uses display screen equipment as a significant part of his or her normal work.

Guidance information states that a person is a DSE user where:

- the individual depends on DSE to do the job because alternative means are unavailable;
- the individual has no discretion as to the use or non-use of the DSE;
- the individual needs particular skills in the use of DSE to do his or her job;
- the individual normally uses the DSE for prolonged spells of more than one hour;
- the individual uses DSE in this way more or less daily;
- fast transfer of information between the user and the screen is an important requirements of the job;
- the performance requirements of the system demand high levels of attention and concentration by the user.

Duties of the employers

In relation to users of display screen equipment, the duties of employers are as follows:

- To assess risks in relation to display screen equipment with particular attention to 'risks to eyesight, physical problems and problems of mental stress'.
- To reduce or eliminate these risks by such means as work redesigning, repositioning of equipment and improved lighting.
- To meet minimum requirements for the workstation in respect of such factors as display screens, keyboards, work surfaces and chairs, lighting, reflections and glare, noise and heat.
- To ensure that employees have the right to eye and eyesight tests and corrective appliances.
- To consult, inform and train employees especially in respect of the recognition and detection of hazards.

13.8.7 Fire precautions

These are covered by the Fire Precautions (Workplace) Regulations 1997. Part II of the Regulations deals with the following aspects of fire precautions in the workplace.

Fire-fighting and fire detection

- A workplace should, to the extent that is appropriate, be equipped with appropriate fire-fighting equipment and with fire detectors and alarms.
- Any non-automatic fire-fighting equipment so provided should be easily accessible, simple to use and indicated by signs.

What is appropriate is determined by the dimensions and use of the building housing the workplace, the equipment it contains and the physical and chemical properties of the substances likely to be present, and the maximum number of people that may be present at any one time.

Employers are responsible for taking appropriate measures, providing equipment and training, and nominating appropriate employees to implement such measures.

Emergency routes and exits

- Emergency exits and routes to emergency exits should be kept clear at all times.
- Emergency routes and exits should lead as directly as possible to a place of safety.
- It must be possible for employees to evacuate the workplace as quickly and safely as possible.
- Emergency doors should open in the direction of the escape, should not be so locked that they cannot be easily and immediately opened, provided (where appropriate) with emergency lighting and indicated by signs.

Maintenance

All equipment is subject to a suitable system of maintenance and should be maintained in efficient working order and in good repair.

Further information

Safety at work is a wide field and readers wishing to obtain further information are advised to contact the following bodies:

Health and Safety Executive

British Safety Council

International Labour Organisation

Royal Society for the Prevention of Accidents

Trades Union Congress

Exercise

Your company makes electrical components of all sizes ranging from small plugs to standard electrical motors weighing up to 0.5 tonne. As a member of a working party appointed to make recommendations for the architect's consideration in connection with the design of a new warehouse for the receipt and dispatch of finished goods, you have been asked to consider what requirements should be specified in respect of working conditions. Under each of the following headings suggest between three and six major factors that the architect should take into account.

1 Illumination

2 Ventilation

3 Heating

4 Noise and vibration

5 Fire precautions

6 Employee welfare facilities

7 Layout factors relevant to health and safety

? Discussion questions

13.1 Discuss the statement that a stores or warehouse is a 'necessary tool'.

13.2 If the emphasis of storage or warehousing has moved from the holding to the movement of stocks, how might the efficiency and effectiveness of stores operations be measured?

13.3 The equipment selection principle states that 'in selecting handling equipment consider all aspects of the material to be handled, the move to be made and the method(s) to be utilised'. State, with reasons, the equipment and methods you might use when moving the following items:

(a) Steel sections in 20 foot lengths from the stockyard to the construction site.

(b) Small electrical motors from stores to the dispatch bay.

(c) Sand from a stockyard to a building site.

(d) Loose apples from goods inwards to a food processing department.

(e) Crates of jam from stores to shelves in a supermarket.

(f) Explosives from a special store to a quarry.

(g) Scrap metal from production to storage.

13.4 The space utilisation principle states that 'optimum use should be made of the building cube'. One application of this principle is that maximum use should be made of height.

(a) What, in general, are the advantages of having high ceiling warehouses?

(b) What may be the disadvantages of high ceilings in stores?

13.5 With regard to location, height, access and security, what recommendations would you make concerning the storage of the following items?

(a) Heavy, bulky items.

(b) Light, easily handled items.

(c) Slow-moving, infrequently required items.

(d) Fast-moving items in constant demand.

(e) Steel tubes too large for internal storage.

(f) Hazardous items such as explosives or easily inflammable supplies.

(g) High value items subject to pilferage.

(h) Production jigs and tools.

13.6 What action would you suggest in respect of the following?

(a) A check on the stock of electrical handtools, e.g. electric drills and screwdrivers, issued to production workers showed that only 60 per cent of the assumed stock could be accounted for.

(b) Steel and wood stored in outside stockyards is sometimes found to be unsuitable for use owing to exposure to the elements.

13.7 The following picture, reproduced by kind permission of the British Safety Council, relates to potential hazards to be found in an office environment. Some of them, however, apply equally to stores.

SPOT THE HAZARDS

(a) See how many hazards you can detect.

(b) List those which apply both to offices and stores/warehouse situations.

13.8 Forklift trucks are the most commonly used item of mobile handling equipment in stores. The generic term 'forklift truck' can include pedestrian operated stacking trucks, reach trucks, counterbalance fork trucks, narrow aisle trucks and order pickers. Suggest at least six points relating to the safe operations of forklift trucks that you would present at a safety training course for forklift truck drivers with no previous experience of mobile handling equipment.

13.9 Torrington and Hall[8] point out that 'Persuading employees to keep to the safety rules is difficult and there often appears to be a general resistance on the part of employees'. In support of this statement they quote from earlier research which observed:

> The management sample saw this 'ideal' safety-conscious operative as a half-witted, slow but reliable person who gave little trouble. They saw him as a worker who could be left safely alone but prone to making trivial complaints. He was certainly not depicted as a worker to be respected. The major construct to emerge from the operatives' data alone was that the ideal safetyman was rather a 'cissy' and somewhat unsociable.

How would you seek to change such negative attitudes?

? Past examination questions

1 Explain how stores layout can impact upon operating costs and explain the factors you would take into account in determining and designing an appropriate layout.

(CIPS, Stores and Inventory Management, November 1997)

2 Explain how you would effectively control and dispose of obsolete, surplus, redundant and waste material.

(CIPS, Introduction to Purchasing and Supply Chain Management, May 1998)

3 Explain the construction and use of a *significant* coding system with which you are familiar and explain the benefits, which an organisation receives from the proper application of such a system.

(CIPS, Stores and Inventory Control, November 1998)

4 Discuss automation in the context of the management of warehouses and distribution centres indicating the benefits which can arise if automation is carried out successfully.

(CIPS, Stores and Inventory Control, November 1998)

5 Explain how you, as stores controller, can productively reduce the occurrence of redundant, obsolete or damaged stock within your warehouse.

(CIPS, Introduction to Purchasing and Supply Chain Management, November 1998)

6 'Warehouse, distribution centres and similar facilities can add value in the supply chain by performing functions beyond simple storage.' Explain this statement, indicating four ways in which the addition of value is facilitated by the warehouse or distribution centre.

(CIPS, Stores and Inventory Control, May 1999)

7 'The quality of the contribution of stores and inventory management operations to an organisation can be assessed in many ways, but two of the most common are service level and stock-turn. Both these should be high but there is a serious difficulty in maximising both factors.' Discuss.

(CIPS, Stores and Inventory Control, May 1999)

8 Explain four of the approaches that might be employed in increasing storage density in a warehouse with a limited floor area and unused vertical space.

(CIPS, Stores and Inventory Control, May 1999)

9 The selection of appropriate storage equipment and appropriate handling machinery are obviously related decisions. Explain the implications for storage facilities and equipment arising from the adoption of counterbalance forklift trucks for warehouse operations.

(CIPS, Stores and Inventory Management, November 1999)

10 Identify, using four detailed examples, how warehouses or stores, or distribution complexes can add value in the supply chain.

(CIPS, Stores and Inventory Management, May 2000)

11 When looking at achieving increased density, various methods are possible. Explain, using appropriate examples, how and in what ways you could make better use of the space available in a warehouse.

(CIPS, Stores and Inventory Management, May 2000)

12 Identify, using four detailed examples, how warehouses, stores or distribution complexes can add value in the supply chain.

(CIPS, *Stores and Inventory Management*, November 2000)

Notes

1. CIMA, *Management Accounting,* Official Terminology, p.91
2. Compton, H.K. and Jessop, D., *Dictionary of Purchasing and Supply Management*, Pitman, 1989, p.134
3. Beesley, A., 'Time compression – new source of competitiveness', *Supply Chain Logistics Focus*, June 1995, p.24
4. Platts, R., *Computing Needs for Automated Materials Handling*, NCC Blackwell, 1989, Ch.1, p.14
5. Firth, K., 'Automated and mechanised warehouses', in Gattorna, J.L. (ed.), *Handbook of Physical Distribution Management*, Gower, 1983, Ch.9, pp.144–5
6. Institute of Logistics, *Principles of Warehouse Design*, 1993
7. Hollier, R.H., and Cooke, C., in *Stock Reduction to Manufacturing*, IFS Publications, 1991, p.111
8. Torrington, D. and Hall, L., *Personnel Management*, 3rd edn, Prentice Hall 1995, Ch.29, p.518

Learning goals

After reading this chapter you should be able to:

- Discuss the factors contributing to a higher demand for transportation.
- Distinguish between strategic, tactical and operational perspectives of transport.
- Differentiate between inbound, outbound and interorganisational logistics.
- State the five principal modern transport modes.
- Define the term 'goods vehicle' as used in road transport.
- State the operating controls on the gross weight of goods vehicles.
- Distinguish between goods lifted and goods moved.
- List some advantages and disadvantages of own account goods vehicle operation.
- State some advantages and disadvantages of road transport.
- Outline some characteristics of the rail transport industry.
- State some advantages and disadvantages of rail freight.
- Outline some characteristics of the air transport industry.
- State some advantages and disadvantages of air transport.
- Outline some characteristics of the inland water transport industry.
- State some advantages and disadvantages of the inland water transport industry.
- State some characteristics of the deep sea transport industry.
- Classify the main types of cargo ship.
- State some advantages and disadvantages of pipelines.
- Define the term 'intermodal freight transport'.
- Provide examples of intermodal freight transport.
- Outline the development of containerisation.
- List the main types of container.
- Name and briefly describe the purposes of some documents used in transportation.

- Define the term 'total distribution cost'.
- Identify the main freight cost elements.
- Outline the development and describe the purpose of Incoterms.
- Describe the format of Incoterms.
- Define the term 'freight agent' or 'forwarder'.
- List and briefly describe the main services provided by freight agents.
- Discuss some future aspects of freight agents and logistics practitioners.

14.1 Transportation and supply chains

Supply chains imply movement, and movement whether of goods or people requires some form of transportation.

An account of the evolution of transport systems is outside the scope of this book. Suffice to say that, since the 1970s, the focus on supply chain management has led to a direct increase in the need for transport services. It has been estimated that between 1970 and 1997, transport as measured in tonne-kilometres increased in the EU by 207 per cent.[1] A study by KPMG[2] attributes this increased demand for transport services to the following factors:

- General economic growth.
- Increased specialisation by companies on specific parts of the value chain.
- Increased outsourcing which has meant that on-site transport has been converted into external transport among different supply chain participants.
- New supply chain management strategies such as JIT and efficient consumer response (ECR) have redefined the demand for transport services as a consequence of shortening replenishment cycles and lower inventory levels.
- Focus, during the 1990s, on the fulfilment of customer demand by the introduction of mass customisation or creation of diversification in product ranges.
- Emphasis on customer service in respect of shorter lead times.
- Quick response systems and higher order fulfilment rates leading to smaller order quantities and increased order frequency, thus increasing the number of deliveries to end users.
- The move to reduced inventory levels leading to centralised inventories, a reduction in the number of stock-keeping locations in the supply chain with a resultant additional demand for transport.
- The shift from make-to-stock to make-to-order.
- The outsourcing of value-added logistics to third-party logistics service providers.
- The change in the geographical scope to logistics from country based to regional, pan-European or global perspectives.

■ Changing distribution concepts such as direct distribution and cross-docking. (Cross-docking refers to the merging of goods flows from several services at a distribution centre before final delivery but without holding any inventory at the distribution centre.)

■ Globalisation and increased competition leading to an increase in the demand for transport services as companies source from the optimal place irrespective of geographical location.

14.2 Transportation and logistics

Transportation is the most important and expensive aspect of logistics, but logistics is more than transportation. The increased usage of the term 'logistics' instead of transportation is, as Willmott[3] observes:

> A reflection that in the need to get the right goods in the right place at the right time, at the right cost, more than just transport was needed.
>   This was certainly the case when the roots of the term [logistics] are traced back to military applications – you need more than transport to put troops, ammunition, food, fuel and equipment in the right place.

Yet, as Gattorna and Walters[4] state, transportation is 'the linkage process in logistics and often consumes much of the resources provided to the logistics function'.

Transport may also be considered from strategic, tactical and operational perspectives. Strategic issues include decisions on what modes of transport to use for which products and whether to invest in company-owned vehicles or use the services of outside hauliers. Tactical issues are concerned with scheduling, routing, carrier selection, etc. Operational matters are those routine decisions relating to vehicle loading, packaging, and load safety and security. The distinction between what is tactical and what is operational is often blurred. Ballou[5] summarises the three approaches as:

> Strategic – what should our distribution service be?
>
> Tactical – how can the distribution service best be utilised?
>
> Operational – lets get the goods out.

14.3 Inbound, outbound and internal movement

Inbound and outbound logistics are two of the five primary activities in Porter's value chain model described in Chapter 3.

14.3.1 Inbound logistics

Transport as an essential element in upstream, goods inward activities is concerned both with the receipt of manufacturing or assembly requirements and with reverse logistics.

Manufacturing or assembly requirements

Important inward transport aspects include those relating to JIT, global sourcing, freight prices and cross-docking.

Reverse logistics

Reverse logistics or 'the transport aspects of returns inwards' is referred to in Chapter 3. Typical reasons for inward returns include:

■ Product returns due to defects, damage etc.

■ Return of crates, pallets, drums and other 'empties'

■ Return of goods over or wrongly delivered.

14.3.2 Outbound logistics

Transport as an essential element in the downstream, goods outwards activity is concerned with:

■ the movement of output from the manufacturer to assembler to the customer;

■ movement of waste or scrap from the source of generation to a source of recycling or disposal.

An alternative name for outbound logistics is physical distribution management, which has been defined as:

> **The study, control and management of all the factors involved in the distribution of materials and finished goods involving an integrated approach to materials handling, protective packaging, freight, transport, warehousing, inventory control and location of depots.**

Important transport aspects of the movement of goods to the customer include the selection of an appropriate transport mode, journey maximisation, JIT deliveries and cross-docking.

The Environmental Protection Act 1990 imposes responsibilities on all concerned with the transport and disposal of what is termed 'directive waste'. Directive waste is defined as:[6]

> **Household, commercial and industrial waste and embraces all waste produced at commercial or industrial premises. It does not include waste from agricultural premises, mines, quarries, explosive waste and most radioactive waste each of which is the subject of separate regulations.**

Section 34 of the Act requires all persons involved to act with a 'duty of care', i.e. to take all reasonable steps to prevent the escape of waste and ensure that it is transferred only to persons authorised to accept it.

14.3.3 Interorganisational logistics

Interorganisational logistics is concerned with logistics issues within the organisation. Important aspects are the following:

■ Transport within the plant or factory, such as the transportation of goods received from the goods inwards location to stores or direct to production, from stores to manufacturing and from manufacturing to assembly to a finished goods warehouse. Some mechanical handling devices used in the internal transportation of production supplies or finished or semi-finished products are described in Chapter 13.

■ Transport exterior to the plant or factory to warehouse or airports or distribution centres owned by the organisation.

14.4   Modes of transport

The five principal modern transport modes are road (goods vehicles), rail, air, water and pipelines. These are dealt with individually in the following sections.

14.5   Road transport

14.5.1   Definitions

A goods vehicle for transport by road is defined as:[7]

A motor vehicle or trailer constructed or adapted for use for the carriage of goods – this includes goods or burden of any description.

The above definition makes no reference to the size or weight of vehicle which can range from a light van to a heavy goods vehicle with or without a trailer. The road traffic freight statistics published by the Department for Transport, Local Government and the Regions however, are estimates of domestic freight activity by British registered heavy goods vehicles over 3.5 tonnes gross vehicle weight. These vehicles pay the goods vehicle rates of vehicle excise duty, are subject to goods vehicle plating, require annual testing and a goods operator's licence. They account for some 95 per cent of road freight activity, with the rest being carried by light goods vehicles less than 3.5 tonnes gross weight.

14.5.2   Vehicle weight groups

Vehicle weight groups reflect some of the operating controls on goods vehicles. For rigid vehicles the maximum allowed gross vehicle weights are: 18 tonnes on 2 axles; 25 tonnes on 3 axles (26 tonnes if fitted with 'road friendly' suspension); and 32 tonnes on 4 axles. For articulated vehicles the limits are: 36 tonnes on 4 axles; 40 tonnes on 5 or more axles; and 44 tonnes on 6 axles.

14.5.3   Freight statistics

As shown in Figure 14.1, freight activity is measured in two ways: goods lifted and goods moved.

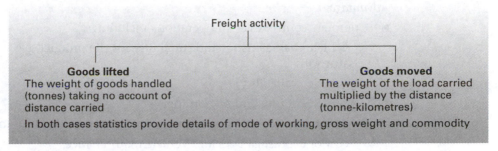

Figure 14.1 Freight statistics

Table 14.1 Freight transport by road: goods lifted by goods vehicles over 3.5 tonnes, 1990–2000 (million tonnes)

Mode of working	1990	1991	1992	1993	1994	1995	1996	1997	1998	1999	2000
Mainly public haulage	978	862	843	911	980	987	1,011	1,044	1,041	991	1,038
Mainly own account	667	643	620	612	618	622	618	599	589	576	556
All modes	1,645	1,505	1,463	1,523	1,597	1,609	1,628	1,643	1,630	1,597	1,593

Source: Department for Transport, Local Government and the Regions

Table 14.2 Freight transport by road: goods moved by goods vehicles over 3.5 tonnes, 1990–2000 (billion tonne-kilometres)

Mode of working	1990	1991	1992	1993	1994	1995	1996	1997	1998	1999	2000
Mainly public haulage	94.7	85.5	86.4	93.2	100.8	106.5	109.1	112.2	114.3	110.9	113.0
Mainly own account	36.0	38.8	34.9	35.4	37.0	37.2	37.7	37.4	37.6	38.3	37.5
All modes	130.6	124.6	121.3	128.6	137.8	143.7	146.8	149.6	151.9	149.2	150.5

Source: Department for Transport, Local Government and the Regions

The respective figures for goods lifted and goods moved over national territory by goods vehicles over 3.5 tonnes for the years 1990 to 2000 are shown in Tables 14.1 and 14.2.

14.5.4 Own account or contract hire

Tables 14.1 and 14.2 distinguish between 'mainly public haulage' and 'mainly own account'. A strategic transport decision for manufacturing and large retail organisations is whether to operate their own vehicle fleets or to concentrate on their core businesses and entrust their road transport to third-party operators under contract hire agreements. The advantages and disadvantages of own account goods vehicle operation are:

Advantages

- Complete control over all operations including:
  - vehicle characteristics and suitability for the product, e.g. tankers, refrigerator vans;
  - vehicle availability;
  - vehicle routing and scheduling;
  - driver recruitment, training, pay and incentives, discipline and performance;
  - cost of depots, garages and vehicle maintenance.
- Flexibility in use of vehicles.
- Promotion of the organisation by vehicle style, advertising and driver uniform, etc.

Disadvantages

- High initial cost of acquiring vehicles and fleet creation.
- High depreciation cost of vehicles and fleet replacement.
- The high fixed and variable cost of transport management, garaging, maintenance and servicing.
- Vehicles are only licensed for own use.
- Legal responsibility for all vehicles operated by the organisation.
- Uneconomic costs of running empty particularly on return journeys or the use of large vehicles for relatively small loads.
- Hidden overheads e.g. cost of recruitment of drivers, wages department, driver sickness etc.

The decision whether to operate on own account or by contract hire requires a careful evaluation of such factors as:

- Return on investment on the capital cost of acquiring vehicles and operating costs of own fleet against the costs of contract hire.
- The extent to which the benefits of flexibility outweigh the cost of operation.
- What added value (if any) accrues to the company and its customers from own account operation.
- The quality and reliability of service offered by contract hirers.
- The strategic advantages of concentrating on the core business rather than the distractions of transport operation.

14.5.5 Advantages and disadvantages of road transport

Advantages

- For distances of 500 kilometres or less, road transport is generally considered to be the least expensive, most flexible and quickest mode of transport.
- The only costs of using roads in the UK are vehicles excise duty, fuel tax and bridge tolls.

- Less stringent packaging requirements.
- High security since consignments are under the control of one driver, delivered on a door-to-door basis and the whereabouts of a vehicle can be monitored.

Disadvantages

- Low load capacities relative to rail and water transport such as barge and coastal vessels.
- High environmental costs due to air pollution, noise, vibration and road damage and road congestion.
- At present some of the largest lorries cannot be fully loaded with heavy goods because of weight restriction and have to run part empty.

14.6 Rail transport

14.6.1 Industry profile

In the EU, rail transport accounts for about 18 per cent of total surface freight transport. Following privatisation of the UK rail transport system and the Channel Tunnel, rail freight is becoming increasingly competitive. In Great Britain train services for moving goods are provided by freight operating companies (FOCs). Unlike passenger train operating companies (TOCs), FOCs are commercial companies with no obligation to provide a given service. Freight business operates in an 'open access' environment in which any operator can run freight trains subject to obtaining a licence and access to the railway network. Customers wishing to move goods by rail can deal directly with an FOC or purchase freight services through an intermediary such as a logistics company or a freight agent or forwarder. National statistics by commodity of freight lifted or moved by rail freight for the years 1990/1 to 2000/01 are shown in Table 14.3.

14.6.2 Advantages and disadvantages of rail freight

The advantages and disadvantages of rail freight are as follows:

Advantages

- For the bulk transit of heavy commodities such as those shown in Table 14.3 rail transport is cheaper per tonne-kilometre than road freight
- Special rates or contracts can be negotiated for train loads of commodities such as coal, oil and aggregates
- Provides a fast transfer between main centres or sometimes direct to users, e.g. coal to power stations
- Freight rail emits only 10 per cent of the carbon dioxide emitted from equivalent road freight kilometres. Ten tonnes of carbon dioxide are emitted from:
  - flying a plane (19 tonnes freight) for 300 km
  - running a lorry (20 tonnes freight) for 9,000 km

Table 14.3   National railways freight, 1990/91–2000/01

	1990/91	1991/92	1992/93	1993/94	1994/95	1995/96	1996/97[b]	1997/98	1998/99	1999/00	2000/01
Freight moved by commodity[a] (billion tonne-kilometres)											
Coal	5.0	5.0	5.4	3.9	3.3	3.6	3.9	4.4	4.5	4.8	4.8
Metals	2.3	2.4	2.3	2.1	1.7	1.7	–	–	2.7	2.9	2.9
Construction	2.7	2.5	2.5	2.3	2.5	2.3	–	–	2.1	2.0	2.4
Oil and petroleum	2.0	2.0	2.0	1.9	1.8	1.8	–	–	1.6	1.5	1.4
Other traffic	3.8	3.4	3.3	3.5	3.8	3.9	11.2	12.5	6.5	6.9	6.6
All traffic	16.0	15.3	15.5	13.8	13.0	13.3	15.1	16.9	17.3	18.2	18.1
Freight lifted by commodity[c] (million tonnes)											
Coal	74.7	75.1	67.9	48.9	42.5	45.2	52.2	50.3	45.3	44.3	45.7
Metals	18.0	17.8	15.9	15.8	16.9	15.1	–	–	–	–	–
Construction	20.2	17.7	15.8	16.1	16.8	11.5	–	–	–	–	–
Oil and petroleum	10.0	10.0	9.5	9.0	8.1	6.3	–	–	–	–	–
Other traffic	15.1	15.3	13.2	13.4	13.0	22.6	49.6	55.1	56.8	47.5	49.7
All traffic	138.2	135.8	122.4	103.2	97.3	100.7	101.8	105.4	102.1	91.9	95.4

[a] Revised series on new basis from 1998/99

[b] Owing to changes in the way freight traffic has been estimated following privatisation, data since 1996/97 are not comparable with those for previous years. Freight excludes parcels and materials carried for rail infrastructure

[c] Break in series from 1999/2000

Source: Department for Transport, Local Government and the Regions

- running a train (700 tonnes freight) for 1,700 km
- 8 times better than road

■ The Channel Tunnel enables freight to be transported to European destinations without transhipment

■ Rail transport is less affected by adverse weather conditions than other modes of land-based transport

■ Relatively high security especially with containers or closed wagons

Disadvantages

■ Host train journeys involve some degree of transhipment due to the distance of the terminus from the final delivery location

■ Time from origin to destination may be long particularly if delivery by road to the departure point and from the destination is required

■ Rail gradients may cause problems for heavy trains

14.7   Air transport

14.7.1   Industry profile

Apart from freight forwarders who provide services to shippers and importers, the main constituents of the air freight industry are airports and airlines.

Airports provide reception, take-off, landing and service facilities for which they receive fees, e.g. landing and parking fees from the airlines and rentals for reception terminals, cargo sheds and maintenance workshops from companies providing such services.

Airlines provide air cargo capacity for the transit of freight both within the UK and abroad. Airlines comprise the following:

■ *Scheduled operators* who provide air cargo capability exclusively on a freight basis or, more usually, in the belly holds of passenger aircraft.

■ *Charter operators* who provide air freight capacity along with the operation of passenger holiday flights on a seasonal basis.

■ *Integrated operators* who use belly hold capacity to transport their 'own' cargo as an express service to importers and exporters of goods.

While, in volume terms, the proportion of total UK trade carried by air freight is insignificant, in value terms air transport accounts for at least one-fifth of the UK trade, amounting in 1998 to £100 billion divided roughly into 54 per cent imports and 46 per cent exports.

Based on Department of the Environment, Transport and the Regions statistics from 1992 to 1998, imports by value comprised North America (39 per cent), Asia (25 per cent), Europe (23 per cent). The corresponding figures for exports were Europe (38 per cent), North America (28 per cent), Asia (18 per cent). In weight terms, the largest import commodity categories were fruit and vegetables (13 per cent), photographic equipment (11 per cent), general and industrial machinery (10 per cent), and telecommunications and audio equipment (9 per cent). For exports, the corresponding categories were: miscellaneous manufactures (15 per cent) and other electrical machinery (15 per cent).

14.7.2 Advantages and disadvantages of air freight

Advantages

- Speed – a few hours contrasted with days for most other forms of transportation.
- Fixed cost of air freight is low in comparison with rail, water and pipeline.
- Particularly applicable to goods of high value or high perishability, e.g. fish, flowers, vegetables.
- Entirely new industries have been created by the availability of air transport, e.g. the export of tropical fruits.
- Facilitates JIT for manufacturers and assemblers who incorporate foreign-sourced components and materials in their products.
- Air transport is more secure from loss, theft or damage. Crating is only used for the most delicate goods.
- Insurance rates may be more competitive than for ocean shipping.
- Overnight provides global freight operation.

Disadvantages

- Cost – air freight costs about 4 times as much per cubic metre as sea freight. For small shipments, however, due to lack of crating charges and documentation, air transport may be cheaper.
- Restrictions on the size and weight of goods carried and the availability of aircraft.
- Considerable diversity between national air traffic control systems and regulations causes difficulty in coordinating operations. The aim, however, is to create a single European sky by 2004.
- Environmental factors including noise and gaseous emissions.
- Airport storage is expensive.

14.8 Inland water transport

14.8.1 Industry profile

A navigable inland waterway is defined as:[8]

> A stretch of water, not part of the sea, over which vessels of a carrying capacity of not less than 60 tonnes can navigate when normally loaded. This term covers the navigable rivers, lakes and navigable canals.

An inland water transport (IWT) vessel is defined as:[9]

A floating craft designed for the carriage of goods or public transport of passengers by navigable inland waterways.

This definition excludes harbour craft, seaport lighters, seaport tugs, ferries, fishery vessels, dredgers, vessels performing hydraulic work and vessels used exclusively for storage, floating workshops, houseboats and pleasure craft. It does, however, include vessels suitable for inland navigation but which are authorised to navigate at sea, i.e. mixed seagoing and inland waterways vessels. Most such vessels are barges which may be self-propelled or 'dumb'. A 'dumb barge' is an IWT vessel designed to be towed which does not have its own means of mechanical propulsion.

British domestic waterways comprise coastal, estuary, river and canal navigations. In 1999 these together accounted for 7 per cent of goods lifted in Britain and 22 per cent of the tonne-kilometres.[10] Traffic on inland waterways, has however, been in decline for many years and now accounts for less than 1 per cent of domestic freight moved.

14.8.2   Advantages and disadvantages of inland water freight

Advantages

- Useful for transporting heavy loads especially liquid bulks, e.g. crude petroleum, and dry bulks e.g. aggregates.

- High capacity vessels and the possibility of barge trains. Barges can carry large bulk loads of up to five times their own weight. Estimates are that the cargo capacity of a barge can be up to 15 times that of one rail wagon and up to 60 times greater than a goods vehicle.[11] To move the same amount of freight as a tow of 15 barges would require a freight train 2.75 miles long or a line of road goods vehicles stretching almost 35 miles.

- Shallow draft water has been shown to be the most energy efficient manner of freight transportation for moving bulk materials. It is much more efficient to move cargo through water than over land.

- Barge transportation has fewer accidents, fatalities and injuries than either road or rail transport.

- Barge transport seldom causes congestion, and gives rise to little noise or pollution.

- Dock dues are not payable on deliveries and from import and export vessels in enclosed docks.

Disadvantages

- The high minimum tonnage fee by barge makes inland water transport uneconomical for small consignments.

- The speed of transport is slow in comparison with road or rail transport and has a limited operational range.

- Specialised loading and terminal facilities are essential.

- Unless the origin and destination of the freight movement is adjacent to a waterway, supplemental haul by road or rail will be required.

14.9   Deep sea transport

14.9.1   Industry profile

The DTLR[12] points out that shipping has an importance for the UK which differentiates it from other industries. Since 95 per cent of UK external trade by weight (77 per cent by value) moves by water, a safe and thriving global shipping industry is vital to the country's economy. British shipping is, however, in decline as evidenced by the reduction in the size of UK-owned trading vessels of over 500 gross tons from a peak of around 50.8 million tonnes dead weight (dwt) in 1975 to 10.8 million dwt in 1997. The UK accounts for about 6 per cent of the world's merchant shipping. World shipping by type of ship over 100 dwt is shown in Table 14.4.

Deep sea shipping lines operate as conference or independent. A 'conference' is an association of shipowners operating in the same trade route who operate under collective conditions and agree on tariff rates. Independent tariffs are those that are not part of a conference system. In recent years it has become increasingly difficult to distinguish between conference and non-conference carriers.

Ships require ports. Nine British ports account for about two-thirds of maritime trade. About one-quarter of trailer or container movements is concentrated into three ports – Felixstowe, Southampton and Thamesport – while continental and coastal traffic is concentrated into Immingham, Felixstowe, Hull, Purfleet, Tessport, Harwich and Dover. In spite of the Channel Tunnel, Dover continues to attract an increased share of Channel port shipping.

14.9.2   Types of cargo ship

Cargo ships may be classified as follows:

Table 14.4   World merchant fleet by type of ship over 100 dwt (total fleet) at 1 January 2000

	Number[a]		dwt (1,000)		
	World	EU flag	World	EU flag	EU control[b]
Oil tankers	7,195	896	296,081	45,163	100,051
Chemical tankers	1,294	201	8,413	1,234	1,833
Liquid gas tankers	1,058	155	17,132	2,004	n.a.
Bulk carriers	5,763	395	255,541	20,597	80,654
Ore/bulk/oil carriers	215	9	16,141	902	5,081
General cargo ships	17,228	1,901	100,061	9,766	27,096
Container ships	2,437	514	63,296	16,064	26,945
			gt (1,000)		
Passenger/cargo ships	3,727	1,071	21,433	7,745	2,006
Cruise ships	243	43	7,772	1,409	n.a.

[a] In addition, in 1998 23,711 fishing vessels (>100 gt) of which EU 3,300, and 1,185 research vessels (>100 gt) of which EU ca. 200 (gt = gross tonnage)
[b] Ships of 1,000 gt and over
Source: Institute of Shipping Economics and Logistics, Bremen

- *Cargo liners* – offer a regular service for general and special cargo sailing, whether fully loaded or not at a scheduled time.
- *Mail and supply ships* – carry mail, supplies and cargo to remote locations.
- *General bulk cargo ships* – carry cargo too large for containers e.g. steel, machinery and boxed goods too small for containerisation.
- *Containerships* – also known as box ships, these carry containers of from 20 to 40 feet in length filled with virtually any type of cargo. 'Refers' or refrigerated containers carry frozen and chilled food.
- *Bulk carriers* – carry coal, grain, phosphates and other loose cargo. Such ships are almost always tramp ships working on a contract basis rather than along regular established routes.
- *Coasters* – small cargo ships travelling along the coast and making many stops in a short period of time. Coasters are often containerships carrying a relatively small number of containers from small to major ports.
- *Ro-ro (roll-on, roll-off)* – these are used to carry motor vehicles loaded by a stern ramp.
- *Tankers* – the International Tanker Owners Pollution Federation (ITOPF) defines a tanker as 'any ship (whether or not self-propelled) designed, constructed or adapted for the carriage by water in bulk of crude petroleum, hydrocarbon products and any other liquid substance.'

14.9.3 Advantages and disadvantages of deep sea transport

Advantages

- Low freight rates.
- Very high capacity.
- Continuous (24 hour) operation.
- Less affected by adverse weather conditions than air transport.
- High security, especially for container cargoes.

Disadvantages

- Relatively low speed especially in comparison with air transport.
- Especially for non-container cargoes the time spent in loading and discharging cargo can be disproportionate to actual travel time.
- Possibly infrequent services.
- More packing required than air transport.

14.10   Pipelines

14.10.1 Industry profile

Transmission pipelines are used to transport such products as crude oil, natural gas and refined petroleum. One of the largest pipeline networks in the UK is that operated by Esso, covering 1,200 kilometres and carrying around 45 million litres of 'white oil products' every day.

Most pipelines carry a number of different products that are introduced at carefully planned intervals and methodically regulated by computer.

14.10.2 Advantages and disadvantages of pipelines

Advantages

■ Underground pipelines are safe, cost effective, efficient and environmentally desirable.

■ Systems can be fully automated and do not interfere with human movement.

■ Pipeline systems are closed and can be operated regardless of weather conditions.

■ Pipelines are cheap to operate.

Disadvantages

■ High initial cost of pipeline construction.

■ Disturbance of land during pipeline construction.

■ Pneumatic pipelines, i.e. those moving capsules through a duct by a vacuum or air pressure, have low efficiency and high noise levels and require booster pumps to transport cargos beyond several miles.

■ Inflexibility, especially when cargos have to be conveyed in greater quantities or if pipelines are no longer required.

14.11 Intermodal freight transport

Intermodal freight transport is defined by the Intermodal Freight Transport Committee[13] (USA) as:

> **All shipments that employ more than one mode in a single through movement from origin to destination. This does not include local pick-up and delivery by truck for other modes.**

Intermodalisation refers to interconnections among modes of transportation, the use of multiple modes for a single trip and coordinated transportation policy and decision making. In 1994 the Final Report of the USA National Commission on Intermodal Transportation identified the following benefits of intermodalism.[14]

■ Lower overall transportation costs by allowing each mode to be used for the portion of the trip to which it is best suited.

■ Increased economic productivity and efficiency thereby enhancing national global competitiveness.

■ Reduced congestion and the burden on overstressed infrastructure components.

■ Generation of higher returns from public and private infrastructure investments.

- Improved mobility for the elderly, disabled, isolated and economically disadvantaged.
- Reduced energy consumption contributing to improved air quality and environmental conditions.

There are possibly nine integrated freight distribution systems: (1) rail–road; (2) rail–water; (3) rail–pipeline; (4) rail–air; (5) road–air; (6) road–pipeline; (7) water–pipeline; (8) water–air and (9) air–pipeline. Ballou[15] points out, however, that not all of these combinations are practical and some have gained little acceptance. Some integrated systems may be other than bimodal. Thus oil transportation may use a combination of pipeline, oil tanker, pipeline and road tanker, to get a product from its source to the final consumer.

Examples of integrated transport modes are 'birdy-back', 'fishy-back' and 'piggyback':

- *Birdy-back* is a form of intermodal transportation where trailers or containers are carried by air.
- *Fishy-back* is a form of intermodal transportation where road or rail containers are carried by barge or ship.
- *Piggyback* is a form of intermodal transportation where trailers or containers are carried on flat railway wagons. Freightliner, Britain's largest intermodal freight operator, uses national road and rail networks to transport over 1 million standard containers yearly and operates over 100 trains and 180 vehicles daily.

14.12   Containers

14.12.1   The development of containerisation

Containerisation is the cornerstone of intermodal transportation. Prior to containerisation all products other than bulk commodities were moved piecemeal. Thus crates were loaded individually onto road vehicles which transported them to a port. At the dockside the crates were unloaded individually and hoisted into a ship's hold. On reaching their destination crates were again unloaded and placed on a goods vehicle or train for delivery. Such freight handling procedures were slow, repetitive and cargos were prone to damage and pilferage.

Containers and containership services introduced in 1956 solved the above problems. A container carrying numerous crates would be loaded at the shippers, sealed, and sent by road or rail to the port of departure where it would simply be lifted into the ship's hold. At the destination the process would be reversed. Thus one giant box which could be handled by road, rail and sea or air transport made the concept of intermodal transportation feasible.

14.12.2   Types of container

Containers are normally built to International Standards Organisation (ISO) specifications. The external dimensions of the containers in general use are:

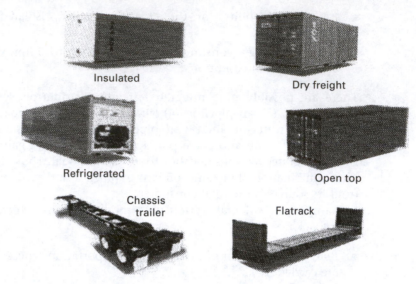

Figure 14.2 Types of container

- 20ft × 7ft 9in wide × 8ft 6in high (average capacity 24 tons)
- 40ft × 7ft 9in wide × 8ft 6in high (average capacity 30 tons)

As shown by Figure 14.2 containers may be:

- Dry freight
- Refrigerated or insulated
- Open top (canvas/open top, top and end loading)
- Flat rack and platform
- Chassis

14.12.3 Advantages and disadvantages of containers

Advantages

- Reduced handling, loss, damage and storage.
- Faster handling times.
- Standardised handling.
- Flexible capabilities.
- Enhanced security and reduction of pilferage.
- Reduced storage space owing to the possibility of multiple stacking.
- Simplified packaging.

Disadvantages

- High cost of containers or container hire.
- High cost of specialised handling equipment such as dedicated cranes.

- The weight of the container adds to the overall freight load. Most containers are of aluminium construction to reduce weight.

- Although minor theft is reduced, 'hijacking' is made easier.

14.13   Transport documentation

The main transportation documents can be classified under the headings of shipping instructions and carriage documentation.

14.13.1   Shipping instructions

Shipping instructions are essential and state exactly what a shipper wants to move, where, at what time and under what terms. The most important documents are standard shipping notes and dangerous goods notes.

Standard shipping note

A standard shipping note (SSN) enables the shipper to complete one standard document for all consignments irrespective of port or inland depot. The document also provides the receiving authority and all those with an interest in the consignment with complete, accurate and timely information at each movement stage, until final loading onto the aircraft or ship.

Dangerous goods note

Dangerous goods legislation is now in place worldwide for all modes of transport. Such legislation aims to protect people, property and the environment by ensuring that packages, tanks and vehicles containing dangerous goods are fully identified throughout transportation. The three main classes of dangerous goods from a transport perspective are inflammable liquids, poisons and corrosives. The key requirement is that dangerous goods in course of transport are properly identified and labelled. When the delivery includes goods classified as dangerous, the SSN should not be used but replaced by the SITPRO dangerous goods note (DGN) which contains the shipper's declaration of dangerous goods. This declaration is, firstly, a legal statement by the shipper that the package containing the dangerous goods has been properly prepared for transport, and secondly, identifies the dangerous goods in the consignment. A special DGN is used for air transport.

14.13.2   Carriage documentation

Bills of lading

A bill of lading is a document issued by a carrier to confirm receipt of goods to be transported to an agreed destination. A bill of lading may serve three purposes:

- As a receipt for goods, certifying that the goods described in the bill are in apparent good order except as noted on the document. The bill should be signed by both the shipper and an agent for the carrier.

- As a contract of carriage identifying the contracting parties and setting out the terms and conditions of the agreement.

- As a transferable document of title effected through endorsement and the passing of the bill from one person to another.

Air and sea waybills

Like a bill of lading, waybills act as a receipt of goods and evidence of carriage. They do not, however, confer a title to the goods. Way bills provide a simple alternative to a bill of lading where the ability to transfer title to the goods is not required.

14.13.3 Customs documentation

Documents that may be required by customs authorities include certificates of origin, consular declarations and pre-shipment inspection certificates.

14.14 Total distribution costs

14.14.1 Definition

The total cost of distribution may be defined as:

The sum total of all the costs incurred in the distribution of goods.

Clearly, costs will differ from organisation to organisation, and a company may have specific 'total' distribution costs which may include such items as a private goods vehicle fleet (either owned or leased) or IT costs for hardware and software to manage the total supply chain operation. In general, however, the total cost of distribution will include such items as transportation charges, inventory carrying costs, service factors, packaging, insurance and miscellaneous costs.

14.14.2 Elements of freight costs

Fixed and variable costs

All costs may be divided into fixed and variable. In relation to the five modes of transport identified earlier, these may be summarised as in Table 14.5.

Critical transport elements

On a five-point scale ranging from 1 (best) to 5 (worst), the critical operating characteristics may be rated as shown in Table 14.6.

Table 14.5   Fixed and variable costs of differing transport modes

Mode of transport	Suitable for	Fixed cost	Variable cost
Road	Medium/light loads	Low	Medium
Rail	Heavy bulk loads	High	Low
Air	High value goods where rapid delivery is important	Low	High
Water	Heavy bulk loads including oil and timber	Medium	Low
Pipelines	Petroleum, chemicals	High	Low

Table 14.6   Operating characteristics of five transport modes

Operating characteristics	Mode of transport				
	Road	Rail	Air	Water	Pipeline
Speed	2	3	1	4	5
Availability	1	2	3	4	5
Dependability	2	3	5	4	1
Capability	3	2	5	4	1
Flexibility	1	3	5	2	5
Environmental	5	3	4	1	1
Composite	14	16	23	19	22

Rates

Rates paid to hire carriers can be classified as follows:

■ *Volume rates in which rates are related to the size of the shipment.* Volume is reflected in the rate structure which may take account of such factors as size of shipments, i.e. consistently high shipments at lower rates than those for smaller shipments. Such special rates are considered deviations from the regular rates that apply to lower volume shipments.

■ *Distance-related rates.* Such rates may be: (i) uniform rates, i.e. one transport rate for all origin–destination distances; (ii) proportional rates in which the rate varies with the distance as, shown in Figure 14.3; (iii) tapering rates in which rates increase with distance but by a decreasing amount (see Figure 14.4); and (iv) blanket rates, i.e. single rates covering a specified area for specified products, e.g. coal, grain. Often, blanket rates are adjusted to meet competition.

■ *Demand-related rates.* These rates are often referred to as charging what the traffic will bear in which the rate is determined by the demand or competition for the particular freight service.

Other factors that may influence rates include: (i) the product, e.g. bulk, volume, fragility; (ii) the freight provider, e.g. conference and independent rates for ocean shipping; (iii) incentive rates, e.g. shippers may be offered reduced rates if an agreed minimum tonnage is moved within a specified period. Conversely,

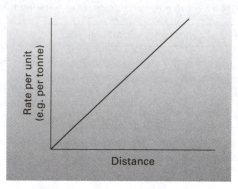

Figure 14.3 Proportional rate

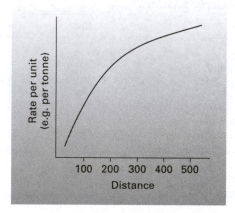

Figure 14.4 Tapering rate

increased rates may be offered to carriers for an assurance that goods will reach their destination ahead of normal times.

Inventory-carrying costs

Inventory-carrying costs were considered in Chapter 8.

Service factors

Transportation costs are strongly influenced by the level of service that a supply chain aims to provide. If, for example, a supplier aims to dispatch goods on the same day an order is received it will have many small outbound loads resulting in high transport costs. Conversely, by aggregating orders over a period it will be able to make larger deliveries at lower transport costs through exploiting economies of scale.

A second factor in transportation costs is the *transportation network*. The achievement of low cost responsiveness depends to a large extent on a well-designed transportation network which provides the infrastructure for efficient vehicle scheduling and routing.

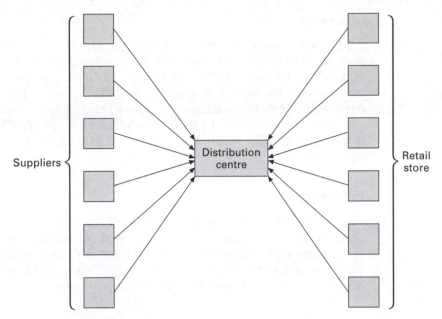

Figure 14.5   Indirect delivery and distribution centre

Networks can be direct or indirect. With *direct delivery* the routing of each consignment is from supplier to customer. Direct delivery, usually by road, is justified when each consignment is large enough so that consignments constitute a full load to each customer. Consignments can be consolidated to enable one vehicle to make drops to a number of customers, e.g. a supplier making deliveries within an area of high customer density.

Indirect delivery is where, instead of making deliveries directly, suppliers make use of distribution centres. Such distribution centres facilitate cross-docking (the merging of goods flows from several sources at a distribution centre before final delivery but without holding any inventory at the distribution centre). Cross-docking, as shown in Figure 14.5, is appropriate when volumes are predictable and enables economies of scale to be achieved by both supplier and customer.

An effective strategy distribution plan will determine the optional network which ensures that customers are provided with the right quantity of goods at the right places, at the right time at the lowest total distribution cost.

Packaging

Packaging influences both the efficiency and effectiveness of logistics implementation. Industrial packaging focuses on such aspects as (i) handling, e.g. palletisation, stock picking; (ii) protection and security, e.g. containerisation; and (iii) communication, e.g. the package content identification, the tracking of goods in transit and in store, and handling instructions relating to such aspects as fragility, hazards and environmental issues.

An important facet of tracking is that the internet can enable the tracking and tracing of consignments by all the parties involved.

Insurance

Suppliers of goods will wish to insure the goods during the period for which they are at their risk. Although such risks end with the passing of title, insurance may also be taken out against contingencies such as stoppage of goods in transit, insolvency of the buyer and refusal of the buyer to accept goods on arrival at their destination. Incoterms, referred to later in this chapter, help to achieve clarity concerning the passing of title of goods in transit. The cost of freight insurance is a specialised field and will vary according to the risks attaching to a specific consignment.

Pilferage

High value and consumer goods especially face an enhanced risk of theft or pilferage. In general, the use of door-to-door intermodal containers significantly reduces the exposure to such risks although container hijacking targeting high value consumer and electrical goods, usually as a result of dishonest 'insider' carrier information, have become increasingly common.

Miscellaneous costs

Additional costs may be incurred for documentation, customs clearance, proof of delivery, delivery outside working hours, cash on delivery, abnormally shaped cargo, hazardous cargo and similar items.

14.14.3 Minimising freight costs

There are numerous ways in which freight costs may be minimised, including:

- Siting manufacturing and assembly processes nearer to customers and suppliers.
- Cross-docking.
- Aggregating loads to prevent part-empty running when delivering.
- Avoiding, if possible, empty vehicles on return journeys.
- Using smaller vehicles, particularly for transportation in urban areas.
- Arranging delivery times at other than peak periods which may necessitate idle or waiting times.
- Negotiating lower rates either directly or through freight forwarders.
- Undertaking a cost analysis of total costs to ascertain where possible economies may be made.
- Requiring reductions in the cost per unit of distance as the distance increases, on the grounds that fixed costs will be spread over a larger distance base.
- Requiring reductions in the cost per unit of weight as the size of the shipment increases, on the grounds that fixed costs can be spread over a larger weight base.
- Analysing the relative importance of such factors as speed, availability, dependability, security, etc., to a particular customer and as a value-adding element for the product and producer. Such an analysis will enable possible trade-offs

to be identified, e.g. speed and cost, cost of carrying inventory and cost of transportation.

14.15   Incoterms

14.15.1   What are Incoterms?

Incoterms refer to the set of international rules for the interpretation of the chief terms used in foreign trade contracts first published by the International Chamber of Trade in 1936 (now International Chamber of Commerce) and amended in 1953, 1967, 1976, 1980, 1990 and 2000.

The reason why Incoterms are periodically revised is to ensure that they represent current practice. In the 1990 version, for example, the clause dealing with the seller's obligation to provide proof of delivery allowed paper documentation to be replaced by e-mail for that purpose.

Although the use of Incoterms is optional, such terms can reduce difficulties encountered by importers and exporters.

14.15.2   Format of Incoterms

Each Incoterm is referred to by a three letter abbreviation. The International Chamber of Commerce (ICC) recommends that Incoterms 2000 be referred to specifically whenever the terms are used together with a location. For example the term FOB (free on board) should always be accompanied by a reference to the exact place to which delivery should be made. An example of the correct use of an Incoterm is 'FOB Liverpool Incoterms 2000'.

Incoterms are grouped into four categories, each denoted by the first letter of the three letter abbreviation:

- Under the E term (EXW) the seller only makes the goods available to the buyer at the seller's own premises. There is only one Incoterm in this category.
- Under the F term (FCA, FAS and FOB) the seller is called upon to deliver the goods to a carrier appointed by the buyer.
- Under the C term (CFR, CIF, CPT and CIP) the seller has to contract for carriage, but without assuming the risk of loss or damage to the goods or additional costs due to events occurring after shipment or dispatch.
- Under the D term (DAF, DES, DEQ, DDU and DDP) the seller has to bear all costs and risks needed to bring the goods to the place of destination.

The most used Incoterms are probably FOB, CIF and FCA. Incoterms suitable for any mode of transport including inter- or multimodal are EXW, FCA, CPT, CIP, DES and DEQ.

14.15.3   Explanation of Incoterms

An explanation of transport obligations, costs and risks attached to each Incoterm is provided by Table 14.7.

Table 14.7 Incoterms

Group	Incoterm	Meaning	Carriage	Risk	Cost
E (i) Departure	EXW	Ex Works (named place) Goods are made available at the seller's premises for collection by the buyer	Arranged by the buyer. Seller does not clear the goods for export or load them onto any collecting vehicle	Transfer from the seller to the buyer when the goods are at the buyer's disposal. Seller's risks are at a minimum	Transfer from seller to buyer when the goods are at the buyer's disposal
F Main carriage not paid by seller but seller must hand over the goods to the buyer's nominated carrier. Free of risk and expense to the buyer	FCA	Free Carrier (named place) Unless otherwise agreed seller arranges export clearance and pays for the pre-carriage in the country of origin	Carriage to be arranged by the buyer or by the seller on the buyer's behalf. If seller's premises chosen, seller is responsible for loading. At any other place seller is not responsible for loading	Transfer from seller to buyer when goods have been delivered to carrier at the named place	Transfer from seller to buyer when goods have been delivered to the carrier at the named place
	FAS	Free Alongside Ship (named port of shipment) Delivery is deemed to have taken place when goods are placed alongside the ship or inland waterway vessel at named port of shipment. Seller clears goods for export (S)	To be arranged by the buyer	Transfer from seller to buyer when the goods have been placed alongside the ship	Transfer from seller to buyer when the goods have been placed alongside the ship
	FOB	Free On Board (named port of shipment) Delivery has taken place when the goods pass the ship's rail at named port of shipment. Seller clears goods for export (S)	To be arranged by the buyer	Transfer from seller to buyer when the goods pass the ship's rail	Transfer from seller to buyer when the goods pass the ship's rail

Code	Description	Carriage / insurance	Risk transfer	Cost transfer
C	Main carriage paid by seller but without assuming the risk of the main carriage. Seller must, however, bear certain costs even after critical point for the division of risk of loss or danger to the goods has been reached			
CFR	Cost and Freight (named port of destination) Seller clears goods for export, delivers to nominated carrier and pays costs and freight to bring them to the named port of destination. Risk and additional costs pass to buyer after time of delivery (S)	Carriage to be arranged by the seller	Transfer from the seller to the buyer after the goods pass the ship's rail	Transfer from the seller to the buyer at port of destination buyer paying such costs as are not for the seller's account under the contract of carriage
CIF	Cost, Insurance and Freight (named port of destination) As CFR with the additional obligation that the seller is required to obtain and pay for minimum cover marine insurance for goods during carriage (S)	Carriage and insurance to be arranged by the seller	Transfer from the seller to the buyer after the goods pass ship's rail	Transfer from the seller to the buyer at port of destination, buyer paying such costs as are not for the seller's account under the contract of carriage
CPT	Carriage Paid To (named port of destination) Seller clears goods for export, delivers to buyer's nominated carrier and pays the cost of carriage to named destination. Buyer bears all risks after delivery. If subsequent carriers are used the risk passes on delivery of goods to the first carrier	Carriage to be arranged by the seller	Transfer from the seller to the buyer when the goods have been delivered to the carrier	Transfer from the seller to the buyer at place of destination, buyer paying such costs as are not for the seller's account under the contract of carriage
CIP	Carriage and Insurance Paid (named port of destination) Seller clears goods for export and delivers to the nominated carrier, paying the costs to bring the goods to the named destination. Seller also obtains and pays for insurance against the buyer's risk of loss or damage to the cargo during carriage on minimum cover. Risk passes when goods delivered to the first carrier	Carriage and insurance to be arranged by the seller	Transfer from the seller to the buyer when the goods have been delivered to the carrier	Transfer from the seller to the buyer at port of destination, buyer paying such costs as are not for the seller's account under the contract of carriage

Table 14.7 (cont'd)

Group	Incoterm	Meaning	Carriage	Risk	Cost
D Seller's cost/risk is maximised since the goods must be made available upon arrival at a stated destination	DAF	Delivered at Frontier (named place) Seller delivers when goods are at the disposal of buyer on the arriving means of transport, cleared for export but not import at the named point of frontier. Contract of sale to state if risk and costs of unloading from arriving means of transport to be borne by seller	Carriage to be arranged by the seller	Transfer from seller to the buyer after the goods have been delivered at the frontier	Transfer from the seller to the buyer when the goods have been delivered to the frontier
	DES	Delivered Ex Ship (named port of destination) Seller delivers when goods are placed at disposal of buyer on board ship not cleared for import. Seller bears all costs and risks to port of destination prior to unloading (S)	Carriage to be arranged by the seller	Transfer from the seller to the buyer when the goods are placed at the disposal of the buyer on board ship	Transfer from the seller to the buyer when the goods are placed at the disposal of the buyer on board ship
	DEQ	Delivered Ex Quay (named port of destination) Delivery takes place when goods, not cleared, are placed at the disposal of the buyer on the quay at the named port of destination. Sellers incurs all costs and risks on boarding goods to the port of destination including cost of unloading. The buyer clears the goods for import and pays all customs-related formalities and duties, contracted sale to specify any further seller obligations upon import (S)	Carriage to be arranged by the seller	Transfer from the seller to the buyer after the goods are placed at the disposal of the buyer on the quay	Transfer from the seller to the buyer after the goods are placed at the disposal of the buyer on the quay

DDU	Delivered Duty Unpaid (named place of destination) Seller delivers goods to buyer not cleared for import and not unloaded from any arriving means of transport at named place of destination. Seller bears costs and risks in bringing goods to this point but not customs formalities or payment of duties. Contract of sale to specify if seller's responsibility extended to customs formalities	Carriage to be arranged by the seller	Transfer from the seller to the buyer when the goods are placed at the disposal of the buyer	Transfer from the seller to the buyer when the goods are placed at the disposal of the buyer
DDP	Delivered Duty Paid (named port of destination) Seller's maximum obligation involving delivery of goods to the buyer, all costs and risks in bringing goods to that point cleared for import and paying duties but not unloaded from arriving means of transport at place of destination. Contract of sale to state if seller is excised from any costs payable in connection with import. Not to be used if seller is unable to obtain import licence	Carriage to be arranged by the seller	Transfer from the seller to the buyer when the goods are placed at the disposal of the buyer	Transfer from the seller to the buyer when the goods are placed at the disposal of the buyer

S = shipbuilding only

14.15.4 Advantages of Incoterms

■ Incoterms are suitable for any mode of transport although six of the terms are intended only for sea and inland waterway transport.

■ If, when drawing up a contract, buyers and sellers specifically refer to one of the ICC Incoterms, they can be sure of defining simply and safely their respective responsibilities especially with regard to passing of title, risks and costs, thus eliminating any possibility of misunderstanding and subsequent dispute. Thus, while Incoterms do not enter into a contract of sale automatically in the same way as local, national or international conventions, they may be incorporated into the contract in five ways: (i) the custom of the trade, (ii) standard forms, (iii) statutory rules, e.g. Sale of Goods Acts, (iv) implied terms, and (v) express intention.

■ Incoterms are subject to regular revision so that they reflect transportation and communication changes: FOB airport and FCA for shipments by aircraft were introduced in 1976 and 1990 respectively. The 1990 revision related FCA, CPT and CID to container vessels.

14.16 Freight agents

Many large companies have their own account transport or logistics functions capable of handling all aspects of transport including import and export requirements. Particularly for international freight, other enterprises will avail themselves of the services of freight agents or forwarders.

14.16.1 What is a freight agent or forwarder?

A freight agent or forwarder is a person or company who, for a reward, undertakes to have goods carried and delivered to a destination. The services of freight agents are normally engaged when the carriage of goods involves successive carriers or the use of successive means of transport.

Traditionally, freight agents make contracts of carriage for their principals. Under the principles of the law of agency, a freight agent is under an obligation to the principal to conclude the contract on the agreed terms. Although, in civil law, freight agents are distinguished from carriers, the latter sometimes act as freight agents.

14.16.2 The services of freight agents

In a 1970 report of the National Economic Development Office,[16] the traditional functions of forwarders were defined as follows:

■ The preparation and handling of documentation. The main types of document with which forwarders are concerned are: bills of lading, air waybills or equivalent, customs papers, certificates of origin, exchange control forms, insurance certificates, shipping notes, calling forward notes, collection orders, port rate forms and help in preparing invoices.

- Planning and costing of the route to give the desired combination of speed, economy and reliability, trading times against cost.
- Booking and coordinating transport and freight space, domestic, international and foreign.
- Arranging any ancillary services, e.g. warehousing, packing.
- Consolidating and paying charges payable to transport, e.g. operators, port authorities, customs, etc.
- Presenting goods for customs clearance, both for imports to the UK and abroad through overseas offices, correspondents etc. for UK exports.
- Advising on special requirements, trade and financial, of foreign countries and providing necessary documents.
- Providing exporters with information to prepare quotations, particularly CIF or delivered importers premises.
- Advising importers of details of and changes in UK import procedures.

Other services offered by forwarders may include:

- Consolidation or groupage, i.e. grouping of consignments from several consignors into a single load.
- Road haulage such as the operation of a cargo collection and delivery service to and from sea or air ports.
- Containers – some forwarders may operate container services or lease containers.
- Provision of warehousing, packing, insurance, financial and market research services.
- Coordination of delivery of multiple consignments.

14.16.3 Freight agents' fees

Freight forwarders are paid a negotiated fee by the shipper or importer depending on the service or documents required. Fees are related to Incoterms in that they depend on the responsibilities undertaken by the Incoterms. They will be lower, for example, if the responsibilities end FOB at the departure port and increase as responsibilities extend DDP to the destination terminal.

14.16.4 Freight agents and the future

Willmott[17] points out that the development of logistics and supply chain management requires 'the services of "logistics practitioners" who can mesh themselves into the overall pattern, not just as suppliers of freight forwarding services but as links that might encompass several business functions'. Such functions are listed by Willmott as:

- Customerisation or tailoring for individual markets or customers.
- Sourcing and delivery of raw materials.
- Allocation of materials and packaging.
- Manufactured and capacity planning.
- Inventory determination and allocation to warehouses.

- International movement by sea, road, rail and air.
- Domestic trunking and primary and multi-drop distribution.
- Order fulfilment, including picking, packing and dispatch/delivery to customer.
- E-commerce support of supply chain visibility.
- Reverse logistics, perhaps involving call centre management and collections for repair/servicing, etc.

Possible developments include:

- The establishing of 'one-stop' entities through the merging of logistics and forwarding services providing wider capabilities as suppliers of materials and components enabling manufacturers to outsource non-core logistic and transport activities.
- The secondment of freight forwarder's staff to major customers to provide on-site freight expertise.
- Whole supply chains will set up in competition with each other rather than individual companies with the consequence that a freight forwarder may become a link in more than one chain.

Case study[18]

You are the newly appointed logistics manager for Electro2000, a large electronics company manufacturing a range of products for both industry and household markets. You have been asked by your managing director to examine the company's international supply chains where he feels there are some significant problems.

Currently your buyers source around a third of the components and assemblies you use at your factory in the London area from a large number of suppliers in the Far East. These imports have a value of £110 million, and are equivalent each year to 800 TEUs (20 ft equivalent container units).

The buyers on return from their sourcing forays to the Far East pass handwritten orders to the shipping department. This is because they have made their purchases in a range of foreign currencies, which your computer system cannot handle.

Your shipping department handles all the order processing, customer clearance and payments, and most of what is bought is on C&F (cost and freight) terms, usually with letters of credit against payment. Paperwork systems are extremely cumbersome, with shipping and bank documents to complete as well as HMC&E (Her Majesty's Customs and Excise) declarations. Once an order is placed, your company usually is not able to track delivery until the goods arrive in the UK. Because of the C&F terms, your suppliers have no obligation to even let you know which ship your goods are on, let alone the date of departure. Nor do you know how much they have built into their pricing structures to cover transport costs, but you suspect it is rather a lot! From landing at port to delivery to your factory also usually takes between 5 days and 3 weeks, with an average of two and half weeks.

Because of the long and vulnerable supply pipeline, your buyers tend to ensure that you have about 2 or 3 months' stock on hand of the purchases from the Far East. However, this stockholding appears to be more than justified by cheap prices they obtain. They are buying at anything up to a 70 per cent discount to comparable prices from UK or European suppliers.

Quality is, however, a continuing problem. A two-stage system is in place, whereby suppliers send Electro samples for testing, and the company also has an agent in the Far East whose job is to monitor quality assurance and check products before dispatch. However, the quality of delivered goods often bears no relation to the samples sent and rigorously tested by you.

And the agent often does not apparently manage to inspect goods before dispatch. At the moment there are products worth around £1 million rejected by Electro's factory quality inspectors with which the company is in dispute with suppliers. Most of these have already been paid for by letters of credit.

Recently attending a meeting of the local Best Practice Club the theme was, fortuitously for you, 'Dealing with Far Eastern Suppliers'. You learned there that Woolworth and Argos, two of the big names on the high street, who themselves sourced globally, had both moved towards appointing freight forwarders in the Far East who acted on their behalf. This seemed to you a good idea, and you determined to assess the arguments for and against.

Questions

1 What would be the advantages to you of a change to buying FOB (free on board)?

2 What are the arguments for and against appointing a freight forwarder in the Far East to handle all of your business?

3 One of the issues you have to deal with in terms of continuing to buy from the Far East is quality. What steps can you take to improve what is currently happening?

? Discussion questions

14.1 Consider the list of factors to which the increased demand for transport in the EU between 1970 and 1997 is attributed. There are 12 such factors. From your reading or experience, give one example of each of the 12 factors listed.

14.2 'You need more than transport to put troops, ammunition, food, fuel and equipment in the right place.' What, in addition to transport, do you need?

14.3 How might transport factors influence JIT? (Consider the example of Japanese transport factors provided by Rhys *et al.* in Chapter 8.)

14.4 Give examples of the reasonable care you would take when arranging for transport of 'directive waste'.

14.5 What are the arguments for and against increasing maximum allowed gross vehicle weights?

14.6 What conclusion do you draw about own account and public haulage working from a study of Tables 14.1 and 14.2?

14.7 From a study of Table 14.3 what conclusions would you draw relating to the demand for coal, metals, construction and oil and petroleum between 1990/91 and 2000/01?

14.8 What are some advantages of delivering coal directly by rail from the colliery to an electricity power station?

14.9 If, in volume terms, the proportion of total UK trade carried by air is insignificant, why does air transport account for at least one-fifth of UK trade in value terms?

14.10 In 1997, the UK government proposed that 3 per cent of all freight currently transported by road should be moved by water. Why do you consider that this proposal has been largely ignored by industry and little support given to the improvement of inland waterways?

14.11 Why is British shipping in decline?

14.12 Identify four commodities that you would send by sea but not by air, and vice versa.

14.13 Your company is a manufacturer of heavy machinery. An important order has been received for shipment to South Africa. Describe how road, rail and sea can be utilised to deliver the machinery to its destination and the role of terminals and containers in the process.

14.14 Describe the purpose(s) of each of the following documents in not more than two sentences. (One of these is not described in the text and you will have to research it independently.)

(a) Air waybill

(b) Bill of lading

(c) Certificate of origin

(d) Dangerous goods note

(e) Sea waybill

(f) Standard shipping note

14.15 Assume that your company is shipping goods valued at £25,000 to an overseas destination. Insert hypothetical figures in the tables below to arrive at the total cost of shipment, EXW, FOB.

Product cost

Material	£
Labour	£
Plant overhead	£
Administration	£
Financing costs	£
Domestic duties	£
Total cost of production	£

Foreign marketing

Travel accommodations	£
Promotion	£
Communications	£
Translation	£
Professional fees	£
Agency marketing costs	£

Total cost of production	£

Preparation for shipping

Labelling	£
Packaging	£
Packing	£
Marking etc.	£

Total shipping preparation costs	£
*Total cost ex works of product	£

International financing

Costs of instruments	£
Export credit insurance	£
Discount on receivables	£
Currency conversion fees	£
Loan interest costs	£

Total international financing	£
Profit mark up	£
Quote ex works price at	£

Calculating an FOB transaction

*Total cost ex works of product	£

Domestic freight

Documentation	£
Factory loading charges	£
Transportation to port	£
Unloading at port	£
Storage	£
Port costs	£
Ship loading charges	£
Freight forwarding fees	£
Total domestic freight	£
Total cost FOB of product	£

International financing

Costs of instruments	£
Export credit insurance	£
Discount on receivables	£
Currency conversion fees	£
Loan interest costs	£
Total international financing	£
Profit mark up	£
Quote FOB price at	£

14.16 Your company has its own fleet of heavy goods lorries that deliver goods in relatively small consignments to customers throughout the country. Customers may be located at distances as little as 2 miles or as great as 300 miles from your factory. Sometimes lorries are only half loaded. Suggest how transport costs can be reduced and what competitive advantages may result from the reduction.

14.17 There are 13 Incoterms. From memory, write down the Incoterms falling into each of the four categories E, F, C and D.

14.18 What criteria would you use to evaluate the services provided by a freight agent or forwarder?

❓ Past examination questions

1 Discuss the advantages and disadvantages of using road transport to distribute goods.

(CIPS, Introduction to Purchasing and Supply Chain Management, May 1998)

2 Write explanatory notes on each of the following pairs of abbreviations:

(a) MRP – DRP

(b) EOQ – JIT

(c) CIF – FOB

(d) VA – VE

(CIPS, Introduction to Purchasing and Supply Chain Management, November 1998)

3 What are the main service components of physical distribution and how would you measure them?

(CIPS, Distribution, November 1998)

4 Select three different modes of transport used to carry freight and compare the benefits and disadvantages of each type.

(CIPS, Introduction to Purchasing and Supply Chain Management, May 1999)

5 With increased road congestion, there is continued interest in using alternatives to road for freight. What are the attractions of using intermodal transport in Europe?

(CIPS, Distribution, May 1999)

6 Explain why, in modern distribution operations, inbound logistics has become just as important as outbound distribution of finished goods to the distribution manager in planning his or her strategy.

(CIPS, Distribution, May 1999)

7 What are the relative benefits for a medium-sized manufacturing company of each of the following distribution alternatives:

(a) In-house

(b) Using a third party distribution company and conventional 3 or 5 year contract

(CIPS, Distribution, November 1999)

8 You are the distribution manager of a fashion chain with 200 ships in the UK and 100 spread across Europe and the Far East. You source products from around the world. What is the role of a freight forwarder in helping you manage your international supply chain?

(CIPS, Distribution, May 2000)

9 You are a distribution manager for a flower growing business in Kenya.

  (a) Explain how you would send cut flowers from your farm to the UK for sale by a major supermarket chain.

  (b) Justify why you have chosen each mode of transport.

  (CIPS, Introduction to Purchasing and
  Supply Chain Management, November 2000)

10 (a) What are the main factors influencing choice of transport mode?

  (b) Discuss why air freight is becoming increasingly popular in servicing the needs of international supply chains.

  (CIPS, Distribution, November 2000)

Notes

1. European Commission, *EU Transport in Figures*, 1998
2. See http://www.iru.org/Publications/OnlinePub/KPMG/KPMG.E.html
3. Willmott, K., *Understanding the Freight Business*, 5th edn, TT Club, 2001, p.202
4. Gattorna, J.L. and Walters, P.W., *Managing the Supply Chain*, Macmillan Business, 1996, Ch.9, p.137
5. Ballou, R.H., *Basic Business Logistics*, 2nd edn, Prentice Hall, 1987, Ch.2, p.26
6. Freight Transport Association, *Yearbook of Transport Law*, 2002, p.287
7. Ibid., p.23
8. Eurostat, *Glossary for Transport Statistics*, 2nd edn, 1997, p.2
9. Ibid.
10. Department for Transport, Local Government and the Regions (DTLR). Note that as of 2002, the Department of Transport is now separate
11. Ship Builders and Ship Repairers' Association, *Waterbound Freight Facts*, 2002, p.1
12. Department for Transport, Local Government and the Regions, *Maritime Statistics*, HMSO
13. IFTC website: http://www.wilbursmith.com/a1605/spc.cfm
14. National Commission on Intermodal Transportation (USA), *Towards a National Intermodal Transportation System*, 1994
15. Ballou, as n.5 above
16. National Economic Development Office, *The Freight Forwarder*, HMSO, 1970 pp.1–3
17. Willmott, as n.3 above, pp.203–4
18. The authors are grateful to the CIPS for permission to reproduce this case study from the May 1998 Distribution examination paper

Strategy, tactics and operations (4): support tools, supplier relationships and purchasing performance

Human resources in the supply chain

Learning goals

After reading this chapter you should be able to:

- Define the term 'human resources management' (HRM).
- Distinguish between HRM and personnel management.
- Identify external and internal factors of importance on HRM planning.
- Define and state the main elements of job analysis.
- State some considerations influencing the decision to recruit.
- Prepare a job description, job specification or role profile.
- State the uses of application forms and CVs.
- Appraise the purposes and criticisms of interviews as a selection method.
- Define and list the aims of performance appraisal and some objections to appraisals.
- Distinguish training from education and development.
- Describe some methods of training and development applicable to purchasing and supply.
- Explain NVQ terms and the application of NVQs to purchasing and supply.
- Outline professional and university qualifications relevant to purchasing and logistics management.
- Describe the aims, benefits, methodology and implementation of Continuing Professional Development.
- Differentiate between pay and the total remuneration package.
- List and explain some sources of information regarding purchasing pay.
- Provide an outline explanation of such concepts as motivation, commitment and empowerment.
- Identify and discuss types of change, resistance to change and the implementation of organisational change.
- Give reasons for team formation and discuss team types, team building, team roles and the characteristics of effective work teams.
- Distinguish between management and leadership.
- List and explain the managerial roles identified by Mintzberg and Drucker.
- Indicate strategic aspects of HRM in a purchasing context.

15.1 Human resources management

15.1.1 Definition

Human resources management (HRM) is defined by Storey[1] as:

> A distinctive approach to employment management which seeks to achieve competitive advantage through the strategic deployment of a highly committed and capable work force, using an integrated array of cultural, structural and personnel techniques.

15.1.2 Comparison with personnel management

As shown in Chapter 3, Porter regards both HRM and procurement as support activities. The use of HRM rather than 'personnel' reflects that those who work for an organisation (not necessarily confined to employees) are considered as a source of comparative advantage to the enterprise in the same way that procurement should be regarded as an added value rather than cost cutting activity. A comparison by Guest,[2] of stereotypes of personnel and HRM is given in Table 15.1.

Purchasing managers need to have an awareness of HRM because they are also managers of personnel. They should also recognise that in the final analysis it is human capability and commitment that distinguish successful organisations from the rest. Purchasing, like other functional managers, are responsible for implementing personnel policies, team briefings, performance appraisals, interviews, target setting, encouraging employee commitment, managing performance-related pay, and similar activities.

Many writers extend the scope of HRM to include organisational behaviour covering such subjects as motivation, interpersonal and group behaviours, attitudes, job satisfaction, leadership communication and organisational change. It is not possible to deal adequately with these areas within the constraints of this

Table 15.1 Stereotypes of personnel management and human resources management

	Personnel management	HRM
Time and planning perspective	Short-term, reactive, ad hoc, marginal	Long-term, proactive, strategic, integrated
Psychological contract	Compliance	Commitment
Control systems	External controls	Self-control
Employee relations	Pluralist, collective, low trust	Unitary, individual, high trust
Preferred structures/ systems	Bureaucratic, mechanistic, centralised, formal defined roles	Organic, devolved, flexible roles
Roles	Specialist/professional	Largely integrated into line management
Evaluation criteria	Cost minimisation	Maximum utilisation (human asset accounting)

book. There are, however, four 'generic' HRM functions that are performed within all organisations: recruitment and selection; appraisal; reward; and training and development. Along with human resources planning and job analysis, the above four activities are considered from the standpoint of the purchasing function.

15.2 Human resources planning

This may be defined as an information and decision-making process designed to ensure that enough competent people with appropriate skills are available to perform jobs where and when they will be needed. For purchasing, as for all other staff, human resources planning will depend on both external and internal factors.

15.2.1 External factors in human resources planning

External factors will depend on the following:

- Whether the organisation operates under conditions of certainty or uncertainty – the more uncertain the environment, the more frequently human resources plans will need to be updated.
- World trade prospects.
- The organisation's competitive position within the industry.
- External changes in technology, equipment and work methods.
- Age trends in the general population.
- Education/skill requirements and their availability.

15.2.2 Internal factors in human resource planning

Internal factors will include a human resources audit including consideration of such factors as the following:

- Ages of the present staff.
- Likely losses through retirement, leaving, etc.
- Labour turnover for each grade of staff employed.
- Anticipated promotions and transfers.
- Skills analysis, regularly updated, in respect of each employee.
- Effects of human resources requirements due to the introduction of technology, organisational planning, etc.
- Temporary losses through illness, pregnancy, training absence, etc.

15.2.3 Other factors in HRM planning

Other internal factors include budget allocations for personnel and training.

Analysis of all the above factors will enable human resources plans to be formulated relating to the positions to be filled in the short, medium and long term; analysis of education and skills likely to be required; and career plans for existing staff with accompanying training and development plans.

15.3 Job analysis

15.3.1 Definition

Job analysis may be defined as:

> the examination of the facts about a certain job to determine its essential component factors and the qualities required by the employee to perform it satisfactorily.

The elements of job analysis, with definitions, are shown in Figure 15.1.

15.3.2 Jobs, positions and occupations

A *job* is a collection of tasks duties and responsibilities, which, as a whole, are assigned to an individual.

A *position* is a series of jobs performed by an individual (e.g. a buyer, purchasing manager).

An *occupation* is a generalised job common to many areas or organisations, e.g. purchasing officer.

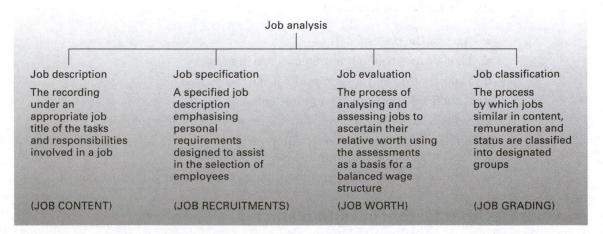

Figure 15.1 The elements of job analysis

15.4 Recruitment and selection

This section looks at deciding whether and how to recruit staff, the preparation of job descriptions and specifications and the attraction and selection of candidates.

15.4.1 Whether and how to recruit

Plumbley[3] has identified the following questions that should be asked before embarking on the recruitment process:

- What is the purpose of the job? Is it necessary? Is it fulfilling the purpose?
- Could it be combined with another job or jobs or could tasks be allocated to make better use of other people in the department?
- Can we learn lessons from the record of the last job incumbent?
- Could the vacancy be used as a temporary training position or to accommodate an employee redundant elsewhere, to provide easier work for an employee approaching retirement or in failing health, or as an opportunity to promote someone?
- Are we certain that no existing employee would be suitable? Could we afford to train someone?
- Is the required type of person easier to recruit locally? Are there aspects of the job analysis (hours of work) or of the person specification which could be adjusted to attract a wider choice of candidates?

To the above, we must add:

- Might it be more advantageous to appoint someone on a short-term consultancy basis?

15.4.2 Job descriptions

A job description defining the overall purpose or role of the employee and the main tasks to be carried out should be prepared for each member of the purchasing function. A typical job description will have the following headings:

- Job title.
- Responsible to – the person or function to whom the jobholder reports.
- Responsible for – a listing of the principal duties and responsibilities of the job.
- Resources controlled.
- Special responsibilities – tasks emphasised as requiring particular attention.
- Limitations on authority – particularly with regard to the amount the jobholder may spend without reference to higher authority.
- Functional contacts – relationship between purchasing and other functions as part of the supply chain.
- Committees – organisational meetings which the jobholder is expected to attend as an ex-officio member

Table 15.2 Samples of job titles relating to purchasing and supply from an analysis of advertised vacancies

Supply Management		Focus	
Job title	No. of vacancies	Job title	No. of vacancies
Asset Manager	1	Buyer	1
Assistant Buyer	1	Category Manager	1
Buyer	5	Category Demand Planner	1
Buyer (Global Sourcing)	1	Category Supply Planner	1
Buyer (Indirects)	1	Contract Manager	2
Buyer/Senior Buyer	1	Director Supply Chain Operations	1
Chief Buyer	1	Food Procurement Manager	1
Commissioner	1	Inventory Control Manager	1
Commodity Buyers (Electronics)	Unspecified	Inventory Manager	1
Commercial Specialist	1	Inventory Schedulers	1
Contracts Buyer	1	Inventory Specialist	1
Contracts Officer	3	Inventory Team Leader	1
Current Model Buyer	1	Logistics Administrator	1
Development Officer	1	Logistics Development Manager	1
Equipment Engineer/Buyer	1	Logistics Executive	1
Fixtures Buyer	1	Logistics Manager	3
Head of Procurement	2	Procurement Planner	1
Ingredients Buyer	1	Production Buyer	1
IT Buyer	1	Replenishment Controller	1
Inventory Controller	1	Senior Buyer	1
Junior Buyer	1	Stock Control Co-ordinator	1
Materials Analyst	1	Stock Control Manager	1
Materials Procurement Analyst	1	Stock Planner	1
Materials Project Manager	1	Supplier Development Manager	1
Packaging Buyer	1	Supply Chain Account Manager	1
Pre-Programme Buyers	Unspecified	Supply Chain Analyst	1
Procurement Advisors	Unspecified	Supply Chain Director	1
Procurement Assistant	1	Supply Chain Management	Unspecified
Procurement Development Officer	1	Supply Chain Manager	3
Procurement Executive	1	Supply Chain Manager/Director	1
Procurement Officer	1	UK Logistics General Manager	1
Produce Buyer	1		
Project Buyer	1		
Purchasing Director	1		
Purchasing Manager	5		
Purchasing and Supply Manager	1		
Senior Buyer	7		
Senior Buyer (Electronics)	1		
Senior Buyer (Operations)	1		
Senior Contracts Manager	1		
Senior Procurement Specialist	1		
Strategic Procurement Manager	1		
Supply Chain Manager	2		
Supply Managers-Non Food	Unspecified		
Vendor Manager	1		

Sources: *Supply Management*, 23 May 2002, CIPS; *Focus*, June 2002, ILT.

15.4.3 Job titles

An analysis of vacancies advertised in the 23 May 2002 issue of *Supply Management*, the journal of the CIPS, and vacancies other than those for Distribution, Operations, Transport and Warehousing (other than Inventory) in the June 2002 issue of *Focus*, the journal of the ILT, provided the samples of job titles relating to purchasing and supply as set out in Table 15.2.

15.4.4 Examples of job descriptions/role profiles

Job descriptions are also referred to as role profiles. Examples of a role profile for the post of strategic sourcing manager and IT purchasing executive are given in Figures 15.2 and 15.3. Both the examples include job specifications indicating the qualifications, experience and attributes ideally required.

15.4.5 Preparation of job descriptions/profiles and specifications

Preparation of a job description requires:

- a thorough knowledge of the job;
- a systematic approach;
- a readiness on the part of those preparing the specifications to challenge their own preoccupations and, in the light of the job description, to see if these are justified.

When drawing up description specifications, role profiles and advertisements it is important to observe the following:

- Specify essential knowledge and skills that the jobholder must possess, e.g. ability to read engineering drawings, knowledge of previous experience with MRP systems.
- Do not overstate requirements. Setting unrealistically high levels of qualification and experience increases the difficulty of attracting candidates.
- Avoid anything that can be construed as discriminatory, e.g. references to age, sex, colour or nationality.

15.4.6 Source of applicants

Once the content of a purchasing job, the ideal characteristics of the jobholder and the reward package relating to the job have been determined, recruitment can begin. Sources and methods of attracting applicants for vacancies include:

- Advertising – which should be in the right media, e.g. quality papers, appropriate journals, e.g. *Purchasing and Supply Management* and *Focus* – respectively the journals of CIPS and the Institute of Logistics and Transport.
- Department of Employment facilities.
- The educational sector, i.e. university appointment boards, career offices.
- Professional organisations, e.g. the Chartered Institute of Purchasing and Supply, the Institute of Logistics and Transport.

ROLE PROFILE
JOB TITLE: Strategic Sourcing Manager

OBJECTIVES:

To manage the development and operation of a successful supplier management strategy and infrastructure relating to agreed supplier spend categories / establish and manage processes to deliver services to customers in keeping with the company's overall procurement strategy and agreed targets for cost/supplier management and service quality enhancements.

KEY ACCOUNTABILITIES:

- For agreed supplier spend categories; develop the category spend strategy, in line with overall procurement strategy and agreed targets for cost and quality.
- To develop a sound level of knowledge of the wider business context in which it operates and of the relevant supply markets to support sourcing strategy.
- To develop the profile for procurement across all areas of the Group, providing effective leadership, guidance and expertise in all aspects of procurement.
- To develop and coordinate supplier selection criteria, working in partnership with key stakeholders/internal customers.
- Communication and acceptance of category spend strategy and effective compliance and measurement thereof across business divisions.
- To select, negotiate, develop and maintain motivated approved supplier relationships that deliver agreed cost, service and quality standards.
- To monitor and manage supplier cost, service and quality performance.

MEASUREMENT CRITERIA:

- Buy in to proposed supplier sourcing strategies from business unit directors and senior management teams.
- Compliance to Sourcing strategies and processes adopted and implemented across the business.
- Suitable selection and application of relevant supplier sourcing and selection criteria.
- Suppliers that see the Group as their customer choice, who deliver and surpass agreed performance criteria and service levels.
- Successful delivery of cost reduction targets against own spend categories.
- Regular feedback and reporting of activities and procurement performance against objectives.
- Positive stakeholder and customer feedback.
- Co-risk exposure issues.

SCOPE and DIMENSIONS:

- Number of positions accountable for categories of spend ranging from £20m to £50m, process design/delivery and gaining buy-in from the businesses.
- Accountable for sourcing, cost management, quality and service performance.
- Team size – no direct reports.
- Team leadership – responsible for coordination and leadership of multidisciplinary project teams.
- Relationships – interrelationships at all levels within the organisation including general management/directors. Externally with supplier base at senior management and director levels.

KEY COMPETENCES:

Leadership and project management
Motivates and empowers others in order to reach organisational goals. Works consultatively and proactively to lead cross-functional/cross-divisional project teams, demonstrating a high level of personal integrity and influence to deliver against procurement and company objectives.

Influencing
Develops coherent and logical arguments based on prior discussion, research and consultation, and can present a case which results in either acceptance, behaviour change or persuasion of others to change their point of view.

Relationship and profile building
Builds and maintains effective relationships with all internal customers and stakeholders. Collaborates with stakeholders, understands their drivers and uses appropriate messages to sell procurement and develop its profile to achieve maximum benefit for the business.

Measurement and results focus
Sets up measures and processes to monitor cost/benefits, supplier and procurement performance and of supplier agreement compliance across the business. Actively delivers against own procurement targets and objectives. Provides regular reporting on activities to senior management and key stakeholders. Gains feedback from key stakeholders on performance.

Market analysis and category planning
Uses and analyses sources of information creatively to understand wider business and market/supplier trends. Formulates category sourcing strategies ensuring the flow-down of organisational/procurement strategy, maintaining clear and unambiguous documentation with contingency plans.

Supplier negotiation
Negotiates with key/critical suppliers in order to deliver against procurement and organisational objectives, on the basis of detailed understanding of supply and successful positioning of RMC as a customer of choice.

Supplier management
Actively manages and develops appropriate business relationships with a range of suppliers to maximise supplier performance, cost, quality and service. Uses structures process and clear measurement criteria for regular supplier performance review, reporting and continuous improvement.

SKILLS AND EXPERIENCE REQUIRED:

- Demonstrate purchasing experience gained within progressive/progressive procurement environments where modern tools/techniques and structures processes and measurement practices are used.
- Strong change management skills, with experience of driving change programmes.
- Effective project management, with experience in leading, motivating and directing multidisciplinary teams.
- Commercially aware, high level of self-motivation and personal integrity.
- Effective influencing and persuasion skills with ability to deal with people at all levels, including senior managers and directors.
- Multi-site experience.
- Prepared to travel within the UK – probably spending 70 per cent of time out of the office at other sites and/or at supplier premises.
- Degree or equivalent calibre.

Figure 15.2 Role profile of strategic sourcing manager

IT PURCHASING EXECUTIVE	
JOB TITLE: IT Purchasing Executive REPORTS TO: IT Purchasing Manager	DEPT: Purchasing and Supply TEAM: IT Purchasing

KEY TASKS

- Work with customers closely to develop sourcing strategies ensuring customer requirements are fully understood and met. This will involve working with various Group businesses, across a wide range of IT (hardware, software and services).
- Take the commercial lead in delivering customer requirements – including negotiation with suppliers and interfacing with Legal.
- Build, maintain and progress relationships with suppliers and internal customers ensuring service standards are achieved, helping to deliver a common message to promote Group Purchasing and Supply Management across the Group and in the market.
- Ensure the timely completion of all procurement deliverables to meet customer requirements.
- Minimises risk by ensuring the organisational, legal and industry rules and standards are met.
- Support manager on higher value/complex projects.

PROFESSIONAL/REGULATORY QUALIFICATIONS REQUIRED TO UNDERTAKE ROLE

- MCIPS or equivalent would be advantageous.

SPECIALIST SKILLS/KNOWLEDGE REQUIRED TO UNDERTAKE ROLE

- Minimum 2 years' procurement relevant experience.
- Understanding of contract law.
- Experience of tendering and evaluation processes..
- Good interpersonal/influencing skills.
- Proficient at negotiation.
- Financial analysis skills.
- Knowledge of IT marketplace would be advantageous.
- Understanding of issues involved in outsourcing.

Figure 15.3   Job description of IT purchasing executive

- Consultants, especially those specialising in the recruitment and selection of purchasing staff.
- Head-hunting through external consultants.
- Internal advertisement.
- The internet.

15.4.7   Application forms and CVs

Application forms and CVs are useful ways of obtaining preliminary information about job applicants and determining whether a particular applicant should be invited for interview.

Application forms

Apart from facilitating the comparison of applicants and the selection of candidates for interview, application forms can:

- provide the basis for a structured interview;
- become part of the permanent personnel record of an employee;
- be the basis of a 'future vacancy' file.

Application forms should be designed with care as they often provide the first direct contact that a potential recruit will have with an organisation. The information required must also receive careful consideration to obviate any change of unfairly discriminating against an applicant.

A well-designed application form will:

- use clear concise wording;
- enable the applicant to complete the form quickly and accurately and the selector to abstract information with a minimum of effort;
- provide adequate space for written answers – to accommodate applicants with large handwriting;
- enable alternatives to be answered by ticking or deleting, thus saving writing time;
- be pre-punched at time of printing for insertion in ring binders.

A modern development is the *competence-based application form*. This requires job applicants to provide evidence, usually limited to about 100 words, of their ability to demonstrate a specified competence. An important purchasing competence, for example, is the ability to enhance the employer's competitive advantage by obtaining supplies of the right quality at the right (not necessarily the cheapest) price. On a competence-based application form, a number of questions will be included, which the candidate will be assisted to complete with the aid of 'prompt questions' similar to those shown in Figure 15.4.

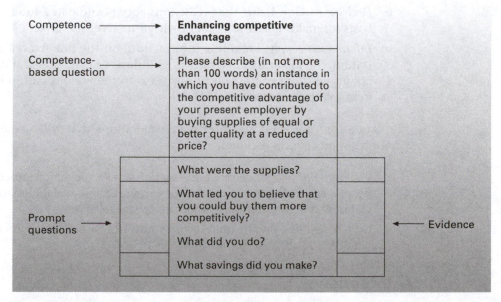

Figure 15.4 Extract from a competence-based application form

The advantages of competence-based application forms, which may be an addition to the standard application form, is that they relate to a specific occupation or job within that occupation. They require a candidate not only to claim competence but also to provide evidence of competence or lack of competence in relation to a particular aspect of a job. They also provide a useful basis for discussion and questioning at a later appointment interview.

CVs

Applicants for senior posts often dislike filling in an application form. The advantage of a CV is that its content and manner of presentation can provide indications about the applicant such as vocabulary, writing style and ability to highlight important information. The disadvantages of CVs is that the required information about an applicant is not presented in a standardised form. The comparison of CVs is therefore a more difficult and time-consuming exercise than the comparison of application forms.

15.4.8   Selection procedures

The preliminary stage of selection involves sifting through the applications received and preparing a shortlist of candidates for interview. Roe and Greuter[4] state that it is important that selection procedures fulfil four main functions:

- *Information gathering*. This involves generating information about the organisation, the job, career paths, employment conditions on the one hand, and, on the other, about candidates, including their experience, qualifications and personal characteristics.
- *Prediction*. Using information on past and present candidates' characteristics as a basis for making predictions about candidates' future behaviour.
- *Decision making*. Using the predictions about candidates' future behaviour as a basis for making decisions about whom to accept or reject.
- *Information supply*. Providing information, on the one hand about the organisation, the job and employment conditions to candidates, and, on the other, about the result of the selection process to the various parties involved – line manager, personnel specialist, etc.

Anderson[5] has stated that other considerations that will shape the design of selection procedures include:

- *The availability of managerial and specialist skills*. Selection procedures must be developed in a way that can be implemented by available managers and specialist staff (e.g. purchasing and supply specialists).
- *Cost/benefit factors*. The quality and soundness of selection procedures must be balanced against the costs involved.

15.4.9   Interviews

Selection will be on the basis of an interview. Interviews may be carried out on an individual or group basis. The purposes of an interview are:

- to provide the applicant with information about the employer and the job;
- to enable the prospective employee to provide the employer with information additional to that given on the application form and enable the employer to assess the suitability of the prospective employee;
- to let the applicant feel that his or her application has been courteously, seriously and fairly considered.

Interviews have been criticised on the grounds of being unreliable, involved and subjective. Torrington and Hall[6] state that the most perceptive criticism is contained in the work of Webster (1964) who, on the basis of extensive research, concluded:

- Interviewers decide to accept or reject a candidate within the first three or four minutes of the interview and then spend the remainder of their time seeking evidence to confirm that their first impression is right.
- Interviews seldom alter the tentative opinion formed by the interviewer based on the application form and appearance of the candidate.
- Interviewers place more weight on evidence that is unfavourable than on evidence that is favourable.
- When interviewers have made up their minds very early on in the interview, their behaviour betrays their decision to the candidate.

To improve the validity of the selection process, interviews may be supplemented by some form of testing, including medical examinations, attainment tests, psychological tests, i.e. intelligence and personality tests, and the observation of candidates in group situations including group tasks, leaderless discussions and simulated business problems.

15.5 Performance appraisal

15.5.1 Definition

Performance appraisal is the assessment of the quality of a person's work and job. Such assessment may be made by:

- the employee's immediate superior – this is the most common method
- the superior's superior
- peers
- subordinates
- an assessment centre
- self-appraisal

15.5.2 Purposes of appraisal

The purposes of performance appraisal differ according to organisational and individual perspectives. From the *organisational* perspective, appraisals may help to determine:

- individual objectives;
- the extent to which individual objectives have been attained;
- employees with promotion potential;
- employees who might be transferred to other work;
- individual training and development needs;
- what an individual actually does, i.e. a comparison of descriptions with what is done;
- career succession and human resources planning;
- salary increases.

From the *individual* perspective, appraisal should be seen as:

- a career development exercise;
- an opportunity to clarify what the organisation expects and how far the job holder is fulfilling those expectations;
- an opportunity to discuss career aspirations and how far these can be met by the organisation;
- a chance to constructively discuss problems relating to the job.

Sometimes, purposes and perspectives conflict. Some writers advocate that performance appraisals and pay reviews should be kept separate.

15.5.3 Objections to appraisals

Appraisals have been criticised on the grounds that they:

- are time consuming;
- generate paperwork;
- do not provide any information not already obtained by daily contact and observation;
- can be confrontational and a source of conflict;
- put the appraiser in the conflicting roles of judge and helper;
- may cause the appraiser to 'fudge' comments to avoid embarrassment inherent in criticising subordinates.

15.5.4 Performance management

Torrington and Hall[7] suggest that the best and most effective use is made of the appraisal process by tying it into the larger and more complete system of performance management which links individual objectives with organisational and functional strategic objectives. Applied to purchasing, the system would be as shown in Figure 15.5.

In this system:

- the objectives set are in terms of results to be achieved which are designed to challenge the individual to perform to his or her potential;

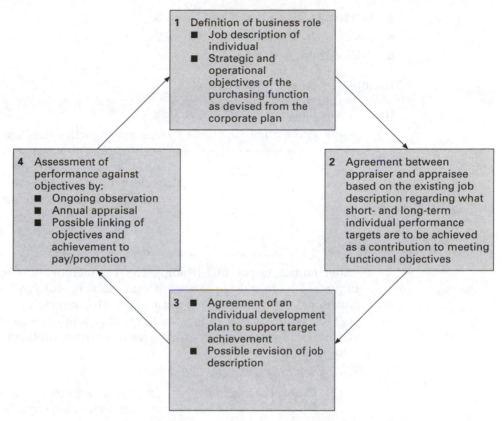

Figure 15.5 The four stages of a representative performance managent system

- the development plan agreed between the appraiser and appraisee emphasises the importance of managerial support and coaching;

- to avoid potential conflict between the openness and development approach aimed at improving job performance and the link with pay, performance and pay reviews are usually separated in time.

15.5.5 Other approaches to appraisal

Other appraisal approaches include:

- Descriptive approaches, i.e. asking the appraiser to provide an unstructured narrative report on the job performance of appraisees.

- Checklists, i.e. a list of key result areas or of behaviour traits on which the appraiser is asked to comment.

- Ratings, in which the appraisee is scored alphabetically or numerically against the checklist.

Stevens[8] provides an example of a detailed rating scale related to buyer perform-ance under three main headings:

- Personal traits, aptitudes and abilities
- Basic purchasing knowledge and skills
- Relationships with people

Examples under each heading are:

(i) *Personal traits, aptitudes and abilities*

(2) Letter writing

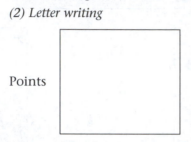

Points

The buyer writes intelligently, concisely and expresses himself well. His grammar and composition are adequate to obtain a clear understanding by his correspondents. In this respect the buyer is:

Excellent	Good	Fair	Poor
10–9	8–6	5–3	2–1

Other ratings under this heading are: (1) memory, (3) telephone techniques, (4) personal appearance, (5) availability, (6) flexibility, (7) grasps situations, (8) aptitudes, (9) persuasion, (10) ethics, (11) independence, (12) follows directions and instructions, (13) weighs problems, (14) accepts criticism, (15) organises work, (16) realises others' problems, (17) attitude, (18) punctuality.

(ii) *Basic purchasing knowledge and skills*

(21) Delay of salesperson

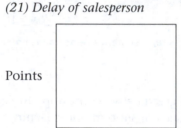

Points

The buyer keeps to a minimum the length of time that salespeople wait to see him He informs them if there is to be a delay. In this respect he is:

Excellent	Good	Fair	Poor
10–9	8–6	5–3	2–1

Other ratings under this heading are: (19) adjustments, (20) materials standards, (22) summary sheets, (23) savings, (24) competition, (25) interviews, (26) delivery, (27) familiarity with items, (28) analysing requisitions, (29) discrepancies, (30) records, (31) order preparations, (32) paperwork, (33) new ideas and new products, (34) stock reductions.

(iii) *Relationships with people*

(37) Other departments

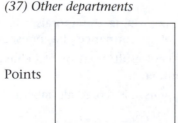

Points

The buyer knows and has the respect of personnel in other departments. He is consulted by them on procurement problems and is cooperative and helpful. In this respect the buyer is:

Excellent	Good	Fair	Poor
10–9	8–6	5–3	2–1

Other ratings under this heading are: (35) supplier's personnel, (36) meetings, (38) own department, (39) supervisor.

In this scheme, by limiting the choice to four categories the tendency for appraisees to pick the middle one when there are an odd number from which to choose is avoided. Although it may be objected that the use of numbers tends to give a falsely scientific and precise air to what is in essence a subjective process, this approach can provide a pay-linked formula and help to provide an analysis of overall performance standards.

15.6   Training and development

15.6.1   Training

Training may be defined as:

> A planned process to modify attitudes, knowledge or skill behaviour through learning experience to achieve effective performance in an activity or range of activities. Its purpose in the work situation is to develop the abilities of the individual and to satisfy the current and future human resource needs of the organisation.

Training is closely associated with education and development, which may be respectively defined as:

> Education – activities which aim at developing the knowledge, skills, moral values and understanding required in all aspects of life, rather than the knowledge and skill relating only to a limited field of activity.

> Development – the growth or realisation of a person's ability through conscious and unconscious learning.

15.6.2   Training needs

Training needs can be identified by a job training analysis. Job training analysis is:

> the process of identifying the purpose of the job and its component parts and the specifying of what must be learnt for there to be effective work performance.

A job analysis will reveal the 'training gap' as shown in Figure 15.6.

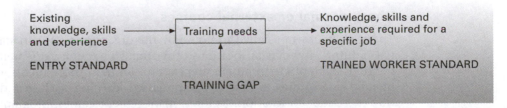

Figure 15.6   The training needs gap

Training needs can be considered from both organisational and individual standpoints. At the *organisational* level, the ascertainment of training needs involves asking such questions as:

- What knowledge and skills are required now and in the future?
- What is the shortfall between staff present capabilities and what they will require in the future?
- How much staff training is required to get to the position we wish to reach?

At the *individual* level, the ascertainment of training needs involves asking such questions as:

- What is your present job?
- How effectively can you do it at present?
- What are your job aspirations?
- What training, if any, do you require to:
  - do the job as effectively as possible?
  - cope with job changes?
  - provide you with confidence and job satisfaction?
  - enable you to meet your long-term aims?

15.6.3 Training and development for purchasing and supply chain management

This may take such forms as practical work experience, short internal and external courses, vocational and professional qualifications, degree studies and continuing professional development.

Practical work experience

Practical work experience may take the following forms:

- Working under the supervision of an experienced colleague or 'mentor'.
- Job rotation, i.e. undertaking a variety of purchasing tasks on a planned basis, e.g. six months in progressing, six months in quality management.
- Understudying, i.e. undertaking the responsibilities of senior staff during their absence through holidays or sickness. Every employee should be encouraged to be both a learner and a teacher (Figure 15.7).

Short internal or external courses

These are courses provided in-house by the organisation's own staff or by external training providers at locations other than the employer's premises. Training methods appropriate to purchasing staff (other than those mentioned elsewhere) include case studies, watching computerised learning packages, discussions, in-tray exercises, job rotation, lectures, management games, programmed learning, role playing, secondment to other organisations, videos and films.

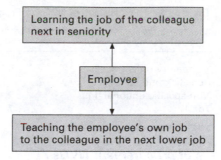

Figure 15.7 Employees should be both learners and teachers

Vocational qualifications

National Vocational Qualifications

National Vocational Qualifications (NVQs) in Procurement are based on national standards developed by the Purchasing and Supply Lead Body (now non-extant) set up by the National Council for Vocational Qualifications (NCVQ) established by the government, along with a similar body for Scotland (SCOTVEC), in 1996 to 'hallmark' qualifications which meet the needs of industry. From October 1997, responsibility for vocational qualifications in England passed to the Qualifications and Curriculum Authority (QCA), with corresponding bodies for Wales and Northern Ireland.

The QCA framework

The QCA is responsible for developing a comprehensive national framework for vocational qualifications in England, Wales and Northern Ireland. As shown in Table 15.3 the QCA framework is related to the NVQ framework set up earlier by the NCVQ. QCA, in partnership with the awarding bodies, is responsible for the quality assurance and marketing of NVQs. The three awarding bodies for NVQs in Procurement are the Edexcel Foundation,[9] Oxford, Cambridge and RSA[10] and the City and Guilds.[11]

Table 15.3 Examples of qualifications in the national framework

Level of qualification	General	Vocationally related	Occupational
5			Level 5 NVQ
	Higher level qualifications[a]		
4			Level 4 NVQ
3 advanced level	A-level	Vocational A-level (Advanced GNVQ)	Level 3 NVQ
2 intermediate level	GCSE grades A–C	Intermediate GNVQ	Level 2 NVQ
1 foundation level	GCSE grades D–G	Foundation GNVQ	Level 1 NVQ
Entry level	Certificate of (educational) achievement		

[a] Responsibility shared with the Quality Assurance Agency (QAA) for higher education.

Table 15.4 The structure of NVQs in Procurement

	Level 2	Level 3	Level 4
Mandatory units	5	4	4
Specific optional units	–	3	3
Non-specific optional units	2	2	3
Total	**7**	**9**	**10**

Structure of procurement NVQs

The levels at which NVQs in Procurement are available is indicated by Table 15.4.

The three levels indicate the competences required with increasing responsibilities. Competence in the NVQ context is defined as:

- 'being able to perform whole work roles': perform – not just know about – whole work roles, rather than just specific skills and tasks
- 'to standards expected in employment': not just 'training' standards or standards divorced from reality
- 'in real working environments', i.e. with all the associated pressures and variations of real work.

For procurement, the applicability of the NVQ qualification at each level are as follows:

- Level 2 – aimed at those who are concerned with the routine aspects of procurement. Candidates will probably be buying within tight spending limits and will be in contact with existing suppliers rather than identifying new suppliers.
- Level 3 – aimed at those who participate in the procurement function, perhaps with supervisory and contract management responsibilities. They may also be participating in determining organisational policies and plans.
- Level 4 – aimed at those who probably have a high level of autonomy and who may manage others in the procurement function. They may also be involved in the developing of procurement plans for the organisation and they will be responsible for planning within their own area of responsibility.

The units required for the Level 4 NVQ in Procurement are shown in Table 15.5. At the time of writing, all NVQ Procurement units are due for revision.

Some other applications of NVQs

The usefulness of the NVQ framework is not confined to qualifications. Together with the appropriate standards for each level the framework can be applied to a number of employment functions including:

- job descriptions
- job grading
- job evaluation
- selection and career development

Table 15.5 Structure and units of the Level 4 NVQ in Procurement

Level and structure	Mandatory units
4 Candidates must complete 9 units in all: 4 mandatory units and 3 from two optional routes: supply and contract management or materials management and 2 further units which may be selected from Group D or any of the remaining units in the two optional routes	**Group A: Mandatory units** **4 components – ALL required** Unit: 01025765 Develop the Effectiveness of Procurement Operations Unit: 01012653 Exchange Information to Solve Problems and Make Decisions Unit: 01012644 Initiate and Implement Change and Improvement in Services, Products and Systems Unit: 01025764 Provide Commercial Input to Decision Making **Group B: Supply and Contract Management** **8 components – 3 required** If candidates select this option route, they must complete 3 units from this group. Candidates may also wish to select from the remaining units the 2 further optional units required to complete this NVQ. Unit: 03025771 Administer the Contract Unit: 01025765 Determine Conditions in the Market for Supplies Unit: 01025770 Establish Contract Strategy and Plan Unit: 01025769 Establish Supplier Status and Secure Improvements in Supplier Performance Unit: 01025768 Establish and Evaluate Current and Future Requirements for Supply Unit: 01025767 Establish and Maintain Strategic Sourcing Arrangements Unit: 01025773 Improve Contract Performance Unit: 01025742 Let Contracts for the Supply of Goods and Services **Group C: Materials Management** **6 components – 3 required** If the candidates select this option route, they must complete 3 units from this group. Candidates may also wish to select from the remaining units the 2 further optional units required to complete this NVQ. Unit: 01025796 Capture and Forecast Demand Unit: 01025777 Define and Establish Production Schedules Unit: 01025799 Determine Inventory Service Levels Unit: 01025797 Manage Materials Requirements Unit: 01025798 Optimum Inventory levels Unit: 01025775 Plan and Reconcile Inventory and Materials Requirements and Capacity **Group D: Non-specific optional units** **6 components – 3 required** Candidates may select to complete the 3 further units required to complete this NVQ from this group and the remaining units from groups B and C. Unit: 01012638 Contribute to Recruitment and Selection of Personnel Unit: 01012649 Develop Teams, Individuals and Self to Enhance Performance Unit: 01025800 Establish and Improve Procurement Systems Unit: 01012650 Plan, Allocate and Evaluate Work Carried Out by Teams, Individuals and Self Unit: 01012677 Recommend, Monitor and Control the Use of Resources Unit: 01012647 Secure Effective Resources Allocation for Activities and Projects

- employee appraisal
- education and training

Professional qualifications

Professional qualifications comprise the qualifications awarded by the Chartered Institute of Purchasing and Supply (CIPS) and the Institute of Logistics and Transport (ILT).

Chartered Institute of Purchasing and Supply

The CIPS provides examinations leading to awards at certificate and graduate diploma levels. Certificate and advanced certificate awards each comprise five modules all of which must be completed. Certificate awards are intended to develop basic skills and knowledge particularly for those new to purchasing and to provide opportunities to advance to the diploma programme.

The graduate diploma is a two-stage programme consisting of a foundation stage of six compulsory modules and a professional stage of eight modules, four of which are a selection from a list of specialist options and modules.

Institute of Logistics and Transport

The ILT offers an introductory certificate, a certification with logistics or transport options, a diploma (logistics or transport options) and an advanced diploma (logistics or transport options). These qualifications are linked to relevant N/SVQs where appropriate and candidates have the opportunity to gain further qualifications. Those achieving the ILT certificate, ILT diploma and ILT advanced diploma with logistics options are eligible for accreditation by the European Certificate Board for Logistics (ECBL).

Both CIPS and ILT qualifications can be obtained by private reading, attendance at further education courses or by distance learning.

Degree studies

Purchasing or logistics can be studied at undergraduate level at a number of universities including Brighton, Coventry, Cranfield (Royal Military College), Liverpool John Moores, North London, and Northumbria.

Postgraduate courses leading to an MBA or MSc in purchasing, procurement, logistics or supply chain management are offered by the universities of Bath, Birmingham, Cardiff, Cranfield, Leicester, Salford, Staffordshire, Strathclyde and Ulster.

15.7 Continuing professional development

15.7.1 Definition

Continuing professional development (CPD) is

A systematic, ongoing, self-directed learning through an active life of service.

The term 'continuing' is used because learning never ceases. 'An active life of service' is a wider term than 'working life': even in retirement, many purchasing professionals continue to make a contribution to their profession and have personal learning goals.

CPD is concerned with development because its goals are to improve personal performance and enhance career progression.

15.7.2 The essential elements of CPD

The essential elements of CPD include:

- Development is a continuous process, not a one-off event; professionals should *always* be actively seeking to improve their own performance.
- The process is owned and managed by the *individual*.
- Development needs must be based on an *analysis of existing skills and knowledge*, and while related to corporate needs, the focus should be on the needs of the individual.
- Clear *objectives* should be established that are realistic, attainable and measurable.
- *Time invested* in identifying and fulfilling personal development needs is as important as its investment in any other activity.

15.7.3 Benefits of CPD

The benefits of CPD include the following:

- The participant's knowledge is current.
- The participant's contribution to the organisation will be enhanced.
- Evidence of CPD may assist in securing exemption from some qualifications.
- The personal CPD plan becomes a plus when job seeking.
- Commitment to CPD ensures that the participant will be adopting the *Kaizen* principle of continuous improvement in small stages.
- The participants plan their own learning which fits in with their identified needs.

15.7.4 Methodology and key factors in a CPD programme

A CPD programme involves six steps, as described below.

1 SWOT analysis of the individual's strengths, weaknesses, opportunities and threats

This analysis is designed to enable participants to identify strengths and weaknesses in:

- the skills and knowledge required to perform their existing job;
- personal qualities;

- anticipated changes in their job during the coming twelve months;
- longer-term career and personal aspirations.

2 Creation of a personal development plan (PDP)

Ideally, the PDP would be drawn up in consultation with the employer. This involves the participant in important decisions, including how to:

- set objectives;
- determine priorities;
- select appropriate development strategies.

3 Implementation of development activities

Participants may need:

- assistance to help overcome an obstacle to learning;
- to seek help in obtaining information;
- to discuss the practical application of techniques/methods;
- resources.

Step 3 is simply putting the plan into action. The plan should be flexible and allow for changed circumstances and unexpected opportunities. Distance learning, for example, has the advantage that a course need not be interrupted even if a person moves to another part of the country.

4 Recording and evaluation

PDP plans should be recorded in a suitable format such as:

- a professional development diary;
- a CPD log or portfolio.

5 Assessment

Persons wishing to claim accreditation of prior learning in respect of NVQs or exemptions from a professional examination will need to submit their diaries, logs or portfolios of evidence to an assessment centre or the professional body concerned or described earlier. They might also be examined orally on the evidence submitted. The CPD scheme of the CIPS, for example, recommends a target of 100 CPD points during a twelve-month period – roughly 35 hours' learning – and lists the activities and associated points set out in Table 15.6. Such points may count towards exemptions from the MCIPS qualifying examination.

6 Evaluation

As indicated by the word 'continuing', CPD is an ongoing process. Participants should review their short-term (up to one year), mid-term (up to five years) and

Table 15.6 CPD activities recommended by the CIPS

Activity	Indicative points for any one activity (3 points for every learning hour)
Secondment or job rotation	20 points
Promotion or career advancement	20 points
Project teams, product groups, cross-functional teams	Up to 20 points for participation in each depending on the specification and outcome
Special assignments or surveys	Up to 40 points depending on the specification and outcome
Presenting or lecturing	10 points for each event providing this is not a normal activity
Coaching, mentoring or teaching	3 points hourly allocation depending on learning outcomes
Published articles	10 points for each article
Peer group meetings, networking, branch meetings, committee work	5 points for each group providing meeting has a business purpose, and an additional 5 points in any one year for chair or other office
Academic or vocational qualifications	Minimum of 100 points for every year of study: additional points will depend on volume and/or assessment methods
Training courses and workshops	Up to 20 points for each full day of training
Conferences and seminars	Up to 20 points for each full day, depending on the learning outcomes
In-company development programmes	100 points per year depending on the volume and outcomes
Research	High points value subject to agreement with author

long-term (lifetime) objectives at least annually and whenever they change jobs or employment as shown by the CIPS activities above. Formal study or attendance at short courses is only part of a much wider range of learning sources which can be grouped under the four headings shown in Table 15.7.

15.8 Purchasing and pay

15.8.1 The basics of pay

A distinction needs to be made between:

- pay, i.e. the actual salary payable less tax and other agreed deductions, and
- the 'total remuneration package' including such fringe benefits as:
  - company cars;
  - loans, normally interest free for such purposes as car purchase or home improvements;
  - employee share schemes – allowing agreed categories of staff to purchase company shares on advantageous schemes;
  - assistance with school fees;

Table 15.7 Opportunities for continuing professional development

Professional work-based activities	Personal activities outside work	Courses, seminars and conferences	Self-directed and informal training
■ Planning and running an in-house training event ■ Advising on unusual or particularly difficult cases or situations (e.g. redundancy, disciplinary or grievance cases) ■ Implementing new systems or techniques ■ Working in a multidisciplinary project team ■ Writing reports and making presentations ■ Coaching or mentoring ■ Secondments to other departments or work projects ■ Learning by observation ■ Understanding or deputising for a senior manager ■ Membership of organisational committees ■ Study visits to other organisations ■ Taking part in schools conventions	■ Public duties – being a school governor, JP, memberships of an industrial tribunal or prison visitor ■ Voluntary work with voluntary/charitable organisations ■ Organising social or sports events or helping in the management of a club or society ■ Providing assistance to family members or friends who have job or career problems or run their own businesses ■ Writing and lecturing	■ Professional education courses leading to relevant recognised qualifications ■ Courses of study for degrees, higher degrees, research and post-qualification studies ■ Training course and seminars ■ Attending conferences including those of your professional organisation ■ Attendance at branch meetings or professional institutes	■ Using your professional journal as a learning source ■ Reading books from your library and building up a personal collection ■ Language courses ■ Courses about running your own business, if your PDD includes this ■ Self-teaching – audio tapes, videos and CD-ROM material

- payment of professional fees;
- discount on purchases of company products.

Pay scales usually involve some form of job grading. Job grading can be related to job specifications so that the grade and pay attached to a job can take into account such factors as:

■ length and variety of experience;

■ general and vocational education;

■ the scope of the job's responsibility;

■ the scope and type of supervision exercised or received by the jobholder;

■ the consequences of mistakes by the jobholder;

■ the physical, mental and social demands of the job;

■ working conditions or job hazards.

The basic principle of a graded salary structure is that jobholders advance within the salary grade for the job as they improve their performance or by securing promotion to a higher grade.

Apart from grading, salaries or remuneration packages may be based on such factors as:

- the actual or potential value of an individual's contribution and performance to the undertaking;

- market rates as affected by supply and demand, general movements in pay levels and particular areas of market pressure;

- salary relativities between jobs within the organisation depending on the values attached to different jobs;

- the influence of trade unions on pay increases and differentials.

15.8.2 Sources of information regarding purchasing pay

Sources of information include the following:

- Informal enquiries from other companies and employers' organisations.

- Job advertisements, remembering that the advertisement is not always indicative of the job requirements and the salary quoted may not always be the salary paid.

- The Department of Employment.

- Professional associations.

- Published salary sources. These are usually only available some time after they have been conducted. Such surveys include:

  - the *Purcon Index*[12] – a specialised survey of the salaries and total remuneration package of purchasing and supplies staff throughout Britain updated in March and September each year. Purchasing earnings are divided into nine industry classifications in eight regional locations and are divided into the six job levels shown in Table 15.8.

  - Remuneration Economics[13] publishes the *National Management Survey* which gives average, median, and lower and upper quartile earnings by sales turnover, number of employees, industry groups, region and age groups for nine levels of management responsibility ranging from senior staff to chief executive.

  - *Reward Group*[14] publishes over fifty salary surveys each year, normally biannually. Reward claims to have the largest salary database in the UK covering over 50,000 job pay records from 4,000 organisations with a combined workforce of almost 5 million employees. It does not, however, specialise in purchasing pay although many of the categories are easily applied to purchasing staff.

Table 15.8 The six job levels of the Purcon Index

Level	Description	Typical job titles
1	Entry level or primarily operational or administrative position. An annual spend of less than £2 million. Focusing on transaction function with little strategic involvement. Frequently engaged in an analysis and research activity and often a development role and first appointment for graduates	■ Assistant Buyer/Purchasing Officer ■ Purchasing/Materials/Supply Chain/Logistics Analyst ■ Contracts Administrator
2	Role for partially experienced supply chain Professionals, typically with two years' plus experience gained outside the supply chain. Roles are primarily operational, and may have some supervisory elements. Responsibility and accountability for given areas of the supply chain, such as defined commodity purchases or inventory categories	■ Buyer ■ Materials Controller ■ Inventory Controller ■ Provisioner ■ Production Controller ■ Contracts Negotiator
3	Roles with a mix of strategic and operational elements including staff responsibility for a small team. Defined portfolio responsibilities are typically allocated including a number of products or commodities. Purchasing spend of up to £15 million or inventory control of up to £10 million	■ Senior Buyer ■ Material Controller ■ Warehouse Supervisor ■ Senior Production Controller ■ Contracts Professional ■ Commodity Specialist
4	Focus on strategic issues. Typically includes significant staff responsibility for a team of up to 10. May be purely strategic or contract based role with less staff. Full functional responsibility for numbers of portfolios of commodities/services. Junior management position as opposed to supervisory position	■ Chief Buyer ■ Senior Purchasing Specialist ■ Deputy Purchasing Manager ■ Contracts Coordinator ■ Planning Controller ■ Logistics Controller
5	Manager for a function operating on a strategic plane with departmental responsibility for up to 30 staff. Alternatively may be senior strategic or developmental position, concentrating on major contracts/project responsibility or operating as a management consultant	■ Purchasing Manager ■ Materials Manager ■ Contracts Manager ■ Logistics Manager ■ Production Control Manager ■ Operations Manager ■ Supply Chain Manager
6	Senior manager or director with board level function or functions. High level of strategic involvement and general management ability. Head function in larger companies	■ Purchasing Director ■ Head of Purchasing ■ Group Materials Manager ■ Materials Director ■ Logistics Director ■ Operations Director ■ Director – Strategic Procurement

15.9 Motivation, commitment and empowerment

Motivation, commitment and empowerment are topics of relevance to any function and can only be discussed in a general way leaving the reader to work out their application to purchasing. Since they are also interrelated it is convenient to discuss them in the order, motivation, reward systems and communication.

Motivation in this context refers to the forces within an individual that account for the level, direction and persistence of effort expended at work.

15.9.1 Theories of motivation

It is inappropriate in a non-specialist book to discuss theories of motivation in detail. Full explanations are given in the many books concerned with organisational behaviour. Sufficient to state that theories of motivation fall into two classes:

■ *Content theories* explain human behaviour in terms of specific human needs or deficiencies that an individual feels some drive to eliminate. The theories associated with Maslow, Alderfer, McClelland and Herzberg are 'content' oriented.

■ *Process theories* endeavour to provide an understanding of the cognitive processes that take place in the minds of individuals and act to influence their behaviour. The equity and expectancy theories associated, respectively, with Adams and Vroom are examples.

15.9.2 General statements regarding motivation

■ Motivation is a complex process because people have different needs.

■ Motivation is linked to leadership because leaders should know what motivates a particular subordinate.

■ Basic needs are related to the satisfaction of physiological, security and social needs. Until such needs are satisfied, so called 'higher-order needs' for esteem and self-actualisation do not normally operate.

■ Money is an important motivator since it provides the means to satisfy a number of needs. Herzberg, however, points out that while lack of money may cause dissatisfaction, its provision does not give lasting satisfaction. Where reward systems are not seen to be fair and equitable, money can demotivate.

■ Motivation at work can be extrinsic, i.e. what is done for employees by employers in order to motivate them (e.g. rewards and punishments), or intrinsic, i.e. self-generated factors that influence people to effort (e.g. self-actualisation, responsibility, achievement, recognition, the work itself).

■ Performance = Ability × Motivation.

Two important concepts associated with motivation are commitment and empowerment.

15.9.3 Commitment

Commitment has been defined by Martin and Nicholls[15] as 'giving all of yourself while at work'. These writers state that the term entails such things as:

■ using all of one's time constructively;

■ not neglecting details;

■ making that extra effort;

■ getting it right the first time;

■ accepting change;

- willingness to try something new;
- making suggestions;
- cooperating with others;
- developing one's talents and abilities;
- not abusing trust;
- being proud of one's abilities;
- seeking constant improvement;
- enjoying one's job;
- giving loyal support where needed.

Martin and Nicholls postulate that creating commitment has three major pillar:

- *Pillar 1 A sense of belonging to the organisation*, derived from:
  - *informing people,* by for example
    - team briefing
    - open disclosure
    - simple language and examples
  - *involving people,* by for example
    - single status conditions
    - consultation
    - outings, visits and jamborees
  - *sharing success with people,* by for example
    - share option schemes
    - productivity gain sharing
    - local lump-sum bonuses
- *Pillar 2 A sense of excitement in the job*, derived from:
  - *creating pride,* by for example
    - responsibility for quality
    - direct identification with output
    - comparison with competitors
  - *creating trust,* by for example
    - abolition of piecework
    - peer-group control
    - removal of demarcation
  - *creating accountability for results,* by for example
    - pushing decision making down the line
    - challenging assignments
    - quality circles
- *Pillar 3 Creating accountability for results*, derived from:
  - *exerting authority,* by for example

- no abdication to shop stewards
- willingness to discipline
- maintenance of standards and objectives

 - *showing dedication*, by for example
   - reduction of management overheads
   - seeking productivity through people
   - attention to commitment
 - *displaying competence*, by for example
   - establishing mission and objectives
   - new management initiatives
   - professional standards

15.9.4 Empowerment

'Empowerment' is a term applied to a number of management approaches aimed at the reduction of employee powerlessness through the satisfaction of worker needs for esteem, self-actualisation, participation and enhanced personal effectiveness.

In a review of empowerment strategies related to employee needs in three countries (Australia, Germany and Japan), Alpander[16] has stated that the common link seen as empowering in all three cases exhibits one or more of the following elements:

- Setting inspirational goals – managers envisage a desired state and show subordinates how to get there; by doing so they establish the basic component of the inspirational process.
- Providing or showing employees how to obtain resources and means to reach their goals.
- Reducing or removing constraints or showing employees how to do so.
- Expressing confidence in subordinates, accompanied by high performance expectations.
- Expressing managerial styles, organisational policies and procedures to enable and empower subordinates to translate intention into action.
- Fostering opportunities to participate in decision making.
- Providing autonomy from bureaucratic constraints.

An empowering manager is therefore one who makes tasks intrinsically satisfying to the individual, not only by fostering in them feelings of self-efficiency but also by eliminating conditions that create feelings of powerlessness. Empowerment is, to some extent, synonymous with enabling. The benefits claimed for empowerment include:

- Enhanced individual responsibility with a consequential motivation to reduce mistakes and improve quality.
- Enlarged opportunities for employees to demonstrate creativity and innovation.

- Improved processes and products through harnessing the skill and knowledge of the workforce.

- Improved customer services by empowering employees nearest to the customer to make rapid decisions.

- Reduced labour turnover and absenteeism deriving from employee loyalty and involvement.

- Increased productivity deriving from employee responsibility for work outcomes.

- Emphasis on a team approach based on cooperation and a breakdown of inter-departmental conflict and barriers.

- Fewer organisational levels.

- Enhanced employee commitment deriving from a sense of belonging to the organisation, sense of excitement in the job and confidence in the management.

- Reduction in quality control procedures and personnel.

- Increased competitiveness.

- Improved labour relationships.

Eccles,[17] however, takes a sceptical view of the practical application of empowerment and points out that its basic techniques derive from suggestion schemes, job enrichment and worker participation approaches which have been available but underused for years. He also claims that in larger (western) organisations, higher involvement occurs, when at all, only at the professional and managerial levels. Outside professional partnerships, empowerment does not extend to strategic power sharing. Eccles concludes:

> The best new thing about empowerment is itself; the word empowerment which is so positive that is has enabled managers to embrace old, well known, more productive ways of managing which have previously languished.

15.9.5 Reward systems

Armstrong[18] points out that the concept of reward management is replacing the essentially static techniques of salary administration because of the need to design remuneration structures which fit into corporate cultures and can operate flexibly in the face of rapid change. Aspects of purchasing remuneration have been touched on in section 15.8; rewards, however, include incentives, which may be financial or non-financial, performance pay and fringe benefits. Some types of performance pay systems are shown in Table 15.9.

In Table 15.11:

- *Individual output systems* link pay to relatively tangible and quantifiable measures of output performance, the unit of production or time saved with piece-work, or sale achieved, with commission. It is also distinguished from *merit pay*, the major individual input scheme, which bases pay upon behavioural traits such as flexibility, cooperation or punctuality, or *skilled-based pay* which

Table 15.9 Types of performance-based pay systems

Type of performance	Unit of performance	
	Individual	Collective
Output	Piecework	Measured daywork
	Commission	Team bonus
	Individual bonus	Profit sharing
	Individual performance-related pay	Gain sharing
Input	Skill-based pay	Employee share
	Merit pay	Ownership schemes

rewards employees for certain physical or mental capacities or capabilities they bring to the job.

■ *Collective output schemes* rely upon a geared relationship between pay and performance of the collective, whether this be the work of the group, the plant or the company, i.e. a stipulated level of performance expressed in terms of profit, sales, savings or added value leads automatically to a pay outrun. In contrast to most individual schemes, those based on collective outputs do not require employee appraisal or the extensive use of managerial discretion and judgement.

■ *Employee share ownership schemes* are more related to questions of ownership and participation than pay.

15.10 The management of change

For examples of change it is unnecessary to look further than those which have taken place since the 1970s in respect of the purchase function itself. A summary of these changes is given in Chapter 3. Change may be *transactional* or *transformational*. Transactional change affects procedures but not the fundamental strategy of the organisation. Transformational change is strategic and fundamentally affects the working of the organisation.

15.10.1 Understanding change

Daft[19] has identified four basic types of change which affect organisations. They can be applied to purchasing or other functions.

■ *Technology*, e.g. computerisation, EDI, CAD/CAM.

■ *The product or service*, e.g. purchasing was mainly an operational function charged with obtaining items for production or internal use. While still carrying out operational tasks, it is now involved in the provision of strategic information and services.

■ *Administrative changes*, e.g. the movement from discrete purchasing 'departments' to cross-functional procedures such as the scanning, screening and selection of supplying partners by purchasing teams of design and production engineers, marketing, procurement and financial specialists.

- *People*, e.g. the need for trained purchasing professionals.

Forces for change may be categorised as:

- *External* – those forces which create pressures on organisations to devise and implement new strategies, e.g. competition.
- *Internal* – those forces from within the organisation which may be the result of changing environmental conditions, e.g. declining competitive advantage, rising production costs or outdated production facilities may create internal pressure for new corporate strategies.

15.10.2 Resistance to change

Resistance to change may also be categorised as:

- *External* – e.g. prior commitments to suppliers; tools owned by suppliers; obligations to customers; government regulations, e.g. the environment.
- *Internal* – e.g. limited organisational resources; incompatibility with existing equipment; inadequate personnel skills or interest; opposition from trade unions.

Organisational culture comprising the leadership style of top management and the values, practices and norms of employees may be a major factor in resistance to change. *Power* and *internal politics* which reflect the different interests of those affected are also important sources of resistance.

15.10.3 Implementing change

With respect to the factors responsible for internal resistance to change, it has been stated that:[20]

> Executives have learned that planning is about 10 per cent of the effort to change an organisation, whereas implementing the plan, the tougher part of the job by far, requires the remaining 90 per cent of the effort.

Readiness for change

For change efforts to be effective they must be supported by favourable conditions. Beer[21] has expressed the most important indicators of readiness for change in a rough formula:

$$C = (D \times S \times P) > X$$

where C stands for change, D dissatisfaction with the current state of affairs, S an identifiable and desired end state, P a practical plan for achieving the desired end state, and X is the cost of change to the organisation. The formula suggests that change is a function of dissatisfaction, a desired goal, a means to obtain the goals and a desired cost.

Strategies for change

Strategies for change may be summarised as:

- *Force change strategy* involves giving orders and enforcing them. This has the advantage of being fast but has the disadvantage of low commitment and high resistance.

- *Educative change strategy* involves convincing people, by the provision of information, of the need for change. This has the advantages of higher commitment and less resistance than force change strategy but the disadvantages of being slow and difficult.

- *Rational or self-interest change strategy* attempts to convince individuals or groups that change will be advantageous. When this approach is successful change will be relatively easy. Implementation of change, however, is rarely to everyone's advantage.

15.10.4   Organisational development

Organisational development (OD) has been defined as 'a planned and systematic attempt to change an organisation'. The individual or group responsible for ensuring that planned change is properly implemented is an internal or external *change agent*. Initially, outside consultants may be used on the grounds that they have greater objectivity and may be more acceptable to those affected. In time, internal staff may take over the change agent role. Change agents may use one or more of the following techniques:

- *Survey feedback* – involving (i) collection of data regarding how the operation operated; (ii) feedback to those from whom data was obtained on the organisational problems discovered; (iii) discussion as to what the findings mean and what steps should be taken; (iv) action to implement the steps required.

- *Team building* – developing effective work teams throughout the organisation.

- *Sensitivity training* – aimed at enabling individuals to develop awareness and sensitivity to themselves and others.

- *Management by objectives* – the facilitation of change by setting attainable goals for individuals and groups and monitoring progress towards goal enrichment.

- *Job enrichment* – making basic changes in the content and responsibility of a job to provide greater responsibilities and challenge to the worker.

- *The Grid Approach* – an approach suggested by Blake and Mouton[22] who defined five major leadership styles and concluded that the most effective is the one that stresses concern for both output and people. The managerial grid provides a framework for assisting an organisation by moving to the best style.

- *Management development* – formal efforts to improve skills and attitudes of present and prospective managers.

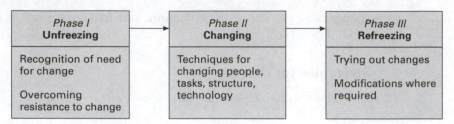

Figure 15.8 Lewin's view of the change process

Kurt Lewin,[23] a behavioural scientist, argues that the process of change involves three basic steps:

- *Unfreezing* efforts to make a person or organisation willing to change.
- *Changing*, i.e. selection of techniques to implement change.
- *Refreezing*, i.e. reinforcing and supporting the change so that it becomes a relatively permanent part of organisational processes.

Lewin's view of the change process is shown in Figure 15.8.

An extension of Lewin's approach is provided by Kotter and Schlesinger[24] who suggest an eight-stage process for the successful implementation of change, the first four stages being directed at the defrosting of a hardened status quo. Stages five and seven introduce new practices and the last stage corresponding to Lewin's 'Refreezing' helps to make them stick. These eight stages are:

1 *Establishing a sense of urgency*. Recognising the need for the enterprise or a function within the enterprise to change if it is to achieve and retain competitive advantage or meet crises and opportunities.

2 *Creating the guiding coalition*. Creating and empowering a group to lead change and encouraging the group to work as a team.

3 *Developing a vision and a strategy*. 'Vision' in this context means having a clear sense of what the future requires and of the strategies required to turn the vision into reality.

4 *Communicating the change vision*. Using every available communication media to create an awareness of the visions and strategies to employees and others affected and secure their cooperation and involvement.

5 *Empowering broad-based action*. Removing obstacles, changing structures or systems and encouraging new approaches.

6 *Generating short-term wins*. Strategies usually involve some shorter-term goals. The achievement of these goals provide encouragement to sustain people in the effort to attain longer-term objectives.

7 *Consolidating gains and producing more change*. Re-invigorating the process with new projects, themes and change agents.

8 *Anchoring new approaches in the culture*. Stabilising change at the new level and reinforcement through such supporting mechanisms as policies, structure or norms.

15.11   Teamwork and multifunctional teams

There are several references to teams in this book in relation to cross-functional structure (section 5.5), design (section 2.11), value analysis (section 7.9), quality circles (section 7.15) negotiation and capital purchases (section 16.11). There are also project teams and 'team buying' which combine the technical skills of the design and production functions with the negotiating and commercial skills of purchasing to determine what shall be bought and the sources from which an important item shall be obtained. A form of team is the 'task force' which is the assembly of a temporary group of staff to work on a short-term project, e.g. the preparation of a specification for outsourcing.

15.11.1   Reasons for team formation

The formation and involvement in procurement matters of multiskilled teams drawn from several functions is due to many factors including:

- The involvement of purchasing in strategic procurement decisions.
- The concept of the supply chain, which emphasises the need to deal with workflow in an integrated way through materials management and logistics approaches.
- Only teams can take full advantage of the vastly increased information availability and ability to communicate effectively provided by information and communications technology.
- The development of approaches such as MRP and JIT together with single and partnership sourcing.
- A recognition that, because of such developments as global purchasing, more complicated price and cost analyses, the need to integrate purchasing processes with those of manufacturing and the enhanced importance of quality, purchasing often needs to have expert advice and support in decision making.
- The recognition, based on research findings, that teams outperform individuals performing alone or in large organisation groupings especially when performance requires multiskills judgements and experiences.

15.11.2   Team types

Teams may be classified as functional, problem solving, cross-functional and autonomous.

Functional teams comprise individuals who work together, usually on a daily basis, on a number of continuing and interrelated tasks necessary to achieve a given objective. The members of a purchasing department where there is a high level of commitment may be a team.

Problem-solving teams are assembled to develop solutions to specific problems and are usually empowered to take action within defined parameters.

Cross-functional teams bring together a number of people with different skills and competences to identify and provide solutions to specified problems.

Autonomous teams are given a goal to achieve and a complete freedom to undertake a number of managerial activities such as task allocation, when to take rest breaks, quality control and so forth. Fully autonomous work teams even select their own positions and evaluate each other's performances. In consequence supervisor positions become less important and may be eliminated.

15.11.3 Teams and their aims

Teams have been defined as:[25]

> **A collection of people who must rely on group collaboration if each member is to experience the optimum of success and goal achievement.**

The growing consensus is that teams are the single best way to achieve the following aims:

- Integrate tasks
- Integrate information
- Maximise competence
- Manage performance
- Manage uncertainty
- Manage resources
- Increase enjoyment and reduce stress
- Total quality management and improvement

15.11.4 Team building

Team building relates to those activities directed towards assisting the individuals who work together or have common organisational goals to combine more effectively. Initially, team building involves two stages:

- Analysing group norms and relationships to identify any factors, especially those of the relationship between the leader (or manager/project leader) and subordinates that may consciously or unconsciously affect the effectiveness of the group.
- Assisting individual members of the group to learn new ways of working together so that their group effectiveness is increased. This may involve helping individuals not only to identify problems but also to smooth group relationships by learning how:
  - to express disagreements without getting into win-lose situations;
  - to provide leadership without dominating others;
  - to express negative feelings in a non-condemnatory way;
  - to tolerate and learn from the opinions of others;
  - to recognise that group tension and conflict can be positive as well as negative.

Team building interventions are, therefore, typically directed towards four areas:

- *Diagnosis* involves the open discussion by the group of the performance to uncover problems that are adversely affecting group performance.
- *Task accomplishment* involves agreement on what the team exists to do, what can be realistically achieved and how it should be accomplished.
- *Team relationships* comprises identifying the role expectations and responsibilities of team members, examining what the leader expects from the group and what the group expects from its leader.
- *Team organisation* is the process of selecting the strongest available team to achieve the identified goals and determining the roles and responsibilities of each member selected.

15.11.5 Team roles

Belbin[26] identified nine types of people that it is useful to have in teams. On the basis of research into team effectiveness carried out at the Henley Management College, he concluded:

> The useful people to have in teams are those who possess strengths and characteristics which serve a need without duplicating those already there. Teams are a question of balance. What is needed is not well-balanced individuals but individuals who balance well with one another. In that way, human faculties can be underpinned and strengths used to full advantage.

Belbin's nine teams roles are listed and elaborated in Table 15.10.

15.11.6 Characteristics of effective work teams

- Clear objectives shared by all team members who are committed to their achievement.
- Participation of all members whose contributions are encouraged and considered.
- Members are encouraged to express their doubts and dissension without fear of reprisal; conflict is regarded as constructive.
- Consensus is sought and tested, and when made, decisions are supported by all team members.
- Problem situations are carefully diagnosed before action is taken; remedies attack the underlying cause.
- Regard is given to the expertise of different team members who become temporary leaders because of their relevant knowledge, skill or experience.
- Members trust and respect each other and are loyal to the team while recognising the need to seek outside help when this is needed.
- The team is flexible and seeks new and better ways of working; individuals change and grow; they are creative.

Table 15.10 Belbin's nine team roles

Roles	Descriptions of team-role contribution	Allowable weaknesses
Plant	Creative, imaginative, unorthodox. Solves difficult problems.	Ignores details. Too preoccupied to communicate effectively.
Resource investigator	Extrovert, enthusiastic, communicative. Explores opportunities. Develops contacts.	Overoptimistic. Loses interest once initial enthusiasm has passed.
Coordinator	Mature, confident, a good chairperson. Clarifies goals, promotes decision-making, delegates well.	Can be seen as manipulative. Delegates personal work.
Shaper	Challenging, dynamic, thrives on pressure. Has the drive and courage to overcome obstacles.	Can provoke others. Hurts people's feelings.
Monitor evaluator	Sober, strategic and discerning. Sees all options. Judges accurately.	Lacks drive and ability to inspire others. Overly critical.
Teamworker	Cooperative, mild, perceptive and diplomatic. Listens, builds, averts friction, calms the waters.	Indecisive in crunch situations. Can be easily influenced.
Implementer	Disciplined, reliable, conservative and efficient. Turns ideas into practical actions.	Somewhat inflexible. Slow to respond to new possibilities.
Completer	Painstaking, conscientious, anxious. Searches out errors and omissions. Delivers on time.	Inclined to worry unduly. Reluctant to delegate. Can be a nit-picker.
Specialist	Single-minded, self-starting, dedicated. Provides knowledge and skills in rare supply.	Contributes on only a narrow front. Dwells on technicalities. Overlooks the 'big picture'.

Source: Belbin, R.M., *Team Roles at Work*, Butterworth-Heinemann, 1997, Ch.3, p.22. The authors gratefully acknowledge the permission of Belbin Associates, to use this table.

15.11.7 Interaction between teams

There are two intervention strategies that focus on improving the process of interactions between two or more groups:

- *Confrontation meetings* – A one-day meeting enabling the interacting groups to share their problems and decide how these can be resolved.
- *Third-party interventions* – in which a third party with a high level of professional expertise regarding social processes acts as a mediator, arbitrator or fact finder.

15.12 Management style and leadership

Leadership is an important element in motivation, communication, teamwork and the management of change.

15.12.1 Management and leadership roles

There is a distinction between management and leadership. Managers may perform tasks radically differently from those traditionally ascribed to leadership. A purchasing manager, for example, may carry out the transactional activities such as placing orders and ensuring their conformance to price, delivery and quality requirements, and not be a leader. Three important qualities that distinguish leaders from managers are vision, innovation and adaptability. Yet leadership in the sense of directing the work of other people to accomplish their assigned tasks is one of the four functions frequently ascribed to management, the other three being:

■ *Planning* – the process of setting performance objectives and identifying the actions needed to accomplish them.

■ *Organising* – the process of dividing up the work to be done and then coordinating results to achieve a desired purpose.

■ *Controlling* – the process of monitoring performance, comparing actual results to objectives, and taking corrective action as necessary.

Broader concepts of managerial work have been provided by Mintzberg[27] and Drucker.[28] Mintzberg states that managerial work encompasses ten roles:

Interpersonal roles (Leading)

1   *Figurehead* – manager as a symbol obliged to carry out social, legal and ceremonial duties.

2   *Leader* – relationship with subordinates especially in allocating tasks, motivating, training, developing, supervising and influencing.

3   *Liaison* – development of a network of contacts outside the vertical chain of command through information and favours which can be traded for mutual benefit.

Informational roles (Administrating)

4   *Monitoring* – seeking and receiving information from a variety of sources which is used to build up a general understanding of the organisation and its environment as a basis for decision making, to determine organisational values and inform outsiders and subordinates.

5   *Disseminator* – sending external information into their organisation and internal information from one subordinate to another.

6   *Spokesperson* – transmitting information to external groups in a public relations capacity, lobbying for the organisation, informing the public about the organisation's performance plans and policies, and providing information to superiors.

Decisional roles (Deciding)

7   *Entrepreneur* – initiating and designing controlled change in the organisation. Initiating 'improvement projects'.

8   *Disturbance handler* – taking charge when their organisations meet situations for which there is no predetermined response. Such situations can include disagreements between subordinates or organisations and the loss of resources or threats thereof.

9 *Resource allocator* – overseeing the allocation of all forms of organisational resources such as money, manpower, machines and materials.

10 *Negotiator* – taking charge in important negotiation activity with other bodies. In such negotiations, managers participate as figurehead, spokesperson and resource allocator.

Drucker analysed the work of a manager into five basic integrated operations: (i) setting objectives; (ii) organising; (iii) motivating and communicating; (iv) measuring, and (v) developing. It should be noted that:

■ almost all the above roles include activities that can be construed as leadership;

■ not all managers perform every role;

■ most roles can apply to non-managerial as well as managerial positions.

It is a useful exercise for readers to identify and provide examples of the roles undertaken by the executive in charge of purchasing in their organisations and those for which they have some personal responsibility.

15.12.2 Management and leadership styles

■ One of the earliest approaches to the study of leadership styles is the distinctions between autocratic, democratic and laissez-faire leadership identified by White and Lippett.[29]

■ An important aspect of leadership style is that of *power sharing*. Tannenbaum and Schmidt[30] suggest that participation and its complement, direction, are based on the amount of authority used by the superior in relation to the amount of freedom permitted to subordinates. As shown by Figure 15.9 this can be represented as a continuum from boss-centred to subordinate-centred leadership.

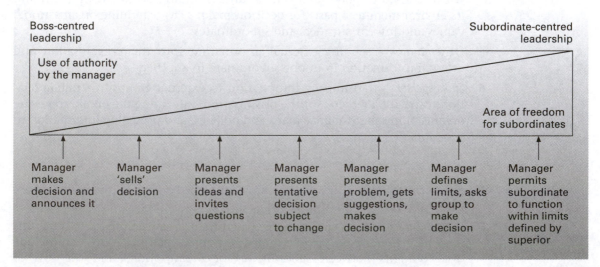

Figure 15.9 Directive versus participative leadership

■ McGregor[31] shows that behind every management decision or action are assumptions about human nature and behaviour which he referred to as Theory X and Theory Y.

Theory X assumes that the average human being dislikes work, prefers to be directed, wishes to avoid responsibility, has little ambition and above all requires security. Because of these factors, most people must be coerced, controlled, directed or threatened with punishment to get them to put forward adequate effort towards achieving organisational objectives.

Theory Y assumes that 'the expenditure of physical and mental effort in work is as natural as rest or play'. Not only are people prepared to exercise self-direction and control, learn, and seek responsibility, but also the capacity to exercise imagination, ingenuity and creativity is widely, not narrowly, distributed in the population.

■ Ouchi[32] draws attention to the influence of culture in determining management style by contrasting Japanese practices with the American traditional and more bureaucratic environment. Ouchi believes that the higher employee motivation, quality and productivity achieved by Japanese enterprises can be attributed to:

■ decision making based on a consensus reached by managers with their subordinates;

■ a participative approach to decision making encouraging the interchange of information between managers and subordinates which encourages trust and democracy;

■ the humanising of work which gives a feeling of significance to all employees.

■ *Contingency approaches* emphasise that there is no one leadership style that can be consistently applied. In addition to organisational culture, variables include: (i) the nature of work; (ii) the formal authority possessed by the leader; (iii) the characteristics of the workgroup, and (iv) the maturity of the subordinates. This latter factor is important. Based on findings of Cousens (1992), Barr[33] notes the 'dramatic increase in the professional and academic qualifications of purchasing personnel' over the decade 1980–1990:

> CIPS training coupled with a substantial rise in the number of graduates entering the profession has greatly increased the overall level of buyer training. Buyers in 1980 were predominantly educated only to O-level standards; whereas in 1991 buyers were found to be predominantly degree or CIPS trained . . . The number of buyers who have CIPS qualifications has increased from 10% in 1980 to 35% in 1991.

This trend has developed even further in the decade 1991–2000. These findings have implications for purchasing management. A study of hospital staff nurses indicated that because of their training, cohesion with colleagues and work technology, the more educated nurses could work autonomously without leadership from the sister in charge.[34] What seems to emerge is that where the task is clear and personnel have extensive professional training and experience, the need for a purchasing manager to play a dominant leadership role is of less significance than where the converse applies.

15.13   Strategic aspects of HRM applied to purchasing

15.13.1   HRM planning

HRM planning must:

- be based on the corporate plan;
- consider both external and internal factors as listed in section 15.2 of this chapter.
- reflect the need for possible redundancy and retraining of staff as indicated by the human resources audit.

15.13.2   Recruitment and selection

- Job descriptions and specifications must reflect the changed nature of purchasing referred to in Chapter 1.
- Emphasis must be placed on:
  - an understanding of strategic purchasing issues;
  - the contribution of purchasing to competitive advantage and the supply chain;
  - understanding and experience of such approaches as JIT, TQM, MRP and EDI;
  - the importance of customer focus
- Possibly there may be a policy of graduate recruitment

15.13.3   Performance appraisal

Performance appraisal must:

- be designed to meet the organisational objectives specified in section 15.5.2 of this chapter;
- relate to criteria appropriate to the job description of the appraisee.

15.13.4   Training and development

Training and development must:

- include provisions for general management training in addition to purely functional (purchasing) aspects;
- be related to national training developments, i.e. into the CIPS examinations scheme, NVQs in Purchasing and Supply, the Management Charter Initiative and ILT qualifications;
- cater for needs arising from the concept of global purchasing, e.g. language training, import and export procedures;
- provide an understanding of functions related to purchasing, e.g. marketing, finance, production and other supply chain activities, e.g. warehousing, transportation;

■ be based on the analysis of the training gap for each individual;

■ improve performance in specific aspects of purchasing, e.g. negotiation, price analysis, legal and financial aspects of purchasing.

15.13.5 Pay

Pay should:

■ be considered from a value added rather than a purely cost standpoint;

■ be competitive as measured by a comparison of information provided by published surveys;

■ be related to job grades and also make provision for individual contributions.

Case study

Lion Trust plc is a conglomerate of twelve companies each of which is allocated to one of three divisions: (1) Mechanical Engineering; (2) Construction, and (3) Domestic Appliances. The twelve companies vary considerably in size and in their individual purchasing spends which range from £70 million to £5 million. The total spend for the group is about £770 million.

Each company undertakes its own purchasing and has its own purchasing staff under the direction of a purchasing manager. This title, irrespective of size of spend, diversity and complexity of purchases, is used throughout the group. In the larger companies the purchasing manager reports to the general manager responsible for that location who in turn reports to the board of the controlling company. In smaller companies the purchasing manager reports to the works manager. Apart from the purchasing managers, the group employs about 170 people exclusively on purchasing and related activities. Some companies have adopted e-purchasing; others have not.

Only recently, as a result of a consultancy exercise, has the Lion board recognised the strategic importance of purchasing and the unsatisfactory nature of the present purchasing arrangements. The board has therefore decided to appoint a chief purchasing executive directly responsible to the group managing director with a remit 'to investigate and rationalise the present purchasing arrangements and procedures, implement them after board approval and substantially improve purchasing performance and profitability'. A small working party headed by the board chairman has been established to make the appointment.

Questions

1 What specialist members do you think should form the working party?

2 How should the working party seek to attract suitable applicants?

3 How might the working party decide on a suitable remuneration package?

4 After selecting a possible shortlist, what procedures might be used to select an applicant?

5 If you were an applicant, make five major recommendations that you would cite at interview regarding how Lion Trust may improve purchasing?

? Discussion questions

15.1 Purchasing managers are also managers of personnel or human resources. List eight aspects of HRM management regarding which your present knowledge and skill might be improved.

15.2 Five out of the twenty people in your purchasing department are expected to retire within the next year. All of these hold senior positions. What factors will you consider when making recommendations how and whether to fill the vacancies created?

15.3 Attempt to write a job description or profile of your own job.

15.4 Take any copy of *Purchasing and Supply Management* or *Logistics Focus*, study and list the job titles attached to the advertised vacancies. Are there any correlation between job titles and the remuneration levels or package offered?

15.5 Draft an example of a competence-based question similar to that in Figure 15.4 that you might include in a competence-based application form.

15.6 Consider the 'objections to appraisals' in section 15.5.3. How do you consider each of the objections listed might be minimised?

15.7 Is study for the CIPS or ILT examinations 'training' or 'education'?

15.8 'You shouldn't teach or share your experience with your subordinates too much otherwise they'll soon be wanting your job.' How would you counter this viewpoint?

15.9 What criticisms could be made of the 'competence' approach with particular reference to NVQs in Purchasing and Supply?

15.10 Gordon has undertaken CPD for the past seven years during which he has acquired his MCIPS, an Open University degree in business studies and an MBA. At a recent appraisal interview, he was told that he is overqualified for the work he is doing and that there are no openings for the foreseeable future for which he will qualify.

    (a) Does his employer owe Gordon something for his diligent pursuit of CPD?

    (b) How should this kind of problem be dealt with to avoid the disappointment and frustration associated with being overqualified for a job?

15.11 How might you use available information on purchasing pay to negotiate an improvement in your present remuneration?

15.12 Recently a football manager of a Premiership club asked, 'How do you motivate a team of millionaires?' How do you?

15.13 What motivations apart from pay may be applicable to purchasing staff?

15.14 Consider the three major pillars of commitment stated by Martin and Nicholls. How might you use these concepts in your working situation?

15.15 With 'empowerment', does a purchasing manager need to be anything more than a 'facilitator'?

15.16 Distinguish between transactional and transformational change. Give examples of transactional and transformational change in purchasing.

15.17 What are the advantages of team buying with special reference to capital equipment and the buying by retail establishments of goods for resale.

15.18 Consider Belbin's team roles. Think of the importance of each role in a value analysis team. Give examples of how an individual may play more than one team role.

15.19 You are the chief purchasing executive of a large company. Give one example of how you might perform each of the ten managerial roles listed by Mintzberg.

Past examination questions

1 The buyer of the future will probably need to be more clearly empowered and able to function effectively within a multifunctional team operating throughout the supply chain. Explain why this is likely to become necessary?

(CIPS, Purchasing and Supply Chain Management I: Strategy, November 1997)

2 It has been said that 'people are the most important asset in business'. Using a model with which you are familiar, discuss the factors which affect the behaviour of people within the strategic management of the supply chain during a period of cultural change within the organisation.

(CIPS, Purchasing and Supply Chain Management I: Strategy, May 1998)

3 Effectively empowered multifunctional teams can contribute to the successful implementation of corporate strategies. Identify factors within an organisation which could prevent a team from working effectively.

(CIPS, Purchasing and Supply Chain Management I: Strategy, November 1998)

4 Fear may motivate staff but it can, at best, only provide a short-term incentive for employees. Discuss this statement.

(CIPS, Management Principles and Practice, May 1999)

5 Explain the external factors which should make organisational change unsuitable.

(CIPS, Management Principles and Practice, November 1999)

6 It may be argued that leadership behaviour is governed by the nature of the task, and the personal characteristics of the manager's subordinates. Explain the reasoning behind this statement.

(CIPS, Management Principles and Practice, May 2000)

Notes

1. Storey, J., *Human Resource Management – A Critical Text*, Routledge, 1995, Ch.1, p.5
2. Guest, D.E., 'Human resource management and industrial relations', *Journal of Management Studies*, Vol.24, no.5, (1987), p.507 (by permission)
3. Plumbley, P., *Recruitment and Selection*, 4th edn, Chartered Institute of Personnel Development, 1985, Ch.1, pp.22–3
4. Roe, R.A. and Greuter, M.J.M., 'Development in personnel selection methodology' in Hambleton, R.K. and Zoal, J. (eds), *Advances in Testing*, Kluwer, 1989

5. Anderson, G., Selection, in Towers B. (ed), *The Handbook of Human Resource Management*, Blackwell, 1992, Ch.9, pp.171–2

6. Torrington, D. and Hall, L. *Personnel Management*, 1995, Ch.15, pp.272–3

7. Ibid., Ch.18, pp.316–30

8. Stevens, J., *Measuring Purchasing Performance*, Business Books, 1978, Ch.8, pp.97–110

9. Edexcel Foundation, Stewart House, 32 Russell Square, London WC1B 5DN (Tel. 0207 393 4540)

10. Oxford, Cambridge and RSA Examinations (OCR), Westwood Way, Coventry CV4 8HS (Tel. 01203 470033)

11. City and Guilds, 1 Giltspur Street, London EC1A 9DD (Tel. 0207 294 2468)

12. Published by Purcon Consultants Ltd, Prospect House, Repton Place, Amersham, Bucks HP7 9LP (Tel. 01494 737300)

13. Remuneration Economics, Survey House, 51 Portland Road, Kingston upon Thames, Surrey KT1 2SH (Tel. 0208 549 8726)

14. Reward Group, Reward House, Diamond Way, Stone Business Park, Stone, Staffordshire, ST15 0SD

15. Martin, P. and Nicholls, J., *Creating a Committed Workforce*, Chartered Institute of Personnel and Development, 1987, Ch.1, p.3

16. Alpander, G.G., Developing managers' ability to empower employees, *Journal of Management Development*, Vol.1, No.3 (1991), pp.13–24

17. Eccles, T., 'The deceptive allure of empowerment', *Long Range Planning*, Vol.26, No.6 (1993), p.5

18. Armstrong, M., *A Handbook of Personnel Management Practice*, 3rd edn, Kogan Page, 1988, p.5

19. Daft, R.L., *Organisation Theory and Design*, West, 1983, quoted in Thompson, J.L., *Strategic Management*, Chapman & Hall, 1990, Ch.24, p.590

20. Burke, W.W., *Organisational Development*, 2nd edn, Addison-Wesley, 1993, Ch.2, p.23

21. Beer, M., reported in Ovmenakis, A., Harvis, M. and Mossholder, K., *Creating Readiness for Large Scale Change, Human Relations*, Vol.46 (1993), pp.681–703

22. Blake, R.R. and Mouton, J.S., *The New Managerial Grid*, Houston: Gulf, 1978

23. Lewin, K., *Field Theory in Social Science*, Harper & Row, 1951

24. Kotter, J.P. and Schlesinger, L.A., 'Choosing strategies for change', *Harvard Business Review*, March–April 1979, pp.107–9

25. Quoted in Gordon, J.R., *Organisational Behaviour*, 3rd edn, Allyn & Bacon, 1991, p.211

26. Belbin, R.M., *Team Roles at Work*, Butterworth-Heinemann, 1997, Ch.3, p.22

27. Mintzberg, H., *The Nature of Managerial Work*, Prentice Hall, 1985

28. Drucker, P.F., *Management Tasks, Responsibilities, Practices*, Harper & Row, 1974

29. White, R. and Lippett, R., 'Leader behaviour and member reactions in three social climates', in Cartwright, D. and Zander, B. (eds) *Group Dynamics, Research and Theory*, Harper & Row, 1968

30. Tannenbaum, R. and Schmidt, W.H., 'How to choose leadership patterns', *Harvard Business Review*, March/April 1958, pp.95–101

31. McGregor, D., *The Human Side of Enterprise*, McGraw-Hill, 1960, Chs 3 and 4

32. Ouchi, W., *Theory 2: How American Business Can Meet the Japanese Challenge*, Addison-Wesley, 1981

33. Barr, C., A code of ethics: good, bad or indifferent? Paper submitted to the Second Purchasing and Supply Education Research Group Conference, Bath, 1993

34. Sheridan, F.E., Vredenburgh, D.J. and Ableson, M.A., 'Contextual model of leadership influence in hospital units', *Academy of Management Journal*, Vol.27 (1984), pp.57–8

Negotiation

After reading this chapter you should be able to:

- Quote and analyse three definitions of negotiation.
- Distinguish between adversarial and partnership negotiation approaches.
- State the main characteristics of adversarial and partnership approaches to negotiation.
- Discuss the applicability of adversarial and partnership approaches to negotiation.
- List and explain some characteristics of an effective negotiation.
- Discuss the main stages of personality, the negotiating situation and time as negotiation factors.
- Identify issues to be considered at the pre-negotiation stage.
- Describe the main stages of the negotiating process.
- Recognise some negotiating skills and ploys.
- List the activities associated with the post-negotiation stage.
- Distinguish between situational and institutional approaches to negotiation with special reference to the work of Ertel.
- Distinguish between positional and principled negotiation with particular reference to the work of Fisher and Ury.
- Discuss the implications of ethical negotiation.

16.1　Introduction

Negotiation has been described[1] as 'perhaps the finest opportunity for the buyer to improve his (or her) company's profits and obtain recognition'.

16.1.1 Definitions

There are numerous definitions of negotiation. Three typical examples are quoted below.

> **The process whereby two or more parties decide what each will give and take in an exchange between them.**[2]

This definition of negotiation highlights (i) its interpersonal nature; (ii) the interdependence of the parties, and (iii) its allocation of resources.

A formal negotiation is:

> **An occasion where one or more representatives of two or more parties interact in an explicit attempt to reach a jointly acceptable position on one or more divisive issues about which they would like to agree.**[3]

This definition highlights that negotiation is:

- *formal* – negotiation restricts the occasion to those in which –
- *representatives of the parties*, e.g. purchaser and supplier –
- *explicitly*, i.e. genuinely and deliberately, attempt to reach an agreement on –
- *divisive issues* about which they would like to agree.

Thirdly, negotiation is:

> **Any form of verbal communication in which the participants seek to exploit their relative competitive advantages and needs to achieve explicit or implicit objectives within the overall purpose of seeking to resolve problems which are barriers to agreement.**[4]

This definition stresses three elements in negotiation:

- Negotiation involves communication, i.e. the exchange of information.
- Negotiation takes place in a context in which the participants use their comparative competitive advantages and the perceived needs of the other party to influence the outcome of the negotiation process.
- Each participant has implicit as well as explicit objectives which determine their negotiating strategies, e.g. a supplier will explicitly wish to obtain the best price but implicitly will be seeking a contribution to fixed overheads and endeavouring to keep the plant and workforce employed.

16.2 Approaches to negotiation

Approaches to negotiation may be classified as adversarial and partnership.

- *Adversarial negotiation*, also referred to as distributive or win–lose negotiation, is an approach in which the focus is on 'positions' staked out by the participants in which the assumption is that every time one party wins the other loses. As a result the other party is regarded as an adversary.

- *Partnership negotiation*, also referred to as integrative or win–win negotiation, is an approach in which the focus is on the merits of the issues identified by the participants in which the assumption is that through creative problem solving one or both parties can gain without the other having to lose. Since the other party is regarded as a partner rather than an adversary the particip-ants may be more willing to share concerns, ideas and expectations.

The characteristics of adversarial and partnership negotiation are summarised in Table 16.1.

Table 16.1   Adversarial and partnership negotiation

Adversarial negotiation	*Partnership negotiation*
■ The emphasis is on competing goals to be attained at the adversary's expense	The emphasis is on ascertaining goals held in common with the other party
■ Strategy is based on secrecy, retention of information and low trust in the perceived adversary	Strategy is based on openness, sharing of information and high trust in the perceived partner
■ The desired outcomes of the negotiation are often misrepresented so that the adversary does not know what the opponent really requires to be the outcome of the negotiation. There is little concern for or empathy with the other party	The desired outcomes of the negotiation are made known so that there are no hidden agendas and issues are clearly understood. Each party is concerned for and has empathy with the other
■ Strategies are unpredictable, based on various negotiating ploys designed to outmanoeuvre or 'throw' the other	Strategies are predictable. While flexible, such strategies are aimed at reaching an agreement acceptable to the other party
■ Parties use threats, bluffs and ultimata with the aim of keeping the adversary on the defensive	Parties refrain from threats, etc. which are seen as counterproductive to the rational solution of perceived problems
■ There is an inflexible adherence to a fixed position which may be defended by both rational and irrational arguments. The approach is basically destructive	The need for flexibility in the positions taken is assumed. The emphasis is on the use of imaginative, creative, logical ideas and approaches to a constructive resolution of differences
■ The approach is basically hostile and aggressive, i.e. 'us against them'. This antagonism may be enhanced in team negotiations where members of the team may seek to outdo their colleagues in displaying macho attitudes	The approach is basically friendly and non-aggressive, 'we are in this together'. This involves downplaying hostility and giving credit to constructive contributions made by either party to the negotiations
■ The unhealthy extreme of an adversarial approach is reached when it is assumed that movement towards one's own goal is facilitated by blocking measures that prevent the other party from attaining the goal	The healthy extreme of the partnership approach is reached when it is assumed that whatever is good for the other party to the negotiation is necessarily good for both
■ The key attitude is that of 'we win, you lose'	The key attitude is how can the respective goals of each party be achieved so that both win
■ If an impasse occurs the negotiation may be broken off	If an impasse occurs this is regarded as a further problem to be solved possibly through the intervention of higher management or an internal or external mediator or arbitrator

An evaluation of adversarial and partnership strategies

Adversarial strategies may, on occasion, be appropriate in the following situations:

- No ongoing relationship or the potential for one exists or is desired, i.e. the deal is a 'one-off'.
- A quick simple solution to a disagreement is required.

Partnership strategies, while more time consuming and difficult to achieve, have the following advantages:

- They are more stable and lead to long-term relationships and creative solutions to mutual problems.
- They may also be the only way of obtaining agreements when both parties to a negotiation have high aspirations and resist making concessions on these issues.

Transforming adversarial attitudes

Fisher and Ury[5] suggest five tactics designed to transform an adversarial into a partnerships approach. These approaches are discussed in section 16.8 on negotiation ethics.

16.3 The content of negotiation

In any negotiation, two goals should receive consideration. These may be referred to as substance goals and relationship goals.

16.3.1 Substance goals

Substance goals are concerned with the content issues of the negotiation. The possible content issues are legion and depend on the requirements relating to a situation. Most negotiations will take place in respect of high-value-usage items, i.e. the 15–20 per cent that constitute the major portion of inventory investment. Negotiation usually relates to non-standard items, although a large use will seek, if possible, to negotiate preferential terms for standard supplies. Most negotiation topics affect price either directly or indirectly. Some of the most commonplace items are:

- Amendments to the quoted or existing price.
- Type of pricing agreement.
- Quantity, cash and trade discounts.
- Terms of payment, e.g. extended credit.
- Basis on which price increases are to be determined.
- Carriage charges.

- Time of delivery.
- Method of delivery, e.g. road versus rail.
- Delivery to prescribed sites.
- Amendments to specifications.
- Amendments to quantities.
- Amendments to delivery dates.
- Packaging requirements, e.g. palletisation.
- Supply and ownership of jigs, moulds, patterns and special tooling.
- Allowances for scrap.
- Trade-in allowances.
- Supply of samples.
- Methods and place of inspection.
- Acceptable quality levels.
- Methods of determining labour, materials and overhead elements in cost-type contracts.
- Charges for use of patents owned by the supplier.
- Sharing of savings due to improved design or production factors.
- Compensation for cancelled orders.
- Buyer's remedies in respect of rejected goods or late delivery.
- Conditions and warranties applicable to the contract.
- Passing of property in the goods.

16.3.2 Relationship goals

Relationship goals are concerned with outcomes relating to how well those involved in the negotiation are able to work together once the process is concluded and how well their respective organisations or 'constituencies' may work together. Some areas for relationship goals include:

- Partnership sourcing.
- Preferred supplier status.
- Supplier involvement in design and development and value analysis.
- Sharing of technology.

16.4 What is effective negotiation?

Effective negotiation may be said to take place when:

- substance issues are satisfactorily resolved, *and*
- working relationships are preserved or even enhanced.

Fisher and Ury[6] identify three criteria for effective negotiation:

- The negotiation produces a *wise agreement*, i.e. one that is satisfactory to both sides.
- The negotiation is *efficient*, i.e. it is no more time consuming or costly than necessary.
- The negotiation is *harmonious*, i.e. it fosters rather than inhibits good interpersonal relationships.

16.5 Factors in negotiation

Three important factors in a negotiation are the negotiators, the negotiating situation and time.

16.5.1 The negotiators

In negotiations, purchasers and suppliers are individuals usually acting as representatives of their respective organisations. Their behaviour in negotiations will be influenced partly by their personalities and partly by the role as representatives.

Personality

Personality may be defined as 'the relatively enduring and stable patterns of behaving, thinking and feeling which characterise an individual'.[7] It should be recognised, however, that there is no universal agreement about the meaning of personality because behavioural scientists define the term from different perspectives. In the present context it can be loosely considered to mean 'how people affect others and how they understand and view themselves'. How people affect others depends primarily on:

- their external appearance (height, facial features, colour and physical aspects);
- their behaviour (vulgar, aggressive, friendly, courteous, etc.)

Studies have shown that personality variables such as authoritarianism, anxiety, dogmatism, risk avoidance, self-esteem and suspiciousness affect the degree of cooperation or competitiveness present in a negotiating situation. The implementation of negotiating strategies may be affected by personality factors, and the mix of personality characteristics of the participants may determine the outcome of negotiations.

Transactional analysis, developed by Eric Berne in the 1950s, has considerable relevance to the understanding of negotiating behaviour. A 'transaction' is the unit of social interaction: 'If two or more people encounter each other . . . sooner or later one of them will speak, or give some other indication of acknowledging the presence of others'. This is called the *transactional stimulus*. Another person will then say or do something which is in some way related to the stimulus and that is called the *transactional response*. Transactions tend to proceed in chains, so that each response is in turn a stimulus. Transactional analysis is based on the concept that persons respond to each other in terms of three ego states, namely parent, adult and child, or frames of mind which lead to certain types of behaviour. For a fuller description of transactional analysis readers should refer to Eric Berne's book *Games People Play*[8] or the later account by T. Harris, *I'm OK – You're OK*.[9]

Negotiators as representatives

In negotiations it is important for participants to know the extent of their authority to commit the organisations they are representing, since such authority prescribes their options and responsibility for the outcome of the negotiations.

The degree of authority may range from that of an emissary commissioned to present, without variation, a position determined by his superiors, to that of a free agent. There is evidence that the fewer constraints imposed on a negotiator the greater will be the scope for his or her personal characteristics such as knowledge, experience and personality to influence the negotiation process. Five sets of conditions prevent negotiators from responding spontaneously to their opposite number:

- When they have little latitude in determining either their positions or posture.
- When they are held responsible for their performance.
- When a negotiator has sole responsibility for the outcome of negotiations.
- When negotiators are responsible to a constituency that is present in the negotiations.
- When negotiators are appointed rather than elected.

In the above situations the behaviour of negotiators will be constrained by their obligations. The more complex and open-ended the negotiations the greater should be the status of the negotiators.

16.5.2 The negotiating situation

This relates to the strengths and weakness of the participants in the negotiation. The factors identified by Porter as affecting the relative strengths of supplier and buyer groups are outlined in Chapter 4.

The buyer's negotiating position

The buyer will be in a strong position in the following situations:

- Demand is not urgent and can be postponed.
- Suppliers are anxious to obtain the business.
- There are many potential suppliers.
- The buyer is in a monopsonistic or semi-monopsonistic position, i.e. the only or one of few firms requiring a particular item.
- Demand can be met by alternatives or substitutes.

- 'Make' as well as 'buy' alternatives are available.
- The buyer has a reputation for fair dealing and prompt payment.
- The buyer is well briefed regarding the supplier's order book, financial situation, manufacturing processes and other relevant intelligence.

The supplier's negotiating position

The supplier will be in a strong position in the following negotiating situations:

- Demand is urgent.
- Suppliers are indifferent about accepting the business.
- The supplier is in a monopolistic or semi-monopolistic position.
- Buyers wish to deal with the supplier because of his or her reputation for quality, reliability, etc.
- The supplier owns the necessary jigs, tools or specialised machinery.
- The supplier is well briefed regarding the buyer's negotiating position.

16.5.3 Time

Senior management, design, production and stores staff should understand that 'necessity never made a good buyer'. They should therefore notify their requirements well in advance to ensure that the purchasing function has adequate procurement and lead time to obviate having to negotiate under the constraint of urgency.

Negotiations may have a past and certainly have a future in addition to a present. The past is important to negotiations for the following reasons:

- Past experience governs expectations and perceptions. It is the expectation of the most likely reaction by the other side on a particular issue which determines whether the bargaining situation is perceived as predominantly integrative or distributive.
- Previous encounters usually produce precedents, conventions, custom and practice, which become identified with a particular relationship and influence the behaviour of the negotiating parties. Where there is no history of negotiation, as in new buy situations, the past can have no direct influence.

16.6 The negotiating process

Negotiation falls into three distinct phases: pre-negotiation, the actual negotiation and post-negotiation. Each phase will be discussed in turn.

16.6.1 Pre-negotiation

'Cases are won in chambers' is the guiding principle in pre-negotiation, i.e. legal victories are often the outcome of the preceding research and planning of strategy on the part of counsel. Buyers can learn much by studying the strategies and tactics of legal, diplomatic and industrial relations and applying them to the purchasing field. The matters to be determined at the pre-negotiation stage are as follows.

Who is to negotiate?

Individual approach

When negotiations are to be between two individuals both should normally have sufficient status to settle unconditionally without reference to higher authority. The majority of rebuy and modified rebuy negotiations are conducted on an inter-personal basis.

Team approach

For important negotiations, especially where complex technical, legal, financial, etc., issues are involved or for new buy or capital purchases, a team approach such as that adopted by Marks and Spencer (see Chapter 11) is usual since an individual buyer is rarely qualified to act as sole negotiator. In team negotiations it is important to:

- *allocate roles* – typical 'players' include:
  - the *spokesperson*, who presents the case and acts as captain of the team in deciding how to respond to the situations arising within the course of the negotiation;
  - the *recorder* who takes notes of the negotiation;
  - the *experts*, e.g. management accountants, engineers or other technical design or production staff, legal advisors who provide back-up to the spokesperson. It is not essential that every member of the team should speak in order to make a useful contribution to the negotiation.

- *avoid disagreement* – there should be no outward disagreement between team members while negotiations are in progress; any differences between members should be resolved in private sessions. The desirability of devising a code of signals enabling team members to communicate imperceptibly during negotiations should be considered.

There are, however, drawbacks to team negotiation. These include:

- The tendency to 'groupthink', i.e. for team members to hold illusions of group invulnerability, stereotyped perceptions of perceived opponents and unquestioning beliefs in group morality.

- The emphasis on win–lose, unless modified by the spokesperson, is greater in team negotiations since team members may wish to demonstrate their 'toughness', inflexibility and ability to demolish rather than consider the merits of proposals made by the other side. The role of spokesperson on each side in setting the tone of the negotiations cannot be overemphasised.

The venue

The buyer should normally expect the vendor to come to him unless there are good reasons to the contrary, e.g. the buyer is seeking concessions or it is desirable to inspect the vendor's facilities. There are advantages in negotiating on home ground. Not only are surroundings familiar but access to files and expert advice is facilitated. The buyer is also under no obligation in respect of hospitality provided by the vendor.

Gathering intelligence

Gathering intelligence normally involves:

■ ascertaining the strengths and weaknesses of the respective negotiating positions;
■ assembling relevant data relating to cost, production, sales, etc.;
■ preparing data which it is intended to present at the negotiation in the form of graphs, charts, tables, etc. so that it can be quickly assimilated.

Determining objectives

Buyers should be clear as to what the negotiations are expected to achieve. A model of bargaining as applied to purchasing is shown in Figure 16.1.
Assuming that the matter under negotiation is price:

■ A–B represents the range of positions that the negotiators may take;
■ IS_B represents the buyer's ideal settlement, i.e. the most favourable price that can, with realism, be achieved in negotiation, i.e. £5;

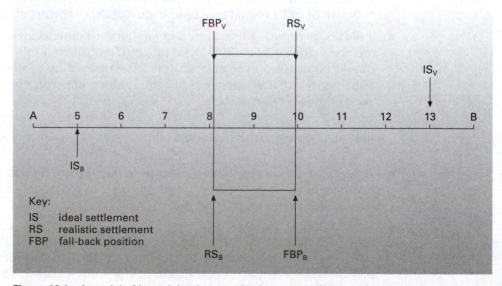

Figure 16.1 A model of bargaining in a purchasing context (see text for explanation)

- IS_V represents the vendor's ideal settlement, i.e. £13.

  (Note: In most cases IS will represent the starting position of each of the negotiators subject, of course, to the point that if there is to be negotiation at all the initial demands must not be too far apart to preclude bargaining.)

- RS_B is the buyer's realistic settlement, i.e. £8 or that point of settlement fully justified by bargaining power which would be reached with reasonable skill in negotiation and no adverse, unforeseen circumstances;

- RS_V is the vendor's realistic settlement, i.e. £10;

- FBP_B is the buyer's fall-back position, i.e. £10, or the price beyond which he will not go. After this point he breaks off negotiations or seeks alternative means of meeting his requirements;

- FBP_V is the vendor's fall-back position, i.e. £8;

- the shaded portion represents the area of settlement. This model is based on the convention that each side will normally be prepared to move from the original position. The negotiated price will be between £8 and £10 depending on the skill of the negotiators and assuming that the bargaining positions are approximately equal.

Before commencing negotiations the buyer should have a clear mandate from his or her superiors to settle at any point not exceeding an agreed fall-back position. It is important to stress the importance of determining in advance what is a *good* agreement. Too often negotiators consider that their goal is to arrive at *an* agreement or even *any* agreement. They therefore should determine what is their own and what is likely to be the other side's BATNA. A BATNA is the 'best alternative to a negotiated agreement', a concept introduced by Fisher and Ury.[10] While BATNAs and fall-back or reservation positions are similar in many respects, they are not the same; e.g. if you are trying to outsource your catering function the BATNA may be to continue to provide this facility in-house.

Tactics and strategy

A tactic is a position, manoeuvre or attitude to be taken or adopted at an appropriate point in the negotiation process. Strategy comprises the overall tactics designed to achieve, as nearly as possible, the objectives of the negotiation. Among the tactics to be decided are the following:

- The order in which the issues to be negotiated shall be dealt with.
- Whether to speak first or allow the opponent to open the negotiations.
- Whether to build in recesses for discussion.
- What concessions to make should the need arise.
- The timing of concessions.
- What issues can be linked, i.e. price and improved quality.
- What the opponent's reaction will be to each tactic.
- What tactics the opponent is likely to adopt and how these can be countered.

The dummy run

Before an important negotiation it is advisable to subject all arguments, tactics and overall strategies to a critical scrutiny.

16.6.2 The actual negotiation

Stages

Even with a philosophy of partnership negotiation, the activities of the participants will change at each stage of the negotiation process. These activities alternate between competition and cooperation. It is useful for a negotiator to recognise this pattern of interaction and to recognise the stage that has been reached in a particular negotiation. The stages of negotiation are indicated in Figure 16.2.

Techniques

Specialised books of negotiation usually list a number of techniques available to negotiators. It is not possible to detail these in this book although a more detailed description of the Fisher and Ury approach is given in section 16.8. Some general findings include:

Stage 1	**Introductions, agreement of an agenda and rules of procedure**
Stage 2	**Ascertaining the 'negotiating range'** i.e. the issues which the negotiation will attempt to resolve With *adversarial* negotiations this may be a lengthy stage since the participants often overstate their opening positions With *partnership* negotiations 'openness saves time'
Stage 3	**Agreement of common goals which must be met if the negotiation is to reach a successful outcome** This will usually require some movement on both sides from the original negotiating range but the movement will be less or unnecessary in partnership negotiations
Stage 4	**Identification of and, when possible, removal of barriers that prevent attainment of agreed common goals** At this stage there will be: ■ problem solving ■ consideration of solutions put forward by each ■ discertainment of what concessions can be made It may also be useful to: ■ review what has been agreed ■ allow a recess for each side to reconsider its position and make proposals or concessions which may enable further progress to be made If no progress can be made it may be decided to: ■ refer the issues back to higher management ■ change the negotiators ■ abandon the negotiations with the least possible damage to relationships
Stage 5	**Agreement and closure** Drafting of a statement setting out as clearly as possible the agreement(s) reached and circulating it to all parties for comment and signature.

Figure 16.2 The negotiating process

- In framing an agenda the more difficult issues should appear later, thus enabling some agreement on less controversial matters to be reached early in the negotiation.

- Questions are a means both of eliciting information and keeping pressure on an opponent. Questions can also be used to control the pattern and progress of the negotiation.

- Concessions are a means of securing movement when negotiations are dead-locked. Research findings show that losers tend to make the first concession and that each concession tends to raise the aspirational level of the opponent. Buyers should avoid a 'pattern of concession' in which, through inadequate preparation, they are forced to concede more and more. The convention is that concession should be reciprocated. While flexibility is essential, there is no compulsion to make a counter-concession and the aim should be to concede less than has been obtained. The outcome tends to be more favourable when the concessions made are small rather than large. An experienced negotiator will often 'throw a sprat to catch a mackerel'.

- Negotiation is between people. It is essential to be able to weigh up the personalities on the other side and the drives that motivate them, e.g. achievement, fear, etc.

Negotiating behaviour

All negotiations involve interpersonal skills. The negotiating styles applicable vary according to the situation. Training in negotiation should, therefore, include training in behaviour analysis, which should lead to an understanding of the responses likely to be evoked by particular behaviour, e.g. shouting usually causes the other person to shout back; humour may diffuse a situation. Lee and Lawrence[11] have identified seven categories of behaviour, all of which may be encountered in negotiations (Table 16.2).

Effect of behaviour on other parties

The main fact that the negotiator can learn from the generalisations in Table 16.2 is that our outward behaviour must be arranged to have the desired effect on those with whom we are negotiating. The desired effect depends upon the negotiator's goals. Thus, development behaviour is more likely than emotional disagreement to persuade the other party to accept our viewpoint. Providing and giving information is indispensable to influencing a group. Sometimes it is better to begin a negotiation by asking questions than by giving information about the subject matter. We should be aware of the different methods of dealing with disagreement.

Ploys

A ploy is a manoeuvre in a negotiation aimed at achieving a particular result. Most of the ploys mentioned below are more appropriate to adversarial than to partnership negotiating. Such ploys are of doubtful utility partly because they are easily recognised and countered by experienced negotiators and partly because

Table 16.2 Types of behaviour and their likely responses

Type of behaviour	Likely response
Proposing behaviour e.g. suggesting actions. 'Shall we look at subcontracting?'	Usually elicits either development behaviour in the form of support or reasoned negative behaviour in the form of difficulty solving
Development behaviour e.g. building on or supporting proposals made by others. 'Having decided to subcontract, whom shall we approach?'	Usually leads to further development behaviour or perhaps a question asking for further explanation
Reasoned negative behaviour e.g. disagreeing with others in a reasoned way, stating difficulties with their ideas. 'Price is likely to be a difficulty because their material costs don't attract our quantity discounts.'	Tends to evoke similar negative behaviour in response, leading to a downward spiral in terms of communications and emotions. This spiral can be avoided by stating difficulties and identifying differences as reasonably as possible, perhaps by further questions
Emotional negative behaviour e.g. attacking others; being critical; defending against attacks in the same way. 'Rubbish.'	In general, attack begets either attack or defence. It can make resumption of constructive negotiation difficult
Clarifying behaviour e.g. checking whether people understand; summarising previous discussion. 'As I see it, this is what we agreed.'	Tends to lead to supportive development behaviour, although there can be disagreement
Seeking information behaviour e.g. seeking facts, opinions, ideas. 'How much discount if we doubled the quantity?' 'What if . . .'	This almost always results in information giving. The certainty of response makes this a powerful shaping behaviour
Giving information behaviour e.g. giving facts, opinions, ideas. 'We need to reach a decision today.'	This is usually a response to other behaviour, especially seeking information. It is uncertain in its effect, since this depends largely on the content of the statement

they are detrimental to long-term relationships. Some ploys identified by Rowntree[12] include:

- The 'time's getting on' ploy – suggesting that a quick settlement is essential.
- The 'yes, but . . .' ploy – acceptance of one part of the opponent's proposal, but in terms that may be unacceptable.
- The 'believe it or not' ploy – straight bluff ('I've already had three lower prices') should be called. ('Why don't you accept one of them').
- The 'or else' ploy – a straight threat (I'll take the business elsewhere'.) Never to be used unless meant.
- The 'hand on the door' ploy – another straight threat ('That is my final offer, if not accepted immediately, I shall leave.') Again, never to be used unless meant.
- The 'divide and rule' ploy – endeavouring to get agreement on issues one by one rather than deferring final agreement on one of the issues at stake until all others have been settled.

- The 'think of your reputation' ploy – suggesting loss of an opponent's credibility unless your proposals are agreed.
- The 'trust me' ploy – accept my proposals now and I'll try to get a better deal later.
- The 'beyond my remit' ploy – suggesting that a settlement cannot be reached until you have had advice from others not represented at the negotiation.

Part of a negotiator's skill is to learn to appraise people and situations quickly. Everything seen and heard should also be taken with a grain of salt. Learn to discern the hidden meaning in the other person's words. Evaluate statements against what you know. Be patient and play for time. Often a little stubbornness can yield high returns.

16.6.3 Post-negotiation

Post-negotiation involves the following activities:

- Drafting a statement detailing as clearly as possible the agreements reached and circulating it to all parties for comment and signature.
- Selling the agreement to the constituents of both parties, i.e. what has been agreed, why it is the best possible agreement, what benefits will accrue.
- Implementing the agreements, e.g. planning contracts, setting up joint implementation teams, etc.
- Establishing procedures for monitoring the implementation of the agreements and dealing with any problems that may arise.

16.7   Negotiation and relationships

16.7.1 Situational and institutional approaches

Ertel[13] states that only rarely do companies think about their negotiating activities as a whole.

> Rather they take a situational view, seeing each negotiation as a separate event, with its own goals, its own tactics and its own measures of success. That approach can produce good results in particular instances, but it can be counterproductive when viewed from a higher, more strategic plane. Hammering out advantageous terms in a procurement contract may torpedo an important long-term relationship with a supplier.

16.7.2 Changing from a situational to an institutional approach

Ertel, therefore, advocates treating negotiation as an institutional capability rather than a series of discrete events. He identifies four changes instituted by companies that had moved away from a situational view of negotiation to a corporate approach concerned with long-term relationships.

- *Creation of a company-wide negotiation infrastructure.* This implies that the outcome of a negotiation does not rely solely on the skill of an individual negotiator. Such negotiators can be supported by databases providing better information to negotiators, drawing lessons from past negotiations, guidance in strategy selection, examples of creative bargaining approaches and evaluation of outcomes. Such an infrastructure not only improves negotiating results but also breaks down the assumption that every negotiation is unique and immune to coordination and control.

- *Broadening the measures used to evaluate the performance of negotiators beyond matters of cost and price.*

  To be judged successful, negotiators have to show, for example, that they explicitly discussed several creative alternatives, used objective criteria to choose among the alternatives and that the final deal fulfils not only the company's interests but the other parties' as well.

  Such an approach forces negotiators to think more broadly and creatively about negotiations both when strategies are initially established and as the bargaining develops.

- *Recognition of the distinction between deals and relationships.* Too frequently, negotiators confuse the deal with the broader relationship. To improve a strained relationship they may offer a price concession. To gain a price concession they may threaten to terminate the relationship. Such approaches, however, are counterproductive in that they create an adversarial climate in which both parties withhold information to protect their bargaining positions thereby creating enhanced suspicion which may adversely affect both the present deal and long-term relationships.

  A previously established climate of trust in which the terms of a deal can be discussed without prejudice to long-term relationships facilitates the free exchange of information and enhanced creative and collaborative problem solving leading to both more valuable deals and stronger trading relationships.

- *Understanding of when to walk away from a deal.* Successful and unsuccessful negotiations are usually evaluated respectively in terms of deals completed or uncompleted. Completion of deals, however, usually involves concessions on the part of one or both parties that may be in the interests of neither. When, however, a deal is struck that is unattractive to the purchaser, supplier, or both, the possibility arises that less time and effort will be invested in working together and consequently relationships will be strained. Companies should therefore encourage their negotiators to see their role not as producing *agreements* that may be mutually unsatisfactory but rather as making good *choices*. Prior to meeting, the negotiators of each side should have established their respective BATNAs or the objective hurdles which any negotiated agreement has to clear. Neither should accept an agreement that is not at least as good as their BATNA. To do so is likely to have an adverse effect upon relationships.

  Before concluding a deal purchasers should consider whether a prospective supplier can possibly meet quality, delivery and other requirements such as the price. If not, they should reject the deal and seek other supply sources. Negotiators should be made aware that rather than arrive at a deal on the basis of concessions that would take the agreement below their BATNA, it is better to walk away.

Ertel points out that not only do executives have to send the right messages internally, they also need to be aware of how external communications may affect negotiations and quotes the following example:

> In an interview published in a widely read magazine the CEO of a large computer company stated that when he was a sales representative he never lost a customer. . . . Imagine how the statement was interpreted by the company's sales force. The CEO was in effect telling the sales reps that they could never say no and signalling to customers that they held all the leverage. The negotiators' BATNAs were instantly rendered inconsequential with one public statement.

16.8 Negotiation ethics

Negotiation ethics is an aspect of the wider subject of purchasing ethics considered in the next chapter and relationships dealt with above. The topic is considered here because ethical perspectives largely determine whether a particular negotiation is adversarial or integrative.

Fisher and Ury[14] distinguish between positional and principled negotiation.

16.8.1 Positional negotiation

Positional negotiation views negotiation as an adversarial or conflict situation in which the other party is the enemy and is based on four assumptions:

- We have the correct and only answer to a particular problem.
- There is a 'fixed price'.
- Opposite positions equal opposite interests.
- It is not our responsibility to solve the problems of the other party.

Positions and interests are closely related. Often negotiators will not move from a fixed position because of psychological pressures or needs. A leader of a negotiating team may refuse to consider alternatives for fear of 'losing face' or being seen by team members to be backing down.

Positional negotiation has at least two drawbacks:

- It is win–lose. It has only two ways to go: forward to victory or backward to defeat.
- From an ethical standpoint, positional negotiation leads to such questionable tactics as:
  - misrepresentation of a position
  - bluffing
  - lying or deception
  - only providing selective information or being economical with the truth
  - threatening
  - manipulating

16.8.2   Principled negotiation

Principled negotiation is fundamentally different from positional bargaining. The very term 'principled' has an ethical connotation. Fisher and Ury criticise positional negotiating on four grounds:

- *Arguing over positions produces unwise agreements.* Compromising, for example, involves both parties giving up something so that neither is completely satisfied with the outcome.
- *Arguing over positions is unwise.* Time is wasted in trying to reconcile extreme positions.
- *Ongoing relationships are endangered.* Anger and resentment result when one side sees itself as forced to bend to the rigid wall of the other.
- *Positional bargaining is worse when there are many partners.* It is harder to change group or constituency positions than those of individuals.

Fisher and Ury also see principled bargaining as an alternative to 'hard' and 'soft' bargaining. Soft bargainers may make concessions to cultivate or maintain relationships. Hard bargainers demand concessions as a condition of the relationship.

The Fisher and Ury principles

Apart from 'don't bargain over positions', Fisher and Ury lay down four elements that parties must follow to obtain an ideal settlement.

Separate the people from the problem

This involves viewing the problem as the central issue to be resolved rather than regarding the other person as an adversary. Failure to do so can lead to antagonism between the parties. Fisher and Ury put forward 18 propositions under four headings – perception, emotion, communication and prevention – of which the following are typical:

Perception
- Put yourself in the other party's shoes.
- Don't blame the other party for your problem.
- Discuss each other's perceptions.
- Look for opportunities to act inconsistently with their perceptions.

Emotion
- First recognise and understand emotions, theirs and yours.
- Allow the other side to let off steam.
- Don't react to emotional outbursts.

Communication
- Listen actively and acknowledge what is being said.
- Speak about how you feel, not how you feel about them.

Prevention

- Where possible, build pre-negotiation relationships that will enable parties to absorb the knocks incurred in the actual negotiation.

Focus on interests not on positions

Positions are symbolic representations of a participant's underlying interests. Each side has multiple needs such as those postulated in Maslow's hierarchy of needs. To find out about interests, ask 'why' and 'why not' questions.

Invent options for mutual gain

Fisher and Ury classify their approaches under five headings: diagnosis, prescription, broadening options, searching for mutual gain, and facilitating the other party's decisions.

Diagnosis. This includes avoiding:

- Premature judgements.
- Searching for a single answer.
- Assuming a 'fixed price'.

Prescription

- Separating inventing from deciding.
- Engaging in brainstorming with the other party.

Broadening options

- Look through the eyes of different experts.
- Invent agreements of different strengths, e.g. substantive versus procedural, permanent versus provisional, etc.

Searching for mutual gain

- Identify shared interests.
- Dovetail differing interests.

Facilitating the other party's decision

- Helping the other party to sell a decision to his or her constituency.
- Look for precedents.
- Provide a range of options.

Insist on using objective criteria

This requires:

- Fair standards, e.g. objective criteria such as market value, professional or moral standards, legal criteria, custom and practice.
- Fair procedures for resolving conflicting interests.
- Reasoning and openness to reasoning.
- Never yielding to pressure but only to principle.

16.8.3 Criticisms of principled negotiation

A number of criticisms have been made of principled negotiation, some of which Fisher and Ury recognise. Thus, where the other party has some negotiating advantage Fisher and Ury suggest that the answer is to improve your BATNA. The only reason we negotiate is to produce something better than the results we could obtain without negotiating. BATNAs offer protection against accepting terms that are too unfavourable and rejecting terms which it would be beneficial to accept.

Where the other party will not play or where it uses dirty tricks, the answer is to insist on principled negotiation in a way that is most acceptable to the competitor. Thus principled negotiators might ask about the other party's concerns to show that they understand such concerns and ask the competitor to recognise all concerns.

Where the other party refuses to play, two techniques are those of (i) 'negotiation jujitsu', in which instead of directly resisting the force of the other party it is channelled into exploring interests, inventing options and searching for independent standards, and (ii) using outside intervention or mediation.

McCarthy[15] offers two main criticisms of the Fisher and Ury approach. The first is that it does not provide an adequate analysis of the role of power. The concept of negotiation jujitsu, for example, does not turn power back on the other party but encourages both parties to ignore dirty tricks and minor power plays. McCarthy holds that the balance of power between the two parties is the key element in determining the limits of a mutually acceptable settlement, and concludes 'in the area of collective bargaining at least I know of no set of maxims or principles that will enable any of us to escape from the limits set by a given power situation'.

McCarthy's second point is that Fisher and Ury assume rather than argue that the factors that make for effective negotiation in widely differing situations, from domestic quarrels to international disputes, are the same. There may be situations in which positional is preferable to principled negotiation.

16.8.4 Can negotiation be ethical?

Arguments that negotiation cannot be completely ethical include the following:

■ It is commonly believed that success in negotiation is enhanced by the successful use of deceptive tactics such as bluffing and outright misrepresentation.

■ Negotiators have the responsibility of obtaining the best results for those they represent.

■ What is ethical is affected by cultural factors, e.g. bribery and deception may be acceptable in some global negotiations. 'When in Rome do as the Romans do.'

■ Self-interest is the most powerful of all motivations. Few negotiations can be wholly altruistic.

■ Ethical negotiation is an idealistic concept that does not work in practice.

■ Sharing information may put a negotiator at a disadvantage.

Crampton and Dees[16] list a number of reasons why it may be possible to gain from deceptive tactics:

- Information asymmetry is great – the greater the information disparity between the two parties the greater the opportunity one has for profitable deception.

- Verification is difficult to verify such as long-term maintenance costs and performance.

- The intention to deceive is difficult to establish. It is hard to distinguish between deception and mistake or oversight.

- The parties have insufficient resources to safeguard adequately against deception.

- Interaction between the parties is infrequent. Deception is more likely in one-off relationships.

- Ex-post redress is too costly. The deceived party may, however, prefer such an effort even when the costs exceed the expected compensation.

- Reputable information is unavailable, unreliable or very costly to communicate.

- The circumstances are unusual in a way that limits inferences about future behaviour. Deceptions are unlikely to damage future negotiations because all negotiations occur in distinctly different circumstances.

- One party has little to lose (or much to gain) from deception. A negotiator may not be concerned about the prospect of being caught provided this does not occur before the deal is closed.

Crampton and Dees state that they cannot recommend a single strategy that will work effectively to promote honesty on all negotiations but they make the following suggestions:

- Assess the situation. This involves considering the incentives for deception. What incentives are there for suppressing or misrepresenting information? What is known about the principals of the other side? What is the competence and character of the other side?

- Build mutual trust. In most cases, the incentive for deception in negotiation is defensive. It arises from the fear that the other party will unfairly exploit any weakness. This also involves building mutual benevolence, creating opportunities for displaying trust and demonstrating trustworthiness.

- Place the negotiation in a long-term context. *Caveat emptor* is reasonable advice for negotiators. Select negotiating partners wisely, verify when you can, request bonds and warranties, get important claims in writing and, where applicable, e.g. in IT and outsourcing negotiations, hire a skilled intermediary.

Ethical negotiation can only take place in a climate of trust. Ascertainment of whether a climate exists requires negotiations to answer two questions: 'can the other party trust us?' and 'can we trust them?' Each party can answer the first question with some certainty although they should beware of self-deception. Not until both sides have established a working relationship can a certain answer be given to the second question. In the interim, both sides should show diligence in obtaining information to provide assurance that the other party will negotiate ethically.

Case study

Your company has patented a vehicle tracking system enabling cars and lorries to be always precisely located. Any interference with the device causes the vehicle to automatically stop and it can only be restarted by entering a secret code into the system. The system has therefore great potential for preventing theft and for driver surveillance in respect of transport. Substantial orders for the system have already been received from vehicle manufacturers both in the UK and abroad. The full sales potential has, however, not been realised because other manufacturers have adopted a 'wait and see' attitude because it is known that one of your competitors will shortly unveil an alternative tracking system that works on different principles but achieves the same results as yours. It is anticipated that this alternative system will be more price competitive than yours although the cost differential will not be substantial.

An important part of your system is a sensor patented by Acme Electronics. This component accounts for 25 per cent of your net manufacturing costs. Apart from the purchase of this component you have had no previous dealings with Acme although you understand that it has a good reputation. You are also having difficulty in meeting delivery dates since demand for your system is beyond the production capacity of your factory. Some manufacturers working on a continuous assembly basis are frustrated by the inability of your company to deliver on time.

As a matter of urgency, your directors have instructed you, as chief purchasing officer, to (i) find additional production capacity and (ii) seek to reduce the cost of bought-out components.

When discussing the latter issue with the representative of Acme Electronics, the representative casually remarks that due to the cancellation of an order his company has a significant amount of spare capacity for which he is trying to obtain orders. After this discussion, you suggest to your directors that both issues of component cost and capacity might be solved by entering into some form of partnership or joint venture with Acme Electronics. Preliminary discussions at director level indicate an interest by both companies in this suggestion and it is agreed that two negotiating teams representative of each company should be set up with the remit of reporting on the possibilities and problems of such a relationship within a timescale of 14 days. You are given the task of arranging and chairing the first meeting to take place in four days' time.

Questions

In preparation for the meeting:

1 Make recommendations regarding the personnel, apart from directors, to be represented on each negotiating team.

2 Prepare an opening statement of the short- and long-term benefits that might accrue to each company from the proposed relationship.

3 Prepare a statement of the principal short- and long-term problems that need to be negotiated between the two companies.

? Discussion questions

16.1 In a negotiation each party knows that the other has some power to influence the outcome. What powers have:

- trade unions and employees in a wage negotiation?
- two superpowers in a negotiation over weapons limitation?
- a monopoly supplier and a customer in a price negotiation?

16.2 Why might an adversarial strategy *not* be appropriate when a quick simple solution to a disagreement is required?

16.3 Why are most negotiations likely to take place in respect of high-value items, i.e. the 15–20 per cent that constitute the major portion of inventory management? Is it possible to agree any substantial expenditure or project, e.g. a construction project, without considerable negotiation?

16.4 Many writers confuse consultation with negotiation. What is the difference between the two concepts?

16.5 It has been said that our personalities are revealed by how we react to given situations. Try to think of six ways in which a person who fails to get his or her own way in a negotiating situation may react. Divide such reactions into those that are productive and those that are counterproductive to the negotiation.

16.6 Why is it important that you should know the limitations to your authority to commit your organisation in negotiations? Why is it equally important for you to know the extent of the authority possessed by your opposite number?

16.7 As a buyer you find yourself in a strong buying position due to a combination of the factors mentioned in section 16.5.2. Why is it essential that you use such power sensitively and responsibly?

16.8 How may time affect your negotiating position with regard to price, quality, negotiating style and future supplier relationship?

16.9 In the industrial relations context it is usual for employees and trade unions to have joint negotiating procedures. Such agreements can contain clauses on such matters as:

(i) the stages in the agreement, i.e. the levels at which the procedure will operate, time limits and provision for adjustments;

(ii) what matters can be dealt with under the negotiating procedure;

(iii) what happens if there is a failure to agree.

What are the possible benefits of an organisation having a negotiating procedure in respect of bargaining relating to the placing of long-term supply or project contracts?

16.10 As part of the preparation for negotiation is it useful to draft ground rules which, if approved by the other party, can provide the framework for a negotiation. What aspects of negotiating would you include within such ground rules?

16.11 Suggest five ways of resolving an apparent deadlock in a negotiation.

16.12 Discuss the following statements:

(a) 'Once you consent to some concession, you can never cancel it and put things back the way they were.'

(b) We cannot negotiate with those who say 'What's mine is mine, what's yours is negotiable.' (John F. Kennedy)

(c) 'Flattery is the infantry of negotiation.' (Lord Chander)

(d) 'Always define your terms.' (Eric Partridge)

? Past examination questions

1 'A buyer is only concerned with negotiating the lowest price with a potential supplier.' Comment on this statement and explain what other factors must be included in negotiations.

(CIPS, Introduction to Purchasing and
Supply Chain Management, May 1997)

2 Assess the value and benefits to the retailer of effective negotiation with suppliers.

(CIPS, Retail Merchandise Management, May 1997)

3 The development of mutual relationships with key suppliers and looking further into the supply chain often requires a major re-think in terms of negotiations methodology and strategy.

Identify how approaches towards negotiations might have to change to achieve such objectives.

(CIPS, Purchasing and Supply Chain Management I:
Strategy, November 1997)

4 Doubt has recently been cast on the concept of so called 'win–win' negotiations on the grounds that, for both parties actually to 'win' is impossible. Express your views of this assertion by explaining how you would conduct negotiations for the supply of an item critical to your production, with a major company operating in a market containing only a few suppliers whose products show a degree of differentiation.

(CIPS, Purchasing, November 1997)

5 Effective negotiation relies heavily on the planning stager and Purchase Price and Cost Analyses are useful tools for the buyer to use in this context. Describe how they could be used to plan a negotiation with the supplier of an important component who wants to renew an existing twelve month contract with you but requires a 15 per cent increase due to increases in raw materials prices. How would you structure the resulting information into your negotiating strategy?

(CIPS, Purchasing and Supply Chain Management II:
Tactics and Operations, May 1997)

6 Describe in detail the information you would gather prior to a major negotiation and show how you would use this information to plan your negotiation. Use any of the generally accepted approaches to negotiation to describe how you would conduct the

negotiation itself and implement the information from the planning phase. State what you believe to be a successful outcome to a negotiation.

(CIPS, Purchasing and Supply Chain Management II: Tactics and Operations, May 1999)

7 In what ways are negotiations with suppliers likely to be affected by such factors as: the maturity of the buyer/seller relationship, stage of purchasing development, and the level of expenditure involved.

Illustrate your answer with appropriate examples.

(CIPS, Purchasing and Supply Chain Management II: Tactics and Operations, May 2000)

Notes

1. Aljian, G.W., *Purchasing Handbook*, 4th edn, McGraw Hill, 1982, Section II, p.115
2. Rubin, J.Z. and Brown, B.R., *The Social Psychology of Bargaining and Negotiation*, Academic Press, 1975
3. Gottschal, R.A.W., 'The background to the negotiating process' in D. Torrington, *Code of Personnel Management*, Gower Press, 1973
4. Lysons, C.K., Modified definition of that in *Purchasing*, 3rd edn, Pitman, 1993
5. Fisher, R. and Ury, W., *Getting to Yes*, Penguin Books, 1983
6. Ibid., pp.4–7
7. Cooper, C.L. and Makin, P., *Psychology for Managers*, British Psychological Society in association with MacMillan, 1988, p.58
8. Berne, E., *Games People Play*, Penguin Books, 1968
9. Harris, T.A., *I'm OK – You're OK*, Pan Macmillan, 1986
10. As n.5 above
11. Lee, R. and Lawrence, P., *Organisational Behaviour: Politics at Work*, Hutchinson, 1988, p.182
12. Rowntree, D., *The Manager's Book of Checklists*, Gower Press, 1989, pp.207–8
13. Ertel, D., 'Turning negotiation into a corporate capability', *Harvard Business Review*, May–June 1999, pp.55–70
14. Fisher and Ury, as n.5 above
15. McCarthy, W., 'The Role of Power and Principle in Getting to Yes', in J.W. Breslin and J.Z. Rubin, *Negotiation Theory and Practice*, Cambridge, 1991, pp.115–22
16. Crampton, P.C. and Dees, J.G., 'Promoting honesty in negotiation', *Journal of Business Ethics*, March 2002, pp.1–28

17 Support tools

After reading this chapter you should be able to:

- Define tendering and state the main types of tender.
- Describe the process of tendering.
- Understand the importance and application of debriefing and post-tender negotiation.
- State some quantitative and qualitative forecasting techniques.
- Identify some techniques of investment appraisal.
- Define and explain the concept of life cycle costing and its methodology.
- Define target costing and describe the application of target costing to purchasing.
- Define absorption based costing and explain the differences between activity-based and absorption costing.
- Define standard costing and the concept of variances.
- Distinguish between budgets and budgetary control and describe the compilation of a purchase budget.
- Explain the concept of a learning curve and the application of learning curves to a purchasing context.
- Identify the main types of project and outline some possible contributions of purchasing to project management.
- Describe the application of Gantt charts and network analysis to project management.
- Define the term 'operational research' (OR) and state some OR techniques and their application to the supplies field.

17.1   Tendering

17.1.1   Definition

Tendering is:

A purchasing procedure whereby potential suppliers are invited to make a firm and unequivocal offer of the price and terms which, on acceptance, shall be the basis of the subsequent contract.

17.1.2   Types of tender

■ *Open tenders*. Prospective suppliers are invited to compete for a contract advertised in the press, the lowest tender generally being accepted although the advertisers usually state that they are not bound to accept the lowest or any tender.

■ *Restricted open tenders*. Prospective suppliers are invited to compete for a contract, the advertising of which is restricted to appropriate technical journals or local newspapers.

■ *Selective tenders*. Tenders are invited from suppliers on an approved list who have been previously vetted regarding their competence and financial standing.

■ *Serial tenders*. Prospective suppliers are requested on either an open or a selective basis to tender for an initial scheme on the basis that, subject to satisfactory performance and unforeseen financial contingencies, a programme of work will be given to the successful contractor, the rates and prices for the first job being the basis of the rest of the programme. Advantages claimed for this system include:

– contractors are given an incentive to maintain a high performance level;

– savings in cost and time by eliminating one-contract negotiations for each stage of a programme;

– teams of employees and plant can be moved to successive jobs without disruption;

– supplier security of contract should enable purchasers to negotiate keener prices.

■ *Negotiated tenders*. A tender is negotiated with only one supplier so that competition is eliminated. This type of contract is unusual. In the case of a local authority it would require the waiving of standing orders.

17.1.3   The application of tendering

Although tendering is used by private sector undertakings, particularly in respect of construction and service contracts, it is in the public sector that tendering is most used to ensure conformity to such principles of public accountability as openness or transparency, avoidance of a conflict of interests and recognition that 'a public office is a public trust'. Guidance regarding public tendering is found in the following places:

■ UK law. Section 135(3) of the Local Government Act 1972, for example, states:

> Standing orders made by a local authority with respect to the supply of goods or materials for the execution of works shall include provision for securing competition for such contracts and for regulating the manner but may exempt from any such provisions contracts for a price below that specified in standing orders and may authorise the authority to exempt any contract from such provision when the authority is satisfied that the exemption is justified by special circumstances.

Part 1 of the Local Government Act 1999 imposes a duty on 'best value authorities' to make arrangements to secure continuous improvement in the way their functions are exercised having regard to 'economy, efficiency and effectiveness'. In addition to local authorities, 'best value authorities' include police, fire, waste disposal, transport, national parks and broads authorities.

■ European law on public sector purchasing (see Chapter 9, section 9.4). Most such law is contained in UK regulations or statutory instruments, e.g. the Public Contracts (Works, Services and Supply) (Amendment) Regulations 2000. Under EC directives it is expected that the majority of public contracts will use open tender procedures. Restricted procedures will apply only where:

– the contract value does not justify the procedural costs of an open tender;

– the product required is highly specific in its nature.

'Negotiated' tenders will normally be allowable only where:

– because bids were irregular or unacceptable, no suitable supplier has been found by open or restricted tender procedures;

– such procedures have resulted in no tender being received;

– the required product is manufactured purely for research and development or experimental purposes;

– for technical or artistic reasons or the existence of exclusive rights, there is only one supplier;

– for urgent reasons, the time limits laid down by competitive tendering cannot be complied with;

– additional deliveries by the original supplier are required, either as part replacement or to extend existing supplies or equipment or where a change of supplier would result in non-compatible equipment or technical differences in terms of operation of maintenance. Contracts of this type should generally not exceed three years.

■ Guidance on good procurement practice given by the Treasury and the Audit Commission.

17.1.4 Tendering procedure

In public purchasing, procedures are usually codified within standing orders which usually prescribe a cash limit above which tenders must be invited, the forms of contract to be used, and to whom and under what circumstances responsibility may be delegated, e.g. to senior officers. In general, the procedure for open tendering involves:

- The issue of a public advertisement inviting tenders.

- Full and identical specifications being issued to each prospective contractor, who is required to submit his or her tender in a sealed and identifiable envelope by a prescribed date.

- On the date arranged for the opening of tenders, appointed officers from the purchasing department and an external department, e.g. treasurer's department, will attend.

- Tenders will be initialled, listed and entered on an analysis sheet showing details of prices, rates, carriage charges, delivery, settlement terms and other information necessary for their evaluation.

- Late tenders are not considered and are usually returned unopened.

- Standing orders frequently give delegated powers to chief officers or the officer in charge of the purchasing function to place orders against tenders up to a specified value. For contracts exceeding this amount, delegated authority is given provided the lowest tender to the specification is accepted. Where the acceptance of the lowest tender is not recommended, standing orders may require the consent of a prescribed committee chairman (e.g. policy and finance) before the tender is accepted.

17.1.5 Disadvantages of tendering

- Contractors may quote a price that is too low, leading to subsequent disputes if goods or services supplied are unsatisfactory.

- Tendering is unsuitable for certain contracts. With plant contracts, for example, consultation with one or more of the more favourable tenderers is often essential to clear up technical points. These often result in the tenderer making suggestions that will result in cheaper running and maintenance costs. The extent to which technical changes can be allowed without affecting the validity of open competition is a matter of difficulty.

- Tendering procedure is too slow for emergencies – this is usually recognised by standing orders.

- Where tenders are accepted on the principle of the lowest price, credit may not be given to suppliers for past performance.

- Tendering procedure, particularly with open tendering, may be expensive from the standpoint of clerical, stationery and postage costs.

- Tendering is expensive to the contractor. For this and the reason above, selective tendering is usually preferable.

17.2   Debriefing

The Central Unit on Procurement (CUP)[1] has pointed out that 'debriefing candidates not selected for a bid list and unsuccessful tenderers is recommended in the Treasury's Public Purchasing Policy: Consolidated Guidelines'. Government departments are also subject to specific requirements for debriefing on contracts for supplies, works and priority services under EC rules and the GATT Agreement on Government Procurement. The GATT Agreement provides, *inter alia*, that:

> Subject to Paragraph 9 below [this relates to disclosure of confidential information] upon request by an unsuccessful tenderer, the procuring entity shall promptly provide that tenderer with pertinent information concerning the reasons why the tender was not selected, including information on the characteristics and the relative advantages of the tender selected, as well as the name of the winning tenderer.[2]

The practice of debriefing might be adopted by private sector purchasers.

17.2.1 The benefits of debriefing

Debriefing can be costly. It is often done verbally rather than by written communication. The Treasury[3] recommends that government departments should balance the resource costs against the likely benefits. The benefits accruing to a purchasing organisation from adopting a policy of responding to requests from unsuccessful tenderers for debriefing information include:

- Establishing a reputation as a fair, honest, 'open' and ethical client.
- Providing unsuccessful tenderers with some benefits for the time and money spent on preparing their tenders. This is likely to be of most value to smaller and newer suppliers. It will help all tenders to be more competitive in the future.

17.2.2 Debriefing topics

The CUP[4] lists the following debriefing topics:

- Cost – actual price or rates offered in tenders are confidential and should never be disclosed. It is permissible, however, to disclose a prospective supplier's ranking in the tender list. The CUP observes that 'if the tenderer was the lowest bidder in cost terms but not selected on VFM [value for money] this need not be disclosed: it is unlikely to lead to constructive debate. The interviewee could, however, be told that although the price was competitive, other factors were more significant in the award decision'.
- Schedules – exceptionally long production and/or construction schedules.
- Design – deficiencies, higher operating costs.
- Organisation/administration weaknesses.
- Experience – where the experience of the tenderer is deemed to be inadequate for the demands of the contract.
- Personnel – where numbers, experience and quality of personnel including management are deemed inadequate.
- Facilities/equipment – outdated equipment or facilities.
- Subcontracting – too much reliance on subcontractors and inadequate control arrangements.
- Cost and schedule control inadequacies.

- Industrial relations – where the tenderer has an unsatisfactory record and no plans for improvement.

- Quality management – where control procedures relating to materials, methods, systems and people are deemed unsatisfactory.

- Contract terms – where these differ fundamentally from those of the client.

- After-sales service – inadequate arrangements for servicing to the supply of spares.

17.2.3 The conduct of debriefing

The Inland Revenue[5] recommends that debriefing:

- should not disclose information about other tenderers which could breach commercial confidentiality;

- should not become arguments about rights or wrongs or attempt to justify the reasons why the contract has been awarded to a particular tenderer;

- should be confined to the unsuccessful bid and the weaknesses that led to its rejection, e.g. cost, delivery dates, inadequate experience, failure to meet quality standards, etc.;

- should indicate the perceived strengths of the unsuccessful tender;

- should conclude by asking for the supplier's view on the debriefing process;

It also recommends that the results of debriefing interviews should be recorded for reference should there be any further audit in the case of follow-up by the unsuccessful bidder or some other party.

17.3 Post-tender negotiation

The disadvantages of traditional tendering procedures have indicated the importance of post-tender negotiation (PTN). PTN is defined by the CIPS as:

> Negotiation after the receipt of formal tenders and before the letting of contract(s) with the Supplier(s) Contractor(s) submitting the lowest acceptable tender(s) with a view to obtaining an improvement in price, delivery of content in circumstances which do not put other tenderers at a disadvantage or affect their confidence or trust in the competitive tendering system.

Post-Tender Negotiation, issued by the CUP, points out that, if it is not considered unethical for a supplier to tender at the highest level that it is considered the purchaser will pay, the converse is that it is not unethical for buyers to challenge the prices tendered.

CUP[6] has stated that PTN can apply to almost any order or contract, although care should be taken to ensure that the cost of negotiation does not outweigh any resultant savings. In particular, PTN is recommended:

- for all orders potentially worth £100,000 or more;
- where the final bid evaluation does not present overwhelming evidence for one tenderer;
- where there is doubt regarding quality or performance or where clarification of terms and conditions is required;
- for all supply agreements made for a period of twelve months or longer.

It is important that the same general questions and propositions are put to shortlisted tenderers although, as stated above, this does not preclude questions asking for clarification. A record should be kept of the negotiation process for audit purposes. Such a record should include:

- date and time of communications (e.g. meetings, telephone calls, correspondence);
- persons present or contacted;
- matters discussed;
- outcomes.

The CUP also identifies eight common areas for direct price negotiation:

- Where single tender action has been authorised.
- Where it is known or suspected that price-fixing or cartel arrangements are operating.
- Where tender prices appear grossly inflated over known or reliably estimated market prices of the price(s) paid for similar or identical items.
- Where, despite competitive tendering, a particular supplier is consistently successful in obtaining the contract.
- Where the enquiry is based on a functional or development specification rather than a detailed specification.
- Where the purchaser needs to justify selections by testing the market.
- Where the quantity to be ordered justifies splitting requirements between more than one supplier.
- To evaluate whether market conditions are in the buyer's favour or otherwise.

The CIPS has issued a statement on PTN in which the following criteria and controls are offered for consideration:

Criteria
- The value of the contract potential for savings and the cost to the buyer of conducting PTN against the likely saving in price.
- Is there time to conduct PTN without delaying the completion date for the contract?
- Effect on the future supply position.
- Is the contract affected by regulations such as EC directives and WTO, which require equality of treatment of potential suppliers?
- Is it or would it be considered ethical?

Controls

- Who will authorise PTN in particular cases and how will that person relate to the person authorised to award the contract?
- Who will take part in and who will lead the negotiations?
- Who will award the contract?
- What documentation is needed to record events before, during and after PTN, and does this provide a satisfactory audit trail?
- How will the conduct and results of PTN be reviewed and by whom?

17.4   Forecasting techniques

Forecasting techniques are methods that can be used to predict future aspects of a business operation. Such methods can be classified as either quantitative or qualitative.

17.4.1   Quantitative techniques

Quanitative techniques are based on an analysis of historical data appertaining to a time series and, possibly, other related time series. The most used quantitative approaches are moving averages, exponential smoothing and trend projection.

Moving averages

Moving averages move in the sense that as new data becomes available it replaces the oldest data in the equation:

$$\text{Moving averages} = \sum \frac{(\text{Most recent data values})}{n}$$

where n is the number of data values.

Exponential smoothing

Exponential smoothing involves the use of a weighted average of past time series as the forecast in the equation:

$$F_{t+1} = aY_1 + (1 - a)F_1$$

where: F_{t+1} = forecast of the time series for period $t + 1$

Y_1 = actual value of the time series in period t

F_1 = forecast of time series for period t

a = smoothing constant $(0 \leq a \leq 1)$

Moving averages and exponential smoothing are also described in section 8.13 of Chapter 8.

Trend projection

Trend projection extrapolates from a time series of data over a given number of periods. If we consider the monthly usage of a product, for example, the trend may be up, down or zero dependent on whether the demand is expanding, contracting or stationary.

17.4.2 Qualitative techniques

Qualitative forecasting methods generally use the judgement of experts to make predictions. Qualitative forecasts are closely related to the planning approaches described in Chapter 4, namely life cycle analysis, scenario planning, systems modelling and strategic issue management.

17.5   Techniques of investment appraisal

Top management, assisted primarily by the management accountant, is responsible for identifying the best assets for an enterprise to acquire in order to achieve its goals and objectives. Barfield et al.[7] state that making such an identification requires answers to the following four questions:

- Is the activity worthy of an investment? An activity's worth is measured by *cost/benefit analysis*. Cost/benefit analysis involves three basic steps:
  - computing the total costs associated with a decision;
  - estimating the total benefits arising from the decision. Often the benefits cannot be quantified in monetary terms, e.g. the refurbishment of an office will not directly improve employee productivity but may do much for morale;
  - comparing the total costs with total anticipated benefits.
- Which assets can be used for the activity? This involves consideration of monetary and non-monetary information for each asset such as initial cost, estimated life, scrap value, raw material and labour requirements, operating costs, output capability, service availability, maintenance cost and revenues (if any) to be generated.
- Of the available assets for each activity, which is the best investment? Deciding which asset is the best investment requires the use of one or more of the evaluation techniques described in Chapter 12, namely payback, average rate of return and net present value.
- Of the 'best investments for all worthwhile activities', in which ones should the enterprise invest? Since investment resources are limited, the enterprise must decide which of several competing assets and activities to fund. This requires the application of sophisticated investment appraisal techniques which allow for the fact that since capital decisions are based on assumptions relating to future occurrences, an amount of risk is involved. Such advanced appraisal techniques are outside the scope of this book.

Rough guides to choosing the best investments are, however, provided by:

- ranking investment possibilities in terms of anticipated profitability based on their net present value;
- ranking investment projects in terms of capital rationing. Capital rationing means that there is an upper limit on the amount of capital available for asset acquisition. Within this amount, money can be allocated according to the following priorities:

  - required by legislation, e.g. pollution control equipment;
  - essential to operating, e.g. assets without which production could not continue;
  - non-essential but income generating, e.g. assets which could provide increased productivity or cost savings;
  - optional improvements, e.g. those which do not produce cost savings or revenue improvements but which make the enterprise run more smoothly, e.g. office refurbishment;
  - miscellaneous, e.g. 'pet projects' of managers.

17.6 Application of costing techniques

No buyer can afford to be unaware of the various cost accounting approaches to make-or-buy decisions, negotiation, price appraisal and purchasing performance, to mention just four such applications. Relevant approaches include life cycle costing, target costing, absorption costing, activity-based costing and standard costing. Marginal cost as applied to make-or-buy decisions is considered in section 9.11 of Chapter 9.

17.7 Life cycle costing

The concept of life cycle analysis with its stages of development – growth, maturity, decline and withdrawal – was introduced in Chapter 4.5. As stated in section 11.3 of Chapter 11, life cycle costing is an important factor in making decisions relating to capital expenditure.

17.7.1 Definition

Life cycle costing has been defined by the Chartered Institute of Management Accountants (CIMA)[8] as:

> **The practice of obtaining over their life time the best use of the physical assets at the lowest cost to the entity (terotechnology). This is achieved through a combination of management, financial, engineering and other disciplines.**

The term 'terotechnology', coined in 1970, is derived from the Greek verb *tereo* and means 'the art and science of caring for things'. Life cycle costs are therefore those associated with acquiring, using, caring for and disposing of physical assets, including feasibility studies, research, development, design, production, maintenance, replacement and disposal, as well as the associated support, training and operating costs incurred over the period in which the asset is owned.

17.7.2 The importance of life cycle costing

Unless life cycle implications are taken into consideration there is a danger that initial cost on delivery will be used as the sole criterion when selecting a physical asset. This simplistic approach can have detrimental implications for the total life cycle cost of the item.

Life cycle costing is of particular importance for products liable to rapid technological styles changes. From the standpoint of producers, rapid technological change may mean that revenue from sales may be insufficient to make the original investment in design and development worthwhile. From the buyer's viewpoint, the asset may, to a greater or lesser extent, be obsolete before the amount invested in its purchase has been recouped.

Purchasing executives concerned with the acquisition of capital items are therefore advised to:

■ ensure that specifications include reference to factors which have a bearing on the cost of ownership of an asset, e.g. maintenance, availability of spares;

■ create a communication bridge with the supplier regarding developments in the particular field;

■ treat initial costs as only one of many factors that contribute to total life cycle costs;

■ ensure that all factors which may have implications for the total life cycle costs are given due consideration before recommending the purchase of a particular asset.

17.7.3 Application of life cycle costing

Apart from the purchase of capital equipment, life cycle costing can be applied to the following:

■ *Acquisition control* – estimating the future costs of large-scale acquisitions.

■ *Optioneering* – comparing the return on a number of expenditure options.

■ *Pricing* – ensuring that, in addition to direct and general overhead cost (not including depreciation), the selling price includes an interest charge that reflects the overall cost of capital required to satisfy all capital providers so that the annual equivalent cost of fixed assets will recover both depreciation and a profit margin that satisfies all providers.

■ *Project analysis* – measurement of the cost of project against targets.

- *Product design* – provision of data that will enable designers to modify or improve designs that will increase consumer satisfaction and give a product greater cost advantage over those of competitors.
- *Replacement decisions* – since the cost of using and repairing physical assets increases with age, life cycle costing can indicate when it is more beneficial to dispose of an asset and purchase a replacement than to meet increasing maintenance costs.
- *Supplier support* – provision by suppliers of comparative life cycle estimates for their products.

17.7.4 Life cycle costing methodology

Life cycle costing methodology involves four basic steps:

- Identify all relevant costs. As shown in Figure 17.1, these are initially broken down into (i) acquisition and (ii) operation and maintenance costs, and then further categorised under each heading.
- Calculate costs over the anticipated life of the asset of all elements identified above. Such costs may be:
  - known rates, e.g. operator wages, maintenance charges;
  - estimated rates based on historical figures or other empirical data;
  - guesstimates based on informed opinion.
- Use discounting to adjust future costs to the present, i.e. the time when the purchase decision is made. This reduces all options to a common base thereby ensuring fair comparison. Discounting is discussed in Chapter 12.
- Draw conclusions from the cost figures obtained by the above procedure.

17.7.5 Annual equivalent cost

By expressing the initial purchase and subsequent running costs of an asset in terms of annual equivalent cost, the life cycle costs of assets with different lives can be compared. The calculation involves dividing the capital cost, i.e. purchase and installation costs, by the relevant cumulative present value factor (obtained from cumulative present value tables) for the specified life and rate of interest. The formula is:

$$\text{Annual equivalent cost} = \frac{\text{Capital cost}}{\text{Cumulative present value factor}}$$

Example 17.1 Annual equivalent cost

A company buys a machine for a capital cost of £10,000 plus £1,000 for installation. The machine has an anticipated life of 5 years and cumulative present value factor of 3.933 representing 8 per cent for 5 years. The annual equivalent cost is therefore:

$$\frac{£11,000}{3.993} = £2,755$$

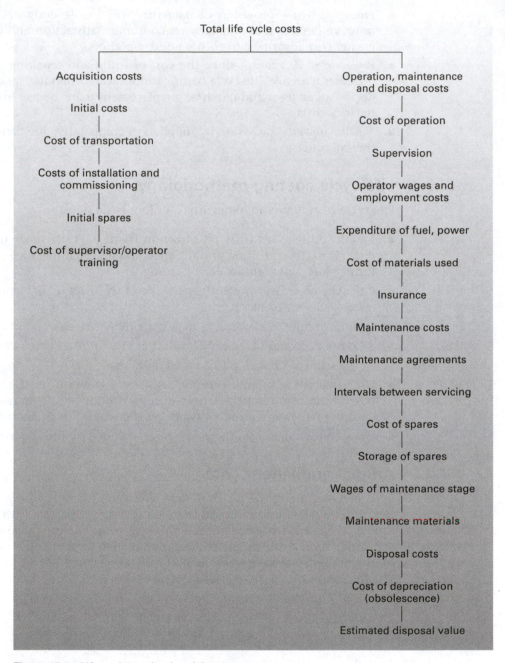

Figure 17.1 Life cycle costing breakdown structure

Example 17.2 Life cycle costing

A department has a requirement for 50 photocopiers capable of producing 40,000 copies per month from each copier.

There are two copiers that fully meet the department's technical specification together with the quality requirements. The anticipated life of the copier is five years.

The metered cost per copy offered by the suppliers includes maintenance charges and all consumables. The two proposals are as follows:

	Copier A	Copier B
Unit price for an order of 50	£10,745	£8,625
Metered cost/copy fixed in cash terms for 5 years	0.9p	1.9p

To ascertain the most cost-effective acquisition in life cost terms an life cycle costing analysis is carried out. A discount rate of 6 per cent in real terms (i.e. after adjusting for inflation) is used in the analysis which gives the following discounting factors:

Year 0	1
Year 1	0.943
Year 2	0.890
Year 3	0.840
Year 4	0.792

The following example sets out the steps involved in this procedure. All costs are expressed at year 0 prices. Staff costs and consumables will almost certainly rise in line with inflation. But any costs which will remain the same in cash terms over the five years will need to be adjusted to year 0 prices using a forecast of inflation which your finance division will be able to give you. In this example, inflation is assumed to be 4 per cent per year. It is also assumed that the machines are deployed at separate locations around the building, not as part of a continuous flow print room. In the case of the latter, it would be necessary to allow for some standby facility to maintain the required level of output.

Step 1: Produce a cost breakdown structure (Figure 17.2)

Step 2: Produce a cost estimate

Acquisition	Copier A	Copier B
Purchase costs	£537.25k	£431.25k
Purchase department costs (2 man/weeks)	£2.5k	£2.5k
(Operator training time required per copier)	(3 hr)	(2 hr)
(2 operators per copier) at £10 per hour × 50 copiers	£3k	£2k
Total acquisition cost	**£542.7k**	**£435.75k**

Operation (5 years)	Copier A	Copier B
	£k	£k
Operator cost		
Year 0	600.0	600.0
Year 1	565.8	565.8
Year 2	534.0	534.0
Year 3	504.0	504.0
Year 4	475.2	475.2
£5 per 1,000		
Year 0	120.0	120.0
Year 1	113.2	113.2
Year 2	106.8	106.8
Year 3	100.8	100.8
Ongoing training	95.0	95.0
	1.5	1.5
Total operation cost	**£3,216.3**	**£3,216.3**

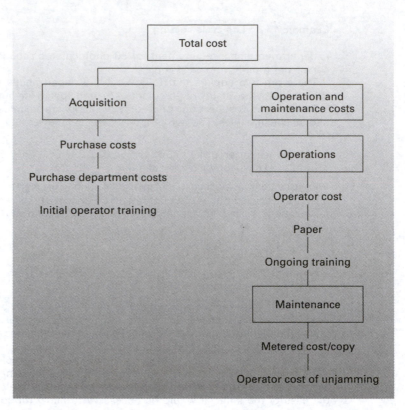

Figure 17.2 Cost breakdown

Maintenance (5 years)				*Copier A*	*Copier B*
Metered cost per copy				0.9p	1.0p

	Adjusted at 4% per year		Then discounted at 6%	
	Copier A	*Copier B*	*Copier A*	*Copier B*
	£k	*£k*	*£k*	*£k*
Year 0	216.0	240.0	216.0	240.0
Year 1	207.7	230.8	196.7	217.4
Year 2	199.7	221.9	177.7	197.2
Year 3	192.0	213.3	161.3	179.2
Year 4	184.6	205.1	146.2	162.5

Operator/supervisor cost of unjamming		
Mean number of copies between jamming		
(source: previous experience)	5,000	3,000
Average downtime	0.5 hr	1 hr

5 year cost at £10/hour	*£k*	*£k*
Year 0	24.0	80.0
Year 1	22.6	75.4
Year 2	21.4	71.2
Year 3	20.2	67.2
Year 4	19.0	63.4
Total maintenance cost	**£1,004.1**	**£1,353.7**

Total 5 year life cycle costing	**£4.831m**	**£5.080m**

Analysis

The example shows that the acquisition cost is far exceeded by the maintenance costs. The cost of operation, although large, is committed by the decision to buy the copier and is not affected by the choice. Therefore, it was unnecessary to discount these costs as they apply equally to both options.

The maintenance costs show the major cost drivers over which the procurer has some control. Not only are the meter costs important but also the time expended by the operator in unjamming the machine.

Before the decision can be fully assessed the options should be evaluated in performance terms. The prime criterion for copiers of equal performance is availability for use. This can be calculated as follows:

$$\text{Availability} = \frac{\text{Uptime}}{\text{Total time}}$$

with the following data:

	Copier A	Copier B
Total possible availability	176 hr	176 hr
Downtime for replacement of consumables/ month/copier (company brochures)	3 hr	4 hr
Downtime for operator unjamming/month/copier (user experience)	4 hr	13.3 hr
Downtime for maintenance engineers/month/copier	5.4 hr	10.8 hr
Average downtime/month/copier	12.4 hr	28.1 hr
$\dfrac{\text{Uptime}}{\text{Total time}}$	$\dfrac{(176 - 12.4)}{176}$	$\dfrac{(176 - 28.1)}{176}$
Availability	**93%**	**84%**

Step 3: Draw conclusions

Copier A, although over £100,000 more expensive to buy, is some £349,000 cheaper to own when considered in life cycle costing terms over five years (i.e. the difference between the operation and maintenance costs of copiers A and B). Additionally, copier A, being a higher quality machine with better reliability than copier B, is on average 9 per cent more available than its competitor, or viewed alternatively, copier B would be unavailable for twice as long as copier A. The additional investment in purchase will be more than recouped during the life of the copiers.

Source: HM Treasury, *Life Cycle Costing*, BCUP Guidance Note 35, pp. 7–8. Reproduced by kind permission of HM Treasury and HMSO.

17.8   Target costing

17.8.1   Definition

Target costing is defined by CIMA[9] as:

A product cost estimate derived from a competitive market price. Used to reduce costs through continuous improvement and replacement of technologies and processes.

17.8.2 Target cost procedures

Target cost, as explained in section 17.8, is simply target price minus target profit. Target costing has the following characteristics:

- It is proactive and forward looking rather than reactive and historical as is the case with standard costs.

- It is dynamic since target costs are revised not only in the design and development stages but throughout the life cycle of a product or service. The emphasis on continuous improvement implies that target costs over this period are expected to decrease.

- It is market driven in the sense that targets are fixed by reference to the costs of competitors.

- It is linked closely to the concept of *functional analysis*. A function is that which a product or service is designed to do, and functional analysis 'contributes to cost management by eliminating or modifying functions of the product or service'.[10] Functional analysis is undertaken by a team comprising representatives of design, engineering, production, purchasing, marketing and management functions, to determine how costs can be managed to meet the desired target. Functional analysis can, on occasion, lead the designer to add new functions if the target profit is greater than the target cost generated by the additional functions.

An initial target cost statement prepared by the supplier would resemble the format shown in Figure 17.3.

Each cost element will be considered by the team to ascertain how target costs can be modified or the competitiveness of the product can be enhanced by:

- improved design specifications;
- improved production techniques;
- alternative materials;
- eliminating or combining functions;

Component X		
Estimated life cycle	5 years	
Estimated annual sales	40,000	
Estimated total sales over life cycle	200,000	
Initial target sales price per unit	£342 (50% on target costs)	
		Target costs
	Per unit	*Total life cycle*
Design and development	£12.50	£2,500,000
Production	£125.50	£25,100,000
Packaging	£10.00	£2,000,000
Marketing	£35.00	£7,000,000
Transportation	£25.00	£5,000,000
After-sales service	£10.00	£2,000,000
	£218.00	£43,600,000

Figure 17.3 Initial target cost statement

- control of packaging, marketing and transportation costs;
- reduction in after-sales service through improved reliability.

17.8.3 Target costing and purchasing

Target costing is primarily associated with the search for competitiveness by product manufacturers and service providers. It is, however, an approach that can be utilised by purchasing particularly in relation to negotiation in such ways as the following:

- Providing suppliers with a target price that the purchaser is prepared to pay.
- Identifying, in association with a supplier, the means by which the target price may be achieved including a fair profit.
- Incorporating improvements into the product or price at agreed intervals or when a contract is due for renewal.
- Providing suppliers with an estimate of the life cycle of parent products in which bought-out components or assemblies will be incorporated. It is then possible to estimate the total demand that a supplier may expect to receive over a defined period of time. This total demand can be used to negotiate quantity discounts, price reviews and learning allowances.

17.8.4 Target and *Kaizen* costing

Kaizen costing is a Japanese approach to cost reduction and management. The principal difference between target and *Kaizen* costing is that target costing applies to the design stage whereas *Kaizen* costing applies to the manufacturing stage of the product life cycle. Target costing focuses on the product and seeks to achieve cost reductions through product design. Thus target costing at Toyota is a rigorous engineering process which uses value engineering to reduce the cost of products. *Kaizen* costing focuses on production processes and cost reduction are achieved through improved manufacturing efficiency. The aim of *Kaizen* costing is to reduce the cost of components and production processes by a specific amount.

17.9   Absorption costing

17.9.1 Definition

Approaches such as life cycle and target costing are approaches to price comparison and price control and reduction rather than day-to-day costing methods. Probably the simplest and best understood method of cost ascertainment is absorption costing defined by CIMA[11] as:

> A principle whereby fixed as well as variable costs are allotted to cost units and total overheads are absorbed according to activity level.
> The term may be applied where (a) production costs only or (b) costs of all functions are allotted.

17.9.2 The elements of cost

Cost is the amount of expenditure incurred on a given item. Costs can be classified in several ways, according to the purpose for which they are required. The most usual classifications are:

■ Direct costs comprising direct wages, materials and expenses that can be allocated to specific cost units or centres.

■ Indirect costs comprising expenses, i.e. indirect wages, materials and expenses, that cannot be allocated but which can be apportioned or absorbed by cost units or centres.

Costs can also be classified as:

■ Fixed, i.e. a cost which tends to be unaffected by variations in volume of output.

■ Variable, i.e. a cost which tends to vary directly with variations in volume of output.

■ Semi-variable, i.e. a cost which is partly fixed and partly variable.

17.9.3 Price composition

The price quoted will therefore be built up as follows:

Direct costs	Materials, labour and expenses	Prime cost
Indirect costs	Works or factory expenses (Production overheads)	Work costs
	Office and administrative expenses (Establishment overheads)	Cost of production (Gross cost)
	Selling and distribution expenses (Selling overheads)	Cost of sales (Selling cost)
Net profit		= Selling price

By price analysis the buyer, with the assistance of the design, production and financial departments, will be able to arrive at a reasonably close estimate of the prime cost of a bought-out item. There will, however, be less precision in arriving at estimates of indirect costs and profit. The preparation of such an estimate is an essential preliminary to negotiation. When presented to a vendor, the estimate puts the prospective supplier in the position either of having to explain why the buyer's estimate is wrong or of providing cost data to support his or her quotation.

The questions that the buyer might raise in analysing the prices quoted by vendors will be peculiar to the item or job. Some examples of questions applicable to each of the elements that constitute selling prices indicate the approach.

Materials costs

Materials costs comprise the quantity of material times the purchase price of material.

- What material is used, i.e. would an alternative material reduce costs?
- What standardisation is possible?
- Is it possible for the buyer to purchase materials on behalf of the vendor at a cheaper cost?
- What weight of material has been allowed for?
- What scrap allowances are included?
- Has scrap any resale value?

Labour costs

Labour costs comprise time multiplied by wage rate.

- What time allocations have been made?
- Has any allowance been included for idle time?
- What element of overtime is included?
- Has any allowance for 'learning' been included? (See section 17.13.)
- What production methods will be used?

Indirect costs

All material, labour and expense costs which cannot be identified as direct costs are termed 'indirect costs' and are usually separated as follows:

- *Production overheads*, i.e. indirect production *materials* (e.g. lubricating oil, spare parts for machinery); indirect *labour* (e.g. supervisory and maintenance wages); and indirect *expenses* (e.g. factory rates and insurance).
- *Administration overheads*, e.g. management, secretarial and office services and related expenditure.
- *Selling overheads*, i.e. costs incurred in securing orders (e.g. salespeople's salaries, commissions and travelling expenses). Overheads may be:
  - *allocated*, i.e. charged against an identifiable cost centre or unit. (A cost centre is a location, function or item of equipment in respect of which costs may be ascertained and related to cost units for control purposes, e.g. the drawing office, the purchasing department.)
  - *apportioned*, i.e. spread over several cost centres on an agreed basis (e.g. rates and lighting may be apportioned on the basis of floor area or space occupied respectively).
  - *absorbed*, i.e. charged to cost units by means of rates separately calculated for each cost centre. In most cases the rates are predetermined.

Production overhead costs

Production overheads costs are usually absorbed in one of six ways shown by the following example:

Total overhead for period	£24,000
Total units produced in period	180
Total direct labour hours for period	3,200
Total direct wages	£6,400
Total direct material used	£12,000
Total machine hours	£4,800

From the above the following overhead absorption rates (OARs) can be calculated:

- Cost unit OAR $= \dfrac{£24,000}{180} = £133.33$ overhead per unit produced

- Direct labour OAR $= \dfrac{£24,000}{180} = £7.50$ per labour hour

- Direct wages OAR $= \dfrac{£24,000}{£6,400} = 375\%$ or £3.75 per £ of wages

- Direct material OAR $= \dfrac{£24,000}{£12,000} =$ or £2 overheads per £ of materials or 200% of materials

- Material hours OAR $= \dfrac{£24,000}{£4,800} = £5$ per machine hour

- Prime cost OAR $= \dfrac{£24,000}{(£6,400 + £12,000)} = 130\%$ or £1.30 per £ of prime use

Non-production costs

Non-production costs are typically absorbed on an arbitrary basis such as:

$$\text{Administration overhead} = \frac{\text{Administration costs}}{\text{Production cost}}$$

$$\text{Selling overheads} = \frac{\text{Selling + Marketing costs}}{\text{Sales value or production cost}}$$

Price analysis in relation to overheads should therefore involve such questions as:

- What is the basis on which indirect costs are allocated, apportioned or absorbed?
- To what extent can the fixed overhead element per unit be reduced by increased quantities?
- What is the vendor's break-even point per item or contract?
- What is the proportion of selling and administrative overhead as a proportion of production cost?
- Attention should also be given to marginal and activity costing approaches as described in Chapter 9 and section 17.10.

Profit

The vendor is entitled to a fair profit, since this is the reason he or she accepted the order. Profit expectation may also provide an incentive to do the work efficiently. The following seven points should be considered when analysing a vendor's anticipated profits:

- *Competitive price*. The buyer who offers lowest price should be allowed what profit he can make provided this is not excessive.
- *Initial orders*. A high profit may be necessary on initial orders to persuade the vendor to undertake the risks of a new line or production.
- *Size of order*. A higher profit may be justified on a small order.
- *Amount of value added to a product*. Vendors who produce all the components incorporated in a product generally make larger profits than assemblers of purchased parts.
- *Management expertise required*. High profits may be required to keep vendors with products requiring a high degree of designer production expertise interested in the buyer's business. Subcontracted items usually require less skill and therefore lower profits.
- *Risks assumed by vendor*. The greater the risk the higher the allowable profit.
- *Efficiency of vendor*. A vendor who has demonstrated reliability with regard to quality and delivery should not be lost because his processes do not allow him adequate profit.

17.10 Activity-based costing and management

17.10.1 Definition

Activity-based costing is:[12]

> A cost attribution to cost units on the basis of benefit received from indirect activities, e.g. ordering, setting up, assuring quality.

17.10.2 Activity management and activity-based costing

Activity-based costing (ABC) is an aspect of activity-based management (ABM). ABM has been defined as:[13]

> A discipline that focuses on the management of activities as a route to improving the value received by the customer and the profit achieved by providing this value.

ABM is based on the principle that 'activities consume costs'. Whereas traditional cost systems focus on the 'worker', ABM systems focus on the work. The field of ABM covers the following activities:

- Activity analysis
- Activity-based budgeting
- Activity-based costing
- Benchmarking
- Business process re-engineering (BPR)
- Cost driver analysis
- Continuous improvement
- Operational control
- Performance evaluation

17.10.3   The distinction between absorption-based costing and ABC

Within traditional absorption costing, overhead costs are assigned to products, services, jobs or other cost objects using one of the approaches indicated in section 17.9 above. Overhead costs are applied in proportion to production volume. With ABC, an overhead is applied to cost objects according to the activities and resources consumed.

17.10.4   Terminology

The following terms are used in relation to ABC.

An *activity* is a repetitive action performed in fulfilment of business functions, e.g. designing, purchasing, production set up, assembly, quality control, packaging and shipping. Activities can be classified as shown in Figure 17.4.

Time, for example, can be classified as production or service inspection, transfer time and idle time such as storage or waiting for materials. Only production or service time adds value. The other categories of time should be reduced to a minimum or eliminated.

A *resource* comprises costs which support activities. The purchasing activity, for example, incurs costs for salaries and benefits, office space, computer time, travelling, training, etc., thus, as Lapsley *et al.*[14] state:

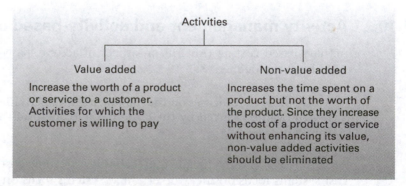

Figure 17.4   Classification of activities for ABC

Activities consume resources
and
Products (or services) consume activities

A *cost object* can be almost anything in respect of which costs are incurred, e.g. products, services, units, batches, jobs, customers, sales territories, etc.

A *cost driver* is a factor that has a direct cause–effect relationship to a cost. Activities creating cost drivers may be either:

- resource drivers, or
- activity drivers.

Resource drivers assign costs to activities thereby forming activity costs pools each containing its appropriate share of resource costs. A number of cost pools can be assigned to an activity cost centre.

For each activity or resource one or more cost drivers must be identified. Cost drivers set activity levels. The cost driver for creating a purchase order, for example, may include the number of orders processed or the number of suppliers.

In general, the appropriate cost driver (i.e. activity and resource driver) is the one that represents the primary output of the activity. Usually a cost driver that captures the *number* of activity transactions is preferable to drivers based on the time duration of monetary amount of the activity transaction because it is (i) readily available; (ii) easy to understand and apply, and (iii) motivates people to act in ways likely to achieve organisational goals.

As Cooper and Kaplan[15] point out:

> A company that wants to reduce the number of unique parts that it processes in order to simplify activities such as vendor selection, purchasing, inspection, maintenance of the bill of materials, storage and accounting may decide to apply the costs of these activities using 'number of part numbers' as the cost driver. Then by evaluating and rewarding product designers according to their ability to design low-cost products, they will be motivated to design products with fewer part numbers.

An *activity cost centre* is a segment of the production or service process for which management wants to separately ascertain the costs of the activities performed, e.g. purchasing, production, marketing. Activity centres should be created where a significant amount of overhead cost is incurred and several key activities are undertaken.

Direct costs inputs as a traditional costing comprise direct labour and direct material and, sometimes, direct technology.

17.10.5   A simple example of ABC

Activity-based costing involves the following steps:

1   Total overhead costs for a given period are computed either prospectively from budgets or retrospectively from departmental and general ledger records.

2   A project team is formed by top management to plan and implement the ABC system. The team, normally led by the management accountant, may comprise

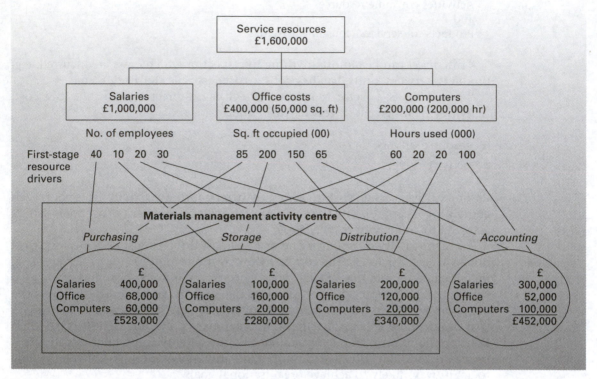

Figure 17.5 Allocation of service resources to cost pools

representatives of the design, production, purchasing/logistics, marketing and financial accounting functions.

3 The estimated or actual total overheads will be divided into service and production categories. Functional managers will then be interviewed and asked questions such as the following:

(a) What activities does your function undertake?

(b) What activities are undertaken by each member of staff in the function?

(c) What are the outputs of each activity?

(d) What equipment and supplies are used for each activity?

(e) What overtime is worked?

(f) Why does idle time occur?

This activity analysis describes what is done by the enterprise and each function within the enterprise, i.e. how resources, including time and effort, are spent and what inputs and outputs are involved.

4 The team will then assign resource costs to activity cost centres and cost pools using first-stage resource drivers as shown in Figure 17.5 (for simplicity only three resources – salaries, office costs and computers – are shown).

5 Second-stage activity drivers, e.g. number of purchaser orders, items stored, deliveries made, will be chosen. These will normally be outputs and are used to assign the cost pools to cost products as shown in Figure 17.5.

6　A bill of activities will be prepared for each product as shown in Table 17.1. This enables the unit cost of each product using ABC to be ascertained.

17.10.6　The application of ABC

Burch[16] states that ABC is especially appropriate in companies where:

- competition is high;
- product mix is diverse in batch sizes, physical sizes, degree of complexity and raw material characteristics;
- product life cycles are short, i.e. three years or less;
- collection and manipulation of data are performed by an integrated computer-based information system (ICBIS).

17.10.7　ABC and purchasing

Barker[17] states that purchasing is 'a key activity for using ABC' and points out that 'much of the literature uses the purchasing and supply function to illustrate how to apply ABC'. Barker identifies a number of ways in which ABC can be implemented within purchasing, including:

- the attribution of purchasing function costs to products;
- provision of information which can be utilised in relation to make-or-buy and sourcing decisions. Ness and Cucuzza[18] note that the introduction of ABC at Chrysler showed that the actual costs of some low-volume parts were as much as 30 times greater than the stated costs. This made clear that the company would be better off outsourcing these parts and making more high-volume parts;
- analysis of the total acquisition cost of purchased items 'may give buyers the information to prove what they have long suspected: paying more often costs less'.

ABC can also:

- highlight procurement activities that do not add value to products, e.g. inspection and storage and which activities should be cut;
- identify ways in which savings in procurement costs can contribute to the competitive advantage of the enterprise, e.g. reduction in the number of suppliers and transactions, elimination of unnecessary purchasing documentation, improve design with fewer and standardised parts;
- control the overall procurement function by regarding it as an activity centre in which all purchasing-activity-related cost pools are aggregated. This may provide data on drivers and rates which allows comparisons to be made across functions and with potential external suppliers;
- make a significant contribution to TQM since costs are a key factor in any decision.

Table 17.1 Bill of activities of products X and Y for the 52 weeks ended 31 March

	Pool driver rate	Product X = 20,000 units			Product Y = 12,000 units		
		Second stage	Activity cost		Activity driver	Activity cost	
		Driver quantity	Activity cost	Unit cost	Quantity	Activity cost	Unit cost
Purchasing	£264 per order	800	£211,200	£10.56	1,200	£316,800	£26.40
Storage	£200 per item stored	600	£120,000	£6.00	800	£160,000	£13.33
Distribution	£10,625 per delivery	200	£212,500	£10.63	120	£127,500	£10.63
Accounting	£200 per a/c	904	£180,800	£9.04	1,356	£271,200	£22.60
Factory administration	£1,000 per factory hour	1,100	£1,100,000	£55.00	1,500	£1,500,000	£125.00
Set-ups	£2,000 per set-up	100	£200,000	£10.00	200	£400,000	£33.34
			£2,024,500			£2,775,500	
Activity costs per unit				£101.23			£231.30
Direct materials cost per unit £65				£65.00			£127.50
Direct labour cost per unit £25				£25.00			£46.20
Total costs per unit				£191.23			£405.00

With traditional absorption costing the overhead rate per unit produced would be £4,800,000/32,000 = £150 per unit. The costs would therefore be:

	Product X	Product Y
Direct materials	£65.00	£127.50
Direct labour	£25.00	£46.20
Overhead	£150.00	£323.70
	£240.00	£497.50

17.11   Standard costing

17.11.1   Definition

Standard costing is defined by CIMA[19] as:

> **A control technique which compares costs and revenues with actual results to obtain variances which are used to stimulate improved performance.**

Standard costing is therefore a technique of comparisons – the actual with the standard. This approach is used mainly in undertakings engaged in repetitive production and assumes the use of materials or components whose design, quality and specifications are standardised. The standard cost of materials comprises quantity, price and variances.

17.11.2   Quantity

Normally this is derived from technical and engineering specifications, frequently as indicated in the bill of materials. Standard quantities normally include allowance for normal losses due to factors such as scrap, breakages, evaporation and the like.

17.11.3   Price

Prices used are the forecast expected prices, normally the latest prices at which the item can be obtained from approved sources in the quantities estimated for the relevant budget period. Another approach which takes into account that an item may have to be bought from several suppliers is to base prices on the average expected to be paid over the period under consideration.

17.11.4   Variances

The difference between the standard and actual cost is termed a 'variance'. The most important material variances are those relating to price and usage. They are calculated by the following formulae:

- *Direct materials price variance*. This is the difference between the standard price and actual purchase price for the quantity of material. It can be calculated at the time of purchase or the time of usage. Generally the former is preferable. The direct materials price variance can be calculated by the formula:

    (Actual purchase quantity × Actual price) – (Actual purchase quantity × Standard price)
- *Direct materials usage variance*. This is the difference between the standard quantity specified for the actual production and the actual quantity used, at standard purchase price. The direct materials usage variance can be calculated by the formula:

    (Actual quantity used for actual production × Standard price) – (Standard quantity for actual production × Standard price)

- The sum of the usage and price variances gives the *direct materials total variance*, defined as:

  (Standard direct materials cost of the actual production volume) –
  (Actual cost of direct materials)

Example 17.3   Calculation of variances

Assume the *standard* quantities and prices of the direct materials used for product X are 75 kg at £3.75 per kg. The *actual* usage and price were 74 kg at £3.85 per kg.
    The direct materials price variance is:

$$(74 \text{ kg} \times £3.85) - (74 \text{ kg} \times £3.75) = £284.90 - £277.50$$
$$= £7.40$$

i.e. an adverse variance of £7.40.
    The direct materials usage variance is:

$$(74 \text{ kg} \times £3.75) - (75 \text{ kg} \times £3.75) = £277.50 - £281.25$$
$$= £3.75$$

i.e. a favourable variance of £3.75.
The direct materials total variance will therefore be:

  (Adverse direct materials total price variance) – (Favourable direct materials usage variance)

$$= £7.40 - £3.75$$
$$= £3.65 \text{ (Adverse)}$$

It is also possible to calculate *direct materials yield and mix variances* in respect of production processes involving the mixing of various materials. For information on these variances and their calculations, reference should be made to any cost accounting text.

17.11.5   Causes of materials price variances

- Actual prices are higher or lower than budgeted.
- Quantity discounts may be lost or gained by buying smaller or larger quantities than expected.
- Prices paid may be affected by buying higher or lower qualities than anticipated.
- Buying substitute material from stockists owing to the non-availability of planned material.

17.11.6   Causes of materials usage variance

- The actual production yield from the material is greater or less than planned.
- The amount of scrap or shortage is greater or less than expected.

Standard costing is an application of the management principle of exceptions. Where a variance exceeds a prescribed level it will be analysed with a view to identifying controllable and uncontrollable factors. Particularly with regard to prices, standard costs provide a widely used measure of purchasing effectiveness.

17.12 Budgets and budgetary control

17.12.1 Definitions

CIMA[20] provides the following definitions:

> A *budget* is a plan quantified in monetary terms, prepared and approved prior to a defined period of time, usually showing planned income to be generated and/or expenditure to be incurred during that period and the capital to be employed to attain a given objective.

> *Budgetary control* is the establishment of budgets relating the responsibilities of executives to the requirements of a policy, and the continuous comparison of actual with budgeted results, either to secure by individual action the object-ive of that policy or to provide a basis for its revision.

17.12.2 Purchasing budgets

Purchasing budgets are derived from the sales and production budgets and will be divided as follows:

- A *materials budget* based on:
  - whole units of products to be completed in the budget period converted into individual direct material requirements expressed in terms of physical quantities and monetary expenditure.
  - the company's end inventory policy based on the availability of materials and components. An example of a materials/components budget is given in Table 17.2.

Table 17.2 A materials/components budget

Materials/components for budget period 2002–2003								
Materials (units)	A	B	C	D	E	F	G	
Stock in hand 1 April 2002	20,000	25,000	16,000	3,500	9,800	7,500	28,600	
Required stock 31 March 2003	18,000	27,000	15,000	4,000	9,000	8,000	25,000	
Std price per unit	£0.06	£0.35	£1.20	£3.25	£0.90	£2.00	£1.20	
Procurement budget for the period 1 April 2002–31 March 2003								
Material (units)	A	B	C	D	E	F	G	Total
Required stock 31 March 2003	18,000	27,000	15,000	4,000	9,000	8,000	25,000	
Budgeted usage during period	125,000	150,000	18,000	24,000	18,000	22,000	137,000	
Totals	143,000	177,000	33,000	28,000	27,000	30,000	162,000	
Stock in hand 1 April 2002	20,000	25,000	16,000	3,500	9,800	7,500	28,600	
Items to be purchased	123,000	152,000	17,000	24,500	17,200	22,500	133,900	
Std price per unit	£0.06	£0.35	£1.20	£3.25	£0.90	£2.00	£1.20	
Value of budgeted purchases (£)	73,800	53,200	20,400	79,625	15,480	45,000	160,680	**448,185**

■ A *purchasing department operating budget* covering projected expenditure for the budget period on salaries, training, computer time, travelling, entertainment, office space occupied, stationery, etc.

Although budgetary control and standard costs are interrelated, the former can be operated in enterprises where the latter is difficult to apply. The value of budgeting is, however, enhanced when it is used with standard costing.

17.13 Learning curves

17.13.1 Definition

A learning curve (sometimes termed a 'skill acquisition or experience curve') is:

A graphical representation of the rate at which skills or knowledge are acquired over a period of time.

17.13.2 The basis of the learning curve

'Skill to do comes by doing.' A task is performed more quickly with each repetition until a point is reached where no further improvement is possible and performance levels out. In industry, cost reduction arising from 'learning' is due to the following factors:

■ Less time required for the operative to 'weigh up' the job.
■ Improved speed and proficiency in performing the actual operations.
■ Reduction in scrap and rectification.
■ Improved operational sequences.
■ Improved tooling as a result of production experience.
■ The application of value engineering and analysis.
■ Larger lot sizes with reduced setting-up costs.

Learning curves are therefore developed on the basis of the following assumptions:[21]

■ The direct labour required to produce the $(n + 1)$th unit will always be less than the direct labour required for the nth unit.
■ Direct labour requirements will decrease at a declining rate as cumulative production increases.
■ The reduction in time will follow an exponential curve.

17.13.3 The learning curve theorem

The learning curve theorem states that each time the number of production units is doubled, the cumulative average labour hours per unit declines by a specific and constant percentage of the previous cumulative average.

Table 17.3   Reduction in the average time taken to produce 1 unit

	Units produced											
	1	*2*	*3*	*4*	*5*	*6*	*7*	*8*	*9*	*10*	*11*	*12*
Time of last unit produced	1.00	0.60	0.51	0.45	0.42	0.39	0.37	0.35	0.34	0.33	0.32	0.31
Total time so far	1.00	1.60	2.11	2.56	2.98	3.37	3.74	4.10	4.44	4.77	5.08	5.39
Cumulative average time	1.00	0.80	0.70	0.64	0.60	0.56	0.53	0.51	0.49	0.48	0.46	0.45

If the learning rate is 80 per cent and the number of items made doubles, the average time per unit is reduced to 80 per cent of its previous value. This is illustrated in Table 17.3. To make 1 unit required 1 day, but to make 2 units required 1.6 days. The average time per unit has fallen to 0.8 days, i.e. 80 per cent of its original value. As you can see from Table 17.3, this does not mean that the second item took 0.8 days.

If the number of units produced is doubled from 2 to 4 and then doubled again to 8, the average time per unit should fall to

$$80\% \times 80\% = 64\%$$

of the average time per unit when only 2 were produced, and then to

$$64\% \times 80\% = 0.512 \approx 0.51$$

of the initial average time per unit. As you can see from the table, this does not mean that the eighth unit took 0.51 days to produce.

It can be shown mathematically that the equation of the learning curve is:

$$y = ax^b$$

where: y = the cumulative average time per unit

x = the number of units produced so far

a = the time taken to produce the first item

$$b = \frac{\log(\text{learning rate})}{\log(2)}$$

It should be noted that learning curves will be affected by the following factors:

■ The complexity of the operation – the learning rate for simple products is less pronounced than for more complex items because the opportunity to improve work is greater with the latter.

■ The opportunity to reduce labour hours in machine-paced operations is limited because the output rate is controlled by the machine.

■ The introduction of automation or improved equipment – because of the variability in learning rates it is necessary, when a number of operations are involved in manufacturing a part, to prepare an aggregate learning curve by multiplying the percentage of the total task for a given operation by the learning rate for that operation. The learning rate for all the operations involved will then be aggregated.

Example 17.4   The learning curve theorem

The manufacture of a product involves four operations:

Operation	Improvement rate (%)	Percentage of task (%)
1	90	30
2	92	20
3	85	20
4	80	30

The aggregate learning curve slope will be:

$(0.90 \times 0.30) + (0.92 \times 0.20) + (0.85 \times 0.20) + (0.80 \times 0.30)$

$= 0.27 + 0.18 + 0.17 + 0.24$

$= 0.86$

17.13.4   Drawing the learning curve

The cumulative average hours per unit could be plotted on arithmetic graph paper, when they would appear as shown in Figure 17.6.

   In practice, log–log paper is used (see Figure 17.7) because it has the following advantages:

■   All lines will be approximately straight.

■   The cumulative total can be plotted within the confines of the paper.

■   For forecasting, a ruler can be laid on the actual line and the results read off.

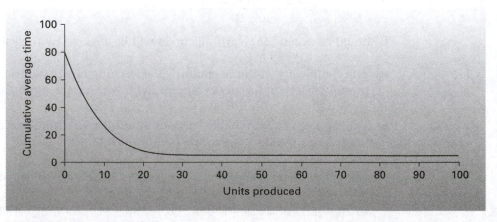

Figure 17.6   Learning curve

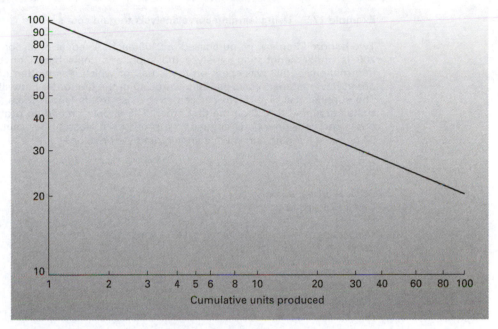

Figure 17.7 An 85 per cent learning curve on log–log scale

17.13.5 The application of learning curves

The greatest potential for savings through learning curve analysis lies in high-cost items, items with a high direct labour content, and items which lie at the beginning of the curve.

Price determination

The learning curve approach indicates the areas on which to concentrate when conducting a price analysis in order to obtain the greatest savings. The method of using learning curves to renegotiate the price for a repeat order is shown by Example 17.5.

Make-or-buy decisions

In comparing the costs of making and buying, the effect of learning on each production run should be determined and taken into consideration as well as the quantity under consideration.

Delivery times

Knowledge of the learning curve principle can enable a supplier to offer improved delivery times. The principle is illustrated by Example 17.6.

17.13.6 When not to use learning curves

- When learning is not constant, i.e. where a straight line cannot be fitted to the data reasonably accurately.

Example 17.5 Using learning curve analysis to gain cost savings

Two hundred items were purchased at £100 each. A repeat order for an additional 200 is under negotiation. Analyse the supplier's costs based on the following information: £2,000 was spent on tools, half of which was written off on the first order. Raw materials costs per item were £40 in the first order but will now be £45. The supplier has given a 10 per cent wage rise to his labour force. Direct labour costs amounted to £50 on the first order. The supplier made no profit on the first order and considers he is entitled to a profit of at least 10 per cent. Assuming a 90 per cent learning curve, what should the new price be?

Solution

	£
Original price per item	100
Deduct Tooling cost	10
	90
Deduct Cost now subject to learning, i.e. raw materials	40
Balance subject to learning	50
Add Wage increase, 10%	5
	55
90% of £55	49.50
Add Half cost of tooling	10.00
Add Materials costs	45.00
	104.50
Add 10% profit	10.45
Price per item for repeat order	114.95

Example 17.6 Using learning curve analysis to promote delivery times

A contract is placed for 100 units of a component. By allocating 7,200 labour hours, the manufacturer expects to produce 10 units in the first month. Assuming that an 80 per cent learning curve applies, how long should it take to complete the order?

Solution
The contract should take just over 5 months, and not 10 months as might be expected from a constant output of 10 units which would be the case if no learning took place.

Month	Capacity (labour hours)	Cumulative average values (80% learning curve) (from tables)	Units produced	Cumulative total
1	7,200	1.00	10	10
2	7,200	0.08	16	26
3	7,200	0.70	21	47
4	7,200	0.64	25	72
5	7,200	0.59	26	98

- Where the direct labour content of the job is small.
- Where the cost/volume does not justify the high expense of periodic time studies or job costing required to obtain the data from which the learning curve is constructed.
- When production is largely automated so that human input is relatively small.

17.14 Project management

17.14.1 Definitions

In the present context, a project may be defined as:[22]

> An activity (or usually, a number of related activities) carried out according to a plan in order to achieve a definite objective within a certain period of time and which will close when the objective is achieved.

Project management is:[23]

> The function of evaluation, planning and controlling a project so that it is finished on time, to specification and within budget.

17.14.2 Types of project

Lock[24] classifies projects under four headings:

- *Civil engineering, construction, petrochemical, mining and quarrying projects*. These are normally undertaken at a site, exposed to the elements and remote from the contractor's office.
- *Manufacturing projects* aimed at the production of a piece of equipment of machinery, ship, aircraft, land vehicle, or some item of specially designed hardware.
- *Management projects*, i.e. operations involving the management and coordination of activities to produce an end result that is not identifiable principally as an item of hardware or construction, e.g. relocation of offices, installation of a new computer system.
- *Research projects* aimed at extending the boundaries of current scientific knowledge. These projects carry high risk because the outcomes are uncertain.

17.14.3 Purchasing and project management

Although not always designated as such, a project manager will have responsibility for the overall direction and control of a particular project and the staff involved. Such staff may be organised on:

- a *matrix* basis, or
- a *functional* or team basis.

Matrix structures and their advantages and disadvantages are described in section 5.5 of Chapter 5. Teamwork is discussed in Chapter 15.

Under either form of organisation, however, purchasing may contribute to ensuring that the project is 'finished on time, to specification and within budget' in such ways as the following:

■ Liaising at each stage with appropriate members of the project organisation (e.g. the project manager, architects, designers, consultants, quantity surveyors, site engineers) with regard to the specification, procurement and scheduling of materials, equipment and services required in connection with the contract.

■ Agreeing where, and by whom, purchasing will be undertaken. Lock[25] points out that:

> The purchasing agent could be an independent organisation in the contractor's purchasing department, or even the client's own purchasing department. There can also be various combinations of these arrangements. In international projects the client's purchasing department might issue purchase orders to local suppliers, with the contractor's head office dealing with other suppliers world wide (possibly operating through purchasing agents overseas where their location and local experience provides for greater efficiency).

■ Advising on the most economic approaches to procurement, e.g. purchase or lease of capital equipment.

■ Assistance with the preparation of tender specifications and negotiation with subcontractors. Typical parts of a project to be subcontracted include: brickwork, civil engineering, drainage, electrical installations, heating and ventilation, painting and decorating, pipework, plumbing and structural steelwork.

■ Evaluating tenders and post-tender negotiation.

■ Placing of orders and subcontracts and ensuring that the terms and conditions are appropriate to the particular contract.

■ Expediting orders placed to ensure deliveries meet scheduled requirements.

■ Inspecting materials received and maintenance of quality records.

■ Dealing with requests from suppliers and subcontractors for price variances.

■ Controlling 'free issue' supplies, i.e. items provided by the customer or client for use in connection with the project. A glass manufacturer might, for example, provide the glass for use in a contract for a new office building.

■ Certifying payment of invoices for goods and services provided by external suppliers and subcontractors.

17.15 Scheduling

Of the above contributions one of the most important is that of ensuring that materials and equipment are on site to obviate delays in meeting the scheduled times for the completion of each part of the project. Two useful scheduling tools are Gantt charts and networks.

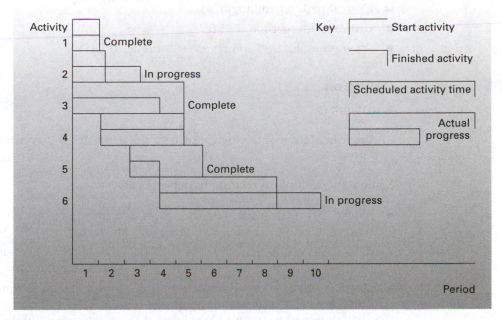

Figure 17.8   Gantt chart

17.15.1   Gantt charts

Devised by Henry L. Gantt in 1917, Gantt charts depict across time the occurrence of the activities comprising a project. An example of a Gantt or bar chart is shown in Figure 17.8.

Gantt activity progress charts perform several functions:

- They show at a glance what project activities are behind schedule (e.g., in Figure 17.8, activities 2 and 6), on time (activities 1 and 4) and ahead of schedule (activities 3 and 5).

- They can facilitate the coordination of activities and labour. Activities represented by overlapping bars can be performed concurrently to the degree that they overlap. Activities shown by non-overlapping bars must be performed in the sequence indicated. Thus activity 4 in Figure 17.8 cannot be started until the completion of activity 1. Activity 4 can, however, be performed concurrently with activities 3 and 5.

- Gantt charts are most useful in scheduling a series of unrelated activities. Where many activities must be correlated network analysis is more appropriate.

17.15.2   Network analysis

Network analysis is the generic term for a family of related techniques developed to aid those planning and controlling projects. This set of techniques is known by a variety of names. The most common are:

- Critical path analysis (CPA)
- Critical path planning (CPP)

- Critical path scheduling (CPS)
- Critical path method (CPM)
- Program evaluation and review techniques (PERT)

Definition

A network is:

> **A representation of the logical sequence of activities and events that constitute a project.**

Some important terms relating to networks are:

- *Activity* – this is a job or task that requires time and resources, e.g. comparing tenders, digging a tunnel, setting up a production line.
- *Event* – this is a point in time at which an activity or a number of activities start or finish, e.g. setting up a production line begins, digging a tunnel completed.
- *Dummy activity* – This is an activity that does not require time or resources. There are strict conventions about the representation of networks. A dummy activity is used to show a logical dependence between activities in such a way that the rules given below are not broken.

Rules for drawing networks

There are two common conventions: activity on arrow and activity on node. The more common activity on arrow convention is outlined below.

1   Each activity is represented by an arrow. The name of the activity is written above the arrow and its duration under the arrow.

2   Events are represented by circles. The circle is divided into three sections as shown. The purpose of each section is given in the section on time analysis.

3   Dummy activities are represented by dotted arrows ----►
4   A network can have only one point of entry, the start event, and only one exit point, the finish event.
5   No activity can start before its tail event occurs.
6   An event cannot occur before all the activities leading to it take place.
7   Every activity must have a preceding tail event and a subsequent head event. Many activities may have the same tail event. Many activities may have the same head event.

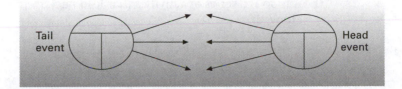

8   However, two activities may not share the same head and the same tail event. This would imply that the two activities must have the same duration and this is an unnecessary assumption. The diagram shown below is not allowed.

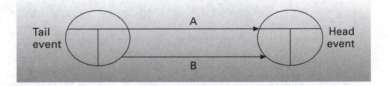

This can be avoided by using a dummy activity as in the diagram below

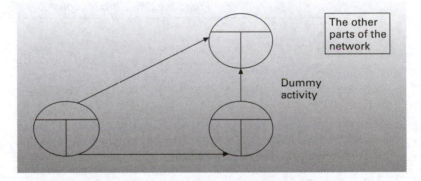

9   Except for the start and finish events, all events are the tail event of an activity and the head event of another activity. An activity that does not contribute to the progression of the project should be discarded. Activities that do not link to the overall project are known as danglers.

Similarly, activities that do not have a tail event are not allowed. The following network is wrong. It has a dangler and an activity with no tail.

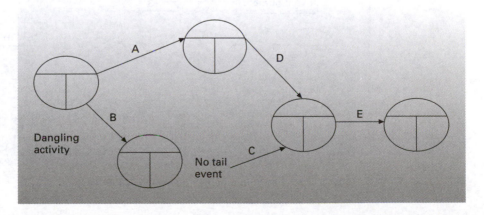

10 A loop is a series of activities that lead back to the same event. Loops are not allowed.

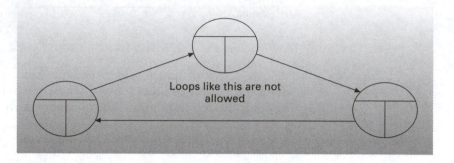

Example 17.7   Network analysis

The activities of a project are shown in the table below.

Activity	Activities that must be complete before this is begun	Estimated duration
A		5
B		6
C	B	4
D	AC	3
E	C	4
F	DE	14

The first stage in analysing this project is drawing the network. There are three steps in drawing the network.

Step 1
Beginning at the entry event 0, draw a diagram that shows the sequence in which the activities must take place and the events that mark the progress of the project.
   In Figure 17.9 the events are numbered sequentially from the left. The identifying number is written in the upper segment of the circle that represents the event.

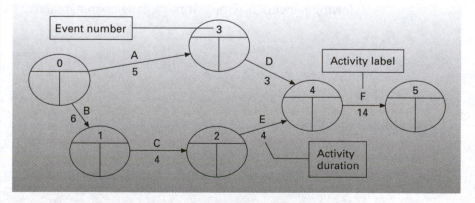

Figure 17.9   Step 1: numbering the events sequentially

Where an event can be given a meaningful name such as 'foundations dug', this name is written in the upper segment.

Step 2
Forward pass (see Figure 17.10): the earliest start times (EST) are calculated by adding to the EST of the tail event the linking activity duration. If there are two or more routes to a node then the longer route must be taken. For example, activity D cannot begin until activities A and C are completed. A is completed at day 5 but C is not completed until day 10. Thus 10 is the EST.

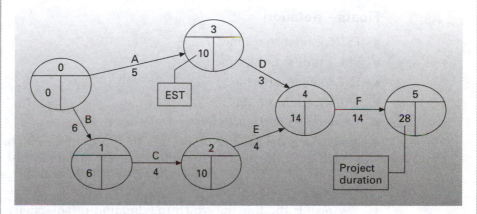

Figure 17.10   Step 2: forward pass

Step 3
Backward pass (see Figure 17.11): in this the latest start time (LST) is found by subtracting the linking event duration from the previously calculated LST. The calculation is started at the right-hand side. In the final node an LST equal to the project duration is entered. (In this case 28, the same as the value found in the forward pass.) The LST for activity E is thus 28 − 14 = 14. If an event can be reached by two routes, the lowest LST is taken. For event 2 the LST is either:

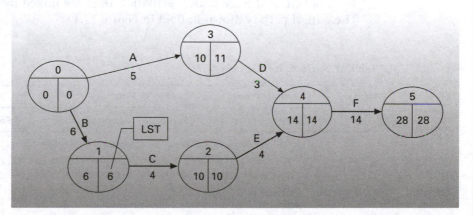

Figure 17.11   Backward pass

■ 14 − 4 = 10 by deducting the duration of activity E from the LST of event 4, or

■ 11 − 0 = 11 by deducting the duration of the dummy activity from the LST of event 3.

Choose 10, the smaller value, for LST since if event 2 did not take place until day 11 event 4 could not take place until day 15 and so on.

The earliest and latest times for each activity have been calculated. The next stage in the analysis is calculating the earliest and latest finish times for each activity. The results should be tabulated.

Floats – notation

■ EST = earliest start time

■ EFT = earliest finish time

■ LST = latest start time

■ LFT = latest finish time

■ *d* = duration of the activity

■ *Total float* is the amount of time a path of activities could be delayed without affecting the duration of the entire project. The total float for an activity is given by LFT − EST − *d*. Table 17.3 shows the total float for the activities in Example 17.7.

■ *Free float* is the time by which the duration of an activity can be increased without affecting the start of subsequent activities at their earliest start time. Free float is given by EFT − EST − *d*. The free floats for Example 17.7 are shown in Table 17.3.

■ *Independent float* is the time by which the duration of an activity can be increased if all preceding activities are completed as late as possible and all subsequent activities take place as early as possible. Independent float is given by EFT − LST − *d*.

■ *Critical path.* Critical activities must be started on time, otherwise the whole project would be delayed. It follows that for such activities LST must equal EST and LFT must equal EFT. These activities have zero floats. Thus in Example 17.7, B, C, E and F are critical activities; they are linked by the critical path. The critical path is shown in bold in Figure 17.11.

Table 17.3 Floats for Example 17.7

Activity	Start time		Finish time		Floats		
	Earliest	Latest	Earliest	Latest	Total	Free	Independent
A	0	0	5	11	6	0	0
B	0	0	6	6	0	0	0
C	6	6	10	10	0	0	0
D	10	11	14	14	1	1	0
E	10	10	14	14	0	0	0
F	14	14	28	28	0	0	0

17.15.3 Network analysis and cost

Time is not the only consideration associated with project management. The cost is of equal importance. What is known as PERT/cost is a technique used to plan, schedule and control project costs and ensure adherence to a specified budget. Basically this involves identifying all the costs associated with a project and then developing a schedule of when the costs are expected to occur. As with other budgets, actual costs are compared with budgeted costs at prescribed intervals, e.g. the end of each activity, and appropriate action taken. Attention to critical activities also indicated how, by the introduction of additional resources, it may be possible to shorten completion times. The cost of introducing such resources has to be weighed against the projected savings. If, for example, a project has high daily fixed costs, it may be profitable to take on extra labour, buy or hire equipment, or subcontract part of the work to reduce the completion time.

17.15.4 CPM and PERT

CPM and PERT use much of the same terminology and many of the same techniques. Both aim to show the logical sequence of activities in a project. CPM, however, was developed mainly for use in industrial projects where activity times could be estimated with reasonable accuracy. In contrast, PERT was devised in the late 1950s in connection with the Polaris missile project where the times could not be forecast because the associated activities had not been previously encountered. Unlike CPM, which provides only one time estimate for each activity, PERT provides three, namely:

- *Normal (m)*, the most realistic assessment of the time required, without allowing for unforeseen contingencies.
- *Pessimistic (p)*, the longest times that will be required, allowing for all foreseeable contingencies.
- *Optimistic (o)*, the shortest duration within which the activity can be accomplished if all circumstances work out favourably.

These three times are used to calculate expected time on the basis of the following weighted average

$$\frac{(4m + p + o)}{6}$$

17.15.5 Network analysis and purchasing

- Generally, network analysis is applicable to large, complex, long-running projects such as construction contracts and to subcontracted work.
- Network analysis provides purchasing with an overview of the complete project and the significance of the contribution of purchasing to its successful completion.
- Network analysis is a team activity to which purchasing contributes essential information such as the availability of materials and the duration of lead times.

- The network enables purchasing to compare actual with promised deliveries and to take early expediting action on slippage to prevent delays in delivery having a cumulative effect on the whole project.

- Purchased items can be scheduled for delivery in the right sequence and to the right location, e.g. materials for construction projects can be delivered direct to site immediately before use, thus reducing the possibility of loss through theft or deterioration.

- In subcontracted work, progress payments can be linked to the completion of specified events.

- Networks can be used to control expenditure on long-running contracts. Computer printouts can show:
  - actual costs incurred at a given date;
  - estimated costs for the rest of the project;
  - statements of future expenditure, e.g. purchase orders outstanding.

17.16 Models and simulation approaches

17.16.1 Definitions

Model

A model is a conceptual framework used to describe a particular aspect of reality.

Thus Newton's law of gravitation is a mathematical model which describes the gravitational interactions of bodies.

Simulations

Simulations are constructions of mathematical models to represent the operation of real-life processes or situations.

The object of a simulation is to explore the effect of different policies on the model to deduce what might happen in reality without going to the expense or risk of trial and error in actuality.

Operational research

Operational research (OR) is defined by the UK Operational Research Society as:

The application of the methods of science to complex problems arising in the direction and management of large systems of men, machine, materials and money in industry, business, government and defence. The distinctive approach is to develop a scientific model of the system incorporating measurement of factors, such as chance and risk, with which to predict and compare the outcomes of alternative decisions, strategies or controls. The purpose is to help management determine its policy and action scientifically.

In this context 'research' has the narrower meaning of 'the application of new mathematical models, methods and techniques to the solution of business or other problems'.

The above definitions emphasise that:

- OR is concerned with problems of organisation and allocation of resources comprising men, machines, materials, and money to achieve a specified objective;
- a model or system can be built;
- OR is a service to management;
- alternative decisions can be evaluated against some measure of effectiveness.

17.16.2   Operational research procedures

The application of quantitative techniques to management practice is known as operational research. The major phases of an OR project have been identified as follows:

- Statement of the problem to which a solution is required.
- Construction of a mathematical model as an analogue (i.e. symbolic model or simulation) of the real system. The general form of an OR model is:

  $$E = f(x_1 y_1)$$

  where E represents the effectiveness of the system, and x and y the controllable variables and non-controllable variables in the system, respectively.
- Deriving an optimum solution from the model either *analytically*, i.e. by the manipulation of the mathematical model, or *numerically* in which a large number of iterations is carried out of possible values of the variables and the equation solved repetitively.
- Testing the model and the solution.
- Establishing controls over the solution, i.e. indicating changes in the values of the uncontrollable variables or the relationships between variables that would render the solution invalid.
- Implementation, i.e. translating the tested solution into a set of operating procedures capable of being understood and applied by those who will be responsible for their use.

17.16.3   Operational research and supplies

Some reference to applications of OR techniques has already been made in this book, namely:

- elementary inventory control (see Chapter 8);
- network analysis (section 17.15 above);
- Materials requirement planning (see Chapter 8);
- Replacement theory and capital expenditure evaluation (see Chapter 11).

Table 17.4 Applications of operational research

Aspect of OR	Typical supplies applications
■ **Linear programming (LP)**. A mathematical technique for determining the optimum allocation of resources such as capital, raw materials or labour, or plan to obtain a desired objective such as minimum cost of operations or maximum profit when there are alternative uses of the resource in question. LP can also help to analyse alternative objectives such as the economics of alternative resources	■ Analysis of quotations from several suppliers who, because of limited resources, can accept only certain combinations of the business offered. LP can indicate the combination of quotations that will minimise purchasing expenditure ■ Determining the relative advantages of a low price and a high probability of late delivery against a higher price with a better chance of delivery time
■ **Queuing theory**. Mathematical analysis and solution of problems in which items requiring or providing service stand idle and in which it is required to optimise either the arrival rate or service rate or both	■ Sequencing and scheduling arrivals of parts or components to achieve minimum costs ■ The most economical staffing of stores to provide the minimum waiting time
■ **Games theory**. A mathematical technique or decision-making fool in a competitive situation in which the outcome depends not only on the actions of a manager but also on those of his or her competitors. The aim of the game is to devise a strategy which maximises returns and minimises losses	Negotiation. Decisions are based on the assumption that the rival is shrewd and will always play to minimise his opponent's gain.
■ **Decision trees**. A decision tree is a type of flowchart or visual aid which summarises the various alternatives and options available in a complex decision process. Decision trees consist of three parts: (i) the initial decision point; (ii) the branches representing various outcomes; (iii) the paths, which may consist of several branches, representing the various probabilities and events of a particular outcome. The whole tree represents the decision problem. The object of decision trees is not to find optimum solutions but to represent visually a wide range of alternatives which can apply to specific policies and procedures	Virtually any supplies problems that can be reduced to: ■ a set of mutually exclusive decisions ■ for each decision, a set of possible outcomes, together with an assessment of the likelihood of each outcome occurring ■ revenues or costs for each outcome
■ **Forecasting**. The process of estimating future quantities required normally using past experience as a basis. OR methods of forecasting include: – exponential smoothing – moving averages – trend analysis – multiple regression analysis – curve fitting	Any supplies problem involving the prediction of future requirements, e.g. stock levels, purchasing expenditure, stores space, purchase of sensitive commodities in various market conditions
■ **Probability theory**. An aspect of forecasting based on mathematical techniques for establishing the likelihood of particular events taking place. The probability of an event ranges from 0 to 1 (0 = event will certainly not occur; 1 = event is certain)	■ The application of statistical techniques, e.g. sampling, as a means of controlling quality ■ Determining the life expectancy of materials and components ■ Predicting the probability of stockouts at given levels of inventory

Many supplies problems can be solved by the application of techniques from such OR fields as linear programming, queuing theory and probability theory. The application of OR to supplies work has been assisted by computerisation which can deal easily with a large number of variables, e.g. many different items of stores in inventory control. In fact, with the increasing use of computers and the availability of specialist software, many OR studies can now be performed by purchasing staff without the need for specialist assistance. In addition to the approaches referred to above, some other applications of OR are given in Table 17.4.

17.16.4 Limitations of operational research

Decision making is the process or activity of selecting a future course of action from a number of possible options. Decision can be classified into different categories such as strategic, operational and administrative, and into those that are programmable and non-programmable. Programmable decisions can be worked out by computer since all the variables are quantifiable and the decision rules or constraints are clearly defined. Non-programmable decisions cannot be quantified and require the exercise of human judgement. It is important therefore to recognise that OR is limited in its effectiveness to the analysis and comparison of relationships between controllable and uncontrollable variables that can be expressed in terms of a mathematical model.

There are times when the subjective judgement of the decision-maker must act contrary to the OR recommendation. OR, for example, can indicate the economic order quantities and most economic inventory levels in respect of raw materials and components, but these recommendations may be disregarded by the purchasing function if it is known that a threatened strike will disrupt production unless sufficient supplies can be obtained to ensure continuity of output at least in the short term.

? Discussion questions and exercises

17.1 Turner[26] records that when Neil Armstrong was being interviewed about the moon landing he was asked to state the most frightening moment: was it as the moon lander came down and might crash; or was it as he stepped off the ladder; or was it when they came to blast off from the moon and the rockets might not be powerful enough. No, he said, the most frightening moment was being on the launch pad at Cape Canaveral and under him were 2,000 components, every single one of which had been bought on minimum price tender. And one of them did fail in 1986.

(a) List the possible dangers of accepting the lowest tender.

(b) If you must accept the lowest tender, how may you seek to ensure that quality or performance does not fall below specified standards?

17.2 In debriefing unsuccessful suppliers, what procedures

(a) would you suggest to ensure that the debriefing session does not become confrontational or recriminative?

(b) How would you respond to requests from an unsuccessful bidder who

(i)   asks for information relating to the tenders of competitors?

(ii)   refers disparagingly to competitive suppliers?

(iii)   asks for copies of the minutes of the meeting at which the decision was made not to accept its tender?

17.3   Opposition to post-tender negotiation (PTN) is usually based on ethical considerations. What arguments would you use to reassure an objector that PTN is honest, open, fair and beneficial to both potential purchasers and suppliers?

17.4   The following figures show the monthly percentages of all deliveries that have been received on time over a period of 12 months.

90 92 94 93 93 94 95 94 92 93 94 93

(a)   Compare a three months' moving average forecast with an exponential smoothing forecast using a smoothing constant of $a = 0.2$.

(b)   Which of the two averages provides the better forecasts?

(c)   What is the forecast for the next month?

17.5   A company is considering the purchase of a new machine and has obtained quotations for alternative models X and Y which have the following costs per machine:

	Machine X	Machine Y
Cost of new machine	3,000	4,000
Cost of installation	200	100
Annual costs		
Maintenance	400	300
Other expenses	400	360
Life of machine	4 years	5 years
The cumulative present value factors are	8% for 4 years	3.312
	8% for 5 years	3.993

Using the equivalent annual cost method of appraisal, which of the two machines do you recommend?

17.6   Your company, a manufacturer of cleaning machinery, has undertaken a market research exercise that has ascertained that the selling price of a new vacuum cleaner must not exceed £350. It also discovers that to be an effective competitor it needs to achieve a profit of £75 per machine sold. A preliminary estimate is that, provided these targets are met, sales over the first three years should be 250,000 units.

A preliminary estimate of costs is as follows:

	£
Development costs	20
Production costs	120
Materials and components	80
Marketing costs	20
Logistics costs	40
Service costs	10
	290

Clearly the initial estimate is above the target cost price of £275. What action would you take to ensure that the target cost is achieved?

17.7 The XYZ Co. Ltd incurred the following overhead costs:

	£
Depreciation of factory buildings	2,000
Repairs and maintenance of buildings	1,200
Factory administrative costs (treat as production overheads)	3,000
Depreciation of machinery	1,600
Insurance of machinery	400
Heating	780
Lighting	200
Canteen	1,800

Information relevant to the factory production and service departments is:

	Production A	Production B	Service C	Service D
Floor space (sq. metres)	2,400	3,200	1,600	800
Volume (cubic metres)	6,000	12,000	4,800	3,200
Number of employees	60	60	30	30
Machinery at book value	£60,000	£40,000	£20,000	£40,000

How do you suggest the overhead costs should be apportioned between departments A, B, C, and D?

17.8 An application of activity-based costing is the measurement of supplier performance. Non-conformance to the purchaser's requirements means that the purchaser has to perform otherwise non-value-adding activities. The management accountant of the XYZ Co. Ltd has assigned labour-hours to non-value activities. Thus material received too early may entail stores disruption and costs estimated at 2 labour-hours, material received too late incurs costs of 8 labour-hours. Each labour-hour is currently costed at £50, so that the cost of a delivery can be obtained by multiplying the labour-hours by the total cost per labour-hour.

The score in £s for each delivery by each supplier is kept in a database and evaluated at six-monthly intervals. This score is used to compute a vendor performance index (VPI) calculated by:

$$VPI = \frac{\text{Cost of purchased items} + \text{Cost of non-value-added activities}}{\text{Cost of purchased supplies}}$$

A score of 1.2 or under is deemed satisfactory. Anything higher may be a factor in deciding to discontinue using the supplier.

The score for supplier A is as shown below. Assuming purchases for the period of £34,542, work out the VPI and decide whether the score is satisfactory or otherwise.

Non-value-added activity	Labour-hours	Cost at £50 per labour-hour
Inspection rejection	0.3	
Paperwork rejection	0.3	
Rework at buyer's premises	5.0	
Materials received too early	2.0	
Materials received too late	8.0	
Excess materials	2.0	
Shortage of materials	4.0	

17.9 The standard materials costs for part number 423 are 50 kg at £5 per kg. During January, 150 units were produced. The actual materials costs for part number 423 for January are direct material purchases 7,000 kg at a cost of £36,400.

    Opening stock of material   1300 kg

    Closing stock of material   850 kg

Calculate (a) the price, (b) the usage and (c) the total materials variances.

17.10 Match the terms on the left with the concepts and definitions on the right

(a) Activity-based costing   (1) Something that increases the worth of a product or service

(b) Life cycle stages   (2) Expected selling price less desired profit

(c) Value-added activity   (3) The process of attaching costs based on activities

(d) Target cost   (4) Idle time, transfer time, storage time

(e) Non-value-added activities   (5) A principle whereby fixed as well as variable costs are allotted to cost units and total overheads are absorbed according to activity level

(f) Variance   (6) Development, introduction, growth, maturity, decline

(g) Absorption costing   (7) Difference between standard and actual prices and quantities

(h) Cost driver   (8) Something that causes or influences costs

17.11 A manufacturing company has just completed the first two units of a new product subject to an 80 per cent learning curve at a labour cost of £20,000. It has received an enquiry for a further two units but the purchaser intimates that a reduced price should be applicable since the learning element involved in the initial two products should be considered. Assuming that variable overheads amount to 20 per cent of direct labour cost, what should be the estimated labour and variable overheads for the two new units?

17.12 Consider the following project network (times in weeks).

(a) Identify the critical path.

(b) How long will it take to complete the project?

(c) Can activity D be delayed without holding up the project? If so, for how many weeks?

(d) Can activity C be delayed without holding up the project? If so, for how many weeks?

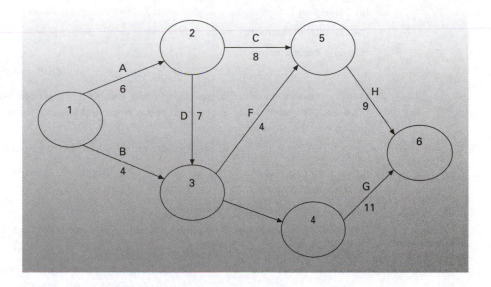

Past examination questions

1 Explain, using a detailed numerical example, the principles of life cycle costing and fully justify its application to a purchasing situation of your choice.

(CIPS, Purchasing, May 1997)

2 As purchasing manager you have recently invited tenders from a selected shortlist of firms for the design, supply, installation and commissioning of a major and important new item of production plant for your factory; value around £250,000. List the factors you would take into account in making an appraisal of the tenders you have received.

(CIPS, Project and Contracts Management, May 1997)

3 The purchase of capital items and the purchase of normal stock differ mainly in the consideration of life cycle cost. Discuss this statement and describe how capital acquisition should be conducted so that all relevant costs are taken into account.

(CIPS, Purchasing and Supply Chain Management II:
Tactics and Operations, November 1997)

4 To what extent does public accountability impact upon the achievement of purchasing objectives in the public sector?

(CIPS, Purchasing, May 1998)

5 Describe the setting up and use of network analysis for project planning. Illustrate your answer with a simple diagram of a project of your choice, which should show the projects critical path.

(CIPS, Projects and Contracts Management, May 1999)

6 Explain how the following buying or appraisal methods are used, giving appropriate examples.

(a)   Hedging

(b)   Capital investment

(c)   Life cycle costing

(CIPS, Purchasing, May 1999)

7   Identify the actions which a purchaser must take and the procedures which he must have established in order to carry out the appraisal of tenders for construction, engineering or consultancy contracts.

(CIPS, Projects and Contract Management, November 2000)

8   It has been suggested that the competitive tendering method could achieve the lowest total acquisition cost.

(a)   Critically appraise this statement.

(b)   Identify situations in which the competitive tendering method is appropriate.

(c)   Identify situations in which the competitive tendering method is *not* appropriate.

(CIPS, Purchasing and Supply Chain Management II:
Tactics and Operations, November 2000)

9   A project to reorganise and move a credit operation to a new office location is represented by the following tasks:

		Immediate predecessors	Expected duration (wks)
A	Select office site	–	3
B	Develop financial plan	–	5
C	Determine personnel requirements	B	3
D	Design office layout	A, C	4
E	Construct office interior	D	8
F	Select personnel to move	C	2
G	Hire new employees	F	4
H	Move records, personnel etc.	F	2
I	Make financial arrangements	B	5
J	Train new personnel	H, E, G	3

(a)   Draw a network to represent the project.

(b)   Calculate earliest start, latest finish and total float for each activity and determine the earliest finish for the project and its critical path.

(c)   One week into the project you are informed that activity F will go late by 4 weeks and activity G will go late by 3 weeks. What will be the effect on the project completion date?

(d)   What would be the order of priority of crashing to reduce the overall project duration?

(CIPS, Operations Management, May 2000)

Notes

1. Central Unit on Procurement, CUP Guidance Note 45, *Debriefing*
2. GATT Agreement on Government Procurement, Article 6, Paragraph 5
3. As n.1 above, pp.2–3
4. Ibid.
5. Inland Revenue, PUM 2840, *Award of Contract Debriefing of Suppliers*
6. Central Unit on Procurement, CUP Guidelines Note 1, *Post-Tender Negotiation*
7. Barfield, J.T., Raiborn, C.A. and Kinney, M.R., *Cost Accounting*, West Publishing Co., 1994, Ch.26, pp.858–83
8. Chartered Institute of Management Accountants, *Management Accounting Official Terminology*, revised 1991, p.44
9. CIMA, as n.8 above, p.49
10. Yoshikawa, Y., Innes, J. and Falconer, M., 'Cost management through functional analysis', in Brinker, B. (ed.) *Emerging Practices in Cost Management*, Warren Gornam Lamont, 1990, p.243
11. CIMA, as n.8 above, p.26
12. Ibid., p.90
13. Raffish, N. and Turney, P.B.B. (eds), 'Glossary of activity based management', *Journal of Cost Management*, Fall 1991, pp.53–63
14. Lapsley, J., Llewellyn, S. and Falconer, H., *Cost Management in the Public Sector*, Longman, 1994, Ch.6, p.90
15. Cooper, R. and Kaplan, R.S., 'How cost accounting systematically distorts product costs', in William, J.B. (ed.), *Accounting and Management Field Study Perspectives*, Harvard Business School, 1987, pp.D–15
16. Burch, J., *Cost and Management Accounting*, West Publishing Co., 1994, Ch.10, p.458
17. Barker, J., How to achieve more effective purchasing through activity based costing, paper presented to Second PSERG Conference, University of Bath, 1993
18. Ness, J.A. and Cucuzza, T.G., 'Tapping the full potential of ABC', *Harvard Business Review*, July/August 1995, pp.130–8
19. CIMA, as n.8 above, p.38
20. CIMA, as n.8 above, p.58
21. Karjewski, L.J. and Ritzman, I.P., *Operations Management*, Addison-Wesley, 1990, Ch.6, p.208
22. French, D. and Saward, H., *Dictionary of Management*, Pan Books, 1975, p.333
23. Lock, D., *Project Management*, Gower, 1994
24. As n.23 above, Ch.1, pp.3–4
25. As n.23 above, Ch.12, p.401
26. Turner, J.R., *The Handbook of Project-based Management*, 2nd edition, McGraw-Hill, 1999, Ch.10, p.234

◆ Solutions to selected exercises

17.4 (a)

Month	Y_1	3 month moving average forecast	(Error)^2	A = 2 forecast	(Error)^2
1	90				
2	92			90.00	4.00
3	94			90.40	12.06
4	93	92.00	1.00	91.12	3.53
5	93	93.00	0.00	91.50	2.25
6	94	93.33	0.45	91.80	4.84
7	95	93.33	2.79	92.24	7.62
8	94	94.00	0.00	92.79	1.46
9	92	94.33	0.43	93.03	1.06
10	93	93.67	0.45	92.83	0.03
11	94	93.00	1.00	92.86	1.30
12	93	93.00	0.00	93.09	0.01
			11.12		39.06

$$\text{Mean square error for 3 months} = \frac{11.12}{9} = 1.24$$

$$\text{Mean square error } (a = 0.2) = \frac{39.06}{11} = 3.55$$

Use 3 months' moving average.

(b) $(93 + 94 + 93) = \dfrac{280}{3} = 93.3$

17.6 The equivalent annual cost for machine X is:

$$\frac{\text{Purchase + Installations cost}}{\text{Cumulative PV factor at 8\%}}$$

$$= \frac{£3,200}{3,312} = £966 \text{ per annum}$$

The equivalent annual cost for machine Y is:

$$\frac{\text{Purchase + Installations cost}}{\text{Cumulative PV factor at 8\%}}$$

$$= \frac{£4,100}{3,992} = £1,027 \text{ per annum}$$

To the above figures must be added the annual running costs:

Machine X: £966 + £800 = £1,766

Machine Y: £1,027 + £760 = £1,787

Taking into account the life of each machine it would seem that machine Y is actually the cheaper.

17.7

Cost	Basis of apportionment	Total	A	B	C	D
Depreciation of factory buildings	Floor area	2,000	600	800	400	200
Repairs and maintenance	Floor area	1,200	360	480	240	120
Factory administration	No. of employees	3,000	1,000	1,000	500	500
Depreciation of machinery	Book value	1,600	600	400	200	400
Insurance of machinery	Book value	400	150	100	50	100
Rates	Volume	780	180	360	144	96
Lighting	Floor area	200	60	80	40	20
Canteen	No. of employees	1,800	600	600	300	300
		£10,980	3,550	3,820	1,874	1,736

17.8

Non-value-added activity	Labour-hours	Cost at £50 per labour-hour
Inspection rejection	0.3	15
Paperwork rejection	0.3	15
Rework at buyer's premises	5.0	250
Materials received too early	2.0	100
Materials received too late	8.0	400
Excess materials	2.0	100
Shortage of materials	4.0	200
		1,080

$$\text{VPI} = \frac{(£34,542 + £1,080)}{£34,542} = \frac{35,622}{34,542} = 1.03$$

Based on a satisfactory score of 1.2 the achieved score is unsatisfactory.

17.9 (a) Materials price variance:

Standards   7,000 kg at £5 = £35,000

Actual   7,000 kg at   = £36,400

Therefore £36,400 – £35,000 = adverse material price variance of £1,400.

(b) Materials usage variance:

Standard for 150 units at 50 kg per unit = 7,500 kg

7,500 × £5   = £37,500

Actual usage

Opening stock	1,300 kg	
Add Purchase	700	
	8,300	
Less Closing stock	850	
	7,450 kg at £5	£37,250
		£250

Materials usage variance = favourable.

(c) Total materials variance = £1,400 + 250 = £1,150 (adverse)

17.11 Cumulative average labour cost for units 1 and 2 was:

$$\frac{£10,000}{2} = £5,000 \text{ per unit}$$

Cumulative average labour cost for first four units will be:

$$\left(\frac{20,000}{4}\right)\left(\frac{80}{100}\right) = \text{£4,000 per unit}$$

Labour cost for the two new units will be computed as follows:

Labour cost for 4 units at £4,000 per unit	£16,000
Less Labour for 2 units at £5,000 per unit	£10,000
Cost for new order of 2 units	£6,000

The estimated cost of the two additional units will be:

Direct labour cost for 2 units	£6,000
Variable overheads (20 per cent of £6,000)	£1,200
	£7,200

17.12 (a) A D F H

(b) 26 weeks

(c) No, since it is a critical activity

(d) Yes, 3 weeks

Purchasing research, performance and ethics

After reading this chapter you should be able to:

- Define the term 'purchasing research' and indicate some aspects of purchasing to which research might be directed.
- State some agencies through which purchasing research may be undertaken.
- Explain the main steps in a research project.
- Define the term 'purchasing performance' and indicate some approaches to the assessment of performance.
- List some aims of performance measurement.
- Discuss the prevalence and importance of performance measurement.
- State the main principles of performance measurement.
- Distinguish between purchasing effectiveness and efficiency and 'traditional' and 'strategic' methods of performance measurement.
- Indicate and explain some accounting approaches to performance measurement.
- Define benchmarking.
- Discuss the types, advantages, topics and process of benchmarking.
- Use ratios to measure purchasing performance.
- Describe the purpose and content of a purchasing audit.
- Explain the concept of management by objectives and the main types of objective.
- Give examples of fraud related to purchasing and some ways or preventing such fraud.
- Define the term 'whistle-blowing' and discuss some ethical, legal and personal aspects of whistle-blowing.
- Define the term 'ethics'.
- Discuss the importance and scope of ethics.
- Critically appraise the benefits of ethical codes.
- Indicate the social responsibilities of purchasing.

- Outline the law relating to corruption and bribery.
- Provide guidelines regarding such individual aspects of purchasing ethics as the receipt of business gifts and reception of representatives.
- Outline the methods and possible content of ethical training related to purchasing.
- Define the term 'environment' and recognise the importance of environmental factors in purchasing.
- Screen suppliers for good environmental performance.
- State the principal EU and ISO standards appertaining to environmental management.

18.1 Purchasing research

18.1.1 Definition

Purchasing research has been defined by Fearon[1] as:

> The systematic gathering, recording and analysing of data about problems relating to the purchasing of goods and services.

The importance of purchasing research has been enhanced by the following:

- Rapid changes in technology and economic circumstances are increasing the complexity of purchasing.
- Much purchasing is undertaken in conditions of uncertainty so that strategic decisions have to be made involving individuals, organisations and events outside the direct control of the purchasing undertaking.
- Electronic data processing provides the facility to store and process vast quantities of data which, when processed, can improve decision making.
- The increased outsourcing of non-critical functions.
- The new focus on partnering and the evaluation of the benefits.
- E-procurement facilitating real-time ordering and payment by line employees.
- Purchasing as a function is increasingly required to quantify its contribution to profitability and its strategic function in the supply chain.

18.1.2 Areas of research

In selecting topics for research, it should be remembered that the greater the area of expenditure the greater is the potential for significant cost savings. Among the most important areas of research are the following:

Materials and commodities

- Trends in respect of the requirements of the undertaking for specific materials.
- Price analysis.
- Substitute materials or items.
- Specifications and standardisation.
- Value analysis.
- Usage analysis.
- Use of learning curves.

Purchasing policies and procedures

- What policies are in need of revision?
- Might it be more economical to make in rather than buy out or vice versa?
- What opportunities exist for the consolidation of purchasing requirements?
- Purchasing contributions to competitive advantage.
- Forms design, distribution and elimination.
- The application of activity-based costing to the purchasing function.
- How can the information made available by electronic data processing be used more effectively?
- Can purchasing organisation for materials be improved by regrouping the purchasing, stores and other related subsystems, e.g. materials or logistics management approaches?
- To what extent can operational research methods be applied to purchasing?
- Internal and external customer satisfaction with the purchasing function.

Suppliers

- Supplier appraisal.
- Supplier performance.
- The possibilities for supplier development.
- Supplier reviews, i.e. how often suppliers are changed and how new suppliers are found.
- Global sourcing.

Staff

- Staff responsibilities.
- Staff turnover, absenteeism, morale.
- What overtime, if any, is worked?
- Staff succession.
- Staff training and development.
- Staff remuneration, facilities and incentives.

Miscellaneous

- Purchasing applications of IT.
- Transportation of bought-out items.
- Securing supplies in conditions of uncertainty.
- Disposal of scrap and obsolete stores equipment.
- Terms and conditions of purchase.
- The measurement of purchasing performance.
- Purchasing ethics.

18.1.3 Organisation for research

Some research is undertaken by all purchasing departments even though this may be only rudimentary, such as consulting directories or the internet to locate possible suppliers of an item not previously bought. Some willingness to initiate research is essential to the development of the status of purchasing. Unless such initiative is taken by purchasing, the research role will be assumed by other functions such as design, marketing and production. Purchasing research may be formal or informal.

Small business units

Small business units may be unable to allocate resources such as personnel and finance to establish a formal purchasing research section. Staff should nevertheless be encouraged to keep up to date by meeting representatives, attending trade exhibitions, attending short courses, having access to and opportunities for studying journals and other relevant literature, and networking with other purchasing staff at meetings of professional bodies such as the CIPS.

Research sections

Systematic research requires time and freedom from distractions. These conditions can best be provided by establishing a special purchasing research section as a centralised staff activity to provide assistance to line members of the purchasing function. Experience has shown that undertakings with formal purchasing research arrangements:

- engage in more research projects;
- do so at a greater depth;
- receive a significant contribution to profitability.

Other approaches

When a specialised research section is not feasible, formalised purchasing research may be undertaken by the following:

- Project teams concerned with a specific problem or range of problems. These teams will probably include staff from outside the purchasing function, e.g. design, production, finance, marketing, as in a value research or engineering project.
- Supplier associations.
- Membership of a research consortium.
- Use of specialised outside research facilities, e.g. the Commodities Research Unit.
- Collaboration with universities. This may be 'contract' or 'collaborative' research. In contract research the agenda for a project is set by the industrial partner, with the university providing a service at a commercial price on the same basis as any other supplier. Collaborative research differs from contract research in that the research goals are jointly defined by both industry and the university. Clubs or networks are often set up by an individual university or consortium of universities to focus on a particular research topic. Companies wishing to become members usually pay an annual subscription. Thus the Centre for Research in Strategic Purchasing and Supply at Bath University claims to work at any time with over 100 companies often organised into project clubs.
- Support of individuals working for higher degrees in purchasing and supply chain management.
- Use of consultants to investigate a specific matter. Some large consultancies also undertake independent research which is made available to industry at a cost. An example is the *Purcon Index*, a biannual survey of the salaries and total remuneration packages of purchasing and supplies staff throughout Britain. Similar research is undertaken by Market Focus Research Ltd.
- Professional institutes – the Institute of Logistics and Transport maintains a Logistics Research Network, a special interest group of academics with some practitioner members. The Network produces the *International Journal of Logistics Research and Applications*. The CIPS supports chairs in purchasing at several universities.

18.1.4 Research methodology

As with all other research, the first step in a purchasing or supply chain investigation is to adopt a plan or model of the research from inception to completion. Sarantakos[2] states that the general assumption made by researchers who employ a research model in their work rests on the following beliefs:

- Research can be perceived as evolving in a series of steps which are closely interrelated and in which the success of one depends on the successful completion of the preceding step.
- The steps must be executed in a given order.
- Planning and execution of the research is more successful if a research model is employed. A typical research model is shown in Figure 18.1.

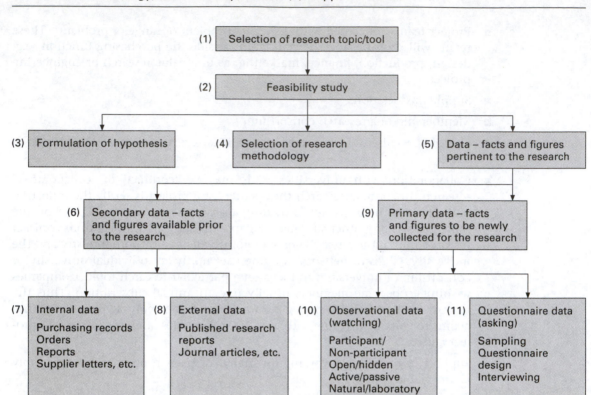

Figure 18.1 A purchasing research model

18.2 Purchasing performance and control

18.2.1 Definition

Purchasing performance may be defined as:

> The quantitative or qualitative assessment of the degree to which the purchasing function and those employed therein achieve the general or specific objectives assigned to them.

18.2.2 Approaches to assessment

Quantitative or qualitative assessment

Assessment may be quantitative or qualitative. Quantitative assessments are objective and measurable whereas qualitative assessments are subjective and intuitive.

Van Weele[3] states that the measures used to evaluate purchasing differ significantly according to whether the status of purchasing within an organisation is that of a clerical or commercial activity or a strategic business function. *Quantitative assessment*, using such measures as number of orders placed, reduction in lead times, price savings, reduction of administrative costs, etc., will tend to be used where purchasing is regarded as a clerical or commercial activity. From this perspective the focus will be on *efficiency*, defined by Van Weele as 'the relationship between planned and actual sacrifices made in order to be able to realise a goal previously agreed upon'. Purchasing performance is therefore 'the extent to which the purchasing function is able to realise its predetermined goals at the sacrifice of a minimum of the company's resources'.

Qualitative assessment, using judgemental impressions regarding the contribution of purchasing to supplier goodwill, partnership sourcing, value analysis and internal customer satisfaction, is applicable when procurement is regarded as a strategic business function. From this perspective the focus will be on *effectiveness*, defined by Van Weele as 'the extent to which by choosing a certain course of action, a previously established goal or standard can be met'. Purchasing performance is therefore the extent to which a goal is reached or not.

General or specific assessment

General or specific assessment may relate to:

- the overall performance of the purchasing function;
- special areas or activities within the function;
- the contributions of individual staff members.

Specific objectives may be corporately prescribed normally in consultation with the head of the purchasing function or set by the latter in consultation with his or her staff.

External or internal assessment

External assessment may be carried out by the executive to whom the head of the purchasing function reports, a group of senior managers, a related function (e.g. finance in respect of budgets, internal audit), outside consultants or by benchmarking. *Internal assessments* can be made by the head of the purchasing function or senior staff.

Individual or functional assessment

Staff appraisal is referred to in Chapter 15. Such *individual appraisals* should refer to the assessment of an employee's performance over a specified period of time and are an essential senior management responsibility.

Functional appraisals, especially those based on quantitative criteria, relate to the results, wholly or in part, of the activity. In the end, however, all performance measurement has an individual element in that the head of the function is accountable for achieving the required results.

18.3 Aims of performance measurement

- To ensure a consensus between individual, functional and corporate aims and objectives.
- To compare actual results with planned performance.
- To ascertain preventable and non-preventable reasons for substandard performance and provide a basis, where required, for improvement.
- To improve decision making.
- To identify and make visible the contribution of the purchasing function to organisational competitive advantage.
- To provide feedback to staff which can improve motivation and encourage the search for improvement and the more efficient and effective discharge of purchasing responsibilities.

18.4 Prevalence and importance of purchasing performance measurement

Measurement of purchasing performance is more usual in the following types of organisation:

- Large enterprises.
- Public purchasing. The Treasury report *Efficiency in Civil Government Procurement* emphasises the role of performance measurement in achieving efficient procurement:

  > Procurement units which measure their activities effectively combine consistent delivery of real savings with low cost efficient operation. They also achieve a greater influence and probity in all areas of departmental spend and conduct effective reviews of projects thus leading to improved performance. At the same time they achieve both a high level of customer satisfaction whilst delivering continuous and sustained improvement.[4]

  The Treasury has issued a Guidance Note on measuring performance in purchasing.[5]

- Enterprises which recognise the strategic importance of the purchasing function. As long ago as 1978, Stevens[6] reported that 'the higher purchasing reports in the organisation the more heavily it uses a spread of evaluators where the percentage material cost/total cost ratio lies between 40 and 60 per cent the more likely purchasing is to use a spread of evaluators and at a fairly high incidence rate.'

Measurement of purchasing performance is, however, important for all organisations for the following reasons:

■ If an activity cannot be measured it cannot be effectively managed and continuous and sustainable improvements cannot be made.

■ Measurement is critical for maintaining the competitive edge of companies in an increasingly crowded global marketplace.

18.5   Principles of performance measurement

The method or methods used to measure performance should be chosen after consideration of the following principles:

■ *Acceptability*. The method of measuring performance should be discussed with and accepted by all the purchasing staff concerned.

■ *Achievability*. The method must use realistic standards of performance otherwise staff will not be motivated to attain them.

■ *Appropriateness*. The methods and factors must be relevant to the work of staff and the department.

■ *Flexibility*. Methods of measurement must be capable of adaptation to meet changing circumstances.

■ *Continuity*. The methods used should be retained over a reasonable period to facilitate comparison between past and present performance.

■ *Comprehension*. The methods adopted should be uncomplicated so that they can easily be communicated to staff.

■ *Credible*. As CUP Guidance Note 14 states: 'The more credible the performance measure, the more acceptable it will be both to those whose performance is being measured and those who are measuring the performance.'

■ *Cost*. The cost of measuring performance should not be out of proportion to the perceived benefit of the exercise.

18.6   Methods of evaluating purchasing performance

18.6.1   Purchasing effectiveness and efficiency

Effectiveness is the ability of a person, function or organisation to accomplish a given goal, purpose or mission.

Efficiency is the ability of a person, function or organisation to maximise productivity with the least amount of effort, time, money or other resources.

Briefly, effectiveness means 'doing the right thing', whereas efficiency means 'doing things right'. Consequently, effectiveness and efficiency are not always synonymous. It is possible to purchase effectively, for example, so that the right supplies of the right quality are available at the right time. Purchasing may not, however, be efficient since the supplies are not purchased at the right price.

18.6.2   Traditional and strategic measures

Because the size, structure and importance of the purchasing function differs widely among organisations it is not feasible to devise a universally applicable measure of purchasing performance. The general principle is that the measures used should reflect the goals of the purchasing function within a particular enterprise. These goals have changed as the focus of purchasing has changed from the traditional role of cutting costs to one aimed at adding value through long-term supplier relationships involving cooperation and benefits to both purchasers and suppliers.

Traditional measures of performance include:

- Savings on cost of purchased supplies.
- Inventory levels.
- Incoming defects, reworking or returns to suppliers.
- On-time deliveries.
- Total cycle time from issue of requisition to delivery to production.
- Costs of placing purchase orders.

Most traditional measurements are now assumed to be part of minimum performance but they cannot be discounted since their achievement is still an important purchasing responsibility.

Strategic performance measures include:

- Supplier management, including a reduced supplier base, supplier development and long-term collaborative relationships.
- Assurance that supplies will arrive just in time for production requirements.
- Acquisition excellence comprising, *inter alia*, quality assurance systems and the communication of quality standards.
- Implementation of strategic purchasing systems to reduce or avoid purchasing costs, including e-procurement, the use of purchase cards and the establishment of world class supplier networks.
- Increased professionalism of purchasing staff and the development of cross-functional teams.
- Financial performance from a total sales perspective.
- The degree of internal customer satisfaction with purchasing services.

The measurement of such factors is more complex, more qualitative and less quantitative than is the case for traditional responsibilities. They are also more difficult to attribute solely to purchasing. Some require the application of such approaches as satisfaction surveys or the use of 360 degree appraisals of purchasing performance.

Such 360 degree appraisals are normally applied in human resources management and aim to obtain performance evaluations of individual employees from multiple perspectives such as superiors, peers and subordinates. The purpose of 360 degree appraisals is to provide feedback to individuals on how their performance is rated by such constituencies as those stated above. The method and purpose is, however, equally applicable to functions such as purchasing.

18.6.3   Approaches to performance measurement

Apart from the above-mentioned approaches that are in practice rarely used, approaches to measuring the effectiveness and efficiency of purchasing performance may be grouped under four main headings:

- Accounting approaches, namely profit centres, activity-based costing, standard costing and budgetary control, and financial audits.
- Comparative approaches, namely benchmarking and ratios.
- The purchasing management audit approach.
- Management by objectives.

18.7   Accounting approaches

18.7.1   The profit centre approach

The profit centre approach regards the purchasing function as a part of the undertaking that controls assets and is responsible not only for expenditure but also for income. The aim of this approach is to demonstrate that the purchasing function is a profit rather than a cost centre.

The approach involves establishing a centralised purchasing organisation that controls assets. The profitability of the centralised purchasing function is generated by an internal accounting transfer of items and services procured by purchasing to other functions at a price above their actual direct cost. In effect, purchasing sells to other functions at what is termed a transfer price. The executive in charge of purchasing is therefore expected to base his or her decisions on profit criteria, and performance is measured by the profits generated by the function.

The profit centre approach is theoretical rather than practical, although it is advocated on the following grounds:

- It provides a measure of the efficiency of the supplies function.
- It allows supplier managers to control their budgets and spend to save money.
- It enhances the status of the supplies function by providing measurable objectives.

Example 18.1   Profit centre approach to performance measurement

Value of assets controlled by the supplies manager:

		£
Inventory		1,500,000
Purchasing function floor space and equipment		250,000
Stores floor space and equipment		750,000
		2,500,000
Annual rate of return required by the undertaking on assets employed	15%	375,000
Estimated annual operating expenses		
Purchasing	150,000	
Stores	475,000	625,000
Total expenses and return (a)		1,000,000
Total purchases for year (b)		20,000,000
(a) + (b)	5%	
Transfer cost of supplies to user function (i.e. internal customers) will therefore be 5 per cent + notional supplies profit (say 1 per cent)	106	
Therefore profit on turnover of £20,000,000		200,000

$$\text{Return on assets controlled by supplies} = \frac{(£200,000 \times 100)}{£2,500,000} = 8\%$$

To reach the expected return of 15 per cent other than by increasing the notional profit the supplies function will have to reduce either the investment in inventory or operating expenses.

18.7.2   Activity-based costing

Activity-based costing (ABC), the basics of which have been described in Chapter 17, contributes to performance measurement in the following ways:

■ *It distinguishes between value adding and non-value-adding activities.* ABC management stresses that the non-value-adding activities must be reduced or eliminated and replaced with those that add value. Just-in-time, while different from ABC management, has similar aims in that both approaches seek to eliminate all wasteful activity by such means as using fewer suppliers, high reliability, minimal paperwork and reduced inventory.

■ *It enables the analysis of cost drivers.* A cost driver is an activity which creates a cost. ABC highlights the fact that complex products require enhanced negotiation expenses, more suppliers and purchase orders, increased administrative costs and similar cost drivers. The following two measures indicate the opportunities for cost savings through simplifying supplier-driven activities.

(i) $\text{Number of suppliers per product} = \dfrac{\text{Number of suppliers}}{\text{Number of products}}$

Assuming 200 suppliers and 10 products this will be:

$\dfrac{200}{10} = 20 \text{ suppliers per product}$

(ii) $\text{Number of orders per product} = \dfrac{\text{Purchase orders}}{\text{Number of products}}$

$$\frac{1,000}{10} = 100 \text{ purchase orders per product}$$

Cost savings can be made by:

- reducing the complexities of bought-out items, i.e. by standardisation;
- reducing the amount of negotiation and number of suppliers by the introduction of single sourcing or an approved supplier list;
- improved design using standard, simplified or fewer parts;
- elimination of unprofitable products.

■ *It enables allocation of overheads to products.* If an ABC analysis shows that product X requires the purchase of items from 12 suppliers whereas product Y involves purchasing from only two suppliers, it is clear that product X will incur a considerably higher proportion of purchasing cost than product Y. This should be reflected in the allocation of purchasing function costs to products which takes place with ABC but not with traditional costing.

18.7.3 Standard costing and budgetary control

Standard costing and budgetary control are described in Chapter 17. *Standard costing* can monitor performance by variance analysis. *Budgetary control* assists performance measurement in the following ways:

■ By defining the results to be achieved by functions and their staff for the purpose of realising overall objectives.

■ By indicating the extent by which actual results have exceeded or fallen below those budgeted.

■ By establishing the extent and causes of budget variations.

■ By appraising budgets to correct adverse trends or to take advantage of favourable conditions.

■ By exercising centralised control in circumstances of decentralised activity.

■ By providing a basis for future policies and, where necessary, the revision of current policies.

18.7.4 Financial audits

Financial audits are considered later under purchasing and fraud (section 18.11).

18.8 Comparative approaches

18.8.1 Benchmarking

Definitions

A benchmark is a fixed point of reference against which measurements and comparisons can be made. In the management context, benchmarking has been defined as:[7]

Measuring your performance against that of best-in-class companies, determining how the best-in-class achieve these performance levels and using the information as a basis for your company's targets, strategies and implementation.

Types of benchmarking

Harrison[8] identifies three types of benchmarking, each of which has its advantages and disadvantages and specific applications:

- *Internal benchmarking.* This is applicable in enterprises with a number of functions, departments or locations carrying out comparable activities. The aim is to ascertain and learn from the best internal role models.

- *Competitive benchmarking.* This involves the systematic comparison of business against that of key competitors. Technically this includes reverse engineering, i.e. the technique of buying and dismantling competitors' products to ascertain their particular features and how they are made.

- *Best practice benchmarking.* This involves comparison against world class enterprises on a function by function or activity by activity basis.

Advantages of benchmarking

- It provides information on what standards must be surpassed in order to achieve a competitive advantage.

- Benchmarking is motivating since it indicates standards and targets that have been achieved by others.

- Resistance to change may be lessened if ideas for improvement come from other enterprises or competitors.

- Benchmarking is broadening in that it prevents insularity, introspection and self-satisfaction.

What is benchmarking

David *et al.*[9] provide the following list of standard benchmarks common to many US industries collected over many years by the Centre for Advanced Purchasing Studies at Arizona State University.

- Purchase dollars as a percentage of sales dollars.
- Purchasing operating expense dollars as a percentage of sales dollars.
- Cost to spend a dollar (purchasing operating expense dollars as a percentage of purchase dollars).
- Purchasing employees as a percentage of company employees.
- Sales dollars per purchasing employee.
- Purchase dollars per purchasing employee.
- Active suppliers per purchasing employee.
- Active suppliers per professional purchasing employee.

- Purchasing dollars spent per active supplier.
- Purchasing operating expense dollars per active supplier.
- Change in purchase dollars spent with minority-owned suppliers.
- Percentage of purchase dollars spent with women-owned suppliers.
- Percentage of active suppliers accounting for 90 per cent of purchase dollars.
- Purchase order cycle time (in days).
- Percentage of purchase transactions processed through electronic commerce.
- Percentage of service purchases handled by the purchasing department.
- Percentage of total purchases handled by the purchasing department.
- Average annual training hours per professional purchasing department.
- Percentage of purchase transactions processed via procurement card.

As can be seen from this list, there is virtually no aspect of purchasing that cannot be the subject of a benchmarking exercise. Benchmarking can apply to prices, delivery, quality, inventory and also to such matters as procurements staffing, training, pay and productivity, e-procurement, administrative procedures and all aspects of purchasing performance.

How to benchmark

The DTI[10] provides the following guidelines on the application of benchmarking to purchasing

Stage 1   Decide what aspects of purchasing/logistics to benchmark

Such aspects may be in areas in which it is considered that the following conditions obtain:

- There are significant gaps between current purchasing policies/procedures/ performance and those of competitors.
- The contribution of purchasing to competitive advantage might be improved.
- Costs are significant.
- Further information on good practice is required.

Stage 2   Plan the benchmarking project

- Appoint a team leader to supervise the project.
- Select a team with appropriate skills.
- Ascertain what information on the selected topics is already available or can be obtained through personal contacts, library research, trade associations, etc.

Stage 3   Create a baseline for benchmarking comparisons

The purpose of this stage is to identify accurately 'where we are now' so that effective comparisons can be made with best-in-class performances. This involves the following activities:

- Identifying the factors that influence performance in the chosen area.
- Determining what factors are important and those that are less important.
- Preparing a statement supported where appropriate by quantitative data of current performance.

Stage 4   Decide whom to benchmark against

The DTI[11] suggests the following important considerations in choosing companies against whom to benchmark:

- Do they know us? (There should already be a good relationship with customers/suppliers.)
- Is their experience really relevant?
- Are they still good at the activity we want to measure?
- Are we legally able to exchange this kind of information? To the above one might add, are they competitors? Competitors are likely to be less willing to share information.

Stage 5   How will we collect the required information?

- Secure cooperation with best-in-class performers often through high level contacts.
- Decide what questions to ask.
- Arrange visits and other means of exchanging information.

Stage 6   Analyse the information obtained

The DTI advises[12] that once it has been identified that other companies have a higher level of performance in a particular activity, the team should

- quantify the information as closely as possible;
- ensure they are comparing like with like;
- decide how much of what has been observed in the other companies is applicable to its own situation.

Stage 7   Use the findings

At this stage the team carries out the following activities:

- Prepares a report on the findings.
- Discusses the findings with senior management and other related functions.
- Sets new performance standards.
- Makes someone in authority responsible for devising an action plan to implement the new standards.
- Monitors progress to ensure that the plan is put into effect.

Further aspects of benchmarking

- Benchmarking is *not* industrial spying but is undertaken openly with the full cooperation of the company against which benchmarking is undertaken.

- Information which may be regarded as confidential or proprietary in content should not be asked for.

- Benchmarking is more than copying the practices of other organisations. All factors must be considered that made the activity successful, e.g. staff training and improvement.

- Benchmarks are not static. The aim should be continual improvement. The Japanese word *dantotsu*, which means striving to be the 'best of the best', is the essence of benchmarking.

- Benchmarking is closely related to activity-based management and total quality management.

18.8.2 Ratios

Ratios show the relationship between two magnitudes or variables and can be used to indicate trends, set standards, control costs and as measures of efficiency. Ratios used to measure purchasing performance include the following:

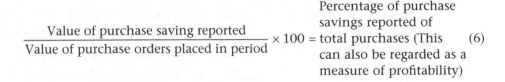

$$\frac{\text{Operating cost of purchasing dept}}{\text{Total value of purchases}} \times 100 = \begin{array}{l}\text{Ratio of operating costs} \\ \text{to procurement costs}\end{array} \tag{1}$$

$$\frac{\text{Operating cost of purchasing dept}}{\text{Number of orders placed in period}} \times 100 = \text{Average cost of orders} \tag{2}$$

$$\frac{\text{Total value of purchases}}{\text{Total value of sales}} \times 100 = \begin{array}{l}\text{Percentage of value of purchases to} \\ \text{value of sales for a given period}\end{array} \tag{3}$$

$$\frac{\text{Value of purchase orders placed in period}}{\text{Number of buyers}} \times 100 = \begin{array}{l}\text{Average value of orders} \\ \text{placed by buyers}\end{array} \tag{4}$$

$$\frac{\text{Value of purchase orders placed in period}}{\text{Number of purchase orders placed in period}} \times 100 = \begin{array}{l}\text{Average value of} \\ \text{purchase orders}\end{array} \tag{5}$$

$$\frac{\text{Value of purchase saving reported}}{\text{Value of purchase orders placed in period}} \times 100 = \begin{array}{l}\text{Percentage of purchase} \\ \text{savings reported of} \\ \text{total purchases (This} \\ \text{can also be regarded as a} \\ \text{measure of profitability)}\end{array} \tag{6}$$

The above ratios are easily derived and are particularly useful as bases of comparison over a number of years. They have the following disadvantages, however:

- In the case of 2, 4 and 5 the ratios show average values which may be distorted, e.g. by one abnormally large order.

- With 1 and 2, the ratio can be improved by increasing the numerator but the aim should be to reduce the total value of purchases and number of orders placed. A fall in the number of orders placed may not be attributable to purchasing.

- With 4, the value of savings reported by the purchasing department may not be wholly attributable to purchasing. The tendency is often to emphasise favourable elements in purchasing performance and minimise or cover up mistakes and losses. A study by the American Management Association[13] noted six areas in which reportable savings can be credited to purchasing:

  - more economical sources of supply developed by the buyer;
  - specification changes at the buyer's suggestion (to obtain lower price, longer life or reduce inventory or installation costs);
  - improved order practice resulting in obtaining a lower price, e.g. combining orders;
  - negotiation of lower price by the buyer;
  - reduction of costs other than material price, e.g. handling or storage costs;
  - increased return from sale of damaged, obsolete or surplus material and scrap.

- the ratios give no indication of sound purchasing judgement.

18.9 Purchasing management audit approach

18.9.1 Definition

An audit may be defined as, *inter alia*, a check or examination. The term 'purchasing management audit' has been defined by Scheuing[14] as:

> **A comprehensive, systematic, independent and periodic examination of a company's purchasing environment, objectives and tactics to identify problems and opportunities and facilitate the development of appropriate action plans.**

Scheuing states that the operative words in this definition are:

- *Comprehensive* – the audit should cover every aspect of purchasing.
- *Systematic* – a standard set of questions should be developed and used.
- *Independent* – purchasing personnel should not evaluate themselves.
- *Periodic* – audits yield the greatest value if they are performed periodically, e.g. annually, thus facilitating comparisons, checks and balances and the evaluation of progress.

18.9.2 Purpose of purchasing management audits

A review of some standard purchasing texts by Evans and Dale[15] indicated that purchasing audits serve four main purposes:

- They police the extent to which the purchasing policies laid down by senior management are adhered to.

- They help to ensure that the organisation is using techniques, procedures and methods which conform to best working practice.
- They monitor and measure the extent to which resources are used effectively.
- They assist in the prevention and detection of fraud and malpractice.

18.9.3   Who should carry out the purchasing management audit?

The audits may be carried out by external or internal auditors, a central purchasing function, a purchasing research function or external management consultants. Two principles are suggested as governing who should carry out the audit:

- The auditors should be external to the function or department which is the subject of the audit.
- The auditors should have a detailed knowledge of the purchasing function which will enable them not only to monitor adherence to policies and procedures but also to understand purchasing perspectives and problems and make recommendations as to how policies, procedures and practice can be improved. External consultants with specialist knowledge and experience are likely to carry greater authority and provide greater objectivity in relation to purchasing audits.

18.9.4   Content of purchasing audits

Suggested headings and typical items for a management as distinct from a financial audit of the purchasing function are given below.

Purchasing perspectives, problems and opportunities

- What are the perceptions of a sample of purchasing staff of:
  - their status in the organisation
  - their involvement in strategic decision making
  - their contribution to profitability and competitive advantage
- What are the job satisfactions and job dissatisfactions identified by the purchasing staff interviewed?
- What are the main problems encountered by purchasing staff in doing their job? To what extent are these problems related to:
  - management
  - colleagues
  - internal customers
  - suppliers
  - information
  - resources
  - other internal or external factors
- What is the level of morale in the purchasing function?

Purchasing organisation

- To whom does the person in charge of the purchasing function report?
- What aspects of purchasing are centralised? Which are decentralised?
- Would any centralised aspects of purchasing benefit from decentralisation, or vice versa?
- With what other functional activities does purchasing interrelate?
- What are the formal mechanisms for coordination of purchasing activities with other functions?
- What is the assessment of purchasing function performance by its internal customers?
- On what interfunctional/departmental committees is the purchasing function represented or could it be represented?
- How might the internal organisation of the purchasing function be improved?
- How might the integration of purchasing with other related functions be improved?

This information will be obtained from organisation charts and formal and informal interviews.

Purchasing personnel

- What staff are employed in the purchasing function?
- What are their grades, qualifications and lengths of service?
- Has every member of the purchasing function an appropriate job description?
- How do actual duties carried out relate to the job descriptions?
- What staff are over/underdeployed?
- Is an attempt made to empower purchasing staff?
- What training and development opportunities are provided for purchasing staff?
- How do salaries and remuneration packages compare with those in similar enterprises/industries?
- What is the staff turnover as measured by the formula:

$$\frac{\text{Number of leavers in function over a specified period (usually 1 year)}}{\text{Average number of employees in function during the same period}} \times 100$$

- What is the stability of employment in the function as measured by the formula:

$$\frac{\text{Number of staff with 1 year's service or more}}{\text{Number employed 1 year ago}} \times 100$$

- What staff will reach retirement age within the next five years?

This information will be obtained from job descriptions or specifications, training documents, human resources plans, and formal and informal interviews.

Purchasing policies

- What written and unwritten policies apply to the purchasing function?
- Is there a purchasing manual? How, and how frequently, is this updated?
- What guidance is provided to purchasing staff in respect of:
  - value to which an individual at a particular grade can commit the enterprise
  - supplier relationships, e.g. disputes, prompt payment
  - conflicts of interest, e.g. gifts and entertainment
  - buying from abroad
  - environmental policies
  - reciprocal, local and intra-company purchasing
- What machinery exists for the investigation and enforcement of reported departures from policy compliance?

This information will be obtained largely from relevant documents, manuals, memoranda, instructions, etc.

Purchasing procedures

- From what sources are requests to purchase obtained?
- How quickly are such requests processed?
- What procedures are laid down for such operational activities as requesting and evaluating quotations, issuing purchase orders, receipt of goods and payment of supplies?
- Are all appropriate procedures computerised?
- To what extent does the purchasing function make use of EDI and e-procurement?
- How are small orders processed?
- What procedures or activities (i) add value, (ii) do not add value?
- How might purchasing documentation be improved, simplified or eliminated?
- How much time do purchasing staff spend on seeing supplier representatives?
- What are the procedures for capital purchases?

Much of this information will be obtained from trailing a sample of purchase orders through from the receipt of the requisition to receipt of goods and payment of the suppliers, and from formal and informal interviews.

Purchasing reports

- What reports are prepared by the purchasing function?
- By whom is each report prepared?
- At what intervals is each report prepared?
- What is the cost of preparing each report?
- To whom is each report sent?

- What use is made of each report by the receiver?
- Is the report really necessary?

Much of this information will be obtained by trailing reports through from their inception to storage or disposal.

Purchases, suppliers and prices

- What is the purchase budget in quantities and value for the period under review?
- What are the principal purchases?
- Who are the principal suppliers?
- What attempts have been made to achieve single and partnership sourcing?
- How and by what criteria are suppliers appraised?
- Are the results of appraisals communicated to suppliers?
- How do prices paid for a sample of purchases compare with what is obtainable in the market?
- In what ways does the purchasing function seek to obtain value for money?
- How and by whom are specifications prepared? Is there any purchasing involvement?
- What savings have been achieved in the period under review and how have these been achieved?

Much of this information will be obtained from the examination of a sample of orders and other purchase documentation, and from formal and informal interviews.

Inventory

- Does the undertaking practise ABC analysis?
- How much inventory is carried: (i) strategic items; (ii) bottleneck items; (iii) leverage items; (iv) non-critical items?
- What is the rate of turnover of a sample of items under each category?
- What items of inventory have been in stock for more than one year?
- What procedures are in place for the identification of obsolescent, slow-moving or damaged inventory and for the prevention of pilferage?
- What procedures are in place for the disposal of surplus stock, obsolete or scrap supplies, or discarded capital items?
- What stockouts have been experienced in the period and why?
- What attempts has the purchasing/supplies function made to reduce inventory investment?

Much of this information will be obtained from an investigation of stores records, physical inspection of inventory and stores procedures, and from formal and informal interviews.

From the above it can be seen that the main tools used in purchasing performance audit include:

- formal and informal interviews;
- sampling;
- trailing a procedure or document through from its inception to its end or storage or disposal;
- observation.

These tools can be supported by such procedures as benchmarking and ratio analysis.

18.9.5 Purchasing management audit reports

On completing the findings, the audit should be presented to senior management in the form of a report with summarised recommendations with supporting reasons. In preparing such reports, auditors should:

- highlight policies, procedures and personnel where efficiency and effectiveness can be improved;
- commend good practice and performance;
- think beyond simple quantitative measures of performance and consider the full consequences, side-effects and reaction likely to occur from their recommendations;
- support constructive proposals made by purchasing staff which may receive greater attention if made by an outside source.

18.10 Management by objectives

Management by objectives (MBO) aims to identify the objectives that a manager or function should be expected to achieve within a given time at the end of which the actual performance will be compared with the desired results. The objectives will be compared with the desired results. The objectives will be agreed by the head of the function in consultation with his or her superior.

One approach to MBO known as *key results analysis* requires functional heads to identify their key tasks, performance standards and control information with a view to suggesting how their individual performance and the performance of their function can be improved. This analysis forms the basis of discussions with both their immediate superiors and their subordinates. The discussions with superiors are to agree functional objectives. When these have been agreed, discussions with subordinates are held to determine what objectives each must achieve if the functional/departmental objectives are to be attained. In this manner overall objectives are cascaded down through the organisation as shown:

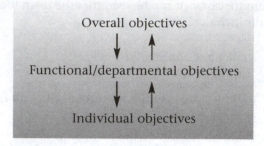

Since, however, functions and individuals participate in the setting of their objectives, MBO also works from the bottom up as well as from the top down.

18.10.1   Types of objective

Three main types of objective can be identified:

- *Improvement objectives.* These seek to improve performance in specific ways in respect of specified factors, e.g. 'to reduce by the next review period the prices paid for all costings used in the assembly of conveyor rollers by 5 per cent'. Such a reduction may be achieved by negotiation with existing suppliers regarding ways of reducing the price (e.g. substituting aluminium for zinc), value analysis, or finding new sources from which to purchase.

- *Personal development objectives.* These appertain to personal growth objectives or to the acquisition of expanded job knowledge, skills and experience, e.g. 'to begin by the next review an approved course of study leading to the examinations of the Chartered Institute of Purchasing and Supply'.

- *Maintenance objectives.* These formally express intentions to maintain performance at its current level, e.g. 'to maintain the present zero defects level of component X purchased from supplier Y'.

The elements of MBO are therefore objectives and feedback.

18.10.2   Objectives and feedback

Objectives should be:

- specific and capable of being expressed precisely in writing;
- measurable;
- time constrained;
- attainable with existing resources or resources to be made available;
- linked vertically and horizontally and with organisational strategies;
- limited in number;
- where possible ranked in order of priority;
- as challenging as possible – there is evidence that difficult objectives produce stronger motivation and a higher level of individual performance than easy objectives

Feedback should:

- be fair;
- distinguish between controllable and uncontrollable reasons for failing to meet objectives;
- when constructive, lead to higher performance;
- include performance-based rewards if objectives have been achieved.

18.11   Purchasing and fraud

Purchasing is a function that is particularly vulnerable to fraud. Evans[16] states that 'fraud is not necessarily restricted to those with the title purchasing officer but may involve anyone in direct contact with suppliers', including engineers, works managers, sales and computer staff. Evans also points out that 'what appears to be fraud may, on occasion, be no more than incompetence'.

18.11.1   Examples of supplies-related fraud

- Buyer/supplier collusion leading to approval for payment of fictitious charges.
- Presentation of false invoices – typically the offender will set up a fictitious company with impressive stationery and invoice the purchaser for goods not supplied.
- Re-presentation of genuine invoices that have not been cancelled at the time the initial cheque was signed.
- Abstraction of tenders or arranging for the lowest tender to come from a desired source.
- Omission of credit notes for goods returned to the supplier.
- Premature scrapping of assets in return for a 'kickback' from a scrap dealer.
- Computer-based frauds which take advantages of inadequate controls or limited understanding of information technology on the part of senior management.

18.11.2   Prevention of fraud

The prevention of fraud in relation to supplies depends on sound internal control, internal and external auditing and the detection of 'give away' signs.

18.11.3   Internal signs of fraud

Internal signs refer to the whole system of controls, financial or otherwise, established by management in order to carry on the enterprise in an orderly fashion, safeguard its assets including money and stock, and secure as far as possible the accuracy and reliability of the records. Such controls include the following:

- Ensuring a separation between recording and custodian duties.

- Only specified employees should have the power to requisition goods, and then only up to an authorised limit which increases with the level of authority. The existence of a separate purchasing department or function considerably strengthens internal control by ensuring that user departments are prevented from ordering items without the order first being independently 'vetted'.

- Conversely, the requisitioning department can act as a check on the purchasing since every order placed should be traceable to a requisition.

- Goods inward should be received in specially designated areas. Control is best established at the gate or entrance. The receipt of all goods should be recorded. Goods received notes, where used, should be serially numbered to reduce the danger of introducing false documents, and copies should be sent to the purchasing and finance departments.

- While it may be unrealistic to check all invoices presented for payment, a sample should be examined on a random basis. A reduction in the supplier base reduces the procedures necessary to prevent fraud.

- The main internal controls in respect of computers can be classified as (i) systems development and control, (ii) organisational controls and (iii) procedural controls. *Systems development controls* are those which ensure that the computer system operates as originally specified and all the relevant documentation has been properly prepared and maintained. *Organisational controls* seek to ensure that an acceptable standard of discipline and efficiency is maintained over the day-to-day running of the computer department. *Procedural controls* are those exercised over each computer application, e.g. purchasing and the payment of suppliers. The purpose is to ensure that the whole of the original data relevant to any application is accurately processed from the point of origin to the final output and that master files used in the application are completely and accurately processed, amended and maintained. The head of the purchasing function should discuss the computerised system with the chief accountant and obtain confirmation that all the above controls appear to be adequate. External auditors should also be asked to pay special attention to computerised purchasing procedures.

- One aim of internal controls is to increase the difficulties of a person who plans to perpetuate a fraud. These difficulties are increased when, not having all the relevant matters under their control, fraudsters have to seek the collusion of others. Persons who may be prepared to undertake fraud themselves are generally unwilling to accept the increased risk of betrayal or detection which exists where there is collusion. Fraud involving collusion is not, however, infrequent.

18.11.4 External auditing

Controls such as the above are complemented by external audits which, in respect of companies (but not sole traders or partnerships) are a statutory requirement under the Companies Acts. Auditors of companies must hold a practising certificate from a professional accountancy body approved by the Department of Trade and Industry.

Contrary to popular belief, it is not an auditor's primary function to prevent fraud but to make an independent examination of the books, accounts and vouchers of a business for the purpose of reporting whether the balance sheet and profit and loss account are properly prepared so as to show a 'true and fair view' of the affairs and profit (or loss) of the business according to the best information and explanations obtained.

An audit may include a physical verification of assets such as inventory and the auditors may also make recommendations which can render the company less susceptible to fraud by its customers, suppliers and employees. Where a fraud is discovered, the auditor is under a duty to prove that fraud to its full extent regardless of the amount in question.

18.11.5   'Give-away' signs

Give-away signs of fraud include the following:

- Unfolded invoices that have not come through the post.
- Too many orders to one supplier other than those where single sourcing arrangements apply.
- Loss of supporting documentation.
- Sudden unexplained affluence.
- Unwillingness of employees to take holidays or accept transfer or promotion to other work.

Evans and Maguire[17] state that the most common source through which fraud is discovered is outside information. These include the reporting of fraudulent practices by colleagues and disgruntled mistresses.

18.12   Whistle-blowing

18.12.1   Definition

Whistle-blowing has been defined by Cannock and Johns[18] as:

> The process of stepping outside one's work role to use irregular or external channels of communication to publicise suspected wrong doing.

18.12.2   Ethical aspects of whistle-blowing

Whistle-blowing involves questions of motivation:

- Whistle-blowing may be motivated by malice.
- There is a danger that incompetent or inadequately performing employees will blow the whistle to avoid facing justified personal sanctions.

Example 18.2   Whistle-blowing

In 1993, George Foxley, the director of procurement at the Ministry of Defence (MoD), was found guilty of twelve charges, involving £1.3 million in backhanders from arms suppliers. Over five years, Foxley had awarded contracts worth more than £30 million to three companies in return for bribes. In all, it is estimated that Foxley's corruption cost the public purse over £100 million. Two other colleagues were also connected.

A report researched for Public Concern,[19] argues that purchasing is at particular risk from corruption and asked the following questions:

■ Was there a culture in the MoD that it was better to mind one's own business?
■ Why did colleagues ask no questions when they noticed Foxley's large homes and lavish lifestyle?
■ Did Foxley and his colleagues discuss bribes with other defence companies?
■ How many purchasing professionals working in a similar situation would have blown the whistle?

■ Whistle-blowers may not be protesting against unlawful or unsafe behaviour but social policies by management against which the whistle-blower is in disagreement.

■ Was the disclosure in return for any reward or profit to the whistle-blower?

18.12.3   Legal issues in whistle-blowing

■ Does whistle-blowing involve a breach of the employment contract, especially express or implied duties of fidelity, trust and cooperation between employer and employee. This is of particular importance where information disclosed has some commercial value.

■ Conversely, it has long been established that 'there is no confidence as to the disclosure of iniquity' from which it is clear that information relating to criminal activity on the part of a person or organisation will never be classed as confidential.

■ A person who fails to disclose wrongdoing may possibly be considered as aiding and abetting the offence.

18.12.4   Public Interest Disclosure Act 1998

Legal protection is given to whistle-blowers by the Public Interest Disclosure Act 1998. This promotes the public interest (i) by outlawing the victimisation of people who blow the whistle and (ii) through its sanctions against the cover-up of serious malpractice. In addition to employees it covers contractors, trainees, agency staff and homeworkers. A disclosure to a manager of an employer will be protected if the whistle-blower has an honest and reasonable suspicion that the malpractice has occurred, is occurring or is likely to occur.

18.12.5   **Whistle-blowing considerations**

Before blowing the whistle, Winfield[20] recommends that answers should be given to the following:

- Is the concern clearly illegal or simply questionable business practice?
- Is the public interest at stake?
- What is the potential damage to the company, its shareholders, clients and colleagues if you blow the whistle?
- Is the whistle-blower prepared for possible rejection by colleagues and friends?
- What are the issues at stake? Can these be prioritised?
- Are there any policy statements relating to the matter?

Other advice includes:

- Submit your concern in writing, with copies of all supporting evidence, to the appropriate authority.
- State that you may expose the issues in the public interest if action is not taken.
- Protect yourself by enlisting the support of colleagues.
- Remember that your own employment record may be reviewed and those exposed may try to discredit you.
- Decide how to publicise the issue as third parties may refuse to act on anonymous information.
- Keep a log of all happenings, particularly at work, from the time you decide to take action.

18.13   Purchasing ethics

18.13.1   Definitions

Purchasing ethics is a subdivision of business ethics which in turn is the application of general ethical principles in a commercial or industrial context.

Sims *et al.*[21] give the following definition of ethics:

> **Ethics is concerned with the moral principles and values which govern our beliefs, actions and decisions.**

Business ethics have been described as:[22]

> **The systematic study of moral (ethical) matters pertaining to business, industry or related activities, institutions or practices, and beliefs can also refer to actual standards, values or practices of beliefs.**

An alternative definition is:[23]

> The way that a business conducts itself in its ordinary, everyday activities, the way the firm deals with its staff and its customers, the way it designs and supports its products, the way it awards contracts and apportions blame . . . these are the key determinants of whether a business is ethical.

18.13.2   The importance of ethics

Ethics is important in purchasing for the following reasons:

- Purchasing staff are the representatives of their organisation in its dealing with suppliers.
- Sound ethical conduct in dealing with suppliers is essential to the creation of long-term relationships and the establishment of supplier goodwill.
- Purchasing staff are probably more exposed to the temptation to act unethically than most other employees.
- It is impossible to claim professional status for purchasing without reference to a consideration of its ethical aspects.

18.13.3   The scope of ethics

Ethics is discussed in most purchasing textbooks from a very narrow perspective as being primarily concerned with such issues as bribes and confidentiality. As the above definition states, however, ethics is also concerned with *values*. 'Values', Donaldson[24] states, 'is a general term relating to those things which people regard as good, bad, right, wrong, desirable, justifiable etc.' Thus, we can speak of 'truth values' (true or false) and of 'false judgements' which are statements about what is valued, sound, deplorable, skilled, etc.

Values are the basis of both individual and organisational ethics and on which we make ethical decisions. Thus individual and business decisions will differ according to which of the following views they are based on:

- *Utilitarian view* – conduct is ethical which secures the greatest good for the greatest number.
- *Individualist view* – conduct is good which promotes *my* personal interests of *my* organisation irrespective of how this affects the interests of other people or organisations.
- *Human rights view* – conduct is good which respects fundamental human rights shared by all human beings.
- *'Justice' view* – justice is the standard for judging legal and moral questions. Conduct is just which is impartial, equal and fair.

18.13.4   Ethical codes

In Chapter 1 it was stated that one of the essentials of a profession is 'integrity maintained by adherence to a code of conduct'. Professions as diverse as medicine, law, accountancy and architecture have issued codes of conduct. The codes of conduct issued by the Chartered Institute of Purchasing and Supply in the UK and the Institute of Supply Management in the USA are reproduced in Appendices 1 and 2 respectively.

Benefits of codes

As membership of the above bodies is not essential for employment in purchasing and logistics. Such ethical codes do not have the same enforcement sanctions as those relating to law or medicine, where to be struck off for unprofessional conduct means the revocation of the right to practice. They are not, however, entirely without value. Manley[25] identified 18 major benefits that a code of conduct provides to a business. Most of these points are directly or indirectly relevant to purchasing, including the following:

- Providing guidance to and inculating the company's values, cultural substance and style in managers and employees.
- Signalling expectations of proper conduct to suppliers and customers.
- Pre-empting legal proceedings.
- Nurturing a business environment of open communication.

It would be tedious and, to some extent, meaningless to quote all Manley's 18 advantages without his supporting comment. A more succinct statement by Karp and Abramms[26] applicable to both organisation and professional codes is that there are advantages in:

- providing a basis for working together – most codes require that people treat each other with respect;
- setting boundaries as to what constitutes ethical behaviour as determined by organisational and professional values. Examples of such boundaries are declarations of interest, confidentiality of information, competition, business gifts and hospitality;
- providing a safe environment for all subscribers – without the guidance provided by a code of ethics employees are always subject to and accountable to the value system of anyone in a higher position;
- providing a commonly held set of guidelines – enabling what is right and wrong in a given situation to be judged on a consistent basis.

Some criticism of codes

Probably, most purchasing people think of ethical codes as remote from the real world. This may be because work often leaves little time for reflection. The requirement to maintain an unimpeachable standard of integrity in all business relationships is fine until one questions the meaning of integrity and to whom the duty of integrity is due. What if there is a clash of loyalties between personal and organisational integrity? Farmer[27] quotes Baumhart[28] who concluded that 'it is easier to be ethical in jobs involving fiduciary relationships such as the accountant's or engineer's than in those jobs involving competitive relationships such as the salesman's or the purchasing agent's.'

It is also a fact that codes of ethics are associated with larger undertakings. In a survey of ethics in management, Brigley[29] considers that codes are easier to introduce and implement in larger organisations than in small undertakings where there is generally a preference for informal approaches to ethical issues. Brigley also reports that, within organisations, senior management's attitudes and tactics and conflicts of values with senior management are the most commonly cited obstacles in managing ethical matters. When there is a conflict between employees' own or their profession's ethical code and the ethics of their organisation or their immediate superior, employees may have to choose between remaining silent or speaking out and facing the consequences of being seen as disloyal. They may even have to face termination of employment which under conditions of redundancy and restructuring is not to be lightly contemplated. Some comments of Brigley's respondents include:

- High unemployment affects your ethics – cynical but true.
- What people say and what people do are very different.
- People suppress their own ethical values to be generally accepted and to get on in business.
- The more senior you are the easier it is to maintain an ethical stance.

The NAPM code, for example, lays down that subscribers must denounce all forms or manifestations of commercial bribery. But, what do you do, knowing full well what happens to whistle-blowers, if you discover that your boss or colleague is receiving bribes? In summary, it seems that to be effective, organisational and professional codes need both to be made more relevant to those to whom they apply and to be supported by administrative procedures designed to assist in creating an ethical culture. This in turn means that, to be effective, purchasing ethics requires appropriate training and education.

18.13.5 Corporate ethics and purchasing

Corporate ethics are statements issued by companies and other organisations describing their general value systems and providing information guidelines for decision making consistent with those principles. Such corporate statements may relate to (i) the social responsibilities of the organisation and (ii) the responsibilities of individual members.

18.13.6 Social responsibility and purchasing

Clutterbuck et al.[30] identify seven key stakeholders or 'communities' who demand attention from socially concerned companies. Those stakeholders are: customers, employees, suppliers, shareholders, the political arena, the broader community, and the environment. In this book, purchasing's social responsibilities to suppliers and the environment are considered (see below and section 18.14).

18.13.7 Social responsibilities to suppliers

Clutterbuck et al.[31] list the following as among an organisation's social responsibilities to its suppliers:

- *Provision of practical help and advice.* This can be provided by:
  - helping suppliers to purchase more effectively and economically;
  - assistance with finding non-competitive customers to prevent too great a reliance on a single big company;
  - providing feedback on unsuccessful bids;
  - providing advice and assistance with design and production;
  - provision of advice and help with regard to training and HRM.
- *Purchasing policy.* This should include:
  - placing a proportion of orders with local suppliers thus assisting the prosperity of the communities in which the company is located;
  - supplier development;
  - measurement of supplier performance and the provision of constructive feedback.
- *Monitoring supplier practice.* The socially responsible organisation should:
  - deal only with suppliers that have high ethical standards;
  - ensure that suppliers have an environmental or 'green' policy where this is appropriate;
  - encourage suppliers to adopt a responsible attitude to various community groups, e.g. disabled personnel, ex-offenders, youth programmes.
- *Prompt payment.* The organisation should help suppliers with cash flow problems by:
  - paying invoices on time;
  - ensuring that both finance and purchasing departments are aware of the policy and adhere to it;
  - dealing with complaints as expeditiously as possible so that payments are not needlessly deferred.
- *Partnership sourcing.* This is dealt with in Chapter 9.

18.13.8 Corporate guidelines in respect of individual purchasing ethics

As shown by the guidance appended to the *Ethical Code of the CIPS*, individual purchasing ethics apply to:

- declaration of interest;
- confidentiality of information;
- fair competition;
- business gifts;
- hospitality.

The ISM (USA) *Principles and Standards of Purchasing Practice* expand the above to include:

- receptivity to competent counsel from colleagues;
- consistent striving for knowledge of materials and processes of manufacture and practical administrative measures;
- According a prompt and courteous reception, so far as conditions will permit, to all who call on a legitimate business mission.

18.13.9 Business gifts and hospitality

Policies with regard to the receipt by purchasing staff of gifts from suppliers especially at Christmas and hospitality at other times vary widely. The three most common policies are:

- Purchasing staff are forbidden to accept gifts of any kind and those received must be returned.
- Purchasing staff may retain gifts that are clearly of an advertising nature, e.g. calendars, diaries, pencils, etc.
- Purchasing staff are allowed to decide for themselves whether a proffered gift of hospitality is an appreciation of cordial business relationships or an attempt at commercial bribery.

The writer's considered view is that the third of the above policies is the best since it regards staff as responsible individuals capable of distinguishing a gift or hospitality from a bribe. There is also the fact that the first two policies encourage subterfuge, e.g. having gifts sent to the buyer's home address. There is, however, the danger that younger, less experienced, lower paid staff are likely to be flattered to receive gifts, the implications of which are not always recognised. For this reason all purchasing staff should have some training in ethics as applied to purchasing. This aspect is referred to in section 18.13.8 above.

18.13.10 The law on corruption and bribery

The Prevention of Corruption Act 1906 deals with the corruptions of agents. The Act defines the term 'agent' but not corruption: an agent is 'any person employed by or acting for another'. As stated below, 'corruption' applies not only to bribery but also to cases involving false documentation.

In *R v Wellburn and others* (1979) the Court of Appeal approved the direction of the Recorder of London that 'corruptly is a simple English adverb and I am not going to explain it to you except to say that it does not mean dishonesty. It is a different word. It means purposefully doing an act which the law forbids as tending to corrupt'.

The Act specifies three aspects of corruption:

- Agents are prohibited from corruptly accepting or obtaining or agreeing to accept or attempting to obtain, any gift or consideration as an inducement or reward for doing or forbearing to do any act, or for showing or forbearing to show favour or disfavour to any person, in relation to his principal's affairs or business.
- It is an offence for any person corruptly to give or agree to give, or offer, any gift or consideration to any agent as an inducement or reward for doing or

forbearing to do, or for having done or forborne to do, any act, or for showing or forbearing to show favour, or disfavour, to any person in relation to his principal's affairs or business.

■ It is also an offence for any person knowingly to give to an agent, or for any agent knowingly to use, with intent to deceive his principal, any receipt, account of other document, in respect of which his principal is interested, and which contains any statement which is false or erroneous or defective in any material particular, and which to his knowledge is intended to mislead the principal.

The Prevention of Corruption Act 1916 creates a presumption of corruption in certain cases prosecuted under the Public Bodies Act 1889 (this is clearly concerned only with public sector corruption) and the 1906 Act if it is proved that any money, gift or other consideration has been paid, given or received by a person in the employment of Her Majesty, or any government, or public body, by or from a person or agent of a person, holding or seeking to obtain a contract from Her Majesty, or any government department or public body, the money, gift or consideration shall be deemed to have been paid or given or received corruptly unless the contrary is proved. A 'public body' includes local and public authorities of all descriptions.

In addition to the above statutes there is also a common law offence of bribery of a public official. This is generally understood to mean:

> The receiving or offering of any undue reward by or to any person whatsoever, in a public office, in order to influence his behaviour in office, and incline him to act contrary to the known rules of honesty and integrity.

The test of corruption in the majority of cases is *secrecy*; the defence against a charge of bribery or corruption is *openness*. It is wise, therefore, for an employee to make a disclosure of gifts offered or received, to his or her employer who then has the responsibility of deciding whether the gift can be accepted or should be returned, and what action, if any, should be taken against the individual or organisation proffering the gift.

18.13.11 The reception of representatives

There is evidence that sales representatives have often a poor opinion of buyers. This is likely to be enhanced where sales representatives are kept waiting unnecessarily. It should be appreciated by purchasing staff that, allowing for travelling time and discussion, a sales representative has a relatively short working day in which to fit in calls. Unsolicited sales calls tend to be unwelcome before 9.30am and after 4.30pm and between 12.15pm and 1.30pm. If kept waiting, the salesperson's whole programme of visits in a particular area may be disrupted. Other factors in the reception of sales representatives should include:

■ a suitable room for interviews;

■ information regarding the times between which representatives will be seen;

■ the provision of honest information.

While purchasing staff should be open to information about new products and suppliers, they should be frank but courteous in informing a representative if there is no possibility of business to avoid future calls. Above all, a buyer should never be patronising, rude or supercilious. Such behaviour demeans both the representative *and* the buyer and is clearly not conducive to establishing supplier goodwill. While there must clearly be an exchange of pleasantries it should be remembered that 'time is money' for both the purchaser and the supplier.

Kennedy[32] instances 22 tactics used by unscrupulous buyers in dealing with representatives. Not only are such tactics unprofessional but they are also the negation of the golden rule: 'always treat others as you would like them to treat you'.[33] This rule is unambiguous and easy to understand; motives for endorsing it may be altruistic but are actually a reflection of precautionary, defensive self-interest.

18.13.12 The promotion of ethical standards

While professional associations issue codes of ethics and companies statements of corporate ethical policy, it is a fact that, as Dubinsky and Gwin[34] suggest, businesspeople tend to employ two sets of ethical standards: a personal set and a business set, and may well have more strict personal than business ethical standards.

How an individual will react with regard to a particular ethical dilemma depends on many factors including:

- family and cultural influences;
- religious or humanistic values;
- the behaviour of superiors;
- the behaviour of peers;
- the prevailing norms and values of society;
- the fear of the consequences of discovery of unethical behaviour.

The findings of an American study in which businessmen were asked to rank the influences which they considered most to ethical or unethical behaviour are shown in Table 18.1.

From Table 18.1 it is clear that an important determinant of both ethical and unethical conduct is the behaviour of an individual's superiors. This highlights the need for purchasing staff at all levels to receive ethical training and for the provision of machinery for ethical policies to be enforced.

Table 18.1 Determinants of ethical behaviour

Factors determining ethical decisions		Factors determining unethical decisions	
Factor	Ave. rank	Factor	Ave. Rank
The individual's personal code of behaviour	1.5	The behaviour of a person's superiors in the company	1.9
The behaviour of a person's superiors in the company	2.8	Ethical climate in the industry	2.6
Formal company policy	3.8	The behaviour of person's equals in the company	3.1
The behaviour of a person's equals in the company	4.0	Lack of company policy	3.3
		Personal financial needs	4.1

18.13.13 Ethical training

Ethical training sessions for purchasing staff can provide a number of benefits. They reinforce the organisation's ethical codes and policies, they remind staff that top management expects participants to consider ethical issues in making purchasing decisions, and they clarify what is and what is not acceptable. Such training can include the following:

- The field of ethics.
- The feasibility of ethics on business.
- How people may rationalise their unethical behaviour. For example:
  - 'I was only doing what I was told.'
  - 'It's not really illegal.'
  - 'It's in everyone's interest.'
  - 'Everybody does it.'
  - 'No one will ever know.'
  - 'The company owes me this because it doesn't pay me enough.'
- Factors to be considered when receiving a gift or the offer of hospitality, including:
  - the motive of the donor, i.e. whether a gift is a token of appreciation or a bribe;
  - the value of the gift or the hospitality – when does it exceed what is permissible;
  - the type of gift or the nature of the hospitality;
  - the manner in which the offer is made, i.e. openly or surreptitiously;
  - what conditions, if any, are attached;
  - what impressions the gift or hospitality will make on superiors, colleagues and subordinates, bearing in mind the human propensity to think the worst;
  - what would be the employer's reaction if the matter was brought to his attention;
  - whether the buyer can honestly be satisfied that the gift will not influence his or her objectivity in dealing with suppliers.

If the buyer has doubts about any of the above the gift or hospitality should be refused.

- Double standards, i.e. some companies offer gifts to the buyers of customers but refuse permission to their own staff to receive gifts.
- What should a member of the purchasing staff do if he discovers his superior, colleagues or subordinates acting contrary to the company's ethical code?
- What are the possible penalties for unethical behaviour?
- Fostering ethical standards:
  - dealing with ethical suppliers;
  - management support for ethical behaviour.

18.14 Environmental aspects of purchasing

18.14.1 Responsibility to the environment

Responsibility to the environment is one aspect of the social responsibility of business and should be a consideration when devising strategies.

According to the Environmental Protection Act 1990, 'the environment consists of all or any of the following media namely, the air, water and land; and the medium of air includes the air within buildings and the air within the natural or man made structures above or below the ground'.

Important areas of environmental concern include the following:

- *More efficient use of raw materials in manufacturing operations.* This applies especially for timber and minerals. Consumer concern about rainforests has had a direct impact on the demand for tropical hardwoods which has affected timber producers, wholesalers and users.

  Of about 80 minerals used by industry, some 18, including lead, sulphur, tungsten and zinc, are in relatively short supply. Such materials will be subject to rising prices and demands for recycling.

- *Pollution and waste.* Pollution is also defined by the Environmental Protection Act 1990 as 'pollution of the environment due to the release (into an environmental medium) from any process of substances which are capable of causing harm to man or any other living organism supported by the environment'.

- *Energy savings.* Energy to power industry is provided by the environment through such sources as wood, fossil fuels, water, sunlight, wind and uranium.

Guidance on the environmental aspects of purchasing issued by Cambridge University[35] point out that the environmental impacts of a product relate not only to its use but also to how it is manufactured, the resources used and its final disposal. This 'cradle to the grave' approach is termed the product's 'life cycle'. The main environmental effects also occur at different times through the life cycle of a product. With a plastic chair, for example, the main impacts arise in manufacture and disposal. A car, using fuel, has impacts throughout its life.

18.14.2 Legislation

Purchasing of supplies is subject to a vast range of international and national environmental legislation and directives.

International legislation

Most international law is enforced through national processes, although EC laws can be enforced through the European Court of Human Rights.

A number of EU environmental directives have been issued relating to quality, water, waste, chemicals, and packaging and packaging waste. European legislation represents minimum environmental demands that are legally binding for all EU member states. A current list of all pertinent legislation is provided by the European an Information Service[36] and the European Information Centres.

National legislation

National legislation includes the Clean Air Act 1956, The Water Act 1989, The Radioactive Substances Act 1993 and the Environmental Protection Act 1990. The latter contains important provisions relating to:

- integrated pollution control;
- best available technology not entailing excessive cost (BATNEEC), requiring companies using major pollution processes to spend as much on clean technology as they can afford;
- air pollution control;
- waste disposal and recycling. Waste is defined in the Act as:
    - (a) Any substance which constitutes a scrap material or an effluent or other unwanted surplus substance from the application of any process
    - (b) Any substance or article which requires to be disposed of as being broken, worn out, contaminated or otherwise spoiled. Anything which is discarded or otherwise dealt with as if it were waste shall be presumed to be waste unless the contrary is proved.
- control of dangerous substances and nuisances.

The Environmental Agency, which combined HM Inspectorate of Pollution, the National Rivers Authority and local authority waste regulators, was established under the Environmental Act 1995 and is responsible for pollution prevention and control in England and Wales.

18.14.3 General purchasing approaches to environmental responsibilities

Two examples may be given. The Department of Environment[37] has stated that:

> The procurement of supplies and equipment is a potent instrument of environmental policy. Careful purchasing gives full weight to environmental considerations in the selection of products and can help improve environmental standards by reducing pollution and waste. It can also, through the natural operation of the market, influence purchasers and suppliers in their pricing policies and product ranges.

The DTI suggests that the following measures should be taken to give practical effect to the above objectives:

- The preparation of an environmental policy statement and ensuring that everyone responsible for purchasing is familiar with it.
- Ensuring that factors such as the scope for waste minimisation and the potential for recycling opportunities are taken into consideration in purchasing decisions.
- Preparing purchasing guidelines which set out clear performance requirements for the procurement of all goods and services (including catering suppliers; furniture and fittings and contracted-out services such as publications).

■ Incorporating environmental performance requirements into purchasing specifications especially in relation to:

- maximum energy efficiency;

- minimum dependence on production and use of ozone-depleting sub-stances, toxic chemicals and other pollutants, e.g. lead, formaldehyde;

- minimum dependence on non-renewable natural resources such as non-sustainably produced hardwoods;

- maximum recyclability;

- maximum use of products based on recycled materials and minimum use of unnecessary packaging and other superfluous material.

■ Ensuring that these guidelines are incorporated into all standard contract conditions for the purchasing of goods and services.

■ Requiring providers of contract services, e.g. cleaning, catering and transportation, to carry out their operations to high standards of environmental performance.

■ Keeping under constant scrutiny purchasing procedures such as stock and inventory control arrangements to discourage unnecessary procurement of supplies and excessive stockholdings.

As a second example of purchasing approaches to environmental responsibilities, the CIPS[38] has listed the following issues that should be included in environmental purchasing and supply management policies to the extent that this is permitted by EC procurement rules.

■ Consider whether the product or service is really needed.

- Could the need be met another way?

- Is a suitable product already available within the organisation?

- Can the requirement be met by renting or sharing rather than purchasing?

- Would a smaller quantity suffice?

■ Select products and services that:

- minimise the amount of material used;

- avoid the use of hazardous materials;

- are obtained from renewable resources;

- minimise the use of consumables;

- minimise energy consumption in use;

- minimise depletion of resources, e.g. their component materials are obtained in a sustainable manner;

- use and emit fewer substances that damage the environment or health;

- can have their life extended by incorporating future proofing elements to maintain or enhance the service provided;

- have options for end-of-life management which minimise environmental impact.

Such green issues need to be clearly identified in product and service specifications.

■ Adopt a whole-life cost approach by assessing the product's environmental impact from its production to disposal costs. These include, for example, the costs of:

- acquisition (total acquisition costs);
- operation;
- maintenance and spares;
- support services;
- staff costs;
- training and training aids;
- health and safety;
- end-of-life management and disposal;
- changes in legislation.

These costs can be simplified to:

- manufacture;
- purchase;
- use;
- disposal.

This holistic approach should be led by the purchasing and supply management professional and become part of most purchasing decisions and thus part of the organisation's culture. Such application of whole-life costs to purchases will ensure best overall value for money. By utilising whole-life costs, the purchasing and supply management professional can demonstrate benefits versus cost in terms of:

- total operating costs;
- quality;
- delivery performance;
- design improvements;
- environmental performance.

18.14.4 Screening suppliers for good environmental performance

Screening of suppliers can be done through questionnaires, requiring compliance with international standards and the use of specialist assessment tools.

Questionnaires

A typical environmental questionnaire used by the Buying Agency, responsible for providing a professional service to government departments and other public bodies, is shown in Figure 18.2.

Compliance standards

Such standards include EU Eco labels and those awarded by the International Organisation for Standardisation (ISO).

Supplier Health and Safety, Environmental Questionnaire

1. **Do you have an Environmental Policy and/or a Health and Safety Policy?**   (please tick box)

   Environmental   Yes ☐   No ☐

   Health and Safety   Yes ☐   No ☐

   If Yes – Please describe or attach copies

   If No – Is it your intention to develop such a policy   Yes ☐   No ☐

2. **Do you operate under an Environmental and/or Health and Safety Management System?**

   Environmental   Yes ☐   No ☐

   Health and Safety   Yes ☐   No ☐

3. **Does your company set environmental objectives and targets (e.g. reduction of waste by a certain percentage by year X, introduction of products which have less environmental impact)?**

   If so, please attach copy or outline of plan   Yes ☐   No ☐

4. **Does your company set health and safety objectives and targets (e.g. monitoring accident performance and setting of improvement targets)?**

   If so, please attach copy or outline of plan   Yes ☐   No ☐

5. **Is there a director/manager(s) appointed who has specific responsibilities for environmental issues and for Health and Safety?**

   Please give relevant details   Yes ☐   No ☐

6. **Has your company been subject to (or pending) any environmental or Health and Safety prosecutions or improvements in the last 5 years**

   Environmental?   Yes ☐   No ☐

   Health and Safety?   Yes ☐   No ☐

   If so, please detail

7. **Are you aware of the activities of the public, environmental or other pressure groups in any aspect of your business?**

   If so, please give the area of concern   Yes ☐   No ☐

   Do you have any measures in place/planned to respond to this?   Yes ☐   No ☐

   If yes, how?

8. **Have you considered the main environmental effects associated with the raw material extraction, manufacture and distribution of the products you intend to supply under this tender (contract)?**

   Yes ☐   No ☐

   If so, please list, in your opinion, which are most significant

9. **Do you have an energy conservation programme?**   Yes ☐   No ☐

   If so, do you have targets?   Yes ☐   No ☐

   What are they?

10. **Do you have in place a programme to improve your environmental and Health and Safety performance?**

    Yes ☐   No ☐

    If so, please give details

11. **To what extent are your employee encouraged to participate in and contribute to, your Environmental and Health and Safety improvement programmes?**

    Do they receive formal environmental and Health and Safety Training?   Yes ☐   No ☐

12. **Does your company have a programme for improving the environmental performance of your suppliers?**

    Yes ☐   No ☐

13. **How often do you formally review your environmental and Health and Safety performance management at senior level?**

Date questionnaire completed
Questionnaire completed by
Position in company
(Please print clearly)

Figure 18.2   Environmental questionnaire

EU Eco labels

The Eco labels scheme has been in operation since 1993 when the first product groups were identified. To be awarded the EU Eco label an individual product must comply with all specified criteria relating to practice and performance. Although aimed primarily at domestic consumers, the scheme can also be useful to professional purchasers.

ISO environmental standards

These are a series of voluntary standards and guideline reference documents which include eco-labelling, environmental evaluation and environmental aspects in performance standards. The focus on management distinguishes them from performance standards. The aim is to help any country to meet the goals of 'sustainable development and environmental friendliness'. Many purchasers of products regard certification to ISO 14001 as an assurance of a supplier's commitment to environmental performance and quality.

The main ISO environmental standards are:

- BS EN ISO 14001 *Environmental Management Systems – Specifications with Guidance for Use*
- BS ISO 14404 *Environmental Management Systems – General Guidelines on Principles, Systems and Supporting Techniques*
- BS EN ISO 14010 *Guidelines for Environmental Auditing – General Principles*
- BS EN ISO 14011 *Guidelines for Environmental Auditing – Audit Procedures*
- BS EN ISO 14012 *Guidelines for Environmental Auditing – Qualification Criteria for Environmental Auditors*
- ISO 14020:1998 *Environmental Labels and Declarations – General Principles*
- BS EN ISO 14040 *Environmental Management Life Cycle Assessment – Principles and Framework*
- BS ISO 14050:1998 *Environmental Management – Vocabulary*
- ISO Guide 64 *Guide for the Inclusion of Environmental Aspects in Production Standards*

The five easy steps of an environmental management system as identified by the British Standards Institution (BSI) are shown in Figure 18.3.

The sixth step, registering under the EU Environmental Management Assessment System (EMAS), which currently only applies to manufacturing industries, power generation, waste disposal and 'approved pilot schemes', involves:

- registration of a specific site rather than the whole organisation;
- the publication and validation of a public environmental statement by an independent, third party, accredited environmental verifier.

Use of specialist assessment tools

A danger with questionnaires is that the answers given by suppliers may receive little or no examination by the issuing purchasing organisation. Reliance on

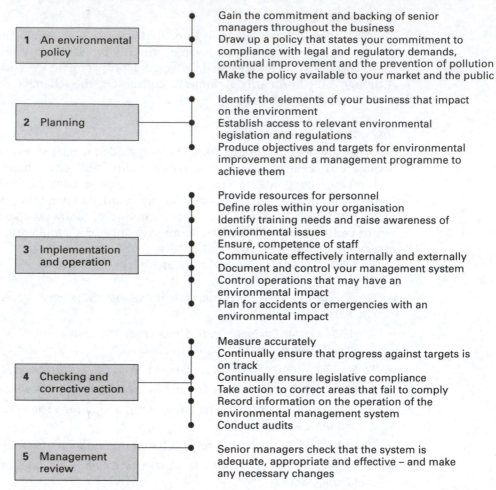

Figure 18.3 The five easy steps of an environmental management system

environmental standards may also be unsatisfactory. Knight[39] provides an example of a timber supplier that gained ISO 14000 because of its methods of wood treatment. 'They had convinced themselves that they were environmentally responsible even though they had never considered where the trees were coming from.'

An example of a tool designed both to provide a more precise evaluation against a benchmark set by the purchasing organisation and to assist suppliers to meet the required environmental standards is EVES – environmental vendor evaluation system – developed by Kileen for Yorkshire Water Services Ltd.[40] This system appraises a supplier's environmental performance against six criteria, namely design, manufacture, in use, legal, management, and measures or controls. Responses to weighted questions provide a score for each of the six areas forming a profile which can be compared against a benchmark as shown in Figure 18.4.

The overall environmental performance of a supplier can be categorised into one of six grades ranging from 1 (leading, best in class) to 6 (environmentally unacceptable – do not use). Areas in which the responses fall below minimum acceptable standard are highlighted enabling corrective action to be taken between prospective purchasers and suppliers.

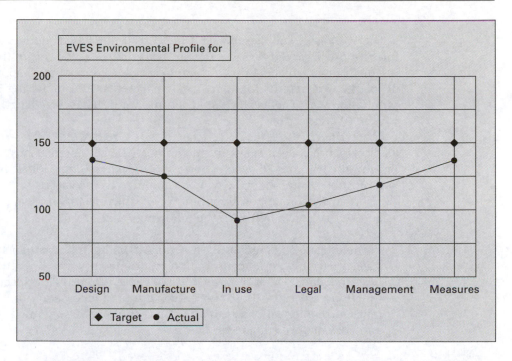

Scores	Design	Manufacture	In use	Legal	Management	Measures	Total score
Max points	150	150	150	150	150	150	900
Actual score	140	125	90	102	120	140	717
Area rates	Design	Construct	In use	Legal	Management	Measures	79.67

Grade 3 – Quite Good, but you can still improve use for small to medium-sized projects

Figure 18.4   Overall vendor environmental rating score

The 2001 operating profit statement of Millingford Manufacturing plc is as follows:

	£	£
Turnover		1,437.7
Less Cost of sales		983.2
Gross margin		454.5
Less Distribution costs	169.9	
Administration costs	209.4	
		379.3
Gross operating profit		75.2

There is a large supplier base and the cost of purchased supplies and assemblies for use in production is £501.4m. The administrative cost of the purchasing function in which 54 staff are employed is £3.28m of which approximately 36 per cent represents total gross staff payments. All purchasing is done by purchasing staff. There is little staff turnover and the average length of service is over 10 years.

Roger Driver, the chief buyer, has recently retired after 32 years' service, all of which has been spent in purchasing. The acting chief buyer is Gilbert Braithwaite who has 26 years' service, also in purchasing. Gilbert is well liked and most of his staff hope he will be appointed to the vacancy.

Before making an appointment, however, the directors have appointed you as an external consultant with the following remit:

To investigate the purchasing function at Millingford Manufacturing with special reference to its contribution to profitability and how the effectiveness and efficiency of the function are viewed from the perspective of user functions, especially those concerned with production and suppliers, and to make recommendations as to how the cost of purchasing might be reduced and performance enhanced.

Questions

1 Use the information given above to demonstrate the importance of purchasing to Millingford and suggest how the contribution might be enhanced.

2 Recommend some quantitative and qualitative measures that may be used to indicate the effectiveness and efficiency of the purchasing function from the perspectives of:

   (a) Internal customers, especially those concerned with production

   (b) External suppliers

3 Recommend how the cost of purchasing might be reduced while improving its effectiveness and efficiency.

? Discussion questions

18.1 A member of your staff who is taking an MBA degree has asked you to suggest some aspects of purchasing that she might research and which might also benefit the company. She also asks for facilities to undertake the research.

   (a) From a consideration of your present post, suggest a suitable research topic giving reasons for your choice with special reference to benefiting the company.

   (b) What conditions would you lay down relating to the investigation and the publication of the results?

18.2 Comment on the following statements:

   (a) 'Much academic research into purchasing is of little practical benefit to practicing purchasing people.'

(b) 'Much academic research is published in journals that practising purchasers never read.'

18.3 Why do many supplier associations tend to lose their initial enthusiasms and impetus and degenerate into 'talking shops'?

18.4 What is the distinction between (a) desk and (b) field research? Give two examples.

18.5 If an undertaking never attempts to measure the performance of purchasing or the supply chain, what does that imply regarding the importance of purchasing or the supply chain in that undertaking?

18.6 Your chief purchasing executive claims that during the previous year savings of 10 per cent have been made in the costs of bought-out materials. What factors would you investigate before giving purchasing exclusive credit for the claimed savings?

18.7 Activities can be distinguished as added-value or non-added-value. Added-value activities increase the worth of a product or service to a customer and the customer is consequently willing to pay. Non-added-value activities increase the time spent on a product or service but do not increase its worth. In the context of purchasing suggest in each year three added-value and three non-added-value activities.

18.8 It has been said that there are two basic types of benchmarking: (a) results and (b) process. Consider David *et al.*'s 19 examples of benchmarks given in section 18.8.1 of this chapter. Decide whether each benchmark can be classified as relating to (a) results or (b) process.

18.9 What practical difficulties would you expect to encounter in carrying out a purchasing management audit such as that described in section 18.9 of this chapter?

18.10 Why, for environmental reasons, may the repair of furniture and similar equipment be preferable to renewal or replacement?

18.11 The CIPS policy statement on environmental purchasing suggests that products or services should be selected that 'use or emit fewer substances that damage the environment or health'. How can you do this if you are not a chemist and have no specialised knowledge of the chemical content or disposal difficulties of the products or materials you are buying?

18.12 Consider how, from an ethical standpoint, you would react in each of the following cases:

(a) A representative telephones you to say that he has left the employment of a supplier from whom you are currently buying large quantities of a component. He knows the price you are paying and states that his new company can undercut your present price by 20 per cent. You have been dealing satisfactorily with your present supplier for a number of years.

(b) You are negotiating on a one-to-one basis with a small machine shop to carry out operations on 100,000 items to relieve capacity on your own production department. You inadvertently mention that you are very pleased with the price and that subject to discussion with your own production manager the subcontractor is likely to receive an order. He then asks, 'Why not let me increase the price by another £1 – 50p for me and 50p for you?'

(c) You can buy cheaper from an overseas supplier but you know he pays starvation wages, and the loss of the order will cause unemployment locally.

(d) You have negotiated and signed a contract with a supplier. When you arrive home you find that an expensive piece of jewellery has been sent anonymously to your wife.

(e) You mention to the representative of a steel stockist that you are proposing to build an extension to your home. He says, 'Why not let us supply you with the steelwork at cost price?'

(f) On two occasions a supplier has delivered substandard components which can nevertheless be used. You telephone the supplier's production manager to complain. He says, 'Don't write about it because it might affect a promotion I'm expecting, Let's keep it to ourselves and I will put it right.'

(g) You inform a potential supplier that, on average, your company buys 100,000 units of a certain item each year and therefore obtains a substantial quanity discount. You know that the average usage is only 50,000 units.

(h) A supplier asks you, in confidence, to give details of competitive quotes, saying that he will beat any price offered and 'that must be good for you'.

(i) A supplier offers you a bribe saying, 'We do exactly the same for your boss and he has no worries.'

(j) One of your subordinates tells you that last night he took his family to a football match and had the use of the hospitality box (including dinner) provided by a company which you know is seeking a share of your business.

What would you do if you were absolutely sure of not being found out?

❓ Past examination questions

1 You are a senior buyer working in a medium-sized organisation. Your managing director has asked you to give a presentation to senior managers on purchasing ethics. Explain the main points you would include.

(CIPS, Introduction to Purchasing and Supply Chain Management, November 1997)

2 Many large organisations have developed their own codes of ethics. The purchasing and supply activity has further extended and refined such codes in its own manuals. Explain why this extension has been necessary and the strategic implications of such ethical codes.

(CIPS, Purchasing and Supply Chain Management I: Strategy, November 1997)

3 From the perspective of an industrial or commercial organisation of your choice, identify the role and contribution likely to be demanded form purchasing in developing an environmentally friendly strategy.

(CIPS, Purchasing and Supply Chain Management I: Strategy, November 1997)

4 As procurement director, explain what you would include in your annual report to the board to show the effectiveness of your purchasing department.

(CIPS, Introduction to Purchasing and Supply Chain Management, May 1998)

5 Purchasing ethics are concerned with how the purchasing activity behaves with suppliers and other internal activities. Explain why purchasing ethics need to be considered in organisations and suggest a strategy for development and implementation of an ethical code of practice for your organisation, or one known to you.

(CIPS, Purchasing and Supply Chain Management I: Strategy, November 1998)

6 Using an example of your choice, show how the purchasing activity can adopt a proactive strategy in terms of environmental (green) issues affecting the supply chain.

(CIPS, Purchasing, November 1998)

7 Describe what efforts a well developed purchasing and supply function could make to help the supply chain become more efficient and effective.

(CIPS, Purchasing and Supply Chain Management I: Strategy, May 1999)

8 Identify and discuss the main ethical and environmental 'green' issues which need to be taken into account when considering commercial relationships.

(CIPS, Commercial Relationships, May 2000)

9 Companies today are paying a great deal of attention to the 'ethical supply chain'. Select and discuss four ethical issues that would be likely to have a bearing upon a company's commercial relationships with its suppliers.

(CIPS, Commercial Relationships, November 2000)

10 There is an old saying in management which says 'If you can't measure it you can't manage it'. Discuss, with reference to relevant techniques, how this saying applies to the management of quality at both the tactical and operational level.

(CIPS, Purchasing and Supply Management II: Tactics and Operations, November 2000)

Notes

1. Fearon, H., *Purchasing Research, Concepts and Current Practice*, American Management Association, 1976, p.5
2. Sarantakos, S., *Social Research*, Macmillan Education, 1993, Ch.4, p.91
3. Van Weele, A.J., 'Purchasing performance measurement and evaluation', *Journal of Purchasing and Materials Management*, Vol.20, No.3 (1984), pp.16–22
4. Quoted in Department for Transport, Local Government and the Regions, *Local Authority Procurement, A Research Report*, 28 June 2001
5. Central Unit on Purchasing, CUP Guidance Note No.14, *Measuring Performance in Purchasing*
6. Stevens, J., *Measuring Purchasing Performance*, Business Books, 1978, Appendix, p.212
7. Pryor, L.S., 'Benchmarking: a self-improvement strategy', *Journal of Business Strategy*, Nov./Dec. 1989, pp.28, 32
8. Harrison, J., 'The role and practice of benchmarking', *Knight Wendling Newsletter*, No.12 (1994), p.9
9. David, J.S., Hwang, Y., Buck, K.W. and Rencau, H., *The Impact of Purchasing on Financial Performance*, Arizona State University, 1999

10. DTI, *Best Practice Benchmarking*, DTI, 1992, pp.7–9

11. Ibid.

12. Ibid.

13. American Management Association, *Evaluating Purchasing Performance*, AMA, 1963

14. Scheuing, E.E., *Purchasing Management*, Prentice Hall, 1989, Ch.6, p.137

15. Evans, E.F. and Dale, B.G., 'The use of audits in purchasing', *International Journal of Physical Distribution and Materials Management*, Vol.18, No.7 (1988), pp.17–23

16. Evans, E., 'Fraud and incompetence in purchasing', *Internal Auditing*, May 1987, pp.132–4

17. Evans, E. and Maguire, R., 'Purchasing fraud – a growing phenomenon', *Purchasing and Supply Management*, May 1993, pp.24–6

18. Cannock, S. and Johns, T., *Ethical Leadership*, Institute of Personnel and Development, 1995, Ch.6, p.121

19. Public Concern at Work, *Blowing the Whistle on Defence Procurement*, 1995, p.2

20. Winfield, M., *Minding Your Own Business*, Social Audit, 1990, Ch.5, pp.23–5

21. Sims, J., Fireman, S. and Gabriel, Y., *Organising and Organisations*, Sage Publications, 1993, p.247

22. Donaldson, J., *Key Issues in Business Ethics*, Academic Press, 1989, p.xii

23. Sternberg, E., *Just Business*, Warner Books, 1994, p.88

24. Donaldson, J., as n.22 above, pp.xvi–xvii

25. Manley, W.W., *The Handbook of Good Business Practice: Corporate Codes of Conduct*, Routledge, 1992, Ch.9

26. Karp, H.B. and Abramms, B., 'Doing the right thing', *Training and Development* (USA), August 1992, pp.37–41

27. Farmer, D., 'Ethical issues in purchasing', in Farmer (ed.) *Purchasing Management Handbook*, Gower, 1985, Ch.22, p.433

28. Baumhart, R., *Ethics in Business*, Holt, Reinhard & Winston, 1968

29. Brigley, S., *Walking the Tightrope: A Survey of Ethics in Management*, Institute of Management/University of Bath, 1994, p.36

30. Clutterbuck, D., Dearlove, D. and Snow, D., *Actions Speak Louder: A Management Guide to Corporate Social Responsibility*, Kogan Page in association with Kingfisher, 1992, Introduction

31. Ibid.

32. Kennedy, G., *Everything is Negotiable*, Business Books, 1989, Ch.18, pp.220–5

33. Matthew 7 verse 12, *New English Bible*

34. Dubinsky, A.J. and Gwin, J.H., 'Business ethics: buyers and sellers', *Journal of Purchasing and Supply Materials Management*, Winter 1981, pp.9–16

35. University of Cambridge, *Guidance on Environmental Aspects of Purchasing*, May 1998

36. European Information Service, Local Government House, Smith Square, London SW1P 3HZ (Tel. 020 7664 3100)

37. Department of the Environment, *Environmental Action Guide for Building and Purchasing Managers*, HMSO, 1991, p.6

38. CIPS, *Policy Statement on Environmental Purchasing and Supply Management*, para. 5.2

39. Knight, A., 'Here today, green tomorrow', *Supply Management*, 11 Dec. 1997

40. This is described in Kileen, P., 'All about EVES', *Supply Management*, 24 Sept 1998. Further details from Peter Kileen, at 5 Cedarwood Close, Lytham St Annes, Lancashire FY8 4DP in whose name the system is copyrighted

Personal Ethical Code of the Chartered Institute of Purchasing and Supply

Introduction

1 Members of the Institute undertake to work to exceed the expectations of the following Code and will regard the Code as the basis of best conduct in the Purchasing and Supply profession.

2 Members should seek the commitment of their employer to the Code and seek to achieve widespread acceptance of it among their fellow employees.

3 Members should raise any matter of concern of an ethical nature with their immediate supervisor or another senior colleague if appropriate, irrespective of whether it is explicitly addressed in the Code.

Principles

4 Members shall always seek to uphold and enhance the standing of the Purchasing and Supply profession and will always act professionally and selflessly by:

(a) maintaining the highest possible standard of integrity in all their business relationships both inside and outside the organisations where they work;

(b) rejecting any business practice which might reasonably be deemed improper and never using their authority for personal gain;

(c) enhancing the proficiency and stature of the profession by acquiring and maintaining current technical knowledge and the highest standards of ethical behaviour;

(d) fostering the highest possible standards of professional competence amongst those for whom they are responsible;

(e) optimising the use of resources which they influence and for which they are responsible to provide the maximum benefit to their employing organisation;

(f) complying both with the letter and the spirit of:
   – the law of the country in which they practise;
   – Institute guidance on professional practice;
   – contractual obligations;

5 Members should never allow themselves to be deflected from these principles.

Guidance

6 In applying these principles, members should follow the guidance set out below:

(a) *Declaration of interest.* Any personal interest which may affect or be seen by others to affect a member's impartiality in any matter relevant to his or her duties should be declared.

(b) *Confidentiality and accuracy of information.* The confidentiality of information received in the course of duty should be respected and should never be used for personal gain. Information given in the course of duty should be honest and clear.

(c) *Competition.* The nature and length of contracts and business relationships with suppliers can vary according to circumstances. These should always be constructed to ensure deliverables and benefits. Arrangements which might in the long term prevent the effective operation of fair competition should be avoided.

(d) *Business gifts.* Business gifts, other than items of very small intrinsic value such as business diaries or calendars, should not be accepted.

(e) *Hospitality.* The recipient should not allow him- or herself to be influenced or be perceived by others to have been influenced in making a business decision as a consequence of accepting hospitality. The frequency and scale of hospitality accepted should be managed openly and with care and should not be greater than the member's employer is able to reciprocate.

Decision and advice

7 When it is not easy to decide between what is and is not acceptable, advice should be sought from the member's supervisor, another senior colleague or the Institute as appropriate. Advice on any aspect of the Code is available from the Institute.

Principles and standards of purchasing practice (ISM)

The following principles are advocated by the Institute of Supply Management (USA):

LOYALTY TO HIS COMPANY
JUSTICE TO THOSE WITH WHOM HE DEALS
FAITH IN HIS PROFESSION

From these principles are derived the ISM standards of purchasing practice:

1   To consider, first, the interests of his company in all transactions and to carry out and believe in its established policies.

2   To be receptive to competent counsel from his colleagues and to be guided by such counsel without impairing the dignity and responsibility of his office.

3   To buy without prejudice, seeking to obtain the maximum ultimate value for each dollar expenditure.

4   To strive consistently for knowledge of the materials and processes of manufacture, and to establish practical methods for the conduct of his office.

5   To subscribe to and work for honesty and truth in buying and selling, and to denounce all forms or manifestations of commercial bribery.

6   To accord a prompt and courteous reception, so far as conditions will permit, to all who call on a legitimate business mission.

7   To respect his obligations and to require that obligations to him and to his concern be respected, consistent with good business practice.

8   To avoid sharp practice.

9   To counsel and assist fellow purchasing agents in the performance of their duties, whenever occasion permits.

10 To cooperate with all organisations and individuals engaged in activities designed to enhance the development and standing of purchasing.

Definitions, acronyms, and foreign words and phrases

Definitions

Acronyms

Foreign words and phrases

caveat emptor (let the buyer beware) 432, 645

dantotsu (best of the best) 723

force majeure (events completely outside the control of the contracting parties) 445

kaizen (ongoing improvement) 144–5
kanban (ticket) An information system in which instructions relating to the type and quality of items to be withdrawn from the preceding manufacturing process are conveyed by a card affixed to a container 298
keiretsu (affiliated chain) used in respect of alliances that extend across the entire supply chain 97, 144–5
kyoryoku kai (supplier organisation) 362

muda (waste) any activity that absorbs resources but creates no value 84

poka-yoke (fool proofing) 208

Index of names and organisations

Subject index